POLITICAL HISTORY
OF AMERICA'S WARS

POLITICAL HISTORY OF AMERICA'S WARS

ALAN AXELROD

CQ PRESS

A DIVISION OF CONGRESSIONAL QUARTERLY INC.

WASHINGTON, D.C.

CQ Press
1255 22nd Street, NW, Suite 400
Washington, DC 20037

Phone: 202-729-1900; toll-free, 1-866-4CQ-PRESS (1-866-427-7737)
Web: www.cqpress.com

Cover photos: *Top left,* an American soldier helps topple a statue of Saddam Hussein in Iraq (AP/Wide World Photos); *Top center,* flag of the Thirty-seventh Pennsylvania Infantry during the Civil War (Brady Collection of the Library of Congress); *Top right,* "The Cuban Melodrama," an 1896 American cartoon from the Spanish-American War (The Granger Collection, New York); *Bottom left,* "The Bostonian's Paying the Excise Man, or Tarring and Feathering," 1774 (National Archives); *Bottom center,* protestors during the Vietnam War (© Leif Skoogfors/Corbis); *Bottom right,* Winston Churchill, Franklin D. Roosevelt, and Joseph Stalin at the Yalta Conference during World War II (© Hulton-Deutsch Collection/Corbis).

Text and interior photo credits are located on pages 553–556.
Cover design: Kimberly Glyder
Interior design and composition: Judy Myers

♾The paper used in this publication exceeds the requirements of the American National Standard for Information Sciences—Permanence of Paper for Printed Library Materials, ANSI Z39.48-1992.

Printed and bound in the United States of America

10 09 08 07 06   1 2 3 4 5

Library of Congress Cataloging-in-Publication Data

Axelrod, Alan
    Political history of America's wars / Alan Axelrod.
        p. cm.
    Includes bibliographical references and index.
    ISBN-13: 978-1-56802-956-6 (hardcover : alk. paper)
    ISBN-10: 1-56802-956-X (hardcover : alk. paper)
    1. United States—History, Military. 2. United States—Politics and government. 3. Politics and war—United States—History. I. Title.

    E181.A945 2006
    355.00973—dc22

                                        2006026340

For Anita and Ian

CONTENTS

KEY HISTORIC DOCUMENTS

BIOGRAPHIES OF
NOTABLE INDIVIDUALS

PREFACE

In the weeks leading up to D-Day, Lieutenant General George S. Patton Jr. delivered to different groups of American soldiers the same speech dozens of times. Although it was unwritten, for the dyslexic Patton never read a prepared speech in public, it was nevertheless virtually identical on each occasion. Actor George C. Scott delivered the same speech on film before a screen-filling American flag in the iconic opening scene of director Franklin Schaffner's 1970 movie *Patton.*

"Americans love to fight," declaimed Patton (and Scott). "All *real* Americans love the sting of battle."

If it was a shocking thing to say in 1944, it was even more jolting in 1970 when the United States was mired in a long, heartbreaking conflict in Vietnam. And it remains provocative today. Even as American soldiers, air force personnel, sailors, and marines fight the twenty-first century's war on terror, including actions in Afghanistan and Iraq, it is difficult for most Americans to think of the United States as a warlike country. Never mind that Americans chose for their national anthem not the pretty song about "spacious skies" and "amber waves of grain" but a British tavern tune that was adapted to praise "the rockets' red glare" and "the bombs bursting in air"—verses written during the War of 1812, which was fought largely at the instigation of sectional and special interests over issues that had already been resolved or were well on their way to peaceful resolution.

Before the age of intercontinental bombers and ballistic missiles, as well as nuclear-powered, nuclear-armed submarines capable of virtually limitless endurance and range, the United States was geographically isolated from most of its potential external enemies. (Hostile Indian tribes displaced by white settlement were effectively defined as internal enemies.)

The United States came to birth in war, the American Revolution (1771–1783), but would not fight another revolutionary conflict until the Civil War (1861–1865), which was regional, economic, and ideological in nature. Shortly after the American Revolution, two insurrections—Shays's Rebellion (1786–1787) and the Whiskey Rebellion (1794)—were quelled by the government. Though minor, they tested the effective authority of the new federal government.

Early in its existence as an independent nation, the United States also fought three conflicts that served to defend its national sovereignty: the Franco-American Quasi-War (1798–1800), essentially over neutrality rights, and the Tripolitan War (1801–1805) and the Algerine War (1815), both against state-sanctioned piracy. The War of 1812 (1812–1815) with Britain was officially fought in defense of U.S. sovereignty, but another compelling motive was national expansion—the most important category of American wars during the nineteenth century. In addition to the War of 1812, all of the Indian Wars (spanning 1786–1891) may be classed as wars of expansion (albeit complicated by racial, cultural, and economic issues), as may the wars with Mexico, including the Fredonian Rebellion (1826–1827), the Texas War of Independence (1835–1836), and the U.S.-Mexican War (1846–1848). (The so-called Aroostook War of 1838–1839 was a border dispute with Canada and never came to actual blows.)

The Indian Wars were contests for control of territory within the United States, and the wars with Mexico were fought for control of territory adjacent to the U.S. border. Other expansionist wars were imperialist in nature, fought over control of territory beyond the North American continent. These cannot be readily categorized as wars of conquest in the European and Asian sense, but aspects of some of them come close. The wars the United States has fought that are most often referred to as "imperialist" are the Spanish-American War (1898) and the associated suppression of the Philippine Insurrections (1896–1902) and the Moro Wars (1901–1913). The suppression of the Boxer Rebellion (1899–1901) in China and arguably every U.S. intervention in Latin American countries (even the Punitive Expedition against Pancho Villa in 1916–1917) were fought to suppress governments unfriendly to U.S. business interests and the U.S. government and to support more compliant governments; these conflicts are therefore also often considered imperialist.

The twentieth century saw the ascension of the United States as a world power, which meant, in part, engaging in "foreign wars." The United States entered World War I (U.S. participation, 1917–1918) largely for ideological reasons, although economics also played a major role. America's entry into World War II (U.S. participation, 1941–1945) was triggered by an actual attack on U.S. territory but is quite reasonably seen as a contest in which democracy itself was at stake.

World War II saw the triumph of democracy over fascism and Nazism, but it also saw the rise and expansion of Soviet and Chinese communism. Almost all of the wars in which the United States became involved after World War II (including Korea and Vietnam) and through the Grenada Invasion of 1983 may be seen as aspects of the Cold War between the United States (allied, in varying degrees, with other democratic powers) and the Soviet Union (and to a lesser extent, the People's Republic of China). These great powers did not fight one another directly but instead attempted to face each other down through proxy wars fought on far-flung battlefields. These confrontations mostly occurred in Asia and Latin America, wherever there was a conflict between a pro-Western democratic government and a pro-Soviet (or pro-Chinese) Communist government.

By the mid-1970s Chinese-American relations had dramatically improved, and a major trading relationship between China and the West largely displaced the enmity of the Cold War era. After a precipitous decline during the 1980s, Soviet communism collapsed entirely in 1991. The Cold War ended, but new regional instabilities developed. Some of these—the War in Bosnia and Herzegovina (1992–1995) and the U.S. Intervention in the Kosovo Crisis (1996–1999)—resulted directly from the sudden removal of Soviet influence from parts of Eastern Europe; others sprang from a complex array of causes, in which culture, religion, and economics played key roles. One can place the U.S. Intervention in the Somali Civil War (1988–1994) and the conflicts in the Middle East and Afghanistan in this latter category. The Persian Gulf War (1991) was fought in part to curb the aggression of Iraq's dictatorial president Saddam Hussein, who had invaded neighboring Kuwait. Beyond issues of stability and sovereignty, however, many saw an imperative to protect sources of oil vital to Western economic interests. The second war in Iraq, Operation Iraqi Freedom, began in 2003 and was most directly a response to the devastating attack on the United States by Muslim (albeit not Iraqi) extremists on September 11, 2001. The same motive—what President George W. Bush called a "war on terror"—lay behind the War in Afghanistan, which began in 2001. The Bush administration also hoped to expand democracy and thereby bring stability to the Middle East region.

Arguably, of all of America's wars, only three were of indisputably urgent necessity to the survival of the nation *as* a nation: the American Revolution, the Civil War, and World War II. The rest may be seen in varying degrees as wars of perceived necessity. The War of 1812, which occasioned "The Star-Spangled Banner," was almost certainly unnecessary (the issues involved were essentially resolved when the fighting began). U.S. entry into World War I was portrayed by the administration of Woodrow Wilson as necessary to protect the sovereign rights of the United States as neutral (a cause also cited for the War of 1812) and to "make the world safe for democracy." Yet in April 1917 a significant number of Americans did not accept Wilson's rationale. Today many historians also reject Wilson's justification, condemning America's entry into the war as unnecessary, a military success but an ideological failure: by ensuring that the British and French succeeded in defeating and humiliating Germany, the United States helped set the stage for a second world war. Other historians interpret America's role in World War I as a triumph against tyranny, a noble effort even if the war failed to be the "war to end all wars" that Wilson had hoped it would be.

The wars of the Cold War era—most notably Korea and Vietnam—were initially seen as vital to stopping the march of communism. They were fought pursuant to the policy of the military, economic, and diplomatic "containment" of communism promulgated by President Harry S. Truman almost immediately after World War II and adopted, in varying degree, by every president who followed, through the administration of George H.W. Bush. The idea was to use every available means, including war (but short of nuclear war), to check any attempt to force Communist control on any free country. Containment stopped being the dominant American postwar policy after the collapse of the Soviet Union.

Like Wilson in 1917, President George W. Bush saw as urgently necessary the war in Iraq, which began in 2003. The war was approved by a substantial majority of Congress, which authorized funding and gave the president wide latitude in conducting military operations. Within months of the war's commencement, however, the chief reasons given for invading Iraq came under intense scrutiny. As of this writing in 2006, public opinion polls show waning support for the ongoing struggle. Yet the government remains deeply divided on whether to continue prosecuting the conflict. Some argue that it has actually heightened America's peril in a world increasingly torn by religious and cultural conflict. But a significant number of decision makers, including the presi-

dent, assert that the war is necessary to protect the United States: In the short term it is better to fight militant extremists in Iraq than to be forced to fight them in the United States. In the long term, the argument continues, the goal of democratizing Iraq will make the United States and the rest of the world safer, because democracies do not attack democracies.

Whether fighting extremists abroad will prevent other radicals from attacking the United States is subject to much dispute. How most historians—and ordinary Americans—will perceive the war in Iraq in the future is a matter of speculation. Some believe that history will strongly condemn the war and, with it, the president. Others, including the president, have expressed confidence that history will bring vindication. If the majority of the wars in this volume are any indication, the writers of history will bring neither definitive condemnation nor definitive vindication; rather, they will perpetuate the current debate.

American history is by no means simply a history of war, but it is a history defined by war. This book provides a survey of the most significant American wars, less from the point of view of the military course of these conflicts than from that of the politics associated with them. It is a *political* history of America's armed conflicts, including wars, rebellions, and insurrections.

Except for minor variations necessitated by thematic coherence, the forty-eight chapters in this book are arranged chronologically. Each chapter treats a particular conflict or, in some cases, a group of related conflicts. With the exception of three chapters—"Introduction to the Indian Wars," "Reconstruction (1865–1877)," and "The United States as Peacemaker"—each chapter begins with a concise statement of the issues involved in the conflict under discussion, followed by a narrative overview of the military course of the conflict, which includes a tabular chronological summary.

After discussing military action, each chapter addresses the political background and antecedents of the conflict, relevant political issues and events during the conflict, and the conflict's political consequences. Included, as necessary, are discussions of

legislation; court decisions; congressional resolutions; executive orders, proclamations, and speeches;
actions by cabinet members and other officials;
public opinion; propaganda efforts; media coverage;
diplomacy; and pre- and postwar treaties and agreements. Although the emphasis here is on interpretive
narrative, relevant original documents are excerpted
in boxes throughout each chapter. Editorial policy
with regard to these documents has been to repro-
duce excerpted sections as faithfully to the original
as possible, including anomalies of spelling, capital-
ization, and grammar. Also included in each chapter
are brief biographies of notable individuals. Each
chapter concludes with a bibliography of works with
which readers can embark upon further study.

I cannot claim that *Political History of America's
Wars* definitively separates the nation's wars of
unambiguous necessity from those of perceived
necessity or choice, let alone definitively identifies
those of dubious choice. Almost certainly there are
very few instances in which such absolute distinctions are possible. Possibly there are none at all.

Even less can I claim that this book explains why
Americans fight or perhaps (as General Patton
asserted) even love to fight. My intention has been
neither to propose nor advance any particular political or moral thesis, although I do present the theses
of others where they are both relevant and prevalent.
After all, it is important to know what American
people, politicians, and historians think and have
thought about the nation's conflicts. It is even more
important that students, teachers, and others interested in American history, politics, and culture have
ready, reliable, and readable access to the historical
tools—the facts, the documents, and the discussions—necessary to make informed assessments
about America's wars and what those wars may suggest concerning the American character. It is to
stimulate and aid such thought that I have written
this book.

Political History of America's Wars was an ambitious
undertaking not only for me, but also for the extraordinarily talented staff of CQ Press. I owe a special
debt of gratitude to acquisitions editor Mary Carpenter, development editor David Arthur, and project
editor Jennifer Campi. Their guidance has been
invariably valuable, their judgment never less than
acute, their encouragement always timely, and their
patience simply breathtaking.

Alan Axelrod
Atlanta, Georgia

CHAPTER **1**

THE AMERICAN REVOLUTION
(1771–1783)

At Issue

Following the passage of a series of laws many of Britain's North American colonists deemed unconstitutional, politically repressive, and economically ruinous, the colonies south of Canada sought independence. Although a significant and growing faction within the British government sympathized with the cause of colonial independence, King George III, his generally conservative ministers, and the Tory majority in Parliament were unwilling to tolerate rebellion. Thus the struggle for American independence became a war.

The Conflict

After Parliament—in which the North American colonies had no direct representation—imposed a series of taxes and laws many colonists perceived as both oppressive and repressive, the British colonies south of Canada simultaneously moved toward union with one another and independence from Britain. In 1774 Massachusetts organized special militia units, including the Minutemen, to resist coercion by British troops. In 1775, after Parliament passed punitive laws aimed at stifling rebellion in New England, Massachusetts girded for war. British general Thomas Gage responded by sending troops from Boston to seize gunpowder stored in Concord. This resulted in skirmishes at Lexington on the morning of April 19, 1775, and later that day at Concord (from which the colonists had already removed the stored powder). The British retreated back to Boston, under sniper fire along their march.

Shortly after the battles at Lexington and Concord, colonial militia forces from all over New England laid siege to the British troops quartered in Boston. In May 1775 Vermont militia leader Ethan Allen's "Green Mountain Boys" took Fort Ticonderoga in New York and Crown Point, on the western shore of Lake Champlain. In June the Second Continental Congress created a Continental army and commissioned George Washington, a veteran of the French and Indian War, to lead it.

As Washington set off for New England to assume command, British general Thomas Gage offered a blanket amnesty to all colonists except Samuel Adams and John Hancock, the principal agitators. In response, the Massachusetts Committee of Safety ordered militia general Artemus Ward to fortify Bunker Hill on Charlestown Heights, overlooking Boston Harbor. Ward instead sent troops to occupy nearby Breed's Hill. On June 17, the British made three attacks, taking Breed's Hill in the third attack, but suffering significant casualties.

In August the British government rebuffed the Continental Congress's Olive Branch Petition, and by December 1775 the Virginia and North Carolina militias had defeated the forces of the royal governor of Virginia. The rebellion was in full swing, its flames fanned by the January 1776 publication of Thomas Paine's stirring pamphlet *Common Sense*. The British, under siege at Boston, withdrew to Halifax, Nova Scotia, in March 1776, and on July 4, the

Continental Congress formally adopted the Declaration of Independence.

At the same time, British forces under General Sir Henry Clinton attempted to rally support from Loyalists (colonists still loyal to the Crown) in the South by bombarding the harbor fortifications of Charleston, South Carolina, but were driven off on June 28, 1776. This defeat brought an end to the British southern offensive for more than two years.

Despite the surprising successes of the Americans against the greatest military power of the time, American victory was far from accomplished. An ill-advised American invasion of Canada failed disastrously by the summer of 1776, and General Sir William Howe (who had replaced Gage as supreme commander of Britain's North American forces) defeated Washington on Long Island, New York, on August 27, 1776. Washington was forced to retreat

CHRONOLOGY OF THE AMERICAN REVOLUTION

1763
Oct. 7 King George III sets the Proclamation Line.

1764
- Parliament passes the Sugar Act and the Currency Act.
- Colonists protest "taxation without representation" and institute their first nonimportation boycott against British goods.

1765
- Parliament passes the Stamp Act and the Quartering Act. The Sons of Liberty and other resistance groups are organized.
- The colonies form the Stamp Act Congress.
- The nonimportation boycott is expanded.

1766
- Parliament repeals the Stamp Act. The colonies end their boycott.
- Parliament passes the Declaratory Act.

1767
- Parliament passes the Townshend Acts. The colonies resume their nonimportation boycott.

1768
- The Massachusetts Circular Letter is promulgated. It presents Samuel Adams's argument against taxation without representation and calls for unified resistance by all the colonies.
- The royal governor of Massachusetts dissolves the colonial legislature, and British troops arrive in Boston.

1769
- The Virginia House of Burgesses condemns Britain's actions against Massachusetts and asserts that only Virginia's governor and legislature may tax its citizens. The Crown orders the Virginia legislature to be dissolved.

1770
Jan. 19 "Battle" of Golden Hill—a clash between citizens and British troops in New York City
Mar. 5 The Boston Massacre—violence between troops and a Boston mob
Apr. 12 Parliament repeals the Townshend taxes, except for the tax on tea.

1772
June The sheriff of Kent County, Rhode Island destroys the *Gaspée,* a royal customs schooner.
Nov. In Boston, Samuel Adams calls for the creation of "Committees of Correspondence."

1773
- Parliament passes the Tea Act.
Dec. 16 Boston Tea Party—a band of Bostonians disguised as Indians board British tea ships held in Boston Harbor and dump the cargo

1774
June 10–Oct. 26 Lord Dunmore's War
- Parliament passes the Coercive Acts.
Sept. 5 The First Continental Congress meets to organize resistance to the Coercive Acts and other examples of British tyranny.
- British troops began to fortify Boston and seize ammunition belonging to Massachusetts.
- Massachusetts creates a Provincial Congress and a Committee of Safety. A colonial citizen militia, dubbed the Minutemen, is organized.

1775
- Parliament passes the New England Restraining Act.

to Manhattan, which also fell to Howe, on September 15, after Washington evacuated to White Plains, Westchester County. Washington next suffered defeat in the Battle of White Plains on October 28. On November 16, Howe attacked the garrison Washington had kept in Manhattan and captured Fort Washington; four days later, he took Fort Lee, in New Jersey. The American army was now split in three: part was in Westchester County; part was far-

ther up the Hudson River at Peekskill, New York; and the main body of troops, under the direct command of Washington, was in a long retreat across New Jersey and (on December 7) into Pennsylvania.

In a bold counterattack, Washington rallied his forces and, on December 26, 1776, won a magnificent victory in the Battle of Trenton, New Jersey. He capped this triumph by taking Princeton on January 3, 1777. With their morale bolstered, the Continental

Apr. 19 Battles of Lexington and Concord, Massachusetts—generally considered the first battles of the American Revolution

May 10 Second Continental Congress convenes in Philadelphia and elects John Hancock president of Congress.

May 10 Patriots capture Fort Ticonderoga, New York.

June 10 Continental Congress creates the Continental Army and appoints George Washington to command it (June 15).

June 17 Battle of Bunker Hill, Massachusetts

July 3 Washington takes command of the Continental army at Cambridge, Massachusetts.

Aug. 23 King George III rebuffs the Olive Branch Petition.

Dec. 31 American forces begin their retreat from Canada.

1776

Jan. 9 Thomas Paine publishes *Common Sense.*

Mar. The British evacuate Boston.

July 4 The Continental Congress declares independence.

Aug. 27 Battle of Long Island, New York

Sept. 15 New York City falls to the British.

Oct. 28 Battle of White Plains, New York

Dec. 26 Battle of Trenton, New Jersey

1777

Jan. 3 Battle of Princeton, New Jersey

Sept. 11 Battle of Brandywine, Pennsylvania

Sept. 26 The British occupy Philadelphia.

Oct. 4 Battle of Germantown, Pennsylvania

Sept.–Oct. Battles of Saratoga, New York (Freeman's Farm, Sept. 19; Bemis Heights, Oct. 7)

Nov. 15 Articles of Confederation are adopted (ratified Mar. 1, 1781).

1778

Winter Continental army endures harsh winter at Valley Forge.

May 4 Congress ratifies a Franco-American alliance.

June 28 Battle of Monmouth Courthouse, New Jersey

Nov. 11 The Cherry Valley Massacre (upstate New York)

Dec. 29 Savannah, Georgia, falls to the British.

1779

• Sailing for the new Continental navy, John Paul Jones compiles a stunning record of victory during 1779–1780.

May Benedict Arnold turns traitor.

June 21 Spain joins France as an American ally against Britain.

Aug. 19 Battle of Stony Point, New York

Sept. 23 *Bonhomme Richard* defeats *Serapis*—John Paul Jones's most famous victory.

1780

May 12 Charleston, South Carolina, falls to the British.

June–Aug. 16 Camden (South Carolina) Campaign

Oct. 7 Battle of Kings Mountain, North Carolina

1781

Jan. 17 Battle of Cowpens, South Carolina

Mar. 15 Battle of Guilford Courthouse, North Carolina

Oct. 6–19 Siege of Yorktown, Virginia, the last major campaign of the American Revolution, virtually ensures American independence

1782

• Peace negotiations take place in Paris.

1783

Sept. 3 The Treaty of Paris is signed—America has won independence.

George Washington
(1732–1799)

George Washington was born in Westmoreland County, Virginia, and after the death of his father in 1743, he was raised by his half-brother, Lawrence. Washington learned the surveyor's trade and from 1749 to 1751 was surveyor for Culpepper County. After Lawrence and Lawrence's daughter Sarah both died in 1752, Washington came into a great inheritance, including Mount Vernon, a fine Virginia plantation estate. As a prominent property holder, he was appointed adjutant for southern Virginia and given the militia rank of major in November 1752. He was additionally named adjutant of Northern Neck—the area between the Rappahannock and Potomac rivers—and the Eastern Shore in 1753.

Late in 1753 Virginia's lieutenant governor, Robert Dinwiddie, sent Washington to assess French military activity in the Ohio Valley and to serve notice on the French that they were trespassing on British territory. The expedition, spanning October 31, 1753, to January 16, 1754, advanced from coastal Williamsburg, Virginia, through the wilderness to Fort Duquesne (on the site of modern Pittsburgh, Pennsylvania). Washington encountered and defeated a small French party at the end of May but was forced to surrender after a larger force attacked on July 3–4, 1754, and killed about half of the troops in his command. These two encounters were the first battles of the French and Indian War.

Washington fought with distinction in the war and was elected to the Virginia House of Burgesses in 1758. On January 6, 1759, he married Martha Dandridge Custis, a wealthy widow with two children. From 1760 to 1774 he served as justice of the peace for Fairfax County while he prospered as a plantation owner.

As the revolutionary movement coalesced, Washington became a key member of the first Virginia Provincial Congress in August 1774 and was chosen to be one of seven Virginia delegates to the First Continental Congress in September 1774. He also served as a member of the Second Continental Congress in May 1775. When the Revolution broke out, the Congress commissioned Washington as general in chief of the Continental forces, and he formally took command of the army at Cambridge, Massachusetts, on July 3, 1775.

Washington was defeated more often than he was victorious, yet his courage, character, leadership, and faith in the cause served to hold the Continental army together to ultimate victory. With French general Jean Baptiste Rochambeau, he planned and executed the Yorktown Campaign (August 21–October 19, 1781), forcing the surrender of Lord Cornwallis's army and effectively ending the war (although the formal peace and British recognition of United States independence did not come until the Treaty of Paris in 1783).

On December 4, 1783, Washington took leave of his troops at Fraunces Tavern in Manhattan, returned to Mount Vernon, and resigned his commission. He continued to work toward uniting the disparate colonies into a single government and was elected president of the Constitutional Convention in Philadelphia in 1787. In February 1789 he was unanimously elected as the first president of the United States and was inaugurated on April 30. He was reelected to a second term in December 1792 but declined a third, thereby establishing a tradition of a two-term limit. This was perhaps the least considerable of the many precedents Washington set. As the first president, he essentially created the office, establishing for it a high and highly democratic standard.

In March 1797 he retired to Mount Vernon but was briefly recalled as commander in chief of the army during a crisis with France (see Chapter 4). In December 1798 Washington took ill with severe laryngitis and died.

Congress rejected the latest surrender terms issued by General Howe, and the fight for independence continued.

British general John Burgoyne led an army from Canada into New York and recaptured Fort Ticonderoga on July 5, 1777, but was defeated at the Battles of Saratoga (September 19 and October 7) and forced to surrender his 6,000 regulars plus various auxiliaries on October 17. In the meantime, however, Howe captured Philadelphia, the American capital, on September 26 and thwarted Washington's attempt to retake the city at the Battle of Germantown on October 4. Despite the American loss at Germantown, French observers were so impressed by Washington's boldness that King Louis XVI decided to enter into a formal alliance against Britain on February 6, 1778. In June 1779 France's ally Spain also recognized the United States and declared war on Britain.

British forces under Charles Cornwallis surrender to George Washington's Continental forces at Yorktown, Virginia, in 1781.

Although the French alliance was a tremendous boon to the American cause, in 1778 the troops of the Continental army endured near-starvation at their winter encampment at Valley Forge, Pennsylvania. However, spring brought new hope to the Americans and war weariness to the British. Resigning his command, Howe turned over the army to Clinton, who withdrew his forces from Philadelphia and sent many of his troops to the Caribbean in anticipation of French action there. Taking advantage of this, Washington pursued Clinton through New Jersey, fighting him to a stand at Monmouth Courthouse on June 28, 1778.

While the regular armies fought along the country's coast, frontier volunteers—Patriots versus Loyalists, with both sides extensively employing Indian allies—conducted a brutal war, especially on the New York–Pennsylvania frontier and in the distant Ohio country, which covered the present state of Ohio as well as parts of eastern Indiana, western Pennsylvania, and northwestern West Virginia. This warfare would continue even after the American Revolution had ended (see Chapter 3, Little Turtle's War [1786–1795]).

In the South, British forces pacified most of Georgia in December 1778. In February 1780 Clinton laid siege to Charleston, South Carolina, which surrendered on May 12. American general Horatio Gates was humiliated at Camden in upper South Carolina on August 16 by troops under Major General Lord Charles Cornwallis, who commanded Britain's southern forces.

Although the coastal South was in British hands, Patriot guerrillas, including the "Swamp Fox" Francis Marion and Thomas Sumter, took the fight inland. On October 7, 1780, Patriot frontiersmen destroyed a force of 1,000 Loyalist troops at the Battle of Kings Mountain, North Carolina. Continental army units, under Major General Nathanael Greene, coordinated with the South Carolina guerrillas, and Greene's subordinate, Brigadier General

Charles Cornwallis

(1738–1805)

The eldest son of the first Earl of Cornwallis, Charles Cornwallis was born in London and educated at Eton. He joined the First Foot Guards as an ensign at the outbreak of the Seven Years' War in 1756 and rose rapidly through the officer ranks. With the outbreak of the American Revolution in 1775, he was promoted to major general and dispatched to America.

Cornwallis landed in the Carolinas during February 1776 and took part in the failed assault on Charleston during June 16–July 28. He served under General Sir Henry Clinton and distinguished himself in fighting on Manhattan Island, New York, where he defeated the American forces at Kip's Bay on September 15. He pursued Washington's forces across the Hudson River, engaging them at Fort Lee in New Jersey on November 18 and taking the fort on the 20th. Washington outmaneuvered him at the Battle of Princeton, however, dealing him a defeat on January 3, 1777.

Frustrated in New Jersey, Cornwallis enthusiastically supported General Sir William Howe's plan to take Philadelphia and led the main attack at the Battle of Brandywine on September 11. Next, he led reinforcements to Germantown (in present-day Philadelphia) to check Washington's counterattack there on October 4.

Following his victories in Philadelphia, Cornwallis returned to England, where he was promoted to lieutenant general in January 1778. In May he sailed back to America as second in command to General Clinton. He fought at the drawn Battle of Monmouth Courthouse, New Jersey on June 28, then went back to England when he received news that his wife was dying. When he once again returned to America, he rejoined Clinton in a new assault on Charleston, South Carolina, during February 11–May 12, 1780.

After Clinton left for New York, Cornwallis assumed command of operations in Charleston and invaded North Carolina, hoping to break the back of the rebellion in the southern theater during the summer of 1780. He achieved a substantial victory at the Battle of Camden, South Carolina, on August 16, but his subordinates failed at Kings Mountain (on the North Carolina–South Carolina border) on October 7 and at the Cowpens, South Carolina, on January 17, 1781. These defeats notwithstanding, Cornwallis doggedly pursued his southern strategy, defeating Major General Nathanael Greene at Guilford Courthouse on March 15 in a Pyrrhic victory that cost him one-third of his men. In defiance of Clinton's orders, Cornwallis next sped to Virginia, determined to wipe out the forces of the Marquis de Lafayette. Lafayette evaded him, and Cornwallis decided to occupy Virginia's Yorktown peninsula in August. There, the combined French and American forces of Washington and the Comte de Rochambeau attacked, prompting his surrender on October 19, 1781. Cornwallis thus had the dubious distinction of losing the decisive battle of the Revolution.

After a brief period as a prisoner of war, Cornwallis was paroled in May 1782 and returned to England. He became governor-general of India on February 23, 1786, and earned a reputation as an excellent and even-handed administrator.

Daniel Morgan, defeated the infamous "Tory Legion" of Lieutenant Colonel Banastre Tarleton at the Battle of Cowpens on January 17, 1781. Cornwallis, however, broke free and pursued Morgan, who linked up with Greene and the main body of the southern army. Together, Morgan and Greene fought Cornwallis to a draw at Guilford Courthouse, North Carolina, on March 15, 1781. This forced Cornwallis to withdraw to the coast while Greene returned to South Carolina and retook every British-held position except Charleston and Savannah.

Cornwallis then withdrew to Virginia's Yorktown peninsula, effectively backing into a cul-de-sac, to which General Washington's Continental troops and Comte de Rochambeau's French army laid siege beginning on October 6, 1781. The British general surrendered his 8,000 troops to the allies' 17,000 on October 19.

Practically and strategically, Yorktown ended the American Revolution by breaking the will of the British government to keep fighting. Although Clinton still occupied key cities and Britain continued to skirmish in the Western hemisphere, mainly with France and Spain, the Yorktown victory gave America's treaty negotiators an advantageous position. The Treaty of Paris, by which Britain recognized the independence of the United States of America, was signed on September 3, 1783, and ratified by the Continental Congress on January 14, 1784.

The End of "Salutary Neglect"

Beginning with the first permanent British colony established at Jamestown, Virginia, in 1607, the British Crown tended to treat both its North American colonies and colonists with what historians have often called "salutary neglect," imposing few restrictions and extending little aid. Wars between the British colonists and the French as well as French-allied Indians—starting at the end of the seventeenth century and spanning the first half of the eighteenth century, culminating in the cataclysm of the French and Indian War (1754–1763)—brought an end to the era of salutary neglect as King George III and Parliament revived dormant tax and revenue laws, known as the "Navigation Acts," and introduced new ones to raise money to defray some of the expense of defending the colonies.

The political flux that accompanied King George III's first years on the throne was critical in determining Britain's relations with the colonies. Just

George III
(1738–1820)

The son of Frederick, Prince of Wales, George was born June 4, 1738, in London. After his father's death in 1751, George became heir to his grandfather, George II, and the Hanoverian crown of England. George was a diligent student in his youth, but his manner was such that many regarded him as slow-witted. He possessed a solid understanding of English law, and he embraced the constitutional limits of the monarchy. When he ascended the throne in 1760, he did so as the first Hanoverian king to be born in England, and he quickly became popular.

King George III presided over England during the Seven Years' War (1756–1763), which was known in North America as the French and Indian War. The war put a dangerous strain on the treasury, prompting the king and Parliament to tax the British colonies to help pay some of the expenses of the war. This policy alienated the colonies and ultimately propelled them toward revolution. Although many people in Britain—possibly a majority—favored releasing the colonies, George argued that simply to let the colonies go would unravel the entire empire. The American Revolution, fought from 1775 to 1783, resulted in the independence of the United States.

With considerably more success, George also prosecuted the Napoleonic Wars (1803–1815), but by 1810 he descended into severe illness characterized by great pain, delirium, and temporary paralysis. Contemporaries believed him insane, but modern physicians believe he was suffering from porphyria, a hereditary metabolic disorder. His son ruled as prince regent during the last decade of his reign.

when the colonies, battered by war, needed a strong and unified government, the king and Parliament offered chaos. The British government was by no means united in supporting the new application of the old Navigation Acts. Prime Minister William Pitt the Elder believed the new economic policy was driving a wedge between the colonies and Britain. The king, however, ousted Pitt in 1761 and replaced him with Lord Bute, a conservative, who enjoyed little support in Parliament and was forced to resign in 1763. After Bute came Lord Grenville, who was soon replaced by Lord Rockingham, who was in turn displaced by the return of Pitt, now advocating a liberal colonial policy. Suffering from increasingly severe mental illness, Pitt was forced into retirement in 1768, and the wholly ineffective Augustus Henry Fitzroy, Duke of Grafton, became prime minister. He was succeeded in 1770 by Lord North.

Frederick, Lord North, served as prime minister for the next twelve years, some of the most eventful in British history, and earned enemies on both sides of the Atlantic. He would do more than any previous prime minister to enforce, amplify, and expand the Navigation Acts with additional legislation that, for the colonies, became a cause for rebellion.

George III's Proclamation of 1763

Rather than an immediate cessation of violence, the end of the French and Indian War in 1763 had brought a brief spasm of even fiercer combat when the Ottawa chief Pontiac attacked Detroit and other western outposts the French had just surrendered to the English. "Pontiac's Rebellion" prompted George III to create a buffer zone between Indians and British colonists. On October 7, 1763, he issued the **Proclamation of 1763,** which drew a line marking the legal western limit of white settlement. The proclamation greatly pleased Pontiac, who made peace with the Crown.

The Proclamation of 1763 pacified the Indians and therefore pleased some colonists, especially those in the well-established Tidewater (coastal)

region, but it outraged the frontier settlers, who wanted no limit on western settlement and freely violated the Proclamation Line, provoking the Indians to resume warfare. The terrorized settlers demanded military aid from colonial authorities, who, ensconced on the coast, were virtually as remote as King George himself. When their demands did not produce results, the settlers appealed to England. Little was sent to aid those who had broken the king's word.

Although the Proclamation of 1763 alienated the colonists on the frontier from the government across the Atlantic, it more immediately and significantly created conflict between colonists in the Piedmont (the interior) and the Tidewater (the coast). Frontier settlers felt betrayed by what today might be called the Eastern Establishment. That "establishment," in turn, resented both the danger in which the Proclamation Line violators had placed the colonies and, increasingly, the ineffectual and apparently indifferent response of king and mother country. Over time, prevailing attitudes in the coastal region became more complex. In 1763 the decision whether to look eastward to England or westward to the frontier was an easy one for most residents of the established East. Britain was mighty, whereas the frontier was weak. But as more and more settlers crossed the Proclamation Line, the West became more influential. Colonial governors generally declined to enforce the Proclamation Line, and, over time, some actively encouraged settlement beyond it.

It would be a mistake to conclude that the American Revolution was born in the conflict created by the Proclamation of 1763, but the proclamation did plant the enmities and alliances that would come to fruition in that rebellion. The proclamation introduced divisions between those who would become rebels and those who would become Loyalists. While different groups, regions, and individuals responded in different ways, the proclamation had one nearly universal effect: an increasingly profound sentiment of unease.

Proclamation of 1763

And whereas it is just and reasonable, and essential to our Interest, and the Security of our Colonies, that the several Nations or Tribes of Indians with whom We are connected, and who live under our Protection, should not be molested or disturbed in the Possession of such Parts of Our Dominions and Territories as, not having been ceded to or purchased by Us, are reserved to them, or any of them, as their Hunting Grounds . . .

And We do hereby strictly forbid, on Pain of our Displeasure, all our loving Subjects from making any Purchases or Settlements whatever, or taking Possession of any of the Lands above reserved, without our especial leave and Licence for that Purpose first obtained.

And We do further strictly enjoin and require all Persons whatever who have either wilfully or inadvertently seated themselves upon any Lands within the Countries above described. or upon any other Lands which, not having been ceded to or purchased by Us, are still reserved to the said Indians as aforesaid, forthwith to remove themselves from such Settlements.

Excerpted from the Avalon Project at Yale Law School, "The Royal Proclamation, October 7, 1763," www.yale.edu/lawweb/avalon/proc1763.htm.

Parliamentary Acts and Actions under Lord Grenville

During the premiership of Lord Grenville (1762–1765), a series of colonial taxation acts were passed. The substantial import and export duties created discontent among the colonists, who had been suffering through a recession in the wake of the French and Indian War, but it was less the taxation that stung than the idea of being taxed without parliamentary representation. This concept became a central cause of the American Revolution. No one on either side of the Atlantic disputed that representation was a basic English right, guaranteed in the Magna Carta of 1215. Even conservative British officials conceded that the king had no right to tax the colonies or anyone else: Parliament alone had the authority to levy taxes. The colonists, as well as Whigs within the British government, argued that the inhabitants of the colonies were not represented in Parliament, whose authority to levy taxes flowed directly from its function as a representative body. It therefore had no authority to tax those whom it did not represent. The Tories and the king countered that Parliament did not, in fact, represent *anyone.* Rather, it represented *estates,* socially and economically defined groups, such as physicians, lawyers, merchants, the landed gentry, and so on. In this sense, then, the colonists were given as much representation as anyone in Britain, inasmuch as the interests of a Philadelphia merchant were no different from those of a London merchant. This sweeping assumption, however, failed to convince a growing majority of colonists, including Boston attorney James Otis. In a speech on February 24, 1761, Otis declared, "Taxation without representation is tyranny," which became one of the great popular slogans that drove the colonies to revolt.

In addition to the long-dormant Navigation Acts of 1645, 1649, and 1651 and the additional Navigation Acts passed between 1660 and 1696, all of which had become subject to enforcement, Parliament revived and began to enforce the Acts of Trade. These included the following acts:

- The Wool Act (1699), which protected the British domestic wool trade by prohibiting the export of wool products from the colonies
- The Naval Stores Acts (1709–1774), which restricted colonial harvesting of raw materials needed by the Royal Navy and the British merchant marine, especially timber

- The Hat Act (1732), which protected the British millinery trade by barring the export of hats from one colony to another
- The Molasses Act (1733), which levied exorbitant duties on sugar and molasses imported into the colonies from French and Dutch islands
- The Iron Acts (1750 and 1757), which restricted the development of the colonial iron industry and fixed Britain as the sole market for colonial iron exports

Lord Grenville further aggravated the situation by also creating a new tax: the American Revenue Act, often called the Sugar Act of 1764, which increased duties on foreign refined sugar and other products imported from countries other than Britain. Administratively, Grenville revitalized the colonial customs system, creating through the Currency Act a new vice admiralty court, whose authority trumped that of local officials. Henceforth, officers of the Crown, not locally appointed or elected officials, would have jurisdiction over matters of taxation and customs. As many colonists saw it, this added the element of outright tyranny to the injustice of taxation without representation.

The Grenville Acts occasioned the first serious, organized, and effective colonial protest against Britain's taxation policy. On May 24, 1764, a Boston town meeting proposed that the colonies unite in a nonimportation agreement by unanimously pledging to boycott a wide variety of English goods. By the end of the year, a number of colonies had joined the boycott. This was significant because, by their nature, the British North American colonies were competitive rather than cooperative. It was in opposition to external force, not of their own internal volition, that they first united. Failing to comprehend this, Grenville next ushered through Parliament the Stamp Act, which was put into force on March 22, 1765.

The Stamp Act taxed all kinds of printed matter, including newspapers, legal documents, and even dice and playing cards. On all such items a government tax stamp was to be affixed. The colonists were infuriated by the Stamp Act, which they regarded as even more egregious than the other taxes. The revenues it generated were earmarked to defray the cost of maintaining British soldiers in the colonies. Colonists had grown to resent the presence of British troops among them, and being required to pay for what many regarded as an occupying army made the Stamp Act all the more galling. As if the situation were not inflammatory enough, the act contained an enforcement clause stipulating that any infringement of the new tax was to be tried in the hated vice admiralty court rather than by local magistrates.

During the Stamp Act crisis of 1765, a colonial newspaper expressed its displeasure with the hated British tax stamps by suggesting they take the form of a skull and crossbones.

Not surprisingly, response to the Stamp Act was swift. In England, Isaac Barré was among a handful of members of Parliament who opposed passage of the Stamp Act, and in a speech he referred to the colonists as "these sons of liberty." The phrase appealed to Samuel Adams, a failed Boston businessperson and brilliant political agitator, who organized one of the first of many secret societies that sprang up in direct response to the Stamp Act. Adams's group, like others that followed, called itself the Sons of Liberty. Members pressured and intimidated the stamp agents and were so successful that every agent they approached resigned. Perhaps more important, the various Sons of Liberty cells communicated with one another and coordinated action. They became a network linking the colonies together.

In Virginia, the passage of the Stamp Act moved Patrick Henry, a lawyer and member of the House of Burgesses, to introduce the seven **Virginia Resolves of 1765,** the seventh of which boldly asserted that Virginia enjoyed, by right, complete legislative autonomy. (This was a vivid precursor of the Declaration of Independence, a document that would not appear for another decade.) Henry pushed his Virginia Resolves through the House of Burgesses with a speech that rang with provocation: "Caesar had his Brutus—Charles the first, his Cromwell—and George the third—may profit by their example. . . . If *this* be treason, make the most of it." The resolves were enacted on May 30, 1765.

Even as the Stamp Act protest gathered momentum, Parliament passed the Mutiny Act of 1765, which included a provision for quartering troops in private houses. At first, outraged colonists took a legalistic approach, pointing out that such quartering did not specifically apply to Britain's overseas possessions. Parliament responded with the Quartering Act of 1765, which eliminated the provision requiring private homeowners to billet soldiers and instead required colonial authorities to furnish, at public expense, barracks and supplies for British troops. The next year, the Quartering Act was extended to require the billeting of soldiers in taverns and inns, again at the expense of the colonists. Colonial legislatures responded by declining to vote funds for the support of troops.

The Stamp Act Congress and Its Effects

Each new protest brought the colonies closer to union. A "Stamp Act Congress" met October 7–25, 1765, in New York City, drawing delegates from

Virginia Resolves of 1765

Resolved, that the first adventurers and settlers of this His Majesty's colony and dominion of Virginia brought with them and transmitted to their posterity, and all others His Majesty's subjects since inhabiting in this His Majesty's colony, all the liberties, privileges, franchises, and immunities that have at any time been held, enjoyed, and possessed by the people of Great Britain.

Resolved, that by two royal charters, granted by King James I, the colonists aforesaid are declared entitled to all liberties, privileges, and immunities of denizens and natural subjects to all intents and purposes as if they had been abiding and born within the Realm of England.

Resolved, that the taxation of the people by themselves, or by persons chosen by themselves to represent them, who can only know what taxes the people are able to bear, or the easiest method of raising them, and must themselves be affected by every tax laid on the people, is the only security against a burdensome taxation, and the distinguishing characteristic of British freedom, without which the ancient constitution cannot exist.

Resolved, that His Majesty's liege people of this his most ancient and loyal colony have without interruption enjoyed the inestimable right of being governed by such laws, respecting their internal policy and taxation, as are derived from their own consent, with the approbation of their sovereign, or his substitute; and that the same has never been forfeited or yielded up, but has been constantly recognized by the kings and people of Great Britain.

Excerpted from the Colonial Williamsburg Foundation, "Virginia Resolves on the Stamp Act, 1765," www.history.org/History/teaching/tchcrvar.cfm.

Resolutions of the Continental Congress, 1765

That it is inseparably essential to the freedom of a people, and the undoubted right of Englishmen, that no taxes be imposed on them, but with their own consent, given personally, or by their representatives.

That the people of these colonies are not, and from their local circumstances cannot be, represented in the House of Commons in Great-Britain.

That the only representatives of the people of these colonies, are persons chosen therein by themselves, and that no taxes ever have been, or can be constitutionally imposed on them, but by their respective legislatures.

That . . . it is unreasonable and inconsistent with the principles and spirit of the British Constitution, for the people of Great-Britain to grant to His Majesty the property of the colonists.

That trial by jury is the inherent and invaluable right of every British subject in these colonies.

That the [Stamp Act] . . . and several other Acts, by extending the jurisdiction of the courts of Admiralty beyond its ancient limits, have a manifest tendency to subvert the rights and liberties of the colonists.

That the duties imposed by several late Acts of Parliament, from the peculiar circumstances of these colonies, will be extremely burthensome and grievous. . .

That as the profits of the trade of these colonies ultimately center in Great-Britain, to pay for the manufactures which they are obliged to take from thence, they eventually contribute very largely to all supplies granted there to the Crown.

That the restrictions imposed . . . on the trade of these colonies, will render them unable to purchase the manufactures of Great-Britain.

That the increase, prosperity, and happiness of these colonies, depend on the full and free enjoyment of their rights and liberties. . . .

That it is the right of the British subjects in these colonies, to petition the King, Or either House of Parliament.

Lastly, That it is the indispensable duty of these colonies . . . to procure the repeal of the Act for granting and applying certain stamp duties.

Excerpted from the Avalon Project at Yale Law School, "Resolutions of the Continental Congress," www.yale.edu/lawweb/avalon/resolu65.htm.

South Carolina, Rhode Island, Connecticut, Pennsylvania, Maryland, New Jersey, Delaware, and New York. (Virginia, New Hampshire, North Carolina, and Georgia declined to participate.) The Congress produced the fourteen-point **Resolutions of the Continental Congress,** which was almost certainly drafted by John Dickinson, a political leader and theorist from Pennsylvania. The document asserted that Parliament had no authority to tax the colonies and that the Crown's vice admiralty courts had no jurisdiction in the colonies. Boldly, the delegates sent the declaration to King George III and to Parliament.

In many quarters, the declaration was received sympathetically. Whigs in Parliament moved to repeal the Stamp Act even before it was scheduled to go into effect. Even Tory members were being pressured by the merchants among their constituencies to repeal the act. Their trade with the colonies, these merchants complained, had plummeted by 25 percent because of the nonimportation boycott begun in 1764 and expanded by the Stamp Act Congress in 1765. In any case, most colonial governments simply refused to enforce the Stamp Act. Only Georgia actually put the law into effect, to a severely limited degree. Frustrated, Grenville refused compromise and instead recommended deploying troops to enforce the Stamp Act. Benjamin Franklin took issue with this. The Boston-born printer and entrepreneur, who had served as a member of the Pennsylvania Assembly, was now a London-based mercantile agent for Pennsylvania. He argued that the colonies should not be obliged to pay the Stamp Tax and, indeed, could not afford to pay it. Moreover, he warned, military intervention would likely provoke outright rebellion.

Partly in response to the persuasive Franklin and partly because of William Pitt the Elder and his faction, Parliament countered Grenville and, on March 18, 1766, repealed the Stamp Act. The enthusiasm of the colonies was muted by a new piece of legislation enacted on the very day of the repeal. The Declaratory Act asserted Parliament's authority to make laws binding on the American colonies "in all cases whatsoever." With one hand, Parliament had acknowledged colonial rights while, with the other hand, it had simultaneously denied them.

The Townshend Acts

In August 1766 Charles Townshend rose to the post of chancellor of the exchequer under Prime Minister William Pitt the Elder. Pitt suffered a mental breakdown soon thereafter, leaving the opportunistic Townshend in control of the cabinet. He ushered through Parliament a series of acts historians generally name for him. These 1767 Townshend Acts included the Townshend Revenue Act, which established a new system of customs commissioners, and an act that suspended the New York Assembly.

The Townshend Revenue Act imposed duties on lead, glass, paint, tea, and paper imported into the colonies, specifying that revenues generated would be used to pay for military expenses in the colonies and the salaries of royal colonial officials. The latter provision was significant in that it took away from colonial legislatures the power of the purse, at least as far as royal colonial officials were concerned. These administrators became answerable only to the Crown. Worse, royal customs commissioners were now free to engage in a form of racketeering in which they would, for a period, purposely refrain from enforcing the complex technicalities governing the duties, and then, without warning, suddenly crack down, seize all merchant vessels that were not in compliance with the hitherto unenforced regulations, and assess huge duties and fines. By law, of all

funds collected, a third went to the royal treasury, a third to the royal governor of the colony, and a third to the customs commissioner himself. If the merchant did not or could not pay, his ship and its cargo were sold at auction.

This tyranny was compounded by the act put into effect on June 15, 1767, suspending the New York colonial assembly because it had refused to authorize funds mandated by the Quartering Act. By law, the assembly would remain suspended until it complied with the act.

The Massachusetts General Court (the colony's legislature) voted to oppose the Townshend Acts as well as to inform the other colonies of what it was doing in the stated hope that other colonies would follow suit. The **Massachusetts Circular Letter,** drafted by James Otis and Samuel Adams, was approved by the General Court on February 11, 1768. It published to the other twelve colonies three revolutionary propositions: first, that the Townshend Acts were "taxation without representation"; second, that governors and judges must not be independent of colonial legislatures; and third, that Americans could never be represented in Parliament.

The idea that Americans could never be adequately represented in Parliament signaled a leap from the former colonial position that taxation without representation constituted tyranny to the position that such taxation constituted a tyranny that could not be remedied simply by providing representation. Parliamentary representation proportionate to colonial population was a practical impossibility—the people of Britain would never stand for it. This proposition left little or no alternative to independence. With that issue on the table, the Circular Letter concluded with a call for proposals of plans for concerted, coordinated resistance. This moved the royal governor of Massachusetts to dissolve the Massachusetts General Court on the grounds of sedition, but the action came too late. Already, New Hampshire, New Jersey, Connecticut, and Virginia had announced their endorsement of the Circular Letter, and the Massachusetts House of Representatives voted overwhelmingly against rescinding it.

Massachusetts Circular Letter, 1768

The House of Representatives of this province have taken into their serious consideration the great difficulties that must accrue to themselves and their constituents by the operation of several Acts of Parliament, imposing duties and taxes on the American colonies. . . .

The House have humbly represented to the ministry their own sentiments, that his Majesty's high court of Parliament is the supreme legislative power over the whole empire; that in all free states the constitution is fixed, and as the supreme legislative derives its power and authority from the constitution, it cannot overleap the bounds of it without destroying its own foundation; that the constitution ascertains and limits both sovereignty and allegiance, and, therefore, his Majesty's American subjects, who acknowledge themselves bound by the ties of allegiance, have an equitable claim to the full enjoyment of the fundamental rules of the British constitution; that it is an essential, unalterable right in nature, engrafted into the British constitution, as a fundamental law, and ever held sacred and irrevocable by the subjects within the realm, that what a man has

honestly acquired is absolutely his own, which he may freely give, but cannot be taken from him without his consent; that the American subjects may, therefore, exclusive of any consideration of charter rights, with a decent firmness, adapted to the character of free men and subjects, assert this natural and constitutional right.

It is, moreover, their humble opinion, which they express with the greatest deference to the wisdom of the Parliament, that the Acts made there, imposing duties on the people of this province, with the sole and express purpose of raising a revenue, are infringements of their natural and constitutional rights; because, as they are not represented in the British Parliament, his Majesty's commons in Britain, by those Acts, grant their property without their consent.

Excerpted from the Avalon Project at Yale Law School, "Massachusetts Circular Letter to the Colonial Legislatures," www.cis.yale.edu/lawweb/avalon/amerrev/amerdocs/mass_circ_let_1768.htm.

Meanwhile, another set of "letters" achieved an even broader readership and made the case of the colonies on a more personal and passionate level and with a significant degree of literary skill. John Dickinson's persuasively reasoned *Letters from a Farmer in Pennsylvania to Inhabitants of the British Colonies* appeared serially during 1767–1768 in the *Pennsylvania Chronicle* and were also widely republished throughout the colonies and in Britain. Dickinson held that Parliament had no authority to tax the colonies solely for revenue—although he conceded that it did have the authority to regulate trade—and he attacked the suspension of the New York Assembly as a grave blow to colonial liberty. He did not so much assert that taxation without representation was morally wrong, as that it was against British law, violating both the rights of colonists and those of all British subjects. This argument advanced colonial

unity and gave British liberals a solid platform on which to build their support for the colonial position.

"Champagne Charlie," as Townshend's parliamentary colleagues called him, did not live to witness all of these effects of his Revenue Act. He contracted typhus, a common scourge of the era, and died the very year the legislation was enacted. Nor did he live to see all of his duties repealed on April 12, 1770, save one: the tax on tea.

Urban Radicals: An "Affair," a "Battle," and a "Massacre"

The repeal of all but one of the Townshend duties had an immediate effect. For a second time, the colonies ended their boycott of English goods. Nevertheless, hard feelings lingered, and for a significant minority of radicals the desire for a break with

England persisted. These radicals were not pleased with the apparent rapprochement brought about by Parliament's repeal.

Just who were the radicals? Three notable incidents from the urban North demonstrate that although many individuals carried the torch of pre-revolutionary radicalism, they had little else in common.

The "Affair"

John Hancock was a prosperous Boston merchant who had inherited his business from an uncle in 1764. As a merchant, Hancock's contact with the royal government was chiefly through its customs officials. What he perceived as their heedless arrogance edged him into radicalism. At first, his acts were hardly revolutionary, but they were subversive. Hancock delighted in annoying, frustrating, and embarrassing royal customs officials. Yet he never broke the law and was always prompt in his payment of taxes and duties. The frustrated customs collectors started looking for something with which to prosecute Hancock. While Hancock's provocatively named sloop *Liberty* was unloading in Boston Harbor, a pair of Crown officers ventured belowdecks, even though the applicable law clearly stipulated that they were not permitted to do so without permission. Hancock withheld his permission and either ordered his crew to eject the officers or, according to Hancock biographer H. L. Allen, sent one official home (apparently drunk) and lodged the other in a cabin with the door nailed shut until the ship had been unloaded. In either case, Hancock's actions prompted the office of the customs collector to complain to the attorney general of the colony, who ruled that Hancock had been within his rights.

In the developing feud, the ante had been raised, and word of the incident spread throughout Boston. In this charged climate, on May 9, 1768, the *Liberty* sailed into Boston with twenty-five pipes (about 3,150 gallons) of Madeira wine. Hancock paid the required duty, unloaded the wine, and took on a new cargo of tar and whale oil. The law specified that a ship's owner had to post bond for a new cargo *before* loading it. In practice, however, customs commissioners always delayed the bond until the ship had cleared port. For Hancock, following that practice rather than the letter of the law was a rare slip. Joseph Harrison, chief collector of customs, pounced on the opportunity, announcing his suspicion that the declared cargo was far below the ship's capacity. Harrison believed he was within his authority to seize the *Liberty*, but, correctly fearing that this might touch off a popular protest, he delayed.

In the meantime, two British warships, the *Romney* and the *St. Lawrence,* entered Boston Harbor. Impressment—the seizure of men for involuntary service aboard His Majesty's ships—had been illegal in American waters for more than a century. Nevertheless, the *Romney*'s captain sent a press gang ashore, where it entered a wharfside tavern and laid hands on an American sailor named Furlong. A crowd responded by stoning the press gang, rushing the sailors, and rescuing Furlong. Duly chastened, the gang returned to the *Romney* empty-handed. In response, the captain beat to quarters (to signal the crew to prepare the ship for battle) and trained his guns on the mob. He held his fire, however, and a standoff developed.

Incredibly, at that very moment customs collector Harrison made the decision to seize Hancock's *Liberty*. Worse, he employed a contingent of armed sailors from the *Romney* to assist him. Furlong's assembled defenders witnessed the seizure of the *Liberty,* which was towed alongside the British warship, under its looming guns. The mob turned its frustrated anger against Harrison, his son, and Benjamin Hallowell, another customs official. The three were savagely beaten; the senior Harrison managed to get away, but his son was dragged by his hair through the streets, and Hallowell was left unconscious in a pool of his own blood. The mob then attacked and broke all the windows of the nearby homes of Harrison, Hallowell, and John Williams, inspector general of customs. Seeing this, other customs workers and officials sought refuge first aboard the *Romney* and then in the royal fortress known as

Castle William (the main fortifications defending Boston from attack).

Samuel Adams and James Otis urgently requested that the governor order the warship out of the harbor in order to prevent the outbreak of a larger riot. Governor Francis Bernard, who served at the pleasure of the Crown, halted the impressment and prevailed upon the customs officials not only to release the *Liberty,* but also to return Hancock's and other merchants' duties. This was sufficient to quell the passion of the mob. Having been thrust center stage in a drama of colonial liberty, however, John Hancock did not allow the case to be dropped. He insisted that the *Liberty* affair run its course through the public courts. Having shown little sense so far, Crown officials prudently responded by withdrawing all claims on March 1, 1769. There would be no day in court.

"The Bostonian's Paying the Excise Man, or Tarring and Feathering." This 1774 British illustration shows the anger, sometimes resulting in violence, that was directed toward the Crown's tax collectors. Tea is dumped into the harbor from the ship in the background.

Townshend's unwise and insensitive taxation policy had failed to subjugate the colonies, but it had succeeded in uniting them, despite their natural economic competitiveness. On the more immediate and local scale of the *Liberty* affair, the actions of Crown officials had created common cause between two poles of colonial society: the prosperous merchants, represented by John Hancock, and the dockside working class. The incident demonstrated the extent of colonial discontent, especially in and around Boston.

The "Battle"

During the 1760s and into the 1770s, New England was a hotbed of revolutionary sentiment. The case was generally different in the Middle Atlantic region, especially New York, where loyalist feelings were far more pervasive. Even there, however, public toleration of perceived tyranny had its limit. In 1766 the New York Assembly was dissolved because it refused to appropriate funds required by the Quartering Act. After the assembly repeatedly declined to support the Quartering Act, the Crown ordered its suspension on October 1, 1767. A new assembly was duly elected, but it also refused to uphold the Quartering Act. Finally, in January 1769, a third assembly yielded to the king's demands, voting £2,000 for the quartering of royal troops.

If the majority of vocal New Englanders were willing to break with Parliament and the king, New Yorkers were polarized: there were those who held their allegiance to the Crown paramount and those who demanded greater liberty for the colonies. Alexander McDougall, a prosperous New York City merchant and leader of the New York chapter of the Sons of Liberty, published on December 16, 1769, a provocative broadside entitled "To the Betrayed Inhabitants of the City and Colony of New York." McDougall's broadside galvanized New York's "Patriot" faction, even as it moved Governor Cadwallader Colden to publish a proclamation denouncing the broadside as "seditious and libelous" and offering a reward of £100 for the arrest of the author and publisher of the offending document.

In the meantime, clashes between citizens and soldiers became frequent. Shortly after the New Year, New York Patriots erected a liberty pole, the symbol of defiance and rebellion, at Golden Hill (in lower Manhattan, approximately at the present-day intersection of John and William streets). On January 13, 1770, British soldiers unsuccessfully attempted to tear it down. They returned on January 17 and managed to remove the offending symbol. Within two days, the Sons of Liberty responded by distributing new broadsides that provoked a riot at the site of the liberty pole on January 19. Between thirty and forty redcoats with bayonets fixed on their muskets were sent to disperse the rioters, who had armed themselves with swords and clubs. In the ensuing clash, people were seriously wounded on both sides, but there were no fatalities.

McDougall was arrested on February 8 on the charge of having written the first provocative broadside. By then, however, Governor Colden had no desire to inflame an already explosive situation, and he offered McDougall the opportunity to post bond. Realizing that his imprisonment made a powerful political statement, McDougall declined and insolently advertised himself as "at home" and invited his many friends to call upon him in jail. (The invitation brought so many callers that they were obliged to make appointments to see him.) On April 29, McDougall was arraigned, entered a plea of not guilty, and was at last released on bail. The state's principal witness died before to the trial began, but McDougall was nevertheless haled before the royal magistrate on December 13 and imprisoned for contempt until April 27, 1771. The "Battle" of Golden Hill was a symptom of colonial discontent.

The "Massacre"

In Boston, the *Liberty* affair had lingering effects. Although Boston customs officials declined to prosecute Hancock, they reported the colony of Massachusetts to be in a state of insurrection. The Crown responded by sending two regiments of British infantry to Boston in October 1768.

Commonly, soldiers, who were miserably paid, sought outside work to fill their off-duty hours; local merchants and tradesmen were generally eager to make use of this cheap, temporary labor. But in 1770 Boston was suffering through the lingering depression that had followed the French and Indian War, and the hard times were compounded by Britain's restrictive trade policies. Employment was scarce. On March 5, 1770, when an off-duty soldier was discovered seeking work at Grey's ropewalk—a wharfside establishment that made ships ropes—a small riot broke out. By about 9:00 p.m., some sixty rioters had gathered before the Customs House, and they began to taunt sentry Hugh White. One young man in the crowd, Edward Garrick, teased White with the news that his company commander was a thief who had not paid Garrick's master for a wig. Incensed, White called on the accuser to step forward. When Garrick did, White struck him in the face with the butt of his musket, and another soldier chased Garrick away at the point of a bayonet.

If this display had been intended to intimidate the crowd, it had the opposite effect. More Bostonians gathered and began to pelt White and other soldiers with icy snowballs. Eventually the soldiers' commanding officers appeared, pleading with the crowd to be calm while they attempted to get control of their men. When the officers were unable to defuse the situation, Captain Thomas Preston arrived with seven soldiers to extricate White from the scene. Henry Knox, proprietor of the London Book-Store (who would later serve as the Continental army general in charge of artillery during the Revolution), intercepted Preston, admonishing him, "For God's sake, take care of your men. If they fire, they die!" Preston replied calmly, "I am sensible of it." He ordered White to fall in with the detail of the seven men he led. White tried to obey, but the mob surged forward to block him. Unable to penetrate the crowd with his troops, Preston ordered his men to form a defensive line where they stood. The mob hurled ice balls at the soldiers and dared them to open fire.

Preston summoned Justice of the Peace James Murray, who read out the Riot Act and received a

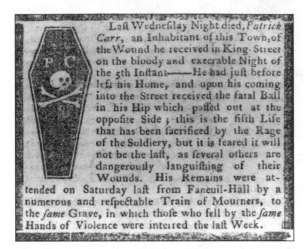

Last Wednesday Night died, *Patrick Carr*, an Inhabitant of this Town, of the Wound he received in King-Street on the bloody and execrable Night of the 5th Instant——He had just before left his Home, and upon his coming into the Street received the fatal Ball in his Hip which passed out at the opposite Side ; this is the fifth Life that has been sacrificed by the Rage of the Soldiery, but it is feared it will not be the last, as several others are dangerously languishing of their Wounds. His Remains were attended on Saturday last from Faneuil-Hall by a numerous and respectable Train of Mourners, to the *same* Grave, in which those who fell by the *same* Hands of Violence were interred the last Week.

This March 1770 newspaper announcement engraved by Paul Revere chronicles the death of Patrick Carr, who was wounded in the Boston Massacre.

pelting of ice balls in reply. Suddenly, a club sailed from out of the crowd and struck Private Hugh Montgomery, knocking him off his feet. Rising, he cocked his musket and fired. The shot hit no one, but a merchant named Richard Palmes responded by striking out at Montgomery with the club he was carrying. Montgomery lunged back with his bayonet, and Palmes fled. Then Private Matthew Killroy leveled his musket at Edward Langford and Samuel Gray. Gray taunted him, Killroy fired, and Gray was mortally wounded.

At this point, another musket shot was heard. Apparently, it was a double load, for Crispus Attucks, a 40-year-old black man from Framingham and presumably a runaway slave, took two rounds in the chest and died where he stood—the first man killed outright in the Boston Massacre, the prelude to a war for liberty. Within moments, more shots were fired, and two more citizens were killed. Another fell with a wound that proved mortal. (Their bodies were carried to Faneuil Hall, where they were accorded the dignity of martyrdom. They lay in state until March 8, when all five victims of the Boston Massacre were consigned to a common grave, despite laws prohibiting the burial of blacks with whites.)

After these volleys, all was silent except for the sounds of reloading. As the crowd again pressed forward, the soldiers leveled their reloaded weapons. Preston, however, strode along the line, knocking each musket barrel skyward and ordering his men not to fire.

Unlike in previous incidents between the Crown and one of its colonies, the participants in the "Boston Massacre" would be tried in a *colonial* court. Preston and six of his men were indicted on charges of murder, and the most prominent member of Boston's Sons of Liberty, Samuel Adams, and the charismatic physician Dr. Joseph Warren mounted a publicity campaign to rouse and maintain Boston's outrage. Fortunately for the redcoats and even more fortunately for the nascent cause of liberty, farther-seeing men stepped to the fore. John Adams and Josiah Quincy, prominent attorneys who were involved in the colonial rights movement, volunteered to defend the accused. A colony protesting tyranny, John Adams believed, must not yield to motives of vengeance and the rule of the mob: "Counsel ought to be the very last thing an accused person should want [lack] in a free country," he remarked. He and Quincy argued that the men, threatened by a mob, had acted in self-defense. The Boston jury acquitted Preston and four of his men. Two others were found guilty, not of murder, but of manslaughter. Both were discharged from military service with a brand on the thumb.

On March 5, 1770, about 400 Bostonians had confronted the British soldiers and suffered five casualties. Samuel Adams and Warren dubbed this a "massacre" and did their best to transform the riot into a cause for revolution. (A minority of historians even argue that Samuel Adams deliberately orchestrated the "Boston Massacre.") Adams and Warren commissioned Paul Revere, a prosperous young Boston silversmith, to create an engraving of the incident. The final engraving was a work of fiction, depicting Preston, his sword upraised, ordering his men to fire on the helpless citizens of Boston. Hundreds of copies were printed and distributed throughout the colonies. Yet despite such efforts, the Boston Massacre failed to become an immediate cause for rebellion. After the soldiers' trial, most people on both sides were mollified by a sense that justice had been served. Moreover, the repeal of the Townshend Acts in April 1770 salved both new wounds and old. Revolution would have to wait.

Backcountry Radicals: The Regulator Movement

During the eighteenth century, people on the frontier tended to be conservative, and many of them felt isolated from the East Coast urban centers, which were their link to Britain. Radicals, insofar as they espoused cutting-edge philosophies, were usually urbanites, in touch with books and lively conversation. However, while the ideas that defined and guided the revolution were formulated, expounded, and published in colonial cities and towns, much of the outrage that fueled rebellion exploded on the frontier. When the king refused to assist those colonists who had violated the Proclamation Line of 1763, frontier people began to perceive that they derived no benefit from the law, so they took the law into their own hands.

About 1768 North Carolinian Herman Husbands organized a band of "Regulators," a group that combined the functions of vigilante and revolutionary protest. They began by protesting a lack of representation in the provincial assembly, as well as what they identified as the misappropriation and outright embezzlement of public funds by officials of the Crown. When their protests were ignored, they acted. On April 8, 1768, seventy Regulators rode into the settlement of Hillsboro, North Carolina, and freed a horse that had been seized from a local man for nonpayment of taxes. By way of signature for this act, they shot up the house of Edmund Fanning, a Crown official.

Fanning petitioned Governor William Tryon for permission to arrest Husbands and another Regulator leader, William Butler. After Fanning had locked the men up, some 700 Regulators marched toward the local jail, and Fanning quite prudently released his prisoners.

In September 1768 Tryon led 1,400 troops against 3,700 Regulators. Despite their superior numbers, the Regulators saw that Tryon's men outgunned them, and they retreated. The movement did not die, however. Early in 1771 a band of Regulators seized and horsewhipped Fanning, ran him out of Hillsboro, and then burned down his house. This provoked the North Carolina Assembly to pass the so-called Bloody Act, which proclaimed the Regulators guilty of treason and made them liable to execution. That spring, acting under authority of the act, Tryon personally led a force to round up the Regulators. On May 14, 1771, he reached the Alamance River, about five miles from a camp of 2,000 Regulators. Tryon had half that number, but he was aware that the Regulators had no real military leader and no artillery. For that matter, many were completely unarmed. On May 16, 1771, therefore, he deployed his men in two lines outside the encampment and demanded that the Regulators surrender. This provoked a debate among the Regulators, who nevertheless assumed defensive positions. After exchanging gunfire for about an hour, the Regulators withdrew; nine men were killed on each side (some records report twenty dead Regulators) and many more were wounded. Tryon advanced and apprehended a number of those identified as prominent in the movement. James Few was executed on May 17, and a dozen other principals were taken back to Hillsboro, tried, and convicted of treason. Six were hanged on June 19; the other six, together with 6,500 settlers in the area, were compelled to swear their allegiance to the Crown.

Following the Battle of Alamance, many of the Regulators migrated west of the Alleghenies. Tryon moved on to new responsibilities. The new royal governor, Josiah Martin, adopted a much more lenient attitude toward the Regulators who remained. In this way, he hoped to secure their loyalty to the Crown. Although the Regulators did not lead another major uprising in North Carolina, their loyalty was another matter. (Most would fight on the side of the Patriots during the Revolution; see Chapter 2 for a discussion of Regulators in Massachusetts after the war.)

The Regulator movement was a preview of things to come. Once the Revolution broke out, most of the fighting took place in the frontier wilderness between irregularly constituted forces like those led by Husbands and typically involved Indians allied with one side or the other.

The *Gaspée* Affair and the Boston Tea Party

In some places, until the repeal of the Stamp Act, the Sons of Liberty had become a kind of shadow government. The Boston Massacre threatened to return them to power, but the furor soon subsided. It was followed, however, by the *Gaspée* affair, which took place in Rhode Island.

The convoluted shoreline of Narragansett Bay, off Rhode Island, was a natural haven for smugglers. In contrast to merchants like Hancock, who protested Crown duties and taxes, these individuals simply evaded them. In June 1772 the Royal Navy dispatched the schooner *Gaspée,* Lieutenant William Dudingston commanding, to police the bay. Dudingston went about his duties with an arrogance that added the insult of insolence to the injury of loss of revenue from smuggled goods. When Rhode Island governor Joseph Wanton, a Patriot, threatened to arrest Dudingston, the Fleet Admiral issued a warning to the colonial official. A heated exchange of letters took place, even as Dudingston and the *Gaspée* continued to raid smugglers. On June 9, Dudingston pursued one smuggler, only to run aground on a sandbar near Providence. In response, Sheriff Abraham Whipple, also a Patriot, assembled a flotilla of small boats and personally led them out to surround the *Gaspée* during the night. He demanded Dudingston's surrender, was refused, and then, with his men, forcibly boarded the *Gaspée.* Dudingston drew his sword on one of the boarders, who reacted by shooting him in the groin. A surgeon stanched the wound, whereupon Dudingston and the rest of his crew were loaded into boats and Whipple and his party set the *Gaspée* aflame.

News of the *Gaspée* affair shot through the colonies: local officials had captured and destroyed a

hated instrument of enforcement of a hated tax. The Crown threatened to try Whipple and the other perpetrators on charges of piracy. With the fires of rebellion reignited, Samuel Adams hastily organized the first Committee of Correspondence, the function of which was to disseminate information and coordinate action among the colonies. The organization was actually a fully revived Sons of Liberty, and it was often called by that name. Recognizing that sentiments were again running high, the king declined to prosecute. Samuel Adams and his circle, however, made sure that the dropping of the case did not calm colonial passions.

By 1773 most of Britain's taxes on import commodities had been repealed—save the tax on tea, which King George III insisted on retaining because he believed that "there must always be one tax" in order to preserve Parliament's right to tax the colonies. In truth, the tax was not terribly burdensome on the colonists because it was easily evaded. Colonial consumers loved their tea, but they did not feel compelled to buy it from English sources. Instead, they purchased smuggled tea from Dutch traders. The result was that the tea tax was harder on the financially ailing East India Company than on the colonials. The cartel of British merchants and shippers needed to pack off to America some of the 17 million pounds of India tea lying in its London warehouses before the whole lot went rotten. Fortunately for the company, its stockholders and ministers had strong ties to the king's prime minister, Lord North, who proposed a program of tax relief: The East India Company actually paid two taxes, one when it landed tea in Britain and tax when it landed a shipment in America. By means of the Tea Act (May 10, 1773), Lord North forgave the first tax and retained only the lesser three-penny-a-pound duty due on landing in America. This priced East India Company tea lower than the smuggled tea.

Lord North reasoned that the colonists would vote with their pocketbooks, but he was mistaken once again. In addition to the tax cut, the Tea Act set up an arrangement whereby East India Company tea would be exclusively consigned to specially designated (and well-connected) brokers in the ports of New

York, Charleston, Philadelphia, and Boston, cutting most American merchants out of the loop. But instead of recapturing the business of American consumers, Lord North's Tea Act drove previously moderate merchants into the camp of the radicals. Under the authority of various local committees of correspondence, colonial activists intimidated into resignation the tea consignees in Philadelphia, New York, and Charleston. Moreover, American captains and harbor pilots refused to handle the East India Company cargo, and tea ships were turned back to London from Philadelphia and New York. One ship was permitted to land in Charleston, South Carolina, but the tea was impounded in a warehouse, where it lay unsold until the revolutionary government auctioned it off in 1776.

In Boston, when three East India Company ships landed in December 1773, Sons of Liberty/Committee of Correspondence members prevented their being unloaded, even as Massachusetts royal governor Thomas Hutchinson refused to issue permits to allow the ships to leave the harbor and return to London. A standoff developed. On December 16, 1773, Samuel Adams and other leaders sent colonial militia captain and tea merchant Francis Rotch to appeal to Hutchinson to grant the permit. While waiting for Rotch to return with the governor's reply, a crowd of about 7,000 people gathered at Boston's Old South Church. Rotch returned at 6:00 p.m. with the governor's adamant response: the ships would *not* be permitted to leave unless the tea was unloaded. At this, Samuel Adams ascended the Old South pulpit, where he declared, "This meeting can do nothing more to save the country."

It was a signal. A loud imitation of a Mohawk war cry was raised outside the church. Three formed troops of fifty colonists each, with their faces painted to simulate Mohawk war markings, left the crowd and raced toward Griffin's Wharf, where they climbed into boats and then rowed out to the three tea ships. Simultaneously, the three troops boarded the tea ships. The Boston Tea Party was under way.

Popular lore portrays the Boston Tea Party as a wild scene of war-whooping ersatz Indians hurling tea chests into the harbor. Actually, the operation was carried out quietly and without interference from the officers and crews of the vessels. Once the cargo had been efficiently jettisoned—342 tea chests valued at £10,000 in colonial currency—the "Indians" quietly climbed back into their boats and rowed ashore.

Most Americans seemed to realize that the Boston Tea Party would have profound consequences. John Adams wrote in his diary that its effects would be "so lasting, that I can't but consider it as an epocha in history." Across the sea in England, liberal voices rose in support of the Americans and called for the repeal of all taxes as well as all the cessation of coercive restraint of trade. The liberal politician and philosopher Edmund Burke urged the House of Commons to "[l]eave the Americans as they anciently stood. . . . Let the memory of all actions in contradiction to that good old mode [of salutary neglect] be extinguished forever. Be content to bind America by laws of trade; you have always done it. . . . Do not burthen them with taxes; you were not used to do so from the beginning." But Burke's and other liberals' voices were drowned out by the conservatives. King George III declared, "We must master them or totally leave them to themselves and treat them as aliens." In effect, it was a declaration of war—for which the stakes were independence.

The Intolerable Acts

The liberal faction in Parliament was significant, but it was in the minority. The government, deeming Massachusetts a hotbed of sedition, passed in 1774 what Parliament called the Coercive Acts and the colonists dubbed the Intolerable Acts. These included the following:

- Closure of the port of Boston
- Abridgment of Massachusetts colonial government, with all members of the bicameral assembly's upper chamber to be royal appointees
- Appointment of most local officials by and at the pleasure of the royal governor

- Restriction of town meetings to one annually
- Abridgment of the jurisdiction and authority of colonial courts, with all capital cases to be tried in England or in another colony
- Extension of the Quartering Act, creating the foundation for the permanent quartering of British troops in Boston

To enforce the Coercive Acts, King George III personally approved the appointment of General Thomas Gage, a veteran of the French and Indian War who had long experience in America, as commander in chief of British forces in America and royal governor of Massachusetts. Gage knew how to deal with rebels; he had participated in the brutal suppression of the Scottish Jacobite Rebellion of 1745–1746. He advised the king that the Americans "will be lions while we are lambs, but if we take the resolute part they will undoubtedly be very meek." Gage arrived back in Boston from England on May 17, 1774. He was greeted by the pealing of church bells, tolling as if for the dead. This continued for weeks, and, in the streets, Bostonians wore black mourning badges. Undeterred, Gage implemented the odious Port Act on June 1, shutting down Boston to overseas traffic as well as seaborne intercolonial shipments. Under this stranglehold, Boston refused to yield. Gage next ordered the removal of the colonial capital from Boston to Salem, at great inconvenience to delegates. Convening in Salem, the General Assembly passed as its first act a resolution changing its name to the Provincial Congress. Gage immediately dispatched a messenger to the "Congress," ordering its dissolution. The delegates responded by barring the doors against the messenger, and while they remained in session, the proscribed Congress voted to convene a *Continental* Congress, with delegates to be drawn from all of the colonies. Once again, coercion spurred solidarity and the creation of a new national identity.

Quebec Act

On May 20, 1774, King George III signed into law the Quebec Act, which extended the Canadian province of Quebec into the Ohio Valley and the Illinois country, the western territory into which many Anglo-American colonists wanted to expand. The Quebec Act, however, decreed that, in this territory, French would be spoken, French-based law would prevail, and the Roman Catholic Church would be officially recognized. Clearly, Parliament and the king were trying to appease the French colonial nationals who still occupied the territories acquired by England as a result of the French and Indian War. But the appeasement of this minority should have been a far lesser priority than avoiding the further provocation of the Anglo-American majority of Britain's North American colonists. Many colonists considered the Quebec Act to be nothing less than the royal abrogation of the Magna Carta. Thus far, the outrages committed against the colonies had been largely economic in basis. The Quebec Act certainly had grave economic implications, but it seemed to many the very essence of tyranny.

Colonial Coalescence

If the Port Act, the most economically destructive of all the Intolerable Acts, had been intended to cut radical Boston off from the rest of America, it had precisely the opposite effect. Most of the other colonies rallied to the support of Boston and Massachusetts generally. In addition, fifty-six delegates from twelve colonies (all except Georgia) answered the call of the Massachusetts Assembly for a Continental Congress, which convened at Carpenter's Hall, Philadelphia, on September 5, 1774.

Once in session, the Continental Congress moved quickly to endorse the **Suffolk Resolves,** a document drafted by Dr. Joseph Warren and adopted by a convention held in Suffolk County, Massachusetts. The Resolves asserted that the Intolerable Acts were unconstitutional and urged Massachusetts to form an independent government and to withhold taxes from the Crown until the acts were repealed. In the meantime, the Suffolk Resolves advised all citizens to arm themselves and to resume a general boycott of English goods.

By a single vote, the Continental Congress defeated "Galloway's Plan of Union," which proposed that the colonies remain loyal to the Crown provided they were granted the semi-independent status of a dominion. Drafted by Joseph Galloway, a Philadelphia lawyer, the plan called for governance of all the colonies by a royally appointed president-general, who would enjoy veto power over acts of a

Suffolk Resolves and Agreement by the Continental Congress, 1774

Whereas the power but not the justice, the vengeance but not the wisdom of Great-Britain, which of old persecuted, scourged, and exiled our fugitive parents from their native shores, now pursues us, their guiltless children, with unrelenting severity. . . . Therefore, we have resolved, and do *resolve*, . . .

3. That the late acts of the British parliament for blocking up the harbour of Boston, for altering the established form of government in this colony, and for screening the most flagitious violators of the laws of the province from a legal trial, are gross infractions of those rights to which we are justly entitled by the laws of nature, the British constitution, and the charter of the province.

4. That no obedience is due from this province to either or any part of the acts above-mentioned, but that they be rejected as the attempts of a wicked administration to enslave America. . . .

10. That the late act of parliament for establishing the Roman Catholic religion and the French laws in that extensive country, now called Canada, is dangerous in an extreme degree to the Protestant religion and to the civil rights and liberties of all America; and, therefore, as men and Protestant Christians, we are indispensably obliged to take all proper measures for our security.

11. That whereas our enemies have flattered themselves that they shall make an easy prey of this numerous, brave and hardy people, from an apprehension that they are unacquainted with military discipline; we, therefore, for the honour, defence and security of this county and province, advise, as it has been recommended to take away all commissions from the officers of the militia, that those who now hold commissions, or such other persons, be elected in each town as officers in the militia, as shall be judged of sufficient capacity for that purpose, and who have evidenced themselves the inflexible friends to the rights of the people; and that the inhabitants of those towns and districts, who are qualified, do use their utmost diligence to acquaint themselves with the art of war as soon as possible, and do, for that purpose, appear under arms at least once every week. . . .

The [Continental] Congress, taking the foregoing into consideration,

Resolved unan, That this assembly deeply feels the suffering of their countrymen in the Massachusetts-Bay, under the operation of the late unjust, cruel, and oppressive acts of the British Parliament—that they most thoroughly approve the wisdom and fortitude with which opposition to these wicked ministerial measures has hitherto been conducted, and they earnestly recommend to their brethren, a perseverance in the same firm and temperate conduct as expressed in the resolutions determined upon, at a [*late*] meeting of the delegates for the county of Suffolk, on Tuesday, the 6th instant, trusting that the effect[*s*] of the united efforts of North America in their behalf, will carry such conviction to the British nation, of the unwise, unjust, and ruinous policy of the present administration, as quickly to introduce better men and wiser measures.

Resolved unan, That contributions from all the colonies for supplying the necessities, and alleviating the distresses of our brethren at Boston, ought to be continued, in such manner, and so long as their occasions may require.

Excerpted from the Library of Congress, "The Suffolk Resolves and Agreement by Continental Congress, September 1774," in *The American Revolution, 1763–1783,* http://memory.loc.gov/learn/features/timeline/amrev/rebelln/suffolk.html.

Grand Council popularly elected by the colonies. The colonial government would have broad authority in civil, commercial, and criminal affairs, as well as veto power over all parliamentary legislation affecting the colonies.

The Continental Congress voted to denounce the Intolerable Acts, the Quebec Act, and other repressive measures, declaring thirteen acts of Parliament passed since 1763 unconstitutional. Each of the delegates pledged his colony's support of economic sanctions against Britain until all the acts were repealed. In a set of ten resolutions, the Continental Congress enumerated the rights of colonists, and the delegates signed a formal Continental Association, a prelude to a formal union. Finally, the Congress prepared addresses of protest to King George III.

After the Continental Congress adjourned, Virginia lawyer and legislator Thomas Jefferson (see biography box in Chapter 4) issued a pamphlet entitled *Summary View of the Rights of British America* and John Adams published a series of letters under the pseudonym "Novanglus" (New Englander), both endorsing and proposing an extreme form of dominion status for the colonies in which the colonies would entirely govern themselves but would acknowledge the king as the head of state. Members of Parliament considered this proposal but rejected it as unacceptably radical. Nevertheless, it prompted liberals in the English government to formulate a plan of conciliation in 1775, which would have granted a considerable degree of self-government to the colonies. This plan was turned down by the House of Lords, a bastion of conservatism, and Parliament as a whole declared Massachusetts to be in rebellion. In effect, it was Parliament, not the colonies, that declared the commencement of a revolution.

While the colonies coalesced, General Gage consolidated and deployed his forces. On September 1, 1774, he sent a detachment from Boston to seize and secure cannons and powder from arsenals in nearby Cambridge and Charles Town. The Salem-based Provincial Congress responded by appropriating £15,627 to buy new military supplies, commissioned John Hancock to form and lead a Committee of

Safety, and further authorized Hancock to call out the militia. The militia members were dubbed "Minutemen," because these citizen-soldiers pledged themselves to be armed, assembled, and prepared for battle on virtually a minute's notice.

Gage was determined to round up more local munitions, but the colonists had developed an extraordinarily extensive and effective network of spies and were able to foil his operation.

Military Prelude to Revolution: Lord Dunmore's War (1774)

Even while the prospect of war between the colonies and Britain loomed, a new colonial war erupted. In addition to the French and Indian War, historians commonly enumerate some thirty-two distinct and significant intertribal and Indian-colonist wars before 1775. The last of these was Lord Dunmore's War, which was a prelude to what would be the complex involvement of Indians in the American Revolution.

John Muir, first earl of Dunmore and popularly known as Lord Dunmore, was the royal governor of Virginia. Early in the 1770s he announced that he would issue patents for land on both sides of the Ohio River in the extensive western territory claimed by his colony. Preparatory to this, in April 1773, he sent out a survey party, whose members shot an unarmed Shawnee named Peshewa (Wild Cat) on May 29, 1773. This provoked a Shawnee reprisal, led by a chief named Black Fish, in which some of the surveyors were killed and one was captured. Black Fish sent that surveyor back to Wheeling (in present-day West Virginia) to warn all the other colonists that any Virginian who attempted to cross the Ohio River would be killed. The man's captors had also told him that they had an ally in the fur trader George Croghan. This persuaded Dr. John Connolly, Dunmore's magistrate of western Pennsylvania, to conclude that a conspiracy was afoot among the Shawnees, fur traders, and Pennsylvanians, who disputed Virginia's claim to the Ohio country. Connolly accordingly secured Dunmore's permission to declare war against the Shawnees.

Like Black Fish, Chief Cornstalk, the principal leader of the Ohio Shawnees, wanted to head off a white invasion, but he also believed that he could not win a war against the colonists. Croghan, who frequently traded with him, invited Cornstalk to travel to Fort Dunmore (formerly known as Fort Pitt and, today, the site of Pittsburgh) to negotiate a peaceful resolution with colonial representatives. There is no record of what was negotiated at Fort Dunmore, but whatever agreement was made became irrelevant: As Cornstalk, his brother Silverheels, and another Shawnee, Non-hel-e-ma, returned from the fort, they were attacked by a party of frontiersmen. Silverheels was fatally wounded in the skirmish, and all hope of peace was thereby shattered.

Believing himself betrayed, Cornstalk sought aid from the Miamis, Wyandots, Ottawas, and Delawares, all of whom declined to offer alliance. Those Mingos, Senecas, and Cayugas who had removed to southern Ohio also expressed a desire to remain neutral, but they were driven to fight by a slaughter instigated by John Cresap, the leader of Dunmore's survey party. Fearing a general Indian uprising, Dunmore officially declared war on June 10, 1774, and raised a militia. On October 10, a sharp and brutal battle took place, in which the Virginians prevailed at the high cost of 222 killed or wounded (out of a force of 1,000). About half as many Indians died before departing the field. Cornstalk and Dunmore concluded a truce on October 26, 1774, and Lord Dunmore's War was ended.

For the settlers of the frontier, the conflict underscored their long-growing sense that royal authority meant little as one traveled farther from the coast. Dunmore was an example of British military leadership at its conventional worst: inept, indecisive, and irresolute. On the eve of revolution, this brief and brutal conflict seemed to offer additional evidence of official indifference and ineffectualness with regard to the welfare of the frontier. Although the people of the colonial frontier tended to be conservative, when confronted with such as Dunmore, they increasingly turned against the distant king and his scarcely less remote representatives and moved toward union with their fellow colonists.

Virginia Joins In

After the Continental Congress appropriated funds for military supplies, called for the organization of the Minutemen, and set up a Committee of Safety, it dissolved itself on December 10, 1774. At this point, the political focus of the brewing revolution shifted south, from Massachusetts to Virginia. On March 20, 1775, a colonial convention met in Richmond. On the fourth day of the convention, local attorney Patrick Henry made his most famous speech and perhaps the most celebrated speech in all American history, concluding:

> Gentlemen may cry, "Peace! Peace!"— but there is no peace. The war is actually begun! The next gale that sweeps from the north will bring to our ears the clash of resounding arms! Our brethren are already in the field! Why stand we here idle? What is it that gentlemen wish? What would they have? Is life so dear, or peace so sweet, as to be purchased at the price of chains and slavery? Forbid it, Almighty God! I know not what course others may take; but as for me, give me liberty or give me death!

No one actually recorded the speech, which has come down through history thanks to Henry's first biographer, William Wirt, and may well be largely compounded of his imagination. Nevertheless, the Virginia convention and Henry's oratory were sufficiently inflammatory to alarm Virginia governor Lord Dunmore, who rattled his saber (largely an empty scabbard, since he had no army at his disposal) and outlawed Patrick Henry—rather too late, since Henry was on his way to Philadelphia and the Second Continental Congress.

In the meantime, the British government, under Lord North, ushered through Parliament a "Conciliatory Plan," by which Parliament did not renounce its right to tax the colonies, but would "forbear" to levy all but regulatory taxes on any American colony that, through its own assembly, taxed itself for the support of defense and civil government. By the time news of this reached Virginia, Dunmore had rallied the colony's Loyalists and even promised slaves their freedom in exchange for military service in the royal cause. Thus the climate was not favorable to the reception of Lord North's Conciliatory Plan, and the Virginia convention rejected it in June 1775. In the weeks and months following this, a series of skirmishes broke out in Virginia, culminating in a naval bombardment of Norfolk. The conflagration, such as it was, spread to neighboring North Carolina, where a band of kilted Scots colonists, loyal to the king, met a colonial militia force at Moore's Creek Bridge on February 27, 1776. The Scotsmen suffered an ignominious defeat—850 were captured—and the royal government of that colony simply fell apart. Virginia and North Carolina were poised for war.

The Olive Branch

The Second Continental Congress convened in Philadelphia on May 10, 1775. Of it, Richard Henry Lee, a delegate from the backcountry of Virginia, wrote: "There never appeared more perfect unanimity among any sett of men." This should either be interpreted as a misstatement or a deliberate distortion or full weight should be given to the word *appeared*. For the delegates were deeply divided over the issue of separation from or reconciliation with England. John Dickinson, whose *Letters from a Farmer in Pennsylvania to Inhabitants of the British Colonies* during 1767–1768 were the most widely read and influential indictment of the Townshend Acts, now drafted what came to be called the **Olive Branch Petition.**

The document, a petition addressed directly to King George III, reiterated all the colonial grievances, but it also professed attachment "to your Majesty's person, family, and Government, with all devotion that principle and affection can inspire." It expressed the colonies' consciousness of being "connected with Great Britain by the strongest ties that can unite societies," and it went on to make an emotional appeal to the king, to "beseech your Majesty, that your royal authority and influence may be graciously interposed to procure us relief from our afflicting fears and jealousies."

John Adams and the other New Englanders objected to the Olive Branch Petition, but the enough members of the Second Continental Congress endorsed the petition to put it into the hands of the highly respected Richard Penn (a descendant of Pennsylvania founder William Penn), who took it to London and awaited an audience with the king. The monarch refused even to receive Penn when he presented himself on August 14, 1775. Without reading the petition, King George proclaimed on August 23 that "our Colonies and Plantations in North America, misled by dangerous and designing men," were in a state of rebellion. The king ordered "all our Officers . . . and all our obedient and loyal subjects, to use their utmost endeavours to withstand and suppress such rebellion."

News traveled slowly across the Atlantic, and it was November before Congress learned that its olive branch had been spurned. Even before receiving this news, however, the Second Continental Congress acted as the Virginia Convention had with regard to Lord North's Conciliatory Plan, rejecting it on July 31, 1775, two days before adjourning.

Back in Parliament, Edmund Burke, always a friend to the American cause, made a speech on November 16 in support of his Motion for a Bill to Compose American Troubles. Having given up on persuading King George to reconcile with the colonies, Burke hoped to obtain for Parliament the direct authority to do so, and his bill accordingly asserted parliamentary supremacy over royal prerogative where the colonies were concerned. This was too radical for Parliament, and the bill failed.

Toward Independence

By the close of 1775, the American colonists were not always divided neatly into "Patriots" (those

Olive Branch Petition, 1775

To the King's Most Excellent Majesty.

MOST GRACIOUS SOVEREIGN:

. . . We shall decline the ungrateful task of describing the irksome variety of artifices practised by many of your Majesty's Ministers, the delusive pretences, fruitless terrours, and unavailing severities, that have, from time to time, been dealt out by them, in their attempts to execute this impolitick plan, or of tracing through a series of years past the progress of the unhappy differences between Great Britain and these Colonies, that have flowed from this fatal source.

Your Majesty's Ministers, persevering in their measures, and proceeding to open hostilities for enforcing them, have compelled us to arm in our own defence, and have engaged us in a controversy so peculiarly abhorrent to the affections of your still faithful Colonists, that when we consider whom we must oppose in this contest, and if it continues, what may be the consequences, our own particular misfortunes are accounted by us only as parts of our distress. . . .

Attached to your Majesty's person, family, and Government, with all devotion that principle and affection can inspire; connected with Great Britain by the strongest ties that can unite societies, and deploring every event that tends in any degree to weaken them, we solemnly assure your Majesty, that we not only most ardently desire the former harmony between her and these Colonies may be restored, but that a concord may be established between them upon so firm a basis as to perpetuate its blessings, uninterrupted by any future dissensions, to succeeding generations in both countries, and to transmit your Majesty's name to posterity, adorned with that signal and lasting glory that has attended the memory of those illustrious personages, whose virtues and abilities have extricated states from dangerous convulsions, and by securing the happiness to others, have erected the most noble and durable monuments to their own fame.

We beg further leave to assure your Majesty, that notwithstanding the sufferings of your loyal Colonists during the course of this present controversy, our breasts retain too tender a regard for the kingdom from which we derive our origin, to request such a reconciliation as might, in any manner, be inconsistent with her dignity or welfare. These, related as we are to her, honour and duty, as well as inclination, induce us to support and advance; and the apprehensions that now oppress our hearts with unspeakable grief, being once removed, your Majesty will find our faithful subject on this Continent ready and willing at all times, as they have ever been with their lives and fortunes, to assert and maintain the rights and interests of your Majesty, and of our Mother Country.

We therefore beseech your Majesty, that your royal authority and influence may be graciously interposed to procure us relief from our afflicting fears and jealousies, occasioned by the system before-mentioned, and to settle peace through every part of our Dominions, with all humility submitting to your Majesty's wise consideration, whether it may not be expedient, for facilitating those important purposes, that your Majesty be pleased to direct some mode, by which the united applications of your faithful Colonists to the Throne, in pursuance of their common counsels, may be improved into a happy and permanent reconciliation; and that, in the mean time, measures may be taken for preventing the further destruction of the lives of your Majesty's subjects; and that such statutes as more immediately distress any of your Majesty's Colonies may be repealed.

Excerpted from America's HomePage, "Olive Branch Petition," in *Historic Documents of the United States,* http://ahp.gatech.edu/olive_branch_1775.html.

favoring independence) and "Loyalists" (those remaining loyal to the Crown), but they were often wracked by considerable doubt, and many found themselves in a gray area between the extremes. The prevailing ambivalence is evident in a November 4, 1775, declaration by the New Jersey Assembly, which denied the reality of the Revolution by asserting that reports of colonists seeking independence were "groundless." The Pennsylvania Assembly had protested the injustice of taxation and other royal policies, but on November 9, the day that word was received of King George's refusal even to receive the Olive Branch Petition, that body instructed its delegates to the Second Continental Congress to "dissent from and utterly reject any propositions . . . that may cause or lead to a separation from our mother country or a change of the form of this government." The Second Continental Congress itself temporized. On December 6, 1775, it issued a response to the rejection of the Olive Branch Petition that reaffirmed colonial allegiance to the Crown but denied the authority of Parliament because the colonies did not—and could never properly—enjoy representation in that assembly.

In some colonies, however, the movers and shakers were eager to write constitutions for themselves. Each of these was, in effect, a declaration of independence. Naturally, Massachusetts made the first move in a characteristic attempt to pull along the other colonies. The Massachusetts Provincial Congress proposed on May 3, 1775, that the Continental Congress write a model constitution for the colonies to adopt individually as well as collectively. Fearing that this would be too bold a leap toward independence, the Continental Congress demurred, whereupon Massachusetts took both a leap forward and a step back. The Provincial Congress created the first *state* constitution by modifying the colonial Charter of 1691 to replace the royal governor with a twenty-eight-member elected council.

On October 18, 1775, New Hampshire asked the Second Continental Congress not for a model constitution, but for a declaration of independence to which it and the other colonies might subscribe. As it had when faced with the Massachusetts proposal, Congress dodged the issue, but it did offer advice. Because New Hampshire had no colonial charter on which to base a constitution, Congress suggested that New Hampshire "establish such a government, as in their judgment will best produce the happiness of the people." On January 5, 1776, therefore, New Hampshire became the first colony to write and

adopt an entirely new state constitution. South Carolina followed New Hampshire with a constitution that its assembly approved on March 26, 1776.

All three of these first constitutions were tentative; none of them asserted a complete break with England. The other colonies would follow with their own state constitutions throughout 1776, which did not sever relations with the Crown but included at least a limited declaration of independence. By the time the Declaration of Independence was adopted by Congress on July 4, 1776, no fewer than seven states were already fully formed with constitutions.

Common Sense

By the end of 1775, the American Revolution was well under way. The Battles of Lexington and Concord had been fought, Boston besieged, and Fort Ticonderoga captured. The Battle of Bunker Hill had been lost, and the Americans had also boldly (if foolishly) assumed the offensive with a daring invasion of Canada. Despite all this, the question of independence was by no means resolved.

Clearly, the colonies were drifting toward a break with Britain. But for those Patriots zealous to create independence, drifting hardly sufficed. They wanted a push. It came in the form of a pamphlet published on January 9, 1776, and written, according to the title page, "by an Englishman."

In 1776 Philadelphia's Benjamin Rush was the most highly respected physician in America and a delegate to the Second Continental Congress. He persuaded Thomas Paine, an acquaintance who had immigrated from England to Philadelphia in November 1774, to write what he hoped would prove a popular pamphlet on the subject of independence. A talented journalist, Paine rapidly completed it and presented it to Rush, who, impressed by its emphatically straightforward eloquence, provided it with the title by which it entered history: *Common Sense.*

The forty-seven-page pamphlet was offered to the public at two shillings a copy. Although the pamphlet's political philosophy was hardly original, *Common Sense* made the argument for independence more

Introduction to Common Sense, 1776

As a long and violent abuse of power, is generally the Means of calling the right of it in question (and in Matters too which might never have been thought of, had not the Sufferers been aggravated into the inquiry) and as the King of England hath undertaken in his own Right, to support the Parliament in what he calls Theirs, and as the good people of this country are grievously oppressed by the combination, they have an undoubted privilege to inquire into the pretensions of both, and equally to reject the usurpations of either.

In the following sheets, the author hath studiously avoided every thing which is personal among ourselves. Compliments as well as censure to individuals make no part thereof. The wise, and the worthy, need not the triumph of a pamphlet; and those whose sentiments are injudicious, or unfriendly, will cease of themselves unless too much pains are bestowed upon their conversion.

The cause of America is in a great measure the cause of all mankind. Many circumstances have, and will arise, which are not local, but universal, and through which the principles of all Lovers of Mankind are affected, and in the Event of which, their Affections are interested. The laying of a Country desolate with Fire and Sword, declaring War against the natural rights of all Mankind, and extirpating the Defenders thereof from the Face of the Earth, is the Concern of every Man to whom Nature hath given the Power of feeling; of which Class, regardless of Party Censure, is the

AUTHOR

Excerpted from Thomas Paine, *Common Sense* (Philadelphia: W. and T. Bradford, 1776), from Bartleby.com, 1999, www.bartleby.com/133.

simply, thoroughly, and persuasively than any document that had come before it. Paine marshaled every argument concisely and incisively. Recognizing the strongly anti-Catholic sentiment that prevailed in the colonies, he compared King George III to the pope. He portrayed the notion of the hereditary succession of the monarchy as an evident absurdity rather than as a product of the natural order; he tore down, one after the other, all arguments favoring reconciliation with England; and he underscored the economic benefits of independence. He developed two central themes, arguing that republican government was inherently superior to government by hereditary monarchy, and that equality of rights was the birthright of humanity, which no just government could abridge or fail to defend. But perhaps the true genius of *Common Sense* was its message of collective destiny:

> O ye that love mankind! Ye that dare oppose not only the tyranny but the tyrant, stand forth! Every spot of the old world is overrun with oppression. Freedom hath been hunted round the globe. Asia and Africa have long expelled her. Europe regards her like a stranger, and England hath given her warning to depart. O receive the fugitive, and prepare in time an asylum for mankind!

Common Sense recast a quarrel between the British colonies and Britain into an event of historic international importance, a veritable epoch in the evolution of humankind. Within ninety days of its publication, the pamphlet sold 120,000 copies, and historians believe that more than half a million copies were in circulation before the end of the American Revolution.

Independence Moves to Debate

Common Sense catalyzed the independence movement. On February 18, 1776, the Second Continental Congress authorized privateers, merchant ships commissioned to prey upon British vessels and take them as prizes. On February 26, Congress passed an embargo on exports to Britain and the British West Indies. On March 3, it sent Silas Deane to France to negotiate for aid. On March 14, Congress took action against the Loyalists by ordering that they be disarmed. Then, on April 6, Congress defied the Crown by officially opening all American ports to the trade of all nations—save Britain.

As Congress had been spurred by *Common Sense* and the consensus it helped to create, so the colonies were encouraged by the acts of Congress. One by one, they voted themselves independent from the Crown. On May 15, the Second Continental Congress enacted a resolution recommending to "the respective Assemblies and Conventions of the United Colonies, where no Government sufficient to the exigencies of their affairs has been hitherto established, to adopt such Government," and on June 7, Richard Henry Lee of Virginia introduced a new resolution:

> That these United Colonies are, and of right ought to be, free and independent States . . . and that all political connection between them and the State of Great Britain is, and ought to be, totally dissolved.

> That it is expedient forthwith to take the most effectual measures for forming foreign alliances.

> That a plan of confederation be prepared and transmitted to the respective Colonies for their consideration and approbation.

Now the Congress of the colonies had its resolution, but even in the wake of *Common Sense,* independence was by no means assured. Loyalists, who opposed independence, were numerous throughout the colonies, especially in the Middle Atlantic region and in the South. Most surprisingly, Loyalist sentiment was very strong on the frontier, the very region that had been the first to raise arms against officials of the Crown. Fortunately for those who advocated

independence, the Loyalists did not organize as a politically unified body or party. Perhaps this was because their opposition to independence sprang from disparate sources. Some were Crown officers whose livelihoods were at stake. Others were Anglican clergymen, attached to Britain through its state religion. Some were simply conservatives of every class. Others were "Dynastic Tories," who believed sincerely in the "rightness" of kings to rule. Some were "Legality Tories," who truly felt it was the right of Parliament to tax even the colonies. Some were "Religious Tories," who believed it a religious duty to fear God and honor the king. Still others were "Factional Tories," who made their decision against independence on the basis of family relationships and personal political alliances and animosities. Once the American Revolution began in earnest, however, Loyalists in various regions banded together, often in militarily effective ways, particularly on the frontier, which became the scene of the bitterest fighting.

The debate on Lee's resolution was postponed three weeks because congressional advocates of independence sensed that the Middle Atlantic colonies were not yet prepared to cut the cords with Britain. They used this time to rally the necessary votes within the assemblies of Delaware, Connecticut, New Hampshire, New Jersey, and Maryland, which instructed their congressional delegates to vote for independence.

On July 1, 1776, the actual debate commenced. Pennsylvania's John Dickinson urged further delay, while John Adams and Lee called for immediate action. On that day, the delegates from South Carolina and Pennsylvania voted against independence. Delaware's delegates, despite instructions from the colonial assembly, remained divided. New York was in the process of reorganizing its government, so its delegates abstained. Therefore, as of July 1, the tally stood at nine to four, in favor of independence.

It was a majority, to be sure, but independence advocates wanted an overwhelming mandate. The most radical members of the Delaware Assembly dispatched one of their number, Caesar Rodney, on an eighty-mile midnight ride from Dover to Philadelphia that was worthy of Paul Revere. He arrived in time to swing the Delaware vote to independence. This moved South Carolina's delegation to change its vote to favor independence, and Pennsylvania followed suit. New York again abstained, but on July 2, the majority was overwhelming.

Declaration of Independence

The Second Continental Congress was not idle during the three-week postponement of the vote on Lee's resolution. It appointed a committee to draft, during the interim, a declaration of independence, naming to it John Adams, Benjamin Franklin, Robert Livingston, Roger Sherman, and Thomas Jefferson. Adams was one of the original movers of revolutionary activity in the independence movement. Benjamin Franklin, the oldest member of the committee, was the only member who possessed an international reputation; he was already celebrated as a scientist, inventor, writer, editor, politician, and, most recently, an emerging statesman. As the scion of a distinguished and well-heeled New York family, Robert Livingston was the aristocrat of the committee and was also highly mindful of his colony's ambivalence. (When the final Declaration of Independence came to a vote, Livingston cast his in opposition, and he absented himself from the signing. Nevertheless, once independence had been declared, Livingston worked tirelessly to execute the will of Congress, and he was an important member of the delegation that negotiated the Treaty of Paris in 1783, ending the Revolution and securing United States sovereignty.) Roger Sherman, a delegate from Connecticut, had risen from his tradesman's roots as a cobbler through omnivorous reading that molded him into a legislator and economic theorist. He was well known as the author of a series of almanacs based on his own astronomical calculations.

The most radical member of the committee, even more so than Adams, was Virginia planter and lawyer Thomas Jefferson. As a colonial politician, Jefferson was dull at the podium; however, he had a certain amiable charm and an impressive presence on the written page. His 1774 *View of the Rights of America* was a direct and highly reasoned attack on the British monarchy. The early leaders of the independence movement had considered it too radical to endorse, although they were impressed by its eloquence.

John Adams had the greatest seniority in the independence movement, and no one would have objected had he nominated himself to be the principal drafter of the declaration. But Adams himself recognized two things: First, he had enemies and tended to provoke jealousies, whereas everyone liked Jefferson. Second, Jefferson was the better writer. At the time, no one on the committee regarded a declaration of independence as particularly momentous. As they saw it, the declaration would put into writing the will of the Second Continental Congress, basically serving the same function as a contract in relation to a business deal. It would make things legal. The document had to present a case for independence that would stand up to the scrutiny of the powers of the world, most notably France, to which the fledgling republic was already in the process of appealing for aid. At Adams's suggestion, the committee delegated the drafting of the Declaration of Independence entirely to Jefferson.

In 1825 Jefferson wrote to Richard Henry Lee that his purpose in writing the declaration was not to "find out new principles, or new arguments, never before thought of . . . but to justify ourselves in the independent stand we are compelled to take" and to "appeal to the tribunal of the world . . . for our justification." The declaration, he explained, neither aimed "at originality of principle or sentiment, nor yet copied from any particular previous writing," rather, it "was intended to be an expression of the American mind. . . . All its authority rests on the harmonizing sentiments of the day, whether expressed in conversation, in letters, printed essays, or in the elementary books of public right, as Aristotle, Cicero, Locke, Sidney, etc."

As many have pointed out, Jefferson's greatest debt was to the seventeenth-century British philosopher John Locke, who had enumerated the basic rights of human beings as life, liberty, and property. Jefferson wrote of "unalienable rights" to life and liberty, but he changed Locke's "property" to the "pursuit of happiness." While some later commentators have pointed out that the word *happiness,* more than any other, reflects the "expression of the American mind," it should be noted that the term had a rather different meaning in the eighteenth century than it does today. In Jefferson's age, it suggested general material well-being, not emotional fulfillment.

The Continental Congress proved to be a stern editor. Jefferson's first draft blamed King George III for forcing slavery upon the colonies; however, this passage was stricken because so many delegates to the Second Continental Congress were committed to preserving the institution of slavery. After this change and others, the Declaration of Independence was approved by Congress on July 4, 1776, and opened for signature. It was published to the new nation on July 8 and provoked boisterous celebration.

John Adams did not confuse the volume of celebration with unanimous support for independence. Writing in 1815, he admitted what he had dared not utter publicly in 1776 or at any time during the Revolution. He believed that one-third of the American population was "averse to the revolution" and another third, "the yeomanry, the soundest part of the nation, always averse to war, were rather lukewarm." This left only a third of the nation fully committed to the war for independence.

Congress as High Command

The colonies had long distrusted standing armies. Despite the colonies' concerns, the Second Continental Congress created the Continental army on June 10, 1775, because it recognized that such an army, established and controlled by a central, legislative body, was not a threat to liberty—it was necessary to obtain and preserve liberty. (Congress also created the Continental navy on October 13, 1775, and authorized, under the navy, a small body of marines.) Although George Washington was commissioned to command the Continental army, he was

the field commander; high command was ultimately the prerogative of the Continental Congress itself. This, however, did not mean that Congress had complete authority over the nation's armed forces. The creation of the Continental army introduced an enduring dual-army tradition into American military history. The national force was complementary to and did not supplant the state militias, which were organized, equipped, trained, and commanded on the local level (in some cases to a degree superior to the Continental army).

The militias recognized the need for coordinated action and generally submitted themselves to the overall command of George Washington. But even Washington's forceful personality could not bring complete harmony and unity to the dual army. The multiplicity of commanders created many problems, the greatest of which was troop availability. During the Revolution, 231,771 men served in the Continental army and 164,087 men served in the various militias. The numbers appear impressive, especially considering that the British regular army deployed to America consisted of about 42,000 troops, plus 29,875 German mercenaries ("Hessians") and perhaps 50,000 American Loyalist troops ("Tories"). Yet enlistment terms varied within the Continental army and were even more irregular in the militias, so that, at any one time, Washington only had about 20,000 men available to him from all of his forces (the later addition of French troops was a tremendous boon). The war plans of both Congress and Washington were greatly influenced, even substantially shaped, by complex and frustratingly fluid issues of troop strength over any particular span of time.

The militia system had its advantages, including local control and the morale-building sense soldiers had that they were defending their homes. Local officers were also better able to purge the militias of Tories or those who had little enthusiasm for independence. Moreover, the omnipresence of militias ensured that enemy forces would get a most unfriendly reception wherever they ventured, making it, at the very least, difficult to maintain an army in the field. British officers were always amazed and chagrined by the numbers of militiamen. These numbers were the product of the democratization of military power in the new country as well as the result of levies. Militia service was often obligatory, unless an individual could pay a commutation fee or hire a substitute to serve in his place.

The disadvantages of the militia system included the great and confusing variety of enlistment terms and the inability of any single militia unit to stand up to a substantial number of regular army opponents. For this reason, militia units typically fought alongside the Continental army units. Another major drawback of the militia was that, generally speaking, these locally raised forces would not venture beyond their locality. The Continental Congress recognized the need for an army that could bring the fight from one colony to another, and that was a major reason for the creation of the *Continental* army.

Washington modeled the Continental army on the British army, as he had come to know it during the French and Indian War. As with the British army, most of the recruits were drawn from the lowest rungs of the social ladder and included vagrants and criminals who joined as an alternative to judicial punishment. Loyalists were sometimes given the option of enlisting or suffering punishment (even including execution). The Continental army was a racially integrated force that counted freed and current slaves among its troops. Although some men joined the Continentals because they clearly had little other choice, most joined for what must have been patriotic reasons. Few colonists became soldiers against their will. In a very real sense, the Continental army was a people's patriotic army and evidence of a very wide popular endorsement of the cause of liberty.

There is no greater evidence of the essential patriotic dedication of the Continentals than their willingness to endure meager, often nonexistent pay and provisioning, shortage of clothing, and paucity of shelter, all thanks to a parsimonious and penniless Congress that lacked both the authority to levy direct taxes and the funds to supply the army. For its part, Congress was also suspicious of the very force it had created,

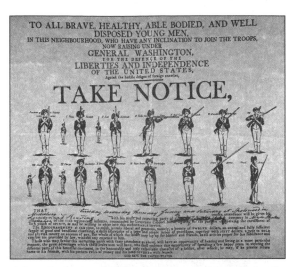

A broadside (circa 1775) soliciting volunteers for the Continental army offers recruits a bounty of $12 as well as an annual supply of "good and handsome clothing," "ample" daily provisions, and $60 per year in "gold and silver money."

ever wary of the evils inherent in a standing army. Congress repeatedly ensured that Washington was mindful of the subordination of his authority to that of the civilian legislature. Fortunately, this was a proposition with which Washington wholeheartedly concurred. As for the individual soldier, although the Continentals were more disciplined and more completely equipped than the various militias, the individual soldiers never considered themselves "regulars" in the European sense. They were willing to be trained to accomplish a mission—independence—and after accomplishing that, they would return to civilian life. They had no intention of becoming professional soldiers attached to a genuine standing army.

Without the power of direct taxation, Congress had to depend on rapidly depreciating paper currency and foreign (mostly French) loans to finance, quite inadequately, the army it had created. And if finance remained an unresolved problem throughout the war, so did administration. While Congress asserted its authority over the military, it was slow to create the machinery to administer the army. Until June 1776, when it formed a five-member Board of

War and Ordnance, Congress threw together committees on an ad hoc basis to address problems as they arose. In October 1777, recognizing the inefficiency of the board, Congress added military officers to it and appointed individuals to oversee quartermaster (supply and provisioning) duties. None of these congressional institutions ever worked very well, and the Continental army was always in the throes of supply and provisioning shortages, which were especially hard during the long winter encampments. The crisis of finance reached its nadir during the winter of 1779–1780, when Congress summarily devolved the bulk of its financial responsibilities on the states, asking each state to finance its own troops in the Continental army. Congress also introduced a quota system by which it directly requisitioned supplies and provisions from the states. The states frequently protested the inequity of the quota system, delayed compliance, and wrought even greater hardship on the troops. As a result, the winter of 1779–1780 was much harsher than the more famous Valley Forge winter of 1778. Three times between January and June 1780, the Continental army mutinied due to the army's truly horrific privations. The mutinies were quelled, but it was not until 1781 that Congress succeeded in rationalizing and centralizing military administration to a workable degree. By then, the fighting was almost over.

Articles of Confederation, 1777

Articles of Confederation and perpetual Union between the states of New Hampshire, Massachusetts-bay Rhode Island and Providence Plantations, Connecticut, New York, New Jersey, Pennsylvania, Delaware, Maryland, Virginia, North Carolina, South Carolina and Georgia.

I.
The Stile of this Confederacy shall be "The United States of America".

II.
Each state retains its sovereignty, freedom, and independence, and every power, jurisdiction, and right, which is not by this Confederation expressly delegated to the United States, in Congress assembled.

III.
The said States hereby severally enter into a firm league of friendship with each other, for their common defense, the security of their liberties, and their mutual and general welfare, binding themselves to assist each other, against all force offered to, or attacks made upon them, or any of them, on account of religion, sovereignty, trade, or any other pretense whatever.

IV.
The better to secure and perpetuate mutual friendship and intercourse among the people of the different States in this Union, the free inhabitants of each of these States . . . shall be entitled to all privileges and immunities of free citizens in the several States; and the people of each State shall free ingress and regress to and from any other State, and shall enjoy therein all the privileges of trade and commerce. . . .

V.
For the most convenient management of the general interests of the United States, delegates shall be annually appointed in such manner as the legislatures of each State shall direct, to meet in Congress on the first Monday in November, in every year. . . .

No State shall be represented in Congress by less than two, nor more than seven members; and no person shall be capable of being a delegate for more than three years in any term of six years; nor shall any person, being a delegate, be capable of holding any office under the United States, for which he, or another for his benefit, receives any salary, fees or emolument of any kind. . . .

VI.
No State, without the consent of the United States in Congress assembled, shall send any embassy to, or receive any embassy from, or enter into any conference, agreement, alliance or treaty with any King, Prince or State. . . .

Articles of Confederation

The Continental Congress was somewhat more efficient in its attempt to define and rationalize the organization of what would formally become the United States than it was in its management of the army. On June 7, 1776, Richard Henry Lee proposed, along with his resolution of independence, the idea of a confederation of states. This proposal was referred to a committee under John Dickinson. A month later, on July 12, 1776, Dickinson presented to the whole Congress the document drafted by his committee: Articles of Confederation and Perpetual Union. The debate on the articles, which was intermittent in the time of war, consumed more than a year before the thirteen **Articles of Confederation** were adopted on November 15, 1777, after Congress agreed that the individual states would bear the expenses of government in proportion to the land area they occupied rather than their population. This solution facilitated congressional adoption, but it delayed ratification by the states, because the two "three-sided states," Virginia and Maryland, laid claims to unspecified expanses of western lands; therefore, their fair share of financial responsibility could not be readily determined. The solution was for these states to cede to the federal government their western land claims. Virginia did not do this until January 2, 1781, and

---

VIII.

All charges of war, and all other expenses that shall be incurred for the common defense or general welfare, and allowed by the United States in Congress assembled, shall be defrayed out of a common treasury, which shall be supplied by the several States in proportion to the value of all land within each State. . . .

The taxes for paying that proportion shall be laid and levied by the authority and direction of the legislatures of the several States within the time agreed upon by the United States in Congress assembled.

IX.

The United States in Congress assembled, shall have the sole and exclusive right and power of determining on peace and war, . . .

The United States in Congress assembled shall also have the sole and exclusive right and power of regulating the alloy and value of coin struck by their own authority, or by that of the respective States — fixing the standards of weights and measures throughout the United States — regulating the trade and managing all affairs with the Indians, not members of any of the States, provided that the legislative right of any State within its own limits be not infringed or violated — establishing or regulating post offices from one State to another, throughout all the United States, and exacting such postage on the papers passing through the same as may be requisite to defray the expenses of the said office — appointing all officers of the land forces, in the service of the United States, excepting regimental officers — appointing all the officers of the naval forces, and commissioning all officers whatever in the service of the United States — making rules for the government and regulation of the said land and naval forces, and directing their operations. . . .

XI.

Canada acceding to this confederation, and adjoining in the measures of the United States, shall be admitted into, and entitled to all the advantages of this Union; but no other colony shall be admitted into the same, unless such admission be agreed to by nine States. . . .

XIII.

Every State shall abide by the determination of the United States in Congress assembled, on all questions which by this confederation are submitted to them.

Excerpted from the Avalon Project at Yale Law School, "Articles of Confederation," www.yale.edu/lawweb/avalon/artconf.htm.

Maryland delayed until February 27, 1781. Final ratification of the Articles of Confederation took place on March 1, 1781. Accordingly, on March 2, the Second Continental Congress became the "United States in Congress Assembled."

The Articles of Confederation did not create a nation—they created a union of individual states. The federal government had powers, most significantly the power to treat with foreign governments on behalf of all the states, yet it lacked the single power that would have created true nationhood: the power of direct taxation. This power was left to the states, and the states, not the people, would in turn render unto the federal government their proportionate share for common expenses. The great weakness of the Articles of Confederation would become apparent after the American Revolution had been won, but the United States would be governed under the document until March 4, 1789, when the Constitution was adopted.

The Franco-American Alliance

The Second Continental Congress could not wait for the ratification of the Articles of Confederation to begin seeking aid and alliance in the Revolution. At the time, Americans had little affection for the French, who had been a bitter enemy in the French and Indian War. Moreover, the United States was overwhelmingly Protestant, Puritan in origin, and biased against Catholics. France was a mostly Catholic nation. Nevertheless, congressional leaders understood that securing from the oldest, most populous, and most important of European nations recognition of American independence was no small matter. They also believed that, because of its long-standing rivalry with England, France had a powerful motive to aid in a war that would diminish British power.

In France, singularly autocratic King Louis XVI had ample incentive not to support a challenge to the authority of a fellow sovereign, but he had even greater desire to contribute to the fall of the British empire. Even so, France dared not rush into an open

alliance. Fighting Britain made sense only if that nation were embroiled in the American war. Neither Louis nor his advisers wanted to risk fighting an unencumbered Britain, which was the greatest military power in Europe. Therefore, the French king took a wait-and-see attitude, biding his time until he was certain of the American commitment to independence and Americans' ability to stay in the fight. This did not preclude individuals, including Baron de Kalb and the Marquis de Lafayette, from rendering military aid on their own, and it did not prevent the French government from supplying secret aid.

In March 1776 Silas Deane joined Benjamin Franklin in Paris to negotiate with representatives of the king. The result was the creation, in May 1776, of Hortalez & Cie., a fictitious French firm conjured up by the French government and masterminded by the highly influential Pierre Augustin Caron. Caron—better known to history as Beaumarchais, the playwright who wrote the libretto for Mozart's *The Marriage of Figaro*—fashioned Hortalez & Cie. into an elaborate means of laundering French funding and supply of the American Revolution. The scheme proved invaluable and enabled Washington and his forces not only to persevere against the British, but also to prevail at Trenton, Princeton, and Saratoga. The victories at Saratoga in September and October 1777 helped persuade French observers to recommend an open and outright Franco-American alliance, but Washington's defeat at the Battle of Germantown on October 4 was even more persuasive. The French were not put off by the American loss there; rather, they were greatly impressed by Washington's daring in assuming the offensive even after suffering a sharp defeat at Brandywine and having lost Philadelphia. Washington's boldness convinced the French that the Americans meant to fight to the finish—all the way through to independence.

On January 8, 1778, the French government informed the American envoys in Paris that it was ready to conclude an alliance, and on May 4, 1778, the Second Continental Congress ratified two treaties: a treaty of amity and commerce, which recognized American independence, and a treaty of military alliance, which would become effective only in the event of war between France and England. Of course, soon after the French ambassador in London informed the British government of the two treaties, that war began—on June 17, 1778.

The war with France motivated the British to attempt to settle with the erstwhile colonists before France entered the American Revolution in earnest, but British peace feelers were spurned. Worse for Britain, a year after the signing of the Franco-American alliance, Spain joined France in the war against England, and a year after that, the Dutch also declared war against the British.

Despite all this international maneuvering, for the first three years of the formal Franco-American alliance, the French provided very little useful and effective military aid to Washington and his fellow commanders. If anything, the mere existence of the alliance tended to inspire among the Americans overconfidence and false expectations, which were somewhat destructive. It was not until a large French expeditionary force under the Comte de Rochambeau arrived on July 11, 1780, that the alliance became truly effective militarily. The alliance ultimately produced the 1781 Yorktown Campaign, by which the issue of American independence was, for all practical purposes, settled.

The Loyalist Factor

Historians agree that there were about 500,000 avowed Loyalists in the colonies at the outbreak of the American Revolution, representing about 20 percent of the colonial population. They estimate that across the colonies, Loyalists contributed about 50,000 troops, both regular and militia, to the British side. Loyalist activity, largely unorganized prior to the war, erupted into what was essentially civil war on the northern frontier and throughout the South (except in Virginia, where organized Loyalist resistance was quickly put down). In New York, a hotbed of Loyalist sentiment, 15,000 colonists enlisted in the regular British army and another 8,000 joined the Loyalist militia. In short, New York supplied more troops to King George III than it did to George Washington.

While the Loyalists troops were of great military value, their presence lulled British military planners into a dangerous optimism. Overdependence on Loyalist aid led the British regular army to overextend itself, for example, in an unsuccessful assault on Charleston, South Carolina, in 1776, and at the battles of Bennington, Vermont, and Kings Mountain, North Carolina, in 1777 and 1780, respectively.

American triumphs at the battles of Trenton (December 26, 1776) and Cowpens (South Carolina, January 17, 1781) must be attributed in part to the overextension of British regular forces to protect the Loyalists, who, without question, needed protection. During the Revolution, the press was strictly controlled to ensure that anti-Crown opinions were circulated widely while any criticism of the Continental Congress or Washington and other commanders was suppressed. Colonial assemblies enacted Test Laws, which required individuals who were either indifferent to or suspected opponents of the Revolution to swear an oath renouncing loyalty to the British government and declaring allegiance to the American cause. While the required oaths varied from state to state, all demanded a pledge not to aid or abet "the enemy." Many of these same state assemblies passed confiscation acts, authorizing the seizure of property belonging to known Loyalists and those actively engaged against the Patriot cause. During the course of the Revolution, approximately 40,000 Loyalists were expelled, by action of law, from the states, and it is estimated that 80,000–100,000 Loyalists left America on their own. In July 1783 the Crown created a commission to examine Loyalist claims for compensation. A total of 4,118 claims were reviewed, and the commission authorized the disbursement of £3.3 million to compensate Loyalist losses.

The Peace Commission and Its Work

On February 15, 1780, a congressional committee issued its report enumerating minimum peace demands. These included, first and foremost, complete and unconditional independence, boundaries established with certainty, withdrawal of the British from all United States territory, certain fishing rights, and free navigation of the Mississippi River. The report was submitted to the full Congress on February 23, and debate ensued about the last two points. In the end, on August 14, Congress approved the demands, with the exception of fishing rights. The list was delivered to John Adams, who was to be the chief negotiator with England. However, on June 11, 1781, Congress decided that the peace should be negotiated by a commission and appointed John Jay, Benjamin Franklin, Henry Laurens, and Thomas Jefferson to serve with Adams. On June 15, 1781, Congress summarily discarded the list of minimum demands, informed the commission that the only essential points were independence and sovereignty, and gave the commission latitude to negotiate whatever else it might. Even as Congress freed up the commission in this way, it tied its hands by instructing the negotiators that they were to act only with the "knowledge and concurrence" of the French ministry. Indeed, they were instructed effectively to subordinate themselves to the French, "ultimately" to govern themselves by the "advice and opinion" of the ministry.

As events played out, Jefferson never left America to join the commission. Laurens was captured at sea and held by the British; he did not arrive in Paris until November 1782. Adams was sidelined in The Hague, on an important mission to secure Dutch recognition of the United States and to arrange a much-needed loan as well as a treaty of amity and commerce. Talks began with Franklin, the only American commissioner present, at Paris on April 12, 1782. By this time, the American Revolution had ended for all practical purposes with Cornwallis's surrender at Yorktown. On September 19, 1782, Richard Oswald, the primary negotiator for the Crown, received authorization to treat with the commissioners of the "13 United States." It was an extraordinary authority because it, in effect, conceded the independence of the entity known as the United States. By this time, Jay had joined Franklin,

and they presented Oswald with a draft of a preliminary treaty on October 5.

On October 26, Adams joined Jay and Franklin, and Henry Strachey joined Oswald two days later. Against the express wishes of Congress, Jay and Adams persuaded Franklin to exclude France from the initial negotiations, and a draft of the negotiated treaty was completed by November 5, 1782.

Treaty of Paris

After a very few additional adjustments, the Treaty of Paris was concluded. Predictably, the French government raised objection to having been excluded from the negotiations, but Franklin, a favorite of the French court, prevented a major breach in Franco-American relations by pointing out that the terms of the treaty were quite favorable to France. Accordingly, on January 20, 1783, at Versailles, representatives of Britain and the United States signed an armistice, the Declaration for Suspension of Arms and Cessation of Hostilities, and on September 3, 1783, they signed the **Treaty of Paris,** which took effect on May 12, 1784. A momentous document in the history of the United States and, indeed, the world, the Treaty of Paris was written in remarkably straightforward language and consisted of a mere ten articles.

Unresolved Postwar Issues

Most Americans were very pleased with the Treaty of Paris, whereas many British subjects were highly dissatisfied. Even those who had accepted the loss of the colonies were outraged over the failure to settle definitively and justly the claims of Loyalists. Worse, although the treaty barred postwar retribution, many Loyalists suffered acts of harassment and persecution, usually financial in nature, but sometimes violent. And although the American negotiators agreed that the federal government would urge the states to restore confiscated Loyalist property, the states overwhelmingly ignored these recommendations.

The most significant issue the Treaty of Paris failed to resolve was the final boundary separating

Treaty of Paris, 1783

Article 1:

His Brittanic Majesty acknowledges the said United States, viz., New Hampshire, Massachusetts Bay, Rhode Island and Providence Plantations, Connecticut, New York, New Jersey, Pennsylvania, Maryland, Virginia, North Carolina, South Carolina and Georgia, to be free sovereign and independent states, that he treats with them as such, and for himself, his heirs, and successors, relinquishes all claims to the government, propriety, and territorial rights of the same and every part thereof.

Article 2:

And that all disputes which might arise in future on the subject of the boundaries of the said United States may be prevented, it is hereby agreed and declared, that the following are and shall be their boundaries. . . .

Article 3:

It is agreed that the people of the United States shall continue to enjoy unmolested the right to take fish of every kind on the Grand Bank and on all the other banks of Newfoundland, also in the Gulf of Saint Lawrence and at all other places in the sea, where the inhabitants of both countries used at any time heretofore to fish. . . .

Article 4:

It is agreed that creditors on either side shall meet with no lawful impediment to the recovery of the full value in sterling money of all bona fide debts heretofore contracted.

Article 5:

It is agreed that Congress shall earnestly recommend it to the legislatures of the respective states to provide for the restitution of all estates, rights, and properties, which have been confiscated belonging to real British subjects; and also of the estates, rights, and properties of persons resident in districts in the possession on his Majesty's arms and who have not borne arms against the said United States. . . .

Article 6:

That there shall be no future confiscations made nor any prosecutions commenced against any person or persons for, or by reason of, the part which he or they may have taken in the present war. . . .

Article 7:

There shall be a firm and perpetual peace between his Brittanic Majesty and the said states, and between the subjects of the one and the citizens of the other, wherefore all hostilities both by sea and land shall from henceforth cease. . . .

Article 8:

The navigation of the river Mississippi, from its source to the ocean, shall forever remain free and open to the subjects of Great Britain and the citizens of the United States.

Article 9:

In case it should so happen that any place or territory belonging to Great Britain or to the United States should have been conquered by the arms of either from the other before the arrival of the said Provisional Articles in America, it is agreed that the same shall be restored without difficulty and without requiring any compensation.

Article 10:

The solemn ratifications of the present treaty expedited in good and due form shall be exchanged between the contracting parties in the space of six months or sooner.

Excerpted from Alan Axelrod, *American Treaties and Alliances* (Washington, D.C.: CQ Press, 2000), 59–62.

the territory of the United States from that of British Canada. In the Northeast, the boundary was finally determined by the Webster-Ashburton Treaty of 1842. In the Northwest, the issue was more problematic. The Oregon Treaty of 1846 averted war between Britain and the United States over this boundary, but it was not until the 1870s that the marine portion of the boundary was definitively established.

Although the American Revolution won independence, it by no means left the United States with a viable government. The Articles of Confederation produced, at best, a loose association of states rather than a genuine country. It would take a full-scale Constitutional Convention in 1787 and a new governing document, the Constitution, to resolve this. The Constitution took effect on March 4, 1789, but even it left one momentous issue unresolved: the contradiction of a government founded on liberty yet condoning and protecting slavery. Through agonized debate and tortured compromise, this issue would stalk the United States of America until the country exploded into civil war in 1861.

BIBLIOGRAPHY

Andrews, Charles M. *The Colonial Period of American History.* 1934–1938. Reprint, New Haven, Conn.: Yale University Press, 1964.

Axelrod, Alan. *American Treaties and Alliances.* Washington, D.C.: CQ Press, 2000.

Boatner, Mark M., III. *Encyclopedia of the American Revolution.* New York: D. McKay Co., 1974.

Commager, Henry S., and Morris, Richard B., eds. *The Spirit of 'Seventy-Six: The Story of the American Revolution as Told by Participants.* New York: Harper & Row, 1976.

Jensen, Merrill. *The New Nation: A History of the United States during the Confederation, 1781–1789.* 1950. Reprint, Boston: Northeastern University Press, 1981.

Leckie, Robert. *George Washington's War: The Saga of the American Revolution.* New York: Harper Perennial, 1992.

Stokesbury, James L. *A Short History of the American Revolution.* New York: William Morrow, 1991.

CHAPTER 2

SHAYS'S REBELLION (1786–1787) AND THE WHISKEY REBELLION (1794)

At Issue in Shays's Rebellion

Disaffected Massachusetts veterans of the American Revolution, burdened by postwar economic depression and heavy state taxation, forcibly prevented local courts from convening to effect pending property foreclosures and seizures.

The Conflict

The Articles of Confederation created at most a loose federation of states, not a nation. The key element missing was the authority of the federal government to raise revenue by direct taxation. Although Congress could enact legislation, it had, in effect, to depend on the goodwill of the individual states to fund any measures it created. An immediate consequence of this federal impotence was the government's inability to compensate adequately and justly the veterans of the American Revolution, who received at most a fraction of the back pay due them. Worse, payment was rendered in "Continental notes," which, due to runaway postwar currency inflation, were of such little value that the phrase "not worth a Continental" entered popular speech. Moreover, the very states that had approved the issue of Continental notes now refused to accept the currency in payment of the taxes they levied.

For a minority of Continental army veterans, namely former officers, crisis was averted when they were compensated with deeds of land in the federal territory of the Ohio country. Enlisted veterans—by far the majority of the disaffected—were excluded and were especially hard pressed in rural Massachusetts, where crops brought dismal prices in the postwar depression economy and the state's conservative governor, James Bowdoin, endorsed heavy taxes. In western Massachusetts, these problems were compounded by the widespread feeling that the state constitution of 1780 had cheated the region of its fair share of representation in the state legislature.

Some westerners banded together in a paramilitary "Regulator" movement consisting of groups of 500–2,000 men who, armed with clubs and muskets, marched on circuit court sessions to intimidate the magistrates into abandoning—or at least postponing until after the next gubernatorial election—pending property seizures. Their hope was that a new, more liberal governor would replace Bowdoin and provide much needed tax relief.

The Regulators were active in Northampton, Springfield, and Worcester as well as in some smaller towns for five months during 1786 and 1787. They succeeded in closing the courts and keeping them closed, and they did so through mere intimidation: not a shot was fired and not a casualty created. If the uprising provided temporary relief for the beleaguered farmers of Massachusetts, it also furnished a case in point for those members of the new national government who favored a strong concentration of federal authority, beyond the bounds of the Articles of Confederation. These individuals pointed to what they called the "rebellion" as evidence of a crisis in government. Henry Knox, secretary of war under the Articles of Confederation (he would also serve in this post in the future cabinet of

Worthless Continental notes, such as the one shown here, helped spark Shays's Rebellion.

CHRONOLOGY OF SHAYS'S REBELLION

1786

- Farmers petition state and federal governments for paper currency, tax relief, and judicial reform.

Aug. 29 Armed Massachusetts farmers halt property seizures and trials for debt.

Sept. 25–28 Former Continental army captain Daniel Shays leads the occupation of the Springfield courthouse, preventing the Supreme Judicial Court of Massachusetts from trying a dozen leaders of the anti-judicial rebellion who had been indicted for sedition.

1787

Jan. 20 Acting under congressional authority, General Benjamin Lincoln defends the debtor court at Worcester.

Jan. 25 The militia successfully defends a federal arsenal at Springfield.

Feb. 3 Lincoln rounds up insurgent ringleaders at Petersham, and the rebellion ends.

George Washington), reported to Congress that "the Regulation" was indeed a full-scale rebellion led by Daniel Shays, a former captain in the Continental army. Knox, a staunch conservative, advocated not only a strong central government but also a strong standing army—something anathema even to most other conservatives. To Congress, he portrayed "Shays's Rebellion" as the work of radicals and anarchists who wanted to abolish private property, to cancel all debts, and generally to incite a civil war. Knox knew full well that neither Massachusetts nor, more to the point, the federal government was in a position to finance an army to oppose the Shaysites. He decided that a practical demonstration of the efficacy of an army was called for and joined forces with Governor Bowdoin, appealing to Boston merchants to fund a force of 4,400 volunteers under the command of General Benjamin Lincoln, a Revolutionary War veteran.

Lincoln's force successfully defended the debtor court in Worcester on January 20, 1787, then marched to the Springfield arsenal, which was already defended by 1,200 local militiamen under William Sheppard, a former Continental army officer. On January 25, 1787, before Lincoln arrived, Sheppard and his men confronted 1,500 Regulators led by Shays, Luke Day, and Eli Parsons. A single cannon shot was fired into the ranks of the Regulators, killing three Regulators and wounding others. Another rebel was killed in the brief skirmish that followed, twenty were wounded, and the others took flight. Arriving with his federal troops, Lincoln gave chase and, on February 3, took a number of Regulator leaders into captivity. The Massachusetts Supreme Judicial Court sentenced fourteen of them, including Shays, to death for treason. Only two of the men, John Bly and Charles Rose, were hanged; the rest, including Shays, who had fled to Vermont, were subsequently pardoned by John Hancock, the newly elected liberal governor of Massachusetts. The Regulator movement came to an abrupt end, apparently for want of new leadership.

But for the final aggression on the part of Lincoln and his force, Shays's Rebellion was nothing more than a series of bloodless intimidations. Knox and others who shared his political views stirred fears that Shays's Rebellion was actually a civil war in the making. These fears provided much of the impetus to convene, in Philadelphia in May 1787, a Constitutional Convention, which scrapped the weak Articles of Confederation in favor of a new Constitution that created a strong central government with the authority to levy taxes and to which the states were subordinate.

Conservative vs. Liberal

Although the rebellion was over quickly and the Regulator movement dissolved as soon as a new governor and liberal-leaning reform legislature came to power, Shays's Rebellion caused a good deal of panic—even among those who should have known better, including George Washington, as his October 22, 1786, letter to David Humphreys suggests:

> But for God's sake tell me what is the cause of all these commotions: do they proceed from licentiousness, British-influence disseminated by the tories, or real grievances which admit of redress? . . . I am mortified beyond expression that in the moment of our acknowledged independence we should by our conduct verify the predictions of our transatlantic foe, and render ourselves ridiculous and contemptible in the eyes of all Europe.

In a similar vein, William Cushing, chief justice of the Massachusetts Supreme Judicial Court, observed in the *Hampshire Gazette* on June 6, 1787, that he feared "evil minded persons, leaders of the insurgents [were warring] against the Commonwealth, to bring the whole government and all the good people of this state, if not continent, under absolute command and subjugation to one or two ignorant, unprincipled, bankrupt, desperate individuals."

Washington's and Cushing's worries reflect the Federalist, or conservative, postwar concern that democracy could degenerate into mob rule. Thomas

---

Daniel Shays
(ca. 1747–1825)

Although others were also involved, the name of Daniel Shays was instantly attached to the 1786–1787 uprising in western and central Massachusetts. During the American Revolution, Shays had been a second lieutenant in Woodbridge's Massachusetts Regiment from May to December 1775 and became a captain in the Fifth Massachusetts Regiment of the Continental army on January 1, 1777.

Shays resigned his commission on October 14, 1780, for unknown reasons. He was acknowledged as a brave and efficient officer who had served from the very beginning of the American Revolution and was promoted for gallantry at Bunker Hill. He also served at Ticonderoga, Saratoga, and Stony Point. No less a figure than Lafayette presented him with a ceremonial sword, which Shays, in his later poverty, was forced to sell.

Jefferson and his protégé James Madison were leading voices among the liberals; they would go on, by the beginning of the nineteenth century, to found the Democratic-Republican Party in opposition to the Federalist Party. On January 30, 1787, commenting on Shays's Rebellion, Jefferson wrote to Madison from Paris, where he was struggling to negotiate a treaty of amity and commerce: "I hold it that a little rebellion now and then is a good thing, and as necessary in the political world as storms in the physical. Unsuccessful rebellions, indeed, generally establish the encroachments on the rights of the people which have produced them. An observation of this truth should render honest republican governors so mild in their punishment of rebellions as not to discourage them too much. It is a medicine necessary for the sound health of the government."

Under Fire: Articles of Confederation

Shays's Rebellion produced four immediate effects: It gave the Federalists a cause and a basis from which to argue for a much stronger central government. It helped to define the divide between conservatives (the Federalists) and liberals (the later Democratic-Republicans). It succeeded in bringing about tax reform in Massachusetts. And it moved Congress to reexamine the Articles of Confederation and ultimately replace them with the Constitution, which gave the federal government the kind of power, including the authority of direct taxation, that theoretically would have provided the funds to compensate the veterans of the American Revolution.

WHISKEY REBELLION

At Issue in the Whiskey Rebellion

A federal excise tax on whiskey, enacted under the new U.S. Constitution, sparked a rebellion that tested the will and competence of federal authority to enforce federal law.

Essential Background

President George Washington's administration, the first to assume office after the ratification of the new Constitution, was essentially conservative, although Secretary of State Thomas Jefferson was liberal. Over Jefferson's vigorous objection, Secretary of the Treasury Alexander Hamilton created a direct taxation plan with the purpose of financing the national debt and supporting a substantial central government that would take precedence over state and other local governments. Jefferson (and other liberals) feared that the federal government would introduce the same kind of oppressive taxation policies that had triggered the Revolution. Furthermore, Jefferson believed that central government was inherently dangerous and inadequately representative of the people governed. By usurping the purse strings, the central government would overpower all local authority. Hamilton (and other conservatives) countered that direct taxation was necessary to pay the national debt, to establish the good faith and credit of the United States both domestically and internationally, and to create a genuine nation rather than a collection of confederated states. Hamilton lobbied for and secured from Congress, on March 3, 1791, a federal excise tax on spirits distilled in the United States.

The Conflict

Popular opposition to the new tax came quickly. Faced with a threat to their livelihood, western Pennsylvania farmers, who turned a portion of their grain crop into the readily saleable and transportable form of alcohol, responded to federal tax collectors with harassment, intimidation, threats, and even assault and arson. The growing violence coalesced into "rebellion" on July 16, 1794, when a mob of about 500 farmers attacked the home of General John Neville, Allegheny County's inspector of the excise. Instead of meekly yielding to intimidation, as so many other officials did, Neville responded by summoning a small detachment of U.S. Army regulars—federal troops—to defend his home. Two attackers were killed and six wounded. However, Neville and his soldiers were outnumbered and had to abandon the house to the mercy of the mob, which first looted and then burned it.

The attack on Neville emboldened the insurgents. On August 1, 1794, nearly 6,000 men assembled at Braddock's Field, near Pittsburgh, only to disperse by August 3. This notwithstanding, George Washington felt about the Whiskey Rebellion much as he had felt about Shays's Rebellion, but this time he was president of a genuinely federal government, and he believed he possessed and was obliged to exercise the power to enforce federal authority by enforcing

Proclamation, 1794

Whereas, combinations to defeat the execution of the laws laying duties upon spirits distilled within the United States and upon stills have from the time of the commencement of those laws existed in some of the western parts of Pennsylvania.

And whereas, the said combinations, proceeding in a manner subversive equally of the just authority of government and of the rights of individuals, have hitherto effected their dangerous and criminal purpose by the influence of certain irregular meetings whose proceedings have tended to encourage and uphold the spirit of opposition by misrepresentations of the laws calculated to render them odious; by endeavors to deter those who might be so disposed from accepting offices under them through fear of public resentment and of injury to person and property, and to compel those who had accepted such offices by actual violence to surrender or forbear the execution of them. . .

And whereas, it is in my judgment necessary under the circumstances of the case to take measures for calling forth the militia in order to suppress the combinations aforesaid, and to cause the laws to be duly executed . . .

Therefore, and in pursuance of the proviso above recited, I. George Washington, President of the United States, do hereby command all persons, being insurgents, as aforesaid, and all others whom it may concern, on or before the 1st day of September next to disperse and retire peaceably to their respective abodes. And I do moreover warn all persons whomsoever against aiding, abetting, or comforting the perpetrators of the aforesaid treasonable acts; and do require all officers and other citizens, according to their respective duties and the laws of the land, to exert their utmost endeavors to prevent and suppress such dangerous proceedings.

Excerpted from the Avalon Project at Yale Law School, "The Whiskey Rebellion," www.yale.edu/lawweb/avalon/presiden/proclamations/gwproc03.htm.

the collection of the excise tax. Therefore, he issued a **Proclamation** on August 7, announcing that he was calling out the militia against "combinations" (that is, organized insurgents), who were "proceeding in a manner subversive equally of the just authority of government and of the rights of individuals." Simultaneously with the issuance of the proclamation, Washington dispatched to western Pennsylvania a team of commissioners to offer amnesty to all who agreed to swear an oath of submission to the United States.

While the countryside remained peaceful, few stepped forward to swear the oath. Frustrated, on September 25, Washington ordered 12,950 militiamen and volunteers from Pennsylvania, New Jersey, Virginia, and Maryland to march to Pittsburgh. This imposing force, led by Washington himself, apprehended in November a few known partic-

CHRONOLOGY OF THE WHISKEY REBELLION

1791

- The federal government institutes a tax on whiskey. Noncompliance and resistance are widespread.

1794

June Local officials order the arrest of those involved in the "Whiskey Rebellion"; farmers in Pennsylvania are incited to open rebellion against tax collectors.

July 16 A mob of 500 attacks the home of General John Neville, a tax collector.

Aug. 1 Some 6,000 whiskey rebels assemble at Braddock's Field, near Pittsburgh, but disperse by Aug. 3.

Aug. 7 Washington issues a proclamation condemning the Whiskey Rebellion.

Aug. 14 Washington orders the governors of Maryland, New Jersey, Pennsylvania, and Virginia to raise a militia against the Whiskey Rebellion.

Nov. 2 Washington arrives with the militia at the scene of the rebellion. Most of the rebels had dispersed or were in hiding. Patrols arrest a few ringleaders, who receive presidential pardons.

A 1794 political cartoon sides with the Pennsylvania organizers of the Whiskey Rebellion who opposed the taxation power of Congress.

ipants in what some were calling the "Whiskey Rebellion," but most of the disaffected farmers, including those prominent in the insurrection, fled and hid. The handful who were arrested were subsequently granted presidential pardons.

Significance

Thomas Jefferson attached little significance to the Whiskey Rebellion. He saw the far greater danger in Washington's response to it, which seemed to him to border on a tyranny that smacked more of George III than of the George who had led the Continental army to victory. Washington, however, was determined to demonstrate both the will and the capacity of the federal government to enforce national laws. Absent such will and capacity, he argued, there was no real government and, therefore, no real nation. It was especially important, Washington believed, to demonstrate the reach of federal authority even into the far corners of the western frontier. But if Washington sought to use the Whiskey Rebellion as an object lesson in federal government, Jefferson, as the third president of the United States, heeded another lesson: the depth and intensity of popular resentment of federal taxa-

tion. In 1801 President Jefferson prevailed upon Congress to repeal the federal excise tax on whiskey.

Origin of the Tax

Many general histories of the United States attribute the tax on whiskey to the desire of Secretary of the Treasury Alexander Hamilton to assert in practice what the Constitution provided for in law: direct taxation by the federal government. Hamilton's further motive, these histories note, was to ensure funding for the repayment of debt incurred by the United States during the American Revolution. Hamilton understood that validation of United States sovereignty over the long run depended as much on sound credit and the perception of a viable *federal* economy as it did upon such ideological concepts as liberty, democracy, and unalienable rights.

While this explanation of the origin of the whiskey tax is accurate as far as it goes, it does not go far enough. Hamilton had negotiated an accord between the states and the federal government by which the federal government agreed to assume all the debts incurred by the states as a result of the American Revolution. Hamilton planned to use this as a means to

Alexander Hamilton

(1755–1804)

The illegitimate son of James Hamilton and Rachel Faucett Lavien, Hamilton was born on the island of Nevis in the British West Indies and was orphaned at age 12. He immigrated to the North American colonies late in 1772, where he enrolled at King's College (now Columbia University) during 1773–1774 and earned a reputation as a pamphleteer promoting the colonial cause.

During the American Revolution, Hamilton served as a captain of artillery and soon attracted the attention of General Washington, who made him his secretary and aide-de-camp. Restless in a staff position, Hamilton served as a field officer during the Yorktown campaign. After the Revolution, his marriage to Elizabeth Schuyler, the daughter of General Philip J. Schuyler, provided the family connections his illegitimate birth and early poverty had denied him, and he became a prosperous New York City lawyer and served as a member of the Continental Congress. He was also a principal architect of a strong central government to replace the weak system under the Articles of Confederation. In 1786 Hamilton proposed a Constitutional Convention be held at Philadelphia the following year, and he served as one of New York's three delegates.

Hamilton was not thoroughly satisfied with the Constitution adopted by the convention; he wanted it to confer even greater power on the central government. Nevertheless, he was instrumental in obtaining its ratification by the states and was an important contributor to *The Federalist Papers,* which so brilliantly presented the case for ratification.

Hamilton was the nation's first secretary of the Treasury in the cabinet of President George Washington. In this capacity, in 1790, he presented a sweeping financial program to the first U.S. Congress, proposing that the debt accumulated by the Continental Congress be paid in full, that the federal government assume all state debts, and that a Bank of the United States be chartered. To raise revenue, Hamilton called for a tariff on imported manufactures and a series of excise taxes. Congress adopted most of Hamilton's program before the Federalists were swept from power in the elections of 1800.

The 1800 contest produced an electoral tie between Jefferson and his running mate, Aaron Burr, leaving the choice of chief executive to the House of Representatives. Hamilton used his influence to ensure that Jefferson (a political adversary whom he nevertheless greatly respected) became president and Burr vice president. In 1804 Hamilton again thwarted Burr, this time in Burr's bid to become governor of New York. Burr accused Hamilton of having insulted his honor and challenged him to a duel. Burr and Hamilton met at Weehawken Heights, New Jersey, on July 11, 1804, where Hamilton was mortally wounded and succumbed the next day.

establish the ascendancy of federal over state sovereignty, even as it provided financial relief for the states. There was another feature to this bargain, however. In return for the assumption of debt, the states agreed to move the federal capital from Philadelphia to land ceded to the government by Virginia and Maryland. The excise tax on whiskey was intended to finance the payment of the newly acquired debt and, indirectly, to enable the establishment of the city that would become Washington, D.C.

Hamilton chose whiskey as the object of his tax because he believed that what today would be called a "sin tax" would meet with the least intense objection. Indeed, Hamilton reasoned, any protest would be confined to the relatively powerless and thinly populated West, the frontier region, where whiskey was a far more important commodity than it was in the East. Westerners produced and drank whiskey; Easterners consumed wines and ports. In effect, Hamilton had hit upon a *federal* tax that was actually *regional* in scope. Jefferson objected to the tax on the grounds that it gave too much power to the central government and promoted regional division with the *United States.*

Public Opinion

What Hamilton did not count on was a western revolt in response to the tax.

By no means was all of the revolt armed or organized. Even in the West, compliance with the tax varied and was proportional to the scale of the production in question. The relatively few large distillers, who saw themselves as being in the business of whiskey production, tended to accept the tax as a cost of doing business. Their volume of sales readily enabled them to pay the annual excise of six cents per gallon. The far more numerous small and casual producers—the western farmers who relied on liquor for their income—were charged at a higher rate of about nine cents per gallon and had to make payments throughout the year. This was perceived as discriminatory, giving large (and usually more prosperous) producers a substantial competitive advantage over small (and typically struggling) producers, and the excise was seen as a tax on the poor that benefited the rich. Compounding this perception of unfairness was the requirement that the tax be paid in cash, the rarest of commodities in the West.

In addition to the violent protest, the people of western Pennsylvania, who believed themselves to be inadequately represented in Congress, formed their own assembly consisting of three to five representatives. This movement toward extralegal representation, more than the violence, posed the most credible threat to the viability of the national government. It was only thanks to the persuasiveness of such Pennsylvania moderates as Hugh Henry Brackenridge and Albert Gallatin that the open rebellion signified by the rogue assembly was ultimately abandoned.

Enduring Consequences

Although Jefferson was alarmed when George Washington sent troops to quell the Whiskey Rebellion, the show of force did end the outright rebellion, if not fully compel compliance with the law. Moreover, the restraint exercised by the troops, together with the pardons issued by the president, softened the blow for the westerners. In the end, President Washington avoided even the appearance of tyranny.

As many historians see it, the most enduring consequence of the Whiskey Rebellion and its suppression was the assertion of federal over local authority. Perhaps even more important, however, was the political division the episode widened and made permanent. If any single event definitively marked the creation of the two major political parties of the early republic, it was the response to the Whiskey Rebellion. The Federalists rallied around Washington, Hamilton, and John Adams, while the party that would be called the Democratic-Republicans formed around Jefferson and Madison.

BIBLIOGRAPHY

Baldwin, Leland. *Whiskey Rebels: The Story of a Frontier Uprising.* Pittsburgh: University of Pittsburgh Press, 1939.

Boyd, Steven R., ed. *The Whiskey Rebellion: Past and Present Perspectives.* Westport, Conn.: Greenwood Press, 1985.

Richards, Leonard L. *Shays's Rebellion: the American Revolution's Final Battle.* Philadelphia: University of Pennsylvania Press, 2002.

Slaughter, Thomas P. *The Whiskey Rebellion: Frontier Epilogue to the American Revolution.* New York: Oxford University Press, 1986.

Starkey, Marion L. *A Little Rebellion.* New York: Alfred A. Knopf, 1955.

CHAPTER 3

LITTLE TURTLE'S WAR

(1786–1795)

At Issue

The expansion of white settlement into Kentucky and the Ohio country created a demand for land possessed by Shawnee, Miami, and allied Indian tribes. The U.S. government deemed the Indians, as allies of the British during the American Revolution, to be a conquered people and therefore demanded the cession of certain lands. When the tribes refused, war began.

The Conflict

The end of the American Revolution coincided with a large influx of settlers into Kentucky and the Ohio country, which covered the present state of Ohio as well as parts of eastern Indiana, western Pennsylvania, and northwestern West Virginia. The U.S. government regarded the Indians of the Old Northwest—chiefly the Shawnee and Miami tribes, who had allied themselves with the British during the Revolution—as a conquered people who had forfeited their civil rights, including the right to occupy their own lands. Despite this policy, the government offered to buy (cheaply) Indian territory of interest to white settlers rather than simply appropriating it as the spoils of war. Some tribes agreed to sell, while others, most notably the Shawnees, resisted. In January 1786 the Shawnee chief Kekewepellethe (Tame Hawk) declared that the contested land was Shawnee and would always be Shawnee. This prompted U.S. treaty commissioner William Butler to reply that, on the contrary, the land in the Ohio country was the sovereign territory of the United States. With his

people suffering from Revolutionary War–induced shortages and the effects of a hard winter, Kekewepellethe agreed to cede the entire Miami Valley rather than provoke renewed war. No sooner had Kekewepellethe signed a treaty of cession than other Shawnee bands, in league with the Miamis, repudiated the agreement.

Shawnee war chief Blue Jacket and his Miami counterpart, Little Turtle, put muscle behind the repudiation by intensifying a campaign of hit-and-run raids on white settlers that had begun during the Revolution. In response, during the fall of 1786, American Revolution hero George Rogers Clark raised a 2,000-man militia in Kentucky and advanced against Shawnees, Miamis, and Ottawas in the Wabash Valley. The expedition dissolved when it failed to encounter the enemy. Soon after, Colonel Benjamin Logan led another 800 militiamen in raids against Shawnee villages on the Miami River but accomplished little. In the summer of 1787, Logan led a more effective raid that destroyed Shawnee provisions. Outrage over Logan's campaign united the Shawnees more closely with the Miamis and other tribes, including Ottawas, Ojibwas (Chippewas), Kickapoos, and Potawatomis. Together, these tribes—sometimes joined by Chickamaugas and Cherokees—retaliated against white settlements along the Cumberland River during 1788.

By 1790 appeals for a federal campaign against the Indians resulted in the creation of the first substantial national army since the Continental army. The First American Regiment was a force of 1,216 federal troops and 1,133 nationalized militiamen, all under the command of General Josiah Harmar. Warned by Major Patrick Murray, the British commandant who still occupied Detroit, that an attack

CHRONOLOGY OF LITTLE TURTLE'S WAR

1786

Jan. Shawnee chief Kekewepellethe (Tame Hawk) cedes territory to the United States. Shawnee war chief Blue Jacket and Miami war chief Little Turtle repudiate the cession and intensify Indian raids on settlers in the region.

Fall George Rogers Clark leads an abortive campaign against the Shawnees, Miamis, and Ottawas.

1787

Summer General Benjamin Logan carries out destructive raids against Shawnee villages, motivating the Shawnee, Miami, Ottawa, Ojibwa (Chippewa), Kickapoo, and Potawatomi tribes to make an alliance.

1788

• Indian raids become epidemic in the Ohio country.

1790

Fall Josiah Harmar leads the First American Regiment and militiamen against Little Turtle and Blue Jacket.

Oct. 19–21 Harmar is defeated with heavy losses.

1791

Winter Shawnee and allied tribes conduct devastating winter raids. Arthur St. Clair leads the enlarged First American Regiment against the Indians.

Nov. 4 St. Clair is devastatingly defeated on the Great Miami River.

1792

Apr. Replacing St. Clair, Major General "Mad Anthony" Wayne recruits and trains the "Legion of the United States."

1794

Aug. 20 Wayne defeats Blue Jacket and Little Turtle at the Battle of Fallen Timbers.

1795

Aug. 3 Wayne concludes the Treaty of Greenville, securing cession of the Ohio country and bringing an unprecedented fifteen years of peace to the region.

was being launched, Little Turtle and his Miami warriors ambushed the advance party of Harmar's force on October 19. His men panic-stricken, Harmar ordered a retreat. On October 21, he sent a small body of regulars and 400 militiamen back to the Indian settlement of Kekionga as a rear guard; that force was also ambushed, this time by Blue Jacket and his Shawnees. Losses on both sides were heavy, and the only thing that saved Harmar's force from total destruction was a lunar eclipse that took place the night following the battle. The Ottawa warriors took this as an evil omen and broke off the fight.

Harmar's defeat enhanced the prestige of the Shawnees, who continued to league with other tribes in a series of winter raids. At the height of the violence in 1791, the British traders in the area volunteered to intercede, but negotiations between British and U.S. authorities broke down. The federal government assembled a new force of 2,300 men, under the command of territorial governor Arthur St. Clair, who built Fort Hamilton near the newly named settlement of Cincinnati. St. Clair was a conventional military leader who moved with agonizing slowness. When even he recognized the need for greater speed, he detached 1,400 men as a "flying column" to move more swiftly against their objective. On November 3, 1791, this reduced force made camp on a plateau above the upper Wabash River. At dawn on November 4, Little Turtle and Blue Jacket led 1,000 warriors against the camp, attacking from three directions. After three hours of one-sided battle, about 500 troops fled, but 623 others were killed, along with twenty-four civilian teamsters. An additional 271 soldiers were wounded. Indian losses were 21 killed and 40 wounded. In proportion to the number of men fielded that day, St. Clair's defeat still stands as the worst loss in the history of the U.S. Army.

St. Clair was replaced by the Revolutionary War general "Mad Anthony" Wayne. In April 1792, after the Shawnees turned down an offer of peace, Wayne recruited and trained an elite force of 1,000 men, which he called the Legion of the United States. He marched westward, recruiting additional troops as peace talks began again, faltered, and broke down.

Wayne built a fort at Greenville, Ohio, and then, farther west, he built an advance position, Fort Recovery, on the very site of St. Clair's defeat. Wayne took his time and prepared his defenses, knowing that for Indian warriors, idleness was always destructive. The great alliance that had grown up around the Shawnees and Miamis began to dissolve.

After two years of desultory and inconclusive peace talks, fearing that more warriors would drift away, Little Turtle and Blue Jacket attacked, hitting a supply pack train on June 30, 1794, routing some 140 legionnaires. Following this small victory, Blue Jacket and the youthful Tecumseh (a brilliant warrior who would earn his greatest fame in the War of 1812; see Chapter 6) recalled their men; however, the Ottawas and other allies refused to break off the attack and insisted on advancing to Fort Recovery. It was a bad mistake, as Wayne's artillery opened up and turned them back. The heavy losses precipitated further disintegration of the Indian alliance.

Even as the Indian forces dwindled, the main body of American troops—2,200 regulars and 1,500 Kentucky militiamen—arrived at Fort Recovery. Proceeding systematically, Wayne ordered a more advanced stockade (Fort Adams) to be built, which was followed by yet another outpost (Fort Defiance) deeper within Indian country. Little Turtle counseled the leaders of his 1,500 remaining warriors that victory over Wayne was now impossible, but Blue Jacket and Tecumseh still refused to yield, and overall command of the Indian forces passed to Blue Jacket. Little Turtle was relegated to leading only his 250 Miamis.

It is a measure of Blue Jacket's daring and desperation that he decided to attack a superior force opposite the rapids of the Maumee River at Fallen Timbers. Wayne deployed scouts, who informed him of the Indians' position. Halting on August 17 a few miles short of Fallen Timbers, Wayne built Fort Deposit, caching inside all that was unnecessary for combat. On August 20, he continued his advance against Blue Jacket. Expecting battle on August 18, the Indians had advanced to Fallen Timbers on the seventeenth without rations—it was their custom to fast immediately before a fight. By the twentieth, they had gone hungry for three days. Some warriors left to look for food; those who remained were weakened. Nevertheless, their first contact with Wayne's advance guard of 150 mounted Kentucky militiamen produced panic, but the charismatic Wayne rallied the main body of his troops and transformed looming defeat into victory, routing Blue Jacket, who surrendered to Wayne. After the battle, Wayne swept through and destroyed all of the Indian towns, which had been abandoned after Blue Jacket's defeat and withdrawal. In August 1795 Blue Jacket signed the **Treaty of Greenville** drawn up by Wayne, which secured white occupancy of lands northwest of the Ohio River. The British, also signatory to the treaty, agreed to vacate the Old Northwest (territory that later became the states of Ohio, Indiana, Illinois, Michigan, part of Minnesota, and Wisconsin). Thus the U.S. government successfully asserted control over an important frontier, and the peace of the Ohio country endured until the outbreak of the War of 1812.

Post-Revolutionary Indian Policy

The Indians who inhabited the western frontier of the newly independent United States had taken no part in the Treaty of Paris, which ended the American Revolution. Nevertheless, the U.S. government asserted that those Indians who had fought alongside the British during the war shared the defeat and were therefore a conquered people, their land forfeit.

While still commanding the Continental army, George Washington outlined proposed Indian policy in a letter of September 7, 1783, to Continental Congress delegate James Duane. Washington began by asserting the necessity of federal laws regulating "Land Jobbers, Speculators, and Monopolisers" as well as "scatter'd settlers," in order to assert the authority of the federal government and to prevent "disputes both with the Savages, and among ourselves." Next, he proposed informing the Indians "that after a Contest of eight years for the Sovereignty of this Country G: Britain has ceded all the Lands of

Treaty of Greenville, 1795

Art. 1:

Henceforth all hostilities shall cease; peace is hereby established, and shall be perpetual; and a friendly intercourse shall take place between the said United States and Indian tribes. . . .

Art. 3:

The general boundary line between the lands of the United States and the lands of the said Indian tribes, shall begin at the mouth of Cayahoga river, and run . . . And in consideration of the peace now established . . . , the said Indian tribes do hereby cede and relinquish forever, all their claims to the lands lying eastwardly and southwardly of the general boundary line now described. . . .

Art. 4:

In consideration of the peace now established, and of the cessions and relinquishments of lands made in the preceding article by the said tribes of Indians, and to manifest the liberality of the United States, as the great means of rendering this peace strong and perpetual, the United States relinquish their claims to all other Indian lands northward of . . .

And for the same considerations and with the same views as above mentioned, the United States now deliver to the said Indian tribes a quantity of goods to the value of twenty thousand dollars. . . .

Art. 6:

If any citizen of the United States, or any other white person or persons, shall presume to settle upon the lands now relinquished by the United States, such citizen or other person shall be out of the protection of the United States; and the Indian tribe, on whose land the settlement shall be made, may drive off the settler, or punish him in such manner as they shall think fit. . . .

Art. 8:

Trade shall be opened with the said Indian tribes; and they do hereby respectively engage to afford protection to such persons, with their property, as shall be duly licensed to reside among them for the purpose of trade; and to their agents and servants; but no person shall be permitted to reside among them for the purpose of trade; and to their agents and servants; but no person shall be permitted to reside at any of their towns or hunting camps, as a trader, who is not furnished with a license for that purpose. . . .

Art. 9:

Lest the firm peace and friendship now established, should be interrupted by the misconduct of individuals, the United States, and the said Indian tribes agree, that for injuries done by individuals on either side, no private revenge or retaliation shall take place; but instead thereof, complaint shall be made by the party injured, to the other.

Excerpted from the Avalon Project at Yale Law School, "Treaty of Greenville 1795," www.yale.edu/lawweb/avalon/greenvil.htm.

the United States within the limits described by . . . the Provisional Treaty." Washington continued:

> [Because the Indians] could not be restrained from acts of Hostility, but were determined to join their Arms to those of G Britain and to share their fortune; so, consequently, with a less generous People than Americans they would be made to share the same fate; and be compelld to retire along with them beyond the [Great] Lakes.

> But as we prefer Peace to a state of Warfare, as we consider them as a deluded People; as we perswade ourselves that they are convinced, from experience, of their error in taking up the Hatchet against us, and that their true Interest and safety must now depend upon *our* friendship. . . . [W]e will from these considerations and from motives of Compn., draw a veil over what is past and establish a boundary line between them and us.

Federal Regulation of White Settlement

Washington's idea of drawing a line to define the limit of white settlement was hardly new. The most famous line was drawn by none other than King George III in his Proclamation of 1763, which set the Alleghenies as the western limit of white settlement. Washington well knew that not only had the Proclamation Line failed to halt westward settlement, but it had also *dared* Americans to defy the Crown. To now propose a new "proclamation line" was a risky business. In his September 7, 1783, letter to James Duane, Washington stressed that, in setting this line, "care should be taken neither to yield nor to grasp at too much," but once the line was established, "a Proclamation . . . Should issue, making it Felony . . . for any person to Survey or Settle beyond the Line."

Washington was willing to chance the dangers of a new proclamation line because he saw the only alternative as "one of two capital evils": he wrote that either "the settling, or rather overspreading [of] the Western Country will take place, by a parcel of Banditti, who will bid defiance to all [federal] Authority," or there will be "a renewal of Hostilities with the Indians, brought about more than probably, by this very means." It is unclear why Washington framed this as an either/or proposition, because his point was that failure to regulate westward settlement would "more than probably" cause both problems: defiance of federal authority *and* Indian hostility. Therefore, despite the danger of constricting liberty, he urged that "[n]o [land] purchase under any pretence whatever should be made by any other authority than that of the Sovereign [federal] power, or the Legislature of the State in which such Lands may happen to be."

On September 22, 1783, the Continental Congress, following Washington's suggestion, issued a proclamation prohibiting "all persons from making settlements on lands inhabited or claimed by Indians . . . without the express authority and directions of the United States in Congress assembled."

"Suffering Officers and Soldiers"

Washington's September 7, 1783, letter also offered another rationale for the regulation of settlement. During a significant portion of the American Revolution, Continental army officers and enlisted men were paid either in all-but-worthless paper currency ("Continentals") or not at all, which had prompted mutinies late in the war. To appease at least the former officers (for enlisted men were ultimately excluded), some in the Continental Congress proposed compensation in the form of grants of western land. Washington worried that unregulated settlement of the western territories would usurp government land promised to the officers—"the many suffering Officers and Soldiers who have fought and bled to obtain it, and are now waiting the decision of Congress to point them to the promised reward of their past dangers and toils"—and possibly provoke new rebellions among them.

Indian Treaties

During the immediate postwar period, the Continental Congress made treaties with many Indian tribes in an effort to secure peace and to define the limits of Indian claims to land. The motive behind these treaties was laudable, but the documents were doomed by three major problems. First, the United States' attempts to treat with Indian tribes as if they were sovereign nations reflected a fundamental misunderstanding of tribal governance. Generally speaking, tribal leaders were respected individuals who exercised influence on the tribe or some portion of the tribe but rarely had true governing authority. The members of the tribe were not legally bound to obey them. Thus, even when Indian leaders signed treaties in good faith, there was no guarantee that others would abide by the terms of the treaty. Second, the Continental Congress, which lacked authority over the state and local governments and controlled no substantial standing army, also had difficulty enforcing on American citizens the terms of the treaties it made. Third, the United States and the Indian signatories often held very different ideas about the meaning of the treaties they signed. Typically, the United States was interested in permanently acquiring land, whereas the Indian signatories, who were interested in receiving gifts and other compensation, tended to regard the land cessions as less absolute.

Typical of the treaties that followed the American Revolution and preceded Little Turtle's War was the **Treaty with the Six Nations (Treaty of Fort Stanwix)** of October 22, 1784, which established a boundary between the land of the Six Nations and that of the United States; additionally, a cession of Indian lands was defined. The treaty also included a provision for "goods to be delivered to the said Six Nations," not as compensation for the cession of lands (which the United States claimed by virtue of the Treaty of Paris), but "in consideration of the present circumstances of the Six Nations, and in execution of the humane and liberal views of the United States."

The Path of Commerce

In his September 7, 1783, letter to Continental Congress delegate James Duane, George Washington expressed his belief that government regulation of trade with the Indians was the most effective way of bringing both the Indians and frontier settlers under the control of the Continental Congress and, therefore, the surest and most efficient path to peace. Washington wrote, "[I]f the Indian Trade was carried on, on Government Acct., and with no greater advance than what would be necessary to defray the expence and risk, and bring in a small profit, . . . it would supply the Indians upon much better terms than they usually are." Washington recommended "engross[ing] their Trade, and fix[ing] them strongly in our Interest." This, he observed, "would be a much better mode of treating them than [the traditional practice] of giving [them] presents," which benefited only "a few" for a limited time.

The Continental Congress agreed with Washington and, on August 7, 1786, passed an **Ordinance for the Regulation of Indian Affairs,** which created a licensing system for white traders' dealings with Indians. Trade licenses were to be restricted to citizens of the United States (thereby excluding British traders who were violating the Treaty of Paris), who

---

Treaty with the Six Nations (Treaty of Fort Stanwix), 1784

The United States of America give peace to the Senecas, Mohawks, Onondagas and Cayugas, and receive them into their protection upon the following conditions:

ARTICLE I.
Six hostages shall be immediately delivered to the commissioners by the said nations, to remain in possession of the United States, till ail [sic] the prisoners, white and black, which were taken by the said Senecas, Mohawks, Onondagas and Cayugas, or by any of them, in the late war, from among the people of the United States, shall be delivered up.

ARTICLE II.
The Oneida and Tuscarora nations shall be secured in the possession of the lands on which they are settled.

ARTICLE III.
A line shall be drawn. . . . [It] shall be the western boundary of the lands of the Six Nations, so that the Six Nations shall and do yield to the United States, all claims to the country west of the said boundary, and then they shall be secured in the peaceful possession of the lands they inhabit east and north of the same. . . .

ARTICLE IV.
The Commissioners of the United States, in consideration of the present circumstances of the Six Nations, and in execution of the humane and liberal views of the United States upon the signing of the above articles, will order goods to be delivered to the said Six Nations for their use and comfort.

Excerpted from Alan Axelrod, *American Treaties and Alliances* (Washington, D.C.: CQ Press, 2000), 28–29.

An Ordinance for the Regulation of Indian Affairs, 1786

Be it ordained by the United States in Congress assembled, That from and after the passing of this ordinance, the Indian department be divided into two districts, viz. The southern, which shall comprehend within its limits, all the nations in the territory of the United States, who reside southward of the river Ohio; and the northern, which shall comprehend all the other Indian nations within the said territory, and westward of Hudson river. . . . That a superintendant be appointed for each of the said districts. . . . The said superintendants, shall attend to the execution of such regulations, as Congress shall from time to time establish respecting Indian affairs. . . . All stores, provisions or other property, which Congress may think necessary for presents to the Indians, shall be in the custody and under the care of the said superintendants, who shall render an annual account of the expenditures of the same, to the Board of Treasury.

And be it further ordained, That none but citizens of the United States, shall be suffered to reside among the Indian nations, or be allowed to trade with any nation of Indians, within the territory of the United States. That no person, citizen or other, under the penalty of five hundred dollars, shall reside among or trade with any Indian or Indian nation, within the territory of the United States, without a license for that purpose.

Excerpted from Francis Paul Prucha, ed., *Documents of United States Indian Policy,* 2d ed. (Lincoln: University of Nebraska Press, 1990), 8–9.

were to be bonded in the amount of $3,000, a very princely sum in 1786.

As with Indian treaties, the ordinance proved difficult to enforce, but its principles would endure as a model for laws enacted in the nineteenth century to regulate trade with the Indian tribes.

Northwest Ordinance of 1787

On July 13, 1787, the Continental Congress enacted the United States' most important piece of pre-Constitutional legislation. The Northwest Ordinance not only ensured that democratic government would prevail within the territories and specified how territories were to become states, but also barred slavery from the territories and, in Article 3, included a statement of good faith and commitment to justice in dealing with the Indians. The article begins with a provision intended to extend the blessings of civilization into the territories: "religion, Morality and knowledge being necessary to good government and the happiness of mankind, Schools and the mans of education shall forever be encouraged." The very next sentence of the article defines relations with the Indians:

The utmost good faith shall always be observed towards the Indians, their lands and property shall never be taken from them without their consent; and in their property, rights and liberty, they never shall be invaded or disturbed, unless in just and lawful wars authorised by Congress; but laws founded in justice and humanity shall from time to time be made, for preventing wrongs being done to them, and for the preservation of peace and friendship with them.

A Conflict of Governments

Although the federal government considered the Indians of the Ohio country to be a people conquered by virtue of the United States victory in the American Revolution, the Northwest Ordinance stepped back from the implications of this assumption and embodied a more generous attitude of good faith toward the Indians and guaranteed them certain rights, especially the right to security in property. The Articles of Confederation, the controlling document under which the federal government and the several states operated, however, established even as it simultaneously undercut the authority of the federal government in Indian matters. Article 6 held that "No State shall engage in any war without the consent of the United States in Congress assembled," but continued, "unless such State be actually invaded by enemies, or shall have received certain advice of a resolution being formed by some nation of Indians to invade such State, and the danger is so imminent as not to admit of a delay till the United States in Congress assembled can be consulted." Thus Article 6 was so vague as to the relative authority of the federal government and the states that conflict was inevitable; states typically felt themselves empowered to act against Indians at will or, yet more destructively, to allow local authorities and even local individuals to act against them.

The Articles of Confederation were similarly vague on the topic of regulating Indian trade, holding that "Congress shall have the sole and exclusive right and power of regulating trade and managing all affairs with the Indians, not members of any of the States," only to continue, "provided that the Legislative right of any State within its own limits be not infringed or violated." The Committee on the Southern Department of the Continental Congress issued a report on August 3, 1787, one month after the Northwest Ordinance was passed, that pointed out the "absurdity" of the Articles on the topic of authority over the Indians and asserted that "the Indian tribes are justly considered the common friends or enemies of the United States, and no particular state can have an exclusive interest in the management of Affairs with any of the tribes, except in some uncommon cases."

Report of Henry Knox on White Outrages, 1788

[The secretary of war reports] That it appears . . . that the white inhabitants on the frontiers of North Carolina in the vicinity of Chota on the Tenessee river, have frequently committed the most unprovoked and direct outrages against the Cherokee indians. . . .

That the unjustifiable conduct of the said inhabitants has most probably been dictated by the avaricious desire of obtaining the fertile lands possessed by the said indians of which and particularly of their ancient town of Chota they are exceedingly tenacious. . . .

That in order to vindicate the sovereignty of the Union from reproach, your secretary is of opinion, that, the sentiments, and decision, of Congress should be fully expressed to the said white inhabitants, who have so flagitiously stained the American name.

That the agent of indian affairs should disperse among the said people a proclamation to be issued by Congress on the subject. . . .

That in case the Proclamation of Congress should be attended with no effect that [a] commanding officer should be directed to move as early in the spring of the next year as the season should admit with a body of three hundred troops to Chota and there to act according to the special instructions he shall receive from the Secretary at War. . . .

Your Secretary begs leave to observe that he is utterly at a loss to devise any other mode of correcting effectually the evils specified than the one herein proposed. That he conceives it of the highest importance to the peace of the frontiers that all the indian tribes should rely with security on the treaties they have made or shall make with the United States. That unless this shall be the case the powerful tribes of the Creeks Choctaws and Chickesaws will be able to keep the frontiers of the southern states constantly embroiled with hostilities, and that all the other tribes will have good grounds not only according to their own opinions but according to the impartial judgements of the civilized part of the human race for waging perpetual war against the citizens of the United States.

Excerpted from Francis Paul Prucha, ed., *Documents of United States Indian Policy,* 2d ed. (Lincoln: University of Nebraska Press, 1990), 11–12.

Extirpation or Peace?

The replacement of the Articles of Confederation with the Constitution in 1789 addressed the conflict between state and federal authority at least in principle, but the question of Indian policy remained: if the federal government somehow managed fully to wrest from the states unambiguous authority over Indian affairs, what should its policy be? Even as Little Turtle's War raged, Secretary of War Henry Knox debated this issue, citing "unprovoked" outrages by "the white inhabitants on the frontiers of North Carolina in the vicinity of Chota on the Tenessee river" against Cherokee Indians there. Knox pointed out that until such outrages were curbed, peace could neither be achieved nor maintained with the Indians (**Report of Henry Knox on White Outrages,** July 18, 1788). In his report on northwestern Indians a year later, Knox asked whether peace with the Indians was a worthwhile objective: "In examining the question how the disturbances on the frontiers are to be quieted, two modes present themselves, by which the object might perhaps be effected; the first of which is by raising an army, and extirpating the refractory tribes entirely, or 2dly by forming treaties of peace with them, in which their rights and limits should be explicitly defined." The second course would require that the United States observe the treaties "with the most rigid justice, by punishing whites, who should violate the same." In the course of his report, Knox ultimately rejected the alternative of extirpation on the grounds that the United States lacked a "clear right [consistent] with the principles of justice and the laws of nature" to "proceed to the destruction or expulsion of the savages"; therefore, he urged a humane and just policy that recognized the Indians' rights to their land and that eschewed the principle of conquest.

The praiseworthy ethics aside, actually persuading the people of the frontier to reject extirpation and conquest would not be easy. Yet when news of General St. Clair's defeat at the hands of Blue Jacket on November 4, 1791, circulated throughout the nation, the prevailing public reaction was not a thirst for vengeance but a weariness with war. Nevertheless, the new Congress authorized the larger army with which "Mad Anthony" Wayne defeated Blue Jacket and Little Turtle.

Treaty of Greenville

The Treaty of Greenville, which ended Little Turtle's War, was concluded on August 3, 1795, at Fort Greenville, Northwest Territory, by Major General Anthony Wayne and ninety representatives of the signatory tribes, most notably the principal war leaders, Blue Jacket of the Shawnees and Little Turtle of the Miamis. The tribes whose representatives signed were the Wyandot, Delaware, Shawnee,

The August 3, 1795, Treaty of Greenville ceded much of the Northwest Territory to the United States. This portion of the treaty shows the signatures of Anthony Wayne and several Wyandot Indian leaders.

Ottawa, Chippewa, Potawatomi, Miami, Kickapoo, Piankeshaw, and Kaskaskia, in addition to two Indian groups known as the Eel River Indians and the Weas. The treaty secured white occupation of lands northwest of the Ohio River, established a "permanent" boundary to white settlement west of the present state of Ohio, and instituted a program of compensation for territory lost by the Indians. The treaty also established peace and "friendly intercourse" between the United States and the signatory tribes and is notable as quite possibly the most successful white-Indian treaty in American history. Although it did not bring the "perpetual peace" hoped for in the text, the treaty was followed by nearly fifteen years of relative quiet, which was more stability than the Old Northwest had known since the French and Indian War during the mid-eighteenth century. Moreover, with the Indian threat neutralized, the British residents of the region acknowledged U.S. authority as well.

The boundaries of settlement established by the Treaty of Greenville proved, however, as futile as any set in previous proclamations and treaties. They were almost instantly violated by white settlers. This fluidity would fuel frontier fighting in the War of 1812.

BIBLIOGRAPHY

Axelrod, Alan. *Chronicle of the Indian War: From Colonial Times to Wounded Knee.* New York: Macmillan General Reference, 1993.

Carter, Harvey Lewis. *The Life and Times of Little Turtle: First Sagamore of the Wabash.* Champagne-Urbana: University of Illinois Press, 1987.

Debo, Angie. *A History of the Indians in the United States.* Norman: University of Oklahoma Press, 1977.

Jensen, Merrill. *The New Nation: A History of the United States during the Confederation, 1781–1789.* 1950. Reprint, Boston: Northeastern University Press, 1981.

Prucha, Francis P. *The Great Father: The United States Government and the American Indians.* Lincoln: University of Nebraska Press, 1984.

Washburn, Wilcomb. *The Indian in America.* New York: Harper and Row, 1975.

At Issue

In a climate of deteriorating Franco-American relations, an undeclared naval war erupted as French vessels violated the rights of American neutrality by interfering with marine commerce.

The Conflict

The cordial relations that developed between France and the United States during the American Revolution deteriorated when American commissioners negotiated the Treaty of Paris, ending the Revolution, without consulting the French ministry. The fall of the Bourbon monarchy during the French Revolution in 1789 created a new crisis, and when war broke out between France and Britain in 1793, the revolutionary French government interpreted U.S. policy as favoring British interests over those of France. This gave rise to the Citizen Genêt Affair (discussed below). American efforts to improve relations with Britain, culminating in the Jay Treaty of 1794, caused further deterioration in Franco-American relations. President John Adams's attempt to patch up relations by sending a commission to France in 1797 produced French demands for what amounted to bribes and tribute, which resulted in the XYZ Affair (discussed below).

By 1793 French naval operations against the British in the West Indies were already beginning to interfere with U.S. shipping. In response, Congress authorized the rapid completion of three great frigates as well as the arming and training of 80,000 militiamen. No less a figure than George Washington was recalled to command the army. Congress also commissioned 1,000 privateers to capture or repel French vessels. An undeclared naval war began, and, on May 3, 1798, Congress created the United States Department of the Navy.

In July 1798 Captain Stephen Decatur, commanding the U.S. sloop *Delaware,* captured the French schooner *Croyable* off the New Jersey coast. Rechristened the *Retaliation,* the vessel sailed with the new U.S. Navy until it was retaken by the French in November 1798 off Guadeloupe. On February 9, 1799, the newly commissioned USS *Constellation* captured the French frigate *Insurgente.* Additional exchanges took place sporadically through 1800, mainly in the Caribbean. Of ten important sea engagements during 1798–1800, the French recapture of *Croyable/Retaliation* was the only American loss.

Despite the successes of the U.S. Navy and American support for the former slave Toussaint Louverture's struggle to obtain Haiti's independence from France (1791–1803), war was never actually declared. When Napoleon Bonaparte assumed the leadership of the French government by his coup d'état of September 10, 1799, he sent unofficial word to American authorities (on November 10) that France wanted to reconcile with the United States. By respecting the rights of neutrals such as the United States, Napoleon hoped to gain the support of neutral Denmark and Sweden, which would lend legitimacy to his new government.

The result of Bonaparte's overtures was the Convention of 1800 between the French Republic and the United States of America, which brought an official end to an unofficial war. The convention clarified the two nations' understanding of the rights of neutrals, reinstated amicable relations, and, equally important, ended any implied military alliance between France and the United States.

Polarization of Pro- and Anti-French Factions

Thomas Jefferson served as U.S. minister to France from 1784 to 1789. During this time, he not only witnessed the beginning of the French Revolution, but, in his zeal to spread democracy worldwide, he also unofficially and more or less secretly supported and helped to foment it. When he returned to the United States in November 1789, he learned—by reading the newspaper—that George Washington had appointed him secretary of state. Jefferson reluctantly accepted.

Jefferson soon found himself the lone liberal voice in a strongly Federalist administration. In the cabinet, he was opposed by Secretary of the Treasury Alexander Hamilton. Jefferson deplored the monarchism of England, while Hamilton favored closer relations between the two nations. Whereas Jefferson applauded the French Revolution and believed that most of the power of government should reside with the people, Hamilton generally distrusted the people and pointed to the French Revolution as proof that any distinction between "the people" and an anarchical "mob" was tenuous at best. Hamilton advocated the creation of an authoritarian central government, more powerful than the one operating under the Articles of Confederation, and had been one of the proponents of the Constitutional Convention. Around Jefferson and Hamilton, as around the poles of a magnet, two political philosophies—and two political parties—soon coalesced.

When the Spanish navy seized some British vessels off Vancouver Island in the spring of 1790, war between England and Spain loomed. Secretary of State Jefferson advised neutrality, but, without consulting Jefferson, Hamilton met with a British secret

---

CHRONOLOGY OF THE FRANCO-AMERICAN QUASI-WAR

1793
- The United States declares neutrality in the War of the First Coalition between Britain (and its allies) and France.
- The Citizen Genêt Affair sours Franco-American relations.

1794
Nov. 19 The Jay Treaty is concluded between the United States and Britain; France construes it as a covert military alliance.

1798
Apr. 3 President John Adams submits the "XYZ correspondence" to Congress, thereby bringing to light the "XYZ Affair," which may be seen as the trigger event for the Quasi-War.
May 3 Congress creates the U.S. Navy during an undeclared naval war with France.
Summer Congress passes the Alien and Sedition Acts, thereby deepening the conservative (Adams-Hamilton) vs. liberal (Jefferson-Madison) political divisions within the nation.

July U.S. Navy captain Stephen Decatur captures the French schooner *Croyable.*
Nov. The *Croyable,* rechristened *Retaliation,* is recaptured by the French off Guadeloupe, West Indies.
Dec. 24 The Virginia Resolutions are enacted.

1799
Feb. 9 The USS *Constellation* captures the French frigate *Insurgente.*
Sept. 10 Napoleon Bonaparte carries off a coup d'état.
Nov. 10 Bonaparte makes peace overtures to the United States.
Nov. 22 The Kentucky Resolutions are enacted.

1800
- Desultory naval action continues through part of the year.
Sept. 30 The convention between the French Republic and the United States ends the Quasi-War.

agent, Major George Beckwith, to discuss the U.S. position on relations between Spain and England. Hamilton assured Beckwith that the United States had no ties with Spain and implied a desire for an Anglo-American alliance. Jefferson was outraged by Hamilton's meddling. The British presence in

Thomas Jefferson
(1743–1826)

Thomas Jefferson was a man of great curiosity, intellect, and achievement. In addition to serving as the third president of the United States, he was governor of Virginia, the first U.S. minister to France, the first U.S. secretary of state, and vice president to John Adams, as well as the author of the Declaration of Independence, the founder of the University of Virginia, an architect, a naturalist, and a minor inventor.

Jefferson was born in Albemarle County, Virginia, attended the College of William and Mary (1760–1762), and afterward apprenticed as a lawyer. In 1769 he was elected to the Virginia House of Burgesses, and in 1774 he wrote *A Summary View of the Rights of British America,* arguing that colonial allegiance to the king was voluntary and could therefore be withdrawn.

Elected to the Second Continental Congress, Jefferson was appointed to draft the Declaration of Independence, a document that made him internationally famous. Back in Virginia, Jefferson served from 1776 to 1779 in the House of Delegates and worked to liberalize and modernize Virginia's laws. His 1779 bill on religious liberty ignited an eight-year dispute before it was finally passed in 1786.

In June 1779 Jefferson was elected governor of Virginia, but he retired from the post in 1781 after months of criticism for his conduct of the state's affairs during the American Revolution. He entered Congress in 1783, where he played a major role in structuring the government of the western territories. A slave owner, Jefferson nevertheless also proposed that slavery be excluded from all of the western territories after 1800.

From 1784 to 1789, Jefferson served as minister to France. On his return to the United States in 1789, Jefferson was appointed secretary of state in the first administration of George Washington. In this post, he was very much at odds with Secretary of the Treasury Alexander Hamilton, whose financial programs he thought both imprudent and unconstitutional. He feared that Hamilton and some other Federalists were monarchist in their zeal to create a strong central government. Jefferson resigned from the cabinet on December 31, 1793, retired to Monticello for three years, and then became the presidential candidate of the new Democratic-Republican Party that he had been instrumental in founding. When Federalist John Adams narrowly won the election, Jefferson (as runner-up) became vice president under the law as it then existed.

At odds with Adams, Jefferson secretly authored the Kentucky Resolutions (1799) in opposition to the Alien and Sedition Acts sponsored by the Federalists in Congress. In 1800 he ran for president again, this time defeating Adams and tying with his running mate, Aaron Burr. The House of Representatives broke the tie in Jefferson's favor, making Burr his vice president. As president, Jefferson reduced internal taxes, permitted the Alien and Sedition Acts to lapse, and made the spectacular Louisiana Purchase (1803). Jefferson won reelection in 1804 and presided over victory in the Tripolitan War (see Chapter 5), but in an effort to resist British (and French) encroachments on U.S. neutrality rights during the Napoleonic Wars, he championed the economically disastrous Embargo Act (December 22, 1807).

After leaving the presidency, Jefferson founded the University of Virginia at Charlottesville in 1819, an institution whose buildings *and* curriculum he designed. It was his last great achievement.

Canada was powerful in North America, as was the Spanish presence in Florida and Louisiana. Jefferson believed that these two North American colonial powers balanced one another, in effect canceling each other out, to the great benefit of the United States. To side with one power or the other would upset this balance, at America's peril.

Although Jefferson endeavored to steer a neutral course between British and Spanish interests in North America, he became an unabashed partisan of France. He recommended that the United States engage in an out-and-out trade war to force Britain to live up to the Treaty of Paris, by which it had agreed to evacuate the forts it still maintained in the Old Northwest, and to pressure Britain into negotiating a fair commercial treaty with the United States. Jefferson went on to advocate increased trade with France at the expense of England. Hamilton not only opposed this plan but also leaked to the British what should have been cabinet secrets.

Jefferson understood that he and Hamilton represented two very different political philosophies, which were vying for dominance over American government. President George Washington, however, vehemently opposed political parties, which, he believed, exacerbated factionalism. Nevertheless, Jefferson, with fellow Virginian James Madison, secretly negotiated with poet Philip Freneau to found and edit the *National Gazette,* an anti-Hamiltonian propaganda sheet. Jefferson supported Freneau—again, covertly—by hiring him as a State Department translator, and he fed Freneau exclusive news stories. By 1792 the *National Gazette* had succeeded in disseminating the anti-Hamiltonian point of view to an ever-increasing readership. Jefferson became widely recognized as the leader of the anti-Hamiltonian coalition, which by 1792 was being called the Republican Party or the Democratic-Republican Party.

Geographically, the new party's adherents tended to come from the South and the West, whereas the Hamiltonians, soon to be formally called the Federalists, were mainly New Englanders. The Democratic-Republicans were ardent democrats and advocates of majority rule and what would later be called states'

rights. In contrast, the Federalists favored strong centralization of governing authority. In international relations, the Democratic-Republicans wanted to reach out to form many foreign ties, and they welcomed the radicalism of the French Revolution; the Federalists tended toward isolationism, feared and condemned the radicalism of the French Revolution, and felt at least a fraternal bond with Britain.

The Citizen Genêt Affair

The Democratic-Republicans backed candidates in the midterm congressional elections of 1792. After much soul searching, Jefferson resolved to remain in Washington's cabinet, even after the president, in 1794, decided to seek a second term. In the meantime, the French Revolution had degenerated into the Reign of Terror and threatened even those members of the nobility who had supported liberty, equality, and fraternity, many of whom had been intimates of Jefferson's social and intellectual circle in Paris. By this time, too, the French Revolution was reaching beyond France to engulf most of Europe and Europe's colonial possessions in war. Still, Jefferson did not abandon the cause. He believed that the defeat of the French Revolution would threaten the American republic, encouraging Hamilton and his party to reshape American government along British lines. Jefferson hoped that the moderate wing of the French Revolution, the Girondists, would prevail against the radical Jacobins to produce a stable, peaceful republic, friendly to the United States.

Yet Jefferson did back off from his earlier extreme partisan stance and counseled strict neutrality as war broke out between France and the First Coalition, made up of Britain, Holland, Spain, Austria, Prussia, and Russia. At the same time, Jefferson maintained that the United States was bound to honor its 1778 Treaty of Alliance with France, which obligated the United States to help France defend its West Indian possessions, should they be menaced. Fearing that this obligation would drag the nation into war against Britain, Hamilton argued that the treaty was null and void because it had been made with the French monarchy, now deposed. Jefferson countered that treaties are made between nations, not between agents of government. In the end, Washington agreed to recognize the French Republic, to honor the treaty of 1778, and (over Hamilton's vigorous protest) to receive its ambassador, Citizen Edmond Genêt. Washington was, however, very particular concerning just how Genêt was to be received: "not with too much warmth or cordiality." Jefferson ignored this instruction and welcomed him quite warmly.

Presumably encouraged by Jefferson's warmth as well as by the generally friendly response of so many Americans, Genêt boldly flouted U.S. neutrality provisions after Washington rejected his request that the United States directly aid France in its war. Genêt commissioned American privateers to prey on British merchant ships in American waters and even began recruiting American volunteers for an amphibious assault against Florida, which at the time was a possession of First Coalition member Spain. Jefferson needed no directive from President Washington to prompt him to issue a warning to Genêt. Genêt responded by insisting that the 1778 treaty gave France the right to equip privateers on American soil and operate them in American waters, then sell any prize vessels in American ports. Jefferson refuted this to Genêt but, confidentially, suggested to Washington that captured prizes were indeed French property and could therefore be sold. Washington responded by summarily ordering all French-commissioned privateers out of U.S. ports.

Genêt's activities culminated in the July 1793 seizure of the British vessel *Little Sarah,* which was towed into the port of Philadelphia, the United States capital, to be fitted out with heavier guns for use as a French privateer. Hamilton supported Secretary of War Henry Knox in his suggestion that a battery of artillery be erected on the Delaware River to prevent the departure of the prize ship. Fearing that this would immediately provoke a war with France, Jefferson objected and proposed that the matter be referred to the Supreme Court—which, however, refused to render an opinion. Finally, after drawing up "Rules Governing Belligerents," the cabinet, on

During the French Revolution, Citizen Edmond Genêt, the ambassador from Republican France to the United States, flouted American neutrality and strained relations between the two countries by commissioning American privateers to prey on British merchant ships.

August 2, recommended to the president that he demand Genêt's recall to France.

By this time in France, the Jacobins had ascended to power through violence and liberal use of the guillotine. The new government did not merely comply with Washington's recall demand, it requested the *extradition* of Genêt, who was a Girondist. Washington refused to appear to endorse the Jacobin government by cooperating with it; therefore, he refused to compel Genêt to return. Citizen Genêt subsequently chose to become an *American* citizen and married the daughter of the governor of New York.

The Jay Treaty

The dispute over Citizen Genêt moved Jefferson to resign from the cabinet and even from politics. But when he saw the text of the **Jay Treaty** (Treaty of Amity, Commerce, and Navigation with Britain), negotiated by Washington's special minister John Jay and signed at London on November 19, 1794, he began a campaign to block its ratification by the Senate.

Motivated by the Washington administration's desire to strengthen Anglo-American bonds, the Jay Treaty laid a firm foundation for Anglo-American trade, obtained a renewed promise of British evacuation of the frontier forts in the Old Northwest, and secured at least the limited right of American ships to trade in the British West Indies. With other liberals, Jefferson protested that the treaty conceded so much to Britain that it was really a covert treaty of alliance. Despite these protests, the Senate ratified the treaty in 1795. It did bring a short-lived improvement in Anglo-American relations, but, as Jefferson had feared, it also produced a precipitous decline in relations between America and France, which regarded the treaty as a de facto Anglo-American alliance.

Jay Treaty, 1794

ARTICLE 1.
There shall be a firm inviolable and universal Peace, and a true and sincere Friendship between His Britannick Majesty, His Heirs and Successors, and the United States of America. . . .

ARTICLE 2.
His Majesty will withdraw all His Troops and Garrisons from all Posts and Places within the Boundary Lines assigned by the Treaty of Peace to the United States. . . .

ARTICLE 3.
It is agreed that it shall at all Times be free to His Majesty's Subjects, and to the Citizens of the United States, and also to the Indians dwelling on either side of the said Boundary Line freely to pass and repass by Land, or Inland Navigation, into the respective Territories and Countries of the Two Parties on the Continent of America (the Country within the Limits of the Hudson's Bay Company only excepted) and to navigate all the Lakes, Rivers, and waters thereof, and freely to carry on trade and commerce with each other. . . .

ARTICLE 4.
Whereas it is uncertain whether the River Mississippi extends so far to the Northward as to be intersected by a Line to be drawn due West from the Lake of the woods in the manner mentioned in the Treaty of Peace between His Majesty and the United States, it is agreed, that measures shall be taken in Concert between His Majesty's Government in America, and the Government of the United States, for making a joint Survey of the said River. . . .

ARTICLE 7.
Whereas Complaints have been made by divers Merchants and others, Citizens of the United States, that during the course of the War in which His Majesty is now engaged they have sustained considerable losses and damage by reason of irregular or illegal Captures or Condemnations of their vessels and other property under Colour of authority or Commissions from His Majesty . . . ; It is agreed that in all such Cases where adequate Compensation cannot for whatever reason be now actually obtained, had and received by the said Merchants and others in the ordinary course of Justice, full and Complete Compensation for the same will be made by the British Government to the said Complainants. . . .

ARTICLE 14.
There shall be between all the Dominions of His Majesty in Europe, and the Territories of the United States, a reciprocal and perfect liberty of Commerce and Navigation. . . .

ARTICLE 19.
And that more abundant Care may be taken for the security of the respective Subjects and Citizens of the Contracting Parties, and to prevent their suffering Injuries by the Men of war, or Privateers of either Party, all Commanders of Ships of war and Privateers and all others the said Subjects and Citizens shall forbear doing any Damage to those of the other party, or committing any Outrage against them, and if they act to the contrary, they shall be punished, and shall also be bound in their Persons and Estates to make satisfaction and reparation for all Damages, and the

Ratification of the Jay Treaty, together with Washington's response to the Whiskey Rebellion (see Chapter 2), persuaded Jefferson to offer himself as the Democratic-Republican's first candidate for the office of president of the United States in the elections of 1796. Because Washington had adamantly refused to stand for a third term, Jefferson's opponent would be John Adams, a Revolutionary War colleague and long-time friend, but, increasingly, his ideological nemesis.

interest thereof, of whatever nature the said Damages may be.

For this cause all Commanders of Privateers before they receive their Commissions shall hereafter be obliged to give before a Competent Judge, sufficient security by at least Two responsible Sureties, who have no interest in the said Privateer, each of whom, together with the said Commander, shall be jointly and severally bound in the Sum of Fifteen hundred pounds Sterling, or if such Ships be provided with above One hundred and fifty Seamen or Soldiers, in the Sum of Three thousand pounds sterling, to satisfy all Damages and Injuries, which the said Privateer or her Officers or Men, or any of them may do or commit during their Cruize contrary to the tenor of this Treaty, or to the Laws and Instructions for regulating their Conduct; and further that in all Cases of Aggressions the said Commissions shall be revoked and annulled.

It is also agreed that whenever a Judge of a Court of Admiralty of either of the Parties, shall pronounce sentence against any Vessel or Goods or Property belonging to the Subjects or Citizens of the other Party a formal and duly authenticated Copy of all the proceedings in the Cause, and of the said Sentence, shall if required be delivered to the Commander of the said Vessel, without the smallest delay, he paying all legal Fees and Demands for the same.

Excerpted from the Avalon Project at Yale Law School, "The Jay Treaty," www.yale.edu/lawweb/avalon/diplomacy/britian/jay.htm.

John Jay
(1745–1829)

John Jay was a brilliant student at King's College (now Columbia University), graduating with highest honors in 1764. After a four-year legal apprenticeship, Jay was admitted to the New York Bar in 1768, and in 1774 he emerged as one of the most active members of the New York Committee of Correspondence and was sent as a delegate to the First Continental Congress. An advocate of reconciliation with Great Britain, he retired from the Congress in 1776 rather than sign the Declaration of Independence.

In 1777 Jay was selected to draft a constitution for New York, after which he served as the state's first chief justice. Reelected to the Continental Congress in 1778, he was voted its president; however, the following year he was appointed minister to Spain, charged with seeking that nation's recognition of American independence and negotiating financial aid and commercial treaties. In 1782 Jay, with John Adams, Benjamin Franklin, and Henry Laurens, was appointed to the commission that concluded the Treaty of Paris with Britain, ending the American Revolution.

Jay authored three of *The Federalist* essays, and President George Washington appointed him chief justice of the Supreme Court under the new Constitution in 1789. Jay stepped down in 1794 to serve as envoy extraordinary to Britain, charged with negotiating improved commercial relations and resolving Anglo-American conflicts on the western frontier. The resulting Jay Treaty was controversial, though approved by the Washington administration.

Jay was elected governor of New York in 1794 and retired from public life in 1801.

The XYZ Affair

The Jay Treaty proved to be the flashpoint issue of the 1796 campaign, a campaign conducted not by the candidates themselves, but by their partisans. (Adams thought personal campaigning unseemly, and Jefferson was more than happy to refrain from it as well.) Adams emerged as a leader who would continue the dignified greatness of Washington, whereas Jefferson was presented as the defender of the rights of the people. In the end, the closeness of the election reflected the deep division of the new nation. Adams prevailed by just three electoral votes, 71 to Jefferson's 68. In the era before the Twelfth Amendment redefined the electoral process, the president and vice president were elected separately. The Federalist vice presidential candidate, Thomas Pinckney, received 48 votes, while Aaron Burr, the Democratic-Republican, received 30. Jefferson had received more votes than Pinckney and, therefore, as runner-up in the presidential contest, was elected vice president.

The first crisis in what would be four stormy years of a combined Federalist and Democratic-Republican administration came just two months after Adams took office. News reached the president that the recently created five-man executive body of France, the Directory, had refused to accept the credentials of Charles Cotesworth Pinckney, who was sent as the new American minister to France. This provoked an indignant speech from Adams, and Federalists began to stir up popular anti-French sentiment. Adams, however, was not interested in provoking a war with France. He commissioned Pinckney, with John Marshall and Elbridge Gerry, to attempt to heal the growing breach in Franco-American relations by negotiating a new treaty of commerce. French prime minister Charles Maurice de Talleyrand-Perigord sent three agents to greet the American commissioners in Paris in October 1797. The agents informed the commissioners that before a treaty could even be discussed, the United States would have to loan France $12 million *and* pay Talleyrand a personal bribe of $250,000.

It was an outrage.

On April 3, 1798, an indignant Adams submitted to Congress the correspondence from the commission, which designated the French agents not by name but as "X," "Y," and "Z." Congress, in turn, published the entire portfolio, and that is how the public learned of the "XYZ Affair." Worse, by the time the XYZ Affair came fully to light, the dispute had become more than diplomatic, as French naval operations against the British in the West Indies had begun to interfere directly with U.S. shipping.

Creation of the United States Navy

Despite Adams's reluctance to come to blows with France, the XYZ Affair brought the United States to the verge of open war with France and may be viewed as the event that triggered an undeclared naval war between the two countries. Congress authorized the rapid completion of three great frigates, recalled George Washington from postpresidential retirement to command the 80,000-troop army it had funded, and commissioned 1,000 privateers to capture or repel French vessels. On May 3, 1798, when the undeclared war was under way, Congress created the United States Department of the Navy.

Alien and Sedition Acts

In the summer of 1798, the undeclared Quasi-War prompted the Federalist-dominated Congress to pass the infamous Alien and Sedition Acts. These included the Naturalization Act (June 18, 1798), which required immigrants seeking U.S. citizenship to be resident in the country fourteen years instead of the originally mandated five; the Alien Act (June 25), which authorized the president to deport by executive order any alien he regarded as dangerous; the Alien Enemies Act (July 6), which authorized the president, in time of war, to arrest, imprison, or deport subjects of any enemy power; and the Sedition Act (July 14), which prohibited any assembly "with intent to oppose any measure . . . of the government" and forbade printing, uttering, or publishing anything "false, scandalous, and malicious" against the government.

In and of itself, the Sedition Act was counterrevolutionary, a bald infringement on the constitutional rights to peaceable assembly and free speech. What made the Alien and Sedition Acts even more insidious was that many of the leading Democratic-Republicans were recent refugees from turbulent Europe who had not been resident in the United States for anything approaching fourteen years. Whatever else the Alien and Sedition Acts were intended to accomplish, they were squarely aimed at reducing the power base of the Democratic-Republican Party.

Jefferson saw the Alien and Sedition Acts as a dangerous step toward a return to monarchy. If they were allowed to stand, he wrote, "we shall immediately see attempted another act of Congress, declaring the President shall continue in office

during life, reserving to another occasion the transfer of the succession to his heirs, and the establishment of the Senate for life." Jefferson set to work on a series of resolutions attacking centralized governmental authority and promoting the sovereignty of the states. Coming from him personally, he believed, the criticism would carry relatively little weight, so he looked for a state legislature willing to publish the resolutions. On November 22, 1799, Kentucky (which had become a state in 1792) published Jefferson's document, which became known as the **Kentucky Resolutions.** On December 24, 1798, Virginia had published ideologically similar resolutions—the Virginia Resolutions—drafted by James Madison.

Both states' resolutions held that the Alien and Sedition Acts were unconstitutional and, therefore, not binding on the states. Jefferson's original draft of the Kentucky Resolutions additionally maintained that a

Kentucky Resolutions, 1799

RESOLVED, That this commonwealth considers the federal union, upon the terms and for the purposes specified in the late compact, as conducive to the liberty and happiness of the several states: That it does now unequivocally declare its attachment to the Union, and to that compact, agreeable to its obvious and real intention, and will be among the last to seek its dissolution: That if those who administer the general government be permitted to transgress the limits fixed by that compact, by a total disregard to the special delegations of power therein contained, annihilation of the state governments, and the erection upon their ruins, of a general consolidated government, will be the inevitable consequence: That the principle and construction contended for by sundry of the state legislatures, that the general government is the exclusive judge of the extent of the powers delegated to it, stop nothing short of despotism; since the discretion of those who adminster the government, and not the constitution, would be the measure of their powers: That the several states who formed that instrument, being sovereign and independent, have the unques-

tionable right to judge of its infraction; and that a nullification, by those sovereignties, of all unauthorized acts done under colour of that instrument, is the rightful remedy: That this commonwealth does upon the most deliberate reconsideration declare, that the said alien and sedition laws, are in their opinion, palpable violations of the said constitution; and however cheerfully it may be disposed to surrender its opinion to a majority of its sister states in matters of ordinary or doubtful policy; yet, in momentous regulations like the present, which so vitally wound the best rights of the citizen, it would consider a silent acquiesecence as highly criminal: That although this commonwealth as a party to the federal compact; will bow to the laws of the Union, yet it does at the same time declare, that it will not now, nor ever hereafter, cease to oppose in a constitutional manner, every attempt from what quarter soever offered, to violate that compact.

Excerpted from The Avalon Project at Yale Law School "The Kentucky Resolutions, 1799," www.yale.edu/lawweb/avalon/kenres.htm.

state had the right not only to judge the constitutionality of acts of Congress, but also to "nullify" any acts it determined to be unconstitutional. The concept of nullification was too radical even for the Kentucky legislature to accept, and it was suppressed in the final draft; however, the nullification principle was implied in both the Kentucky and Virginia resolutions.

The Kentucky and Virginia resolutions did not bring about the immediate repeal of the Alien and Sedition Acts. They did set forth the Democratic-Republican opposition to autocratic power, and they ensured that even in an atmosphere of international crisis and armed conflict, the Alien and Sedition Acts would be short lived. The Sedition Act was repealed in 1801, and the Alien and Naturalization Acts expired without renewal in 1802. Only the Alien Enemies Act occasionally resurfaced in American political life, most notably during World Wars I and II (see Chapters 34 and 36).

The Kentucky and Virginia resolutions made Jefferson a popular political figure at the expense of the Federalists. The concept of nullification lingered to haunt American history and, as resurrected by South Carolina's John C. Calhoun, would serve as a political rationale for secession and the Civil War (see Chapter 17).

Convention with France

The Quasi-War ended as quickly as it had begun when, on September 30, 1800, French and American representatives signed the **Convention between the French Republic and the United States of America.** Simple and straightforward, the document sought to ensure freedom of navigation for American and French vessels; interference with this freedom had been the principal proximate cause of the Quasi-War.

The convention reinstated amicable relations between France and the United States. It also ended any implied *military* alliance between the two nations, in effect canceling any moral debt the United States might have accrued when it had accepted French aid during the American Revolution.

Convention between the French Republic and the United States of America, 1800

ARTICLE I
There shall be a firm, inviolable, and universal peace, and a true and sincere Friendship between the French Republic, and the United States of America. . . .

ARTICLE III
The Public Ships, which have been taken on one part, and the other, or which may be taken before the exchange of ratifications shall be restored.

ARTICLE IV
Property captured . . . shall be mutually restored. . . .

ARTICLE V
The debts contracted by one of the two nations, with individuals of the other, or by the individuals of one, with the individuals of the other shall be paid. . . .

ARTICLE VI
Commerce between the Parties shall be free . . . and in general the two parties shall enjoy in the ports of each other, in regard to commerce, and navigation, the priviledges of the most favoured nation.

Excerpted from The Avalon Project at Yale Law School, "France – Convention of 1800: Text of the Treaty," www.yale.edu/lawweb/avalon/diplomacy/france/fr1800.htm.

BIBLIOGRAPHY

DeConde, Alexander. *The Quasi-War: The Politics and Diplomacy of the Undeclared War with France 1797–1801.* New York: Scribner, 1966.

Palmer, Michael A., ed. *Stoddert's War: Naval Operations During the Quasi-War with France, 1798–1801.* Annapolis, Md.: Naval Institute Press, 2000.

CHAPTER 5

TRIPOLITAN WAR (1801–1805) AND ALGERINE WAR (1815)

At Issue in the Tripolitan War

The United States sought to end the piracy and extortion sanctioned by the "Barbary States."

The Conflict

The "Barbary pirates" were Muslim seafarers who had been operating for centuries off the coast of North Africa from the so-called Barbary (or Berber) states, including present-day Morocco, Algeria, Tunisia, and Libya. Financed by the region's wealthy merchants and rulers, the piracy was state-sanctioned, its victims exclusively so-called Christian nations plying the North African waters. These nations customarily paid extortionary tribute to the Barbary States as protection money. The refusal of the United States to continue paying tribute spawned a series of limited naval wars to suppress the Barbary pirates. Collectively called the "Barbary Wars," they spanned 1801–1815, with the most concentrated action occurring in the Tripolitan War of 1801–1805.

Shortly after the inauguration of Thomas Jefferson as the third U.S. president in 1801, Pasha Yusuf Qaramanli of Tripoli abrogated a 1796 treaty by demanding resumption of tribute payments to Tripoli in the amount of $225,000. Jefferson refused, whereupon the pasha unofficially declared war against the United States. Jefferson quickly formed a coalition with Sweden, Sicily, Malta, Portugal, and Morocco against Tripoli. Faced with the combined strength of the coalition, Algiers and Tunis ceased piracy, but Morocco and, under Qaramanli, Tripoli refused to commit. For the next two years, therefore, one U.S. frigate and several smaller U.S. Navy vessels patrolled the Tripolitan coast in an effort to suppress piracy. During most of 1803, a flotilla under Commodore Edward Preble interdicted pirates and periodically bombarded Tripoli. In October 1803 one of Preble's ships, the frigate USS *Philadelphia,* ran aground and was boarded by Tripolitan sailors, who captured 300 U.S. sailors, took the ship as a prize, and prepared to use it against the Americans. In February 1804 naval lieutenant Stephen Decatur stealthily entered Tripoli Harbor aboard a captured native ketch and burned the *Philadelphia,* thereby depriving the pasha of his prize. Decatur was hailed as an American naval hero.

While Preble continued the naval bombardment of Tripoli, William Eaton, U.S. consul at Tunis, proposed an alliance with Ahmed Qaramanli, the brother Yusuf had deposed in 1795. Eaton also recruited an army of Arabs and Greeks and joined these to a contingent of U.S. Marines to support the restoration of Ahmed as ruler of Tripoli. Eaton's force captured the port city of Derne in a battle that spanned April 27–May 13, 1805, just as the Jefferson administration, which had neither opposed nor supported the Eaton plan, was concluding a treaty of peace with Yusuf. The June 4, 1805, treaty ransomed

After running aground at Tripoli in 1803, the frigate USS Philadelphia *was captured and some 300 U.S. sailors were taken prisoner. In February 1804 Lieutenant Stephen Decatur led a dashing raid to burn the ship.*

CHRONOLOGY OF THE TRIPOLITAN WAR

1801
- Pasha Yusuf Qaramanli of Tripoli unofficially declares war on the United States.
- Jefferson forms a coalition of nations to oppose Tripolitan piracy; the U.S. Navy begins patrolling North African waters.

1803
Oct. The USS *Philadelphia* runs aground at Tripoli and is captured; 300 U.S. sailors are held prisoner.

1804
Feb. 16 Lieutenant Stephen Decatur leads a dashing raid and burns the captured *Philadelphia.*

1805
Apr. 27–May 13 William Eaton captures the port city of Derne.
June 4 The United States concludes a new treaty with Tripoli, ending the war.

the *Philadelphia* crew for $60,000 and ended the practice of tribute payment by establishing free and unhindered commerce between the United States and Tripoli.

Background of the Barbary Pirates

The coast of North Africa had been the site of piracy since the decline of the Roman Empire. Organized, state-sanctioned piracy developed in the sixteenth century and reached its height in the seventeenth. The European states generally responded by paying tribute, but, at various times, they actually encouraged the pirates to prey on rival states. For instance, during much of the eighteenth century, the British found Barbary piracy useful in suppressing trade competition from weaker Mediterranean nations. At the end of the eighteenth century and early in the nineteenth, especially during the period of the War of 1812 (see Chapter 6), Britain actively encouraged piracy against U.S. shipping.

Tribute Treaties and Public Response

In 1785 the British encouraged Algerian pirates to capture two American vessels. Thomas Jefferson, who was then United States minister plenipotentiary to France, attempted to build a coalition among Portugal, Naples, Sardinia, Russia, and France to combat the piracy. France, the linchpin of the proposed coalition, soon left the alliance, whereupon the British encouraged further Algerian action in which a dozen American merchant vessels were captured and more than 100 American sailors were imprisoned.

Lacking the naval and military means to mount a credible resistance against the Barbary pirates, especially when they were supported by a European power, the American government concluded a series of treaties:

- The Treaty of Peace and Friendship with Morocco (1786) stipulated the establishment of commerce between the United States and Morocco "on the same footing as is the Commerce with Spain or as that with the most favored Nation . . . and their Citizens shall be respected and esteemed and have full Liberty to pass and repass our Country and Sea Ports whenever they please without interruption." On the face of it, this did away with extortion; but it proved ineffective.
- The Treaty of Peace and Amity with Algiers (1795) stipulated an end to piracy but acknowledged the payment of tribute money, referring to it as "the usual duties . . . paid by all nations at Peace with this Regency." Thus the understanding was that the United States would pay the same tribute as other nations, no more and no less.
- The Treaty of Peace and Friendship with Tripoli (1796) sought to end Tripolitan-sanctioned piracy with a lump-sum tribute payment. Soon after signing the treaty, the dey of Tripoli repudiated it and demanded additional tribute. The United States initially agreed to pay additional money, but President Jefferson then refused, thereby provoking the Tripolitan War.
- The Treaty with Tunis (1797) defined what was, in fact, extortionary tribute as a schedule of "duties and other taxes" to be paid by U.S. vessels entering Tunisian ports. Despite the treaty, Tunis continued to make increased tribute demands.

Sanitizing extortion by calling it "duties and taxes" was an attempt to preserve American pride and, more important in a legal sense, U.S. sovereignty. It was also a sop thrown to the American public, which

almost universally bridled at the thought of their nation paying protection money. As the treaties proved ineffective because the Barbary rulers concluded them in bad faith, so they also reflected a certain bad faith on the part of the American negotiators. They were dodges intended to rationalize the compromise of American rights of trade. But Congress, the Republic, and even President Thomas Jefferson, who had drastically reduced funding for the U.S. Navy, could not tolerate the deception for long, especially since it failed to appease the governments that sanctioned the Barbary pirates.

Jefferson Builds a Coalition

In May 1801 Pasha Yusuf Qaramanli unofficially declared war after Jefferson refused his demand for tribute. Before he became president, Jefferson had proposed a military solution to deal with the Barbary pirates. He always met with objections that the cheaper course was simply to pay the ransoms and tributes demanded, which, after all, was what other nations did. As president, Jefferson responded to the pasha's bellicosity by assembling a naval squadron at Norfolk. Before sending it off to Tripoli, however, he convened his cabinet and put before its members two questions: First, should the squadron be sent to deal with the pirates? Second, did the president, while Congress was adjourned (as it was at the time), have the authority to commit an act that might lead to war? The cabinet was unanimous in its opinion that the squadron should be sent, but the members were divided on the question of the president's authority to act without congressional approval. Attorney General Levi Lincoln expressed the gravest doubts, arguing that in the absence of a congressional declaration of war, U.S. warships could legally do nothing more than defend themselves; they could not act aggressively. The rest of the cabinet members were persuaded to agree with Jefferson that he had the authority to act against the Barbary pirates.

Jefferson's decision put him at odds with his own political ideology. He was, first and foremost, a man of peace, who now advocated military force. He also believed passionately in the subordination of the executive branch to the legislative, but he was about to take what he realized would be a precedent-setting action by assuming an executive prerogative that neither Washington nor Adams had ever dared assume. Nevertheless, Jefferson unilaterally ordered the squadron to set sail for the Mediterranean, to locate Barbary pirate vessels, and to destroy them, wherever they might be found.

An American Hero

Jefferson's stand against the pasha of Tripoli and extortion was very popular. Americans were proud of their young nation, and they were also gratified

---

Stephen Decatur
(1779–1820)

Born on Maryland's Eastern Shore, Decatur was raised in Philadelphia, where he attended the University of Pennsylvania, which he left to join the navy as a midshipman in April 1798. In 1799 he was promoted to lieutenant and saw action (as first lieutenant aboard the USS *Essex*) during the Quasi-War (see Chapter 4). Given command of the sloop *Delaware,* he captured the French schooner *Croyable* off the New Jersey coast in one of the signal actions of the conflict.

Decatur's greater fame came during the Tripolitan War. While commanding the twelve-gun *Enterprise,* Decatur captured a pirate ketch (which he renamed *Intrepid*) and used it to lead a small band of sailors and marines into Tripoli Harbor on February 16, 1804, to set fire to the captured 36-gun frigate *Philadelphia*. British admiral Horatio Nelson pronounced this exploit the "most bold and daring act of the age," and the feat earned Decatur a promotion to captain in May—at age twenty-five, he was (and remains) the youngest man ever promoted to this rank. He was also presented with a sword of honor by Congress. Decatur continued to fight with gallantry throughout the war and took part in the negotiations with the dey of Tunis that ended the war.

Decatur served in the 1808 court-martial that suspended Captain James Barron for negligence in the *Chesapeake-Leopard* incident of June 22, 1807, in which the U.S. warship *Chesapeake* was stopped by the British frigate *Leopard* off Norfolk, Virginia, and four seamen were "impressed" (forcibly removed) into the British service and others killed in an exchange of gunfire. Impressment proved to be one of the precipitating factors in the War of 1812 (see Chapter 6), which saw Decatur commanding the 44-gun frigate *United States,* which captured the 38-gun British frigate *Macedonian* in a battle on October 25, 1812.

Promoted to commodore, Decatur was responsible for the defense of New York Harbor (1813). During June 13–15, 1813, he attempted to run the British blockade of the harbor in the 44-gun USS *President*. Although he engaged and damaged the 24-gun HMS *Endymion,* he was compelled to surrender to superior British forces; he was taken prisoner but subsequently paroled.

With the outbreak of the Algerine War in May 1815 (discussed in this chapter), Decatur was again dispatched to the Mediterranean to fight the Barbary pirates. Decatur personally dictated highly favorable peace terms, securing release of all U.S. prisoners, ending U.S. tribute payments to Algiers, and obtaining an indemnity.

On his return to the United States, Decatur was appointed to the newly created Board of Naval Commissioners in November 1815. Five years later, James Barron, embittered by the disgrace he had suffered in the *Chesapeake-Leopard* court-martial, mortally wounded Decatur in a duel on March 22, 1820, at Bladensburg, Maryland.

by what many saw as a crusade against an enemy of Christianity. The American people also found in Stephen Decatur a hero personifying the republic's courageous and daring ideals. His spectacular foray into the harbor of Tripoli, aboard a seized pirate ketch, to burn the captured *Philadelphia* succeeded under fire at the cost of only one man wounded.

On his return to the United States after the end of the hostilities, Decatur found himself the focus of celebration. Even before he died in an 1820 duel, several American cities and towns had already renamed themselves in his honor.

Treaty of 1805

The Treaty of Tripoli, which ended the Tripolitan War, was signed on June 4, 1805, at Tripoli, Barbary (present-day Libya), and ratified by the U.S. Senate on April 17, 1806. The treaty established free and unhindered commerce between the United States and Tripoli. It deliberately avoided mention of tribute money, because the U.S. treaty commissioners did not want to appear to legitimate an act of extortion; however, by guaranteeing free and unmolested commerce by sea, the practice of tribute was ended. The treaty did provide for a $60,000 ransom to be paid for the release of American prisoners, mainly the captured crew of the *Philadelphia,* held in Tripoli. Recognizing that the basis for centuries of Barbary piracy was at least in part religious—the Muslim Barbary pirates preyed exclusively on the shipping of "Christian nations"—Article 14 of the treaty sought to avoid further conflict arising from religion:

> As the Government of the United States of America, has in itself no character of enmity against the Laws, Religion or Tranquility of Musselmen, and as the said States never have entered into any voluntary war or act of hostility against any Mahometan Nation, except in the defence of their just rights to freely navigate the High Seas: It is declared by the contracting parties that no pretext arising from Religious Opinions, shall ever produce an interruption of the Harmony existing between the two Nations; And the Consuls and Agents of both Nations respectively, shall have liberty to exercise his Religion in his own house; all slaves of the same Religion shall not be Impeded in going to said Consuls house at hours of Prayer.

While victory in the Tripolitan War and the resulting Treaty of Tripoli greatly enhanced the prestige of the young American republic, both among its own citizens and among the family of nations, neither the victory nor the treaty put an end to all Barbary Coast piracy. The Algerine War (discussed next) was fought to end Algerian-sanctioned piracy and was quite successful; however, it was not until France captured and colonized Algiers in 1830 that the piracy ended permanently.

At Issue in the Algerine War

Like the Tripolitan War fought between 1800 and 1805, the Algerine War was fought by the United States to end state-sanctioned piracy by the "Barbary States" of North Africa's coast.

The Conflict

The American naval victory in the Tripolitan War greatly curbed (but did not end) the activity of the "Barbary pirates," and the outbreak of the War of 1812 (see Chapter 6) prompted the withdrawal of the U.S.

warships that had been keeping the Barbary pirates in check. This not only encouraged the dey of Algiers to resume preying on American commerce in the region, but also emboldened him to expel the U.S. consul and imprison or enslave U.S. nationals. He then declared war on the United States for its having violated a 1795 treaty pledging to render tribute to the dey.

At the end of the War of 1812 and in response to the declaration of war by Algiers, Commodore Stephen Decatur led a ten-ship squadron into the Mediterranean. Between March 3 and June 30, 1815, he captured two Algerian warships and then sailed into the harbor of Algiers. With his artillery trained on the city, Decatur demanded the cancellation of tribute and the release of all U.S. prisoners without ransom. The June 30 Treaty of Peace with Algiers also incorporated the dey's pledge to end state-sanctioned piracy.

From Algiers, Decatur sailed to Tunis and Tripoli, where he compelled similar treaties from the rulers of these countries and also obtained compensation for American vessels that had been seized at the urging of the British during the War of 1812.

Algerine War Context: The Operative Treaty

The United States counted on its victory in the Tripolitan War to discourage the other Barbary

States from engaging in piracy against American merchant vessels plying North African waters; however, the new dey of Algiers, Hadji Muhammad, seeking to establish his prestige, did not merely sanction the resumption of pirate activity, but boldly declared war on the United States. He cited the Treaty of Peace and Amity with Algiers, concluded on September 5, 1795, and in force from March 7, 1796, by which the United States had agreed to pay tribute money to Algeria—although the document referred to the extortionary protection money as "the usual duties . . . paid by all nations at Peace with this Regency." The United States never formally repudiated the treaty but simply refused to continue paying the "duties," which it did not consider legal.

Outrages of the Algerine Dey

Hadji Muhammad was not content merely to resume piracy. He ejected the U.S. consul, then rounded up all members of the small American mercantile community in Algiers and held them hostage along with captured ships' crews and passengers. The idea of a Muslim ruler holding Christian civilians, including women, for ransom created a great sentiment of outrage in the United States, which moved President James Madison to ask Congress for a declaration of war against Algiers.

Negotiation at the "Mouth of a Cannon"

The declaration of war with Algiers was approved by both houses on March 2, 1815, and Stephen Decatur sailed from New York with the frigates *Guerriere, Constellation,* and *Macedonian,* as well as seven smaller warships.

Decatur won a very quick naval victory, and the Algerine War, such as it was, ended when he captured the Algerian flagship *Machuda.* Decatur sailed his squadron into Algiers and, with the ships riding at anchor off the coast, Decatur negotiated the Treaty of Peace with Algiers on June 30, 1815, "at the mouth of a cannon."

CHRONOLOGY OF THE ALGERINE WAR

1815

Mar. 2   At the request of President Madison, Congress declares war on Algiers.

Mar. 3–June 30   Stephen Decatur captures two Algerian warships, then sails into the harbor of Algiers.

June 30–July 3   A new peace treaty is concluded with Algiers, ending the brief war, calling for an end to piracy, and ending tribute. Decatur proceeds to Tunis and Tripoli and compels rulers there to sign similar treaties

1816

Dec. 22–23   Revised treaty with Algiers is signed.

The 1815 treaty secured the release of all captives, ended the payment of all duties, taxes, and tributes, and levied a substantial indemnity against the dey. Decatur immediately went on to secure new treaties from the dey of Tunis and the pasha of Tripoli, obliging them also to pay the United States an indemnity for ships captured and cargoes plundered. On December 22–23, 1816, a revised **Treaty of Peace and Amity with Algiers** was signed. Both sides felt that the 1815 treaty—concluded hastily as well as under duress—was imperfect, and the new treaty was drawn up to "restore and maintain upon a stable and permanent footing" of peace and amity.

Like the earlier Tripolitan War, the brief Algerine War greatly enhanced the prestige of the young American republic. The United States was the first "Christian nation" to make an effective stand against the centuries-old practice of Barbary Coast piracy. This notwithstanding, Algerian piracy remained a threat, albeit diminished, to the shipping of the United States and other non-Muslim nations until France captured Algiers in 1830.

Treaty of Peace and Amity with Algiers, 1816

ARTICLE 1st
There shall be from the conclusion of this Treaty, a firm, perpetual, inviolable and universal peace and friendship between the President and Citizens of the United States of America on the one part, and the Dey and subjects of the Regency of Algiers in Barbary on the other. . . .

ARTICLE 2d
It is distinctly understood between the contracting parties, that no tribute, either as biennial presents or under any other form, or name whatever, shall be required by the Dey and Regency of Algiers from the United States of America on any pretext whatever. . . .

ARTICLE 6th
If any citizens or subjects belonging to either party shall be found on board a prize-vessel taken from an enemy by the other party, such citizens or subjects shall be liberated immediately and in no case, or on any presence whatever shall any American citizen be kept in captivity or confinement. . . .

ARTICLE 9th
Vessels of either of the contracting parties, putting into the ports of the other, and having need of provisions or other supplies shall be furnished at the Market price, and if any such vessel should so put in from a disaster at sea, and have occasion to repair, she shall be at liberty to land and reembark her cargo, without paying any customs or duties whatever; but in no case shall be compelled to land her cargo.

ARTICLE 10th
Should a vessel of either of the contracting parties be cast on shore within the territories of the other, all proper assistance shall be given to her and her crew; no pillage shall be allowed. . . .

ARTICLE 11th
If a vessel of either of the contracting parties shall be attacked by an enemy party within cannon-shot of the forts of the other, she shall be protected as much as is possible. . . .

ARTICLE 12th
The commerce between the United States of America and the Regency of Algiers, the protections to be given to Merchants, Masters of vessels, and seamen, the reciprocal rights of establishing consuls in each country, the privileges, immunities, and jurisdictions to be enjoyed by such consuls, are declared to be on the same footing in every respect with the most favoured nations respectively.

Excerpted from Alan Axelrod, *American Treaties and Alliances* (Washington, D.C.: CQ Press, 2000), 70.

BIBLIOGRAPHY

Chidsey, Donald Barr. *The Wars in Barbary: Arab Piracy and the United States Navy.* New York: Crown, 1971.

Lambert, Franklin. *The Barbary Wars: American Independence in the Atlantic World.* New York: Hill and Wang, 2005.

Nash, Howard Prevear. *The Forgotten Wars: The Role of the U.S. Navy in the Quasi-War with France and the Barbary Wars, 1798–1805.* South Brunswick, N.J.: A. S. Barnes, 1968.

United States Office of Naval Records and Library. *Naval Documents Related to the United States Wars with the Barbary Powers . . . Including Diplomatic Background.* Washington, D.C.: U.S. Government Printing Office, 1939–1944.

Wheelan, Joseph. *Jefferson's War: America's First War on Terror 1801–1805.* New York: Carroll and Graf, 2004.

CHAPTER 6

WAR OF 1812 AND THE CREEK WAR
(1812–1815)

At Issue

Ostensibly, the United States declared war to compel Great Britain to respect its maritime and other rights as a neutral nation; however, a more significant motive for war was the territorial ambitions of certain American factions and regional interests.

The Conflicts

War of 1812

Much of the action of the War of 1812 took place along the U.S.-Canadian border in the frontier region between Detroit and Lake Champlain. Although the United States claimed only to defend its sovereignty, the initial American strategy included an invasion of Canada, with the objective of incorporating parts of the country into the United States. The British, defending their territory, wanted to fight the war in the United States rather than in Canada, and their forces therefore expanded the theater of operations to include the mid-Atlantic coast and the U.S. territories around the Gulf of Mexico. As a result, the War of 1812 came to encompass a large portion of North America, extending from Canada to New Orleans.

The United States entered the war with a standing army of only 12,000 regular troops, who were distributed over a vast territory and supplemented by state-based militia. Troop leadership was uneven, many generals having attained their rank through political connections rather than military aptitude. U.S. Navy officers were generally of a higher caliber

than those of the army, but the tiny force could not be expected to prevail against Britain's Royal Navy, the dominant military force of its day. Despite the lack of resources and absence of preparation, American strategists devised a three-pronged invasion of Canada: one prong penetrating from Lake Champlain to Montreal, another crossing the Niagara frontier, and a third advancing into Upper Canada from Detroit.

Michigan territorial governor William Hull commanded U.S. forces north of the Ohio River. Hull led his regular and militia troops across the Detroit River into Canada on July 12, 1812, intending to take Fort Malden, which guarded the entrance to Lake Erie. Believing himself outnumbered (in fact, he had the superior force), Hull delayed his assault, which allowed British major general Isaac Brock time to capture Fort Michilimackinac, the U.S. border fort guarding the Mackinac Straits between Lake Huron and Lake Michigan, without a fight on July 17, 1812. On August 2, the Shawnee Indian leader Tecumseh ambushed Hull's columns, prompting Hull to retreat to Fort Detroit. Brock and Tecumseh marched on Fort Detroit and intimidated Hull into surrendering without a shot on August 16. The day before, on August 15, Fort Dearborn (at the site of present-day Chicago) also surrendered to a mixed force of British soldiers and Indians. As U.S. troops and settlers left the fort, Potawatomi Indians attacked and then tortured and killed thirty-five men, women, and children.

In the Northeast, New York militia general Stephen Van Rensselaer led 2,270 militiamen and

900 regulars in an October 13 assault on Queenston Heights, Canada, just across the Niagara River.

CHRONOLOGY OF THE WAR OF 1812 AND THE CREEK WAR

1812
June 1   President Madison recommends a declaration of war.
June 18   The U.S. Senate passes the House bill declaring war against Britain; Madison signs it.
July 17   Fort Michilimackinac falls to the British.
Aug. 15   Fort Dearborn massacre
Aug. 16   Fort Detroit falls to the British.
Oct. 13   Battle of Queenston Heights, Canada
Nov. 23   The U.S. invasion of Canada collapses.
Dec. 26   Britain begins its blockade of the Chesapeake and Delaware Bays.

1813
Jan. 23   Raisin River massacre
Apr. 27   Battle of York
May 27   Battle of Fort George, Ontario, Canada
Aug. 30   Battle of Fort Mims, Alabama
Sept. 10   Battle of Lake Erie
Oct. 5   The Indian leader Tecumseh falls at the Battle of the Thames in Ontario, Canada.
Nov. 9   Battle of Talladega, Alabama

1814
Jan. 22   Battle of Emuckfaw and Enotachopco Creek, Alabama
Mar. 27   Battle of Horseshoe Bend, Alabama
Aug. 8   Peace talks begin in Ghent, Belgium.
Aug. 9   The United States and the Creek nation sign the Treaty of Fort Jackson, ending the Creek War.
Aug. 24   As part of a British campaign in the Chesapeake Bay area, U.S. forces are badly defeated at the Battle of Bladensburg, Maryland.
Aug. 24   British general Ross burns Washington.
Sept. 13–14   Battle of Baltimore, Maryland
Sept. 14   Francis Scott Key writes "The Star-Spangled Banner."
Dec. 24   Treaty of Ghent is signed.

1815
Jan. 8   Battle of New Orleans, Louisiana
Feb. 11   Treaty of Ghent reaches the United States.
Feb. 17   Senate ratifies the Treaty of Ghent. The war ends.

When some of the militiamen refused to cross the international border, part of the force was stranded in Canada. The result was another humiliating American defeat. Although British losses were slight, Isaac Brock, the most capable British commander in North America, fell in battle.

In November U.S. major general Henry Dearborn led 5,000 troops to the Canadian border. Once again, the militia refused to fight in a foreign country, Dearborn withdrew, and the grand American plan to invade Canada was aborted.

The fall of Forts Detroit and Dearborn, coupled with the collapse of the Canadian campaign, laid the Ohio country open to Indian and British attack. The Shawnee and allied tribes believed that a British victory would push the American invaders out of their territory. Yet despite intense guerrilla warfare, neither the British nor their Indian allies scored a decisive victory in 1812. Although most of the Ohio country fell under Indian control, a coordinated British assault, which might have brought the War of 1812 to a quick and devastating end, failed to materialize, and U.S. general William Henry Harrison mounted effective counterattacks against the Miami Indians near Fort Wayne, Indiana.

In January 1813 Harrison advanced across frozen Lake Erie and was defeated by combined British and "Red Stick" Creek forces. Little Warrior led the Red Sticks in a devastating attack on a detachment at Frenchtown (present-day Monroe, Michigan), on the Raisin River on January 23. Of 960 American troops engaged, only 33 evaded death or capture. After this, Harrison's larger force was also mauled. Yet the British, under Henry Proctor, again failed to capitalize on their victory. This prompted Proctor's Indian allies to desert him, which gave the Americans a badly needed reprieve.

While U.S. land forces suffered one defeat after another during 1812, the tiny U.S. Navy was often victorious in single-ship engagements. The most famous of these were the battles between the USS *Constitution* ("Old Ironsides") and the British frigate *Guerriere,* off the coast of Massachusetts on August 19, 1812, and between the *Constitution* and the

Tecumseh

(ca. 1768–1813)

Tecumseh was born of a Shawnee father and a Creek mother, probably in the Shawnee village of Old Piqua (modern Springfield, Ohio). After his father was killed in Lord Dunmore's War (see Chapter 1) in 1774, Tecumseh was raised by the Shawnee chief Blackfish.

In his youth, Tecumseh acquired a reputation as a formidable warrior, fighting on the side of the British during the later years of the American Revolution (Chapter 1), from about 1780 to 1783, then organizing Shawnee resistance during Little Turtle's War (Chapter 3) in the 1790s. Tecumseh was defeated at the Battle of Fallen Timbers on August 20, 1794, but refused to sign the Treaty of Greenville (Ohio), which ceded (for cash) much Indian land to the federal government. Instead he moved to Indian territory along the Wabash River. There, with his brother Tenskwatawa—known as "the Prophet"—he labored to unite several tribes in order to offer effective resistance to the ongoing invasion by white settlers. A brilliant orator, Tecumseh recruited adherents throughout Iowa, New York, and, to a lesser extent, the Southeast.

While Tecumseh was absent from his village on the Wabash River, his brother attacked a force under Ohio territorial governor William Henry Harrison at Tippecanoe on November 7, 1811, and was defeated. The Prophet was disgraced, and the union Tecumseh had created was largely destroyed. When Tecumseh returned, he led his remaining followers to Canada, where they joined with British army forces at the outbreak of the War of 1812 in June 1812.

Tecumseh fought brilliantly in the war but was hampered by the conventional timidity of his British allies. He was killed at the Battle of the Thames in Ontario, Canada, on October 5, 1813. With him died perhaps the last great hope of forming a politically and militarily effective union of Indian tribes.

British frigate *Java,* off the Brazilian coast on December 29, 1812.

In 1813, after the disaster at Fort Malden, Harrison rebuilt and enlarged his army, which grew into a force of 8,000 by the late summer. Simultaneously, U.S. Navy officer Oliver Hazard Perry built an inland navy at Presque Isle (present-day Erie), Pennsylvania. On September 10, Perry defeated the British fleet on Lake Erie. His triumph cut British supply lines, forcing them to abandon Forts Malden and Detroit. On October 5, 1813, Harrison overtook the retreating British columns and their Indian allies on the banks of the Thames River in Ontario, Canada, defeating them and killing Tecumseh.

The Battles of Lake Erie and the Thames were brilliant victories, but the sudden end of the Napoleonic Wars in Europe (Napoleon abdicated on April 4, 1814) released more British soldiers for duty in America. British commanders drew up plans to attack in three principal areas: in New York, along Lake Champlain and the Hudson River, which would sever New England from the rest of the nation; at New Orleans, which would block the vital Mississippi artery; and in the Chesapeake Bay, to threaten Washington, D.C., and to create a diversion that would draw off and pin down U.S. military resources.

The objective of the British offensive was to force a peace that would include major territorial concessions from the United States. Despite the victories of 1813, the nation was strangled by the British blockade that had begun on December 26, 1812, and was drifting toward economic ruin. Late in the summer of 1814, American resistance to the attack in

Oliver Hazard Perry
(1785–1819)

Born at Rocky Brook, Rhode Island, Oliver H. Perry joined the navy in his youth, sailing in 1799 as a midshipman under his father, Christopher R. Perry, captain of the 28-gun frigate USS *General Greene*. Promoted to lieutenant in 1802, Perry served in the Mediterranean during the Tripolitan War (see Chapter 5). On his return to the United States after the war, Perry directed the building of gunboats for the fledgling U.S. Navy and also sailed on enforcement patrols pursuant to President Thomas Jefferson's Embargo Act during 1807–1809.

Given command of the Newport gunboat flotilla when the War of 1812 commenced, Perry was sent to Lake Erie to serve under Commodore Isaac Chauncey on February 17, 1813. He arrived at Presque Isle, Pennsylvania, and finding that there were no American ships on the lake, he set to work building a flotilla of gunships. By the spring, he had completed nine vessels. On May 27, Perry assisted in the capture of Fort George (Ontario), then returned to his gunboats, slipping them out of Presque Isle Harbor during August 1–4. After defeating the British blockading fleet on Lake Erie on September 10, he sent a message to General William Henry Harrison, who was waiting to commence the land attack at the Battle of the Thames: "We have met the enemy and they are ours. Two ships, two brigs, one schooner, one sloop." Perry then went ashore to serve under Harrison in the ensuing land battle.

Perry was promoted to captain and was given the thanks of Congress in January 1814. After the War of 1812 Perry commanded the captured 44-gun British frigate *Java* in the Mediterranean during 1816–1817. In 1819 he commanded a diplomatic mission to the new republic of Venezuela. While there he contracted yellow fever, from which he died.

---

the Chesapeake Bay folded, and the British, under Major General Robert Ross, brushed aside inept defenders at the Battle of Bladensburg, Maryland (August 24), marched on Washington, and burned most of the public buildings, including the Capitol and the White House. From Washington, Ross advanced north, by ship, on Baltimore. The supporting British fleet bombarded Fort McHenry, in Baltimore Harbor, during September 13–14, 1814 (an event witnessed by Francis Scott Key, who composed the "Star-Spangled Banner" during the bombardment). Failing to take the fort and confronted by effective militia resistance, the British withdrew. Ross fell in the battle.

The salvation of Baltimore was a relief, but some 10,000 British veterans of the Napoleonic Wars were still advancing into the United States from Montreal.

Opposing them on land was an inferior American force, but on September 11, 1814, U.S. naval captain Thomas MacDonough destroyed the British squadron on Lake Champlain, forcing a British retreat. Peace talks, which had begun earlier, suddenly became more focused, and the Treaty of Ghent, signed on December 24, 1814, ended the war.

Word of the Treaty of Ghent did not reach General Andrew Jackson, who was marching on New Orleans, having defeated the Red Stick Creeks in the Creek War (discussed below), which was an integral part of the War of 1812. Nor had it reached British general Edward Pakenham as he made his way with 5,300 British regulars to capture New Orleans. With a mixed force of 4,700 men (including "free colored" volunteers), Jackson was determined to drive off Pakenham. His first attempt, on December 23,

1814, failed, but when Pakenham launched his principal attack, against Jackson's line on the east bank of the Mississippi on January 8, 1815, Jackson violently repulsed the British, inflicting casualties of 2,400 killed and wounded. Among the dead were Pakenham and his two senior subordinates. Jackson lost no more than 70 men and had forced the British to withdraw. Even though the battle took place after the war had officially ended, the glorious victory at New Orleans made most Americans feel that they had won the War of 1812.

The Creek War

In fighting the War of 1812, the British employed Indian allies, as they had done during the American Revolution. In the deep South, particularly along the Gulf Coast, white-Indian warfare was nearly a separate war fought simultaneously with the War of 1812. The Indians often acted independently of the British but, like them, were determined to defeat the Americans. The Creek War may also be viewed as an intratribal conflict—a civil war between Creek tribal factions known as the Red Sticks and White Sticks—in which American interests became involved.

In Georgia, Tennessee, and the Mississippi Territory, the so-called Creek confederacy suffered violent dissension between those who advocated cooperation with whites (the Lower Creeks) and those determined to expel white settlers from Creek lands (the Upper Creeks). The Lower Creeks, also called the White Sticks, lived mainly in Georgia. The Upper Creeks, or Red Sticks, lived to the west. The Red Stick leader Little Warrior fought alongside the British at the

Raisin River, on January 23, 1813, and also raided settlers along the Ohio River on his way home from that battle. However, Little Warrior was ambushed by the White Stick chief Big Warrior, who took him captive and then killed him. This precipitated the intratribal combat.

On August 30, 1813, William Weatherford (Red Eagle), a Red Stick half-breed partisan of Tecumseh, attacked Fort Mims, located north of Mobile, Alabama. More than 400 white settlers were killed. In response, the Tennessee legislature commissioned Major General Andrew Jackson to lead 5,000 Tennessee militia troops, nineteen companies of friendly Cherokee warriors, and 200 White Sticks into Red Stick country. Early in November 1813, a detachment under Colonel John Coffee (including the soon-to-become-legendary Davy Crockett) ambushed a large contingent of Red Sticks at Tallashatchee, Alabama. On November 9, Jackson

Red Eagle, also known as William Weatherford, surrenders to Andrew Jackson, ending the Creek War. The resulting Treaty of Fort Jackson ceded two-thirds of the Creeks' tribal lands to the United States, including land of the "White Sticks," who were allies of the Americans.

marched to the relief of Talladega, a White Stick fort that had been held under siege. It was reported that

290 Red Sticks died in this engagement. Jackson and General William Claiborne then fruitlessly pursued

Andrew Jackson

(1767–1845)

Both North and South Carolina lay claim to being the birthplace of Andrew Jackson, but it is most likely that he was born on the South Carolina side of the Waxhaws settlement. His father, a poor Scotch-Irish immigrant, died before Jackson was born. During the British invasion of the Carolinas in 1780, Jackson lost a brother and his mother. He himself was beaten by a British officer.

After the war, Jackson dissipated his modest inheritance, then studied law, gaining admission to the North Carolina bar. He moved to Nashville, Tennessee, where, in 1791, he became attorney general for the Southwest Territory and, subsequently, the circuit-riding solicitor in the Nashville area. In 1791 he married Rachel Donelson Robards; both he and Rachel believed that she and her first husband had been legally divorced. When this proved not to be the case, they remarried in 1794, but the incident haunted Jackson's private and political life for many years, ultimately becoming the cause of a duel in 1806.

Jackson served as a delegate to the Tennessee Constitutional Convention in 1796 and was elected to Congress, where he served from 1796 to 1797. He was a fierce opponent of the Washington administration's conciliatory stance toward Great Britain and the Indian tribes that had sided with the British during the Revolution. In 1797 Jackson was appointed to serve out the senatorial term of his political mentor, William Blount, who had been expelled from the Senate as a result of his involvement in a British plan to seize Florida and Louisiana from Spain.

In 1798, on the verge of bankruptcy, Jackson resigned from the Senate and returned to Tennessee, where he served as a Tennessee superior court judge until 1804, then stepped down to devote himself full-time to building his fortune. During this period he built his famous plantation, the Hermitage, outside Nashville.

Blount, now governor of Tennessee, commissioned Jackson a major general of volunteers in the War of 1812. Jackson's most distinguished service came toward the end of the war against the proBritish Red Stick Creeks, whom he defeated in the decisive Battle of Horseshoe Bend on March 27, 1814. By the Treaty of Horseshoe Bend, Jackson compelled all of the Indians of the region—hostiles, neutrals, and even allies—to cede enormous tracts of land throughout Alabama and Georgia.

Jackson was quickly appointed to command of the defense of New Orleans, which was imperiled by the British. His brilliant defense resulted in the total defeat of the British assault on January 8, 1815, and made Jackson a national hero.

Jackson continued his military career in 1817–1818, when he led the nation's first war against the Seminole Indians. He not only fought Indians, but also audaciously evicted Spanish colonial authorities from Spanish Florida, which led to the Adams-Oñis treaty of 1819, by which Spain formally ceded Florida to the United States.

Jackson resigned his army commission in 1821 to become provisional territorial governor of Florida. The following year, the Tennessee legislature nominated him for the presidency, and then elected him to the U.S. Senate in 1823. In 1824 Jackson was narrowly defeated by John Quincy Adams in a bitterly contested presidential election. He ran again in 1828 and won by a comfortable margin, serving two terms and bringing about such profound changes in American government that the era became known as the Age of Jackson.

Red Eagle for two months. In January 1814, after receiving fresh troops, Jackson engaged the Red Sticks at Emuckfaw and at Enotachopco Creek, Alabama, and ruthlessly destroyed Red Stick towns.

By March, Jackson's militia had been augmented by U.S. Army regulars. He attacked Horseshoe Bend, a peninsula on the Tallapoosa River, on March 27, 1814, scoring a stunning victory that ended the Creek War. Jackson imposed a treaty that extorted 23 million acres of land from the Red Sticks *as well as* the White Sticks, even though the latter group had fought as allies of the Americans. The Creeks thus collectively ceded two-thirds of their tribal lands.

Cause of War: Deteriorating Anglo-American Relations

Two main reasons are traditionally cited as causes of the War of 1812: First, despite the Treaty of Paris, which ended the American Revolution (see Chapter 1), and the Jay Treaty, which resolved certain territorial disputes (see Chapter 4), British fur trappers and traders repeatedly "invaded" U.S. territory on the western frontier. Moreover, during the election year of 1810, Democratic-Republicans and other liberals stirred fears that Britain was actually planning to support an Indian confederacy to create an Indian nation-state on the western frontier. (The initial British demands during peace talks at the end of the War of 1812 demonstrated that these fears were by no means groundless.) Second, Britain's wars against Napoleon created a great demand for sailors, which the Royal Navy sought to satisfy by "impressing" seamen from the ships of other nations whenever a Royal Navy boarding party could assert (plausibly or not) that the personnel thus abducted were really navy deserters or, at the very least, Englishmen. In the years before the War of 1812, some 6,200 American sailors, unilaterally deemed to be British subjects liable for service, were impressed. On June 16, 1812, Britain agreed to end impressment on the high seas, effective June 23. Although this should have made impressment a non-issue, war was declared anyway.

The Congressional Debate: War Hawks

That war was declared is actually quite remarkable, because neither Britain nor the United States was eager or even prepared for conflict. Heavily engaged against Napoleon, the last thing the British wanted was another war. As for the Americans, although the "War Hawks" (mostly western and southern congressmen) loudly rattled their sabers, the pro-British Federalists were steadfastly opposed to war. Only when war seemed inevitable early in 1812 did Congress vote to increase the strength of the regular army to 35,000 and to provide for 50,000 volunteers as well as a militia of 100,000. Even so, by the time war was declared, the regulars numbered just 12,000 and the volunteers and militia had yet to be organized. As for naval strength, the United States had 16 ships versus the Royal Navy's fleet of about 1,000.

What, then, would compel the United States to declare war?

The *single* most pressing origin of the conflict was an insatiable hunger for new territory, especially on the part of southerners and westerners—the constituency of the War Hawks. The most attractive parcel of new land was Spanish Florida. Because Spain was an ally of Britain against Napoleon, the War Hawks reasoned that victory in a war against Britain would ultimately result in the acquisition of its ally's territory, which would be joined to the vast western territories acquired by the Louisiana Purchase of 1803. Those who advanced the cause of war in Congress were Henry Clay and Richard M. Johnson of Kentucky; Felix Grundy of Tennessee; Langdon Cheeves, William Lowndes, David R. Williams, and John C. Calhoun of South Carolina; and George M. Troup of Georgia.

The Congressional Debate: Opposition

Opposed to the War Hawks were the New England Federalists (the most numerous and important opponents to the war), a handful of upper-class, northern

Democratic-Republicans derisively dubbed "the Invisibles," and an even smaller coterie of Democratic-Republicans from the southern Tidewater planter aristocracy. Whereas the War Hawks called for war to defend U.S. sovereignty, to end British encroachments and depredations in the West, to protect the right of the United States (as a neutral in the Napoleonic Wars) to ply the seas unmolested, and to acquire new territory, the Federalists and other opponents predicted that economic disaster would accompany war and that the British would interdict merchant vessels. In addition, they argued that Britain was the great bulwark of conservative stability in a world that was menaced by the dangerous radicalism of revolutionary France and might be overrun by the imperial ambitions of Napoleon. These were both sound arguments, but not very exciting, and the War Hawks enjoyed substantial majorities in the House as well as the Senate.

The President Moves toward War

President James Madison, like his mentor and predecessor Thomas Jefferson, was hardly hawkish by inclination, but his party, the Democratic-Republicans, supported the war as a means of gaining ascendancy over the Federalists. Like Jefferson, Madison believed in a minimalist federal government run on the cheap and abhorred the idea of a standing army. He also opposed the accrual of a national debt. All three of these principles were incompatible with waging a major war against a major power. Nevertheless, carried by the tide of his own party's War Hawks, Madison asked Congress for a declaration of war on June 1, 1812.

Congress Acts

Under unremitting pressure from the War Hawks, the House of Representatives voted for a declaration of war on June 4. The Senate approved the House bill two weeks later, and it was presented to Madison for his signature. Every Federalist in both chambers had voted against it.

Passage of "An Act Declaring War Between the United Kingdom of Great Britain and Ireland and the Dependencies Thereof and the United States of America and Their Territories" on June 18, 1812, by no means brought national unity on the subject of war. Within Congress, the Federalists and the relatively few Democratic-Republicans who had opposed the war not only continued to do so, but they also became increasingly adamant and bitter in their opposition. Even within Madison's own cabinet there was little unity. Some cabinet members continued to debate the wisdom of the war, while those who supported the war argued fiercely over just how it should be fought. Finally, within the high command of the army there was a combination of dissension and incompetence.

Regionalism and Its Discontents

President Madison's idea was to wage an offensive campaign aimed at the singularly quixotic objective of conquering Canada. Just how much northern territory Madison hoped to gain is not clear, but his intention was to use possession of Canadian territory as a means of forcing Britain into concessions regarding issues of sovereignty and high seas commerce; Madison believed the British would yield in order to regain captured territory.

The problems with this strategy were many. First and foremost, the U.S. military establishment was hardly sufficient to conquer a nation. Second, there was no means within either the army or the navy to coordinate strategic action on a high level. Third, there was no government administrative bureau to oversee military operations and to harmonize the work of the army and navy.

Fourth—and most troublesome of all—there were the problems wrought by regionalism. Just as differing regional interests created a debate over the war to begin with, so regionalism conflicted with any notion of a *national* strategy. Coastal and maritime areas were concerned only with stopping British depredations at sea; in the Southwest, settlers saw the enemy not as the British, but as the Indians, especially the Red Stick Creeks. In the Old Northwest, Tecumseh and his Indian "confederacy" posed the biggest threat—the British were important only as instigators of Indian depredations. Finally, in the West and parts of the South, territorial expansion was the primary motive for going to war. Thus the War of 1812 lacked a single, unified American war aim.

In Federalist New England, factionalism became the most intense. The region refused to become reconciled to the war, and some of its residents carried on an illicit commerce with Britain, actually providing materiel to British armies in Canada. New England, the richest region in the nation, also withheld financial support for what New Englanders called "Mr. Madison's war." The Madison administration was forced to borrow some $40 million from the people, of which a mere $3 million came from New Englanders. Worse, New England's Federalist governors typically refused to mobilize state militias. Madison protested that, under the Constitution, the president had the authority to determine when a national exigency warranted the call-up of the militia. The governors denied that such an exigency existed or that the president had the authority to identify one. Withholding from federal service the nation's best-trained, best-equipped militias, who had access to a strategic route into Canada, crippled the war effort. The constitutional issue regarding the president's authority was not settled until an 1827 decision by the Supreme Court, which ruled that the president had the authority both to determine when an emergency existed and to call up the militia for national service in such a case.

The Prisoner of War Cartel

Mindful of the often appalling treatment of prisoners of war during the American Revolution, which included the confinement of American prisoners aboard overcrowded, disease-ridden ships ("prison hulks") riding at anchor off the occupied coast, U.S. and British officials concluded the **Cartel for the Exchange of Prisoners of War Between Great Britain and the United States of America** on November 28, 1812, at Halifax, Nova Scotia. In principle, the cartel anticipated the Geneva Conventions of the twentieth century. It called for humane treatment and speedy exchange or parole of prisoners.

A Movement to Secede: The Hartford Convention

Whereas the American defeats of 1812 were deeply depressing, the victories of 1813 gave reason for hope. Yet even in the face of these triumphs, United

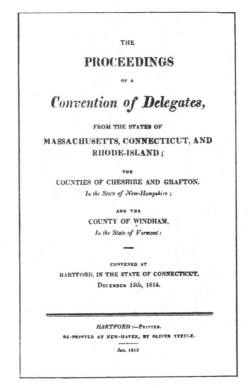

With New England's mercantile economy suffering under a long British siege, opponents of the War of 1812 from five New England states gathered at the Hartford Convention in Connecticut to protest the conduct of the war. Although their formal consideration of secession never got very far, the secretive, closed-door meetings raised alarms nationwide.

Cartel for the Exchange of Prisoners of War between Great Britain and the United States of America, 1812

Article I

The Prisoners taken at sea or on land on both sides shall be treated with humanity conformable to the usage and practice of the most civilized nations during war; and such prisoners shall without delay, and as speedily as circumstances will admit, be exchanged on the following terms and conditions. That is to say—An admiral or a General commanding in chief shall be exchanged for officers of equal rank or for sixty men each: a vice admiral or a Lieutenant General for officers of equal rank or for forty men each, a Rear Admiral or a Major General, for officers of equal rank, or for thirty men each; a Commodore with a broad pendant and a Captain under him or a Brigadier General for officers of equal rank or for twenty men each; a Captain of a line of Battle ship or a Colonel for officers of equal rank or for fifteen men each; a Captain of a frigate, or Lieutenant Colonel for officers of equal rank or for ten men each; Commanders of sloops of war, Bomb Catches, fire ships, and Packets or a Major for officers of equal rank, or for eight men each; Lieutenants or masters in the navy, or Captains in the army, for officers of equal rank, or for six men each; Masters-Mates, or Lieutenants in the army for officers of equal rank, or for four men each; Midshipmen, warrant officers, Masters of merchant vessels, and Captains of private armed vessels, or sub Lieutenants and Ensigns for officers of equal rank, or for three Men each: Lieutenants and mates of private armed vessels Mates of merchant vessels and all petty officers of ships of war, or all non commissioned officers of the army, for officers of equal rank, or for two men each seamen and private soldiers one for the other. . . .

Article VII

No prisoner shall be struck with the hand, whip, stick or any other weapon whatever, the complaints of the prisoners shall be attended to, and real grievances redressed; and if they behave disorderly, they may be closely confined, and kept on two thirds allowance for a reasonable time not exceeding ten days. They are to be furnished by the government in whose possession they may be, with a subsistence of sound and wholesome provisions, consisting of, one pound of beef, or twelve ounces of pork; one pound of wheaten bread, and a quarter of a pint of pease, or six ounces of rice, or a pound of potatoes, per day to each man; and of salt and vinegar in the proportion of two quarts of salt and four quarts of vinegar to every hundred days subsistence.

Excerpted from Alan Axelrod, *American Treaties and Alliances* (Washington, D.C.: CQ Press, 2000), 68.

States commerce was being strangled by the British blockade, and the nation was drifting toward economic ruin. By 1814 America's merchant trade had declined to approximately 17 percent of its 1811 level. In addition, as if the blockade were not bad enough, beginning in 1813, British raiders regularly hit coastal settlements, committing arson and other acts of destruction.

In New England, where the mercantile economy was suffering under the long British siege, opponents of "Mr. Madison's war" began discussing the possibility of seceding from the Union. From December 15, 1814, through January 5, 1815, twenty-six delegates from five New England states gathered in Connecticut at the Hartford Convention to protest what they deemed the disastrous Democratic-Republican conduct of the war. Although formal consideration of secession never got very far, the secretive, closed-door meetings raised alarms nationwide. To many citizens, the country seemed to be falling apart. Whether he realized it or not, however, President Madison had reason to find satisfaction in the Hartford Convention: It would stain the Federalists with the taint of treason, from which the party would never recover—especially after Andrew Jackson's victory at the Battle of New Orleans made the entire war seem to most Americans like a glorious triumph. In short, among the casualties of the War of 1812 was the Federalist Party.

Washington and Baltimore: Evacuation and the "Star-Spangled Banner"

It says something about the self-perception of the federal government that Secretary of War John Armstrong thought Washington, D.C., to be of such slight strategic importance that he deliberately chose not to fortify the city. The British, however, did not share his view. After the abdication of Napoleon freed more British troops for North American service, the center of a three-pronged offensive against the United States in 1814 was aimed directly at Washington. At the last possible moment, the administration organized a defense under the thoroughly incompetent General William H. Winder. He deployed about 6,000 troops, mostly militia, in three defensive lines for a stand at Bladensburg, Maryland. With him also were a handful of regulars, 500 U.S. Navy sailors, and a small contingent of marines. The attacking British force consisted of some 4,000 veterans of the Peninsular Campaign of the Napoleonic Wars, led by General Robert Ross.

On August 24, 1814, at the first attack of the British, the militia and regulars crumbled in a disgraceful defeat. Only the sailors and marines made a valiant stand and bought the capital a few precious hours to effect an evacuation. Ross marched on Washington, sending Madison and the city's other inhabitants fleeing across the Potomac into Virginia. The British set fire to most of Washington's public buildings, including the White House and Capitol.

It was a shocking and demoralizing event, and to opponents of the war it seemed to cap a series of unmitigated and needless disasters. Yet most Americans devoted little time to brooding about the raid on the capital as their attention turned to Ross's unsuccessful bombardment of Fort McHenry in Baltimore Harbor on September 13–14. At about the same time, a 3,200-man militia force under General John

Stricker had engaged Ross's army at Godly Wood on September 12. Although the Americans were pushed back, they took a heavy toll on the British, killing or wounding 346. Among the fallen was General Ross. The British survivors advanced to the heights at the outskirts of Baltimore and found them heavily defended. They also saw that Fort McHenry had not been reduced and, therefore, abandoned the assault on the city.

During the heavy, nightlong bombardment of Fort McHenry, a young Baltimore attorney detained aboard a British warship watched through the night, expecting to see the fort surrender. When the "dawn's early light" revealed that the "star-spangled banner" still flew above the fort, Francis Scott Key jotted down the verses that, after some revision, would be set to a popular British tavern song, "To Anacreon in Heaven," and unofficially adopted as the "national air" of the United States. (On March 3, 1931, President Herbert Hoover signed into law a congressional bill making "The Star-Spangled Banner" the national anthem of the United States.)

Key's verse is a barometer of the patriotic fervor that prevailed in most quarters during the War of 1812, despite the many military failures and the unwavering opposition of the Federalists. It was the salvation of Baltimore, not the arson at Washington, that most Americans bore in mind as the war continued.

Peace Talks

The bellicosity of the War Hawks and the prevalence of patriotic sentiment notwithstanding, the Madison administration and British officials spent much of the war engaged in talks aimed at finding a way to extricate themselves from the hostilities. As early as March 1813 President Madison accepted the offer of Russian czar Alexander I to mediate. Although the British rejected the mediation in July 1813, they made separate peace overtures, to which Madison responded favorably in January 1814. As the course of the war began to improve for the British after the fall of Napoleon, English diplomats managed to delay the commencement of negotiations until August. The talks finally convened at Ghent, Belgium, and Britain made its demands: the establishment of an Indian buffer state in the U.S. Northwest and U.S. territorial cessions to be made along the Canadian border. The American treaty commissioners rejected these demands out of hand. In the meantime, the U.S. victory at the Battle of Lake Champlain on September 11 significantly strengthened the American bargaining position. This advantage was coupled with the refusal of the Duke of Wellington—victor over Napoleon at Waterloo—to assume command in Canada. He commented that British forces would not be defeated, but neither could they inflict any disaster sufficient to force the surrender of the United States.

Treaty of Ghent

With the British will to fight having waned, the Crown's negotiators ultimately decided to forgo territorial demands, whereupon the United States withdrew its chief demand that Britain formally recog-

nize America's rights as a neutral. The Napoleonic Wars having ended, the British were no longer interested in impressing American seamen into service with the Royal Navy, nor with interfering in American maritime commerce in any other way, so the issue was, at least to a degree, moot. However, impressment had been the most visible justification for war, and because it was excluded from the **Treaty of Ghent**—signed on Christmas Eve 1814 and unanimously ratified by the U.S. Senate on February 17, 1815—some Americans felt dissatisfied and even betrayed by the outcome of the war.

Indeed, beyond ending the war, little was resolved by the Treaty of Ghent. It did establish a joint U.S.-British commission to set a definitive boundary between the United States and Canada, but these issues would not be satisfactorily resolved until the Webster-Ashburton Treaty of August 9, 1842 (see Chapter 7). The signatories also agreed to "engage to put an end . . . to hostilities with all the Tribes or Nations of Indians with whom they may be at war . . . and forthwith to restore to such Tribes or Nations respectively all the possessions, rights, and privi-

Treaty of Ghent, 1814

ARTICLE THE FIRST.
There shall be a firm and universal Peace between His Britannic Majesty and the United States. . . .

ARTICLE THE THIRD.
All Prisoners of war taken on either side as well by land as by sea shall be restored. . . .

ARTICLE THE NINTH.
The United States of America engage to put an end immediately after the Ratification of the present Treaty to hostilities with all the Tribes or Nations of Indians with whom they may be at war at the time of such Ratification, and forthwith to restore to such Tribes or Nations respectively all the possessions, rights, and privileges which they may have enjoyed or been entitled to in one thousand eight hundred and eleven previous to such hostilities. . . . Provided

always that such Tribes or Nations shall agree to desist from all hostilities against His Britannic Majesty and His Subjects upon the Ratification of the present Treaty being notified to such Tribes or Nations, and shall so desist accordingly.

ARTICLE THE TENTH.
Whereas the Traffic in Slaves is irreconcilable with the principles of humanity and Justice, and whereas both His Majesty and the United States are desirous of continuing their efforts to promote its entire abolition, it is hereby agreed that both the contracting parties shall use their best endeavours to accomplish so desirable an object.

Excerpted from the Avalon Project at Yale Law School, "Treaty of Ghent," www.yale.edu/lawweb/avalon/diplomacy/britain/ghent.htm.

leges which they may have enjoyed or been entitled to in one thousand eight hundred and eleven previous to [the War of 1812]." (The United States would notably fail to live up to this provision, both in letter and spirit.) Article X of the treaty included a clause concerning abolition of the slave trade. While the United States did cooperate in the suppression of the international slave trade, it made no move to end slavery within the nation itself.

To say that the War of 1812 risked much and achieved little is not entirely accurate, for the United States was not the same after the war as it had been

Treaty of Fort Jackson, 1814

WHEREAS an unprovoked, inhuman, and sanguinary war, waged by the hostile Creeks against the United States, hath been repelled, prosecuted and determined, successfully, on the part of the said States, in conformity with principles of national justice and honorable warfare— And whereas consideration is due to the rectitude of proceeding dictated by instructions relating to the re-establishment of peace: Be it remembered, that prior to the conquest of that part of the Creek nation hostile to the United States, numberless aggressions had been committed against the peace, the property, and the lives of citizens of the United States, and those of the Creek nation in amity with her, at the mouth of Duck river, Fort Mimms, and elsewhere, contrary to national faith, and the regard due to an article of the treaty concluded at New-York, in the year seventeen hundred ninety, between the two nations: That the United States, previously to the perpetration of such outrages, did, in order to ensure future amity and concord between the Creek nation and the said states, in conformity with the stipulations of former treaties, fulfill, with punctuality and good faith, her engagements to the said nation: that more than two-thirds of the whole number of chiefs and warriors of the Creek nation, disregarding the genuine spirit of existing treaties, suffered themselves to be instigated to violations of their national honor, and the respect due to a part of their own nation faithful to the United States and the principles of humanity, by impostures [impostors,] denominating themselves Prophets, and by the duplicity and misrepresentation of foreign emissaries, whose governments are at war, open or understood, with the United States. Wherefore,

1st—The United States demand an equivalent for all expenses incurred in prosecuting the war to its termination, by a cession of all the territory belonging to the Creek nation within the territories of the United States, lying west, south, and south-eastwardly, of a line to be run and described by persons duly authorized and appointed by the President of the United States. . . .

2nd—The United States will guarantee to the Creek nation, the integrity of all their territory eastwardly and northwardly of the said line to be run and described as mentioned in the first article.

3d—The United States demand, that the Creek nation abandon all communication, and cease to hold any intercourse with any British or Spanish post, garrison, or town. . . .

7th—The Creek nation being reduced to extreme want, and not at present having the means of subsistence, the United States, from motives of humanity, will continue to furnish gratuitously the necessaries of life, until the crops of corn can be considered competent to yield the nation a supply, and will establish trading houses in the nation, at the discretion of the President of the United States, and at such places as he shall direct, to enable the nation, by industry and economy, to procure clothing.

8th—A permanent peace shall ensue from the date of these presents forever, between the Creek nation and the United States, and between the Creek nation and the Cherokee, Chickasaw, and Choctaw nations.

Excerpted from the Carl Vinson Institute of Government, GeorgiaInfo, "Treaty of Fort Jackson," www.cviog.uga.edu/Projects/gainfo/creektre.htm/ftjackso.htm.

before. The economic depression created by the British blockade endured for years and was crippling; however, the nation also benefited from the end of British interference in western trade and Britain's withdrawal of support for "hostile" Indians. In this respect, the war made the West that much more attractive for continued expansion. Finally, most Americans came away from the War of 1812 feeling that they had actually defeated Britain. In one sense, this was true. Even if declaring war had been most ill advised, by surviving the war and by refusing to yield, the United States reaffirmed its independence and sovereignty and may well have gained an added measure of respect in the international community.

Indian Policy: The Treaty of Fort Jackson

The feeling of American triumph had very little to do with the Treaty of Ghent and everything to do with the exploits of one man, Andrew Jackson. A natural soldier and commander, Jackson performed both brilliantly and brutally against the Red Sticks in the Creek War, achieving a stunning victory at the Battle of Horseshoe Bend on March 27, 1814. This ended the Creek War and resulted in the Treaty of Horseshoe Bend, which, in a more formal revision, became the **Treaty of Fort Jackson,** signed on August 9, 1814.

The guarantee of the Indians' possession of their unceded territory was almost immediately violated by the state of Georgia and, subsequently, by the Indian Removal Act of 1830, passed by Congress during the presidential administration of Andrew Jackson. The "means of subsistence" promised in the treaty were delivered, but only very irregularly through the federal government's indifferent, inadequate, and corrupt Indian agency system.

Andrew Jackson's War Dividend

Andrew Jackson's victory against the Creeks returned him dramatically to public notice. He was a frontier hero, the true embodiment of the American martial spirit, a representative of the vigorous West versus the effete East, and a welcome contrast to superannuated and inept commanders, such as William Hull, and colorless chief executives, namely James Madison.

At New Orleans Jackson was brilliant in his military leadership, and also exhibited a flair for the dramatic, exclaiming on December 23, 1815, when he was told that British troops were just nine miles from the city, "By the Eternal, they shall not sleep on our soil!" It was the name of Andrew Jackson that was inseparable from the victory at New Orleans and linked to the "triumphal" conclusion of the entire bitter war. His fateful path to the White House had surely been paved by his performance in the War of 1812, and *that* is the most enduring political legacy of the conflict.

BIBLIOGRAPHY

Carter, Alden R. *The War of 1812: Second Fight for Independence.* New York: Franklin Watts, 1992.

Gay, Kathlyn. *War of 1812.* New York : Twenty-First Century Books, 1995.

Hicky, Donald R. *The War of 1812: A Forgotten Conflict.* Urbana and Chicago: University of Illinois Press, 1990.

Katcher, Philip R. *The American War, 1812–1814.* London: Osprey, 1990.

Nardo, Don. *The War of 1812.* San Diego, Calif.: Lucent Books, 1999.

Prucha, Francis P. *The Great Father: The United States Government and the American Indians.* Lincoln: University of Nebraska Press, 1984.

At Issue in the Fredonian Rebellion

When the Mexican government revoked a land charter, an American entrepreneur who was attempting to found a colony in Texas (Mexican territory at the time) responded by declaring independence from Mexico in a rebellion that was both abortive and bloodless.

The Conflict

American entrepreneur Moses Austin obtained a grant from the Spanish government in 1820 to establish a colony of American settlers in Texas, which was at the time a territorial possession of the Spanish empire. He fell ill and died in 1821, and his son Stephen F. Austin assumed the grant and resolved to establish the colony. By this time, Mexico had won independence from Spain (Revolution of 1821), and it was the Mexican government that enacted legislation in 1824 authorizing a fixed number of American families to settle in what had become the Mexican territory of Texas. A subsequent agreement in 1825 brought more colonists (and agreements in 1827 and 1828, yet more).

In 1825 another American, Hayden (or Haden) Edwards, secured a contract or charter from the Mexican government to establish a colony in east Texas, near Nacogdoches. Edwards's claim conflicted with claims of certain Mexican nationals, most of whom were unable to produce legal proof of title. Edwards demanded that the Mexican nationals pay him for the value of the acreage they claimed or vacate it. As the dispute verged on violence, Austin warned Edwards that he was creating a crisis for all American colonists. Ignoring the warning, Edwards pressed his demands. In response, the Mexican claimants petitioned their government to intervene.

In May 1826, leaving his brother Benjamin in charge of the colony, Edwards traveled to Louisiana to recruit more settlers. In June the Mexican government revoked Edwards's contract and ordered him and his colonists out of the country. Benjamin Edwards responded by leading thirty volunteers into a building known as the Old Stone Fort. They hoisted over the building a flag bearing the legend "Independence, Liberty, and Justice," and Benjamin Edwards grandiosely proclaimed the independent republic of Fredonia.

Nothing more happened for weeks. On December 21, 1826, Benjamin and Hayden Edwards, with a handful of followers, drew up a declaration of independence and a constitution. However, as Mexican troops approached Nacogdoches, the Edwards brothers and their volunteers, then numbering about 200, fled Texas on January 31, 1827. The bloodless Fredonian Rebellion had lasted six weeks.

Hayden (or Haden) Edwards
(1771–1849)

Born in Stafford County, Virginia, Edwards moved with his family in 1780 to Bourbon County, Kentucky (then part of Virginia). Edwards was educated to be a lawyer but devoted himself to land speculation instead. In 1820 Edwards and his bride, Susanna Beall of Maryland, moved to the area of Jackson, Mississippi, where he acquired a plantation with his brother Benjamin W. Edwards and fathered thirteen children.

Hearing of Moses Austin's plans for Texas colonization, in 1823 Edwards traveled to Mexico City, where he joined Stephen F. Austin, Robert Leftwich, and others in a three-year attempt to persuade successive Mexican governments to authorize American settlement. Edwards provided much of Austin's financing. Thanks to their efforts, colonization laws were passed in 1824 and 1825, allowing American *empresarios* (land agents) to colonize Texas.

Edwards soon fell out with Austin. Edwards's own grant was in the vicinity of Nacogdoches, where he was authorized to settle 800 families. Like other *empresarios,* Edwards agreed to honor preexisting grants and claims made by Spanish or Mexican officials. Edwards's violation of this pledge led to the Fredonian Rebellion, during part of which Edwards took refuge in Louisiana, returning to Texas during the Texas War of Independence (see Chapter 9). He lived in Nacogdoches until his death on August 14, 1849.

CHRONOLOGY OF THE FREDONIAN REBELLION

1825

- Hayden Edwards secures a grant of land in Nacogdoches; conflicts with the claims of Mexican nationals develop.

1826

May Hayden Edwards travels to Louisiana to recruit settlers; he leaves his brother Benjamin in charge of the Texas colony.

June The Mexican government revokes the Edwards' land contract; Benjamin Edwards responds by proclaiming the independent Republic of Fredonia.

Dec. 20 The Edwards brothers conclude a treaty of alliance with the Cherokee, agreeing to divide Texas between the whites and the Indians and jointly make war against Mexico.

Dec. 21 The Edwards brothers and some of their followers draw up and sign a declaration of independence and a constitution.

1827

Jan. 31 At the approach of a large Mexican army, the Fredonian rebels flee Texas, and the Fredonian Rebellion ends.

Moses Austin's Grant, Stephen Austin's Pledge

The Louisiana Purchase of 1803 created great interest in Texas, then a possession of the Spanish Empire, prompting several American entrepreneurs to attempt colonization. In 1820 Connecticut-born Moses Austin, a prosperous merchant, lead miner, and colonial entrepreneur (in 1798, he had established the first Anglo-American settlement west of the Mississippi River, on the site of modern Potosi, Missouri), traveled to San Antonio, where he succeeded in securing a grant from the Spanish government. The prospects appeared bright, but in 1821 Austin suddenly took ill before he could begin the settlement. On his deathbed, he persuaded his son, Stephen F. Austin, to bring his unrealized plans to fruition. At the same time, Spain's imperial hold on Mexico also died as Mexico won independence in the revolution of 1821. After much wrangling, the new Mexican government agreed to honor the grant the Spanish colonial government had given Moses

Austin. Stephen Austin was permitted initially to bring 300 American families to Texas. (Colonization would prove so successful that by 1836, when the Texas War of Independence was fought [see Chapter 9], the American population of Texas stood at 50,000, while that of the Mexican nationals was a mere 3,500.)

Important conditions of the Mexican grant included the acceptance, by each settler, of Mexican citizenship and conversion to the Roman Catholic faith. In return, each colonist received title to vast amounts of land—as much as 4,428 acres to each family who planned to raise stock. It is important to note that while accepting Mexican citizenship disturbed few of the colonists, the conversion to Roman Catholicism was repugnant to many settlers of Protestant stock. Unresolved issues of ethnicity and religion would fester in the Texas colony, leading after a few years to the Texas War of Independence.

Hayden Edwards's Charter

Hayden (or Haden) Edwards was a Virginia pioneer and land speculator, who was living on a plantation in Jackson, Mississippi, when he heard of Moses Austin's plans for colonization in Texas. In 1823 Edwards traveled to Mexico City, where he joined Stephen F. Austin and others in an effort to persuade the Mexican government to authorize American colonies in Texas. A wealthy man, Edwards frequently extended financial support to Austin, and it was he who maintained him in Mexico City. Ultimately, Austin's and Edwards's lobbying resulted in the passage of the colonization laws of 1824 (in Mexico City) and 1825 (in Saltillo).

Edwards received a charter for land in the vicinity of Nacogdoches, on which he was authorized to locate as many as 800 families. Like all other *empresarios* (as the American grantees were called), Edwards agreed to honor all existing grants and claims made by Spanish or Mexican officials. It seems, however, that Edwards's grant was encumbered by many more such claims than those of other *empresarios,* including Austin. This led to him to

reject claims in cases where the claimants could not produce documentary evidence of legal title. Indeed, few of the claimants were able to produce such evidence, although the families of many had occupied the land for as long as a century. Responding to a petition of the claimants, the Mexican government revoked Edwards's contract and ordered him to leave Nacogdoches. At this time, however, Edwards was absent—he had gone to Louisiana to recruit more settlers. His brother Benjamin responded by proclaiming the independent republic of Fredonia.

Response to Fredonia

The Edwards brothers expected that a significant number of Americans would rally to the cause of Fredonian independence. This belief was a combination of wishful thinking and their sense of the powerful anti-Mexican, anti-Catholic prejudice prevailing in the United States. When virtually no one in the United States came to their aid, however, the Edwards brothers and Harmon B. Mayo, representing the rebellious Americans, and Richard Fields and John Dunn Hunter, purporting to represent the Cherokees, concluded on December 20, 1826, a treaty of alliance by which they divided the territory of Texas between the Indians and whites and agreed to prosecute together the war against Mexico until they had won independence. (In the end, however, only about 200 men, mostly the settlers Hayden Edwards had originally attracted, formed the army of Fredonia.) On the next day, the Edwardses, Mayo, and other followers drew up a formal **Declaration of Independence.**

Stephen Austin persuaded his fellow *empresarios* that the Edwardses' defiance of the Mexican government was dangerous to all American colonial enterprises in Texas. He counseled patiently seeking redress of grievances through legal Mexican channels. Acting on his own authority, Austin sent three of his colonists as commissioners to attempt to persuade the disaffected Fredonian colonists to abandon any notion of rebellion. When the commission failed, Austin prevailed on the Mexican government to offer

Fredonian Declaration of Independence, 1826

Whereas, the Government of the Mexican United States, have by repeated insults, treachery and oppression, reduced the White and Red emigrants from the United States of North America, now living in the Province of Texas, within the Territory of the said Government, into which they have been deluded by promises solemnly made, and most basely broken, to the dreadful alternative of either submitting their freeborn necks to the yoke of an imbecile, faithless, and despotic government, miscalled a Republic; or of taking up arms in defence of their unalienable rights and asserting their Independence. . . .

1. The above named contracting parties, bind themselves to a solemn Union, League and Confederation, in Peace and War, to establish and defend their mutual independence of the Mexican United States.

2. The contracting parties guaranty, mutually, to the extent of their power, the integrity of their respective Territories, as now agreed upon and described. . . .

4. It is distinctly understood by the contracting parties, that the Territory apportioned to the Red people, is intended as well for the benefit of the Tribes now settled within the Territory apportioned to the White people, as for those living in the former Territory, and that it is incumbent upon the contracting parties for the Red people to offer the said Tribes a participation in the same. . . .

7. The contracting parties mutually stipulate that they will direct all their resources to the prosecution of the Heaven-inspired cause which has given birth to this solemn Union, League and Confederation, firmly relying upon their united efforts, and the strong arm of Heaven, for success.

Excerpted from H. P. N. Gammel, *The Laws of Texas–Volume 1 [1822–1838],* University of North Texas Libraries, http://texashistory.unt.edu/permalink/meta-pth-5872:115.

the hostile colonists amnesty in return for their compliance with Mexican law. An amnesty was granted, but the Edwards brothers pressed on with the Fredonian Rebellion, which the Mexicans suppressed, bloodlessly, by a show of military strength.

The Fredonian Rebellion made relatively little stir in the United States, but it did serve to alert the more perceptive members of the American and Mexican governments, as well as the Texas colonists, that a crisis in Mexican-American relations might not be far off.

AROOSTOOK WAR

At Issue in the Aroostook War

A small number of Americans and Canadians disputed the international boundary between Maine and New Brunswick, Canada.

The Conflict

Neither the Treaty of Paris, which ended the American Revolution in 1783 (see Chapter 1), nor the Jay Treaty of 1794 (see Chapter 4) definitively resolved the question of precisely where the U.S.-Canadian border lay. In 1838 the border between Maine and New Brunswick became a heated issue when Maine farmers sought to cultivate land in the Aroostook River Valley, which was claimed by Canadian lumber interests as Canadian territory. In February 1839 Maine land agents were arrested by Canadian officials for attempting to force the lumbermen off a tract in the disputed area. In response to the arrest, Maine officials called out the state militia and New Brunswick responded in kind. At this point, the two *national* governments were not involved.

Fearing the outbreak of a shooting war between the forces of Maine (known as "Red Shirts") and those of New Brunswick (nicknamed "Blue Noses"),

Webster-Ashburton Treaty, 1842

Whereas certain portions of the line of boundary between the United States of America and the British Dominions in North America . . . have not yet been ascertained and determined . . . , and whereas it is now thought to be for the interest of both Parties, that, . . . they should agree on a conventional line in said portions of the said boundary, such as may be convenient to both Parties. . . .

ARTICLE I.

It is hereby agreed and declared that the line of boundary shall be as follows. . . .

ARTICLE III.

In order to promote the interests and encourage the industry of all the inhabitants of the countries watered by the river St. John and its tributaries . . . it is agreed that, where, by the provisions of the present treaty, the river St. John is declared to be the line of boundary, the navigation of the said river shall be free and open to both Parties. . . .

ARTICLE VII.

It is further agreed, that the channels in the river St. Lawrence, on both sides of the Long Sault Islands and of Barnhart Island; the channels in the river Detroit, on both sides of the Island Bois Blanc, and between that Island and both the American and Canadian shores; and all the several channels and passages between the various Islands lying near the junction of the river St. Clair with the lake of that name, shall be equally free and open to the ships, vessels, and boats of both Parties.

ARTICLE VIII.

The Parties mutually stipulate that each shall prepare, equip, and maintain in service, on the coast of Africa, a sufficient and adequate squadron, or naval force of vessels, of suitable numbers and descriptions, to carry in all not less than eighty guns, to enforce, separately and respectively, the laws rights and obligations of each of the two countries, for the suppression of the Slave Trade. . . .

ARTICLE X.

It is agreed that the United States and Her Britannic Majesty shall, upon mutual requisitions by them, or their Ministers, Officers, or authorities, respectively made, deliver up to justice, all persons who, being charged with the crime of murder, or assault with intent to commit murder, or Piracy, or arson, or robbery, or Forgery, or the utterance of forged paper, committed within the jurisdiction of either, shall seek an asylum, or shall be found, within the territories of the other.

Excerpted from the Avalon Project at Yale Law School, "The Webster-Ashburton Treaty," www.yale.edu/lawweb/avalon/diplomacy/britian/br-1842.htm.

CHRONOLOGY OF THE AROOSTOOK WAR

1838
- Maine farmers ("Red Shirts") dispute with New Brunswick (Canada) lumbermen ("Blue Noses") over land both claim as lying within their respective countries.

1839
Feb. Canadian authorities arrest a band of Maine land agents for attempting to force lumbermen off a tract in the disputed area. In response, the Maine governor calls out the militia; New Brunswick responds in kind.

Mar. A small U.S. Army force under General Winfield Scott intervenes. Scott averts armed conflict by pledging the creation of a boundary commission to settle the disputed international border.

1842
Aug. 9 The Webster-Ashburton Treaty fixes the disputed border.

as well as a dispute over state versus federal authority, President Martin Van Buren dispatched a small force of army regulars under General Winfield Scott to the Aroostook Valley in March. Backed by a modest show of force, Scott interceded to negotiate an agreement between officials of Maine and New Brunswick that averted armed conflict and sent the opposing militia forces home.

The Scott Agreement

Scott's intercession consisted of the promise that an impartial boundary commission would be convened to determine the boundary once and for all. This determination would then be solemnized in a treaty.

Webster-Ashburton Treaty of 1842

The **Webster-Ashburton Treaty,** which set the boundary per the Scott Agreement, was not concluded until 1842. The formally titled "Treaty to settle and define the Boundaries between the Territories of the United States and the possessions of Her Britannic Majesty, in North America: For the final Suppression of the African Slave Trade: and For the giving up of Criminals fugitive from justice, in certain cases" was signed on August 9, 1842, in Washington, D.C., and went into force on November 10.

The treaty was negotiated between U.S. secretary of state Daniel Webster and Alexander Baring, the first Baron Ashburton. The first two articles defined the boundary, and the third specified that the St. John River, separating New Brunswick from Maine, would be free for purposes of navigation and trade by both Canadians and Americans. Articles VIII and IX set out a program for Anglo-American cooperation in suppressing the slave trade, and Article X was an agreement for the extradition of fugitive felons. Thus a bloodless boundary war between a handful of Maine farmers and New Brunswick lumbermen occasioned not just an international boundary settlement, but also international cooperation to suppress the slave trade and to ensure the extradition of fugitives.

BIBLIOGRAPHY

Brands, H. W. *Lone Star Nation: The Epic Story of the Battle for Texas Independence.* New York: Anchor, 2005.

Davis, William C. *Lone Star Rising.* New York: Free Press, 2003.

Day, Clarence Albert. *Aroostook, The First Sixty Years: A History of Maine's Largest County, From Its Earliest Beginning Up Through the Bloodless Aroostook War.* Presque Isle: University of Maine at Presque Isle, 1981.

CHAPTER 8
SEMINOLE AND BLACK HAWK WARS
(1817–1858)

At Issue

At issue in the three Seminole Wars and the Black Hawk War was possession of lands disputed by the Indians and the federal government.

The Conflicts

First Seminole War (1817–1818)

After the War of 1812 ended, an abandoned British fort at Prospect Bluff on the Apalachicola River was occupied by Seminoles and served as a refuge for fugitive slaves; the fort became known to locals as "Negro Fort" and was deemed to be a threat to the navigation of three rivers. In spring 1816 the U.S. Army intervened, building Fort Scott on the Flint River fork of the Apalachicola River in Georgia. From this fort, on July 27, an attack was launched against Negro Fort with land forces supported by two gunboats. Using a common practice, the captain of one of these vessels ordered a cannonball heated before firing it. The red-hot projectile hit the fort's powder magazine, touching off a catastrophic explosion that killed about 300 fugitive slaves (men, women, and children) and thirty Seminoles. Recognizing that the attack and explosion would push the Seminoles to the brink of war, Lieutenant Colonel Duncan Lamont Clinch rushed the fort after the explosion to disarm the Seminoles. Instead of preventing war, however, Clinch's action provoked it, although the Seminoles made no aggressive gesture until November 1817, when Chief Neamathia warned Brigadier General Edmund Gaines to keep all whites out of his village, Fowl Town. Gaines responded by sending 250 men under Major David E. Twiggs to Fowl Town to arrest Neamathia. Twiggs attacked and Neamathia escaped, but Fowl Town was razed. Seminoles and the closely allied "Red Stick" Creeks (led by Peter McQueen) retaliated by attacking a party of 40 soldiers, some of whom were traveling with their families (seven wives, four children). All except four men (who escaped) and one woman (who was taken captive) were killed.

Following these events, General Andrew Jackson mustered a force of 800 regulars, 900 Georgia volunteers, and a significant number of "White Stick" Creeks, rivals of the Red Sticks. In March 1818 they rebuilt Negro Fort, renamed it Fort Gadsden, and established it as a base from which to mount a full-scale war against the Seminoles. Marching out from Fort Gadsden, Jackson flushed the hostiles from the Mikasuki Seminole villages around present-day Tallahassee, Florida, pursuing them to Saint Marks, a Spanish fort and town where they sought refuge. By the time Jackson's forces reached Saint Marks, the Indians had already fled. Nevertheless, with complete disregard for Spanish sovereignty, Jackson claimed possession of the town on April 7, 1818. Two days later, he and his army departed for Suwannee Town, 107 miles to the east, to attack warriors under Chief Boleck (a name the whites corrupted to "Billy Bowlegs"). En route, Jackson located McQueen in a swamp near the Econfina River. Jackson attacked McQueen's camp on April 12, killing thirty-seven warriors and taking many of the others captive, including the women and children. (Among those captured was the future Creek-Seminole war leader Osceola, aged fourteen at the time.)

McQueen and approximately 100 warriors escaped, but Jackson induced McQueen's sister to betray his whereabouts in exchange for the release of the women and children. As with much extorted information, the intelligence proved unreliable. In search of McQueen, Jackson marched to Suwannee Town (which he found deserted) and thence to Pensacola, which he claimed for the United States on May 26,

1818, again without acknowledging Spanish sovereignty. A diplomatic crisis erupted but was quickly ended by the Spanish cession of all Florida to the United States in February 1819. The cession brought a rush of new white settlement, and it was this sudden influx of settlers, rather than further military action, that ended the First Seminole War by forcing local Seminoles and Red Sticks to withdraw into hiding. Peter McQueen was never captured. He lived the rest of his life, peacefully, in the Tampa Bay area.

CHRONOLOGY OF THE SEMINOLE AND BLACK HAWK WARS

1804

Nov. 3   By a fraudulent treaty, the Sac and Fox Indians cede vast tracts to the United States.

1812–1814

• Chief Black Hawk and his "British Band" side with the British during the War of 1812

1815

• "Negro Fort" is established along the Apalachicola River in Florida.

1816

July 27   Forces under Andrew Jackson attack Negro Fort, inflicting heavy casualties.

1817

Nov.   Seminole chief Neamathia issues a provocative threat; the chief's village, Fowl Town, is destroyed; the Seminoles and Creeks attack Fort Scott

1818

Mar.   Using the former Negro Fort as a base, Andrew Jackson leads a punitive force against the Seminoles and Red Stick Creeks.

Apr. 7   Jackson seizes St. Marks, violating Spanish sovereignty.

Apr. 12   Jackson attacks the camp of Creek leader Peter McQueen.

May 26   Jackson seizes Pensacola, again violating Spanish sovereignty.

1819

Feb. 22   By the Adams-Oñis Treaty, Spain cedes Florida to the United States, triggering an influx of white settlement, which ends the First Seminole War

1829

• Black Hawk is dispossessed by white settlers, who occupy his home territory; he leads his British Band west of the Mississippi.

1832

Apr.   With the British Band, Black Hawk returns to the east bank of the Mississippi in search of food. This triggers a militia call-up and the Black Hawk War.

May 9   Seminole leaders sign a provisional removal treaty; subsequently, they are coerced into signing a final treaty binding the tribe to leave Florida by 1837. A majority of the tribe repudiates the treaty as fraudulent.

May   After "Stillman's Run," Black Hawk raids along the Mississippi in Illinois. A mixed force of U.S. Army regulars and militia pursue Black Hawk and his British Band.

June   Black Hawk lays siege to a fort on the Apple River.

Aug. 1   Forces under Colonel Henry L. Dodge attack the British Band, inflicting heavy casualties and prompting an abortive surrender attempt.

Aug. 3   The British Band is decimated at the Battle of the Bad Axe River.

Sept. 19   The United States signs the Treaty of Fort Armstrong with the Sac and Fox tribes.

1835

Oct.   The Seminoles plan war under Chiefs Osceola, Jumper, King Philip, and Alligator.

Nov.   Osceola assassinates Charley Emathla, a Seminole chief who favors removal.

Dec.   Osceola and his lieutenants terrorize white settlers in Florida.

Black Hawk War (1832)

The Indian Removal Act of 1830 primarily affected the Indians of the Southeast, but the policy of removal also applied in the upper Midwest, where it resulted in the brief but violent Black Hawk War of 1832.

Black Hawk was a chief of the Sac (also spelled Sauk) and Fox Indians, separate but closely allied tribes living mostly in Illinois and Wisconsin along the east bank of the Mississippi River. Black Hawk was duped into affirming the Treaty with the Sauk and Foxes of November 3, 1804 by which the tribes had ceded 50 million acres to the federal government. Upon discovering that he had been deceived, Black Hawk fought alongside Tecumseh as an ally of the British in the War of 1812. After that war, he and his people came into frequent conflict with white settlers, who not only claimed Sac and Fox lands, but also freely pillaged their villages, fenced their cornfields, and even plowed up their burial grounds. Black Hawk protested to U.S. Indian agents at Rock Island, Illinois, but was told that his only remedy was to move west of the Mississippi. In 1829, when he returned from a hunting trip across that river, he found a white family newly settled in his own lodge. The U.S. General Land Office had declared the entire

Black Hawk, a chief of the Sac and Fox Indians, frequently came into conflict with white settlers, leading to the Black Hawk War of 1832.

Dec. 18 Osceola defeats the militia in the Battle of Black Point.

Dec. 31 Osceola ambushes troops under General Duncan Clinch at Withlacoochee River.

1837

Oct. 21 General Thomas Jesup takes Osceola prisoner; Alligator and Chief Boleck (Billy Bowlegs) continue a guerrilla war through 1842.

1838

Jan. 30 Osceola dies in prison.

1838–1839

Winter Cherokees are marched to Indian Territory along 1,200-mile "Trail of Tears."

1842

- Having forced the removal to Indian Territory of some 3,000 Seminoles between 1835

and 1842, the U.S. government ceases military action, thus ending the Second Seminole War.

1855–1857

- A dispute between surveyors and Chief Boleck provokes a low-level conflict consisting of hit-and-run-Indian raids. Outraged U.S. citizens demand army and militia intervention. Fitful combat ensues.

1857

Mar. 5 Boleck and 165 followers agree to leave Florida in exchange for a cash settlement of several thousand dollars.

1858

May 8 The United States unilaterally declares the end of the Third Seminole War.

Black Hawk
(Ma-ka-tai-me-she-kia-kiak)
(1767–1838)

During the War of 1812 (see Chapter 6), Black Hawk allied himself and members of the Sac and Fox tribes with the British, hoping thereby to eject American settlers from tribal lands in Illinois country. After the war, in response to Black Hawk's British alliance, U.S. government officials favored and negotiated with Black Hawk's rival chief, Keokuk. This drove Black Hawk to further hostility toward the government, and he became de facto leader of about 2,000 Sac and Fox dissidents known as the British Band.

In 1831 white encroachment pushed Black Hawk and his followers across the Mississippi River into Iowa. He led the British Band back into Illinois in 1832 and planted crops on land already settled by whites. This provoked the Black Hawk War.

Despite Black Hawk's initial success in the war, other tribes did not offer assistance. Black Hawk was forced into retreat, ultimately to the Bad Axe River in Wisconsin, where the final battle of the conflict took place. Black Hawk fled but was soon captured. He was confined to Jefferson Barracks, Missouri, and, subsequently, to Fortress Monroe, Virginia. In 1833 he was paroled to his rival Keokuk, an act he took as the final insult, but it was not. After he died five years later and was buried at Iowaville on the Des Moines River, his bones were stolen and ended up on display at a local historical society.

and winters west of the river. Clearly dissatisfied with this attempt at a compromise, in April 1832 Black Hawk, in search of food, headed east across the river with a large group of 2,000 men, women, and children. His followers, known as the British Band because of their allegiance to the British during the War of 1812, were attached politically to Black Hawk and guided spiritually by a charismatic figure known as the Winnebago Prophet.

A rival Sac and Fox faction was led by Chief Keokuk, who favored accommodation of the federal government. Keokuk alerted Indian agent Felix St. Vrain to the approach of the British Band and, complying with General Henry Atkinson's request, attempted to persuade Black Hawk to return to the West. Black Hawk refused. On April 28, Atkinson marched 2,000 U.S. Army and Illinois militia troops to Yellow Banks on the Mississippi, but Black Hawk professed to be unimpressed by this show of force and refused to withdraw to the west bank of the river. In response, on May 1, 1832, Atkinson mustered into federal service 1,500 mounted militiamen and 200 infantry volunteers, who joined 340 infantry regulars under Colonel Zachary Taylor. On May 9, Atkinson ordered the mounted militia, under General Samuel Whiteside, to march up the Rock River via the village of the Winnebago Prophet while he sailed up the river with his mixed infantry.

While these movements were taking place, two additional militia battalions also patrolled the area. Major Isaac Stillman's force ranged east from the Mississippi, while Major David Bailey's troops patrolled the territory between the Rock River and settlements along the Illinois River. Stillman camped near the mouth of the Kyte River on May 14.

Aware of these gathering forces and realizing that he would get no help from either the Winnebago or Potawatomi Indians, Black Hawk sent three warriors under a white flag to Stillman's camp. The inexperienced militia troops panicked at their approach and fired on the delegation. In response, Black Hawk attacked and, with just forty warriors, defeated 275 well-armed Illinois militiamen in a battle dubbed "Stillman's Run."

region, including Black Hawk's land, subject to public sale.

Black Hawk attempted to live among the intruders, spending summers east of the Mississippi

Emboldened, Black Hawk led his warriors on violent raids throughout the region, the worst of which was the Indian Creek Massacre, in which fifteen settlers were murdered and mutilated and two girls abducted. Responding to the crisis, Atkinson mustered additional militia forces and drew Indian auxiliaries from the Sioux and Menominee tribes. He led his mixed force in pursuit of Black Hawk, pushing him toward the headwaters of the Rock River. A band of Winnebagos, impressed by the British Band's victories, offered Black Hawk and his followers refuge near the Four Lakes in present-day Dane County, Wisconsin. From there, he continued his raids, often humiliating the militia.

Late in June, Potawatomis and Winnebagos friendly to the white settlers reported Black Hawk's whereabouts above Lake Koshkonong. Atkinson now commanded 3,000 militiamen and 400 regulars, but he was reluctant to begin an offensive. An impatient President Andrew Jackson ordered Major General Winfield Scott to coordinate with Atkinson. Scott brought 800 more regulars, plus six companies of rangers and various militia bands, to Chicago. In the meantime, however, Black Hawk and 200 warriors attacked a fort on the Apple River, approximately fourteen miles from Galena, Illinois. The twenty-five-man garrison held off the attack for about twelve hours before the Indians finally withdrew and plundered the surrounding area.

Atkinson commenced operations at the beginning of July, but by the second week of the month, he had yet to locate the British Band and his troops were running low on supplies. Moreover, militiamen began to drop out of the campaign as their brief enlistments ended. (Abraham Lincoln was among them.) Scott's army was bogged down in Chicago, stricken by a cholera epidemic.

Black Hawk and the British Band were also suffering, subsisting on a starvation diet and hiding so far from white settlements that they had no one to raid and loot. Although he had started the war because he refused to settle west of the Mississippi, Black Hawk now decided that escape across the river was the only means of saving his force. On July 11, however, Winnebagos revealed to Colonel Henry L. Dodge that Black Hawk was camped on the rapids of the Rock River. Dodge gave chase and, on July 24, Atkinson and 1,300 handpicked men joined him. On August 1, 1832, the much-reduced British Band—now numbering about 500—was camped at the junction of the Bad Axe and Mississippi rivers. Some had begun to cross the Mississippi in canoes and rafts, but most were still on the east bank as the steamboat *Warrior* approached. A few abortive attempts were made at negotiation, after which the *Warrior* opened fire, bombarding the British Band for two hours and killing twenty-three Indians. The others were delayed in crossing the river. Black Hawk and a few of his closest followers fled northward to what they hoped would be refuge among the Winnebagos.

On August 3, the combined command of Atkinson and Dodge reached the Bad Axe–Mississippi junction. Those Indians remaining on the east bank of the Mississippi attempted to surrender, but the troops responded with a general attack in the eight-hour Battle of the Bad Axe River. About 200 of the British Band Indians did reach the west bank, but they were intercepted by white-allied Sioux, who captured or killed them. Black Hawk, who had headed north, was again betrayed by the Winnebagos. Arrested and imprisoned by U.S. troops, he took no part in the Treaty of Fort Armstrong, which General Scott concluded with the survivors of the British Band on September 19, 1832. The treaty ceded 6 million acres to the United States. Black Hawk remained in prison for a year before he was permitted, in exchange for his pledge never again to act as their chief, to rejoin what was left of his people.

Second Seminole War (1835–1842)

The Second Seminole War was provoked by the Jackson administration's policy of Indian removal pursuant to the Indian Removal Act of 1830. Determined to force the Seminoles, Creeks, and Cherokees living in Georgia and Florida to accept removal to "Indian Territory" in the West, the Jackson administration made no attempt to intervene in the actions

*Osceola, leader of the Seminoles, was a skillful strate-
gist and tactician who used the swamplands of Florida
to his advantage in the grim guerrilla warfare of the
Second Seminole War.*

and policies of local authorities, who persecuted the
Indians. In 1831–1832 drought accomplished what
harrassment could not. On May 9, 1832, a large
group of Seminoles signed a preliminary treaty,
which gave them the right to approve, prior to their
actual removal, the site selected for their resettlement. Before Seminole representatives had an
opportunity to inspect the site, however, a U.S.
Indian agent coerced tribal authorities into signing a
final treaty, which bound the Seminoles to leave the
Southeast by 1837. This provoked a resistance movement led by Osceola.

Osceola approached the local Indian agent, Wiley
Thompson, and agreed to removal, but asked that it
be delayed until January 15, 1836. Thompson

agreed; however, he was suspicious of Osceola's
motives and ordered the suspension of the sale of
gunpowder to the Indians, which caused friction
between the two men. In October 1835 Osceola convened a secret council of war and discovered that six
of sixteen chiefs favored accepting removal. Osceola
threatened them with death, and, late in November,
he and twelve other warriors assassinated the most
important of the pro-removal faction chiefs, Charley
Emathla. This was the formal beginning of the
Second Seminole War.

As the Seminoles' war chief, Osceola led raids
across a large part of central Florida. With considerable military sophistication, he particularly targeted
roads and bridges, knowing that these were essential
to the movement of troops, supplies, and the one military asset against which he was powerless: artillery.

The first formal military encounter of the war was
the Battle of Black Point on December 18, 1835,
west of the village of Micanopy. Osceola and eighty
warriors raided a wagon train. Thirty mounted militiamen who stumbled on the scene were ordered to
attack, but they balked and retreated. In the action,
eight militia troops were killed and six wounded.

Next, while King Philip, another Seminole leader,
drew off army strength with his raids on area plantations, Osceola sent his lieutenant, Alligator, with 250
warriors to intercept General Clinch, who was
marching with 550 mounted Florida militiamen and
200 federal regulars on a Seminole village near the
Withlacoochee River. At noon on December 31,
1835, the Indians ambushed Clinch's superior force
(killing four men and wounding fifty-two, one mortally), forcing Clinch to abort his campaign.

The Battle of Black Point and the ambush at the
Withlacoochee were the only actions of the Second
Seminole War that might be called formal battles.
Over a period of seven years, the war consisted of
raids and mostly fruitless pursuits, punctuated by
short, sharp guerrilla exchanges. A series of commanders—Edmund Gaines, Duncan Clinch, Winfield Scott, Robert Call, Thomas Jesup, Zachary
Taylor, Alexander McComb, Walker Armistead, and

Osceola

(1804–1838)

Osceola, variously identified as a Red Stick Creek or a Seminole, emerged as a leader of the Seminole tribe during the Second Seminole War. Born on the Tallapoosa River in Alabama, Osceola was probably the son of a Creek mother and an English father, William Powell. Whites generally called him Billy Powell or simply Powell. (Some historians believe that William Powell was Osceola's stepfather and that his natural father was a Creek. Osceola himself claimed to be a full-blooded Indian.)

Osceola was introduced to warfare during the First Seminole War. He was among those Andrew Jackson captured in an attack on the camp of Red Stick leader Peter McQueen. Young Osceola, probably about fourteen years old at the time, was held only briefly. His band of Red Sticks later moved to Tampa Bay, and it is probable that Osceola served for a time as an Indian agency police officer, responsible for apprehending Indians who strayed from the reservation.

By 1833–1834, as tribal debate over the mandated removal to Indian Territory grew heated, Osceola emerged as a powerful voice in the resistance movement. In an 1834 council with Indian agent Wiley Thompson, Osceola was the principal spokesperson for the cause. He was at the forefront again in April 1835, when President Jackson convened a large council to settle the matter of removal once and for all. It is said that, at this council, sixteen Seminole chiefs signed a document reaffirming their agreement to remove to Indian Territory, but that Osceola pinned the paper to the table with his knife, declaring that *this* would be the only mark he would make. (No official record of this incident exists.) In November 1835 Osceola committed his now-sizable following to action when he murdered Charley Emathla, a Seminole chief who had agreed to move west. Late the next month, in a raid on Fort King, Osceola and his warriors killed Agent Wiley Thompson and four others.

Against regular troops as well as militia, Osceola proved to be a skillful strategist and tactician who used the impenetrable swamplands of Florida as a powerful ally in a grim guerrilla war. He also exercised a combination of powerful verbal persuasion and ruthless strong-arm tactics to keep the various chiefs loyal to the resistance. Osceola repeatedly eluded capture and was taken, at last, only by treachery.

William Worth—all failed to drive the Seminoles out of Florida. Jesup managed to capture Osceola on October 21, 1837, by violating a truce. Imprisoned at Fort Moultrie, South Carolina, Osceola fell ill and died on January 30, 1838. Alligator and the Red Stick leader Boleck (Billy Bowlegs) continued to lead the Seminole resistance after Osceola's death, but it was increasingly perceived among the Indians as a lost cause. Between 1835 and 1842, about 3,000 Seminoles submitted to removal and were marched to Indian Territory. Some 1,500 federal troops died in the war, and the government spent $20 million to fight it. The war ended in 1842 not in victory, but exhaustion. The federal government simply ceased military operations.

Third Seminole War (1855–1858)

A new Seminole war erupted in 1855 after a surveying party working in the Great Cypress Swamp stole or vandalized crops belonging to followers of Chief Boleck (Billy Bowlegs). The chief and others demanded compensation and an apology from the surveyors. Rebuffed, the Indians withdrew, only to begin raiding local settlers and settlements. The fighting was sporadic and involved some federal troops and militia forces. Eventually exhausted, Boleck agreed on March 5, 1857, to leave Florida in exchange for a cash settlement of several thousand dollars. He took with him to Indian Territory 165 followers, leaving behind 120 Seminoles, whose descendants remain in Florida today. The United States unilaterally declared the Third Seminole War ended on May 8, 1858.

Toward a Policy of Indian Removal

"Indian removal," the policy of removing Native Americans from lands east of the Mississippi River to territory reserved for their exclusive occupation in the West, is inextricably associated with the administration of President Andrew Jackson. However, while the Indian Removal Act of 1830 was endorsed by Jackson and was enacted during his administration, the idea of segregating whites and Indians went back as far as the administration of George Washington. Washington envisioned what he called a "Chinese Wall" that might separate Indians and whites, although he never specified just how such an absolute separation might be effected.

The nation's third president, Thomas Jefferson, concluded the Louisiana Purchase in large part because he believed the vast new western territory could be used for the resettlement of the Indians, with plenty of room left over for an ample buffer zone. Jefferson's successor, James Madison, also discussed exchanging newly acquired western lands for the Indians' eastern holdings. John C. Calhoun, secretary of war under James Monroe, who followed Madison into office, proposed an act of Congress to mandate removal. Monroe's successor, President John Quincy Adams, laid additional groundwork for the removal legislation that was finally enacted during the Jackson administration.

Washington and the presidents that followed him, including Jackson, suggested well-regulated trade as a means of producing a workable living arrangement for whites and Indians; yet even as these chief exec-utives advocated the healing virtues of commerce, they all espoused the far more radical solution of separation—of Indian "removal."

Diplomatic Crisis with Spain: The Adams-Oñis Treaty

The Indians were not the only occupants of southeastern lands coveted by American settlers. Spain possessed Florida and other lands east of the Mississippi at the time of the First Seminole War (1817–1818). General Andrew Jackson, in pursuit of recalcitrant Seminoles and the Red Stick Creek leader Peter McQueen, seized the settlements of Saint Marks and Pensacola without any regard for Spanish sovereignty. This high-handedness precipitated a diplomatic crisis, which was deftly resolved by the diplomacy of John Quincy Adams, secretary of state in the cabinet of President James Monroe. On February 22, 1819, Adams negotiated with Luis Oñis, Spain's foreign secretary, the "Transcontinental Treaty," better known as the **Adams-Oñis Treaty.** The treaty confirmed and defined the Spanish cession of Florida to the United States and also provided for Spanish renunciation of the Oregon country in exchange for U.S. recognition of Spanish sovereignty over Texas. Broadly speaking, by this treaty, the United States and Spain divided their North American claims along a line from the southeastern corner of what is now Louisiana north and west to what is now Wyoming, and thence due west along the latitude 42° north to the Pacific. The treaty also resolved once and for all the so-called West Florida controversy, which had been created by the Spanish cession of Louisiana to France in 1800 and the Louisiana Purchase by the United States in 1803. Spain had held that its cession to France comprehended only the territory that was generally called Louisiana at the time of the cession, whereas the United States claimed that the Louisiana Territory encompassed much more, including all of the territory finally specified by the Adams-Oñis Treaty.

As a result of the Spanish cession of Florida, many white Americans rushed into the lower South-

Adams-Oñis Treaty, 1819

Treaty of Amity, Settlement, and Limits Between the United States of America and His Catholic Majesty. 1819

ARTICLE I

There shall be a firm and inviolable peace and sincere friendship between the United States and their citizens and His Catholic Majesty, his successors and subjects, without exception of persons or places.

ARTICLE II

His Catholic Majesty cedes to the United States, in full property and sovereignty, all the territories which belong to him, situated to the eastward of the Mississippi, known by the name of East and West Florida. . . .

ARTICLE V

The inhabitants of the ceded territories shall be secured in the free exercise of their religion, without any restriction; and all those who may desire to remove to the Spanish dominions shall be permitted to sell or export their effects, at any time whatever, without being subject, in either case, to duties.

ARTICLE VI

The inhabitants of the territories which His Catholic Majesty cedes to the United States, by this treaty, shall be incorporated in the Union of the United States as soon as may be consistent with the principles of the Federal Constitution, and admitted to the enjoyment of all the privileges, rights, and immunities of the citizens of the United States.

Excerpted from the Avalon Project at Yale Law School, "Treaty of Amity, Settlement, and Limits Between the United States of America and His Catholic Majesty," www.yale.edu/lawweb/avalon/diplomacy/spain/sp1819.htm.

---

east—so many, in fact, that the hostile Seminoles waging war against federal and local forces suddenly withdrew into hiding and broke off all military action. It was this withdrawal, triggered by the cession formalized in the Adams-Oñis Treaty, that ended the First Seminole War, not any U.S. military victory.

The Indian Removal Act of 1830

The **Indian Removal Act** was officially titled "An Act to Provide for an Exchange of Lands with the Indians Residing in Any of the States or Territories, and for Their Removal West of the River Mississippi," and the congressional debate over the bill reflected ethical divisions within the nation. The language of the proposed law implied that the process of Indian "removal" was to be, on the part of the Indians, an entirely voluntary exchange of eastern lands for western lands. Proponents of the bill argued, with little regard for the facts of the matter, that Indians were nomadic hunters, whereas white settlers were farmers, and held that these two ways of life could not coexist: whereas agriculture was a prerequisite for the advance of civilization, hunting was atavistic, an antisocial throwback to the past, and therefore inherently uncivilized. The future development of the United States, removal proponents argued, depended on the removal and segregation of the Indians, who were to be regarded as wards of the state. Removal to a defined Indian Territory would include government subsidies, which would ensure the physical welfare of the Indians.

Opponents of the Indian Removal Act countered that, despite the language of the bill, removal would be effectively compulsory, a matter of eminent domain. They pointed out that tribal decisions often failed to reflect the will of the majority of the tribe and argued that it was morally repugnant to force individuals to abide by the will of the majority in such matters as place of residence, as if the tribe possessed a human mind and will. The leading congressional voice in opposition to Indian removal was

New Jersey senator Theodore Frelinghuysen, whose long speech of April 9, 1830, presented the main arguments against the policy. Frelinghuysen made a powerful appeal to a morality of common-law, commonsense justice, which reflected the position of many Americans at the time:

> God, in his providence, planted these tribes on this Western continent, so far as we know, before Great Britain herself had a political existence. I believe, sir, it is not now seriously denied that the Indians are men, endowed with kindred faculties and powers with ourselves; that they have a place in human sympathy, and are justly entitled to a share in the common bounties of a benignant Providence. And, with this conceded, I ask in what code of the law of nations, or by what process of abstract deduction, their rights have been extinguished?
>
> Where is the decree or ordinance that has stripped these early and first lords of the soil? Sir, no record of such measure can be found.

After much bitter debate, the Indian Removal Act was passed and signed into law on May 28, 1830.

The Law in Letter and Execution

In principle, the Indian Removal Act provided for a voluntary, equitable exchange of western land for eastern land; in practice, however, the law was applied poorly, cynically, and often in bad faith. Indian tribes were typically coerced or duped into removal by officials who secured the agreement of Indian leaders known to be compliant. The government deemed these leaders as representative of the tribe and considered their compliance binding on all members of the tribe, regardless of what the majority of members of their tribes might or might not desire. Once a removal treaty was concluded, the government assumed the right to move all Indians off of the land, by force if necessary.

Some of the northern tribes were peacefully resettled in "Indian Territory," land west of the Mississippi River, most of it in present-day Oklahoma. Among the tribes of the Southeast (especially the so-called Five Civilized Tribes: Chickasaw, Choctaw, Seminole, Cherokee, and Creek), resistance was bitter and sometimes fierce. Ultimately, about 100,000 southeastern Indians were marched to Indian Territory during the 1830s. The conditions of the marches were usually harsh: Preparation, provisions, and supplies were often inadequate. Abuse at the hands of the soldiers assigned as escorts was

Indian Removal Act, 1830

That it shall and may be lawful for the President of the United States to cause so much of any territory belonging to the United States, west of the river Mississippi, not included in any state of organized territory, and to which the Indian title has been extinguished, as he may judge necessary, to be divided into a suitable number of districts, for the reception of such tribes or nations of Indians as may choose to exchange the lands where they now reside, and remove there. . . .

. . . That upon the making of any such exchange as is contemplated by this act, it shall and may be lawful for the President to cause such aid and assistance to be furnished to the emigrants as may be necessary and proper to enable them to remove to, and settle in, the country for which they may have exchanged; and also, to give them such aid and assistance as may be necessary for their support and subsistence for the first year after their removal.

Excerpted from Alan Axelrod, *American Treaties and Alliances* (Washington, D.C.: CQ Press, 2000), 38–39.

commonplace. Approximately one quarter of those removed died en route.

Cherokee Politics

Of all the southeastern tribes, the Cherokees, who had close commercial and cultural ties to their white neighbors, were the most politically sophisticated. They skillfully attempted to work within the legal system to resist removal.

The tribe was dominated by two political factions: the Nationalist Party, which favored legal means to prevent removal and represented about 17,000 of the 18,000 Cherokees living in the Southeast, and the Treaty Party, which was willing to accept removal and represented no more than 1,000 southeastern Cherokees. While the Nationalists fought removal in the courts, Jackson administration officials negotiated a removal treaty with the Treaty Party. On December 29, 1835, federal negotiators concluded with representatives of the Treaty Party the **Treaty of New Echota,** for the removal of the Cherokees. Although negotiated with a small minority of the tribe, it was deemed binding on all Cherokees. President Jackson acted to check resistance by issuing an executive order barring the Cherokee National Party from convening any meetings to discuss the treaty or alternative courses of action. Despite this, under the leadership of a prominent Cherokee named John Ross, the Nationalist Party managed to postpone removal until the fall and winter of 1838 and 1839.

The Supreme Court Rules: *Cherokee Nation v. Georgia* and *Worcester v. Georgia*

The Indian Removal Act was implemented even as the Cherokees appealed to the courts for aid in resisting removal. The state of Georgia moved most aggressively against the Cherokees by unilaterally extending state laws over Cherokee lands. The Cherokees brought suit against Georgia, but the U.S. Supreme Court refused to accept jurisdiction on the grounds that the Cherokee Nation was not a "foreign nation" as that concept was contemplated in the Constitution. In *Cherokee Nation v. Georgia* (1831), Chief Justice John Marshall defined the Cherokees and all other Indian tribes as "domestic dependent nations." This greatly reduced the legal standing of all the tribes.

In 1832, however, the Supreme Court seemed to reverse itself in the case of *Worcester v. Georgia.* Samuel A. Worcester, a white missionary among the Cherokees, was arrested and jailed for his defiance of a Georgia law forbidding whites from living in Cherokee country without obtaining a state permit that required an oath of allegiance to the state. In deciding in favor of Worcester, the Court defined the Cherokees as a "nation" not subject to the jurisdiction of the state. This was not necessarily a repudiation of the 1831 definition of the tribe as a "domestic dependent nation," but it did enhance the functional meaning of that definition by giving the Cherokees and other Indian tribes a legally sanctioned degree of sovereignty.

President Jackson Defies the Court

The decision in *Worcester v. Georgia* proved to be a hollow triumph for the Cherokees because President Jackson refused to employ federal authority to enforce the decision—that is, to deny Georgia's jurisdiction over the Cherokees. In 1833 Jackson would take a momentous stand against South Carolina in the Nullification Crisis, threatening to use force to compel the state to comply with a federal tariff to which it objected. In 1832, however, he protested that the federal government was powerless to interfere in the affairs of an individual state. To the Cherokees, Jackson pointedly suggested that their only remedy was acceptance of removal.

The Seminole Response

In contrast to the Cherokees and their legal approach, the Seminoles resisted by means of war. The First Seminole War (1817–1818) was an outgrowth of developments during the War of 1812 and

Treaty of New Echota, 1835

WHEREAS the Cherokees are anxious to make some arrangements with the Government of the United States whereby the difficulties they have experienced by a residence within the settled parts of the United States under the jurisdiction and laws of the State Governments may be terminated and adjusted; and with a view to reuniting their people in one body and securing a permanent home for themselves and their posterity in the country selected by their forefathers without the territorial limits of the State sovereignties, and where they can establish and enjoy a government of their choice and perpetuate such a state of society as may be most consonant with their views, habits and condition; and as may tend to their individual comfort and their advancement in civilization . . .

And whereas the Cherokee people at their last October council at Red Clay, fully authorized and empowered a delegation or committee of twenty persons of their nation to enter into and conclude a treaty with the United States commissioner then present . . .

Therefore the following articles of a treaty are agreed upon and concluded. . . .

ARTICLE 1.
The Cherokee nation hereby cede relinquish and convey to the United States all the lands owned claimed or possessed by them east of the Mississippi river, and hereby release all their claims upon the United States for spoliations of every kind for and in consideration of the sum of five millions of dollars. . . .

ARTICLE 7.
The Cherokee nation having already made great progress in civilization and deeming it important that every proper and laudable inducement should be offered to their people to improve their condition . . . it is stipulated that they shall be entitled to a delegate in the House of Representatives of the United States whenever Congress shall make provision for the same.

ARTICLE 8.
The United States also agree and stipulate to remove the Cherokees to their new homes and to subsist them one year after their arrival there and that a sufficient number of steamboats and baggage-wagons shall be furnished to remove them comfortably, and so as not to endanger their health, and that a physician well supplied with medicines shall accompany each detachment of emigrants removed by the Government. . . .

ARTICLE 10.
The President of the United States shall invest in some safe and most productive public stocks of the country for the benefit of the whole Cherokee nation who have removed or shall remove to the lands assigned by this treaty to the Cherokee nation west of the Mississippi the following sums as a permanent fund. . . .

ARTICLE 12.
Those individuals and families of the Cherokee nation that are averse to a removal to the Cherokee country west of the Mississippi and are desirous to become citizens of the States where they reside and such as are qualified to take care of themselves and their property shall be entitled to receive their due portion of all the personal benefits accruing under this treaty for their claims, improvements and *per capita;* as soon as an appropriation is made for this treaty.

Excerpted from Charles J. Kappler, ed., *Indian Affairs: Laws and Treaties,* vol. II, *Treaties* (Washington, D.C.: U.S. Government Printing Office, 1904), 439–449, available from the Oklahoma State University Library, http://digital.library. okstate.edu/kappler/Vol2/treaties/che0439.htm.

the Creek War: the cession of Spanish Florida and of Red Stick and White Stick Creek lands, both of which brought a massive influx of white settlement into what had been Indian territory. The Second Seminole War (1835–1842) corresponded to the period during which the Indian Removal Act of 1830 was most vigorously executed. The Seminoles did not wish to suffer the fate of the Cherokees, who were dispossessed and then marched to alien lands along the infamous and often lethal "Trail of Tears." It should also be observed that pursuing the legal course attempted by the Cherokees was never a viable option for the Seminoles. In contrast to the Cherokees, whose daily lives and commerce were intimately tied to the white community, the Seminoles tended to live apart from white society. Unlike the Cherokees, who defined themselves as Americans, the Seminoles felt that they had very little stake in the legal and political system of the United States.

The Epoch of the Trail of Tears

In the face of all opposition, President Jackson remained staunch in his endorsement of the removal policy. Addressing Congress on December 7, 1835, he held that "all preceding experiments for the improvement of the Indians have failed. It now seems an established fact that they cannot live in contact with a civilized community and prosper." He argued that removal was "founded upon the knowledge we have gained from their character and habits" and that the policy was "dictated by a spirit of enlarged liberality" as demonstrated by the fact that a "territory exceeding in extent that relinquished has been granted to each tribe."

The truth was that "Indian Territory," encompassing present-day Oklahoma and parts of Nebraska, Kansas, and the Dakotas, bore little resemblance to the lush, green southeastern homelands of the removed tribes. Much of the stubborn soil in this mostly semiarid region was highly resistant to cultivation and quite unsuited to the type of agriculture the Indians had practiced in the East. The problems of climate and soil were compounded by a general failure of the federal system that had obligated itself by treaty to aid and support the "resettled" Indians. The Indian agency system was corrupt, callous, and inefficient. Many of the removed Indians quickly died of malnutrition and privation, not to mention what might best be described as broken hearts.

The journey to Indian Territory was, for many, a death march. By 1838 Cherokees were herded into

Worcester v. Georgia, *1832*

Chief Justice MARSHALL delivered the opinion of the Court.

This cause, in every point of view in which it can be placed, is of the deepest interest. . . .

The Cherokee Nation . . . is a distinct community occupying its own territory, with boundaries accurately described, in which the laws of Georgia can have no force. . . .

The act of the State of Georgia, under which the plaintiff in error was prosecuted, is consequently void, and the judgment a nullity. . . . [T]he acts of Georgia are repugnant to the Constitution, laws, and treaties of the United States.

Excerpted from FindLaw, *Worcester v. State of Ga.,* 31 U.S. 515 (1832), http://caselaw.lp.findlaw.com/scripts/getcase.pl?court=US&vol=31&invol=515.

holding camps, where they spent a miserable and sickly summer before being herded along what came to be called the 1,200-mile "Trail of Tears" during the fall and winter of 1838 and 1839. Cold, short of rations, and subject to the abuse of their military guards, 4,000 of the 15,000 who began the journey died before reaching its end. Many Americans were outraged, but even many of those who objected to the cruelty with which removal was executed agreed with President Jackson that all other "experiments" in the coexistence of whites and Indians had failed.

Sac and Fox Cession of 1804

Indian removal was less extensive in the upper Midwest than in the Southeast, but it began earlier. On November 3, 1804, William Henry Harrison, territorial governor of Indiana and the "district of Louisiana," concluded the **Treaty with the Sauk and Foxes (1804),** by which a few Indians ceded most of their lands—a vast tract of the upper Midwest—in return for a payment of $2,234.50 and an annuity of

Treaty with the Sauk and Foxes, 1804

ARTICLE 1. The United States receive the united Sac and Fox tribes into their friendship and protection, and the said tribes agree to consider themselves under the protection of the United States, and of no other power whatsoever. . . .

ARTICLE 3. In consideration of the cession and relinquishment of land . . . the United States will deliver to the said tribes . . . yearly and every year goods suited to the circumstances of the Indians of the value of one thousand dollars (six hundred of which are intended for the Sacs and four hundred for the Foxes). . . .

ARTICLE 4. The United States will never interrupt the said tribes in the possession of the lands which they rightfully claim, but will on the contrary protect them in the quiet enjoyment of the same.

Excerpted from the University of Tulsa College of Law, "Treaty with the Sauk and Foxes," www.utulsa.edu/law/classes/rice/treaties/07_stat_084_sauk_fox.htm.

$1,000 in "goods suited to the circumstances of the Indians." In a manner typical of treaties between the government and Indian tribes, although the government negotiated only with the most compliant tribal faction, it held the treaty as binding on the entire tribe. Black Hawk and his followers had been duped into affirming the treaty, and they ultimately resisted all government actions flowing from it. As whites moved onto the disputed land, the result was the Black Hawk War.

The Treaty of 1832

On September 19, 1832, General Winfield Scott concluded the **Treaty of Fort Armstrong** with the survivors of the Black Hawk War. Black Hawk himself, having been imprisoned, took no part in this treaty

whose terms were dictated rather than negotiated. Added to the cessions of the 1804 Treaty with the Sauk and Foxes was a requirement that the tribe cede a strip of land fifty miles wide, running the entire length of Iowa's Mississippi River frontage, representing about 6 million acres. The treaty further mandated the total removal of the Indians by June 1, 1833, and required a pledge that the Sac and Fox tribes would never return to the lands they had ceded. In return, the United States paid them annuities amounting to $660,000.

Organization of the Department of Indian Affairs

The flurry of treaties, cessions, and forced removals that preceded and followed the Indian Removal Act of 1830 was accompanied by war and surrounded by confusion. In an attempt to introduce order and a measure of justice into this chaotic situation,

Treaty of Fort Armstrong, 1832

WHEREAS, under certain lawless and desperate leaders, a formidable band, constituting a large portion of the Sac and Fox nation, left their country in April last, and, in violation of treaties, commenced an unprovoked war upon unsuspecting and defenseless citizens of the United States, sparing neither age nor sex; and whereas, the United States, at a great expense of treasure, have subdued the said hostile band, killing or capturing all its principal Chiefs and Warriors—the said States, partly as indemnity for the expense incurred, and partly to secure the future safety and tranquillity of the invaded frontier, demand of the said tribes, to the use of the United States, a cession of a tract of the Sac and Fox country, bordering on said frontier, more than proportional to the numbers of the hostile band who have been so conquered and subdued.

Excerpted from Alan Axelrod, *American Treaties and Alliances* (Washington, D.C.: CQ Press, 2000), 41.

Congress passed "An Act to Provide for the Organization of the Department of Indian Affairs," which was signed into law on June 30, 1834. The act federalized and centralized the administration of Indian affairs, removing it from the hands of the territorial governors and making it the responsibility of regional superintendents of Indian affairs. Appointed by and reporting to the president of the United States, the superintendents were charged with "general supervision and control over the official conduct and accounts of all officers and persons employed by the government in the Indian department." The act further established a system of Indian agents and agencies throughout Indian country; the agents were to be appointed by the president (with the advice and consent of the Senate) for a term of four years. The act attempted to put an end to the corruption that had plagued earlier attempts to administer Indian affairs by barring any Indian agent or other official of the Department of Indian Affairs from having "any interest or concern in any trade with the Indians." The legislation was much needed, and it was enacted in good faith; however, in practice, it did little to end corruption, inefficiency, and indifference in the administration of an increasingly far-flung and chronically underfunded network of Indian agencies and reservations. Indeed, the legislation was merely one act in a long series that inexorably institutionalized Indian dependency on a federal government that, more often than not, lacked the will or the capacity to care adequately for a people it had made so entirely dependent. Thus this act, with others that followed, also effectively institutionalized a more or less permanent state of war between many Indian tribes and the United States.

BIBLIOGRAPHY

Black Hawk. *Life of Black Hawk*. New York: Dover, 1994.

Knetsch, Joe. *Florida's Seminole Wars, 1817–1858*. Mount Pleasant, S.C.: Arcadia Publishing, 2003.

Mahon, John K. *History of the Second Seminole War, 1835–1842*. Gainesville: University Press of Florida, 1991.

Missall, John, and Mary Lou Missall. *The Seminole Wars: America's Longest Indian Conflict*. Gainesville: University Press of Florida, 2004.

Whitney, Ellen M. *The Black Hawk War, 1831–1832: Part 1 and Part 2*. Springfield: Illinois State Historical Society, 1973.

At Issue

When the burgeoning colonies of Americans in the Mexican state of Coahuila y Tejas posed a threat to Mexico's governance of its northern provinces, Mexico moved not only to curb further Anglo colonization, but also to assert political control over Texas. The Texans rebelled and declared independence.

The Conflict

By the mid-1820s, colonial entrepreneur Stephen F. Austin and others had established colonies of Americans in the Mexican province of Coahuila y Tejas. Within a decade, the Anglo population of these colonies outnumbered the population of Mexican nationals, and the colonists sought independence from the Mexican government.

The first armed uprising occurred in June 1835, when thirty Texans forced the surrender of the small garrison and customs house at Anáhuac. Although the various Texas colonies were by no means united in their desire for independence, other Texas communities refused to turn the rebels over to Mexican authorities. The incipient rebellion and defiance gave Mexican president Antonio López de Santa Anna a pretext for assuming dictatorial powers within Mexico proper and for taking a stronger hand in Texas affairs. He sent Mexican cavalry forces under General Martín Perfecto de Cós into Texas on October 2, 1835, and demanded the surrender of a cannon in the possession of Texans at Gonzales. Instead of giving up the piece, settlers attacked the cavalry, which retreated to San Antonio. The next month, Austin, having assembled 500 men, laid siege to San Antonio.

As the rebellion developed in piecemeal fashion, representatives of the dozen American colonies in Texas convened to decide on a united course of action and a war aim: either full independence or a return to Mexican rule under the provisions of the liberal 1824 constitution, which Santa Anna had repudiated. The rebels compromised by creating a provisional government, which would appeal to liberal elements in the Mexican government for full statehood within a constitutionally governed Mexico. In order to leave all options open, however, Austin led a delegation to Washington, D.C., to discuss with President Andrew Jackson the prospects for annexation to the United States.

In the meantime, when the Anglo troops laying siege to Cós in San Antonio decided to withdraw to winter quarters at Gonzales, frontiersman Ben Milam rallied them for a do-or-die assault on the town. "Who will go with old Ben Milam?" became the first rallying cry of the Texas revolution. On December 5, 1835, a force of 5,300 Texans stormed San Antonio, fighting the outnumbered Cós in the streets. Gathering 1,100 troops about him, Cós took refuge in a tumbledown fortress that had been converted from the town's disused namesake mission. Officially called Mission San Antonio de Valero, the compound was more familiarly known as the Alamo. The Texans pounded the old mission's walls with artillery; after Cós surrendered on December 9, they occupied the fortress, which they then set about repairing for their own defensive use.

With a revolution suddenly under way, two Texas leaders, Samuel Houston and Henry Smith, urged unity in a commitment to independence. They met with objections from land speculators, who, having amassed their holdings by bribing Mexican legislators, feared that independence would nullify their claims. This faction favored sending a force to seize Matamoros, a Mexican town at the mouth of the Rio Grande that was a center of anti–Santa Anna activity, and then make common cause with the Mexican liberals, depose Santa Anna, and restore the liberal federalism of the 1824 Mexican constitution. The mission to Matamoros, however, was cut short due to dissension in the ranks and never reached its destination. Instead, its leader, Colonel J. W. Fannin, established his forces in a fort at Goliad, Texas.

In January 1836 Santa Anna led 5,000 well-equipped Mexican regulars on a punitive expedition against the Texas rebels. At this time, word came from the Alamo that the unpaid Texas garrison there was tired and hungry. Houston advised them to withdraw, as there was little point in defending a remote outpost. He favored making a stand closer to San Felipe de Austin (modern Austin, Texas), which offered ground that was both easier to defend and simply more difficult to attack. In the meantime, Fannin proposed leaving Goliad to attack Matamoros, as had been proposed earlier. Houston objected that this would allow Santa Anna free passage into the Texas interior. Choosing the lesser of two evils, Houston decided to concentrate his main forces not where he really wanted them—near Austin—but sixty miles east of San Antonio, at Gonzales. He dispatched Jim Bowie to San Antonio to order the evacuation and the destruction of the Alamo and to see to the transportation of its artillery. No sooner did Bowie arrive at the Alamo, however, than he decided to ignore Houston's orders. With Alamo garrison commander Colonel James C. Neill, Bowie resolved to use the fortress as a defense against Santa Anna's farther advance.

Neill and Bowie could muster little more than 100 men to garrison the Alamo. Colonel William B. Travis, a longtime leader of the Texas war faction, arrived with a handful of reinforcements, as did the colorful David (Davy) Crockett, who led a dozen volunteers from Tennessee. On February 11, 1836, Neill left the Alamo and turned over command of about 150 men to Bowie and Travis. All clung to the hope that Santa Anna would wait until spring before marching through the barren and forbidding desert country south of San Antonio. This would give ample time for reinforcements from all over the United States to answer Travis's rallying pleas. But neither Bowie nor Travis had reckoned on Santa Anna's willingness to sacrifice his men to a hard winter march. He entered San Antonio on February 25, 1836, with a force that had been reduced by the rigors of the march to about 2,000 troops fit for duty. As the Mexicans approached, a number of noncombatants—mostly women and children—took refuge with the Alamo garrison, adding to the defenders' responsibilities and representing more mouths to feed. Further, Travis, chronically ill with tuberculosis, had sustained injuries while placing a cannon and was confined to bed with a high fever. At the last minute, and against Houston's orders, twenty-five reinforcements arrived, bringing the number of Alamo defenders to 187.

Santa Anna bombarded the Alamo for a week, failing to kill a single Texan, even as the defenders'

CHRONOLOGY OF THE TEXAS WAR OF INDEPENDENCE

1835
- *June* Seizure of Anáhuac
- *Oct. 2* Battle of Gonzales
- *Oct. 9* Battle of Goliad
- *Dec. 9* Siege of Bexar (San Antonio) ends.

1836
- *Mar. 1* Convention of 1836 gathers to sign a Texas constitution and form a new government.
- *Mar. 2* Texas Declaration of Independence
- *Mar. 6* The Alamo falls.
- *Mar. 27* The Goliad Massacre
- *Apr. 21* The Battle of San Jacinto secures Texas Independence.

Sam Houston

(1793–1863)

Sam Houston was born near Lexington, Virginia, and was raised in Virginia and Tennessee. He lived among the Cherokees from 1808 to 1811, taught school briefly, and then, as a junior U.S. Army officer, served under Andrew Jackson during the Creek War phase of the War of 1812 (Chapter 6). Houston was promoted to first lieutenant in 1818, but he abruptly resigned his commission in 1818 after Secretary of War John C. Calhoun chastised him for affecting Indian dress and for making what he considered an impertinent inquiry that called into question Calhoun's integrity.

Houston studied law and was admitted to the bar in Nashville, Tennessee, late in 1818. He was chosen major general of the state militia in 1821 and in 1823 was elected to Congress, where he served until 1827, when he was elected governor of Tennessee. He was reelected in 1829, but he resigned in April after his bride of three months deserted him. Emotionally shattered, he moved west and again took up residence among the Cherokees, who formally adopted him into their tribe in October 1829. Houston then campaigned in Washington, D.C., for the better treatment of the Cherokee and other tribes.

Jackson commissioned Houston to negotiate with several Indian tribes in Texas during 1832.

While he was there, Houston became increasingly involved in local politics and participated in the San Felipe Convention of April 1833, which drew up a Texas constitution as well as a petition to the Mexican government for Mexican statehood. After settling in Texas, Houston was appointed commander of the small Texas army in November 1835.

Houston was a participant in the convention at which Texas declared independence on March 2, 1836. After leading the Texas victory at the Battle of San Jacinto on April 21, 1836, Houston coerced Santa Anna into signing the Treaty of Velasco, which granted Texas independence from Mexico.

Houston was twice elected president of the Republic of Texas, serving from 1836 to 1838 and from 1841 to 1844. After Texas was admitted to the Union, Houston was elected senator in 1846 and was reappointed to the Senate in 1852. A staunch Unionist, he was not returned to the Senate in the elections of 1858, but was elected governor in 1859 and tried to block secession in 1861. When, despite his efforts, Texas seceded, Houston refused to swear allegiance to the Confederacy in March 1861 and was removed from office. He retired to Huntsville, Texas, where he died two years later.

grapeshot and rifle fire took a heavy toll among the attackers. The artillery broke down the Alamo's walls, however, and on March 6, 1,800 of Santa Anna's men stormed the fortress. It was a remarkably inept attack in which about 600 Mexicans were killed. But after ninety minutes of combat, almost all of the Alamo's defenders had fallen, and Santa Anna seized the fort. Crockett and the few other prisoners Santa Anna took were summarily executed. The women and children were released, and Santa Anna directed one of them, Susannah Dickerson, to tell all

of Texas what had happened at the Alamo. He believed this would crush any further rebellion.

Santa Anna's assault on the Alamo was a tactical victory, but a strategic defeat. The "massacre" gave the Texas revolution a pantheon of martyrs that brought sudden unity to the struggle under the rallying cry of "Remember the Alamo!"

After the fall of the Alamo, Houston ordered Fannin to destroy the fortress at Goliad and retreat. Fannin complied on March 18, but it was too late. Surrounded by a Mexican force of 1,400 under General

José Urrea, Fannin surrendered on March 20. On Santa Anna's orders, all of Urrea's prisoners were executed on March 27. By responding to the rebellion with an iron fist, adding the "Goliad Massacre" to the Alamo slaughter, Santa Anna believed the rebellion would end. Indeed, in what became known as the "Runaway Scrape," thousands of Texans did flee east to the U.S. border, and the Texas provisional government likewise evacuated. Houston, however, dubbed this flight a mere strategic retreat and, by April, had raised and trained an army of 740 handpicked and highly determined men, whom he deployed on April 21, 1836, against Santa Anna and some 700 troops on an open plain west of the San Jacinto River, near Galveston Bay. Last-minute reinforcements brought Santa Anna's forces to 1,600 men. Now outnumbered more than two to one, Houston nevertheless ordered the attack. The Battle of San Jacinto was over in just eighteen minutes and was an overwhelming victory for the Texans, who killed 630 Mexicans. Santa Anna was captured and brought before Houston, who compelled him, in exchange for his life, to sign the Treaty of Velasco, by which Texas became independent.

When Texas declared its independence from Mexico in 1836, Mexican president Antonio López de Santa Anna personally led his army to the Alamo, killing its defenders and thereby inadvertently galvanizing the cause of Texas independence.

Stephen Austin's Mexican Grants

Before losing Mexico in the Revolution of 1821, Spain had been eager to attract American colonists to the province known as Coahuila y Tejas. The Spanish monarchy believed that the colonists, who were compelled to renounce their American citizenship and swear allegiance to Spain, would act as a buffer against Indian raids on the one hand and United States expansionism on the other. After gaining its independence, Mexico resumed a colonization policy that was similar to that of Spain. The Colonization Law of 1824 was generous toward colonists, guaranteeing them land, security, and a four-year exemption from taxes. As Spain had required a pledge of allegiance, so did Mexico.

Assuming grants Spain had promised to his father, Stephen Austin became the foremost *"empresario"* (as the colonial grantees, or land agents, were called) among the several that came to Texas. Austin intended to honor his colony's commitments to Mexico, but he could not control other *empresarios* and often could not even control all of his own colonists. Although most "Texians" (as they called themselves) were willing to pledge allegiance to Mexico, they never stopped thinking of themselves as Americans. To them, being "American" meant being a white Anglo-Saxon Protestant, whereas Mexico was a land of Catholic Hispanics. In addition, Americans who were daring enough to leave the United States for "colonial" Mexico tended to be adventurers with a propensity for hair-trigger violence. They were not people easy to manage.

John Quincy Adams Proposes a Deal

In the years immediately following independence from Spain, Mexico was highly unstable, and those

Antonio López de Santa Anna

(1794–1876)

Born in Jalapa, Veracruz, to a minor colonial official, Antonio López de Santa Anna joined the Spanish army in Mexico as a young man and rose to the rank of captain. An adept political opportunist, Santa Anna supported Augustin de Iturbide in the war for Mexican Independence during 1821, then, two years later, was instrumental in Iturbide's overthrow. In 1828 he supported Vicente Guerrero in his bid for the presidency, only to conspire in a coup against him. Santa Anna became a popular hero in 1829, when he led Mexican forces against Spain's attempt to recover Mexico. He was elected president of Mexico in 1833 and quickly assumed the authority of a dictator.

When Texas declared its independence from Mexico in 1836, Santa Anna personally led the Mexican army to the Alamo, killing all of its defenders and thereby inadvertently galvanizing the cause of Texas independence. Defeated at the Battle of San Jacinto on April 21, 1836, he signed the Treaty of Velasco, by which Texas gained its independence. Santa Anna resigned from the Mexican presidency and retired to private life. In 1838, however, when French forces landed at Veracruz to claim reparation for injuries to French citizens living in Mexico, Santa Anna led an expedition against the French. By the time he arrived, however, the French fleet was already in the process of departing. There was a brief skirmish in which Santa Anna was wounded—he lost his leg, but rehabilitated his image among the Mexican people. He became dictator of Mexico for a few months in 1839, while the duly elected president was absent, then led a coup d'état in 1841. He held the reins of government until 1845, when he was driven into exile in Cuba.

With the outbreak of the U.S.-Mexican War (Chapter 10) in 1846, Santa Anna persuaded U.S. president James K. Polk to transport him from Cuba to Mexico aboard an American ship so that he could broker peace between Mexico and the United States. Polk complied, but no sooner had Santa Anna arrived than he took command of the Mexican army and led the war against the United States. He was defeated in every engagement and again retired in 1847, before the war had been officially ended by the Treaty of Guadalupe Hidalgo.

Santa Anna lived briefly in Jamaica and New Granada (modern Colombia), returning to Mexico as dictator during 1854–1855. Exiled yet again, he settled on the island of Nassau in the Bahamas. When France's Napoleon III installed Archduke Maximilian of Austria as emperor of Mexico in 1863, Santa Anna appealed to the United States to support him in an attempt to remove the emperor—even as he simultaneously offered Maximilian his support against Mexican nationalists. Both the American president and Maximilian rejected his proposals, and Santa Anna remained in exile until 1874, when, impoverished and blind, he was allowed to return to Mexico. He died in Mexico City two years later.

who attempted to govern it were not eager to acquire yet another group of rebellious citizens. The Fredonian Rebellion of 1826 (see Chapter 7) made the Mexican government increasingly wary of the Texans. They saw the Fredonian episode as an attempt by the United States to seize Mexico's northern borderlands, a perception reinforced when President John Quincy Adams offered to purchase Texas for $1 million in 1826. Adams wanted to defuse the volatile Texas situation while also expanding the country and ensuring that Texas stayed out of the hands of British or even French interests. The lowball offer was spurned, and, four years later, on April 6, 1830, Mexico barred further American immigration into Texas.

Andrew Jackson Ups the Ante

In 1830 Adams's successor to the White House, Andrew Jackson, raised the buyout offer to $5 million. When this offer was also turned down, Jackson recalled his negotiator, Joel Poinsett, an upright and honorable diplomat, and replaced him with the far more morally pliable Anthony Butler. Butler tried to make a backdoor deal by foisting on Mexico a usurious loan with Texas as collateral. The loan was structured such that it was virtually unpayable, and so Texas would be forfeit by default. If the Mexican government attempted to repudiate the terms of the loan, Butler pointed out to Jackson, the United States would have a legitimate basis for simply going to war to claim its collateral. The deal, however, was never consummated.

Congressional Qualms

If Texans were difficult to unite either in obedience to the Mexican government or in rebellion against it, so the will of the people of the United States, as represented in Congress, was likewise deeply divided. Congress was reluctant to provoke war with Mexico or to annex a territory populated mainly by southern slaveholders, who would seek Texas's admission to the union as a slave state and thereby threaten the always-delicate congressional balance between slave and free states.

In the United States, civil war was held at bay by continual and increasingly difficult compromises aimed at maintaining a balance between free and slave states. From the 1820s until the U.S.-Mexican War of 1846–1848 (Chapter 10)—even after Texas won its independence in 1836—congressional and presidential ambivalence about the question of annexation and statehood prevailed.

The Changing Political Climate of Texas

While the attitude toward Texas annexation was increasingly ambivalent in the United States, the attitude of the growing population of Texans toward Mexico was increasingly hostile, especially by the beginning of the 1830s. Some historians account for the rise in hostility on religious grounds, arguing that the predominantly southern Protestant colonists deeply resented having to answer to predominantly Catholic Mexico and feared that they would lose their freedom of religion. While religious sentiment undoubtedly played a role in the deteriorating relations, the Mexican government did seek to reassure the colonists by enacting legislation in 1834 that guaranteed religious freedom as well as the liberty to express "political opinions."

Other historians see the slavery issue as the chief cause of colonial disaffection. Many Texans brought slaves with them to the colony (the slave population was nearly equal to the free population), and they made no secret of requiring more slaves as their land holdings increased. Having already abolished slavery throughout Mexico proper, the Mexican government proposed eventual emancipation for Texas as well; however, in 1829 the Mexican president yielded to Texan demands by issuing an exemption from the general abolition decree.

Still other historians have pointed to issues of trade and taxation as the causes of colonial discontent. The colonists wanted to trade freely with both Mexico and the United States. Texans also complained that the Mexican government was inefficient. Its legal system, in particular, was slow, Byzantine in its complexity, subject to extreme corruption, and just plain arbitrary.

All of these issues contributed to discontent with how Mexico administered the Texas colonies, but the independence movement was, above all, cultural and ethnic in motivation. The Texans thought of themselves as in every way superior to the Mexicans, who, they believed, were lazy, servile, corrupt, and enslaved to their Catholic priests. By 1835–1836 the

Anglo population of Texas had reached 30,000 (with almost as many slaves), while Mexican nationals in Texas numbered a mere 3,500. Texans questioned whether a superior majority should have to answer to an inferior minority. Looking at the population numbers, many Texans quite reasonably saw Texas as having already become American. Some believed that the colony should be granted a large degree of autonomy as a Mexican state. Others sought outright independence—and most of these did so with an eye toward eventual annexation to the United States. Although the factions favoring Mexican statehood and those favoring independence were significantly split, they shared a desire to be out from under the thumb of absolute Mexican rule.

Factionalism in Texas, Revolt in Mexico

The evolution of factionalism within Texas requires somewhat closer examination. It initially developed as a rift between the early settlers and the ever-growing stream of newcomers. The newer settlers favored independence, whereas the more established colonists wanted to continue to pursue a practical compromise with the Mexican government. The factionalism within Texas occurred during a period of intense instability in Mexican politics, as Antonio López de Santa Anna sought the overthrow of the government of Anastasio Bustamante. Stephen Austin, dean of the more established Texans, saw in the struggle between Santa Anna and Bustamante an opportunity to achieve greater autonomy within Mexico without resorting to armed rebellion. Santa Anna indicated to Austin a willingness to accommodate Texan demands for greater autonomy. Accordingly, Austin negotiated peace with him and pledged the support of Texas in Santa Anna's bid for control of the Mexican government. Because Austin by no means controlled all of Texas, it was a bold pledge; however, Santa Anna did prevail over Bustamante in 1832, and Austin seized upon this as an opening to take the next step toward enlarged autonomy: full and formal statehood within Mexico. In the mean-

time, Sam Houston, a veteran of Andrew Jackson's command in the War of 1812 (Chapter 6) and former congressman and governor of Tennessee, arrived in Texas. With Jackson's encouragement, he took charge of a Texas volunteer army, then drafted a state constitution, which Austin took to Mexico City in 1833, along with a petition for Mexican statehood.

The Radicalization of Stephen Austin

Once he had succeeded in overthrowing Bustamante, Santa Anna was no longer eager to encourage Texan autonomy. He kept Austin waiting for five months before even granting him an audience to discuss the petition and constitution. Then Santa Anna was both conciliatory and cagey, promising to remedy all of Texas's grievances, doing everything Austin asked—short of allowing Texas to become a separate state. Austin left the audience and Mexico City feeling that although he had hardly achieved all that he had hoped for, he had made progress. Then, while passing through Saltillo, he was suddenly and unaccountably arrested, escorted back to Mexico City, and imprisoned there on a charge of having written a letter urging Texas statehood while he was in Mexico. Santa Anna deemed it a seditious violation of Austin's pledge of allegiance. Without trial, Austin spent nearly two years in prison. When he was released in 1835, he was embittered and broken in health.

If his object had been to crush an incipient rebellion, Santa Anna had blundered by imprisoning the most important moderate voice among the Texans. While Austin was in a Mexican jail, the most aggressive pro-independence faction in Texas, the "War Dogs," had significantly increased in number and influence. Even though most Texans repudiated the assault on the Mexican garrison at Anáhuac in June 1835, no one in Texas would surrender any of the thirty rebels to Mexican authorities. Austin, radicalized by his treatment at the hands of Santa Anna, now called for a revolution. He urged Texans to "Americanize" the territory and, in violation of the limits imposed by his grants from the Mexican government, invited Americans to pour into Texas, "passports or no passports . . . each man with his rifle. . . . War," he declared, "is our only recourse."

"Remember the Alamo!"

As discussed earlier, the war for independence began in earnest on October 2, 1835, when General Martín Perfecto de Cós crossed the Rio Grande to demand the surrender of a cannon in Gonzales. It reached its major crisis on March 6, 1835, with the fall of the Alamo. Until this time, the "War Dogs" had failed to stir much popular support in the United States for the cause of Texas independence. During the siege of the Alamo, however, commanding officer Colonel William Travis managed to send by messenger repeated messages to the outside world. Travis's most famous **Message from the Alamo,** addressed to "Fellow Citizens and Compatriots," was widely published in U.S. newspapers immediately following the fall of the Alamo.

Travis's plea produced no assistance from the United States, but it was one of several elements that transformed the tragic and ill-advised defense of a minor Texas outpost into a symbolic event that rallied Texans to the cause of independence and that still holds the American popular imagination. Travis had revealed acute insight when he wrote of defending "everything dear to the American character." For it was a collective self-perception that ultimately drove the fight for independence from Mexico and, later, that provoked the U.S.-Mexican

Travis's Message from the Alamo, 1836

Commandancy of the Alamo
Bexar, Fby. 24th, 1836

To the People of Texas & all Americans in the world
Fellow Citizens & Compatriots

I am besieged by a thousand or more of the Mexicans under Santa Anna. I have sustained a continual bombardment & cannonade for 24 hours & have not lost a man. The enemy has demanded a surrender at discretion, otherwise the garrison are to be put to the sword if the fort is taken. I have answered the demand with a cannon shot, and our flag still waves proudly from the walls. I *shall never surrender nor retreat.*

Then, I call on you in the name of Liberty, of patriotism, & of everything dear to the American character, to come to our aid with all dispatch. The enemy is receiving reinforcements daily & will no doubt increase to three or four thousand in four or five days. If this call is neglected, I am determined to sustain myself as long as possible & die like a soldier who never forgets what is due to his own honor & that of his country.

Victory or Death

William Barret Travis
Lt. Col. Comdt.

P. S. The Lord is on our side. When the enemy appeared in sight we had not three bushels of corn. We have since found in deserted houses 80 or 90 bushels & got into the walls 20 or 30 head of Beeves.

Travis

Excerpted from Lone Star Junction, "Travis' Appeal for Aid at the Alamo," www.lsjunction.com/docs/appeal.htm.

War (Chapter 10). Most Texas colonists, like many other Americans, perceived fundamental differences of culture, religion, and ethnicity between themselves and the Mexicans, and these differences were sufficient to motivate both wars.

The Treaty of Velasco

Following his victory at the eighteen-minute Battle of San Jacinto on April 21, 1836, Houston issued an ultimatum to the captive Santa Anna: either evacuate Texas and acknowledge its independence or be shot. Santa Anna signed the **Treaty of Velasco,** which obligated him to withdraw all troops from Texas and thereby grant the former province full independence.

The government of Mexico repudiated the Treaty of Velasco as an extorted agreement, and the repudiation would figure as one of the causes of the U.S.-Mexican War (Chapter 10). Nevertheless, the United States and most other nations recognized the treaty, and the Republic of Texas was born.

Treaty of Velasco, 1836

Article 1st
General Antonio Lopez de Santa Anna agrees that he will not take up arms, nor will he exercise his influence to cause them to be taken up against the people of Texas, during the present war of Independence.

Article 2nd
All hostilities between the mexican and texian troops will cease immediately both on land and water.

Article 3rd
The mexican troops will evacuate the Territory of Texas, passing to the other side of the Rio Grande del Norte.

Excerpted from the Avalon Project at Yale Law School, "Treaty of Velasco," www.yale.edu/lawweb/avalon/velasco.htm.

The United States Responds

Personally, Andrew Jackson wholeheartedly favored Texas independence followed by annexation to the United States. He encouraged Sam Houston, and he applauded those few Americans who did go to the aid of the rebellion. Publicly, however, Jackson restrained himself for the same reasons that his successors—Martin Van Buren, the short-lived William Henry Harrison, John Tyler, and, initially, James K. Polk—temporized on the subject of annexation. He did not want to provoke a war with Mexico, and he did not want to upset the balance in Congress between slave and free states. In his message to Congress on December 21, 1836, the president urged the exercise of "prudence" with a wait-and-see attitude, even after Congress had passed resolutions to recognize the Republic of Texas "whenever satisfactory information should be received that it had in successful operation a civil government capable of performing the duties and fulfilling the obligations of an independent power." The swelling tide of public support for what was seen as the heroic struggle of Texas finally persuaded Jackson to recognize the Republic of Texas by appointing a chargé d'affaires (not a more exalted minister or ambassador) on March 3, 1837. By this time, Congress, motivated by an awareness that the British were establishing commercial ties with the new republic, had voted funding for a full U.S. diplomatic mission.

Generally, from the moment of Texas independence, the representatives of the southern and western states favored more or less immediate annexation, despite the dangers of provoking war with Mexico. The representatives of the northern states almost unanimously opposed annexation. In addition, Congress was flooded with thousands of individual protests, among them the eloquent **Protest of William Ellery Channing,** one of New England's literary luminaries and a prominent abolitionist. Channing had read *The War in Texas,* a widely circulated pamphlet by William Lundy, which portrayed the Texans as avaricious "adventurers" and "outcasts." Appalled that such "criminals" were to form a

Protest of William Ellery Channing, 1837

[B]y this act our country will enter on a career of encroachment, war, and crime, and will merit and incur the punishment and woe of aggravated wrongdoing. The seizure of Texas will not stand alone. It will darken our future history. It will be linked by an iron necessity to long continued deeds of rapine and blood. . . .

In attaching Texas to ourselves, we provoke hostilities, and at the same time expose new points of attack to our foes. . . .

A country has no right to adopt a policy, however gainful, which, as it may foresee, will determine it to a career of war. A nation, like an individual, is bound to seek, even by sacrifices, a position which will favor peace, justice, and the exercise of a beneficent influence on the world. A nation provoking war by cupidity, by encroachment, and, above all, by efforts to propagate the curse of slavery, is alike false to itself, to God, and to the human race.

Excerpted from William Ellery Channing, "Against the Annexation of Texas," in *Annals of America,* ed. Mortimer J. Adler and Charles Van Doren (Chicago: Encyclopaedia Britannica, 1976), 6:357–362.

new state of the union, Channing, on August 1, 1837, sent his protest to Henry Clay, representative from Tennessee and a strong proponent of annexation. The protest enumerated three principal objections to annexation: First, that the rebellion was illegal and that annexation constituted an illegal and immoral seizure. Second, that annexation would plunge the United States into war with Mexico, which would be bad enough in and of itself, but which would also require the United States to amass and finance a large standing army on a permanent basis. Third, that Texas would come into the union as yet another slaveholding state. The United States, Channing and other abolitionists argued, should not be in the business of extending the institution of slavery.

In the long run, the position of Channing and other opponents was doomed; however, the agitation against annexation was so intense that, on August 4, 1837, when the government of Texas formally proposed annexation to the United States, President Martin Van Buren rejected the proposal. Annexation would be delayed almost a decade, until 1846.

BIBLIOGRAPHY

Binkley, William C. *The Texas Revolution.* Baton Rouge: Louisiana State University Press, 1952.

Hardin, Stephen L. *Texian Iliad: A Military History of the Texas Revolution.* Austin: University of Texas Press, 1994.

Lack, Paul D. *The Texas Revolutionary Experience: A Political and Social History.* College Station: Texas A&M University Press, 1992.

Vigness, David M. *The Revolutionary Decades: The Saga of Texas, 1810–1836.* Austin, Texas: Steck-Vaughn, 1965.

At Issue

The U.S.-Mexican War was principally the product of the United States' southwestern expansion at the expense of Mexico and was provoked chiefly by the annexation of Mexico's former territory, Texas, to the United States. Beyond its principal motives for war, the United States identified as provocations Mexico's refusal to make restitution to U.S. citizens for losses suffered during various Mexican uprisings and the Mexican government's refusal to negotiate the U.S. purchase of Upper California. For its part, Mexico sought to restrain U.S. expansion and to punish what it saw as the "insolence" of the American government. Finally, the war played out against a backdrop of mutual ethnic, cultural, and religious prejudice.

The Conflict

On March 1, 1845, Congress resolved to admit the independent republic of Texas into the Union. The Mexican government responded by severing diplomatic relations with the United States. Despite the diplomatic break, President James K. Polk continued to pursue negotiation of the Texas-Mexican boundary and the purchase of Alta (or Upper) California. Rebuffed, Polk, anticipating Mexican aggression as soon as the Texas congress approved annexation on July 4, ordered Brigadier General Zachary Taylor to deploy forces near the Rio Grande after the annexation to repel invasion. On July 23, 1845, Taylor arrived with 1,500 men at the mouth of the Nueces River near Corpus Christi.

During the summer and into the fall, Taylor's border force increased to about 4,000 men. In February 1846 U.S.-Mexican negotiations collapsed, and Taylor advanced 100 miles down the coast to the Rio Grande. He deployed most of his combat troops on the river, opposite the Mexican town of Matamoros, where he erected Fort Texas.

Mexican Attack

On April 25, 1846, Mexican general Mariano Arista invaded Texas, sweeping aside a U.S. detachment of sixty dragoons (mounted infantry who fought dismounted) as he advanced on Taylor's main position. Taylor reported to President Polk that hostilities had commenced. He appealed to Texas and Louisiana for 5,000 militia volunteers to supplement his 4,000 regulars. Seeking to safeguard his supplies nearby, Taylor withdrew to Point Isabel with the bulk of his troops, strengthened his fortifications, resupplied his army, and then marched back to Fort Texas with 2,300 men on May 7.

Battle of Palo Alto

En route to Fort Texas on May 8, Taylor's 2,300-man force (part of which was far to the rear) encountered Arista's 4,000 soldiers at Palo Alto. In addition to a two-to-one advantage in numbers, Arista also enjoyed terrain favorable to his cavalry, whereas Taylor had mostly dragoons. Taylor had some advantages of his own, however, including superior artillery and excellent young officers (future Civil

War generals Ulysses S. Grant and George G. Meade formed part of the force). Despite their superior numbers, the Mexicans had only obsolete, small cannon with which to return the artillery fire; consequently, they suffered devastating losses and retreated. Taylor, a conservative commander, did not immediately pursue the retreating forces, but paused to strengthen defenses around his supply train.

Battle of Resaca de la Palma

On May 9, Taylor reached Resaca de la Palma, where his scouts reported that the Mexican forces were entrenched in a nearby ravine called Resaca de la Guerra. Taylor flushed the Mexican forces out, but the battle seesawed until the Mexicans finally fell back on Matamoros. At least 547 Mexican soldiers were killed or wounded, whereas Taylor's losses were 33 killed and 89 wounded. Once again, Taylor chose not to give chase after a hard-won victory. He delayed crossing the Rio Grande until May 18, by which time Arista's army had retreated well into the interior of Mexico.

Declaration of War

With the war already well under way, Congress passed a declaration of war, which President Polk signed on May 13, 1846.

Strategy

After the formal declaration of war, one of the army's senior commanders, Major General Winfield Scott, drew up a three-pronged plan. Taylor was to march west from Matamoros to take Monterrey, Mexico. Capture of this city would open all of northern Mexico to attack. Simultaneous with this movement, Brigadier General John E. Wool was tasked with marching from San Antonio to Chihuahua, Mexico; he would then advance farther south to Saltillo, ultimately linking up with Taylor's force at Monterrey. Finally, Colonel Stephen Watts Kearney was to march out of Fort Leavenworth,

Kansas, to take Santa Fe. After accomplishing this mission, he would continue all the way to San Diego, California. (Kearny's mission was later modified when part of his force, Missouri volunteers under Colonel Alexander W. Doniphan, advanced deep into Mexico, via Chihuahua to Parras.)

As originally conceived, no deeper penetration of Mexico, including the capture of Mexico City, was planned. The hope was that the initial three attacks would force Mexico to come to terms. In July Polk and his secretary of war, William L. Marcy, endorsed (but held in abeyance) an additional plan to take

CHRONOLOGY OF THE U.S.-MEXICAN WAR

1846

Apr. 25 Mexican troops cross the Rio Grande to attack U.S. dragoons commanded by Zachary Taylor.

May 8 Battle of Palo Alto

May 9 Battle of Resaca de la Palma

May 13 Declaration of war on Mexico

May 18 U.S. occupation of Matamoros

July 7 U.S. naval occupation of Monterey, California

July 14 U.S. occupation of Camargo

Aug. 16 With U.S. assistance, Santa Anna returns to Mexico from exile in Cuba.

Aug. 18 U.S. occupation of Santa Fe (in modern New Mexico)

Sept. 21–23 Battle of Monterrey, Mexico

Sept. 24 Taylor agrees to armistice.

Nov. 14 U.S. naval seizure of Tampico

Nov. 16 U.S. occupation of Saltillo

1847

Feb. 3–4 Battle of Pueblo de Taos, New Mexico

Feb. 22–23 Battle of Buena Vista

Mar. 9 U.S. amphibious landing at Veracruz

Mar. 9–29 Siege and surrender of Veracruz

Apr. 18 Battle of Cerro Gordo

Aug. 19–20 Battles of Contreras and Churubusco

Sept. 8 Battle of El Molino del Rey

Sept. 13 Battle of Chapultepec

Sept. 13–14 Battle for Mexico City

Sept. 14 Surrender of Mexico City

1848

Feb. 2 Treaty of Guadalupe Hidalgo

Zachary Taylor
(1784–1850)

Born in Orange County, Virginia, Taylor grew up near Louisville, Kentucky. He joined the Kentucky militia as a short-term volunteer in 1806, received a regular army commission in March 1808, and went on to serve under General William Henry Harrison against Tecumseh's band of Shawnee and other Indians of the Old Northwest in 1811. During the opening phase of the War of 1812 (Chapter 6), Taylor's valiant defense of Fort Harrison earned him a brevet promotion to major. During the war he served on the frontier and commanded an expedition that advanced down the Mississippi River.

In the postwar rush to demobilize, Taylor was reduced in rank to captain in June 1815, which prompted his resignation. Through the personal intervention of President James Madison, he was restored to the rank of major and served garrison duty from 1817 to 1819 in Wisconsin Territory, then assumed command of Fort Winnebago. Promoted to lieutenant colonel in April 1819, he transferred to Louisiana in 1822, where he built Fort Jesup, near Natchitoches. During 1829–1832, Taylor commanded Fort Snelling (present-day St. Paul, Minnesota) and served as superintendent of Indian affairs for the region.

During the Black Hawk War (see Chapter 8), Taylor fought in the Battle of Bad Axe River on August 2, 1832. In July 1837 Taylor fought the Seminoles (Chapter 8), scoring a major victory at Lake Okeechobee, Florida, on Christmas day. Brevetted to brigadier general the following year, Taylor had no further success against the Seminoles. He requested to be relieved in April 1840, served in Louisiana again, then was named commander of the Second Department, Western Division, at Fort Smith, Arkansas in May 1841.

During the U.S.-Mexican War, Taylor compiled a victorious record of victory tempered by excessive caution. Ordered to send most of his experienced men to General Winfield Scott, whose army was in the process of invading central Mexico during the winter of 1846–1847, Taylor used his remaining troops—4,600 inexperienced volunteers—to defeat 15,000 men under Santa Anna at Buena Vista on February 22–23. This battle made Taylor a national hero, and he became the Whig candidate for president in June 1848. Winning by a wide margin, he took office in March 1849 but succumbed to heatstroke the following year. Vice President Millard Fillmore served out the balance of his term.

Mexico City by means of what would be the army's first-ever amphibious landing, at Veracruz.

Advance on Monterrey

With about 6,200 men, Taylor reached Monterrey on September 19, 1846. The city was defended by 7,000 Mexican troops fighting from well-prepared positions and equipped with modern British-made heavy artillery. Undaunted, Taylor deployed engineers to reconnoiter the fortifications, then commenced his attack on September 21. By September 22, Taylor

had breached the Mexican defenses and was fighting in the city's streets. By the next day, the defenders had contracted their perimeter to the town's central plaza. With the enemy thus concentrated, Taylor directed all artillery fire on the plaza, which forced a surrender. Remarkably, Taylor allowed the Mexican commander to withdraw and together they declared an eight-week armistice.

Taylor hoped that the armistice would demonstrate good will and therefore be conducive to negotiations; he knew that President Polk had just agreed to a proposal from Santa Anna, who offered his services as a paid intermediary. Santa Anna had been living in Cuban exile since a rebellion ended his dictatorship in Mexico following the Texas War of Independence (see Chapter 9). Although Polk declined to give Santa Anna the $30,000,000 he requested, he did guarantee him safe conduct to Mexico to help negotiate a treaty. Santa Anna, however, had no intention of honoring the deal he made with Polk. No sooner did he arrive in Mexico than he began raising an army to defeat Zachary Taylor.

On October 11, Polk condemned Taylor for allowing the Mexican army to withdraw intact, and he ordered an immediate end to the armistice. In response to the new orders, on November 13, Taylor dispatched 1,000 men to Saltillo to seize control of the only road to Mexico City from the north as well as the road to Chihuahua. On November 14, U.S. naval forces took Tampico, and in December Brigadier General Wool arrived at that port from San Antonio with 2,500 men. Headed for Chihuahua, Wool learned that the Mexicans had abandoned the town, so he united with Taylor's main force at Monterrey.

Taylor received a message that President Polk had authorized Major General Winfield Scott to conduct an amphibious assault on Veracruz, and 8,000 of Taylor's troops were to be detached to join Scott's force. With only 7,000 men left, mostly volunteers, Taylor was ordered to evacuate Saltillo and defend Monterrey. He decided, however, to interpret these orders as merely "advice" and, leaving modest garrisons at Monterrey and Saltillo, he marched 4,650 men eighteen miles south of Saltillo to Agua Nueva.

James K. Polk

(1795–1849)

Born in rural North Carolina, Polk moved with his family at age 11 to a prosperous farm in Tennessee. Polk graduated from the University of North Carolina in 1818, then returned to Tennessee to practice law in Nashville. He quickly earned a reputation as a fine orator and was christened the "Napoleon of the stump." In 1823 he was elected to the state House of Representatives, where he served until 1825. His marriage to socially prominent and politically astute Sarah Childress in 1824 helped ensure his rise in Democratic politics. He was elected to the U.S. House of Representatives in 1825 and served until 1839, becoming Speaker of the House and an advocate of the programs and policies of President Andrew Jackson.

Polk was elected governor of Tennessee in 1839, but was twice defeated for reelection. During the highly contentious Democratic National Convention of 1844, he emerged as the "dark horse" presidential candidate—and, to the surprise of many, he won election as the nation's eleventh chief executive (with George Mifflin as vice president).

During his campaign, Polk had been an outspoken advocate for the annexation of Texas and even bellicose in his demand for all of Oregon, rejecting compromise with Britain, which contested the territory. His campaign slogan—"Fifty-four forty or fight" (reflecting the demand that the U.S. border in Oregon be extended as far north as latitude 54°40')—became one of the most famous in American history.

Under President Polk, the United States vastly expanded its western territory, annexing Texas, fighting the U.S.-Mexican War (and acquiring most of the Southwest as a result), and ultimately resolving the Oregon boundary with Britain. Polk also oversaw the negotiation of a treaty with New Granada (Colombia), giving U.S. citizens the right of passage across the Isthmus of Panama.

Winfield Scott
(1786–1866)

Winfield Scott was born near Petersburg, Virginia, briefly attended the College of William and Mary in 1805, and then was apprenticed to a lawyer. He enlisted in a local cavalry troop in 1807 and was commissioned a captain of light artillery and dispatched to New Orleans in May 1808. After a dispute with his commanding officer, he was suspended from 1809 to 1810 but returned to service in New Orleans during 1811–1812. He served valiantly and brilliantly in the War of 1812 (Chapter 6), became a national hero, was promoted to brigadier general in March 1814, performed with exceptional valor at the Battle of Lundy's Lane on July 25, 1814 (in which he was twice wounded), and was brevetted to major general.

After the war, Scott was named to command of the army's Northern Department in 1815 and was made commander of the Eastern Division in 1829. He was called on to lead a force during the Black Hawk War of 1832 (see Chapter 8), but cholera swept through his ranks and Scott did not arrive in Wisconsin until Black Hawk had surrendered. Nevertheless, he was instrumental in negotiating the Treaty of Fort Armstrong with the Sac and Fox tribes on September 21, 1832.

In 1836 Scott was sent to Florida to fight the Seminoles (Chapter 8), but plagued by ill-trained troops and a lack of supplies, he was relieved and brought up on charges before a board of inquiry. The board cleared him in 1837, and in 1838 he was assigned to oversee the forcible removal of the Cherokees from Georgia, South Carolina, and Tennessee to Indian Territory.

On July 5, 1841, Scott was appointed general in chief of the army. During the U.S.-Mexican War, he prosecuted a bold campaign of invasion, taking Mexico City on September 14. He emerged as a national hero and narrowly lost the Whig presidential nomination to Zachary Taylor in 1848.

Brevetted to lieutenant general in February 1855, Scott made strenuous but vain efforts to prepare the U.S. Army for what he saw as an inevitable civil war. He supervised the opening engagements of the Civil War; however, aged, infirm, and rotund, he retired from the army on November 1, 1861, and was replaced as general in chief by George B. McClellan.

Battle of Buena Vista

Taylor's scouts spotted the advance guard of Santa Anna's army on February 21, 1847. Taylor withdrew to a defensive position at Buena Vista, just south of Saltillo. Outnumbered three to one, he nevertheless refused Santa Anna's surrender demand on February 22, and the Battle of Buena Vista began. After initial gains, Santa Anna's forces were pushed back. Reinforced by a fresh division of reserves, Santa Anna regained the initiative on February 23 but was soon repulsed. After losing as many as 2,000 men killed or wounded, Santa Anna retreated toward San Luis Potosi. American losses were 264 troops killed and 450 wounded. The spectacular upset victory at Buena Vista neutralized the Mexican army as a threat to the lower Rio Grande.

Kearny's Advance

While Taylor fought in Mexico, Colonel Stephen Watts Kearny led the long march from Fort Leavenworth, Kansas, to Santa Fe, New Mexico. After the failure of an ambush attempt at Apache Canyon, the Mexican provincial governor surrendered Santa Fe to Kearny on August 19 without firing a shot. From Santa

Fe, Kearny marched on to California, reaching San Diego in December 1846 only to find that a U.S. Navy squadron had already secured the California ports.

Doniphan's March

In November 1846 Colonel Alexander Doniphan detached 856 Missouri volunteers from Kearny's main force in Santa Fe and marched south to pacify the upper Rio Grande region. In a remarkable series of operations after crossing the river at El Paso, he defeated a total of 1,200 Mexican troops, and then, on February 27, 1847, approached Chihuahua. The city was defended by 2,700 Mexican regulars and perhaps 1,000 civilian volunteers. Doniphan deployed his greatly outnumbered forces to outflank the defenders and won the Battle of Sacramento (named after the nearby river) in two hours.

Veracruz Landing

Winfield Scott began amphibious operations at Veracruz on March 2, 1847, and landed 10,000 men during the night of March 9. He began bombardment of the walled city on March 22, his artillery supplemented by that of the navy. The city surrendered on March 29.

Battle of Cerro Gordo

After taking Veracruz, Scott advanced on Jalapa, seventy-four miles along the national highway to Mexico City. Along the way, at Cerro Gordo, Santa Anna had placed artillery and 12,000 men, all poised to attack along the rocky defile through which the highway passed. Santa Anna was confident that this was the only means by which Scott could transport his artillery. Scott, however, dispatched Captain Robert E. Lee, then an army engineer, to scout Mexican artillery emplacements. Lee discovered a rugged, undefended pass by which Scott could bring his artillery to bear on the Mexican rear without using the national highway. Taking this alternate route, Scott began the attack the next morning with a rocket battery. Santa Anna's large army panicked and fled. More than 1,000 Mexicans were killed or wounded in the attack, which cost the Americans 417 casualties, including 64 killed.

Advance on Mexico City

After Cerro Gordo, Scott advanced to Jalapa and then to Puebla, the second-largest city in Mexico. The citizens of Puebla hated Santa Anna, so they surrendered to Scott without resistance on May 15, 1847.

While Scott prepared to march out of Puebla to Mexico City, State Department official Nicholas P. Trist opened peace negotiations with Santa Anna. President Polk wanted Scott to advance on Mexico City as quickly as possible to put pressure on Santa Anna. Accordingly, Scott decided to commit all of his troops to the advance, taking the grave risk of leaving his line of communication, from Vera Cruz to Puebla, undefended.

By August 10 Scott was just fourteen miles from the city. Seeing that the principal road was heavily defended, he shifted to the south and approached Mexico City from the west via Pedregal, a fifteen-mile-wide lava bed. Considered by the Mexicans impassable, it had been left undefended, but Robert E. Lee found a mule path through it to the village of Contreras. An initial assault on Contreras was beaten back on August 19, but a reinforced attack the next day resulted in a rout. Some 700 Mexicans were killed in the battle, and 800 more were captured, including four general officers. Scott lost sixty troops killed or wounded.

In contrast to the conservative Taylor, Scott was highly aggressive and ordered an immediate pursuit. Remarkably, Santa Anna managed to regroup and keep his army intact, deploying his troops in defensive positions at Churubusco. Here, on August 20, Santa Anna fought the most vigorous defense of the war, significantly slowing Scott's progress. Nevertheless, the Battle of Churubusco cost nearly 4,000 Mexican casualties. Scott lost 155 killed and 876 wounded. This hard-won victory brought a request from Santa Anna to reopen peace negotiations. Scott granted a cease-fire, and for the next two weeks, Trist and the Mexicans parleyed, until it became apparent to Scott that Santa Anna was negotiating in bad faith and merely playing for time. On September 6, therefore, Scott ended the armistice and commenced his final approach to Mexico City.

Battle of Chapultepec

Scott had 8,000 men fit for duty against Santa Anna's 15,000 defending Mexico City. Despite the disparity in numbers, on September 8, Scott stormed and seized El Molino del Rey, which erroneous intelligence reported to be home to an important cannon foundry. Early on September 13, he began his assault on Chapultepec with an artillery barrage, then sent three columns over the approaches to the hilltop fortress. The Americans overran Chapultepec by 9:30 in the morning.

Fall of Mexico City

Approximately 1,800 Mexicans were killed or wounded at the Battle of Chapultepec, which cost Scott 130 dead and 703 wounded. The exhausted defenders fought house to house before surrendering Mexico City on September 14, 1847.

Manifest Destiny

The U.S.-Mexican War developed in an era of U.S. expansionism, which was articulated in 1844 in the platform of the Democratic Party. The Democrats spoke of effecting the "re-occupation of Oregon and the re-annexation of Texas" and called these "great American measures." The word *reoccupation* is significant because it represents a fabrication or, more precisely, a verbal fiat. The United States had never previously occupied these places. By using the word, however, the party asserted a non-existent right, advancing an imperialist agenda without incurring a charge of imperialism. The idea was to court the support of expansionists without alienating the more reticent or scrupulous.

A year later, a famous article published in the *United States Magazine and Democratic Review* in July 1845 echoed the Democrats' platform. In **"Annexation,"** *New York*

An 1844 pro-Democrat cartoon forecast the collapse of Whig Party opposition to the annexation of Texas. Expansionist presidential candidate James K. Polk beckons Texans Stephen Austin and Sam Houston aboard the vessel "Texas." Meanwhile, Whig candidate Henry Clay and his anti-annexation allies flounder in the water below.

Under Democratic president James K. Polk, the United States vastly expanded its western territory, by annexing Texas, fighting the U.S.-Mexican War (and acquiring most of the Southwest as a result), and resolving the Oregon boundary with Britain.

Whig presidential candidate Henry Clay lost the election of 1844 to James K. Polk after misreading the public's majority support for the annexation of Texas.

Post editor John L. O'Sullivan wrote, "It is our manifest destiny to overspread and possess the whole of the continent which Providence has given us for the development of the great experiment of liberty and federated self-government entrusted to us." O'Sullivan put into memorable words a sentiment of many Americans since the days of the Pilgrims and Puritans: that America was a chosen land and that it was the providential destiny of white, Christian Americans to possess the entire American continent as part of God's plan. The implication was that any war fought to realize this "manifest destiny" would be a just war—indeed, a holy war.

The election of James K. Polk to the presidency in 1844 by a narrow margin was seen by the Democrats, including Polk himself, as a mandate to acquire not only Oregon and Texas, but California and New Mexico as well. Polk justified this as a reaffirmation of the Monroe Doctrine in his December 2, 1845, **Message to Congress.** Indeed, the Polk administration courted the calamity of a two-front war by provoking both Mexico and Great Britain. There was a bitter dispute as to the boundary between British Canada and Oregon. Many expansionist Democrats clamored for U.S. possession of "all Oregon," and Polk himself had called for the international boundary to be established at the parallel of 54°40' north, far into British Canada (prompting his catchy campaign slogan, "Fifty-four-forty or fight!"). War was averted by the 1846 Treaty of Oregon, which compromised at the forty-ninth parallel. It was a significant gain over the original British claim of a

"Annexation," 1845

It is time now for opposition to the annexation of Texas to cease. . . . It is time for the common duty of patriotism to the country to succeed; or if this claim will not be recognized, it is at least time for common sense to acquiesce with decent grace in the inevitable and the irrevocable.

Texas is now ours. . . .

She is no longer to us a mere geographical space—a certain combination of coast, plain, mountain, valley, forest, and stream. She is no longer to us a mere country on the map. She comes within the dear and sacred designation of our country. . . .

It is time then that all should cease to treat her as alien, and even adverse—cease to denounce and vilify all and everything connected with her accession—cease to thwart and oppose the remaining steps for its consummation; or where such efforts are felt to be unavailing, at least to embitter the hour of reception by all the most ungracious frowns of aversion and words of unwelcome. . . .

Why, were other reasoning wanting, in favor of now elevating this question of the reception of Texas into the Union, out of the lower region of our past party dissensions, up to its proper level of a high and broad nationality, it surely is to be found, found abundantly, in the manner in which other nations have undertaken to intrude themselves into it, between us and the proper parties to the case, in a spirit of hostile interference against us, for the avowed object of thwarting our policy and hampering our power, limiting our greatness and checking the fulfillment of our manifest destiny to overspread the continent allotted by Providence for the free development of our yearly multiplying millions. This we have seen done by England, our old rival and enemy; and by France.

Excerpted from John L. O'Sullivan, "Annexation," in *Annals of America,* ed. Mortimer J. Adler and Charles Van Doren (Chicago: Encyclopaedia Britannica, 1976), 7:288–289.

border at the fortieth parallel, but far short of the boundary for which Polk had pledged to fight. There would be no similar compromise with Mexico.

Texas Statehood

Texas won its independence from Mexico in 1836 (see Chapter 9) and proclaimed itself a sovereign republic; however, most Texans favored annexation to the United States over independence. For a full decade, a succession of presidents and Congresses temporized on annexation. They understood that annexation would bring war with Mexico, which (America and the rest of the world judged) had a fine army, large in comparison to the limited professional forces of the United States. Most Americans wanted to avoid such a war. The presidents and most of the legislators also wanted to avoid upsetting the delicate balance in Congress between slave and free states, and they knew that Texas would certainly seek

admission as a slave state. Thus Presidents Jackson and Van Buren had simply refused to act on the matter. William Henry Harrison did not live long enough in office to tackle the issue, but his successor, John Tyler, was finally ready to initiate annexation. His second secretary of state, John C. Calhoun, made such an issue of states' rights and slavery, however, that he alienated many northerners, so the annexation bill at last presented to the Senate in June 1844 was defeated.

Yet the elections of 1844 proved that the senators, as well as presidential hopefuls Martin Van Buren and Henry Clay, both opposed to annexation, had misread public opinion. A majority of Americans, although hardly an overwhelming majority, were caught up in the "manifest destiny" movement and favored the annexation of Texas toward the realization of that destiny, regardless of such consequences as slavery and war with Mexico. Accordingly, the Democratic Party passed over Van Buren in favor of James K. Polk, who favored annexation (which became a key plank of the party platform), and Polk went on to defeat the Whig candidate, Clay. Days before his term ended, Tyler, interpreting Polk's victory as a mandate, asked Congress to consider a joint resolution on Texas statehood. The resolution was passed on March 1, 1845, and approved by the Congress of the Republic of Texas on July 4. On December 29, Texas was formally admitted to the union.

Diplomatic Crisis with Mexico

The slavery issue would be addressed as it had been in the past—unsatisfactorily—through tortured legislative compromise that would ultimately lead to civil war. The crisis with Mexico created by annexation was more immediate. After annexation, the government of Mexico severed diplomatic relations with the United States, but Polk continued to pursue diplomacy with attempts to negotiate the purchase of California and New Mexico and to persuade Mexico to accept the Rio Grande rather than the Nueces

River as the international boundary with Texas. When Polk learned that his envoy had failed, he ordered Zachary Taylor on January 13, 1846, to lead troops to a position "on or near" the Rio Grande. The cautious Taylor advanced only as far as the mouth of the Nueces at Corpus Christi. Polk declined to order him to advance farther. While Polk believed he was prudently deploying troops in an advanced defensive position, the Mexicans saw Taylor's approach as an invasion, which they met with an army under General Mariano Arista. It was Mexican forces that crossed the Rio Grande first in April, invading (as most Americans saw it) Texas—now sovereign American territory.

British and French Interest in Texas

Historians have generally ascribed the annexation of Texas to motives of manifest destiny, but there was also a more immediate impetus. During the long delay between Texas independence and annexation, France and Britain both began making overtures to

Polk's Message to Congress, December 2, 1845

The rapid extension of our settlements over our territories heretofore unoccupied, the addition of new states to our confederacy, the expansion of free principles, and our rising greatness as a nation are attracting the attention of the powers of Europe, and lately the doctrine has been broached in some of them of a "balance of power" on this continent to check our advancement. The United States, sincerely desirous of preserving relations of good understanding with all nations, cannot in silence permit any European interference on the North American continent, and should any such interference be attempted will be ready to resist it at any and all hazards. . . .

The American system of government is entirely different from that of Europe. Jealousy among the different sovereigns of Europe, lest any one of them might become too powerful for the rest, has caused them anxiously to desire the establishment of what

they term the "balance of power." It cannot be permitted to have any application on the North American continent, and especially to the United States. We must ever maintain the principle that the people of this continent alone have the right to decide their own destiny. Should any portion of them, constituting an independent state, propose to unite themselves with our confederacy, this will be a question for them and us to determine without any foreign interposition. We can never consent that European powers shall interfere to prevent such a union because it might disturb the "balance of power" which they may desire to maintain upon this continent.

Excerpted from James K. Polk, "Reaffirmation of the Monroe Doctrine," in *Annals of America,* ed. Mortimer J. Adler and Charles Van Doren (Chicago: Encyclopaedia Britannica, 1976), 7:302.

the Republic of Texas, eying it as a prospective ally, perhaps a client state, or even a colonial possession. These dangers contributed to President Tyler's decision to appeal to Congress for a joint annexation resolution.

The Slidell Mission and Its Rebuff

As President Tyler had acted to thwart foreign plans for Texas, so his successor acted in California. In 1845 Polk sent John Slidell to Mexico City to negotiate the purchase of Upper California for the sum of $40,000,000. Mexican president José Joaquin Herrera did not even deign to grant Slidell an audience, let alone consider the offer. Outraged, Polk commissioned Thomas O. Larkin, the U.S. consul at Monterey, California, to organize—covertly—California's small but prosperous and influential American community into a separatist movement sympathetic to annexation.

California's Bear Flag Rebellion (June–July 1846)

At this point, events overtook Polk's efforts at manipulation and intrigue. Given sufficient time, Larkin might have succeeded in the mission Polk had assigned him, but the president was nervous about rumors that the British vice consul in San Francisco was successfully wooing Southern California's governor, Pio Pico, to the notion of accepting a British protectorate. What is unclear is whether Polk authorized what happened next or merely acquiesced in it.

At the very least, Polk's growing impatience coincided with the activities in California of John Charles Frémont, an army officer on assignment to survey prospective transcontinental railroad routes for the U.S. Bureau of Topographical Engineers. Frémont was camped with sixty armed men close to the fort John A. Sutter had built in Northern California, near Sacramento. From this fort, even a modest military force could effectively control the thinly populated Northern California region. Mindful of this, Mexico's governor of Northern California, José

Castro, summarily ordered Frémont and his men out of the territory. Frémont responded with theatrical defiance, moving his men to a hilltop known as Hawk's Peak, over which he raised the Stars and Stripes. Fearing that Frémont's actions would bring about a premature revolt, which the Mexicans could easily crush, Larkin intervened in an attempt to defuse the situation. He persuaded Frémont and his men to withdraw to the lower Sacramento Valley. Frémont was about to leave California when Lieutenant Archibald Gillespie delivered a letter from Frémont's powerful father-in-law, Missouri senator Thomas Hart Benton, as well as news that war between the United States and Mexico was imminent. Gillespie told Frémont that the U.S. Navy ship *Portsmouth* was anchored in San Francisco Bay, that the rest of the Pacific fleet was anchored off Mazatlán, Mexico, primed for attack, and that American and Mexican troops faced each other across the Texas border. In a later account of this encounter, Frémont claimed that Gillespie delivered one more item: secret orders from President Polk explicitly authorizing him to lead a rebellion in California. Most historians do not believe Frémont's claim, concluding that he turned back to California on his own initiative and assumed command of what would be called the Bear Flag Rebellion. Whatever the truth may be, Polk never repudiated what happened next.

Frémont returned to the American settlements around Sutter's Fort. Agitated by rumors of an impending Mexican attack, many of the settlers—among them hunters, trappers, and merchant sailors who had jumped ship—gathered at Frémont's camp for protection and to formulate a plan of action. This group was loosely led by a man named Ezekiel Merritt, who reported to Frémont that he had been told that a herd of horses was being driven to the Mexican militia for use in a campaign against the settlers. Frémont approved Merritt's intention to intercept the horses and bring them to the American camp. Merritt and his band duly performed their mission and, anticipating Mexican reprisals, decided to exceed their orders by continuing the offensive. Joining forces with another Anglo-Californian leader,

William B. Ide, Merritt and thirty men rode to Sonoma on June 14, 1846, to capture the chief settlement in the area. The party surrounded the home of Mariano G. Vallejo, a retired Mexican army colonel and the town's leading citizen. When Merritt informed Vallejo that he was now a prisoner of war, the old colonel welcomed the news: he was a supporter of California annexation to the United States and celebrated the arrival of Merritt and Ide with a hearty breakfast of a freshly killed bull, over which the men could negotiate "surrender" terms. The negotiation turned into a drinking party, at which Ide was the only man sober enough to complete the instrument of surrender. He roused the stuporous Vallejo to countersign it, and in this way Sonoma fell to the rebellion.

Ide assigned twenty-five men to garrison Sonoma. His handful of followers then named him president of the California Republic, and on June 15 they raised over Sonoma's plaza a flag emblazoned with the image of a grizzly bear. It was from this flag, subsequently adopted as the state flag of California, that the Bear Flag Rebellion took its name.

Sending Vallejo off to Frémont, Ide continued the rebellion. On June 24, in a brief exchange dubbed, with some exaggeration, the Battle of Olompali, Ide drove off the small force Governor Castro had managed to mount against the Bear Flaggers. Two American lives were lost in the fighting. In the meantime, by consenting to receive Vallejo as a prisoner of war, Frémont had dropped any pretense to neutrality in the Bear Flag Rebellion. On June 25, he marched his small force into Sonoma, summarily assumed command from Ide, and set out with 134 men to avenge the two deaths suffered at Olompali. The vengeance consisted of murdering three Mexicans his party encountered along his march south. The rest of Castro's small force fled before Frémont's approach, offering no resistance. In a bloodless battle on July 1, Frémont took the Presidio, the military fortress at San Francisco that had not been garrisoned for many years. In a gesture both grandiose and superfluous, Frémont spiked the fort's single Spanish cannon, even though it had not been fired for at least half a century.

California Annexation

The Texas Republic lasted a decade before it was annexed to the United States. The Republic of California endured less than a month. On July 7, 1846, Commodore John D. Sloat of the U.S. Navy landed at Monterey, California. He took the harbor and the town without firing a shot, raised the Stars and Stripes, and claimed possession of California in the name of the United States. None of the Bear Flaggers protested. Frémont was named commander of the "California Battalion" and went on to fight in the larger war with Mexico, into which the Bear Flag Rebellion merged.

Although the Bear Flag Republic ceased to exist, Congress was caught in a deadlock over whether California and the other territories gained in the war with Mexico would be admitted as slave or free states. The issue was not resolved until the Compromise of 1850, a collection of acts passed by Congress during August and September 1850.

Debate and Polarization

After the Texas War of Independence, the combined issues of Texas statehood, territorial expansion, and war with Mexico provoked polarization and debate. For the most part, those Americans who strongly opposed slavery, especially New Englanders, also opposed the annexation of Texas, territorial expansion at the expense of Mexico, and war with Mexico. (Charles Sumner, at the time a Massachusetts state legislator, expressed the essence of northern opposition in his 1847 **Resolves on the War with Mexico.**) Southerners generally favored expansion and all it entailed. Westerners were divided: those who opposed slavery tended to oppose any war fought as a result of acquiring a slave state, whereas those who were most concerned to continue the western advance of U.S. territory favored annexation, expansion, and, if necessary, war. Coloring the debate were the same cultural and religious biases that had been active during the Texas War of Independence. Many in the predominantly white Anglo-Saxon Protestant

Resolves on the War with Mexico, 1847

Resolved, that the present war with Mexico has its primary origin in the unconstitutional annexation to the United States of *the* foreign state of Texas, while the same was still at war with Mexico; that it was unconstitutionally commenced by the order of the President, to General Taylor, to take military possession of territory in dispute between the United States and Mexico, *and in the occupation of Mexico;* and that it is now waged ingloriously,—by a powerful action against a weak neighbor,—unnecessarily and without just cause, at immense cost of treasure and life, for the dismemberment of Mexico, and for the conquest of a portion of her territory, from which slavery has already been excluded, with the triple object of extending slavery, of strengthening the "Slave Power," and of obtaining the control of the Free States, under the Constitution of the United States.

Resolved, that such a war of conquest, so hateful in its objects, so wanton, unjust, and unconstitutional in its origin and character, must be regarded as a war against freedom, against humanity, against justice, against the Union, against the Constitution, and *against the Free States.* . . .

Resolved, that our attention is directed anew to the wrong and "enormity" of slavery, and to the tyranny and usurpation of the "Slave Power," as displayed in the history of our country, particularly in the annexation of Texas, and the present war with Mexico.

Excerpted from Charles Sumner, "A War to Strengthen the Slavery Interests," in *Annals of America,* ed. Mortimer J. Adler and Charles Van Doren (Chicago: Encyclopaedia Britannica, 1976), 7:365.

United States considered the Catholic and racially mixed (Indian and Spanish) Mexicans uncivilized, even barbaric. In this respect, a war of "manifest destiny" took on an even more pronounced character as something of a holy war.

Ultimately, events outran the debate. War in Texas broke out before a declaration, allowing President Polk to assume war powers previously reserved to Congress. Indeed, John C. Calhoun, a southerner, a supporter of slavery, and one of the prime architects of the doctrine of states' rights, opposed the war on the ground that Polk exercised unrestrained and therefore unconstitutional war powers. (See Calhoun's January 26, 1846, speech, **Against General Resolutions on Foreign Affairs.**) Because American troops were already engaged in desperate battle, Polk's request for a congressional war resolution met with nothing more than token opposition. It was quickly passed on May 13, 1846.

That war was declared by Congress only after war was under way belies the fact that the Polk administration actually prepared very thoroughly for war. Fully six months before the hostilities, Polk worked closely with his cabinet and senior military officers to conduct extensive strategic planning, the first instance of such prewar planning in the nation's history. Moreover, although Polk was not a military man, he enthusiastically assumed the role of commander in chief, exercising very tight and direct control over the war. In this, he did set the very precedent Calhoun had feared: the president, not Congress, directed the conduct of the war.

The Antiwar Movement

There was an important antiwar movement during the U.S.-Mexican War, but it had remarkably little effect on the course or duration of the conflict. Abolitionists objected to the war, which they thought of as a struggle to preserve and spread slavery. Pacifists and others driven by ethical considerations regarded the war as a violation of Christian doctrine and a blatantly immoral example of unconscionable imperialism. The Whig Party generally condemned "Mr. Polk's war" as a deliberately provoked imperialist venture; however, most Whigs supported the war once it was under way, because it was both the patriotic and politically expedient thing to do. A small faction within the party, known as "Conscience" Whigs, did actively resist the war by voting against military appropriations. Even some Democrats denounced the war, including partisans of former president Van Buren and those of South Carolina senator and presidential hopeful John C. Calhoun. The Van Buren Democrats saw the war as a ploy to expand slavery, and they feared that Polk was assuming dictatorial powers. Calhoun and his followers supported slavery, but nevertheless feared that its expansion as a result of the war would move the nation toward civil war. Calhoun also vigorously objected to the war powers he believed Polk had usurped.

Although the antiwar movement was vocal and significant, it had virtually no impact on the war. Service in the military was voluntary—no one was forced to fight. The war was financed not by direct taxes as much as by government loans, so, for the most part, even the financing of the war was voluntary. The most memorable antiwar protestor did not see it this way, however. In July 1846 Henry David Thoreau, a young but crusty resident of Concord, Massachusetts, was arrested for failure to pay his poll tax. He refused to pay, he said, because the money was being used to finance an unjust war. Thoreau's modest protest failed to spark public debate over the war, but it did occasion one the most influential essays of modern times, "Civil Disobedience" (1849), which inspired the likes of Mohandas Gandhi and Martin Luther King Jr. Although occasioned by the war, this document, written and published after the war in 1849, was not truly an antiwar protest, but a manifesto of nonviolent resistance to injustice.

War Aims

Polk had two major objectives in fighting the war: to secure a Rio Grande boundary for Texas and to obtain all Mexican territory north of the Rio Grande and Gila River, all the way west to the Pacific Ocean. He thought these objectives could be obtained

"Against General Resolutions on Foreign Affairs," 1846

As to Texas, Mr. President, as far as I had any share in the management of that particular question, I can only say that the declaration of Mr. Monroe had not the weight of that piece of paper; and if a thousand such declarations, in even stronger terms, had been made and passed the Senate, they would not have had that weight. Declarations, sir, are easily made. The affairs of nations are not controlled by mere declarations. . . .

But we must meet interference in our affairs in another way. We must meet it as it was met in the case of Texas—decidedly, boldly, and practically. We must meet each particular case by itself, and according to its own merits, always taking care not to assert our rights until we feel ourselves able to sustain our assertions. As to general abstract declarations of that kind, I would not give a farthing for a thousand of them. They do more harm than good, or rather no good at all, but a great deal of harm.

Excerpted from John C. Calhoun, "Against General Resolutions on Foreign Affairs," in *Annals of America,*, ed. Mortimer J. Adler and Charles Van Doren (Chicago: Encyclopaedia Britannica, 1976), 7:337–338.

quickly by a shallow invasion of Mexico. Originally, invasion plans did not even contemplate penetrating as far as Mexico City, the capital, because Polk and his advisers believed that the combination of a naval blockade and partial invasion would create sufficient economic hardship that Mexico would soon negotiate a favorable end to the war. Militarily, the United States was very successful on land and on the sea (there were no naval engagements, but the Gulf blockade proved highly effective); however, much as the Mexicans had miscalculated the power of United States nationalism, so Polk had failed to appreciate Mexican national pride. In the end, war plans had to be revised to include an amphibious assault (the first in U.S. military history) on Veracruz and an invasion of Mexico City.

As the United States piled one military triumph upon another—though without ending the war—there arose a clamor from some Democrats for the conquest of "all Mexico." By this time, however, treaty negotiations were already in progress. Many Democrats were dissatisfied with the final Treaty of Guadalupe Hidalgo, which ended the war, because it failed to treat Mexico as a conquered nation

Political Conduct of the War

Although the conduct of the war was directed by the White House, Congress cooperated by authorizing increases in military strength. On May 13, 1846, Congress extended the term of service of the militia from three to six months and authorized President Polk to double the strength of the regular army by increasing the number of privates. Congress also called for 50,000 volunteers to serve for twelve months or for the duration of the war, at the discretion of the president. Surprisingly, after assuming so much direct control of the military, Polk left to each state the decision as to whether volunteers raised from that state would serve for twelve months or the duration. In February 1847 Congress voted to add ten new regiments to the regular army; nevertheless, the war was fought by a small core of regular army personnel and a large body of short-term militiamen and longer-term volunteers.

Overall command fell to two officers. Zachary Taylor, nicknamed "Old Rough and Ready," was a brave and calm leader, whose besetting flaw was his conservatism, which often led to a lack of aggressiveness. Nevertheless, his men loved him and were loyal. Winfield Scott, a hero of the War of 1812, possessed the tactical and strategic abilities Taylor lacked. While he was a more formal officer than Taylor (his nickname was "Old Fuss and Feathers") and did not possess Taylor's personal rapport with troops, he was daringly aggressive as well as imaginative.

Both Taylor and Scott were Whigs, and therefore both were prospective political opponents of the

Democrat Polk and his successors. Seeking to avoid making either man a politically bankable hero, Polk considered elevating a Democrat over both Taylor and Scott, who were major generals. Congress, however, refused to create the rank of lieutenant general, so Polk had no choice but to conduct the war with men whose political ambitions he did not trust and sought to squelch. With good reason, neither Taylor nor Scott felt confident that their commander in chief was giving them his full support. Scott believed he was menaced both by "fire, in front, from the Mexicans" and "a fire upon my rear, from Washington."

When it became apparent that the shallow invasion strategy, using Taylor's forces in northern Mexico, had succeeded militarily yet failed to bring Mexico to the negotiating table, Polk decided to execute a temporarily shelved plan for an amphibious invasion of Veracruz, from which troops would march inland to take Mexico City. Polk had hoped to make Senator Thomas Hart Benton a lieutenant general and assign command of this complex operation to him, but he was blocked by Congress. Polk then considered two Democratic major generals, Robert Patterson and William O. Butler. Patterson, however, had been born abroad, so he was ineligible to run for president, and it would be a waste of resources to make a hero of him. Butler was native born, but he was an unknown quantity to whom Polk was loath to entrust a major command. That left Whigs Taylor and Scott, and in choosing Scott, Polk made a wise choice based at least in part on an objective military assessment.

Enter Santa Anna

Despite his lack of military experience, Polk proved to be a competent manager of the military aspects of the war—except for logistics and a failure to understand the culture of the enemy. In part due to Polk's parsimonious management, troops were chronically undersupplied. Moreover, the president and his advisers also consistently failed to appreciate the depth of the national pride that motivated Mexico's conduct of the war and its refusal to negotiate, even in the face of one defeat after another. This is best illustrated by Polk's response to an overture from Antonio López de Santa Anna. Following his defeat in the Texas War of Independence, Santa Anna had been forced into retirement, only to reemerge in a skirmish with the French navy at Veracruz in 1838. Gaining prestige from this exchange, in which he lost a leg, Santa Anna briefly became dictator of Mexico from March to July 1839 in the absence of the president. In 1841 he led a coup d'état and took over the government until he, too, was overthrown in 1845 and driven into exile on Cuba. From his exile, Santa Anna contacted President Polk with an offer to mediate a favorable peace, including a Rio Grande boundary for Texas and the sale of California. In return, Santa Anna asked for the staggering sum of $30,000,000 and safe conduct to Mexico. True to character, Polk balked at the money, but he did send a ship for Santa Anna and duly took him to Mexico. Once there, Santa Anna hardly worked toward peace. Instead, he recruited an army to defeat the invaders.

Polk had inadvertently reinvigorated Mexican resistance by transporting Santa Anna to Mexico, an action that gave the nation's army a single, well-known leader, whose charisma was beyond Polk's understanding. Fortunately for the U.S. war effort, Santa Anna proved as poor a general as he had during the Texas War of Independence (see Chapter 9).

The Trist Mission

In April 1847 Polk sent Nicholas P. Trist, a relatively junior State Department official, to accompany Scott's army with an offer to negotiate peace. Polk's instructions to Trist were, essentially, to secure the Rio Grande as the southern border of Texas and to negotiate the cession, by purchase, of territory encompassing what is now the U.S. Southwest. The talks began on August 27, 1847, and were broken off by the Mexicans on September 7, before the invasion of Mexico City. On September 14, 1847, General Scott took the capital and accepted Santa Anna's surrender, ending the fighting, but not the war. National

pride, that quality Polk had so underestimated, stayed the Mexicans' hand. The Mexican government was also aware that antiwar sentiment in the United States was on the rise. The hope dawned that continued resistance, perhaps of a guerrilla nature, might yield more favorable terms from apparently war-weary Americans.

The situation in Mexico worried Scott, who was concerned about a possible protracted guerrilla war, especially in the absence of a stable government. Indeed, Scott feared there soon would be no legitimately recognized Mexican government with which to negotiate anything. Far from the scene, however, Polk, having received news of one victory after another, was revising his war aims. He now pondered demanding an indemnity consisting of more territory than he had originally sought, but instead of altering Trist's instructions, Polk issued an order in October for his recall. Acting on Scott's advice and, like Scott, persuaded that the Mexican situation was rapidly deteriorating, Trist ignored Polk's recall. Scott, in the meantime, managed to persuade Polk that Mexico was so unstable that it was absolutely necessary to conclude a treaty swiftly. When the order to resume negotiations came, Trist did not even take the time to assemble a formal board of treaty commissioners. Talks with Mexico resumed on November 22, and over nearly three months, Trist negotiated peace on Polk's original terms.

The Treaty of Guadalupe Hidalgo

Considering the magnitude of the American victory, the terms of the February 2, 1848, **Treaty of Guadalupe Hidalgo** were very generous. In return for the cession to the United States of "New Mexico"—the present state of New Mexico and portions of the present states of Utah, Nevada, Arizona, and Colorado—and Alta California, as well as the renunciation of claims to Texas above the Rio Grande, the United States paid Mexico $15,000,000 and assumed all claims of U.S. citizens against Mexico, which (as later determined by a specially appointed commission) amounted to an additional

Treaty of Guadalupe Hidalgo, 1848

ARTICLE I

There shall be firm and universal peace between the United States of America and the Mexican Republic. . . .

ARTICLE V

The boundary line between the two Republics shall commence in the Gulf of Mexico . . . to the point where it strikes the southern boundary of New Mexico; thence, westwardly, along the whole southern boundary of New Mexico (which runs north of the town called Paso) to its western termination; thence, northward, along the western line of New Mexico, until it intersects the first branch of the river Gila; . . . thence down the middle of the said branch and of the said river, until it empties into the Rio Colorado; thence across the Rio Colorado, following the division line between Upper and Lower California, to the Pacific Ocean. . . .

ARTICLE VIII

Mexicans now established in territories previously belonging to Mexico, and which remain for the future within the limits of the United States, as defined by the present treaty, shall be free to continue where they now reside, or to remove at any time to the Mexican Republic. . . .

Those who shall prefer to remain in the said territories may either retain the title and rights of Mexican citizens, or acquire those of citizens of the United States. But they shall be under the obligation to make their election within one year from the date of the exchange of ratifications of this treaty; and those who shall remain in the said territories after the expiration of that year, without having declared their intention to retain the character of Mexicans, shall be considered to have elected to become citizens of the United States.

In the said territories, property of every kind, now belonging to Mexicans not established there, shall be inviolably respected. . . .

ARTICLE IX

The Mexicans who, in the territories aforesaid, shall not preserve the character of citizens of the Mexican Republic, conformably with what is stipulated in the preceding article, shall be incorporated into the Union of the United States. and be admitted at the proper time (to be judged of by the Congress of the United States) to the enjoyment of all the rights of citizens of the United States, according to the principles of the Constitution; and in the mean time, shall be maintained and protected in the free enjoyment of their liberty and property, and secured in the free exercise of their religion without; restriction. . . .

ARTICLE XII

In consideration of the extension acquired by the boundaries of the United States, as defined in the fifth article of the present treaty, the Government of the United States engages to pay to that of the Mexican Republic the sum of fifteen millions of dollars.

Excerpted from the Avalon Project at Yale Law School, "Treaty of Guadalupe Hidalgo; February 2, 1848," www.yale.edu/lawweb/avalon/diplomacy/mexico/guadhida.htm.

$3,250,000. In addition, the United States agreed to make restitution for customs duties Mexico had been unable to collect because of the blockade in effect during the war.

Although neither government was wholly satisfied with the treaty—Polk in particular was disappointed—the Senate ratified the document on March 10, 1848. After considerable rancor, Mexico exchanged final ratifications with the United States on May 25.

Coda: The Gadsden Purchase

The Treaty of Guadalupe Hidalgo was modified by the **Gadsden Treaty** of 1853, which formalized the Gadsden Purchase, through which the United States acquired additional territory from Mexico. The Gadsden Treaty also abrogated Article XI of the Treaty of Guadalupe Hidalgo, in which the United States had pledged to prevent Indians from leaving territory acquired as a result of that treaty and settling (or raiding) in territory still held by Mexico. The Gadsden Treaty reflected a U.S. finding that enforcement of Article XI was unfeasible and probably unconstitutional.

Crisis: The Slavery Issue

The territorial windfall produced by the U.S.-Mexican War predictably upset the delicate balance between slave- and free-state representation in Congress. Pursuant to the Missouri Compromise of 1820, Missouri had been admitted as a slave state, but the compromise barred slavery in territories above the latitude of 36°30'. By the end of the war with Mexico, thanks to the work of abolitionists, most northerners were unwilling to accept slavery in new territories regardless of whether they lay above or below the Missouri Compromise line. In an effort to resolve the issue with regard to the new southwestern territories acquired as the result of the war, Senator Lewis Cass of Michigan introduced the doctrine of "popular sovereignty," which held that the new territories would be organized by the federal government without reference to slavery. At such time as a territory became eligible for admission to statehood, the people of the territory would write the prospective state's constitution and decide whether the state would be free or slave. California, a special case, would be admitted to the Union directly—presumably, through popular sovereignty—as a free state. This caused great consternation among southern senators and representatives. Senators Henry Clay and Daniel Webster proposed a new compromise by which California was to be admitted as a free state and the other territories subject to popular sovereignty. In addition, slave trading was to be discontinued in the District of Columbia. To appease the South, however, the Compromise of 1850 included a new, much stronger Fugitive Slave Law, which strictly forbade northerners (or anyone else) from giving refuge to escaped slaves. Finally, the federal government agreed to assume the debts incurred by Texas (which had been admitted as a slave state in 1845) when it was a republic.

No one was truly pleased with the Compromise of 1850. Southerners saw it as pushing the representa-

Gadsden Treaty, 1853

ARTICLE I

The Mexican Republic agrees to designate the following as her true limits with the United States for the future: retaining the same dividing line between the two Californias as already defined and established, according to the 5th article of the treaty of Guadalupe Hidalgo, the limits between the two republics shall be as follows. . . .

ARTICLE III

In consideration of the foregoing stipulations, the Government of the United States agrees to pay to the government of Mexico, in the city of New York, the sum of ten millions of dollars.

Excerpted from the Avalon Project at Yale Law School, "Gadsden Purchase Treaty," www.yale.edu/lawweb/avalon/diplomacy/mexico/mx1853.htm.

tional balance inexorably northward, and abolitionists were outraged by the Fugitive Slave Law. Four years after it was passed, the compromise was repealed and replaced by the Kansas-Nebraska Act, which left the issue of slavery in these two territories seeking statehood entirely to popular sovereignty. The immediate result was a savage guerilla war in Kansas, which heralded the great Civil War to come.

BIBLIOGRAPHY

Dufour, Charles L. *The Mexican War: A Compact History, 1846–1848.* New York: Hawthorn Books, 1968.

Eisenhower, John S. D. *So Far from God: The U.S. War with Mexico, 1846–1848.* New York: Random House, 1989.

Jones, Okah L., Jr. *Santa Anna.* New York: Twayne, 1968.

Nevin, David. *The Mexican War.* Alexandria, Va.: Time-Life Books, 1978.

Schroeder, John H. *Mr. Polk's War: American Opposition and Dissent, 1846–1848.* Madison: University of Wisconsin Press, 1973.

CHAPTER 11

INTRODUCTION TO THE INDIAN WARS

No historic label in the study of American warfare is used more vaguely than the "Indian Wars." Some historians attach the phrase to every white-Indian conflict since the first clash between the Spanish and native people on Hispaniola in 1493, whereas others apply it only to the U.S. Army's battles with the Plains Indians from 1865 to Wounded Knee in December 1890. The latter usage is officially sanctioned by U.S. Army historians, because "Indian Wars" was a label the army created for the conflicts of 1865–1891 in order to qualify soldiers who participated for wartime decorations and pay benefits. For the purposes of this book, however, "Indian Wars" will encompass all of the white-Indian conflicts from 1850 to 1891. Together, these conflicts are coherently defined by a region—the American West, including the Northwest, Southwest, and Great Plains—and by their more-or-less continuous or chronic nature. They are also conflicts in which the U.S. Army, not just militia and other volunteer forces, took part. Finally, while varied, they are conflicts that may be understood in the context of the same broad set of themes, which this chapter briefly discusses.

The fighting in this period was characterized by very few traditional "set-piece" battles. Typically, each of the "wars" consisted of raids by relatively small bands of Indians against settlers or simply refusal by tribes or tribal subgroups to accept confinement on reservations. The government's response both to raids and resistance was typically the same: a punitive military mission or, on a larger scale, expedition. Most of the time, the punitive mission failed to result in a showdown battle, but instead consisted of long, often fruitless pursuits punctuated by brief running exchanges of fire. Because actual battles were relatively rare, most military action consisted of destroying "hostile" villages, including Indian ponies and stores of crops and other provisions. Moreover, although the Indian Wars have beginning and ending dates (albeit often vague), they were not formally declared wars, and the army's "peacetime" routine between the wars was not very different from its practices during them. The U.S. Army, deployed across far-flung western outposts, was essentially a police force.

Although the U.S. Army rarely enjoyed clear-cut victories in the Indian Wars, the Indians did suffer certain and definitive defeat. This was not so much the result of military action as the outcome of population change. The Indians were inexorably outnumbered by the growing white population settling on their traditional lands. At most, the actions of the U.S. Army during 1850–1891 accelerated the decline of Indian hegemony by keeping "hostile" tribes on the run and thereby wearing them down through attrition.

U.S. Indian Policy

The Indian Wars were fought within the context of the struggle of the U.S. government to accommodate and to promote the westward expansion of the nation while treating the Indian population with an acceptable degree of humanity. It was never the avowed intention of the U.S. government to commit genocide against the Indians. Chapter 8, "Seminole and Black Hawk Wars (1817-1858)," discusses the evolution of the policy of Indian "removal," which culminated in the Indian Removal Act of 1830. The spirit behind this policy continued to inform U.S. Indian policy during 1850–1887 as the government endeavored to confine Indians either to "Indian Territory" (which originally encompassed the present state of Oklahoma and parts of adjacent states) or to reservations set aside for them. They were to be treated as wards of the federal government and furnished with the basic means of sustenance and other provisions. Those Indians who resisted removal and confinement were to be persuaded by force of arms, if necessary. In 1887 passage of the **Dawes Severalty Act** began to reverse the policy of segregation by at least partially dissolving the reservation system.

Problems Inherent in U.S. Indian Policy

During the period of the Indian Wars, U.S. Indian policy was characterized far more by failure than success. Its most basic problem was the nature of its dual mission: to support and promote the westward expansion of the white population without encroaching on the rights of the Indian population. The fact was that white settlement came at the expense of the Indians. Thus the very essence of U.S. Indian policy was unjust or, at the very least, coercive. It was virtually destined to create war.

Although doomed in this basic and critical manner, Indian policy was nevertheless often motivated by sincerely humane intentions. These were more often than not hampered and distorted in execution by such factors as racism, failure to understand the variety of Indian cultures, and failure to respect and accommodate Indian ways of life, as well as by political expedience and greed. Most important, the federal government had little authority with which to enforce even its best-intentioned policies. States, territories, individual military commanders, militia forces, and even settlers frequently took matters into their own hands and violated the provisions of agreements between the federal government and Indian tribes or groups. Moreover, the Bureau of Indian Affairs, charged since 1849 with administering federal Indian policy, was

Dawes Severalty Act, 1887

Chap. 119.– An act to provide for the allotment of lands in severalty to Indians on the various reservations, and to extend the protection of the laws of the United States and the Territories over the Indians, and for other purposes.

Be it enacted by the Senate and House of Representatives of the United States of America in Congress assembled, That in all cases where any tribe or band of Indians has been, or shall hereafter be, located upon any reservation created for their use, either by treaty stipulation or by virtue of an act of Congress or executive order setting apart the same for their use, the President of the United States be, and he hereby is, authorized, whenever in his opinion any reservation or any part thereof of such Indians is advantageous for agricultural and grazing purposes, to cause said reservation, or any part thereof, to be surveyed, or resurveyed if necessary, and to allot the lands in said reservation in severalty to any Indian located thereon in quantities as follows:

> To each head of a family, one-quarter of a section;
>
> To each single person over eighteen years of age, one-eighth of a section;
>
> To each orphan child under eighteen years of age, one-eighth of a section; and
>
> To each other single person under eighteen years now living, or who may be born prior to the date of the order of the President directing an allotment of the lands embraced in any reservation, one-sixteenth of a section.

Excerpted from University of Denver, Sturm College of Law, "Dawes Severalty Act," www.law.du.edu/russell/lh/alh/docs/dawesact.html.

notoriously underfunded, corrupt, inept, and insensitive, even heartless. Finally, U.S. Indian policy tended to shift with each presidential administration. A conciliatory policy might suddenly give way to an aggressive or punitive policy as the occupant of the White House changed. In sum, the chasm between stated federal Indian policy and the actual treatment of Indians by government representatives created resentment, hatred, violence, and outright warfare.

The Treaty System

Even if the very best intentions had prevailed on all sides, a clash of white and Indian cultures would probably have been inevitable. The system by which treaties were made illustrates the way that cultural differences led to armed conflict.

All of the European powers that colonized parts of the New World made treaties with Native American peoples. The practice was based on the uncritical—and invalid—assumption that Indian tribes were like nations, sovereign entities with rulers who were the equivalent of heads of state. In legal terms, however, neither a tribe nor a chief was competent to enter into a treaty. The mere fact that a chief, who typically led (if at all) by influence rather than by force of law or even custom, signed a treaty did not necessarily bind the rest of the tribe to it. Over the years, this became apparent to the various governments that concluded treaties with the Indians.

In addition, the U.S. government lacked the authority and the means to enforce its side of the treaties. State and local authorities, as well as individual military commanders and settlers, violated treaty obligations routinely and with impunity. Nevertheless, treaty making continued, although essentially in bad faith. Treaties were drawn up, signed, and, in due course, broken—which gave the white government in question a "legal" and "ethical" justification for war. White-Indian treaties, more often than not, served as instruments of war rather than instruments of peace.

If, by the nineteenth century, treaties were entered into in bad faith, they were also often concluded in a nakedly cynical and opportunistic manner. For instance, when the administration of Andrew Jackson wished to conclude a "removal" treaty with the Cherokees, it did so with a small faction of the tribe that favored removal (see Chapter 8). Once signed, the Treaty of New Echota was simply—and fraudulently—declared binding on the entire tribe.

Further, treaties wholly ignored basic cultural differences between white governments and Indian societies. In addition to the insistence on equating tribes with sovereign states, government negotiators refused to acknowledge that whites and Indians typically attached very different degrees of significance to treaty making. For whites, a treaty was a solemn, binding contract. For Indians, it was often little more than a means of obtaining the gifts and other ceremonial items that typically accompanied treaty-signing ceremonies. Finally, in many cases, the Indians did not enter into the treaties freely. U.S. treaty commissioners were usually accompanied by a substantial military force, which delivered the message that annihilation was the only alternative to signing the proffered treaty.

After concluding a long series of almost universally failed treaties with various tribes, the U.S. Congress, on March 3, 1871, passed the **Indian Appropriation Act,** by which all future treaty making was banned, all current treaties summarily nullified, and all Indians declared wards of the federal government.

Reform Movement

By the 1840s, it became clear even to the most optimistic observers that white-Indian relations were doomed to a permanent state of crisis. The expansion of white settlement was proceeding so quickly and over such an expanse that the idea of segregating white and Indian populations seemed impossible. The Civil War in the 1860s temporarily delayed serious debate on the future of U.S. Indian policy, but after that conflict ended, people in and out of the government began calling for policies that treated Indians more effectively, humanely, and justly. Some

Indian Appropriation Act, 1871

An Act *making Appropriations for the current and contingent Expenses of the Indian Department. . . .*

. . . Yankton Tribe of Sioux.— . . . For insurance and transportation of goods for the Yanktons, one thousand five hundred dollars: *Provided,* That hereafter no Indian nation or tribe within the territory of the United States shall be acknowledged or recognized as an independent nation, tribe, or power with whom the United States may contract by treaty: *Provided, further,* That nothing herein contained shall be construed to invalidate or impair the obligation of any treaty heretofore lawfully made and ratified with any such Indian nation or tribe.

Excerpted from George P. Sanger, *U.S. Statutes at Large* (Boston: Little, Brown, 1871), 16:566.

thought that the quickest way to accomplish this was to grant Indians immediate citizenship. Others believed that transitional programs were required to "civilize" the Indians before they could be made ready for citizenship: one faction called for a gradual, evolutionary process of education, whereas the other, including part of the military, believed the process should be accelerated and enforced by compulsion of arms. The majority of authorities within the government believed that the reservation system should be maintained only as a means of controlling Indian populations as they were gradually trained in the arts of "civilization."

Within this broad spectrum of approaches was one common assumption: white civilization was superior to the Indians' ways of life, and, one way or another, the Indians would have to accept and be assimilated into white civilization. Within this common assumption, of course, was yet another source of conflict. Many tribes had no desire to forsake the traditions sacred to them.

Grant's "Peace Policy" and "Civilization" Programs

In 1871 the government embraced reform with the Indian Appropriation Act and the so-called Peace Policy endorsed by President Ulysses S. Grant (see Chapter 21). The legislation transformed the Indians' status from members of sovereign nations to members of "dependent domestic nations"—that is,

noncitizen wards of the federal government. Grant's policy, which went along with this change in legal status, perpetuated the isolation of Indians on reservations in order to facilitate their education, transition to the ways of white civilization, and eventual integration into white American society.

Grant's Peace Policy had the positive effect of cleaning up at least some of the corruption and inefficiency of the Bureau of Indian Affairs; however, it also triggered a battle between the U.S. Army and government-sanctioned civilian philanthropists for control over Indian policy and its implementation. This meant that institutions and agents of the government often worked at cross-purposes with regard to the Indians. As a result, the government frequently seemed duplicitous to the Indians. The philanthropists' plan was not always welcomed by the Indians, either. The process of "civilization," as the white social engineers saw it, meant transforming the typically nomadic members of the Plains tribes into sedentary farmers. This was a cultural change so elemental and repugnant that many Indians resisted it—violently.

"Severalty" and Assimilation

The irony that Grant's Peace Policy coincided with perhaps the most intense phase of the Indian Wars was not lost on contemporaries. Humanitarian reformers began to argue that the failure of the Peace Policy demonstrated that only by granting the

Indians the full rights of citizenship, including individual land ownership, would peaceful white-Indian relations become a reality. The 1870s and 1880s saw the creation of a variety of white-sponsored Indian rights organizations. These groups agitated for "severalty," the dissolution of reservations (lands jointly held by tribes) in favor of the allotment of Indian lands to individual Indians, with each Indian family owning its own parcel of land in fee simple. The title to each parcel would be exactly equivalent to any title held by a white person—a universally and legally valid document.

To the reformers, severalty was appealing because it gave the Indians a basic right of citizenship and seemed a most humane step. Moreover, it would encourage (rather than coerce) the Indians to become settled, sedentary farmers because they would have a peaceful stake in a legally specified piece of property. Expansion-minded white westerners also found the concept of severalty attractive, because it would break up the reservations and potentially open new lands to them. If a parcel of land could be owned in fee simple, it could also be sold—outright and without tribal encumbrance. The concept of severalty therefore united two opposing streams of Indian policy and resulted in passage of the Dawes Severalty

Act in 1887 (see Chapter 27). By the early twentieth century, 60 percent of land claimed by individual Indians had been sold to whites. The process of dispossession, which proceeded during the late nineteenth century, triggered the last of the Indian Wars, culminating in the "Battle" of Wounded Knee in December 1890 and, on January 15, 1891, the final surrender of the Sioux nation.

BIBLIOGRAPHY

Axelrod, Alan. *Chronicle of the Indian Wars: From Colonial Times to Wounded Knee.* New York: Macmillan General Reference, 1993.

Debo, Angie. *A History of the Indians in the United States.* Norman: University of Oklahoma Press, 1977.

Lamar, Howard R. *The Reader's Encyclopedia of the American West.* New York: Crowell, 1977.

Phillips, Charles, and Alan Axelrod, eds. *The Encyclopedia of the American West.* 4 vols. New York: Macmillan General Reference, 1996.

Prucha, Francis P. *The Great Father: The United States Government and the American Indians.* Lincoln: University of Nebraska Press, 1984.

CHAPTER 12

EARLY INDIAN WARS IN CALIFORNIA (1850–1860)

At Issue

All of the wars between whites and Indians in California during this ten-year period were caused, directly or indirectly, by disputes over territory. Indians perceived white miners, farmers, and other settlers as having encroached on their traditional homelands.

The Conflicts

The California Indian Wars during this decade included the Mariposa War (1850–1851), the Yuma and Mojave Uprising (1851–1852), and the Paiute War (1860).

Indian Policy after the Transfer of Indian Affairs to the Department of the Interior (1849)

Following the tumultuous 1830s, which witnessed the Indian Removal Act of 1830 (see Chapter 8), the 1840s were relatively tranquil on the frontier. In this somewhat settled climate, responsibility for Indian affairs was transferred from the Department of War to the newly created Department of the Interior. Accordingly, Congress passed **An Act to Establish the Home Department** on March 3, 1849.

An attempt at general reform of Indian policy resulted, with an emphasis on equitable and humane treatment, education, and enhanced subsidies intended to integrate the Indians into white "civilization." This new approach effectively acknowledged that the policy of removal was destined to fail as white settlement continually overspread lands reserved for the Indians. However, the army never reconciled itself to the transfer of authority, and local commanders continued to wield considerable independent authority to police the Indians as they saw fit. Local white populations also were generally dissatisfied with the new policy. Thus the Department

An Act to Establish the Home Department, 1849

Be it enacted . . . , That, from and after the passage of this act, there shall be created a new executive department of the government of the United States, to be called the Department of the Interior; the head of which department shall be called the Secretary of the Interior, who shall be appointed by the President of the United States, by and with the advice and consent of the Senate, and who shall hold his office by the same tenure, and receive the same salary, as the Secretaries of the other executive departments, and who shall perform all the duties assigned to him by this act. . . .

SEC. 5. *And be it further enacted,* That the Secretary of the Interior shall exercise the supervisory and appellate powers now exercised by the Secretary of the War Department, in relation to all the acts of the Commissioner of Indian Affairs.

Excerpted from Francis Paul Prucha, ed., *Documents of United States Indian Policy,* 2d ed. (Lincoln: University of Nebraska Press, 1990), 80.

of the Interior's policies often were not carried out or, when they were, they were implemented half-heartedly, inconsistently, or in bad faith.

Mariposa War (1850–1851)

This brief conflict began in May 1850, when the Miwok and Yokut Indians, who lived in the Sierra Nevada foothills and the San Joaquin Valley of California, attacked gold prospectors who were encroaching into their territory. The first significant incident was an attack led by a chief known as Tenaya against isolated miners. During the attack, Tenaya torched trading posts owned by entrepreneur James D. Savage, who responded by recruiting a pri-vate militia, called the Mariposa Battalion (after Mariposa County), which he led in a campaign against the Miwoks and Yokuts during 1851.

Tenaya and about 350 warriors evaded Savage's first foray, but were captured during a second campaign. This ended the Mariposa War. The presence of the miners proved temporary. They left Miwok and Yokut country as the gold rapidly petered out.

Modifications to the Indian Department (1851)

Following the transfer of responsibility for Indian affairs from the Department of War to the Department of the Interior, Congress passed **An Act**

CHRONOLOGY OF THE EARLY INDIAN WARS IN CALIFORNIA

1850

May Miwok and Yokut Indians raid gold miners, thereby beginning the Mariposa War.

1851

Mar. 25 Chief Tenaya begins peace talks, but breaks them off.

May The Mariposa Battalion captures Chief Tenaya and a peace is concluded.

July 1 The Mariposa Battalion musters out, officially ending the Mariposa War.

Nov. Antonio Garra, chief of the Cupanga-kitoms, unites with tribes in southeastern California and southwestern Arizona in a rebellion.

Nov. 11 Yuma and Mojave warriors attack sheep drovers near Yuma Crossing on the Colorado River.

Nov. 12 Lieutenant Thomas "Fighting Tom" Sweeny resists the Indian attack at Yuma Crossing, creating Camp Independence.

Nov. 23 Indians raid Warner's Ranch outside of San Diego; white residents respond with a major campaign.

Dec. 6 Sweeny withdraws from Camp Independence. Also this month, Antonio Garra is captured and executed provoking renewed violence.

Dec. 25 Major H. P. Heintzelmann defeats a band of Yuma "rebels," and a peace treaty is concluded; however, a significant number of holdouts remain at Yuma Crossing.

1852

Feb. Regular army troops and militia volunteers flush the remaining "rebels" from Yuma Crossing.

Mar.–Apr. Army and militia forces raid and raze Indian villages in the area.

Sept. 29 Attack on Yuma holdouts

Oct. 2 The Yumas agree to peace and are granted pardons. The Yuma and Mojave Uprising ends.

1860

Early May Miners in the Comstock mining region of Nevada abduct and rape two Paiute girls. Paiutes rescue the girls and burn the Williams Station trading post, kill the five white employees.

May 8 Word of the "Williams Station Massacre" reaches Virginia City, where some 2,000 miners organize a militia. The force dissolves as quickly as it was formed.

May 12 Major William M. Ormsby leads 105 men into Pyramid Lake in Paiute country where, ambushed by Paiutes, he and 45 of his men are killed. Panic sweeps the Comstock region.

Late May A force of about 800 infantry regulars, militiamen, and volunteers battles the Paiutes at Pinnacle Mountain, killing some 25 Indians and ending the Paiute War.

AN ACCOUNT OF

CALIFORNIA,
AND THE
WONDERFUL GOLD REGIONS.

A New Arrival at the Gold Diggings.

WITH A DESCRIPTION OF

The Different Routes to California;

Information about the Country, and the Ancient and Modern Discoveries of Gold;

How to Test Precious Metals; Accounts of Gold Hunters;

TOGETHER WITH MUCH OTHER

Useful Reading for those going to California, or having Friends there.

ILLUSTRATED WITH MAPS AND ENGRAVINGS.

BOSTON:
PUBLISHED BY J. B. HALL, 66 CORNHILL.
For Sale at Skinner's Publication Rooms, 60½ Cornhill.

Price, 12½ cents.

Beginning in 1849, the lure of gold drew waves of white settlers to California, resulting in numerous confrontations with Indians over territory.

An Act Making Appropriations for the Current and Contingent Expenses of the Indian Department, 1851

SEC. 2. *And be it further enacted,* That from and after the thirtieth day of June next, all laws or parts of laws now in force, providing for the appointment or employment of superintendents of Indian affairs, of whatever character, for any of the Indian tribes east of the Rocky Mountains, and north of New Mexico and Texas, shall be, and the same are hereby repealed; and that the President be, and he is hereby, authorized by and with the advice and consent of the Senate, to appoint three superintendents of Indian affairs. . . .

SEC. 3. *And be it further enacted,* That hereafter all Indian treaties shall be negotiated by such officers and agents of the Indian department as the President of the United States may designate. . . .

SEC. 6. *And be it further enacted,* That the superintendents and agents to be appointed under the provisions of this act, before entering upon the duties of their respective offices, shall give bond in such penalties and with such security, as the President or Secretary of the Interior may require, and shall hold their offices respectively for the term of four years.

Excerpted from Francis Paul Prucha, ed., *Documents of United States Indian Policy,* 2d ed. (Lincoln: University of Nebraska Press, 1990), 83–84.

Making Appropriations for the Current and Contingent Expenses of the Indian Department on February 27, 1851. It streamlined the Indian superintendencies and agencies east of the Rocky Mountains and north of New Mexico and Texas while authorizing agents for the newly established New Mexico and Utah territories. The act empowered agents (and other officers the president might appoint) to negotiate all necessary treaties with the Indians of these regions, and it specifically extended current laws governing Indian trade and intercourse to cover New Mexico and Utah.

The Commissioner's Report (1851)

Even though there were disturbances in California, the civilian commissioner of Indian affairs, Luke Lea, declared in his November 27, 1851, **Annual Report of the Commissioner of Indian Affairs** that the "civilization of the Indians" was a "cherished object of the government." Despite the positive tone of the report, which reflected the public opinion of the majority of Americans at the time, Lea failed to specify the process by which civilization was to be accomplished. Thus he recommended continuing the reservation system as a stopgap measure pending a "satisfactory answer" to the question of how to "civilize" the Indians.

Yuma and Mojave Uprising (1851–1852)

Following the 1849 gold rush, the settlement of California was greatly accelerated, prompting the Yuma

Annual Report of the Commissioner of Indian Affairs, 1851

The civilization of the Indians . . . is a cherished object of the government. . . . There are not wanting those, who, judging from the apparently little success which in some instances has attended the instrumentalities employed, doubt the practicability of the measure. It should be remembered, however, that to change a savage people from their barbarous habits to those of civilized life, is, in its nature, a work of time, and the results already attained, as evinced in the improved condition of several of our tribes, are sufficient to silence the most skeptical, and warrant the assurance that perseverance in the cause will achieve success.

The history of the Indian furnishes abundant proof that he possesses all the elements essential to his elevation . . . He is intellectual, proud, brave, generous; and in his devotion to his family, his country, and the graves of his fathers, it is clearly shown that the kind affections and the impulses of patriotism animate his heart. That his inferiority is a necessity of his nature, is neither taught by philosophy nor attested by experience. Prejudice against him, originating in error of opinion on this subject, has doubtless been a formidable obstacle in the way of his improvement. . . .

On the general subject of the civilization of the Indians, many and diversified opinions have been put forth; but, unfortunately, like the race to which they relate, they are too wild to be of much utility. The great question, How shall the Indians be civilized? yet remains without a satisfactory answer.

Francis Paul Prucha, ed., *Documents of United States Indian Policy,* 2d ed. (Lincoln: University of Nebraska Press, 1990), 85–86.

and Mojave Indians of southwestern Arizona and southwestern California to launch an armed resistance against the settlers, whom they regarded as invaders. While prospectors did not work the Yuma and Mojave lands extensively, they did traverse these lands in substantial numbers via the Overland Trail. This infringement was sufficient to provoke tribal violence.

In contrast to most other wars between whites and Indians, the Yuma and Mojave Uprising had the characteristics of a genuine revolution. The Yumas in particular suffered abuses from those who passed through the so-called Yuma Crossing, a natural ford across the Colorado River near the mouth of the Gila. Outraged by the abuses, Antonio Garra, leader of a Yuma tribe that called itself the Cupangakitoms, notified San Diego County authorities in 1851 that his people would not pay taxes the county had assessed upon them. By November 1851 this act of defiance prompted other local Indian leaders to talk of outright revolution against the white government. Chief Geronimo of the New River Kamias, Captain Alleche of the Cahuillas, and Chief Fernando of the Chemehuevis joined Garra in calling on all Yuma leaders to plan a full-scale uprising along with the Mojaves and Yokuts of the San Joaquin Valley and smaller tribes in the Mexican territory of Baja California.

On November 10, 1851, a party of white sheep drovers entered the Yuma Crossing. The next day the party divided: five men led the sheep while the others remained in camp under the protection of a one-armed army lieutenant, Thomas "Fighting Tom" Sweeny, and a small detachment of soldiers. Before the end of the day, 400 Yumas had surrounded Sweeny's camp of about 100 men, withdrawing when Sweeny trained his 12-pound howitzer on them. This bought time for reinforcements to arrive on November 12, but Camp Independence, as Sweeny named his improvised outpost, was continually under siege throughout November and into early December. At last, on December 6, Sweeny and his men withdrew.

Elsewhere, encounters were considerably more violent. The most serious exchange took place on November 23, when Indians led by Garra raided Warner's Ranch outside of San Diego. This moved the local settlers to raise a militia, but it was not this band that succeeded in capturing Garra. He was snared in December by Cahuilla Indians who had refused to take part in the uprising. They turned him over to white authorities, who tried and executed Garra and other "rebels." The executions provoked the "rebel" Cahuillas to attack the village of those who had captured Garra, but U.S. Army major H. P. Heintzelmann led eighty cavalry troopers against the rebels, defeating them in battle on Christmas Day 1851. A peace treaty was hastily concluded.

Along the Colorado River, Sweeny's departure from Camp Independence encouraged the Yumas to declare their control of the region and to exclude whites from the area. With about 400 men, Heintzelmann marched against 500 Yumas, then began a punitive campaign during March and April that consisted of raids against Indian villages.

In August 1852 Heintzelmann and Sweeny learned that an all-out attack on Fort Yuma was being planned. Instead of attacking, however, Yuma leaders asked for peace talks. Sweeny agreed, and the Indians assembled near the Colorado River. Heintzelmann, however, ordered three companies of troopers to fix their bayonets and charge into the assembly. The Indians retreated and again asked for peace talks. Persuaded of their sincerity, Heintzelmann met with them, this time in earnest, on August 27. A truce was concluded, but when a treaty failed to emerge from tedious talks, Heintzelmann renewed his campaign, attacking a band of Yumas near present-day Blythe, California, on September 29. Rather than offer battle, the Indians fled and, on October 2, concluded a lasting peace.

Creation of a Superintendent of Indian Affairs for California (1852)

To government officials, the Mariposa War and the Yuma and Mojave Uprising indicated an urgent need for a superintendent of Indian affairs to be appointed specifically for California. Accordingly, on March 3, 1852, Congress passed **An Act to Provide for the Appointment of a Superintendent of Indian Affairs in California.** The superintendent's mission would be to administer the regulation of trade and intercourse with the Indians and to "preserve peace on the frontiers."

An Act to Provide for the Appointment of a Superintendent of Indian Affairs in California, 1852

Be it enacted . . . , That the sixth section of an act approved May sixth, eighteen hundred and twenty-two, entitled "An act to amend an act entitled An act to regulate trade and intercourse with the Indian tribes, and to preserve peace on the frontiers, approved the thirtieth March, eighteen hundred and two;" also, the fifth section of an act approved May twenty-fifth, eighteen hundred and twenty-four, entitled "An act to enable the President to hold treaties with certain Indian tribes, and for other purposes," be and the same hereby are revived, and extended to the State of California, for the purpose of establishing a superintendency of Indian affairs for said State, and that the President, by and with the advice and consent of the Senate, be, and he hereby is authorized to appoint a superintendent of Indian Affairs to reside in said State, who shall possess the same powers, and be subject to the same duties within his superintendency as belong to the Superintendent of Indian Affairs at St. Louis, in the State of Missouri, with the power also of exercising administrative examination over all claims, and accounts and vouchers for disbursements, connected with Indian affairs in the said State of California, which shall be transmitted to the Commissioner of Indian Affairs for final adjudication, and by him passed to the proper accounting officers of the treasury for settlement.

Excerpted from Francis Paul Prucha, ed., *Documents of United States Indian Policy,* 2d ed. (Lincoln: University of Nebraska Press, 1990), 86–87.

Evolving Reservation Policy (1858)

In the **Annual Report of the Commissioner of Indian Affairs** for 1858, Commissioner Charles E. Mix asserted that the entire reservation system had been a mistake. His plan for correcting the error, however, was to perpetuate the reservation system even more strictly, ensuring more rigorous segrega-

tion of white and Indian populations except as regulated by law, so that, in a gradual and controlled manner, Indians could become civilized. The civilization process, he wrote, was to be accompanied and promoted by severalty, the breakup of commonly held tribal reservations in favor of the allotment of parcels of land to Indians as individuals.

Mix's report reflects the ideological flux of Indian policy in the decade prior to the Civil War. There prevailed a general sense that policy had been a failure so far but that no rapid remedy was available. Change would have to come as a matter of evolution. In the meantime, Indian policy would have to consist mainly of policing both the Indian and white populations in an effort to avoid armed violence.

Annual Report of the Commissioner of Indian Affairs, 1858

The policy of concentrating the Indians on small reservations of land, and of sustaining them there for a limited period, until they can be induced to make the necessary exertions to support themselves, was commenced in 1853, with those in California. It is, in fact, the only course compatible with the obligations of justice and humanity. . . .

The operations thus far, in carrying out the reservation system, can properly be regarded as only experimental. Time and experience were required to develop any defects connected with it, and to demonstrate the proper remedies therefor. From a careful examination of the subject, and the best information in the possession of the department in regard to it, I am satisfied that serious errors have been committed; that a much larger amount has been expended than was necessary, and with but limited and insufficient results. . . .

No more reservations should be established than are absolutely necessary for such Indians as have been, or it may be necessary to displace, in consequence of the extension of our settlements, and whose resources have thereby been cut off or so diminished that they cannot sustain themselves in their accustomed manner. Great care should be taken in the selection of the reservations, so as to isolate the Indians for a time from contact and interference from the whites.

Excerpted from Francis Paul Prucha, ed., *Documents of United States Indian Policy,* 2d ed. (Lincoln: University of Nebraska Press, 1990), 94–95.

Paiute War (1860)

Also called the Pyramid Lake War (after the region in Nevada), the Paiute War began as a quest to avenge the abduction and rape of two Indian girls. White residents saw the violence not as an act of vengeance for a crime, but as an "uprising," and they reacted accordingly.

In May 1860 miners abducted and raped two girls of the Southern Paiute tribe. Paiute warriors rescued the girls, then retaliated by burning down Williams Station, one of two trading posts in the Carson Valley along the California Trail. The five men who staffed the station were killed. By May 8, word of the "Williams Station Massacre" reached Virginia City, Nevada. Immediately, some 2,000 miners formed themselves into a militia force and telegraphed the territorial governor for arms. Their enthusiasm rapidly evaporated as they waited for a reply, however, and the force dissolved without seeing action. Miner Henry Meredith recruited a new force. At Dayton, Nevada, these men joined Major William M. Ormsby, who was leading volunteers from Carson City.

Ormsby assumed command of a combined force numbering just 105 men and led them to Pyramid Lake, in Paiute country, where they were ambushed at the Big Bend of the Truckee River Valley on May 12. The Paiutes killed Ormsby and 45 of his men with their traditional poison-dipped arrows. Survivors spread tales of the ambush throughout the region of the Comstock Lode, prompting the governor to send militia troops under the command of Colonel Jack Hays (or Hayes), a former Texas Ranger. The U.S. Army added a small detachment of infantry regulars out of San Francisco. Joined by local volunteers, Hays's command ultimately consisted of about 800 men, who headed for the Truckee River late in May.

Hays's force skirmished with Paiutes near the site of the Ormsby ambush, then pursued the Indians to Pinnacle Mountain, a Paiute stronghold. In the Battle of Pinnacle Mountain, Hays's command killed about twenty-five warriors and, with that, the brief and ugly war abruptly ended.

Evolving Reservation Policy (1862)

The Paiute War was a minor conflict, but it spread disproportionate panic throughout California. Alarmed whites cited the conflict as evidence that Indians were inherently uncivilized and uncivilizable. Such local reactions and opinions notwithstanding, the Bureau of Indian Affairs continued to favor strict enforcement of confinement to reservations with the purpose of ultimately integrating Indians into white civilization through a combination of education and gradual severalty. Commissioner of Indian Affairs William P. Dole made this clear in his **Annual Report of the Commissioner of Indian Affairs** for 1862.

Annual Report of the Commissioner of Indian Affairs, 1862

Another year has but served to strengthen my conviction that the policy, recently adopted, of confining the Indians to reservations, and, from time to time, as they are gradually taught and become accustomed to the idea of individual property, allotting to them lands to be held in severalty, is the best method yet devised for their reclamation and advancement in civilization. . . .

[The Indians] find themselves in the pathway of a race they are wholly unable to stay, and on whose sense of justice they can alone rely for a redress of their real or imaginary grievances. Surrounded by this [white] race, compelled by inevitable necessity to abandon all their former modes of gaining a livelihood, and starting out in pursuits which to them are new and untried experiments, they are brought in active competition with their superiors in intelligence and those acquirements which we consider so essential to success. In addition to these disadvantages, they find themselves amenable to a system of local and federal laws, as well as their treaty stipulations, all of which are to the vast majority of them wholly unintelligible. If a white man does them an injury, redress is often beyond their reach; or, if obtained, is only had after delays and vexations which are themselves cruel injustice.

Excerpted from Francis Paul Prucha, ed., *Documents of United States Indian Policy,* 2d ed. (Lincoln: University of Nebraska Press, 1990), 95–96.

BIBLIOGRAPHY

Axelrod, Alan. *Chronicle of the Indian Wars: From Colonial Times to Wounded Knee.* New York: Macmillan General Reference, 1993.

Debo, Angie. *A History of the Indians in the United States.* Norman: University of Oklahoma Press, 1977.

McDermott , John D. *A Guide to the Indian Wars of the West.* Lincoln: University of Nebraska Press, 1998.

Michno, Gregory F. *Encyclopedia of Indian Wars: Western Battles and Skirmishes 1850–1890.* Missoula, Mont: Mountain Press Publishing Company, 2003.

Phillips, Charles, and Alan Axelrod, eds. *The Encyclopedia of the American West.* 4 vols. New York: Macmillan General Reference, 1996.

Prucha, Francis P. *The Great Father: The United States Government and the American Indians.* Lincoln: University of Nebraska Press, 1984.

Utley, Robert M. *Indian Wars.* New York: Mariner Books, 2002.

At Issue

As with the other Indian Wars, those in the Pacific Northwest during 1855–1858 had at their root a conflict over territory. They were also based on a powerful element of cultural conflict between the Christian missionary zeal of some pioneering white settlers and the prevailing way of life of the indigenous people.

The Conflicts

Three wars occurred in this region during the period: the Rogue River War (1855–1856), the Yakima War (1855), and the Coeur d'Alene War (1858).

Catalyst: The Whitman Massacre (1847) and Response

In 1835 Marcus Whitman, a physician and Presbyterian minister, established a mission near present-day Walla Walla, Washington. He and his wife, Narcissa Prentice Whitman, also provided medical care to the Indians and mountain men—local hunters and trappers. Dr. Whitman selflessly attended to the medical needs of the Cayuse Indians, for which they were grateful, but his demand that the Cayuses who sought his aid convert to his religion provoked much resentment among the Indians.

In the fall of 1847, a measles epidemic devastated the Indian population near Walla Walla. Influential tribal leaders attributed the epidemic to the growing presence of whites in the area. One of these whites,

a French Canadian settler named Joe Lewis, sought to deflect the simmering Indian hostility away from himself and began spreading a rumor that the measles epidemic had been brought deliberately by Whitman in an effort to steal the Indians' land. This provoked two Cayuse Indians to attack Whitman's mission on November 29, 1847, killing the doctor, his wife, and (by most accounts) fourteen others, as well as abducting 53 women and children.

Word of the "Whitman Massacre" moved a local man, Cornelius Gilliam, to organize 550 militiamen in a punitive campaign. His unit killed perhaps twenty Indians in indiscriminate attacks on random Cayuses. In the meantime, the territorial governor appointed a three-man peace commission in an effort to contain the violence, but Gilliam continued his attacks, provoking a retaliation in which ten of his militiamen were wounded and Gilliam was killed when he accidentally shot himself. Despite the loss of their "colonel," the militia continued to stalk Cayuses, rousing the neighboring Walla Wallas, Umatillas, Palouses, and Nez Perces to violence.

Federal Indian Statutes for Oregon Territory

In response to the Cayuse attack on the Whitman mission, famed mountain man Joe Meek, father of Helen Meek, who was slain at the mission, traveled to Washington, D.C. On May 28, 1848, he petitioned his cousin-in-law, President James K. Polk, to organize Oregon as a territory of the Untied States, an act that would entitle Oregon to the full protection of the federal government. On August 14, the Oregon Territory, which encompassed the present states of Oregon and Washington, was created.

While Oregon quickly received territorial status, the federal government was slow to intervene in Indian affairs there. It was not until June 5, 1850, almost two years later, that Congress passed **An Act Authorizing the Negotiation of Treaties with the Indian Tribes in the Territory of Oregon, for the Extinguishment of Their Claims to Lands Lying West of the Cascade Mountains, and for Other Purposes.**

In 1853 Washington Territory was separated from Oregon Territory, and Isaac Stevens was appointed governor of Washington. Armed with the act created for the original territory, Stevens rapidly concluded treaties to "extinguish" Indian claims to the territory. The "other purposes" alluded to in the act's title included the appointment of a superintendent of Indian affairs and one or more Indian agents, as well as the extension of current trade and intercourse laws and regulations to the area.

Rogue River War (1855–1856)

After the "Whitman Massacre" and the militia reprisals of Cornelius Gilliam, relations so deteriorated that whites and Indians in Oregon and Washington territory routinely shot one another on sight. Because the region was a federal territory, the white community called on the federal government for aid. This thrust Major General John E. Wool,

---

CHRONOLOGY OF THE EARLY INDIAN WARS IN THE PACIFIC NORTHWEST

1835
- Marcus Whitman establishes a mission near present-day Walla Walla, Washington.

1847
Nov. 29 Cayuse Indians massacre Whitman and others. In response, Cornelius Gilliam organizes militiamen in a campaign against the Cayuse.

1848
Aug. 14 Oregon Territory, encompassing the present states of Oregon and Washington, is created.

1850
June 5 Congress passes an act to authorize treaty negotiations with Indians in Oregon Territory.

1853
- Washington Territory is separated from Oregon Territory, and Isaac Stevens is appointed governor of Washington Territory.

1855
Aug. The Rogue River War begins.
Mid-Sept. Qualchin, nephew of the Yakima chief Kamiakin, leads an attack that kills six prospectors and A. J. Bolen, the local Indian agent. Kamiakin warns that all whites who venture east of the Cascades will meet a similar fate.

Oct. 16 Whites raid a Rogue camp, killing twenty-three Indians, including old men, women, and children.
Oct. 17 Indian war parties avenge the raid of Oct. 16, killing twenty-seven settlers in the Rogue Valley.
Oct. Major Granville O. Haller plans to coordinate an attack with men out of Fort Steilacoom under Lieutenant W. A. Slaughter, but Haller is ambushed by warriors under Kamiakin. Slaughter withdraws to Puget Sound.

1856
Early spring Colonel George H. Wright marches against Kamiakin, but discovers that all warriors have withdrawn. The Yakima War is declared over.
May 28 The Rogues are defeated at the Battle of Big Meadows, which ends the Rogue River War.

1858
May 17 The Coeur d'Alene War begins when Coeur d'Alene and allied tribes attack a U.S. Army column under Lieutenant Edward J. Steptoe.
Sept. 1 Ordered to avenge the attack on Steptoe's column, Colonel George Wright defeats the Coeur d'Alene and allied tribes at the Battle of Spokane Plain.
Sept. 5 Wright's victory at the Battle of Four Lakes ends the Coeur d'Alene War.

Marcus Whitman
(1802–1847)

Born in Rushville, New York, Marcus Whitman was trained as a physician and practiced in Canada and New York. In 1835 he became a missionary under the auspices of the American Board of Commissioners for Foreign Missions. The board sent him, with fellow missionary Samuel Parker, to explore the potential for creating missions in Oregon, which was then jointly occupied by the United States and Britain. Encouraged, Whitman and Parker recruited other missionaries, assistants, and settlers. After marrying Narcissa Prentiss, Whitman set out with her (in company with the Reverend Henry H. Spalding and his wife, Eliza, as well as two single men) for Oregon.

Despite Whitman's success, the board abandoned Oregon in 1842 to focus on missions established near modern Spokane, Washington. Whitman returned to Boston during 1842–1843 and successfully lobbied for reestablishment of his missions at Waiilatpu and Lapwai, then rode to Washington, D.C., to report to federal officials on conditions in the Oregon country. Government authorities pledged aid to promote immigration. When he returned to the West in 1843, Whitman accompanied a wagon train of 1,000 Oregon-bound immigrants—the first wave of what became known as the "Great Migration."

Whitman's missionary work was plagued by the Indians' general indifference to Protestant Christianity, their attraction to Roman Catholicism, and the bad influence of lawless white settlers. In 1847 a deadly measles epidemic swept the vicinity of the mission. Whitman worked valiantly to nurse the sick, but many Indians blamed him for the onset of the epidemic, believing it to be a form of sorcery and a scheme to purge the country of Indians. On November 29, 1847, Indians attacked the mission, killing (by most accounts) sixteen whites, including Marcus and Narcissa Whitman, and abducting the fifty-three women and children who lived there.

An Act Authorizing the Negotiation of Treaties with the Indian Tribes in the Territory of Oregon, 1850

Be it enacted . . . , That the President be authorized to appoint one or more commissioners to negotiate treaties with the several Indian tribes in the Territory of Oregon, for the extinguishment of their claims to lands lying west of the Cascade Mountains; and, if found expedient and practicable, for their removal east of said mountains. . . .

SEC. 2. *And be it further enacted,* That the President be authorized, by and with the advice and consent of the Senate, to appoint a Superintendent of Indian Affairs for the Territory of Oregon. . . .

SEC. 5. *And be it further enacted,* That the law regulating trade and intercourse with the Indian tribes east of the Rocky Mountains, or such provisions of the same as may be applicable, be extended over the Indian tribes in the Territory of Oregon.

Excerpted from Francis Paul Prucha, ed., *Documents of United States Indian Policy,* 2d. ed. (Lincoln: University of Nebraska Press, 1990), 81.

commanding officer of the U.S. Army's Department of the Pacific, into a difficult position. In contrast to most settlers and army officers, Wool believed in a policy of moderation toward the Indians. He was caught between the settlers, who demanded nothing less than the annihilation of the Indians, and the Indians themselves.

The whites in the territory called the Takelma and Tutuni Indians who lived along the Oregon-California border "Rogue" Indians because they chronically attacked travelers along the Siskiyou Trail near the Rogue River.

The 1847 murders of physician and minister Marcus Whitman, his wife, and other whites in his missionary settlement led to a punitive campaign against the Cayuse Indians by Oregon militiamen and the creation of the Oregon Territory.

When some drunken Rogues killed ten or eleven miners along the Klammath River in August 1855, local whites retaliated by killing about twenty-five Indians—albeit not those who had slain the miners. This incident began the Rogue River War.

By September the violence of the Rogue River War had intensified after rumors circulated concerning a possible new war with the Yakima Indians east of the Cascades. The rumors incited local settlers to escalate the violence against the Rogues to the point that Captain Andrew Jackson Smith, commanding officer of Fort Lane, felt obliged to open the fort to the Indians to provide them with protection from trigger-happy settlers. This was barely effective and increased distrust between the settlers and the army. Despite Smith's efforts to protect the Rogues, settlers raided a camp on October 16, killing twenty-three Rogues, including old men, women, and children. The next day, Indian war parties took their revenge, killing twenty-seven settlers in the Rogue Valley and razing the village of Gallice Creek to the ground.

Smith found himself in a precarious position—typical for a small standing army of the West, whose limited resources were thinly spread across vast expanses of territory. Wool's main body of regulars was engaged in what had become the Yakima War, and Smith could do little more than hope to keep his small, isolated garrison from being overrun in the conflict that the local whites had escalated.

Fortunately, by the time reinforcements were scheduled to arrive at Fort Lane, the Rogue River War seemed to be winding down due to the mutual exhaustion of both sides. Indeed, the Takelma and Tutuni chiefs the whites knew as Limpy, Old John, and George had all agreed to surrender to Captain Smith at a place called Big Meadows. Yet, possibly at the last minute, the chiefs reconsidered and instead assembled about 200 warriors to attack Smith's fifty dragoons (troops who ride to battle, but fight on foot) and thirty infantry troops. A pair of Indian women revealed to Smith the chiefs' change of heart, however, so that when the captain reached Big Meadows, instead of riding into the open, he deployed his troops on a commanding hilltop. When the chiefs attacked, the outnumbered Smith dug in. By the end of the first day of battle, twenty-five of his men had been killed or wounded. On the next day, May 28, 1856, the Rogues assembled for a final assault, only to be met by the timely arrival of reinforcements under Captain Christopher C. Augur. Routed, the Rogues withdrew and, by the end of the month, submitted to confinement on a local reservation.

Governor Stevens Makes and Breaks Treaties

In 1853 Isaac Stevens, a bold young adventurer, led a surveying party from Minnesota to Puget Sound, Washington, scouting out a route for the proposed transcontinental railroad. Later in the year, he was appointed Washington's first territorial governor, and in his zeal to clear the right of way for the planned Northern Pacific Railroad linking Minnesota and Washington, he aggressively made treaties with the Indians, seeking to gather up as much land as he could. Historically, the best of white-Indian treaties rarely endured, and those Stevens made were far from the best. He concluded treaties with the Yakima and thirteen other tribes, binding the Indians to cede their lands in exchange for internment on large reservations, where they would be provided with homes, schools, horses, livestock, and a large tribal annuity. Most important, he guaranteed that the removal to the reservation would be delayed for two or three years after the treaties were signed. For their part, the tribes were largely convinced of the futility of resisting the settlers in their ever-increasing numbers and believed that the deal Stevens offered was the best they could get. Within a dozen days of concluding the last treaty, however, Stevens unilaterally proclaimed the former Indian territory "open" to white settlement.

Emergence of Kamiakin

Stevens's treachery did not surprise Kamiakin, a Yakima chief, who had been among the minority of chiefs refusing to sign Stevens's treaties. Greatly revered by Indians throughout the Pacific Northwest, Kamiakin forged an alliance among the Yakima, Walla Walla, Umatilla, and Cayuse tribes. This

Isaac Stevens
(1818–1862)

Born in Andover, Massachusetts, Isaac Stevens graduated from West Point in 1839. His service as an engineer in the army included the U.S.-Mexican War (Chapter 10). In 1847, while still an army officer, he was appointed Indian agent for Washington Territory. In 1853 President Franklin Pierce appointed him governor of the territory, with responsibilities that included serving as superintendent of the territory's Indian affairs.

Stevens served as territorial delegate to Congress in 1857. During the Civil War, he accepted a commission as a major general in the Union army. He fell in the Battle of Chantilly, Virginia, on September 1, 1862.

accomplished, he waited patiently to build up his forces and plan an attack. But Kamiakin soon learned the limits of his authority. Without authorization, a band of five young braves led by his own nephew Qualchin killed a party of six prospectors during mid-September 1855. A. J. Bolen, the local Indian agent investigating the incident was also killed. Although he was appalled by these precipitate acts, Kamiakin made the most of them and issued a warning to whites that a similar fate awaited any who dared travel east of the Cascades.

Yakima War (1855)

In October 1855, despite Kamiakin's warning, U.S. Army major Granville O. Haller led a force of eighty-four regulars to reconnoiter the east face of the Cascades in order to plan a joint attack with Lieutenant W. A. Slaughter's command in the area. Kamiakin's warriors ambushed Haller, however, killing five soldiers and forcing the column to abandon its howitzer during the retreat to Fort Dalles. The withdrawal left the area around Seattle unprotected, and local Indians raided freely along the White River, north of Seattle. Nine settlers were killed, and others fled in panic to Seattle, where citizens erected a hasty stockade. A subsequent counterattack led by Slaughter (who was fatally wounded) drove the Indians out of Seattle.

Governor Stevens, who was in Montana making more treaties, received a greatly exaggerated account of the extent of combat and rushed back to Washington, where he quickly raised two militia companies, which, however, failed to engage the enemy. Major General John E. Wool, commander of the army's Department of the Pacific, found himself locked in a bitter dispute with Governor Stevens, of whose amateur military ventures he strongly disapproved, pointing out that they served only to inflame the Indians. For his part, Stevens protested that *someone* had to fight the Indians and that he would do it if the U.S. Army was reluctant to. At last, early in spring 1856, after continual pressure from Stevens, Wool sent reinforcements to Captain Andrew Jackson Smith, who was pinned down at Fort Lane (see the discussion of the Rogue War, above). He also assembled a force of 500 regulars under George H. Wright to march against Chief Kamiakin.

By the time Wright led his men in pursuit, Kamiakin had withdrawn eastward, and Wright could find only peaceful Indian fishermen. Persuaded that they meant no harm, Wright duly reported the facts to Wool, who simply declared the Yakima War to be at an end. Although sporadic fighting actually continued, Kamiakin was nowhere to be found. As the military and citizens of the territory were about to discover, he was busily inciting the Coeur d'Alene and Spokane Indians to begin a whole new war.

The Death of Peo-Peo-Mox-Mox and Its Consequences

Among the hundred or so victims of the Yakima War was Peo-Peo-Mox-Mox, a Walla Walla chief whose death illustrates the injustice and confusion that characterized many of the Indian Wars. At the Walla Walla Council of 1855, convened by Governor Stevens to conclude land-cession treaties with the Walla Walla and Palouse Indians, Peo-Peo-Mox-Mox was among the tribal minority who spoke out against the treaties; yet he was also instrumental in restraining his warriors from joining in the Yakima War, which broke out later that year. In December 1855 Oregon volunteers skirmished with the Walla Wallas, Umatillas, and Cayuses. During this time, Peo-Peo-Mox-Mox led five warriors under a flag of truce in an attempt to broker a peace. Instead of honoring the white flag, the volunteers killed the truce party and proudly displayed the ears and scalp of Peo-Peo-Mox-Mox.

It was precisely such senseless barbarity, routinely practiced by untrained volunteers, that so angered Major General Wool. The army lacked sufficient personnel to prevent such outrages, which made a mockery of attempts to negotiate peace. Predictably, Kamiakin seized on the slaying and mutilation of Peo-Peo-Mox-Mox to justify the Yakima War and, subsequently, to rally other tribes in the Coeur d'Alene War.

The Miners Appeal, the Army Responds

During the Indian Wars, the thinly spread U.S. Army usually functioned less as a traditional military organization than it did as a police force. Combat units often answered calls that came directly from citizens. This made centralized command all but impossible and further complicated both the formulation and implementation of Indian policy. For example, late in 1857 miners in Colville, Washington, terrorized by Indian raids, appealed directly to the commander of Fort Walla Walla for help. In May 1858, after considerable delay—a fatal flaw in carrying out any police mission—158 troopers were dispatched under Lieutenant Edward J. Steptoe.

Steptoe's assignment was to march to the Colville gold camp and do his best to overawe the hostile

Indians, including members of the Palouse, Spokane, and Coeur d'Alene tribes, with the army's might. Steptoe assumed the Indians were just making trouble for a few miners, when they were actually desperate to stop a proposed Missouri-to-Columbia River road—a much bigger issue. Through no fault of his own, therefore, Steptoe proceeded, utterly unaware of the big picture. Unprepared for a major campaign, his men carried obsolescent arms and were so short of pack animals that they had to jettison their ammunition boxes to make room for other baggage. This lack of preparation was typical of the Indian Wars. Operations were frequently executed on the fly, with little cognizance of larger political and strategic issues.

Coeur d'Alene War (1858)

About twenty miles south of the present-day city of Spokane, Steptoe's column was intercepted by more than 1,000 warriors, who forced him into retreat, following him all the way. On May 17, 1858, they suddenly attacked in full force, killing two officers. Steptoe led his men to a hilltop, then crept away with his force under cover of darkness. Anxious to avenge what he considered a profound humiliation, Major General Newman S. Clarke ordered Colonel George Wright to conduct a punitive campaign against the Coeur d'Alene and allied tribes. Perhaps encouraged by their easy triumph over Steptoe, some 600 warriors arrayed themselves in the open on two battlefields: Spokane Plain (September 1) and Four Lakes (September 5). Wright commanded superior numbers, and his men were armed with modern carbines and rifles. Even more important, combat on an open field was precisely the kind of fighting at which the army excelled but, during the Indian Wars, rarely had the opportunity to engage in. The Indians were defeated in both encounters, and Wright sent a detachment from one Indian camp to another, demanding delivery of those responsible for attacking Steptoe. A number of braves were handed over, fifteen of whom were summarily hanged.

Kamiakin, who had been instrumental in the attack on Steptoe as well as in the two subsequent battles, escaped to Canada.

A Policy of Unmitigated Aggression

Wright's punitive expedition reflected a short-lived policy of unmitigated aggression directed against the Coeur d'Alene and other tribes. The policy was not the product of politicians, civilian administrators, or even of the army high command, but of an army field officer, Newman Clarke. It was motivated by Clarke's anger over the humiliation of Steptoe and his column, rather than by any cogent strategic plan. This essentially emotional pattern would come to typify many of the Indian Wars: policy was frequently formulated on impulse, provoked by nothing more than a perceived affront to honor or ego and a visceral desire for punitive vengeance.

With Kamiakin having escaped to Canada, Wright turned his wrath on the chief's brother-in-law, Owhi. When Owhi approached Wright with a peace offer, the colonel arrested him and forced him to summon his son, the warrior leader Qualchin, whom Wright hanged in his presence. Owhi, heartbroken, attempted a desperate escape and was gunned down. Often such brutality incited further warfare, but just as often it served to demoralize the Indian warriors. That is what happened in this case. Following the deaths of Qualchin and Owhi, the tribes of the Columbia Basin surrendered en masse.

The Stevens Treaties Ratified and Enforced

After the sudden and definitive conclusion of the Coeur d'Alene War, the U.S. Senate rushed to ratify the host of treaties Governor Stevens had concluded, often fraudulently, among the tribes of the Pacific Northwest. These were collectively ushered through ratification on March 8, 1859, thereby ending the early period of Indian Wars in the Pacific Northwest.

BIBLIOGRAPHY

Axelrod, Alan. *Chronicle of the Indian Wars: From Colonial Times to Wounded Knee.* New York: Macmillan General Reference, 1993.

Cozzens, Peter, ed. *The Wars for the Pacific Northwest.* Mechanicsburg, Pa.: Stackpole Books, 2002.

Debo, Angie. *A History of the Indians in the United States.* Norman: University of Oklahoma Press, 1977.

McDermott , John D. *A Guide to the Indian Wars of the West.* Lincoln: University of Nebraska Press, 1998.

Michno, Gregory F. *Encyclopedia of Indian Wars: Western Battles and Skirmishes 1850–1890.* Missoula, Mont: Mountain Press Publishing Company, 2003.

Phillips, Charles, and Alan Axelrod, eds. *The Encyclopedia of the American West.* 4 vols. New York: Macmillan General Reference, 1996.

Prucha, Francis P. *The Great Father: The United States Government and the American Indians.* Lincoln: University of Nebraska Press, 1984.

Utley, Robert M. *Indian Wars.* New York: Mariner Books, 2002.

At Issue

During this period, federal officials sought to confine the Apaches and Navajos to reservations. The Indians resisted throughout the Arizona Territory.

The Conflict

War with the Apaches and Navajos began when the Chiricahua Apache chief Cochise was falsely accused of participating in a raid on John Ward's Arizona ranch during which cattle were taken and a boy was abducted. On February 4, 1861, Cochise, together with his brother, two nephews, and a woman and child, voluntarily answered Second Lieutenant George N. Bascom's summons to meet him at Apache Pass. (Some sources report that Cochise was accompanied by an additional party of six or seven warriors.) Bascom suddenly announced that he would hold Cochise and his party until the kidnapped boy and purloined stock were returned. Drawing a knife, Cochise slit the canvas of the conference tent and escaped. At least five others remained behind and one (according to some reports) was killed.

Cochise

(ca. 1812–1874)

Nothing is known of the birth or early life of this influential Chiricahua Apache chief. Cochise was at peace with white settlers and authorities until the Bascom Affair in 1861, after which he swore vengeance on the whites for having killed his friends. He was such an effective military leader that he forced the U.S. Army and the settlers it was assigned to protect to withdraw from Apache country. In the power vacuum created by the Civil War, Cochise and followers virtually controlled all of the Arizona Territory.

Cochise became principal chief of the Apaches after the death of his father-in-law, Mangas Col_oradas (Red Sleeves) in 1863. He led highly destructive raids and, with about 200 followers, eluded the army for nearly a decade before surrendering to General George Crook in September 1871. Rather than submit to life on the Tularosa Reservation, he escaped in spring 1872 but returned when a dedicated Chiricahua Reservation was created that summer.

Though greatly feared throughout Arizona, Cochise earned the respect of other Indians and the U.S. Army for his daring and skill at arms.

After his escape, Cochise gathered warriors and raided a station on the stage line, killing one employee and taking another hostage. He also captured a passing wagon train, taking eight Mexicans and two Americans prisoner. The Mexicans he immediately burned alive, and he offered his three American captives to Bascom in a prisoner exchange. When Bascom refused, Cochise killed them. On February 14, 1861, Bascom retaliated by hanging his prisoners. This prompted Cochise to vow to exterminate all Americans in Arizona Territory. According to the U.S. Army, the resulting "Apache Uprising" lasted from 1861 to 1863; in fact, violence between whites and Apaches spanned a quarter century.

As war with the Apaches had begun with an incident that should have been readily contained, so war with the Navajos began over a trivial matter. Fort Lyon (formerly Fort Fauntleroy), New Mexico Territory, served as a distribution point for rations guaranteed by treaty to local Navajos. In September 1861 the fort also became the site of a series of "friendly" horse races between Indians and militia members. A dispute over one race resulted in the shooting deaths of thirty to forty Indians, including women and children. This incident incited a general war, which was fought simultaneously with the Apache Uprising. Given the army's depleted strength in the region due to the outbreak of the Civil War in April 1861, both Indian wars proved protracted and very destructive. (The area was also left vulnerable to raids by the Utes, Comanches, and Kiowas.)

The Apache Uprising brought terror to the settlements and trade routes between El Paso and Tucson, both at the hands of Cochise and his ally and father-in-law, the Mimbreño Apache chief Mangas Coloradas. When federal troops largely withdrew from the region to avoid being overwhelmed by superior Confederate troops who had invaded Arizona and New Mexico, Cochise and Mangas Coloradas incor-

CHRONOLOGY OF THE APACHE AND NAVAJO WAR

1860

- Pinal Apaches raid John Ward's ranch near Fort Buchanan, Arizona.

1861

Feb. 4 Cochise, a prominent Apache leader, and others are falsely arrested for the raid on Ward's ranch. Cochise escapes, swears vengeance, and the Apache phase of the Apache and Navajo War begins.

Feb. 14 Cochise kills three hostages, and members of Cochise's family are hanged in response. Cochise vows to kill all Americans in Arizona Territory.

Apr. 12 The American Civil War begins.

July Mescalero Apaches begin routinely raiding the herds of Arizona ranchers.

Sept. A disputed horse race between the Navajo chief Manuelito and a militia officer at Fort Lyon, New Mexico, starts the Navajo phase of the Apache and Navajo War.

1862

July 15 Cochise ambushes the advance guard of Brigadier General James Henry Carleton's "California Column."

1863

Jan. 17 During a truce, the Apache war leader Mangas Coloradas is captured and killed. The war intensifies.

June Carleton sets a deadline of July 20, 1863, for all Navajos to withdraw to the reservation.

July 20 Carleton sends Kit Carson with a regiment to make war on the Navajos.

Sept. Navajos begin to surrender.

1864

Jan. 12 Carson and Captain Albert H. Pfeiffer attack the Navajo stronghold at Canyon de Chelly, Arizona.

Jan. 15 Navajos surrender in large numbers and march off to the Bosque Redondo reservation.

Late 1864 The Bosque Redondo becomes dangerously overcrowded and undersupplied.

1868

June 1 A treaty allows the Navajos to return to their homeland, now designated as their new reservation. The Apache and Navajo War ends, although raiding continues sporadically.

This is the only known authentic portrait of Apache chief Cochise. Respected and feared for his courage and military prowess, Cochise was a relentless foe of white settlers and authorities in Arizona Territory from 1861 to 1871.

rectly assumed that they were withdrawing from fear of them. Emboldened, beginning in July 1861, the Mescalero Apaches raided the herds of local settlers. At last, in July 1862, the Indians saw the approach of 119 infantry soldiers and 7 cavalrymen equipped with two howitzers under the command of Captain Thomas L. Roberts. This was the vanguard of a newly raised federal force, the so-called California Column, organized and commanded by Brigadier General James Henry Carleton. On July 15, these 126 men entered Apache Pass, where they were ambushed by 700 warriors under Cochise. All that saved the badly outnumbered soldiers was their artillery, which held the attackers at bay. In a chance exchange of rifle fire, Mangas Coloradas was wounded. He subsequently recovered, but his wounding was sufficient to break off the battle.

No more was heard from Mangas Coloradas until January 17, 1863, when he agreed to meet with Captain E. D. Shirland, who was serving under Brigadier General Joseph R. West, commander of the southern sector of the Department of New Mexico. Despite his flag of truce, the chief was seized and delivered to West's camp, where he was killed, either while trying to escape or by deliberate execution. This, predictably, intensified the fighting.

Mangas Coloradas

(ca. 1795–1863)

Likely born in territory that is now southern New Mexico, Mangas Coloradas became principal chief of the Mimbreño Apaches by 1837 and was a powerful figure who united the Apaches in resistance to white incursions brought on by the California Gold Rush of 1849.

Mangas Coloradas especially hated the Mexicans, who preyed upon the Mimbreños in order to claim scalp bounties offered by the Mexican government. During the U.S.-Mexican War (Chapter 10), he offered to aid the Americans, but was rebuffed. When the demands of the Civil War removed most U.S. troops from Arizona and New Mexico, Mangas Coloradas joined his son-in-law Cochise in raiding the territories. He was captured in January 1863 and killed (according to official reports) while trying to escape. Most historians believe that he was murdered, perhaps on the orders of an army officer.

Carleton soon became commander of the Department of New Mexico when his predecessor, Edward R. S. Canby, was transferred east to fight the Civil War. Carleton called on the celebrated Indian fighter Kit Carson to pursue the Mescalero Apaches mercilessly. Carson followed orders, but, holding an abiding respect for the Mescaleros, he also arranged for five chiefs to visit Santa Fe for peace talks with Carleton. En route, two of the chiefs met a detachment of soldiers commanded by Captain James (Paddy) Graydon. Graydon offered the chiefs beef and flour for the journey, and the two parties continued along their separate ways. A short time later, however, they met once again in one of those incidents of senseless brutality that were repeated with heartbreaking regularity throughout the history of Indian-white relations. Graydon went into the chiefs' camp, shared a drink with them and then, unaccountably, shot and killed both of them. When the other three chiefs Carson had sent to Carleton reached the commander, they told him that they no longer had the heart to fight and threw themselves on his mercy. Carleton proposed to send them and all other Navajos to a forty-square-mile reservation at the Bosque Redondo on the Pecos River in New Mexico. Some agreed to retire to the reservation, but others fled to Mexico.

While Kit Carson pursued and fought the Mescaleros, four companies of his First New Mexico Volunteer Cavalry established Fort Wingate on the border of Navajo country. This induced eighteen Navajo chiefs, including prominent leaders and brothers Delgadito and Barboncito, to call on Carleton at Santa Fe. To their proposals of peace, Carleton replied that their only alternative to continued war was to lead their people to the Bosque Redondo. He set a deadline of July 20, 1863, for this removal, after which, he warned, every Navajo would be regarded as hostile. Barboncito replied that rather than live on the desolate Bosque, he would die.

When the July 20 deadline came and went, Kit Carson marched out of Fort Wingate with 736 men and officers to make war on the Navajos. From the end of September 1863 through January 1864, the Indians retreated to the Bosque Redondo, and by late 1864 three-quarters of the Navajo tribe had accepted concentration on the reservation, which was now overcrowded and undersupplied. In 1868 Manuelito, Barboncito, and other chiefs were permitted to journey to Washington, D.C., to explain the horrors of the reservation to President Andrew Johnson. A month later, peace commissioners visited the Bosque Redondo and concluded that conditions were desperate. This motivated a treaty on June 1, 1868, which returned the Indians to the heart of their homeland, Canyon de Chelly. With this, the war ended, although sporadic raids and fighting continued for years.

Official Responses to the Cochise Incident and the Bascom Affair

History records the "Bascom Affair"—Second Lieutenant George N. Bascom's unjustified arrest of Cochise and the execution of his prisoners—as the brash bumbling of an inexperienced young officer, which started the Apache Uprising phase of the Apache and Navajo War and initiated nearly a quarter century of chronic violence between whites and Apaches. Bascom's superiors, however, commended the young second lieutenant and promoted him to captain, a rank he enjoyed briefly before being killed by Confederate troops at the Battle of Valverde, New Mexico, in 1862. Bascom's promotion vividly illustrates the military attitude toward Indians: the army typically identified them as the enemy, period, and rarely attempted to understand their side of a given dispute, let alone find an alternative to armed conflict. Not only was this attitude inherently unjust, it usually led to costly and senseless warfare.

Enforcing Indian Policy in the West: The Impact of the Civil War

The Civil War was fought mainly east of the Mississippi; however, it had a profound effect on white-Indian relations in the American West. The officer corps of the U.S. Army, tiny as it was at the outbreak of the war, was reduced even further as significant numbers of officers resigned their commissions to join the Confederate forces. The West was especially hard hit: approximately two-thirds of the officers in the region left the U.S. Army. Moreover, many of the best remaining officers were tapped for service back east. The general withdrawal of army garrisons from western outposts left the region open to Indian raids and other depredations. In most places, the implementation of Indian policy had to be suspended. Many Indians interpreted the withdrawal of so many "bluecoats" as surrender to *them,* thus encouraging more raids.

Although white residents of the Southwest suffered significantly during this period, their plight received little attention from a government and public preoccupied with the Civil War. Likewise, the single-minded determination of James Henry Carleton was overlooked, and he was thereby allowed to pursue the impractical and inhumane course of forcibly herding large numbers of people onto a reservation completely inadequate to support them.

Reservation Policy and the Commissioner's Report of 1862

The crisis of white-Indian violence in the Southwest produced two effects, as the 1862 Annual Report of the Commissioner of Indian Affairs (see Chapter 12) reveals. Indian affairs commissioner William P. Dole called for the strictest possible confinement of Indians to reservations. He specified, however, that such confinement was to last only until the Indians had been "gradually taught [to become] accustomed to the idea of individual property." When this was achieved, Dole advised, the Indians should be allotted lands in severalty and thereby integrated into white "civilization."

Dole's report suggests the degree to which Indian policy during the 1860s was largely a matter of wishful thinking masking the most repressive measures. On the one hand, the policy proposed integration into civilization and full citizenship for the Indians. Vaguely, the policy suggested that this integration would be achieved through education. Yet, on the other hand, confinement to reservations was to be strictly enforced in the meantime. How the Indians were to be educated and integrated into the larger white society while they were confined by force simply was not discussed in official documents.

Report of the Doolittle Committee (1867)

With the end of the Civil War, the federal government turned its attention back to the subject of Indian policy. Even before the war ended, Congress created, on March 3, 1865, a joint special committee to study the condition of the Indians and to make recommendations for Indian policy. The chairman of the committee, Wisconsin senator James Doolittle, submitted the report, **Condition of the Indian Tribes,** on January 26, 1867. The document reflects the increasingly reformist tenor of federal Indian policy during the administrations of presidents Andrew Johnson and Ulysses S. Grant.

The first issue the committee studied was the rapid decline in the numbers of "Indians everywhere, with the exception of the tribes within the Indian Territory." The committee concluded that the reduction in population was caused by disease, "intemperance," wars ("among themselves and with the whites"), and "by the steady and resistless emigration of white men into the territories of the west." This influx, the committee concluded, confines "the Indians to still narrower limits [and] destroys that game which, in their normal state, constitutes their principal means of subsistence." To this empirical observation, the committee added a conclusion reflecting the racism that prevailed even among those with the best of intentions: the diminution of the Indians resulted from "the irrepressible conflict between a superior and inferior race when brought in presence of each other."

Whatever else the committee concluded, the report asserted that conflict between whites and Indians was both *natural* and *inevitable.* Despite this

Condition of the Indian Tribes, 1867

Second. The committee are of opinion that in a large majority of cases Indian wars are to be traced to the aggressions of lawless white men, always to be found upon the frontier. . . . Such is the rule of savage warfare, and it is difficult if not impossible to restrain white men, especially white men upon the frontiers, from adopting the same mode of warfare against the Indians. The indiscriminate slaughter of men, women, and children has frequently occurred in the history of Indian wars. . . .

Third. Another potent cause of [the Indians'] decay is to be found in the loss of their hunting grounds and in the destruction of that game upon which the Indian subsists. This cause, always powerful, has of late greatly increased. . . .

. . . [T]he discovery of gold and silver in California, and in all the mountain territories, poured a flood of hardy and adventurous miners across those plains, and into all the valleys and gorges of the mountains from the east.

Two lines of railroad are rapidly crossing the plains, one by the valley of the Platte, and the other by the Smoky Hill. They will soon reach the Rocky mountains, crossing the centre of the great buffalo range in two lines from east to west. It is to be doubted if the buffalo in his migrations will many times cross a railroad where trains are passing and repassing, and with the disappearance of the buffalo from this immense region, all the powerful tribes of the plains will inevitably disappear. . . .

On the other hand, the emigration from California and Oregon into the Territories from the west is filling every valley and gorge of the mountains with the most energetic and fearless men in the world. In those wild regions, where no civil law has ever been administered, and where our military forces have scarcely penetrated, these adventurers are practically without any law, except such as they impose upon themselves, viz: the law of necessity and of self-defence.

Even after territorial governments are established over them in form by Congress, the population is so sparse and the administration of the civil law so feeble that the people are practically without any law but their own whim. In their eager search for gold or fertile tracts of land, the boundaries of Indian reservations are wholly disregarded; conflicts ensue; exterminating wars follow, in which the Indian is, of course, at the last, overwhelmed if not destroyed.

Excerpted from Francis Paul Prucha, ed., *Documents of United States Indian Policy,* 2d ed. (Lincoln: University of Nebraska Press, 1990), 103.

---

controlling assertion, the committee boldly stated what to many observers had long been obvious: "The committee are of opinion that in a large majority of cases Indian wars are to be traced to the aggressions of lawless white men, always to be found upon the frontier." Enforcement of federal laws, the committee concluded, was essential to stopping this aggression. However, the committee upheld the inclusion of the Bureau of Indian Affairs in the Department of the Interior rather than in the Department of War. The committee believed that this would produce a more impartial attitude with regard to resolving conflicts between Indians and local whites, and that it would also result in more humane treatment of the Indians themselves. In practice, retaining authority for Indian affairs within the civilian Department of the Interior created friction with local military officials, which contributed to inadequate and often grudging enforcement of policy in the field.

Finally, the committee recognized that, regardless of policy, government officers charged with administering Indian affairs were often inefficient, uncaring, or downright corrupt. The committee recommended the creation of boards of inspection to reform the Bureau of Indian Affairs and its practices.

The Work of the Indian Peace Commission (1867–1868)

The ascension of the "Radical Republican" wing in Congress at the end of the Civil War brought with it not only a zeal to reform the South through an aggressive program of Reconstruction, but also a new determination to "solve" the problems of white-Indian relations in the West once and for all. The violence of the Civil War era in the Southwest (and throughout the Plains) moved Congress to launch what might be described as a major "peace offensive." On July 20, 1867, Congress passed **An Act to Establish Peace with Certain Hostile Indian Tribes.** The legislation created a peace commission composed of high-ranking army officers and civilian officials with the power to make treaties as well as to identify new sites for reservations and to obtain them as "permanent homes" for Indians not yet confined to reservations. The act stipulated that the Indians domiciled on the new reservations were to "support themselves by agricultural and pastoral pursuits."

Although the brief of the peace commission and the implementation of the "peace offensive" were ambitious, the policy behind them was little different from earlier attempts at reform. Establishing peace still was seen as requiring the separation of whites and Indians, which meant confinement of the Indians to reservations. Moreover, the Indians' conversion to a sedentary reservation life required their acceptance of "agricultural and pastoral pursuits," a way of life eminently unsuited to most of the Plains tribes.

On January 7, 1868, the Peace Commission issued its first report (**Report of the Indian Peace Commission**). The commissioners reported that, in making treaties with the Indians, "We have done the best we could under the circumstances, but it is now rather late in the day to think of obliterating from the minds of the present generation the remembrance of wrong. . . . Have we been uniformly unjust? We answer, unhesitatingly, yes!"

To redress the long history of injustice and the grossly inadequate or corrupt implementation of policy, the commission recommended a more vig-

An Act to Establish Peace with Certain Hostile Indian Tribes, 1867

Be it enacted . . . , That the President of the United States be, and he is hereby, authorized to appoint a commission . . . to call together the chiefs and headmen of such bands or tribes of Indians as are now waging war against the United States or committing depredations upon the people thereof, to ascertain the alleged reasons for their acts of hostility, and in their discretion, under the direction of the President, to make and conclude with said bands or tribes such treaty stipulations, subject to the action of the Senate, as may remove all just causes of complaint on their part, and at the same time establish security for person and property along the lines of railroad now being constructed to the Pacific and other thoroughfares of travel to the western Territories, and such as will most likely insure civilization for the Indians and peace and safety for the whites.

Sec. 2. *And be it further enacted,* That said commissioners are required to examine and select a district or districts of country having sufficient area to receive all the Indian tribes now occupying territory east of the Rocky mountains, not now peacefully residing on permanent reservations under treaty stipulations, to which the government has the right of occupation or to which said commissioners can obtain the right of occupation, and in which district or districts there shall be sufficient tillable or grazing land to enable the said tribes, respectively, to support themselves by agricultural and pastoral pursuits.

Excerpted from Francis Paul Prucha, ed., *Documents of United States Indian Policy,* 2d ed. (Lincoln: University of Nebraska Press, 1990), 105–106.

orous policy aimed at bringing the Indians into white civilization more quickly. This was to be effected simply by creating more humane reservations, governed by more liberal policies. The commissioners were appalled by conditions at the Bosque Redondo, where, they said, the Navajos were "held as prisoners." But, they said, the Bosque was just the most egregious example of how the reservation had been universally perverted from places where Indians were expected to learn to be self-supporting members of civilization to cruel and profoundly inhumane prison camps.

In the case of the Navajos, the commissioners recommended making a treaty with them "or their consent in some way [be] obtained, to remove [them from the Bosque Redondo] to the southern district selected by us, where they may soon be made self-supporting."

Congressional Debate on Indian Treaties

At the height of the reform movement in Indian policy, while the Peace Commission was making its treaties, the House of Representatives opened a debate on treaty making itself. The debate was ignited by a treaty negotiated with the Osage Indians of Kansas, by which vast lands ceded by the Osage were immediately turned over to a railroad corporation. Representatives Sidney Clarke of Kansas and Glenni W. Scofield of Pennsylvania argued on June 18, 1868, that such use of Indian lands, instead of properly turning them to the public domain, was inherently wrong and the result of the corruption of the treaty-making authority given to the superintendents of Indian affairs. Through the superintendents, tribes could be made vulnerable to the overtures of special interests, who could thereby acquire Indian lands under cover of a federal treaty. Scofield declared, "I intend never to give my consent to allowing the treaty-making power to add to or diminish the domain of this country. It has no power either to cede away the State of Maine to Great Britain or to acquire new territory on the Northwest"; therefore, Scofield implied, treaty making could not be used for the cession or the acquisition of land.

Report of the Indian Peace Commission, 1868

In making treaties it was enjoined on us to remove, if possible, the causes of complaint on the part of the Indians. This would be no easy task. We have done the best we could under the circumstances, but it is now rather late in the day to think of obliterating from the minds of the present generation the remembrance of wrong. Among civilized men war usually springs from a sense of injustice. The best possible way then to avoid war is to do no act of injustice. When we learn that the same rule holds good with Indians, the chief difficulty is removed. But, it is said our wars with them have been almost constant. Have we been uniformly unjust? We answer, unhesitatingly, yes! We are aware that the masses of our people have felt kindly toward them, and the legislation of Congress has always been conceived in the best intentions, but it has been erroneous in fact or perverted in execution. Nobody pays any attention to Indian matters. This is a deplorable fact. Members of Congress understand the negro question, and talk learnedly of finance, and other problems of political economy, but when the progress of settlement reaches the Indian's home, the only question considered is, "how best to get his lands." When they are obtained the Indian is lost sight of. While our missionary societies and benevolent associations have annually collected thousands of dollars from the charitable, to be sent to Asia and Africa for purposes of civilization, scarcely a dollar is expended or a thought bestowed on the civilization of Indians at our very doors. Is it because the Indians are not worth the effort at civilization? Or is it because our people, who have grown rich in the occupation of their former lands—too often taken by force or procured in fraud—will not contribute?

Excerpted from Francis Paul Prucha, ed., *Documents of United States Indian Policy,* 2d ed. (Lincoln: University of Nebraska Press), 106–107.

As a result of this debate, opposition to all treaty making with the Indians grew, and in 1871 Congress legislated both an end to treaty making and summarily nullified all existing treaties. The fiction that Indian tribes effectively constituted foreign nations was abandoned, and the tribes were redefined as special internal domestic nations. Along with the Dawes Severalty Act of 1887 (see Chapter 27), calling a halt to treaty making was the boldest step Congress took toward the integration of Indians into what the legislators understood as "civilization."

BIBLIOGRAPHY

Axelrod, Alan. *Chronicle of the Indian Wars: From Colonial Times to Wounded Knee.* New York: Macmillan General Reference, 1993.

Debo, Angie. *A History of the Indians in the United States.* Norman: University of Oklahoma Press, 1977.

McDermott, John D. *A Guide to the Indian Wars of the West.* Lincoln: University of Nebraska Press, 1998.

McNitt, Frank. *Navajo Wars: Military Campaigns, Slave Raids, and Reprisals.* Albuquerque: University of New Mexico Press, 1990.

Michno, Gregory F. *Encyclopedia of Indian Wars: Western Battles and Skirmishes 1850–1890.* Missoula, Mont: Mountain Press Publishing Company, 2003.

Phillips, Charles, and Alan Axelrod, eds. *The Encyclopedia of the American West.* 4 vols. New York: Macmillan General Reference, 1996.

Prucha, Francis P. *The Great Father: The United States Government and the American Indians.* Lincoln: University of Nebraska Press, 1984.

Reedstrom, Ernest Lisle. *Apache Wars: An Illustrated Battle History.* New York: Barnes & Noble Books, 1995.

Utley, Robert M. *Indian Wars.* New York: Mariner Books, 2002.

CHAPTER 15

CIVIL WAR PRELUDE

(1854–1861)

At Issue

During the turbulent decade leading up to the Civil War, the Kansas-Nebraska Act introduced "popular sovereignty," making the question of whether a territory would enter the Union as a slave state or a free state a matter for the local population, not the federal government, to decide. Proslavery and antislavery settlers in Kansas wanted to ensure, by any means necessary, that the issue would be decided in their favor.

The Conflict

On May 30, 1854, President Franklin Pierce signed into law the Kansas-Nebraska Act, thereby abrogating federal authority over slavery and empowering Kansans and Nebraskans to decide whether they would enter the Union as slave or free states. No one doubted that Nebraska would vote itself free, but Kansas was very much in play. Eastern abolitionists organized the Emigrant Aid Society to finance antislavery settlers in Kansas. In response, thousands of proslavery Missourians streamed across the border into Kansas in March 1855 to vote—illegally—in favor of a proslavery territorial legislature. Having cast their ballots, they returned home. The number of interlopers overwhelmed that of legitimate Kansas residents and voted in a proslavery territorial legislature. In response, thousands of "Free Soilers" poured into Kansas and set up their own legislature and capital in the town of Lawrence. Despite federal recognition of the proslavery legislature, the Free Soil legislature petitioned Congress for admission to the Union as a free state. Violence soon broke out, beginning with the murder of a prominent abolitionist in November 1855.

The conflict was first called the Wakarusa War because a number of armed clashes occurred along the Wakarusa River near Lawrence from November 26 to December 7, 1855; casualties, however, were light. David R. Atchison, a proslavery senator, resigned his Senate seat to organize and lead an army of proslavery Missourians into Kansas to raid Lawrence on May 21, 1856. These "border ruffians" put a hotel and a few houses to the torch, destroyed an abolitionist printing press, and "arrested" several Free Soil leaders and killed three others. A fanatical abolitionist named John Brown retaliated three days later by leading a saber-wielding band in an attack against five proslavery settlers on the Pottawatomie Creek. The hapless five men were hacked to death and then mutilated, even though none of them had been involved in the Lawrence raid. The "Sack of Lawrence" and the "Pottawatomie Massacre" threw Kansas into years of chaotic guerrilla warfare and anarchic civil insurrection. With the help of federal troops brought in by Kansas governor John Geary in the fall of 1856, the first wave of violence was gradually quelled, but not before some 200 people had been killed.

Although the physical violence abated, an ideological war continued as the Kansas legislature, still dominated by proslavery representatives, set up a constitutional convention over Governor Geary's veto. Held in the town of Lecompton in November

1857, it issued the so-called Lecompton Constitution, while the legislature prepared a popular referendum phrased such that *either* a yes or no vote would result in adoption of the Lecompton document. Not surprisingly, the constitution was adopted on December 21, 1857, and not only legalized slavery, but also made it permanent by forbidding future voters from ever outlawing the institution. Although the Free Soilers had boycotted the referendum, the proslavery faction submitted the constitution to Congress with an application for statehood. President James Buchanan accepted the Lecompton Constitution, but Senator Stephen Douglas of Illinois denounced it as a fraud and led an opposition movement in Congress, and the issue became deadlocked. This led to renewed violence in what the nation now called "Bleeding Kansas," and, once again, federal troops were called in early in 1858.

Order was largely restored by 1860, but a low level of violence continued until the outbreak of the Civil War in April 1861. During the Civil War, Kansas was frequently the scene of guerrilla-style combat.

Missouri Compromise (1820)

The Louisiana Purchase of 1803 added a huge territory to the United States, which would eventually have to be divided into states. The admission of each new state to the Union was an assault on the delicate congressional balance between representatives of slave states and free states. In 1818–1819 the petition of the Missouri Territory for admission to statehood as a slave state created a major crisis. At the time, the U.S. Senate consisted of twenty-two senators from northern states and twenty-two from southern states. The addition of a new slaveholding

---

CHRONOLOGY OF THE CIVIL WAR PRELUDE

1854

May 30 The Kansas-Nebraska Act is signed.

Aug. 1 Twenty-nine northern emigrants (mostly from Massachusetts and Vermont) are the first to arrive in Lawrence, Kansas.

1855

Mar. Proslavery Missourians cross into Kansas to elect a proslavery Kansas territorial legislature.

Oct. 7 Abolitionist John Brown arrives in Osawatomie, Kansas.

1856

Apr. A federal congressional investigating committee finds the Kansas elections fraudulent and concludes that the free-state government represents the will of the majority. The federal government does not accept the conclusion and continues to recognize the proslavery legislature.

May 21 Five hundred proslavery advocates raid Lawrence, destroying the Free State Hotel, smashing the presses of two Lawrence newspapers, "arresting" some, and killing three people.

May 24 In retaliation for the Lawrence raid, John Brown leads a band that murders five proslavery men in the Pottawatomie massacre.

Aug. Osawatomie is attacked by 400 proslavery Missourians. John Brown and forty other men defend the town, but it is sacked. Brown's son Frederick is killed.

1857–1860

- Guerilla warfare seizes Kansas.

1859

July A constitutional convention—the territory's fourth—gathers at Wyandotte. For the first time, a free-state majority is in control.

Oct. The free-state constitution is accepted by a vote of the people.

Oct. 16 Brown's Raid on Harpers Ferry (Virginia)

1860

Feb. 23 The territorial legislature passes a bill, over the governor's veto, abolishing slavery in Kansas.

1862

Jan. 29 Kansas, having voted itself free, becomes the thirty-fourth state.

state would suddenly shift the balance. Seeking a means of blunting the impact of Missouri statehood, Representative James Tallmadge of New York introduced an amendment to the Missouri statehood bill that called for a ban on introducing additional slaves into the state, while maintaining slaves in their current status. Slaves subsequently born in the state would be automatically emancipated at age twenty-five. In this way, by attrition, slavery would be eliminated from Missouri.

The House passed the Tallmadge amendment, but the Senate rejected it, adjourning without reaching a decision on Missouri statehood. When the Senate reconvened, a long and tortured debate began. Northern senators held that Congress had the right to ban slavery in new states, whereas southerners asserted that the people of the new states had the same right as those of the original thirteen: to determine for themselves whether they would allow slavery. Finally, in March 1820, the Missouri Compromise was cobbled together. Missouri was admitted to the Union as a slave state, but Maine (until then a part of Massachusetts) was admitted as a free state at the same time. This maintained the slave state–free state balance in Congress. As for the future, the Missouri Compromise called for a line to be drawn across the territory of the Louisiana Purchase at latitude 36 degrees, 30 minutes. North of this line, slavery would be permanently banned—except in the case of Missouri.

Compromise of 1850

Like the Louisiana Purchase of 1803, the U.S.-Mexican War of 1846–1848 (Chapter 10) created a crisis because new territory was acquired. The war was popular with most Americans, but during its first year, Congress sought a means of hastening its end with a bill to appropriate $2 million to compensate Mexico for what the lawmakers euphemistically termed "territorial adjustments." Pennsylvania representative David Wilmot introduced an amendment to the bill that would have barred the introduction of slavery into any land acquired by the United States as

Abolitionist John Brown, shown here in the winter of 1856–1857, helped throw Kansas into bloody civil insurrection. He is best known for his raid on Harpers Ferry in October 1859.

a result of the war. The proposed "Wilmot Proviso" incited South Carolina's John C. Calhoun to counter with four proposed resolutions: first, that all territories, including those acquired as a result of the war, would be regarded as the common and joint property of the states; second, that Congress acted as an agent for the states and could, therefore, make no law discriminating among the states or depriving any state of its rights with regard to any territory; third, that the enactment of any national law regarding slavery violated the Constitution and the doctrine of states' rights; and, fourth, that the people had the right to form their state governments as they wished, provided that the proposed government was republican in principle. Calhoun warned that if these resolutions were not accepted, a civil war would surely result.

The purchase of the Mexican land never came to pass, and the Wilmot Proviso was defeated. For the next three years, however, Congress debated how the fragile Missouri Compromise could be bolstered and perpetuated. A stalemate developed, which Senator Lewis Cass of Michigan sought to break by introducing the doctrine of "popular sovereignty." It abrogated federal authority over slavery by providing for the organization of new territories without mention of slavery one way or the other. Only when the territory applied for admission to statehood would the people of the territory itself vote the proposed state slave or free. As for California, acquired as a result of the U.S.-Mexican War, it would be admitted to the Union directly instead of going through the customary interim territorial status. Southerners objected, arguing that California would vote itself free, as would New Mexico (another territory acquired as a result of the war). To address these objections, Senators Henry Clay of Kentucky and Daniel Webster of Massachusetts proposed a new compromise. California would be admitted as a free state, but the other territories acquired as a result of the Mexican War would be subject to popular sovereignty. This meant greatly modifying the Missouri Compromise and its ban on slavery north of latitude 36 degrees, 30 minutes. However, Clay and Webster added a provision ending the slave market in the District of Columbia, which, operating in plain sight of foreign diplomats, was an embarrassment. To sweeten the deal for the South, the Compromise of 1850 package included a strong fugitive slave law, which barred northerners from providing refuge to escaped slaves. The federal government also agreed to assume debts Texas (admitted as a slave state in 1845) had incurred before it was annexed to the United States.

Kansas-Nebraska Act (1854)

The Compromise of 1850 substantially diluted the Missouri Compromise. Four years later, in response to the statehood application of the territories of Kansas and Nebraska, Congress repealed the Missouri Compromise altogether and passed in its stead the **Kansas-Nebraska Act.** This new law extended the doctrine of popular sovereignty to *all* new territories and was not restricted to territories acquired as a result of the U.S.-Mexican War. The Missouri Compromise's artificial geographical boundary between slavery and freedom was eliminated. In this way, the federal government sought to remove itself almost entirely from the slavery issue.

Popular sovereignty was sure to result in a free state of Nebraska, but Kansas, to its south, could go either way. The act was an invitation to conflict, and it touched off a bloody civil war within the territory of Kansas as pro- and antislavery factions fought one another for control.

Kansas-Nebraska Act, 1854

Be it enacted by the Senate and House of Representatives of the United States of America in Congress assembled, That . . . when admitted as a State or States, the said [Kansas-Nebraska] Territory or any portion of the same, shall be received into the Union with or without slavery, as their constitution may prescribe at the time of the admission: Provided, That nothing in this act contained shall be construed to inhibit the government of the United States from dividing said Territory into two or more Territories, in such manner and at such time as Congress shall deem convenient and proper . . . : Provided further, That nothing in this act contained shall be construed to impair the rights of person or property now pertaining the Indians in said Territory' so long as such rights shall remain unextinguished by treaty between the United States and such Indians.

Excerpted from the Avalon Project at Yale Law School, "An Act to Organize the Territories of Nebraska and Kansas," www.yale.edu/lawweb/avalon/kanneb.htm.

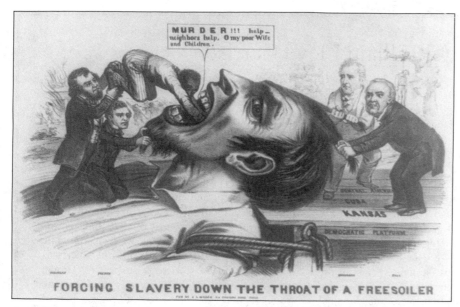

An 1856 cartoon of "Bleeding Kansas" in the wake of the Kansas-Nebraska Act blames the Democrats for the violence unleashed upon antislavery settlers. Democratic senator Stephen A. Douglas and president Franklin Pierce are shown forcing a black man down the throat of a "freesoiler" who is being restrained by presidential nominee James Buchanan and Democratic senator Lewis Cass.

The Abolitionist Movement

The first organized opposition to slavery in America came from the Quakers, who issued a statement against the institution as early as 1724. During the colonial period, slavery was practiced in the North as well as in the South, but the agricultural economy of the northern colonies was built upon small, family-run farms rather than the large plantations found in the South. For this reason, the North had few economic motives for slavery, whereas in the South the institution became an economic imperative. In the North, the absence of the economic incentive was combined with an increasingly widespread moral revulsion to slavery that promoted abolitionism. Rhode Island abolished the institution in 1774, on the eve of the Revolution, and several states outlawed slavery after the war had ended.

The first major abolition group was the American Colonization Society, founded in 1816, which led antislavery protests and mounted a campaign to relocate freed slaves to Liberia, Africa. Three years after the establishment of the American Colonization Society, Quaker abolitionist Elihu Embree began publishing the first periodical devoted to the abolitionist cause, a weekly newspaper in Jonesborough, Tennessee, and in 1820 he added a monthly journal, the *Emancipator*. It was not until 1831, however, when William Lloyd Garrison of Massachusetts began publication of the *Liberator*, his weekly newspaper, that the organized abolition movement became national.

Garrison called for immediate and universal emancipation—an extreme position at the time—and he further called for blacks to be accorded the same political and economic rights whites enjoyed. Garrison and the *Liberator* inspired the four most prominent antislavery interest groups—the Philadelphia Quakers, New York reformers, New England partisans of Garrison, and freed slaves—to form the American Anti-Slavery Society in 1833. Garrison led the society, which demanded the immediate emancipation of slaves without compensation to slave owners. Garrison and his followers made an uncompromising moral appeal, and from 1833 until the Civil War, the abolition movement was divided between radical followers of Garrison and those who advocated various more gradual approaches to emancipation.

William Lloyd Garrison

(1805–1879)

William Lloyd Garrison was raised in the progressive social climate of New England. He became editor of the Boston-based *National Philanthropist* in 1828 and the *Journal of the Times* (Bennington, Vermont). Beginning in 1829, he directed his energies to the cause of abolition, becoming coeditor, with Benjamin Lundy, of the Baltimore-based *Genius of Universal Emancipation.* Garrison's passion for abolition soon outgrew the *Genius,* and in 1831 he founded the *Liberator,* which emerged as the most radical of the American abolitionist journals.

Garrison called for an immediate, unconditional end to slavery as atonement for a "national sin." The year after beginning the *Liberator,* Garrison founded the New England Anti-Slavery Society, and in 1833 he also became a founding member of the American Anti-Slavery Society. Garrison took his radicalism even further in 1837 when he proclaimed advocacy of what he called "Christian perfectionism," which took in the causes of abolition, the rights of women, and nonviolent civil disobedience with regard to the laws of what he deemed a corrupt society. In 1844 he went so far as to call for the peaceful secession of the free northern states from the states of the slaveholding South.

Garrison's radicalism was divisive within the abolitionist movement, and many individuals broke away from the American Anti-Slavery Society to form the American and Foreign Anti-Slavery Society and the Liberty Party. Garrison persisted in his uncompromising course, denouncing the Compromise of 1850, the Kansas-Nebraska Act, and the *Dred Scott* decision, while celebrating John Brown's raid on Harpers Ferry as holy work. Indeed, Garrison's support for Brown marked a break with his former pacifism; he would support Abraham Lincoln's prosecution of the Civil War.

Garrison enthusiastically welcomed the Emancipation Proclamation in 1862 and 1863, but once emancipation had been accomplished, he suddenly turned away from radicalism, backpedaling from his earlier strident call for the immediate integration of "freedmen" (freed slaves) into American society. He also attempted, without success, to dissolve the American Anti-Slavery Society in 1865, and in December of that year, he published the last issue of the *Liberator,* then withdrew entirely from the abolitionist cause and retired from public life.

Responses to Abolitionism

Resistance to abolition was rife in the South, of course, but also in much of the North. Violence was frequent, but it was usually directed against free blacks rather than white abolitionists. There was also dissension among abolitionist groups. The American Anti-Slavery Society, which called for immediate emancipation, was opposed by the American Colonization Society, which promoted a back-to-Africa program as the only feasible means of ending slavery.

Such was the opposition they faced that Garrison and his followers decided to take steps to better integrate blacks into white society. Working with black churches, the abolitionists developed programs to educate blacks in order to facilitate their acceptance by whites. Many whites opposed such programs, however, fearing that educated blacks would take white jobs and would even intermarry with whites. The abolitionist task then became a campaign to change the basic attitudes of whites. Some of the nation's leading literary voices participated, among them the poets James Russell Lowell and John Greenleaf Whittier, as did members of another major emerging interest group, the advocates of women's rights. By the 1840s, the causes of women's rights (including suffrage) and abolition were becoming increasingly intertwined. There was also an increasing demand for free black speakers and writers, especially former slaves. The most prominent of this group were Frederick Douglass, a former fugitive slave from Maryland, and Sojourner Truth, a freed slave from New York.

As abolitionism spread throughout the North and became, in many places, increasingly militant—by actively aiding the escape of slaves by means of the Underground Railroad—the movement all but disappeared in the South, where social pressure and intimidation as well as formalized legislation operated against it. Most southern legislatures went so far as to outlaw the publication and distribution of antislavery literature.

Bleeding Kansas: The Nation Watches

Americans watched the contest between pro- and antislavery forces in Kansas with a mixture of horror and hope. Abolitionist and poet John Greenleaf Whittier celebrated the immigration of northern Free Soilers into the territory in his 1854 poem "The

Kansas Immigrants," which described these settlers as latter-day "Pilgrims," crossing the prairie "sea / To make the West . . . / The homestead of the free!"

Proslavery advocates faced a paradox with regard to slavery in the territories. While they recognized that the institution was not economically feasible in the arid West, where high-production plantations would never be established, they craved the political power the addition of new slave states represented. Accordingly, southern endorsements of the Kansas-Nebraska Act emphasized the constitutional right of slave ownership and (as in the **Arkansas Resolutions on the Kansas-Nebraska Act,** passed on February 9, 1855) accused abolitionists of making "war with the letter and spirit of the Constitution" by aiming "a traitorous blow . . . at the rights of the South and the perpetuity of the Union."

The leaders of the Lafayette (Missouri) Emigration Society published a typical **"Appeal to Southerners to Settle Kansas"** in *De Bow's Review* in May 1856. In the U.S. Senate, Charles Sumner of Massachusetts delivered a long and impassioned speech, **"The Crime against Kansas,"** during May 19–20, 1856, calling the Kansas-Nebraska Act a "swindle" and condemning the illegal influx of proslavery

---

Arkansas Resolutions on the Kansas-Nebraska Act, 1855

Whereas the right of property in slaves is expressly recognized by the Constitution of the United States and is, by virtue of such recognition, guaranteed against unfriendly action on behalf of the general government. *And whereas* each state of the Union, by the fact of being a party to the federal compact, is also a party to the recognition and guarantee aforesaid. *And whereas* the citizens of each state are, in consequence of such citizenship, under the most sacred obligation to conform to the terms and tenor of the compact to which their state is a party: Therefore

1. *Be it resolved by the General Assembly of the State of Arkansas,* that the legislation of Congress repealing the misnamed "compromise" of 1820, and asserting the doctrine of noninterference with

slavery, alike in states and territories, is in strict accordance with the Constitution, and in itself just and expedient, and is for these reasons cordially approved by the people of Arkansas.

2. *Resolved,* that the opposition of Northern states to the legislation above mentioned is at war with the letter and spirit of the Constitution, is grossly violative of plighted faith, and is a traitorous blow aimed at the rights of the South and the perpetuity of the Union.

Excerpted from "Arkansas Resolutions on the Kansas-Nebraska Act," in *Annals of America,* ed. Mortimer J. Adler and Charles Van Doren (Chicago: Encyclopaedia Britannica, 1976), 8: 354.

Missourians into the territory for the purpose of electing a proslavery legislature. On May 22, Representative Preston S. Brooks of South Carolina stormed into the Senate chamber and assaulted Sumner, beating him so severely with his cane that the Massachusetts senator did not recover for nearly three years.

The *Dred Scott* Case and Decision (1857)

While guerrilla warfare raged in Kansas, the Supreme Court handed down its decision on March 6, 1857, in the case of **Dred Scott v. Sandford.** Dred Scott was a fugitive Missouri slave who had belonged to army surgeon John Emerson of St. Louis. Transferred first to Illinois and then to Wisconsin Territory, Emerson took Scott with him to each of these posts. After Emerson's death in 1846, Scott returned to St. Louis, where he sued Emerson's widow for his freedom, arguing that he was now a citizen of Missouri, having been made free by virtue of his terms of residence in Illinois, where slavery was banned by the Northwest Ordinance, and in Wisconsin Territory, where the provisions of the Missouri Compromise made slavery illegal. After a Missouri state court ruled against Scott, his lawyers appealed to the U.S. Supreme Court. The Court's antislavery northern justices, predictably, sided with Scott, whereas the proslavery Southerners upheld the Missouri court's decision. Chief Justice Roger B. Taney, a native of the slaveholding state of Maryland, had the final word.

Taney held that neither free nor enslaved blacks were citizens of the United States and, therefore, could not sue in federal court. This alone would have settled the case, but Taney intended the case to stand as a landmark slavery ruling. He further stated that the Illinois law banning slavery had no force on Scott once he returned to Missouri, a slave state, and that the law in Wisconsin was likewise without force, because the Missouri Compromise was unconstitu-

"An Appeal to Southerners to Settle Kansas," 1856

To the People of the South:

On the undersigned, managers of the "Lafayette Emigration Society," has devolved the important duty of calling the attention of the people of the slaveholding rates to the absolute necessity of immediate action on their part in relation to the settlement of Kansas Territory. The crisis is at hand. Prompt and decisive measures must be adopted, or farewell to Southern rights and independence.

. . . [T]he Abolitionists, staking their all upon the Kansas issue, and hesitating at no means, fair or foul, are moving heaven and earth to render that beautiful territory not only a free state, so-called, but a den of Negro thieves and "higher law" incendiaries.

. . . It requires no great foresight to perceive that if the "higher law" men succeed in this crusade, it will be but the commencement of a war upon the institutions of the South, which will continue until slavery shall cease to exist in any of the states or the Union is dissolved.

How, then, shall these impending evils be avoided? The answer is obvious. *Settle the territory with emigrants from the South.* The population of the territory at this time is about equal—as many proslavery settlers as Abolitionists; but the fanatics have emissaries in all the free states—in almost every village—and by misrepresentation and falsehood are engaged in collecting money and enlisting men to tyrannize over the South. Is it in the nature of Southern men to submit without resistance, to look to the North for their laws and institutions? We do not believe it!

Excerpted from "Appeal to Southerners to Settle Kansas," in *Annals of America,* ed. Mortimer J. Adler and Charles Van Doren (Chicago: Encyclopaedia Britannica, 1976), 8:365–366.

"The Crime against Kansas," 1856

It belongs to me now, in the first place, to expose the Crime Against Kansas in its origin and extent. Logically this is the beginning of the argument. I say crime, and deliberately adopt this strongest term as better than any other denoting the consummate transgression. I would go further if language could further go. It is the *crime of crimes* — passing far the old *crimen majestatis,* pursued with vengeance by the laws of Rome, and containing all other crimes, as the greater stains the less. I do not go too far when I call it the *crime against nature,* from which soul recoils and which language refuses to describe. . . .

Sir, the Nebraska Bill was in every respect a swindle. It was a swindle by the South of the North. It was, on the part of those who had already completely enjoyed their share of the Missouri Compromise, a swindle of those whose share was yet absolutely untouched; and the plea of unconstitutionality set up—like the plea of usury after the borrowed money has been enjoyed—did not make it less a swindle. Urged as a bill of peace, it was a swindle of the whole country. Urged as opening the doors to slave masters with their slaves, it was a swindle of the asserted doctrine of popular sovereignty. Urged as

sanctioning popular sovereignty, it was a swindle of the asserted rights of slave masters. It was a swindle of a broad territory, thus cheated of protection against slavery. It was a swindle of a great cause, early espoused by Washington, Franklin, and Jefferson, surrounded by the best fathers of the republic. Sir, it was a swindle of God-given inalienable rights. Turn it over; look at it on all sides, and it is everywhere a swindle; and if the word I now employ has not the authority of classical usage, it has, on this occasion, the indubitable authority of fitness. No other word will adequately express the mingled meanness and wickedness of the cheat.

. . . Time does not allow, nor does the occasion require that I should stop to dwell on this transparent device [popular sovereignty] to cover a transcendent wrong. Suffice it to say that slavery is in itself an arrogant denial of human rights, and by no human reason can the power to establish such a wrong be placed among the attributes of any just sovereignty.

Excerpted from Charles Sumner, "The Crime against Kansas," in *Annals of America* ed. Mortimer J. Adler and Charles Van Doren (Chicago: Encyclopaedia Britannica, 1976), 8:367–368.

tional—a violation of the Fifth Amendment, barring the government from depriving an individual of "life, liberty, or property" without due process of law.

The *Dred Scott* decision galvanized the abolitionist movement, which asserted that the highest court in the land had been so corrupted by slave interests that it misused the Bill of Rights to *deny* freedom. More important, the decision made further compromises impossible. By defining slavery as an issue of property, a Fifth Amendment issue, the decision mandated the protection of slavery in all the states, regardless of whether a given state permitted slavery. As abolitionists saw it, if the rights of slaveholders had to be upheld universally as long as slavery existed, then slavery had to be abolished universally.

Creation of the Republican Party

In 1840 the abolitionist movement produced a political party, the Liberty Party, which nominated James G. Birney, a former slaveholder born in Kentucky, as its first candidate for president. Birney ran in 1840 and 1844. The abolitionist movement also spawned the Free Soil Party, which fielded candidates in the elections of 1848. In 1854 the Republican Party absorbed the Free Soil Party and other reform and antislavery parties. It became the abolitionist's party of choice and rapidly developed into a major political force.

John Brown's Raid on Harpers Ferry

The fighting in "Bleeding Kansas" produced a dramatic national figure who embodied the most

Supreme Court Decision in Dred Scott v. Sandford (1857)

Can a negro, whose ancestors were imported into this country, and sold as slaves, become a member of the political community formed and brought into existence by the Constitution of the United States, and as such become entitled to all the rights, and privileges, and immunities, guarantied by that instrument to the citizen? One of which rights is the privilege of suing in a court of the United States in the cases specified in the Constitution.

We think [people of African ancestry] are not [citizens], and that they are not included, and were not intended to be included, under the word "citizens" in the Constitution, and can therefore claim none of the rights and privileges which that instrument provides for and secures to citizens of the United States.

. . . [T]he legislation and histories of the times, and the language used in the Declaration of Independence, show, that neither the class of persons who had been imported as slaves, nor their descendants, whether they had become free or not, were then acknowledged as a part of the people, nor intended to be included in the general words used in that memorable instrument. . . .

The act of Congress, upon which the plaintiff relies, declares that slavery and involuntary servitude, except as a punishment for crime, shall be forever prohibited in all that part of the territory ceded by France, under the name of Louisiana, which lies north of thirty-six degrees thirty minutes north latitude, and not included within the limits of Missouri. And the difficulty which meets us at the threshold of this part of the inquiry is, whether Congress was

authorized to pass this law under any of the powers granted to it by the Constitution; for if the authority is not given by that instrument, it is the duty of this court to declare it void and inoperative, and incapable of conferring freedom upon any one who is held as a slave under the laws of any one of the States.

There is certainly no power given by the Constitution to the Federal Government to establish or maintain colonies bordering on the United States or at a distance, to be ruled and governed at its own pleasure; nor to enlarge its territorial limits in any way, except by the admission of new States. That power is plainly given; and if a new State is admitted, it needs no further legislation by Congress, because the Constitution itself defines the relative rights and powers, and duties of the State, and the citizens of the State, and the Federal Government. But no power is given to acquire a Territory to be held and governed permanently in that character.

. . . [I]t may be safely assumed that citizens of the United States who migrate to a Territory belonging to the people of the United States, cannot be ruled as mere colonists, dependent upon the will of the General Government. . . .

. . . The powers of the Government and the rights and privileges of the citizen are regulated and plainly defined by the Constitution itself. And when the Territory becomes a part of the United States, the Federal Government enters into possession in the character impressed upon it by those who created it. It enters upon it with its powers over the citizen strictly defined, and limited by the Constitution. . . . It has no

extreme aspects of radical abolitionism. John Brown had been a drifter, unable to find a meaningful life for himself or his family, until he discovered the cause of abolition in Kansas. After rising to command the territory's so-called Free Soil Militia, in 1857 Brown moved from Kansas to Boston. There, with the support of six prominent abolitionists—Samuel Gridley Rowe, Thomas Wentworth Higginson, Theodore Parker, Franklin Sanborn, George L. Stearns, and Gerrit Smith—he raised the cash to

finance a raid he was planning on the federal arsenal at Harpers Ferry, Virginia (present-day West Virginia). His plan was to use the guns and ammunition appropriated from the arsenal to arm the slaves of the South for a massive rebellion.

Brown led sixteen white men and five black men to the federal arsenal and armory at the confluence of the Shenandoah and Potomac rivers during the night of October 16, 1859. He and his band quickly took the armory and Hall's Rifle Works nearby, then hun-

power of any kind beyond it; and it cannot, when it enters a Territory of the United States, put off its character, and assume discretionary or despotic powers which the Constitution has denied to it.

. . . [T]he rights of private property have been guarded with . . . care. Thus the rights of property are united with the rights of person, and placed on the same ground by the fifth amendment to the Constitution, which provides that no person shall be deprived of life, liberty, and property, without due process of law. And an act of Congress which deprives a citizen of the United States of his liberty or property, merely because he came himself or brought his property into a particular Territory of the United States, and who had committed no offence against the laws, could hardly be dignified with the name of due process of law.

Upon these considerations, it is the opinion of the court that the act of Congress which prohibited a citizen from holding and owning property of this kind in the territory of the United States north of the line therein mentioned, is not warranted by the Constitution, and is therefore void; and that neither Dred Scott himself, nor any of his family, were made free by being carried into this territory; even if they had been carried there by the owner, with the intention of becoming a permanent resident.

But there is another point in the case which depends on State power and State law. And it is contended, on the part of the plaintiff, that he is made free by being taken to Rock Island, in the State of Illinois, independently of his residence in the territory of the United States; and being so made free, he was not again reduced to a state of slavery by being brought back to Missouri.

. . . [I]n the case of Strader et al. *v.* Graham . . . the slaves had been taken from Kentucky to Ohio, with the consent of the owner, and afterwards brought back to Kentucky. And this court held that their status or condition, as free or slave, depended upon the laws of Kentucky, when they were brought back into that State, and not of Ohio. . . .

So in this case. As Scott was a slave when taken into the State of Illinois by his owner, and was there held as such, and brought back in that character, his status, as free or slave, depended on the laws of Missouri, and not of Illinois.

Upon the whole, therefore, it is the judgment of this court, that it appears by the record before us that the plaintiff in error is not a citizen of Missouri, in the sense in which that word is used in the Constitution; and that the Circuit Court of the United States, for that reason, had no jurisdiction in the case, and could give no judgment in it. Its judgment for the defendant must, consequently, be reversed, and a mandate issued, directing the suit to be dismissed for want of jurisdiction.

Excerpted from Street Law and the Supreme Court Historical Society, "*Dred Scott v. Sandford,*" in *Landmark Cases of the Supreme Court,* www.landmarkcases.org/dredscott/majority.html.

---

kered down to defend their prize, holding hostage some sixty residents of Harpers Ferry, including the great-grandnephew of George Washington. Brown dispatched two of his black "soldiers" to alert local slaves in the belief that they would incite thousands to rise up in rebellion.

Nothing of the kind occurred, however, and the citizens of Harpers Ferry surrounded the arsenal, opened fire, and killed two of the abolitionist's sons. Sporadic combat continued throughout the morning and afternoon, when the survivors barricaded themselves and their hostages in a firehouse adjacent to the armory. Lieutenant Colonel Robert E. Lee, U.S. Army, and his former West Point student, Lieutenant James Ewell Brown "Jeb" Stuart, arrived, commanding the nearest available troops, a company of marines.

On the morning of the October 18, Lee sent Stuart under a flag of truce to demand Brown's surrender. When Brown refused, Stuart signaled for the

John Brown

(1800–1859)

A native of Torrington, Connecticut, Brown grew up to be a drifter, settling for brief periods in Ohio, Pennsylvania, Massachusetts, and New York and finding catch-as-catch-can employment as a sheep drover, tanner, wool trader, farmer, and land speculator. Brown, who was white, settled his family in a black community founded at North Elba, New York, in 1849 on land donated by the abolitionist philanthropist Gerrit Smith. It was while he lived at North Elba that Brown resolved to take bold action to end slavery. With this in mind, he and five of his sons moved to Kansas Territory in 1855 to join forces with the antislavery settlers vying with proslavery settlers for control of the territory.

Brown settled at Osawatomie, where he became leader of local Free Soil guerrillas. In the spring of 1858, Brown presided over a meeting of blacks and whites in Chatham, Ontario, Canada, where he outlined a plan to create in the hills of Maryland and Virginia a stronghold for fugitive slaves that would serve as the headquarters of a national slave rebellion. The meeting also produced a revised antislavery constitution for the United States and elected Brown commander in chief of a new provisional government for the United States. Brown secured the financial backing of prominent Boston abolitionists and in 1859, at the head of an "army" of sixteen white men and five blacks, he raided the federal arsenal at Harpers Ferry, Virginia. The massive slave rebellion Brown envisioned failed to materialize, and his small band was defeated. Found guilty of charges including treason, he was hanged on December 2, 1859.

assault to begin, and within a matter of three minutes, the battle was over. Brown sustained a saber wound, and all but four of the raiders in the firehouse were killed. One marine and four citizens of Harpers Ferry, including the town's mayor, also died.

The state of Virginia charged Brown and his surviving followers with treason, conspiracy to foment servile insurrection, and murder. All were found guilty and sentenced to hang. At his sentencing, Brown spoke calmly and eloquently, arguing that he had behaved in harmony with the New Testament injunction to "remember them that are in bonds, as bound with them." He concluded: "Now, if it is deemed necessary that I should forfeit my life for the furtherance of the ends of justice, and mingle my blood further with the blood of my children and with the blood of millions in this slave country whose rights are disregarded by wicked, cruel, and unjust enactments—I submit; so let it be done."

On December 2, 1859, the day of Brown's execution, the nation's most respected philosopher and man of letters, Ralph Waldo Emerson, joined William Lloyd Garrison to memorialize Brown before a mass gathering of abolitionists in Boston. From "Bleeding Kansas" by way of Harpers Ferry, Virginia, the abolitionist cause now had a martyr who seemed to many both harbinger of and justification for the coming civil war

BIBLIOGRAPHY

Corder, Eric. *Prelude to Civil War: Kansas-Missouri.* New York: Crowell-Collier Press, 1990.

McCandless, Perry. *A History of Missouri: Volume 2, 1820–1860.* Columbia: University of Missouri Press, 1972.

Monaghan, Jay. *Civil War on the Western Border, 1854–1864.* Lincoln: University of Nebraska Press, 1985.

Parish, William E. *A History of Missouri, Volume 3: 1860–1875.* Columbia: University of Missouri Press, 1973.

At Issue

The Santee Sioux (a subgroup of the Sioux often called the Dakota, consisting of the Mdewakantons, Wahpekutes, Sissetons, and Wahpetons) generally accepted reservation life. However, confined to a narrow strip of land along the upper Minnesota River, they found themselves hemmed in by growing numbers of Scandinavian and German immigrants before suffering a catastrophic crop failure. The difficult situation was made worse when they did not receive federal money and provisions they had been promised.

The Conflict

Santee rage exploded when money and provisions guaranteed them by the 1851 **Treaty of Fort Laramie** were withheld. In a climate of desperation, on Sunday, August 17, 1862, four young Mdewakanton men robbed and killed five white settlers.

Treaty of Fort Laramie, 1851

ARTICLE 1. The aforesaid nations, parties to this treaty, having assembled for the purpose of establishing and confirming peaceful relations amongst themselves, do hereby covenant and agree to abstain in future from all hostilities whatever against each other, to maintain good faith and friendship in all their mutual intercourse, and to make an effective and lasting peace.

ARTICLE 2. The aforesaid nations do hereby recognize the right of the United States Government to establish roads, military and other posts, within their respective territories.

ARTICLE 3. In consideration of the rights and privileges acknowledged in the preceding article, the United States bind themselves to protect the aforesaid Indian nations against the commission of all depredations by the people of the said United States, after the ratification of this treaty. . . .

ARTICLE 7. In consideration of the treaty stipulations, and for the damages which have or may occur by reason thereof to the Indian nations, parties hereto, and for their maintenance and the improvement of their moral and social customs, the United States bind themselves to deliver to the said Indian nations the sum of fifty thousand dollars per annum for the term of ten years, with the right to continue the same at the discretion of the President of the United States for a period not exceeding five years thereafter, in provisions merchandise, domestic animals, and agricultural implements, in such proportions as may be deemed best adapted to their condition by the President of the United States, to be distributed in proportion to the population of the aforesaid Indian nations.

Excerpted from Little Big Horn Associates, "Treaty of Fort Laramie," www.lbha.org/Research/lara51.htm.

The Mdewakanton chief Little Crow disapproved of the act, but, feeling that the die had been cast, personally led an August 18 attack on a local trader's store. Simultaneously with this raid (in which trader Andrew J. Myrick was killed), other war parties swept across the Minnesota countryside. The Santee Sioux Uprising had begun.

Minnesota, like other states and territories in the West, suffered a critical shortage of military personnel during the Civil War as troops were drawn off to fight in the East. As Santee braves raided throughout Minnesota on August 18, settlers fled, many seeking refuge at Fort Ridgely, an installation commanded by Captain John S. Marsh and manned by a garrison of only 76 troops. The garrison received minimal reinforcements, and the fort remained vulnerable. An assault on Fort Ridgely, led

CHRONOLOGY OF THE MINNESOTA SANTEE SIOUX UPRISING

1862

Aug. 17 Four Mdewakanton men rob and kill five local settlers.

Aug. 18 Chief Little Crow leads warriors in an attack on Andrew J. Myrick's trading post, killing Myrick; other war parties sweep across Minnesota; refugees begin arriving at Fort Ridgely.

Aug. 20 Chiefs Little Crow, Mankato, and Big Eagle attack New Ulm and are repulsed. Little Crow attacks Fort Ridgely and is again repulsed.

Aug. 23 Little Crow renews the assault on New Ulm, burning most of the town. Two thousand citizens are evacuated to Mankato.

Sept. 2–3 Battle of Birch Coulee

Sept. 23 Battle of Wood Lake

Sept. 26 Santees and other Indians begin to surrender. The uprising itself ends, but fighting spreads beyond Minnesota.

1863

July 26–29 Battle of Devil's Lake, Dakota Territory

Sept. 3 Battle of Whitestone Hill, Dakota Territory

1864

July 28 Battle of Killdeer Mountain

by chiefs Little Crow, Mankato, and Big Eagle, seemed inevitable on August 19. However, the attackers halted in front of the fort, only to turn away and head for the nearby settlement of New Ulm. For the army, it was a reprieve, as reinforcements soon increased the number of defenders to 180. On the afternoon of August 20, a Santee war party attacked New Ulm. When the militia and townspeople put up a gallant defense, Little Crow turned the attack back against Fort Ridgely, but was repulsed by the reinforced garrison, now under the command of Lieutenant Thomas P. Gere. (Marsh had been ambushed and killed on his way to the Santee reservation.) On August 23, Little Crow renewed the assault on New Ulm, reducing most of the town to smoldering ruins. Some 2,000 citizens evacuated to Mankato.

On September 2, warriors under Big Eagle, Mankato, and Gray Bird attacked Captain Hiram P. Grant's camp at the head of a deep gulch called Birch Coulee. Digging in, the troops held their position until September 3, when a large militia contingent under Colonel Henry Hastings Sibley arrived. Grant had been forced to withstand a thirty-one-hour siege, prompting criticism that Sibley was not responding aggressively to an uprising that now extended beyond the borders of Minnesota into Wisconsin and Dakota Territory. Sibley responded to his critics that he needed more soliders and time to train the raw militia troops currently in his command. Thus it was not until September 19 that Sibley, commanding 1,619 soldiers, felt ready to begin a counteroffensive. By this time, the Indians had seized the initiative, mounting an ambush with 700 warriors on September 23. The warriors attacked prematurely, though, and the Battle of Wood Lake resulted in the deaths of 7 troopers and about 30 Indians. This was enough to discourage Little Crow's army, which disintegrated. Beginning on September 26, Sibley accepted the surrender of some 2,000 Indians.

The Battle of Wood Lake ended the Minnesota Santee Sioux Uprising, but hostilities on the Plains continued throughout the Civil War period; the theater of war shifted from Minnesota to Dakota Territory. In July 1863 a major battle was fought at

Devil's Lake, Dakota Territory, against Sisseton and Teton Sioux as well as some Hunkpapas and Blackfeet. The running battle raged from July 26 to July 29, when the army broke off pursuit of the withdrawing Indians. On September 3, near Whitestone Hill (northwest of present-day Ellendale, North Dakota), four companies of the Sixth Iowa Cavalry under Major Albert E. House

This photograph was taken by photographer Adrian J. Ebell on August 21, 1862, as he and his assistant fled the Minnesota Santee Sioux Uprising with the missionaries and their families pictured here.

encountered a superior number of Sioux led by Inkpaduta. Reinforcements arrived in time to prevent House's defeat, and after a fierce battle, Inkpaduta fled. Still, fighting continued. On July 28, 1864, 3,000 troops reached Killdeer Mountain, where (according to the official army account) they faced some 6,000 warriors. (Indian accounts say no more than 1,600 warriors were engaged.) Whatever the actual numbers, army losses were surprisingly light: 5 killed, 10 wounded. The Indians lost 150 warriors, according to the army (only 31 according to Indian sources). Following the battle, troopers pursued the retreating warriors, but conflicts on the upper Plains largely dissipated until after the Civil War.

Indian Policy and Public Opinion: The Civil War Years

The years leading up to the Civil War saw the emergence of a reform movement in federal Indian policy. While this movement advocated the integration of Indians into white "civilization"—including the institution of severalty (the breakup of reservations so that Indians could hold individual title to their lands), programs of education, the conversion to a sedentary agricultural lifestyle, and full citizenship—the move-

ment also paradoxically called for stricter confinement of Indians to reservations during a vague and unspecified period of transition. The onset of the Civil War, which drew off military resources from the West, made implementation of any consistent Indian policy nearly impossible. Although advocates continued to preach reform during the war, there was little the government could do to enforce confinement to reservations, and the implementation of Indian policy was allowed to drift.

Throughout the Plains, raiding became widespread. News of Indian "depredations" did not change the minds of reformers, but did turn much of the public against reform. The raids reinforced stereotypes of Indians as incorrigible savages who could never be civilized and opened a gulf between developing public policy on the one hand and prevailing public opinion on the other.

In the years immediately following the Civil War, during the administrations of Andrew Johnson and Ulysses S. Grant, federal policy would support a general "peace offensive" with regard to the Plains Indians, even though the public had come to favor a sterner military approach (see Chapter 21). This set the stage for the later phase of the Indian Wars during the 1870s and 1880s.

Confederate Indian Policy

During the Civil War, Union loyalists in the West feared that the Confederates planned to recruit Indian warriors to their cause. In fact, the Confederacy did find some allies among the Caddos, Osages, Wichitas, Delawares, Shawnees, Senecas, and Quapaws. (Both the Confederacy and the Union recruited troops from the Cherokees, Chickasaws, Choctaws, Creeks, Seminoles, and other tribes.) Stand Watie, a Cherokee leader, was commissioned a brigadier general in the Confederate army, served heroically, and became the very last general to formally surrender—a full month after General Robert E. Lee surrendered at Appomattox (see Chapter 17). Confederate commanders also armed the Comanches and Kiowas on the southern Plains. But the Confederates never made the concerted effort that the Unionists feared they would and so failed to win large numbers of Indians to the Southern cause.

The Reservation System: Policy vs. Execution

As previously observed, a frequent cause of white-Indian violence was the failure of the reservation system, not so much at the policy level as in the execution. Living conditions were often deplorable. Promised annuity payments, supplies, and provisions regularly failed to materialize. The annuities, which were inadequate to begin with, were frequently diverted by inefficient or corrupt administrators and agents. A closer look at the incident that triggered the Santee Sioux Uprising offers a dramatic example of the great gulf that lay between policy and implementation.

In the months before the uprising, the Santees had repeatedly appealed to the local Indian agent to release the funds and food stores promised them by treaty. In June 1862 they were told that the payment and distribution of rations would be delayed because the government had not determined whether to make the annuity disbursement in gold or in currency. The Indians agreed to wait for the annuity, but pointed

out that the food supplies were already stored in a warehouse at the Yellow Medicine Agency and demanded that the rations be distributed without delay. Indian agent Thomas J. Galbraith replied that bookkeeping requirements as well as reservation custom obliged him to distribute the food at the same time as the money. He advised the Indians to go on a hunt and return to the agency in a month's time.

They returned a month later, on July 14, to discover that the money had still not arrived and that Galbraith was, therefore, still refusing to distribute the food. On August 4, a band of mounted warriors broke into the Yellow Medicine Agency warehouse and looted sacks of flour. A garrison detachment under Lieutenant Timothy J. Sheehan dispersed the looters, but Sheehan also appealed to Galbraith to release at least some of the rations. A few days later, Little Crow and other leaders met with local traders and agency officials near New Ulm. Little Crow asked for the release of the rations, commenting that "When men are hungry they help themselves." Instead of simply releasing the rations, Galbraith deferred to the assembled traders. The most prominent among them, Andrew J. Myrick, offended by Little Crow's veiled threat, replied, "So far as I am concerned, if they are hungry, let them eat grass." This remark nearly sparked a riot, which was defused only by the promise to commence food distribution immediately. However, on August 15, after Galbraith observed what he judged to be an abundant harvest in the Lower Agency section of the Santee reservation, he announced that the distribution would, after all, be delayed until the arrival of the money. This betrayal created the climate in which four young disaffected Mdewakanton men, returning from a fruitless hunting trip, murdered five settlers on August 17, thereby prompting Little Crow into a headlong war with the whites of Minnesota.

President Lincoln's Response to the Uprising

President Abraham Lincoln first became aware of the scope of the Minnesota uprising in August, when he

Little Crow (Taoyateduta)

(ca. 1810–1863)

The son of a chief of the Mdewakanton Santee Sioux, Little Crow became a chief on the death of his father in 1834. He led his band in generally amiable relations with neighboring whites and in 1851 signed the Treaty of Mendota, by which the Santee ceded much of their land in exchange for a reservation on the upper Minnesota River plus annuities. By the end of the 1850s, however, tensions between the Santee and whites steadily mounted as white settlement increasingly encroached on Sioux hunting grounds and as federal distribution of annuities, supplies, and provisions became increasingly irregular and subject to corruption. Little Crow did all he could to keep his younger warriors from going to war, but after young braves killed five settlers, Little Crow became instrumental in organizing the Santee uprising in August 1862.

After suffering defeat at the Battle of Wood Lake on September 23, 1862, Little Crow fled and found protection among the Sioux in Dakota Territory. In May 1863 he sought the help of the British at Fort Garry (Winnipeg, Manitoba), but was rebuffed. The next month he led a horse-stealing expedition back to Minnesota, and on July 3, near Hutchinson, he was killed by settlers while picking berries with his sixteen-year-old son. Little Crow's body was discarded at a local slaughterhouse; the Minnesota Historical Society later acquired his skeleton and scalp, which were put on display. Much later, these items were returned to the Sioux for burial at a Santee cemetery on the Flandreau Reservation in South Dakota.

received a telegram from Governor Alexander Ramsey asking for an extension of the deadline for meeting his state's quota for Union army conscripts. Lincoln replied, "If the draft cannot proceed of course it will not proceed," adding a quotation from Publius Syrus, a Roman philosopher of the first century B.C.: "Necessity knows no law."

The president again became involved in the uprising in November 1862, after a military tribunal ordered the execution of 303 Santees who had been found guilty of killing settlers. Doubting the justice as well as the wisdom of the tribunal, Lincoln personally reviewed each of the sentences. On December 6, the president notified General Sibley that he should proceed with the execution of only 39 of the 303 convicted, and the rest were to be held subject to further orders. The 38 Indians who were hanged—Lincoln gave one additional last-minute reprieve—constituted the largest mass execution in American history. All were hanged simultaneously, except for one man whose rope broke; he had to be hanged separately. The thousands who had gathered to witness the executions cheered. The bodies were buried in a mass grave, which was quickly looted by area physicians in search of medical cadavers. An administrative error caused the hanging of two Indians who were not on Lincoln's list, and the error was not admitted for nine years. Reportedly, among those wrongfully executed was an Indian who had saved a woman's life during the raids.

Aftermath

The uprising moved Congress in April 1863 to pass legislation enabling the forcible removal of all Sioux from Minnesota. Most were moved to present-day South Dakota. On March 22, 1866, President Andrew Johnson ordered the release of the 177 surviving

Indian prisoners. These individuals were moved to the Santee Reservation near Niobrara, Nebraska. Little Crow, however, was neither among the prisoners nor the condemned. In 1863, with about 150 followers, he escaped to present-day North Dakota and then to Canada. In June 1863 he returned to Minnesota. On July 3, a farmer recognized Little Crow, took aim, and shot him while he picked berries with his son near Hutchinson. The state presented the farmer with a $500 reward.

BIBLIOGRAPHY

Keenan, Jerry. *The Great Sioux Uprising: Rebellion on the Plains August–September 1862*. New York: Da Capo Press, 2003.

Salberg, Chris. *The Santee Sioux: Before and after the Uprising of 1862*. Lincoln: University of Nebraska, 1978.

Schultz, Duane. *Over the Earth I Come : The Great Sioux Uprising of 1862*. New York: St. Martin's, 1993.

At Issue

After years of tortuous compromise on the issue of slavery collapsed, the slaveholding Southern states seceded from the United States. United as the "Confederate States of America" they fought for "states' rights," the concept that the sovereignty of the individual states trumps the authority of the federal government (such state sovereignty would allow the perpetuation of slavery in any state that elected to allow the institution). The Northern (nonslaveholding) states fought to preserve the Union and to assert the sovereignty of the federal government over that of the states; additionally, many Northerners were inspired to fight in order to bring about a permanent end to slavery in the United States.

The Conflict

Outbreak

The election of Abraham Lincoln as president in November 1860 provoked seven Southern states—South Carolina, Mississippi, Florida, Alabama, Georgia, Louisiana, and Texas—to secede from the Union. About a month after Lincoln's inauguration, at 4:30 on the morning of April 12, 1861, Confederate artillery under Brigadier General P. G. T. Beauregard (who, like most Southern commanders, had resigned

from the U.S. Army to join the Confederate forces) opened fire on Fort Sumter in the harbor of Charleston, South Carolina, thereby beginning the Civil War. The fort surrendered on April 13.

Scott's Anaconda

Lieutenant General Winfield Scott, aged hero of the War of 1812 (Chapter 6) and the U.S.-Mexican War (Chapter 10), was the senior commander of the U.S. Army. To gain time to recruit and organize

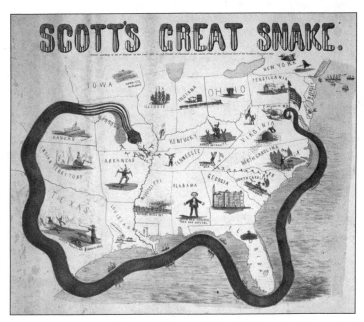

This 1861 cartoon illustrates General Winfield Scott's "Anaconda" plan to strangle the Confederacy by blockading the Atlantic and Gulf coasts and controlling the Mississippi River.

a combat-ready army, he proposed a naval blockade of the Confederacy. He planned to cut off Atlantic and Gulf ports while sending 60,000 troops and a flotilla of gunboats down the Mississippi to capture New Orleans, Louisiana. He believed this would cut off the South economically and divide it geographically, east from west, strangling the Confederacy as an anaconda constricts its prey. The press and the public, on both sides, derided the plan as "Scott's Anaconda." Many saw it as a less-than-

CHRONOLOGY OF THE CIVIL WAR

1861

Apr. 13 Fort Sumter surrenders to the Confederates (it is evacuated on Apr. 14).

July 21 First Battle of Bull Run, Virginia

1862

Feb. 16 Fort Donelson falls to Brigadier General Ulysses S. Grant.

Apr. 6–7 Battle of Shiloh, Tennessee

May 1 New Orleans, Louisiana, falls to combined Union army and naval forces (the army under Major General Benjamin F. Butler, USA; the navy under Flag Officer David Farragut, USN).

Mar 23–June 9 Confederate major general Thomas J. "Stonewall" Jackson triumphs in the Shenandoah Valley, Virginia.

June 25–July 1 The "Seven Days" Campaign, Virginia

Aug. 28–30 Second Battle of Bull Run, Virginia

Sept. 4 General Robert E. Lee's Confederates invade Maryland.

Sept. 17 Battle of Antietam, Maryland

Sept. 22 Abraham Lincoln issues the Preliminary Emancipation Proclamation.

Dec. 13 Battle of Fredericksburg, Virginia

1863

Jan. 1 The Emancipation Proclamation takes effect.

May 1–4 Battle of Chancellorsville, Virginia

July 1–3 Battle of Gettysburg, Pennsylvania, the turning point in favor of the Union

July 4 Vicksburg, Mississippi, falls to Major General U. S. Grant.

Sept. 19–20 Battle of Chickamauga, Georgia

Nov. 23–25 Battles of Chattanooga and Lookout Mountain, Tennessee

1864

Mar. 9 Newly promoted Lieutenant General U.S. Grant assumes overall command of the Union armies.

May 5–6 Battle of the Wilderness, Virginia

May 8–21 Battle of Spotsylvania, Virginia

May 31–June 12 Battle of Cold Harbor, Virginia

June 15 The siege of Petersburg, Virginia, begins.

July 20 The Battle of Peachtree Creek, Georgia, opens Union major general William T. Sherman's Atlanta Campaign.

Aug. 5 Union naval victory in the Battle of Mobile Bay

Sept. 2 Sherman occupies Atlanta, Georgia.

Nov. 8 Abraham Lincoln is reelected.

Nov. 15 Atlanta burns; Sherman begins his "March to the Sea."

Nov. 30–Dec. 16 Battles of Franklin and Nashville, Tennessee

Dec. 21 Savannah, Georgia, falls to Sherman.

1865

Jan. 31 Congress sends the Thirteenth Amendment, abolishing slavery, for state ratification.

Feb. 17 Columbia, South Carolina, falls to the Union.

Feb. 18 Confederates evacuate Fort Sumter.

Apr. 1 Battle of Five Forks, Virginia

Apr. 2 Grant breaks through the Confederate lines at Petersburg, Virginia.

Apr. 2–3 The Confederate government flees Richmond; the Union army occupies the city.

Apr. 9 Lee surrenders the Army of Northern Virginia to Grant at Appomattox Court House, Virginia.

Apr. 14–15 Abraham Lincoln is shot (April 14) and dies (April 15).

Apr. 26 Joseph Johnston accepts armistice and surrenders the Army of Tennessee in North Carolina

May 26 General Edmund Kirby Smith surrenders Confederate troops west of the Mississippi, thereby ending the war.

honorable approach to a war that should be a forthright duel between North and South. Others saw it as simply ineffective, because the Union navy did not have enough ships to carry out the blockade. In fact, as the Union embarked on a rapid shipbuilding program, the "Anaconda" proved increasingly effective, although not decisive, as the war progressed.

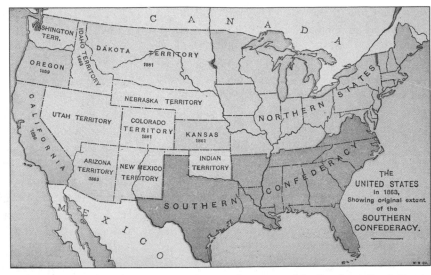

An 1863 map of the United States, showing the extent of the Southern Confederacy.

The "Border States"

Delaware, Kentucky, Missouri, and Maryland (as well as West Virginia, which would be created in 1863 from three western counties that broke away from Virginia) were slave states, but they remained loyal to the Union and did not secede. Lincoln believed that if the Union should lose these so-called border states, the war itself would be lost. The population of these states was a mix of pro-Union, pro-Confederate, and neutral individuals; some states contributed soldiers to both sides. The most precarious of the border states was Missouri. Its legislature was pro-Union, but its governor was a secessionist. Although Missouri ultimately did not secede, it was the site of guerrilla warfare throughout the Civil War.

Overview

Before it ended in the spring of 1865, the Civil War would pit 1,082,119 Confederate soldiers against 2,128,948 Union troops. Casualties would be staggering: an estimated 258,000 Confederate troops killed and 225,000 wounded; 359,528 Union soldiers killed and 275,175 wounded. It remains the deadliest war in American history.

The Civil War engulfed virtually the entire nation. Although the most intense fighting took place in the Eastern Theater, encompassing Maryland, North Carolina, Pennsylvania, South Carolina, Virginia, and West Virginia, the action in the Western Theater was also crucial, because it was in large part a contest for control of the nation's vital transportation artery, the Mississippi River. This theater included Alabama, Arkansas, Georgia, Louisiana, Mississippi, and Tennessee. Farther west was the Trans-Mississippi Theater, which encompassed Arizona, Arkansas, Indian Territory (modern Oklahoma), Kansas, Missouri, New Mexico, and Texas. The fighting there was sporadic, often merging into the already chronic combat between whites and Indians. Finally, although a civil war is by definition largely a land-based war, the two sides also fought each other at sea, especially along the Atlantic seaboard and Gulf Coast, as well as in the Caribbean and on the high seas, as Confederate commerce raiders preyed on Union shipping.

First Battle of Bull Run

In July 1861 Brigadier General Irvin McDowell, USA, led a force of 37,000 men from Alexandria, Virginia, to attack Confederates under Brigadier General P. G. T. Beauregard just east of Manassas Junction along Bull Run in Virginia. The battle commenced on July 21, at which time the Confederate forces had been reinforced to a strength of approximately 35,000. McDowell enjoyed initial success; however, Brigadier General Thomas J. Jackson, CSA, rallied his Virginia troops, who steadfastly stood their ground, earning him the nickname "Stonewall." The battle ended with a Confederate counterthrust (led by Jackson) that broke the Union lines, sending the panic-stricken bluecoats running back toward Washington.

A New Commander

After Bull Run, President Lincoln relieved McDowell as commander of the Army of the Potomac and replaced him with Major General George Brinton McClellan. McClellan transformed the Army of the Potomac from a demoralized, ill-disciplined bunch into an army. Nevertheless, his troops were defeated at the Battle of Ball's Bluff, Virginia (October 21, 1861), his first engagement as commander of the force. Aside from this action, McClellan devoted a great deal of time to organizing and training his troops and avoided major engagements.

Opening Battles in the West

In the summer of 1861, Major General John Charles Frémont, USA, built a gunboat fleet to operate on the Mississippi, Tennessee, and Cumberland rivers and, in August, assigned Brigadier General Ulysses S. Grant to command the highly strategic position of Cairo, Illinois, where the Ohio River joins the Mississippi River. When, in September 1861, Kentucky proclaimed loyalty to the Union, Major General Leonidas Polk, CSA, invaded the state. He occupied Columbus, Kentucky, on the bluffs above the Mississippi. Grant responded by taking Paducah, Kentucky, which gave him control of the mouths of the Tennessee and Cumberland rivers. General Albert Sidney Johnston, CSA, whose line stretched across the length of Tennessee, reinforced Columbus and fortified his positions in northwestern Tennessee on the Cumberland and Tennessee rivers, building Fort Henry on the Tennessee and Fort Donelson on the Cumberland.

In November 1861 Major General Henry Wager Halleck, USA, assumed command of Union forces west of the Cumberland, and Brigadier General Don Carlos Buell, USA, assumed command east of the river. Brigadier General George H. Thomas, USA, defeated a Confederate force at Mill Springs, Kentucky, on January 19, 1862, after which Halleck sent Grant to take Fort Henry on the Tennessee. The fort fell on February 6, whereupon Grant marched twelve miles east, attacking Fort Donelson on the Cumberland River in concert with Flag Officer Andrew Foote's U.S. Navy gunboats. That fort surrendered on February 16, 1862, after a three-day battle, breaking Johnston's line and forcing him to evacuate Nashville. The fall of Forts Henry and Donelson marked the first major victory for the Union in the Civil War and boosted Northern morale.

Shiloh

On April 6, 1862, at Pittsburg Landing, Tennessee, Confederate generals Albert Sidney Johnston and P. G. T. Beauregard attacked 42,000 troops under Grant, who was headquartered near a Methodist meeting house called Shiloh Chapel. For the first twelve hours, the Battle of Shiloh was one-sided, as the 40,000 Confederates drove the Union troops nearly into the Tennessee River. Grant's subordinate, Brigadier General William Tecumseh Sherman, rallied his command, averting a rout. An effective Union defense was organized, Johnston suffered a fatal wound, and, after fighting another ten hours on April 7, Beauregard withdrew to Corinth, Mississippi, from where the Confederates had come. What had begun as a Union disaster ended as a hairbreadth Union victory. The cost—staggering and unprecedented in American warfare—was almost 24,000 casualties on both sides.

The Peninsula Campaign

The war was going well for the Union in the Western Theater, but in the East, it stalled as George B. McClellan failed to assume the offensive. Exasperated, President Lincoln, on March 11, 1862,

Ulysses S. Grant

(1822–1885)

As general in chief of the Union army, Grant led the North to victory in the Civil War. Born at Point Pleasant, Ohio, as Hiram Ulysses Grant, the son of a farmer, he enrolled at West Point in 1839. When he learned that he was listed on the academy's roster as Ulysses Simpson (his mother's maiden name) Grant, he accepted this as his name thereafter.

After graduating in 1843, twenty-first of a class of thirty-nine, Grant was commissioned a second lieutenant of infantry and fought with distinction in the major battles of the U.S.-Mexican War (Chapter 10).

After the war, Grant married Julia Dent and served variously in New York, Michigan, California, and Oregon during 1848–1854. Although he was promoted to captain in August 1853, he grew impatient with the glacial pace of peacetime army advancement, resigned his commission, and tried and failed at a series of business endeavors. In 1860 he moved to Galena, Illinois, where he joined his father and brothers in the family tannery. Although he was a clerk when the Civil War began in April 1861, because of his military experience he was chosen to train the Galena militia company. After this, he served in the state adjutant general's office at Springfield until June 1861, when he was appointed colonel of the Twenty-first Illinois Volunteer Infantry Regiment. Promoted to brigadier general of volunteers in August, he was given command of the District of Southeast Missouri, headquartered at Cairo, the southernmost tip of Illinois.

In contrast to most Union officers, Grant was bold and, on his own initiative, captured Paducah, Kentucky, on September 6, 1861. He went on to various victories in the war's Western Theater, culminating in the capture of Vicksburg, Mississippi, on July 4, 1863, which put the Mississippi River firmly under Union control. The July 3 Union victory at Gettysburg and the victory at Vicksburg the next day together became the turning point of the Civil War.

Following Vicksburg, Grant was promoted to major general in the regular army and was assigned command of the Military Division of the Mississippi on October 4, 1863. He and his subordinates defeated Confederate general Braxton Bragg's Army of Tennessee at Lookout Mountain and Missionary Ridge (at Chattanooga) during November 23–25, 1863. These and his other victories prompted Abraham Lincoln to promote Grant to lieutenant general and, early in 1864, to appoint him general in chief of all Union armies.

Grant set as his objective not the capture of territory, but the destruction of Robert E. Lee's Army of Northern Virginia. In a series of horrific battles in Virginia, Grant, although often defeated by Lee, persisted in advancing southward and in wearing the Confederate commander down and draining his resources. Grant knew that Lee did not have the resources to replace his casualties. Grant's success lay in his own willingness to trade casualties for strategic objectives. The inevitable conclusion came at Appomattox Courthouse, where Grant accepted Lee's surrender on April 9, 1865.

After the war, Grant was promoted to the newly created rank of general of the army in July 1866. He served briefly as interim secretary of war under President Andrew Johnson during 1867–1868, then embraced the unyielding Reconstruction policies of the radical Republicans and easily achieved the party's nomination for president in 1868. He served two terms in the White House but proved to be an ineffectual president whose administration was engulfed in corruption and scandal (although Grant's own ethics were above reproach).

After his second term ended, Grant settled in New York City in 1881 and suffered a series of financial reverses that left him virtually bankrupt by 1884. An offer from the humorist Mark Twain, who owned a successful publishing company, induced the impoverished Grant to write his *Memoirs*. Completed just four days before his death from throat cancer, it is a work of great historical and literary distinction.

restricted him to command of the Army of the Potomac, which Lincoln urged him to lead in an advance on Richmond. Instead, McClellan proposed and executed a roundabout plan whereby he would transport his army in ships to a position southeast of Richmond and Confederate general Joseph E. Johnston's lines. This would outflank the main Confederate force at Fredericksburg by sea and thereby avoid a major battle.

Ninety thousand men of the Army of the Potomac landed near Fortress Monroe, Virginia, on April 4, 1862, and advanced northwest on Yorktown the next day. McClellan did not attack the city directly, but instead laid siege in the mistaken belief that he was outnumbered. McClellan's failure to attack gave Johnston time to construct a stout defense of Richmond. The Union had lost the initiative.

Jackson's Shenandoah Campaign

Confederate strategy at this point in the war was to menace Washington, D.C., which, it was believed, the Union would defend at all costs. Confederate general Thomas J. "Stonewall" Jackson swept through Virginia's Shenandoah Valley in a move intended to persuade the Northern commanders that an invasion of the capital was imminent and to prompt them to divide the Union forces, thereby reducing the number of troops available to advance on Richmond. Indeed, 35,000 men were detached from McClellan's command to reinforce the defenses of Washington.

Despite some defeats and disappointments, Jackson's Shenandoah Valley Campaign was a brilliant success. In battles at Kernstown, McDowell, Front Royal, Winchester, Cross Keys, and Port Republic, Virginia, his 17,000 men forced the diversion of more than 50,000 Union soldiers (including the 35,000 sent to guard Washington).

New Orleans

In mid-April 1862 Flag Officer David Farragut, USN, led a Mississippi River fleet in an assault on New Orleans. By April 24, Farragut had bypassed the city's defensive forts, and Major General Benjamin F. Butler, USA, occupied the surrendered city on May 1. The loss of this major gulf port was a severe blow to the Confederacy.

Fair Oaks and Seven Pines

At the end of May 1862, after minor skirmishing at Yorktown and Williamsburg, Virginia, most of McClellan's army was north of the Chickahominy River, except for a corps under Major General Erasmus Darwin Keyes. Confederate general Joseph E. Johnston attacked this isolated corps at Fair Oaks and Seven Pines, Virginia, on May 31, resulting in an inconclusive but costly battle. Casualties exceeded 11,000 soldiers of the roughly 80,000 engaged on both sides. Most notably, Johnston was so severely wounded that he had to be replaced by Robert E. Lee (who had served up to this time chiefly as personal military adviser to Confederate president Jefferson Davis). This seemingly chance occurrence would change the course of the war.

Stuart's Ride

On June 12–15, 1862, Brigadier General James Ewell Brown (J.E.B.) Stuart led 1,200 Confederate cavalrymen in a spectacular reconnaissance that completely circled the Union positions in Virginia. "Stuart's Ride" humiliated McClellan, who at last decided to attack Richmond in earnest. He met fierce resistance at Oak Grove, near Mechanicsville, along the Chickahominy River (June 25).

"The Seven Days"

General Robert E. Lee planned to bring most of the Army of Northern Virginia, about 65,000 troops, to the north bank of the Chickahominy at Mechanicsville to overwhelm Union general Fitz-John Porter and his 25,000 Union troops, who were isolated on that side of the river. It was a gamble, because it would leave few troops to defend Richmond, south

Robert E. Lee

(1807–1870)

Robert E. Lee commanded the Confederate Army of Northern Virginia through most of the Civil War and is generally regarded as the war's greatest commander. He was born into the Virginia "aristocracy" at Stratford, Virginia, a son of Revolutionary War hero Henry "Light Horse Harry" Lee, who died when Lee was eleven, leaving the family in strained financial circumstances. Studious and intellectual, young Lee could not afford a college education, so he enrolled at West Point and graduated second in the class of 1829. Commissioned in the Corps of Engineers, Lee served along the southeast coast, where he met and married Mary Custis, the great-granddaughter of Martha Washington. The couple raised a large and loving family, which included three sons and four daughters.

A brilliant military engineer, Lee served in this capacity during the U.S.-Mexican War (Chapter 10) and as a staff officer under Winfield Scott. After the war, Lee was appointed superintendent of West Point, where he served from 1852 to 1855. Promoted to colonel, he was given command of the Second Cavalry and served in Texas and the Southwest before he was recalled to Virginia after the death of his father-in-law in 1857. Lee was still in Virginia when he was ordered to Harpers Ferry to put down John Brown's raid on the federal arsenal there on October 18, 1859.

From February 1860 to February 1861, Lee commanded the Department of Texas, then was recalled to Washington on February 4. It is widely believed, though no hard evidence has been found, that, on April 20, 1861, Abraham Lincoln offered Lee command of the Federal forces. But Lee, who opposed secession, resigned his commission when Virginia seceded, declaring it his duty to participate in the "defense of [his] native state." He accepted command of Virginia's military and naval forces and soon thereafter became one of Confederate president Jefferson Davis's principal military advisers. After Joseph E. Johnston was wounded at the Battle of Seven Pines during May 31–June 1, 1862, Lee took command of Johnston's forces, renamed them the Army of Northern Virginia, and led a successful defense of Richmond against McClellan in the Seven Days Campaign (June 25–July 1). For the next year, Lee proceeded to outgeneral the Union's top generals, among them John Pope, George McClellan, Ambrose Burnside, and Joseph Hooker. He followed his triumphs at Antietam, Fredericksburg, and Chancellorsville with a second invasion of the North and was defeated by George G. Meade at the Battle of Gettysburg (July 1–3, 1863). Lee was forced to withdraw into Virginia, where inconclusive fighting continued until Grant became Union general in chief on March 9, 1864.

Against Grant, Lee employed a brilliantly successful defense at the Battle of the Wilderness (May 5–6, 1864) and thwarted Grant again at Spotsylvania (May 8–21), but he was forced out of his entrenchments at the North Anna River on May 23 when Grant outflanked him. At Cold Harbor, on June 3, Lee again repulsed Grant, only to be forced back across the James River, which Grant crossed during June 12–16. Lee then mounted a defense of Petersburg and endured a siege that lasted nine months.

Jefferson Davis named Lee general in chief of the Confederate armies on February 3, 1865, but Lee was forced to withdraw from Richmond and Petersburg during April 2–3, 1865. He surrendered the Army of Northern Virginia to Grant at Appomattox Court House on April 9, 1865.

Lee, who suffered from heart failure, spent months recuperating from the strain of combat but was unable to return to his beloved home, Arlington, which had become a national military cemetery. In September 1865 he became president of Washington College (later renamed Washington and Lee University) in Lexington, Virginia, and spent the last five years of his life there as an educator, a role he cherished.

of the river. Lee's decision began the Battle of Beaver Dam Creek, the second in a series of battles that had started with Oak Grove. These were followed by the battles of Gaines' Mill, Garnett's and Golding's Farm, Savage's Station, White Oak Swamp, Glendale, and Malvern Hill. Collectively, these encounters—known as the "Seven Days," spanning June 25–July 1, 1862—prompted McClellan to retreat east from Richmond to the James River, where he remained until mid-August. Although the Seven Days battles were a costly strategic failure for the Union army, the Northerners did gain a tactical advantage. Richmond had been saved, but whereas McClellan suffered about 16,000 casualties, Lee's smaller force lost nearly 20,000.

Despite the casualties he had inflicted, McClellan was discredited. He remained, for the moment, in command of the Army of the Potomac, although its numbers were gradually reduced to reinforce Major General John Pope's Army of Virginia, which was operating in Central Virginia.

Cedar Mountain, Catlett's Station, and Second Bull Run

General John Pope's first major battle as commander in chief of the Army of Virginia was at Cedar Mountain, near Culpepper, Virginia, on August 9. Both armies withdrew soon after the Confederate victory—Stonewall Jackson south of the Rapidan (Aug. 11) and Pope to Culpepper. Lee, displaying a tendency for which he would become famous, acted audaciously and divided his army, putting half his forces under the command of Major General James Longstreet to occupy Pope's front and sending the other half, under Jackson, to make a surprise attack on the rear of Pope's army. While Lee maneuvered, the two sides traded raids. During the last one, forces under Jackson destroyed Pope's supply depot at Manassas Junction, Virginia, and severed rail and telegraph communications with the North.

Pope pursued Jackson, resulting eventually in the Second Battle of Bull Run, beginning on August 28, 1862. On August 30, Longstreet rushed the Union flank along a two-mile front, inflicting another embarrassing Union loss. Commanding 75,696 Union soldiers against the Confederates' 48,527, Pope was forced to retreat. He was soon relieved as commander of the Army of Virginia, and that army was incorporated into the Army of the Potomac, under the command of McClellan.

Antietam

Lee saw Pope's defeat as an opportunity to invade the demoralized North and achieve several goals. Militarily, he hoped to maneuver Union forces into a defensive posture to protect Washington and Baltimore and to locate food for his own army in the Maryland countryside, thereby relieving Virginia farmers beleaguered by combat. Politically, he hoped that Maryland's proslavery population would rally to his side, that the invasion would influence Northern voters in the 1862 congressional elections to elect Democratic candidates who would negotiate a peace recognizing the Confederacy, and that a clear victory on Northern soil would bring diplomatic recognition of the Confederacy by European governments. On September 4, 1862, Lee led his 55,000-man Army of Northern Virginia into Maryland. In a stroke of luck, one of McClellan's soldiers stumbled upon an apparently forgotten copy of Lee's invasion plan, Special Order 191, in an abandoned Confederate campsite. Even with this information, however, McClellan again grossly overestimated his enemy's number and declined to act decisively. Instead, he took a half-measure by sending elements of his army against the Confederate rearguard posted at three gaps along South Mountain. The indecisive encounter gave Lee ample time to set up a strong defensive line at the western Maryland town of Sharpsburg, behind Antietam Creek. McClellan had sacrificed the element of surprise.

McClellan resolved to attack both of Lee's flanks, then drive through the center with his reserves. A ferocious battle commenced on September 17, lasting from dawn to dusk. Late in the day Union forces nearly flanked Lee in a move that would have blocked his route of retreat to Virginia, but Confederate reinforcements arrived from Harpers Ferry, West Virginia, just in time to save the Southerners. On September 18, both armies occupied the battlefield without fighting, and Lee began to withdraw back to Virginia that evening. Yet McClellan made no effort to attack the Confederates as they retreated across the Potomac River; he allowed the Army of Northern Virginia to survive.

The carnage at Antietam (where a section of the battlefield was dubbed the "Bloody Lane") was stunning. Approximately 23,000 Union and Confederate soldiers were killed or wounded in the bloodiest single day of fighting in American history. Although profoundly disappointed that Lee's army was not destroyed, President Lincoln seized on the successful ejection of Lee's army from Northern soil as the occasion to publish the Preliminary Emancipation Proclamation on September 22, freeing all slaves held in unoccupied Confederate territory (see "The Emancipation Proclamation," below).

Fredericksburg

On November 7, 1862, McClellan was again relieved of command of the Army of the Potomac. His replacement was Maj. Gen. Ambrose Burnside. Where McClellan had been reluctant to act, Burnside was eager. On December 13, 1862, he ineptly mounted a massive frontal attack on well-defended Fredericksburg, Virginia, culminating in fourteen suicidal charges against a virtually impregnable Confederate hilltop position. Union forces suffered more than twice the casualties of the Confederates. Lincoln relieved Burnside on January 26, 1863, replacing him with Major General Joseph "Fighting Joe" Hooker.

Chancellorsville

Under Hooker, the Army of the Potomac was reinforced to 130,000 men, more than twice the strength of Lee's Army of Northern Virginia. Hooker planned a three-pronged attack across the Rappahannock

above Lee's Chancellorsville, Virginia, entrenchments. It was a sound plan, but Lee guessed Hooker's intentions. Once again daring to divide his army in the face of a numerically superior enemy, Lee sent forces under Stonewall Jackson to launch a surprise attack on Hooker's exposed right flank at dawn on May 3, initiating a battle that culminated the next day in Hooker's retreat. Facing a force less than half the strength of his, Hooker suffered 17,000 casualties. Lee also lost heavily, incurring 13,000 casualties, including Jackson, who was wounded by friendly fire and died of his injuries.

Invasion of the North

For the North, Chancellorsville was a terrible defeat, but for the South it was a Pyrrhic victory. Whereas the North could replace its lost troops, the South lacked the resources to do so—and no one could take the place of Stonewall Jackson. Lee decided that the Confederacy's only hope was to try another raid into the North to break the will of the Union and force a negotiated peace.

Beginning on June 3, 1863, to compensate for the loss of Jackson, Lee reorganized his army from two into three corps, two of which would be led by generals new to corps-level command. At the head of the movement north was a corps commanded by Lee's senior subordinate, Lieutenant General James Longstreet.

Hooker observed these movements but proposed ignoring them to advance against Richmond, which would be thinly defended. Lincoln rejected the plan as too dangerous and ordered Hooker to assume the defensive and follow Lee. This led to the Battle of Brandy Station on June 9, 1863, which was the largest cavalry engagement ever fought in North America, involving about 20,000 mounted troops fighting for twelve hours. In the end, Brandy Station remained in Confederate hands, but Hooker now knew that Lee was heading north.

On June 15, elements of the Army of Northern Virginia crossed the Potomac into Maryland, with Jeb Stuart artfully deploying his cavalry in a counter-reconnaissance screen that led to cavalry duels at Aldie, Virginia (June 17), Middleburg, Virginia (June 19), and Upperville, Virginia (June 21). Then, on June 24, Stuart wheeled east, riding around Hooker's rear and flank, disrupting his supply lines, capturing 125 U.S. Army wagons at Rockville, Maryland, and taking a total of 400 prisoners at various locations.

Stuart's so-called Gettysburg Raid—which took him to skirmishes at Rockville and Westminster, Maryland; Fairfax, Virginia; and Hanover and Carlisle, Pennsylvania—was spectacular, but the operation took longer than planned and therefore deprived Lee of the reconnaissance he needed to determine the whereabouts of the Union forces. It was not until June 28 that Lee learned—belatedly, from other scouts—that the entire Army of the Potomac was concentrated around Frederick, Maryland, and that Hooker had been replaced as commander of the Army of the Potomac by Major General George Gordon Meade. The two armies were about to meet at a place neither of them had planned to use as a battlefield: Gettysburg, Pennsylvania.

Gettysburg

On June 30, a Confederate infantry brigade under Brigadier General Richard S. Ewell stumbled across a Union cavalry brigade under Brigadier General John Buford near Gettysburg, Pennsylvania. Although outnumbered, Buford decided to fight it out in order to hold the high ground he occupied. Thus the Battle of Gettysburg began at 9:00 a.m. on July 1, 1863. By the time Union reinforcements arrived, the Confederates were on the offensive. By midday the situation was thoroughly confused. After much back and forth the Confederates finally drove the Union army back into the streets of Gettysburg, fighting hand-to-hand before the Northerners withdrew southeast of town along the Baltimore Pike. Lacking a definitive command from Lee to exploit what he had gained, Ewell broke off pursuit. This gave the Union time to establish a new position on high ground: East Cemetery Hill, Cemetery Ridge, and Culp's Hill.

On the morning of July 2, Lee, still without Stuart, was unsure how many Union troops were massing, but he was eager to maintain the offensive. General Longstreet argued that they would be facing most of the Army of the Potomac and advised assuming defensive positions. Longstreet wanted to withdraw southward and attack the enemy from the rear. Lee overruled him, refusing to take what he deemed the demoralizing step of withdrawing after the previous day's victory.

Major General Meade, the Union commander, occupied high ground that gave him clear fields of view and fire. He also had nearly 90,000 men assembled opposing 75,000 Confederates. Meade's Union line resembled a giant fishhook, with the barb just south of Culp's Hill, the hook's curve at Cemetery Hill, the shaft running along Cemetery Ridge, and the tie-end of the shaft at two hills south of town, Little Round Top and Big Round Top. Lee ordered Longstreet to attack the Union left. Ewell was to swing down to smash into the Union's right.

One of Longstreet's subordinates, Major General John Bell Hood, attacked through an area called the Devil's Den and drove Meade's left backward. Realizing that the Confederates would seize undefended high ground on a pair of hills known as the Round Tops and therefore be in a position to flank the Union line, Meade's chief engineer, Brigadier General Gouverneur K. Warren, sent in reinforcements. At the extreme south end of the Union flank was Colonel Joshua Lawrence Chamberlain's Twentieth Maine Regiment, which had lost half its strength in the previous day's fighting. Chamberlain, in desperation, ordered a downhill bayonet charge into a superior Confederate force that saved the Union's flank and, thereby, the battle.

By the morning of July 3, Lee believed he had worn down the enemy sufficiently to attempt a vast infantry charge. Longstreet vehemently opposed the move but nevertheless ordered his commanders to execute it. Remembered as "Pickett's Charge"—although Pickett commanded just three of the nine brigades involved—it is perhaps the single most celebrated action of the war. At 1:45 p.m., 12,000–15,000 Confederates advanced in close order across a hilly but largely open plain. They walked into a withering fire that decimated their number; nearly sixty percent of those charging became casualties. Only a handful of Confederates managed to penetrate the Union line.

On July 4, the armies held their positions but did not fight. That night, Lee began retreating back to Virginia, his second invasion of the North ending much like the first. As at Antietam, the Union commander again failed to deal the Confederacy a fatal blow. Meade declined to aggressively pursue Lee's army even though the retreating Confederates were pinned against a rain-swollen Potomac River. To Meade, Lincoln wrote, "Your golden opportunity is gone, and I am distressed immeasurably because of it." More than 50,000 men were killed or wounded during the three days of battle. Nevertheless, the victory at Gettysburg heartened a war-weary North.

Vicksburg

Meanwhile, in the West, Ulysses S. Grant culminated an arduous campaign by laying siege to Vicksburg, Mississippi, a strategic Confederate fortress town. From late May through the beginning of July, Union artillery continuously pounded Vicksburg until the starving and shell-shocked inhabitants finally surrendered on July 4, 1863. Vicksburg's fall put all of the Mississippi River into Union hands. Vicksburg and the Battle of Gettysburg are together viewed by most historians as the turning point of the Civil War. For the South, the simultaneous defeats ended hope for European recognition or for an imminent negotiated peace.

Chattanooga Taken

Union general William Starke Rosecrans, commanding the Army of the Cumberland, had been sparring with Braxton Bragg, general in command of the Confederate Army of Tennessee, since the end of October 1862. Lincoln called on Rosecrans to seize

the initiative by taking Chattanooga, then Knoxville. Ambrose Burnside took Knoxville on September 3, 1863, and Rosecrans cut off Bragg's supply and communications line to Atlanta, prompting him to evacuate Chattanooga, which fell to Rosecrans without further resistance on September 8, 1863.

Chickamauga

Rosecrans pursued Bragg, but the Union commander's three exhausted corps became separated in the thickly forested mountain passes. Bragg halted at La Fayette, Georgia, twenty-five miles south of Chattanooga, where he was reinforced, and then moved on. Suddenly, on September 19, he turned on Rosecrans at Chickamauga Creek, in Georgia, twelve miles south of Chattanooga.

It was a terrible place for a battle—densely wooded and trackless. The September 19–20 battle was both confusing and horrendously bloody. After the first day of intense combat, neither side had gained an advantage. During the night, both sides dug in, and at 9:00 a.m. on September 20, Bragg and the Confederates attacked. The terrain was so bewildering that Rosecrans was never able to obtain an accurate picture of how his own units were deployed. He believed that there was a gap in his right flank and ordered troops from what he believed was the left to plug it. The unintended result was that he *created* the very gap he had meant to plug. It looked as if the Battle of Chickamauga would end in a Union disaster even greater than Fredericksburg. Believing all was lost, Rosecrans and two of his corps commanders, Major General Thomas Leonidas Crittenden and Major General Alexander McDowell McCook, fled to Chattanooga. Only Major General George Henry Thomas remained. Subsequently hailed as the "Rock of Chickamauga," Thomas held the field until nightfall, thereby saving the Union's Army of the Cumberland from annihilation. The Battle of Chickamauga was another Pyrrhic tactical victory for Confederates, because Confederate losses exceeded those of the Union, and Bragg had made no strategic gain.

Chattanooga Besieged

Following Chickamauga, the Army of the Cumberland withdrew to Chattanooga, where Bragg laid it under siege. Two Union army corps under Major General Joseph Hooker were detached from Meade's Army of the Potomac to help break the siege. They arrived on October 2, while Major General William T. Sherman led elements of the Army of the Tennessee east from Memphis. Major General Ulysses S. Grant, now commanding all military operations west of the Alleghenies, broke through a Confederate outpost on the Tennessee River west of Lookout Mountain and opened up a supply route to beleaguered Chattanooga.

Lookout Mountain and Missionary Ridge

Sherman arrived at the Union rallying point—Bridgeport, Alabama—on November 15. On November 23, Union forces pushed the Confederates off Orchard Knob near Lookout Mountain, Tennessee. On November 24, Grant ordered Hooker to take Lookout Mountain. He dutifully commenced an uphill battle until, early on the morning of November 25, federal soldiers from the Eighth Kentucky Regiment scrambled up to the summit and planted the Stars and Stripes. The sun had just broken through the fog, creating a spectacle that war correspondents dubbed the "Battle above the Clouds."

That afternoon, Grant ordered Thomas to lead the Army of the Cumberland forward to take the Confederate rifle pits at the base of Missionary Ridge, south of Chattanooga and just to the east of Lookout Mountain. Having been bottled up under siege so long in Chattanooga, Thomas's men were eager to prove themselves. With unbridled zeal, they not only took the rifle pits, but also charged all the way up the steep slope of Missionary Ridge, sweeping away the Confederate forces before them and breaking Bragg's line where it was the strongest. The Battle of Missionary Ridge was the culmination of Union victory in the middle South.

Grant Assumes Command

On March 9, 1864, Ulysses S. Grant, promoted to lieutenant general, was appointed supreme commander of all the Union armies. He immediately revised Northern war plans to focus on the mission of destroying Robert E. Lee's Army of Northern Virginia rather than capturing the Confederate capital of Richmond. He assigned Sherman to pursue the Army of Tennessee, now retreating under the command of Joseph E. Johnston (recovered from wounds sustained in the Peninsular Campaign), who had replaced Bragg. Sherman was to advance against Atlanta and, in the process, destroy the Army of Tennessee.

Grant's principal force was the Army of the Potomac. Additionally, he directed two smaller forces: the Army of the James (33,000 troops under Major General Benjamin F. Butler) and a force in the Shenandoah Valley (led by Major General Franz Sigel) against Richmond. The entire operation began on May 4, 1864.

Lee's Desperate Strategy

After Gettysburg and the defeats in Tennessee, Robert E. Lee realized that the Confederacy could no longer prevail in the Civil War. His hope, however, was to prolong the fight in a manner that would break the will of the North to continue the war. Abraham Lincoln would be up for reelection in November 1864. Opposing him was former Union general in chief George B. McClellan, who was believed (erroneously, as it turned out) to favor an immediate armistice followed by a negotiated peace. If Lee could score victories that would discredit Lincoln and bring McClellan into office, perhaps the South could negotiate a favorable peace.

Wilderness Campaign

On May 4, 1864, Grant marched the 120,000-troop Army of the Potomac across the Rapidan River. Lee had just 66,000 troops remaining in his Army of Northern Virginia, yet he seized the initiative by attacking Grant's columns as they passed through the tangled and densely forested Virginia area known as the Wilderness. It was a brilliant move on Lee's part—without an open field of fire, Grant would be unable to bring his superior strength to bear on Lee and his artillery would be useless.

The principal combat spanned May 5–6 but continued through May 8. Grant was forced to withdraw, with losses of 17,666 casualties of 101,895 engaged. The Confederates lost 7,500 of 61,025 troops engaged. Among them was Lee's senior corps commander, James Longstreet, who was severely wounded in a friendly fire incident eerily similar to that which had killed Stonewall Jackson one year earlier at Chancellorsville.

Spotsylvania

In defeat, Grant advanced instead of retreating, forcing Lee to fight at Spotsylvania Court House, which occupied a crossroads on the way to Richmond. Lee beat Grant to Spotsylvania, and after preliminary skirmishing on May 8, the two armies were locked in a death grip, through May 21.

Yellow Tavern

Meanwhile, Major General Philip Sheridan, who commanded the Army of the Potomac's 10,000-man cavalry, proposed a raid toward Richmond to draw out Jeb Stuart's Confederate cavalry, thereby depriving Lee of much needed reconnaissance. Stuart, however, outmaneuvered Sheridan, positioning his 4,500 cavalrymen between Sheridan and Richmond at the Yellow Tavern, an abandoned wayside inn only six miles north of the Confederate capital.

The Battle of Yellow Tavern was fought on May 11, and although Sheridan enjoyed a two-to-one manpower advantage, he was forced to withdraw—albeit not before a Union sniper shot and killed Stuart. For Lee, the death of Stuart, coming on the heels of Longstreet's wounding, meant a great loss of experienced leadership.

North Anna River

After Spotsylvania, which had been bloody but indecisive, Grant disengaged from Lee and again both armies shadowed each other southward, halting at the North Anna River on May 24. Here Lee's defensive positions proved too strong to overrun, but Grant battered them nonetheless, eager for any opportunity to bleed Lee.

From the North Anna, Grant moved yet closer to Richmond. At Totopotomoy Creek (May 26–30), he once again struck at the Confederate defenses, which, once again, held—although their strength was diminished.

Cold Harbor

During the night of May 31–June 1, 1864, Grant and Lee raced one another to Cold Harbor, a crossroads just six miles northeast of Richmond. Lee got there first and dug in. During June 1–2, Grant sacrificed 5,000 men in a fruitless assault against the Confederate entrenchments. On June 3, he mounted a charge with 60,000 troops, who were decimated—about 7,000 fell in a single hour.

Petersburg

Grant withdrew from Cold Harbor under cover of darkness on June 12 and crossed the Chickahominy River. Lee did not know where Grant was going but assumed that he was heading for Richmond. Therefore, he sent most of his troops to the outskirts of the city. Instead of advancing on Richmond, however, Grant shifted his objective to Petersburg, a key rail junction. He reasoned that by taking Petersburg, Richmond would be cut off from the rest of the Confederacy and would therefore fall.

The 16,000 Federal troops who arrived at Petersburg on June 15 were opposed by just 3,000 Confederates, under General P. G. T. Beauregard. Had Major General William Farrar "Baldy" Smith been able to rally his tired bluecoats, they would doubtless have overwhelmed the Confederates and taken

Petersburg. But Smith so mishandled his assaults against Petersburg during June 15–18 that Beauregard held his position. Grant was compelled to settle in for a long and costly siege.

Atlanta

Grant was not happy about the failure to break through at Petersburg, but he also understood that the siege would cost Lee more than it cost him. In the meantime, Major General William T. Sherman began his advance on Atlanta, the principal railway junction of the South. Sherman's 100,000 troops marched out of Chattanooga, Tennessee, and into Georgia on May 7, 1864. General Joseph E. Johnston, with 62,000 men, withdrew before Sherman's advance but acquired some reinforcements in the process.

Johnston's retreat was both tactical and strategic. In a head-on fight, he knew that he could not defeat Sherman's superior numbers, but if he could keep his own army intact, thereby delaying the fall of Atlanta, Lincoln might lose his reelection bid to McClellan, who might negotiate a favorable peace. However, Johnston's strategy did not sit well with Confederate president Jefferson Davis, who, on July 17, replaced him with the impetuous Lieutenant General John Bell Hood. Hood meant to fight.

Seeing that Atlanta was well defended by earthworks, Sherman decided against a frontal assault. Instead, he cut the four major rail lines into the city, intending to draw the Confederates out for a fight. It was a good plan; however, in executing it, a gap developed between the Union forces. Seeing this, Hood attacked on July 20, and the fierce Battle of Peachtree Creek commenced. Union major general George H. Thomas's Army of the Cumberland offered a deft defense, which both saved his army and allowed him to close the deadly gap. This victory led to the major Battle of Atlanta.

On July 22, Hood hit Major General James McPherson's Army of the Tennessee and very nearly flanked it by swinging around it to the east. McPherson fell in the battle, and his army was attacked simultaneously from the front and the rear.

Despite this, the Union troops rallied and, using their superior numbers, drove Hood back into his defensive works. But on July 28, Hood emerged to attack the Army of the Tennessee, now commanded by O. O. Howard, in the Battle of Ezra Church, just west of Atlanta. Howard repulsed Hood, inflicting heavy losses on the Confederates.

At the end of July, Hood held Atlanta with 37,000 Confederate infantry troops reinforced by 5,000 Georgia militiamen. Sherman had 85,000 infantry troops, and the city seemed clearly within his grasp. Yet in an exchange of skirmishes and ineffective raids, the days of August slipped by. Sherman was well aware that if Hood managed to hold him off long enough, Confederate cavalry under Major General Nathan Bedford Forrest might attack from the rear. Feeling vulnerable, Sherman broke off action and ceased bombardment of Hood's entrenchments on August 25. By the next day, most of his army had simply disappeared. Hood, prone to wishful thinking, assumed Sherman had retreated.

Sherman had done no such thing. Swinging south, he cut the Macon and Western Railroad, the last rail connection into the city. Forrest was still too far to the northwest to come to Hood's aid, and, on September 1, Hood at last grasped what Sherman had done. To avoid being hopelessly trapped in Atlanta, Hood evacuated without a fight on September 1, and Union forces occupied Atlanta on September 2. Sherman ordered all civilians out of the city (relatively few complied) and transformed it into a fortress. Sherman's victory in Atlanta not only deprived the Confederacy of a major rail center, but it also helped guarantee Lincoln's reelection, which ended for the South any hope (however illusory) of a negotiated peace.

Sherman saw that the Confederacy was rapidly falling apart. This inspired him to turn away from Hood and take 60,000 of his troops on a long march southeast to Savannah, Georgia, a "March to the Sea." He would thus cut the Confederacy in two, north and south, and would position himself to attack Lee's Army of Northern Virginia from the south even as Grant continued to bear down on it from the north.

Moreover, the March to the Sea would cut a wide swath through the South, undermining civilians' will to continue the fight and demonstrating that their government was utterly unable to defend them. On November 11, 1864, just before he left, Sherman ordered everything of military significance in Atlanta destroyed. The result, by November 15, was a blaze that consumed virtually all of the city. As Sherman marched to the sea, Hood headed toward Nashville, intending to join forces with Nathan Bedford Forrest in order to overwhelm the 30,000 men under Thomas, who were clearing Confederates out of Tennessee. By menacing Thomas, Hood gambled that Sherman would be forced to change his plans and come to the rescue. But Sherman did not change his plans, and Thomas was left to fight—and defeat—Hood at Franklin and at Nashville. After the December 16 Battle of Nashville, Hood fell back and then withdrew from Tennessee into Mississippi on Christmas Day. At his own request, he was relieved of command of the Army of Tennessee.

March to the Sea

Sherman cut his swath of destruction, reaching Savannah on December 21. The city surrendered without a fight. On February 16, 1865, Sherman marched into Columbia, the capital of South Carolina. That city surrendered on February 17, and fires consumed half the town. The next day, the Confederates evacuated Fort Sumter in Charleston's harbor, where the war had begun.

Five Forks and the End of the Petersburg Siege

With the Confederate defenders of Petersburg near starvation, Lee persuaded Jefferson Davis that the only alternative to unconditional surrender was to break out from Petersburg and retreat southeast via the junction at Five Forks to unite the Army of Northern Virginia with what remained of General Joseph E. Johnston's Army of Tennessee in North Carolina, where the army could obtain desperately needed supplies. This would mean the loss of Richmond, but the army would remain intact, thereby offering hope for a negotiated peace. Davis approved the plan.

Philip Sheridan anticipated Lee's move, however. On March 31, back from the Shenandoah Valley with 12,000 cavalry troops, the Union general rode for Five Forks. Lee sent 19,000 (some estimates put this figure at only 10,000) troops under Major General George Pickett to hold the junction, but Sheridan, now reinforced by an infantry corps, routed Pickett, taking 5,000 prisoners in a battle on April 1.

On April 2, Lee's breakthrough attempt at Petersburg failed. Grant finally penetrated the Confederate lines here, forcing Lee to fall back on the town of Petersburg and then to retreat west toward Amelia Court House. On the same day, Jefferson Davis ordered the Confederate government to evacuate Richmond for Danville, Virginia.

Endgame

With fewer than 50,000 troops remaining in the Army of Northern Virginia, Lee marched west, intending to reach Amelia Court House, where he expected to find supplies and board the Danville and Richmond Railroad, which would transport his army to Johnston's position. By April 5, most of Lee's force was concentrated at Amelia Court House. Not only did the anticipated rations fail to materialize here, but Sheridan and others prevented Lee from moving toward North Carolina. Instead, he was forced to turn to the southwest, toward Rice Station, where there was another possibility of resupply. Grant ordered an interception, which led to a fight at Little Sayler's Creek and then at High Bridge, near Farmville.

By April 8, Lee's army was halted between Appomattox Station, on the rail line, and Appomattox Court House, a few miles to the northeast. Blocked from further movement, his depleted army starving, Lee sent word to Grant that he was prepared to surrender. On April 9, 1865, the two men met in the

McLean farmhouse at Appomattox Court House and negotiated the terms of the surrender of the Army of Northern Virginia.

Lee had the authority to surrender the Army of Northern Virginia and nothing more, but his surrender effectively meant the end of the war. Montgomery, Alabama, fell on April 12, and Federal troops entered Mobile the same day. On April 13, Sherman occupied Raleigh, North Carolina, where, during April 17–18, he hammered out a broad armistice with Joseph Johnston. However, Andrew Johnson became president after Abraham Lincoln's death on April 15 and repudiated the agreement Sherman and Johnston had concluded, finding it too lenient. On April 26, Johnston accepted an armistice with terms identical to those that Grant had offered Lee. On this date as well, the Confederate cabinet met to dissolve itself. Early in May, the Confederate army's Department of East Louisiana, Mississippi, and Alabama surrendered, and on May 10, President Johnson declared that armed resistance was "virtually at an end." Three days later, at Palmito Ranch, near Brownsville, Texas, Confederate troops under Edmund Kirby Smith skirmished with Union troops. It was the last fighting of the war. Smith surrendered the Confederate army west of the Mississippi on May 26, but the very last Confederate commander to surrender was the Cherokee Stand Watie, a brigadier general, who laid down arms on June 23, 1865, at Doakville, Indian Territory.

Prewar Policy under President Buchanan

James Buchanan, the moderate Democrat who occupied the White House from 1857 to 1861, had served in the House of Representatives from 1821 to 1831 and in the Senate from 1834 to 1845. Although he was a Pennsylvanian, in Congress he tended to side with the South. Personally, he found slavery morally repugnant but feared that the means necessary to eliminate the institution would introduce what he called "evils infinitely greater." Thus, in the years leading up to the Civil War, Buchanan exemplified the deep conflict in the national mentality that abhorred slavery, yet believed the Constitution protected it. Not surprisingly, he was a strong supporter of the 1846 Wilmot Proviso, which would have prohibited the extension of slavery into the U.S. territories, and the Compromise of 1850, which sought to maintain a balance of Senate seats between slave and free states as new territories applied for statehood.

By 1856 the Democratic Party saw in Buchanan the ideal moderate compromise candidate for president, and he easily won over the antislavery Republican John C. Frémont as well as American ("Know-Nothing") Party candidate Millard Fillmore. As president, Buchanan lacked the intellectual and personal qualities that might have worked to reconcile the North and the South. His moderation proved to be nothing more than ineffectual temporizing in a crisis that continued to grow. His goal was to preserve the Union, but the only substantive steps he took toward that end were to attempt to suppress antislavery agitation and activity in the North and to insist on the rigorous enforcement of the Fugitive Slave Act of 1850. During the guerrilla warfare crisis of Bleeding Kansas in 1854–1859 (Chapter 15), he spoke out in favor of the unpopular and illegitimate Lecompton Constitution, which would have permitted slavery in the state and (as Buchanan saw it) thereby would have removed another cause of Southern discontent.

As the years of his presidency elapsed, Buchanan's "moderate" course succeeded only in emboldening the South through appeasement while building in the North a greater consensus for a stronger stand against slavery. Buchanan did not offer himself as a candidate for his party's nomination in 1860, and the party split regionally, the northern faction nominating Senator Stephen A. Douglas of Illinois and the southern, Vice President John C. Breckinridge. The Democratic split gave the Republican candidate, Abraham Lincoln, a plurality victory in the November elections. This precipitated the secession crisis, which began on December 20, 1860, when South Carolina voted to leave the Union. Days earlier, on December 3, 1860, in his **Final Mes-**

sage to Congress, Buchanan had continued to temporize, protesting lamely that the federal government was constitutionally powerless to prevent secession.

Having announced his position that the federal government had no authority to act against the secession of the states, Buchanan did nothing but observe and denounce the secession of seven Southern states by February 1, 1861. His own cabinet began to splinter as five of its seven members resigned. Buchanan did draw the line at Southern demands for the surrender of federal forts, and he ordered the reinforcement and resupply of menaced Fort Sumter in the harbor of Charleston, South Carolina. However, when the unarmed supply ship he sent was fired upon by Southern shore batteries, the vessel turned back, and Buchanan did not act again. Instead, he waited, counting the minutes before he could turn the entire crisis over to Abraham Lincoln.

Campaign and Election of 1860

Chapter 15 includes an account of the creation of the Republican Party after the passage of the Kansas-Nebraska Act and of how the *Dred Scott* decision took the nation beyond compromise on the issue of slavery. It was in this context that the campaign and election of 1860 played out among the two candidates of the Democratic Party, Stephen A. Douglas (of the northern faction) and John C. Breckenridge (of the southern faction), and Republican candidate Abraham Lincoln.

In truth, there was remarkably little difference between the stands Lincoln and Douglas took on slavery. While both favored banning it in the territories, neither believed that the Constitution allowed the abolition of slavery by federal political action in the states where it already existed (see **Party Platforms, 1860**). Because Douglas refused to defend slavery in any positive terms, the breakaway Southern Democratic Party nominated Breckenridge. Had they presented a united front and a single candidate, the Democrats would probably have defeated Lincoln in 1860. Splintered (and further diminished by a third breakaway group, the Constitutional Union

---

Buchanan's Final Message to Congress, December 3, 1860

The question fairly stated is: Has the Constitution delegated to Congress the power to coerce a state into submission which is attempting to withdraw or has actually withdrawn from the confederacy? If answered in the affirmative, it must be on the principle that the power has been conferred upon Congress to declare and to make war against a state. After much serious reflection, I have arrived at the conclusion that no such power has been delegated to Congress or to any other department of the federal government. It is manifest upon an inspection of the Constitution that this is not among the specific and enumerated powers granted to Congress, and it is equally apparent that its exercise is not "necessary and proper for carrying into execution" any one of these powers. So far from this power having been delegated to Congress, it was expressly refused by the Convention which framed the Constitution.

Excerpted from "The Impending Disruption of the Union," in *Annals of America*, ed. Mortimer J. Adler and Charles Van Doren (Chicago: Encyclopaedia Britannica, 1976), 9:217.

Party), the Democrats ended up with 123 electoral votes divided among their candidates, whereas the Republicans and Lincoln commanded 180. Lincoln captured only a minority of the total popular vote—1,866,452 popular ballots against 2,815,617 cast for his combined opponents—and thus eked out a plurality rather than a majority victory.

Secession

Various leaders in the South had threatened secession if Lincoln were elected president. South Carolina was the first state to make good on this threat,

Party Platforms, 1860

From the Republican Party Platform:

5. [That] the present Democratic administration has far exceeded our worst apprehensions, in its measureless subserviency to the exactions of a sectional interest, as especially evinced in its desperate exertions to force the infamous Lecompton Constitution upon the protesting people of Kansas; in construing the personal relations between master and servant to involve an unqualified property in persons; in its attempted enforcement everywhere, on land and sea, through the intervention of Congress and of the federal courts, of the extreme pretensions of a purely local interest; and in its general and unvarying abuse of the power entrusted to it by a confiding people. . . .

7. That the new dogma that the Constitution, of its own force, carries slavery into any or all of the territories of the United States is a dangerous political heresy, at variance with the explicit provisions of that instrument itself, with contemporaneous exposition, and with legislative and judicial precedent; is revolutionary in its tendency and subversive of the peace and harmony of the country.

8. That the normal condition of all the territory of the United States is that of freedom; that as our republican fathers, when they had abolished slavery in all our national territory, ordained that "no person should be deprived of life, liberty, or property without due process of law," it becomes our duty, by legislation, whenever such legislation is necessary, to maintain this provision of the Constitution against all attempts to violate it; and we deny the authority of Congress, of a territorial legislature, or of any individuals to give legal existence to slavery in any territory of the United States.

From the Democratic Party Platform (Douglas):

Inasmuch as difference of opinion exists in the Democratic Party as to the nature and extent of the powers of a territorial legislature, and as to the powers and duties of Congress, under the Constitution of the United States, over the institution of slavery within the territories, . . .

2. *Resolved,* that the Democratic Party will abide by the decision of the Supreme Court of the United States upon the questions of constitutional law.

From the Southern Democratic Party Platform (Breckinridge):

1. That the government of a territory organized by an act of Congress is provisional and temporary, and during its existence all citizens of the United States have an equal right to settle with their property in a territory, without their rights either of person or property being destroyed or impaired by congressional or territorial legislation.

2. That it is the duty of the federal government, in all its departments, to protect, when necessary, the rights of persons and property in the territories and wherever else its constitutional authority extends.

Excerpted from "Party Platforms of 1860," in *Annals of America,* ed. Mortimer J. Adler and Charles Van Doren (Chicago: Encyclopaedia Britannica, 1976), 9:189–191.

issuing a **Secession Declaration** on December 20, 1860. Within six weeks, five other states followed suit—Mississippi (January 9, 1861), Florida (January 10), Alabama (January 11), Georgia (January 19), and Louisiana (January 26). Delegates from these six states met in Montgomery, Alabama, in February 1861 to form a new government, and the "Confederate States of America" adopted a constitution modeled on that of the United States. The delegates named Jefferson Davis and Alexander H. Stephens provisional president and vice president, respectively, subject to confirmation by elections to be held in November 1861. None of the border states —eight of them, from Virginia to Missouri— seceded or joined the Confederacy immediately. Although most of the people in these states disliked the new administration in Washington, they were not sufficiently discontent to break with the United States. Indeed, there was a prevailing sentiment that the "cotton states" were playing an extreme form of politics, using secession to intimidate the federal government into making concessions that would guarantee Southern "rights." When the concessions were obtained, the majority believed, the seceding six would return.

But this did not come to pass. On February 1, 1861, Texas seceded. Virginia held out until May 4, 1861, after the shooting war had already begun and the Confederate States of America had agreed to transfer its capital from Montgomery, Alabama, to Richmond, Virginia. Arkansas and Tennessee seceded on May 6, and North Carolina followed on May 20.

Crittenden Compromise

On December 18, 1860, before James Buchanan left office, Senator John J. Crittenden of the border state of Kentucky proposed what he conceived of as a last-ditch alternative to war. The so-called **Crittenden Compromise** was a set of six irrevocable constitutional amendments to protect slavery while limiting its spread.

Senator John J. Crittenden of Kentucky attempted to avert war with his unsuccessful "Crittenden Compromise."

South Carolina Secession Declaration, 1860

The ends for which this Constitution was framed are declared by itself to be "to form a more perfect union, to establish justice, insure domestic tranquility, provide for the common defense, promote the general welfare, and secure the blessings of liberty to ourselves and our posterity." These ends it endeavored to accomplish by a federal government in which each state was recognized as an equal and had separate control over its own institutions. The right of property in slaves was recognized by giving to free persons distinct political rights; by giving them the right to represent, and burdening them with direct taxes for, three-fifths of their slaves; by authorizing the importation of slaves for twenty years; and by stipulating for the rendition of fugitives from labor.

We affirm that these ends for which this government was instituted have been defeated, and the government itself has been destructive of them by the action of the nonslaveholding states. Those states have assumed the right of deciding upon the propriety of our domestic institutions; and have denied the rights of property established in fifteen of the states and recognized by the Constitution. They have denounced as sinful the institution of slavery; they have permitted the open establishment among them of societies, whose avowed object is to disturb the peace of and eloign the property of the citizens of other states. They have encouraged and assisted thousands of our slaves to leave their homes; and, those who remain, have been incited by emissaries, books, and pictures to servile insurrection.

Excerpted from "Southern Secession," in *Annals of America,* ed. Mortimer J. Adler and Charles Van Doren (Chicago: Encyclopaedia Britannica, 1976), 9:208.

Crittenden Compromise, 1860

ARTICLE I.
In all the territory of the United States now held, or hereafter acquired, situated north of latitude 36° 30', slavery or involuntary servitude, except as a punishment for crime, is prohibited while such territory shall remain under territorial government. In all the territory south of said line of latitude, slavery of the African race is hereby recognized as existing, and shall not be interfered with by Congress, but shall be protected as property by all the departments of the territorial government during its continuance. . . .

ARTICLE II.
Congress shall have no power to abolish slavery in places under its exclusive jurisdiction, and situate within the limits of States that permit the holding of slaves.

ARTICLE III.
Congress shall have no power to abolish slavery within the District of Columbia. . . .

ARTICLE IV.
Congress shall have no power to prohibit or hinder the transportation of slaves from one State to another, or to a Territory in which slaves are by law permitted to be held. . . .

ARTICLE VI.
No future amendment of the Constitution shall affect the five preceding articles; nor the third paragraph of the second section of the first article of the Constitution, nor the third paragraph of the second section of the fourth article of said Constitution and no amendment shall be made to the Constitution which shall authorize or give to Congress any power to abolish or interfere with slavery in any of the States by whose laws it is, or may be allowed or permitted.

Excerpted from the Avalon Project at Yale Law School, "Amendments Proposed in Congress by Senator John J. Crittenden, December 18, 1860," www.yale.edu/lawweb/avalon/amerdoc/critten.htm.

Pleading his lame-duck status, President Buchanan made no comment for or against the Crittenden Compromise, and President-elect Lincoln also declined to address the proposal directly. Without support from either the outgoing or incoming president, the proposal died. In January 1861 Crittenden tried to get a public hearing on the compromise, but the Senate declined to act on the resolution he introduced.

The Silence of the President-Elect

President-elect Lincoln learned that Jefferson Davis, the president of the Confederacy, was eager to negotiate peaceful relations with the United States. He was also well aware of the Crittenden Compromise. Yet he kept resolutely silent about all issues relating to secession, impending war, and slavery in the belief that until he actually assumed office he should voice no opinion on these momentous matters.

Lincoln's silence might have done little enough harm had he not permitted others to attribute positions to him. When Radical Republicans—the Republican faction that was absolutely committed to abolition—voiced what they claimed was Lincoln's unalterable opposition to compromise on the slavery issue, Lincoln said nothing, even though his primary objective was not to end or even limit slavery, but to save the Union. As Lincoln subsequently made clear when he took office, in order to save the Union, he was willing to consider protecting slavery where it existed—even by constitutional amendment, if necessary—and he also believed that the Fugitive Slave Act, because it was a duly enacted law, had to be enforced. If Lincoln had spoken out on these issues, he might have placated Southern extremists and even staved off war, at least for a while. But his silence between the election and the inauguration conveyed the impression that he shared the Radical Republican opposition to compromise.

The Peace Convention

On February 4, 1861, barely a month before Lincoln's inauguration, the state of Virginia sponsored a "Peace Convention" at Willard's Hotel in Washington, D.C. Presided over by former president John Tyler (a Virginian), the convention included 131 delegates from twenty-one states—including Southern states that had not seceded—and drafted a number of proposals on March 1, which failed even to receive congressional attention.

Morrill Tariff

In what seemed an instance of colossally bad timing, Congress passed the Morrill Tariff Act on March 2, 1861. This protectionist tariff—sponsored by Senator Justin S. Morrill, one of the founders of the Republican Party—blocked importation of a large number of manufactured goods. It was a boon to Northern industry, but by altering the balance of trade between Europe and the South (the South traded raw goods for European manufactured

Abraham Lincoln

(1809–1865)

Abraham Lincoln was born on February 12, 1809, in a log cabin in Hardin (now Larue) County, Kentucky. In 1816 his family moved to Indiana before finally settling in Illinois in 1830. Mostly self-taught, Lincoln tried his hand at various occupations and unsuccessfully ran for the Illinois legislature in March 1832. In April of that year, he enlisted as a militiaman in the Black Hawk War (Chapter 8). He had little appetite for military life, but after being elected captain of his militia company, he found that he had a natural aptitude for leadership.

Lincoln ran for the Illinois state legislature again in 1834 and was elected to the first of four consecutive terms (1834–1841). He practiced law in Springfield, the state capital, served a term (1847–1849) in the U.S. House of Representatives, and then returned to his law practice, having apparently lost interest in politics.

What revived his interest was the Kansas-Nebraska Act of 1854 (see Chapter 15). Lincoln believed that its doctrine of popular sovereignty potentially opened vast new territories to slavery, which seemed to the young lawyer both immoral and destructive to the nation. He believed that the Constitution protected slavery in states where it already existed, but he also thought that the Founders had unmistakably put slavery on the way to extinction with the Northwest Ordinance, which

barred its spread to new territories. Lincoln ran unsuccessfully for the U.S. Senate in 1855, then, in 1856, left the Whig party to join the newly formed Republicans. He ran for the Senate again in 1858, against Illinois incumbent, Democrat Stephen A. Douglas, accepting his party's nomination on June 16, 1858, with a powerful speech that accused Douglas, Chief Justice Roger B. Taney, and Democratic presidents Franklin Pierce and James Buchanan of conspiring to nationalize slavery. Declaring the Kansas-Nebraska Act doomed, Lincoln predicted that the nation would inevitably become either all slave or all free. Paraphrasing the Gospel of Mark, he declared, "A house divided against itself cannot stand."

Nominated by the Republican Party as its 1860 presidential candidate, Lincoln won a plurality victory and spent the next four years fighting the Civil War. Although he lacked significant military experience, Lincoln proved to have a sound native understanding of military strategy and tactics. As a war leader, he sought to prosecute the struggle to total victory, yet he proposed a policy of absolute reconciliation once that victory was won. He was elected to a second term at the end of 1864, and he lived to see the certain approach of that victory before he was fatally wounded by the bullet of John Wilkes Booth on April 14, 1865. He died the following morning.

goods), the tariff would also sharply curtail exports of the raw goods—especially cotton—that the Southern economy relied on. A similar, though less restrictive, tariff had triggered the secession crisis of 1832–1833, and the Morrill Tariff seemed to dare more cotton states to leave the Union.

Lincoln's First Inaugural Address

Abraham Lincoln finally broke his silence on his inauguration day, March 4, 1861. His reasoning on this occasion was brilliantly clear, and yet the regional responses were diametrically opposed. Whereas Northern newspapers reported the **First Inaugural Address** as a plea for peace and an offer of reconciliation, Southern editors interpreted it as nothing less than a call to war.

Davis and His Cabinet (1861)

Like Lincoln, Jefferson Davis, president of the Confederacy, was a product of the American frontier, born—like Lincoln—in a Kentucky log cabin. But while Lincoln's father remained a poor back-

---

Lincoln's First Inaugural Address, 1861

I have no purpose, directly or indirectly, to interfere with the institution of slavery in the States where it exists. I believe I have no lawful right to do so, and I have no inclination to do so. . . .

I hold that in contemplation of universal law and of the Constitution the Union of these States is perpetual. Perpetuity is implied, if not expressed, in the fundamental law of all national governments. It is safe to assert that no government proper ever had a provision in its organic law for its own termination. . . .

It follows from these views that no State upon its own mere motion can lawfully get out of the Union. . . .

. . . But no organic law can ever be framed with a provision specifically applicable to every question which may occur in practical administration. Shall fugitives from labor be surrendered by national or State authority? The Constitution does not expressly say. Must Congress protect slavery in the Territories? The Constitution does not expressly say.

From questions of this class spring all our constitutional controversies, and we divide upon them into majorities and minorities. If the minority will not acquiesce, the majority must, or the Government must cease. There is no other alternative, for continuing the Government is acquiescence on one side or the other. If a minority in such case will secede rather than acquiesce, they make a precedent which in turn will divide and ruin them, for a minority of their own will secede from them whenever a majority refuses to be controlled by such minority. . . .

Plainly the central idea of secession is the essence of anarchy. A majority held in restraint by constitutional checks and limitations, and always changing easily with deliberate changes of popular opinions and sentiments, is the only true sovereign of a free people. Whoever rejects it does of necessity fly to anarchy or to despotism. Unanimity is impossible. The rule of a minority, as a permanent arrangement, is wholly inadmissible; so that, rejecting the majority principle, anarchy or despotism in some form is all that is left. . . .

In your hands, my dissatisfied fellow-countrymen, and not in mine, is the momentous issue of civil war. The Government will not assail you. You can have no conflict without being yourselves the aggressors. You have no oath registered in heaven to destroy the Government, while I shall have the most solemn one to "preserve, protect and defend it."

I am loath to close. We are not enemies, but friends. We must not be enemies. Though passion may have strained it must not break our bonds of affection. The mystic chords of memory, stretching from every battlefield and patriot grave to every living heart and hearthstone all over this broad land, will yet swell the chorus of the Union, when again touched, as surely they will be, by the better angels of our nature.

Excerpted from the Avalon Project at Yale Law School, "First Inaugural Address of Abraham Lincoln," www.yale.edu/lawweb/avalon/presiden/inaug/lincoln1.htm.

woodsman, Davis's became a wealthy planter, and the boy grew up on a plantation named Rosemont, near Woodville, Mississippi. Whereas Lincoln was largely self-educated, Davis was the product of Transylvania College (Lexington, Kentucky) and West Point. After completing his military service, Davis became a planter near Vicksburg, Mississippi. After the death of his bride of three months, he devoted himself to the study of philosophy and the law, particularly constitutional law. In 1845 he was elected to the U.S. House of Representatives and also remarried, but in 1846 he resigned his seat to serve in the U.S.-Mexican War as colonel of the First Mississippi Volunteers. The brilliant victory he led at the Battle of Buena Vista in 1847 earned him an international military reputation. After the war, he was elected to the Senate, where he served as chairman of the Military Affairs Committee, and in 1853 he was appointed secretary of war by President Franklin Pierce.

Strangely enough, Jefferson Davis was not a secessionist. As civil war approached, he frequently spoke of reconciliation and compromise, and he continued to oppose secession even after South Carolina left the Union in December 1860. Yet while he was opposed to secession, he did believe that the Constitution gave the states the right to secede, and, like many others in the South, he believed that Abraham Lincoln, if elected, would force the South to end slavery, thereby bringing economic disaster upon the region. Therefore, on January 21, 1861, a dozen days after his home state of Mississippi seceded, Davis bade farewell to his Senate colleagues, made a final plea for peace, and then accepted a commission as major general in command of Mississippi's army. He was chosen as provisional president of the Confederacy shortly afterward.

One of Davis's first acts as president of the Confederacy was to send a peace commission to Washington, D.C., on February 18, 1861. However, President Lincoln believed that receiving the commission would constitute a tacit acknowledgment of the Confederacy as a sovereign nation, so he refused even to see the commissioners.

In prosecuting the war and governing the Confederacy, Davis faced even more problems than Lincoln did. His tasks were contradictions: he was to fight a conservative revolution—a rebellion not to change, but to preserve the status quo. To do this, he had to create an instant government with central authority powerful enough to fight a war—a war, in large part, opposing the powerful authority of a central government. It was a philosophically, politically, and economically daunting task, perhaps doomed from the start.

International Response to the Civil War

The U.S. Navy blockade of Confederate ports, known as "Scott's Anaconda," became increasingly effective as the United States launched more ships each month. The South had limited industrial capacity, compared with the North, and needed to import most manufactured goods, including arms. The blockade interfered directly with these import shipments. Even more important was the economically crippling effect of the blockade on Southern exports of cotton and other raw materials.

The Confederate government hoped to gain the support of European nations, if not by way of outright military alliance, at least in the form of liberal credit. The most important of the European powers, France and England, had come to regard the South as a major trading partner. Cloth manufacturers in both countries—but especially Britain—needed Southern cotton, and the South figured as a key market for both French and British exports; however, individuals in the Confederate government tended to overestimate the importance to France and Britain of Southern trade. These nations, after all, traded even more extensively with the North, and the grain produced on the plains of the Northern states was, especially for Britain, as important as Southern cotton. Nevertheless, there was another factor that tended to prejudice Britain and France in favor of the Confederate cause. At this time, both European powers were monarchies that prevailed in a part of the world recently swept by republican revolutions. While it was true that the American Civil War was yet another rebellion, it was a rebellion of an essentially aristocratic order (the Southern planter class) against the more egalitarian and radically democratic government of the North. A Confederate victory would be a triumph of a hereditary landed aristocracy.

Despite the economic and political considerations, the greatest obstacle to an alliance with France, Britain, or virtually any other major European power was slavery: European governments would not support a slaveholding state. Before the Emancipation Proclamation became final on January 1, 1863, however, the Lincoln administration had insisted that the issue of the Civil War was the preservation of the Union, not the abolition of slavery. Confederate diplomats could therefore attempt to argue that the British and French governments could aid the Confederacy without becoming involved in a fight to preserve slavery.

Relations with England

President Davis appointed James M. Mason of Virginia minister to Britain and John Slidell of Louisiana minister to France. They sailed out of Charleston harbor early in October 1861 and landed at Havana, Cuba, where they boarded the British mail packet *Trent.* By happenstance, Captain Charles Wilkes of the USS *San Jacinto,* in port at Havana, learned that Mason and Slidell were aboard the *Trent* and steamed out to intercept the British ship. Encountering the *Trent* on November 8, Wilkes fired two shots across her bow, boarded the vessel, and removed Mason and Slidell. Congress reacted jubilantly, but the British government demanded an apology as well as the release of the prisoners. Secretary of State William Seward advised President Lincoln to stand firm, even to the point of war with Britain, suggesting that such a war might serve to reunite the nation. Lincoln refused to fight two wars, ordered the release of Mason and Slidell, and personally composed a note of apology to the British government.

Although a major crisis with Britain was averted, the British continued to observe official neutrality with regard to the Civil War while also showing favoritism to the Confederacy. British officials consistently turned a blind eye toward English munitions works and shipyards that were violating neutrality laws by selling materiel to the South.

The Alabama Claims

Among the exports proscribed by the British Neutrality Act of 1819 were ships of war, but British shipyards more-or-less covertly sold the Confederacy vessels to be used as commerce raiders—fast craft deliberately designed to prey upon the commercial shipping of the North. Typically, these vessels were built in Britain, sold to dummy owners, and then sailed to Caribbean ports, where they were armed and commissioned in the Confederate States Navy. The most famous of these commerce raiders was the CSS *Alabama,* launched from a Liverpool shipyard in the summer of 1862. Skippered by the brilliant and dashing Raphael Semmes, the *Alabama* took nearly seventy U.S. merchant ships as prizes before the USS *Kearsarge* sank her in a spectacular battle on June 19, 1864.

The United States did not press damage claims against the British government until the conclusion of the Civil War. After much wrangling, the United States and Britain concluded the Treaty of Washington on May 8, 1871, which called for the creation of an international panel to arbitrate settlement of the "*Alabama* claims." Pursuant to the treaty, a panel of U.S., British, Brazilian, Swiss, and Italian arbitrators met in 1872 in Geneva and awarded the United States $15.5 million in damages, payable by the British government. In addition to resolving this particular case, the treaty had the more enduring effect of defining rules of conduct and commerce for neutrals in time of war.

Suspension of Habeas Corpus and Its Consequences

Although international threats were serious, Lincoln's more immediate problems were, of course, much closer to home. On April 19, 1861, the Sixth

Massachusetts Regiment was traveling by rail to Washington to garrison the menaced capital. The troops were obliged to change trains in Baltimore, a city rife with Confederate sympathizers, some of whom mobbed the Massachusetts troops, bombarding them with stones and bricks in a riot that resulted in the deaths of four soldiers and the wounding of many more. The troops opened fire, killing twelve civilians and wounding others.

Three days after the Baltimore riot, a citizens' committee called on President Lincoln to protest what they deemed the "pollution" of Maryland soil by the passage of Union troops. Lincoln responded without sympathy, and Baltimoreans continued their rebellion by cutting telegraph lines, sabotaging railroad tracks, and tearing down bridges. For a time, this was sufficient to sever Washington from communication with the North.

During this crisis, Lincoln ordered Major General Benjamin F. Butler to occupy Baltimore. The president authorized him to arrest and jail all secessionist sympathizers, including nine members of the state legislature, Mayor William Brown, and the city's chief of police. For the first time in American history, Lincoln ordered the suspension of one the most basic of democratic rights, inherited from the body of English common law: habeas corpus, the protection from imprisonment without due process of law. For this, many in the North as well as the South condemned Lincoln as a dictator. Despite the public outcry and opposition from Chief Justice Roger B. Taney, Lincoln would suspend habeas corpus on two more occasions. As a result, in the course of the Civil War, more than 13,000 Americans were held for varying periods without charges, hearings, or trials.

The President and the Committee on the Conduct of the War

For the most part, Congress was less concerned that President Lincoln might become a tyrant than with how he was prosecuting the war. Opposition to Lincoln's policies came not from moderate congressional Republicans nor even from those in the Democratic Party, but from the powerful Radical Republicans, who, on December 20, 1861, organized the Committee on the Conduct of the War.

The Committee on the Conduct of the War was a joint committee of Congress created explicitly to invigorate what Radical Republicans described as a timid administration. It was chaired by Senator Benjamin Franklin Wade, a Radical Republican from Massachusetts, who consistently criticized Lincoln's prosecution of the war as insufficiently aggressive and his attitude toward the Confederates as overly conciliatory. Other committee members included Senators Zachariah Chandler (a Radical Republican from Michigan) and Andrew Johnson (a moderate Tennessee Democrat who would be Lincoln's running mate in the 1864 election) and Representatives Daniel W. Gooch (a moderate Massachusetts Republican and legal expert), John Covode (a Pennsylvania Radical Republican who favored harsh treatment for the South), George Julian (an Indiana Republican, and perhaps the most extreme of the committee's Radical Republicans), and Moses Fowler Odell (a New York Democrat). Thus the majority of the committee was Radical Republican, highly combative, and determined to crush the Confederacy.

The committee's self-assigned mission was oversight of military contracts (an area subject to much corruption and inefficiency), trade with the enemy, and treatment of the wounded. Most important, however, was the committee's role as investigator of Union military failures. This role soon translated into collective advocacy of an increasingly vigorous war effort. The committee continually attempted to outflank President Lincoln by endorsing emancipation before he did, by agitating for the enlistment of black troops, and by pushing for the appointment of "fighting generals," commanders who were deemed to be unrelentingly aggressive. Ostensibly a watchdog group, the Committee on the Conduct of the War often cast itself in the role of shadow commander in chief, not only undermining the president's constitutionally mandated authority, but, as Lincoln saw it, also unnecessarily alienating the population of the border states as well as those Southerners who lived in regions of the Confederacy occupied by Union forces. In many instances, the committee worked directly with military commanders, violating the chain of command by bypassing the president altogether.

In creating and conducting the Committee on the Conduct of the War, Congress encroached on the prerogatives of the president, which was in itself damaging. Most modern scholars believe that, on balance, the activities of the committee, although well intended, were detrimental to the war effort. They tended to polarize Congress and the army and to demoralize the top commanders. The committee often inflated the reputations of mediocre commanders based solely on demonstrated or perceived aggressiveness and zeal. Moreover, the committee's insistence on a continual maintenance of an offensive posture limited strategic options.

Emancipation

From the very beginning of the war, the Radical Republicans agitated for the universal emancipation of the slaves. Abraham Lincoln, whom schoolbook histories would later celebrate as the "great emancipator," did not share this zeal. As president, Lincoln understood that he had sworn an oath to "preserve, protect and defend" the Constitution, which, as it existed in 1861, unmistakably protected slavery as a property right. In this, Lincoln was consonant with a majority of Northerners and even most other members of the Republican Party. He did not believe that the outbreak of the war gave him the legal authority simply to abolish slavery.

Some generals and crusading newspaper editors took positions that contrasted sharply with Lincoln's moderation. In May 1861 Major General Benjamin F. Butler, USA, commanding Fort Monroe, Virginia, refused to return to their owners runaway slaves who had sought asylum at the fort. Lincoln believed Butler had acted contrary to the Constitution but, yielding to the advice of his cabinet, chose not to reprimand him. Three months later, when Major General John C. Frémont, commanding Union army

forces in St. Louis, unilaterally announced the emancipation of all slaves owned by Confederates in Missouri, Lincoln ordered Frémont to restrict his proclamation to slaves owned by Missourians actively fighting for the Confederacy. Frémont refused, and Lincoln revoked the emancipation.

In May 1862 Brigadier General David Hunter, USA, began enlisting black soldiers in the occupied coastal areas of Georgia, Florida, and South Carolina that were under his control. In doing this, he declared the emancipation of all slaves in this region. Lincoln responded by ordering the black regiment disbanded. This order prompted *New York Tribune* editor Horace Greeley to address an open letter to Lincoln in the pages of his paper. Greeley unjustifiably claimed to write on behalf of the 20 million citizens of the loyal states who (he asserted) called for abolition to become an explicit objective of the war. Lincoln replied in the *Tribune* on August 22, 1862:

> My paramount object in this struggle is to save the Union, and is not either to save or destroy Slavery. If I could save the Union without freeing any slave, I would do it; and if I could save it by freeing all the slaves, I would do it; and if I could do it by freeing some and leaving others alone, I would also do that. What I do about Slavery and the colored race, I do because I believe it helps to save this Union; and what I forbear, I forbear because I do not believe it would help to save the Union.

There can be no question that Lincoln personally abhorred slavery, but he would not act against it in what he believed to be violation of the Constitution and the rule of law. Most of all, he would not act against it if doing so threatened the preservation (or restoration) of the Union. The dissolution of the Union was an immediate crisis, whereas the abolition of slavery could be effected over time.

Before he took office as president and prior to the outbreak of the Civil War, Lincoln had contemplated alternatives to emancipation by executive order or fiat. One idea he entertained was a policy of gradual emancipation, to be carried out in accordance with the Constitution by compensating slave owners for the release of their "property." He would, moreover, attempt to institute this policy not on the federal level, but rather on a state-by-state basis, beginning with the legislatures of the Northern slaveholding states where slavery was already weak, such as Delaware. This, Lincoln had believed, was the only hope of staving off civil war as well as keeping the emancipation issue out of the federal courts, where a negative decision might forever block *any* attempt to abolish slavery.

Once in office and even after seven states had seceded, Lincoln still held on to the possibility of legislated emancipation. When Senator John J. Crittenden of Kentucky reintroduced for consideration part of his failed "Crittenden Compromise"—the constitutional amendment barring the federal government from ever interfering with the institution of slavery, even by some future amendment—in an attempt to lure the errant states back into the Union, Lincoln withheld objection, even as he refused to consider any legislation permitting the expansion of slavery. His hope was that by containing slavery and preventing its expansion into the federal territories, he could still prevail upon state legislatures to introduce gradual, compensated emancipation by which slavery would peacefully wither away over time. Lincoln further believed that this more-or-less natural reduction of slavery was precisely what the Founders had envisioned.

When secession led to war, Lincoln turned to the border states, which were always key to him. He believed that his best chance for both ending slavery and restoring the Union lay with them. For that reason, he did not want to risk alienating them with a forceful policy of emancipation, which might drive them into the embrace of the Confederacy. Lincoln hoped that if he could demonstrate to them the viability and desirability of compensated emancipation, perhaps the rebellion itself would end and the Union be restored. Even if persuasion by example failed, Lincoln believed it possible that the combination of Union military success and compensated emancipa-

tion in the border states would bring about the collapse of the rebellion.

Yet all of the border state legislatures ultimately rejected Lincoln's proposals for compensated emancipation—and they did so in 1862, at a time when the war was not going well for the North. The combination of the border states' rejection of voluntary abolition and the stalemate of the war persuaded Lincoln that time had run out for the cause of gradual emancipation. Lincoln realized that the combination of military failure and a failure to push for emancipation would be perceived by the South as a vindication of slavery. The president therefore decided that he could no longer temporize on the issue of emancipation; however, it was also clear to him that only a military victory could drive the abolition of slavery.

Of course, there was still the danger that emancipation would alienate the border states. Also, a presidential emancipation proclamation might be challenged in the federal courts, which were conservative and might hand down a decision protecting slavery forever. Moreover, emancipation might truly be unconstitutional, open to legal challenge even after a successful conclusion to the Civil War. Finally, the border states were not alone in believing that blacks were an inherently inferior race. Many people in the North, soldiers included, were willing to fight a war to preserve the Union but did not want to sacrifice their lives to free slave members of a "lesser race." But Lincoln had decided that the risks were worth taking, especially if emancipation would provide the moral impetus that might finally drive the people of the North to achieve victory. Lincoln therefore consulted William Whiting, a War Department lawyer, on the question of the president's legal authority to declare emancipation. Whiting reported his opinion that the chief executive's war powers conferred the necessary authority. Lincoln consulted with his vice president, Hannibal Hamlin, and set about writing an emancipation proclamation that would claim the moral high ground without alienating the border states or anyone else, and without doing violence to the Constitution.

On July 22, 1862, Lincoln announced to his cabinet his intention of issuing a proclamation freeing the slaves, but only in the unconquered parts of the Confederacy. This would put off the issue in the border states and even in those parts of the Confederacy occupied by the North. Postmaster General Montgomery Blair argued that such a proclamation would bring about the collapse of the Republican Party, but Secretary of State William Seward supported the idea; however, he reinforced Lincoln's sense that issuing the proclamation on the heels of so many military defeats would undercut it fatally, making it seem an empty gesture or even an act of desperation. Seward advised Lincoln to delay the proclamation until the army had won a significant military victory.

Lincoln waited until September 17, 1862, when Union forces eked out a narrow and tremendously bloody victory at the Battle of Antietam. Betraying Lincoln's eagerness to avoid any immediate or future legal challenges as well as his determination to alienate no one who was still willing to be considered loyal, the Preliminary Emancipation Proclamation published on September 22, 1862, freed not a single slave. Rather, it merely served warning on slave owners living in states "still in rebellion on January 1, 1863" that their slave property would be declared "forever free." Lincoln duly awaited the January 1 deadline before issuing the final **Emancipation Proclamation,** which freed only those slaves in areas still "in rebellion"—that is, those slaves who lived in parts of the Confederacy that were not yet under the control of the Union army. Elsewhere, where it existed, slavery continued.

The Draft: North and South

Although the North and South both resorted to conscription, both armies were largely volunteer forces. Of the 2.1 million men who served in the Union army, only 52,068 were draftees. Another 42,581 men enlisted as paid substitutes for draftees, and 86,724 men who were subject to the draft each paid a $300 commutation fee to receive an exemption from service. The legal commutation fee represented a hefty (and discriminatory) sum in an age when common laborers earned about a dollar a day.

The Confederacy enacted a conscription law on April 16, 1862, almost a full year before the Union did so. Though exact numbers are not known due to poor record keeping and the loss of records, in the Confederate states all white men between the ages of eighteen and thirty-five who were not legally exempt were conscripted for three years' service. In September 1862 the upper age limit was raised to forty-five, and in February 1864 it went up to fifty, while the lower limit was pushed down to seventeen. A gauge of the desperate state of the South's military manpower crisis was the February 1864 authorization by the Confederate Congress of the conscription of free blacks and slaves for "auxiliary" (noncombat) military service. On March 13, 1865, the "Negro Soldier Law" authorized the voluntary recruitment of slaves for combat. These troops could remain slaves or, with the "consent of the owners and of the States," could be emancipated. Although a few companies of black Confederate soldiers were enrolled, the war ended before any saw combat.

The Confederate conscription laws, like those enacted later in the North, were inherently unjust. Those with enough money could pay a commutation fee or hire a substitute; moreover, men who owned or oversaw twenty or more slaves were automatically exempt from conscription, although many joined voluntarily. Draft evasion was common in the South, and by the end of the war, desertion reached epidemic proportions.

Enthusiasm for the war was hardly uniform, either in the North or the South. In New York City, where support for the war had never been strong—early in the war, Mayor Fernando Wood had proposed declaring New York and Long Island independent of both the United States *and* the Confederacy—the large immigrant population was terrified and enraged over the prospect of an influx of liberated slaves, who they believed would take their jobs. This fear was especially strong among the city's 200,000 Irish immigrants, many of whom had fled

Emancipation Proclamation, 1863

Whereas, on the twenty-second day of September, in the year of our Lord one thousand eight hundred and sixty-two, a proclamation was issued by the President of the United States, containing, among other things, the following, to wit:

"That on the first day of January, in the year of our Lord one thousand eight hundred and sixty-three, all persons held as slaves within any State or designated part of a State, the people whereof shall then be in rebellion against the United States, shall be then, thenceforward, and forever free; and the Executive Government of the United States, including the military and naval authority thereof, will recognize and maintain the freedom of such persons, and will do no act or acts to repress such persons, or any of them, in any efforts they may make for their actual freedom.

"That the Executive will, on the first day of January aforesaid, by proclamation, designate the States and parts of States, if any, in which the people thereof, respectively, shall then be in rebellion against the United States; and the fact that any State, or the people thereof, shall on that day be, in good faith, represented in the Congress of the United States by members chosen thereto at elections wherein a majority of the qualified voters of such State shall have participated, shall, in the absence of strong countervailing testimony, be deemed conclusive evidence that such State, and the people thereof, are not then in rebellion against the United States."

Now, therefore I, Abraham Lincoln, President of the United States, by virtue of the power in me vested as Commander-in-Chief, of the Army and Navy of the United States in time of actual armed rebellion against the authority and government of the United States, and as a fit and necessary war measure for suppressing said rebellion, do, on this first day of January, in the year of our Lord one thousand eight hundred and sixty-three, and in accordance with my purpose so to do publicly proclaimed for the full period of one hundred days, from the day first above mentioned, order and designate as the States and parts of States wherein the people thereof respectively, are this day in rebellion against the United States. . . .

And by virtue of the power, and for the purpose aforesaid, I do order and declare that all persons held as slaves within said designated States, and parts of States, are, and henceforward shall be free; and that the Executive government of the United States, including the military and naval authorities thereof, will recognize and maintain the freedom of said persons. . . .

And I further declare and make known, that such persons of suitable condition, will be received into the armed service of the United States to garrison forts, positions, stations, and other places, and to man vessels of all sorts in said service.

Excerpted from the Avalon Project at Yale Law School, "Emancipation Proclamation: January 1, 1863," www.yale.edu/lawweb/avalon/emancipa.htm.

---

the Potato Famine that had starved their native land in 1848. The federal Conscription Act, passed in March 1863, seemed crafted to force the Irish to fight and die to free the very slaves who would steal the bread from their mouths. When the draft commenced in New York City on Saturday, July 11, a massive riot, mostly carried out by Irish immigrants, broke out and lasted through Wednesday evening, when a detachment of Gettysburg veterans marched into the city to restore order. The Irish chiefly targeted the city's black community, so the "Draft Riot" was, in large part, a race riot. No accurate estimate was ever made of the casualties of the New York Draft Riot, but historians believe that 300–1,000 or more people died.

Troops quickly put down the New York riot, but war weariness gripped many parts of the North. Sporadic violence flared in nearby Brooklyn, Jamaica, and Staten Island, New York, as well as in Jersey City and Newark, New Jersey. Albany and Troy, New York; Boston, Massachusetts; Portsmouth, New Hampshire; Columbia and Bucks counties, Pennsylvania;

and parts of Kentucky, Iowa, Illinois, Indiana, Ohio, and Wisconsin all saw rioting. Some riots protested the draft itself, but most objected specifically to being drafted in order to free black slaves.

Copperheads and Confederate Terrorists

The draft riots sparked Northern fears—and Confederate hopes—of a general rebellion throughout large parts of the North, fomented by Northerners politely referred to as "Peace Democrats." These individuals advocated immediate restoration of the Union through a generous negotiated settlement with the South. Their opponents called them "Copperheads," a term that first appeared in a *New York Tribune* article on July 20, 1861, comparing them to the venomous snake that strikes lethally without warning.

Copperheads opposed not only the Conscription Act, but also the Emancipation Proclamation, which, they protested, changed the Civil War from a struggle to preserve the Union to a "war for the Negro." The most extreme Copperheads organized themselves into secret societies, which were modeled on the "Southern Rights clubs" that had come into existence during the Nullification Crisis of the 1830s, when the cotton states had threatened to secede rather than abide by adverse tariff legislation. In 1854 George W. L. Bickley, a self-proclaimed physician, founded the Knights of the Golden Circle, which was headquartered in Cincinnati, Ohio. Renamed during the war the Order of the American Knights and, still later, the Order of the Sons of Liberty, this Copperhead secret society gave rise to satellite lodges, called "castles," throughout Kentucky, Missouri, Iowa, Illinois, Indiana, and Ohio.

If the Copperheads rallied around any particular leader, it was Clement Vallandigham, who was renowned throughout Ohio as a prosperous and virtually unbeatable defense attorney. Vallandigham served a term as lieutenant governor of Ohio, then was elected to Congress as an anti-Abolitionist Democrat, but was defeated for reelection in 1862. His parting speech before Congress called on his countrymen to lay down their arms. Many regarded the speech as treasonous, and a significant number of Copperheads were emboldened by it.

Governor Oliver Morton of Indiana so feared Copperhead subversion in his state that he prevailed on Secretary of War Edwin Stanton to send Brigadier General Henry B. Carrington to Indianapolis to organize undercover government agents to infiltrate the "castles" beginning in November 1862. Although Carrington did discover widespread Copperhead activity, his superiors in Washington dismissed it all as the ravings of harmless fanatics. Carrington responded by pointing out that some Copperheads actively aided the Confederate guerrilla leader John Hunt Morgan in his destructive raids throughout the Midwest and Kentucky during the summer of 1863.

In the wake of Morgan's raids, Major General Ambrose Burnside, who had been named commander of the Army of the Ohio (after he was relieved as commander in chief of the Army of the Potomac following the catastrophic Battle of Fredericksburg), issued Order No. 38 on April 13, 1863, which authorized the death penalty for couriers carrying secret mails, for enemy agents operating behind Union lines, and for anyone recruiting members for secret societies. Vallandigham responded to this in a May Day address before an audience of Democrats assembled at Mount Vernon, Ohio. He spat on a copy of the order, cursed Burnside as a tyrant, and accused the Republicans of prolonging the war for the sole purpose of destroying the Democratic Party. Burnside, in turn, arrested Vallandigham—a precipitous act that touched off riots in Dayton, Ohio, and elsewhere in the Midwest. Even many moderate newspapers defended Vallandigham's right of free speech, and he was catapulted into national prominence.

Vallandigham was tried and sentenced to imprisonment for the duration of the war, but President Lincoln commuted the sentence to banishment to the South. When Confederate authorities insisted that Vallandigham renounce his loyalty to the Union before he would be admitted to Confederate territory, he refused, sailed for the Caribbean, and then turned north to Nova Scotia. Despite his banishment, the

Ohio Democratic Party defiantly nominated him as its candidate for governor, and Vallandigham ran his campaign from the Canadian side of Niagara Falls.

In the end, Vallandigham was not elected, and the influence of the Copperheads waned, although rumors of insurrection persisted through the summer of 1864, when there was talk of their liberating Confederate POWs from a large prison camp outside of Chicago. This plot, if it ever actually existed, came to nothing.

Emergence of Black Troops

As early as August 1861, Frederick Douglass, the eloquent former slave who had earned national fame as an advocate of abolition, spoke in favor of the enlistment of black soldiers in the Union army. The initial response was unyielding resistance. Some objected that blacks were inherently untrainable and cowardly, while others were simply unwilling to trust them with firearms. In addition to the racist basis for resistance, there was a fear among many military men that the presence of black soldiers in the Union army would serve to boost Confederate morale and possibly incite Confederate troops to acts of atrocity and vengeance. Even President Lincoln resisted recruiting black troops, for fear of alienating the population of the border states.

Despite social, political, and military resistance, a group of free blacks who had formed a (never-activated) Confederate regiment in 1861 offered their services to Union general Benjamin F. Butler after New Orleans fell to the Union in the spring of 1862. At first Butler declined the offer, but under imminent threat of a Confederate attack in August, he quickly recruited three black regiments as the Louisiana Native Guard, or Corps d'Afrique. The War Department refused to muster them in, but Butler nevertheless deployed them in November 1862. Also during spring 1862, on Union-occupied islands off the coast of South Carolina, Major General David Hunter raised a black regiment consisting of volunteers as well as men he "drafted" into service. When the War Department refused to sanction the regiment, Hunter disbanded all but a single company of troops by

August. In perpetually violent Kansas, between July 1862 and October 1863, James H. Lane, a major general of the local militia, raised two regiments of fugitive slaves and free blacks that were officially recognized by the War Department in 1863.

As the Union suffered one defeat after another early in the war, Congress passed the **Second Confiscation Act** of July 17, 1862, which authorized the president to "employ as many persons of African descent as he may deem necessary and proper for the suppression of this rebellion." Simultaneously, another act passed on this date repealed a 1792 law barring blacks from serving in the armed forces and explicitly authorized the recruitment of free blacks and freedmen.

On August 25, 1862, the War Department authorized the military governor of the South Carolina Sea Islands to raise five regiments of black troops, to be commanded by white officers. The unit was mustered in on November 7, 1862, as the First South Carolina Volunteers. After the final Emancipation Proclamation was issued on January 1, 1863, President Lincoln personally called for four black regiments, and by war's end, 178,985 blacks were serving in 166 regiments. This represented about 10 percent of the Union army at its peak strength.

The acceptance of blacks into the army was a major step, but the majority of white soldiers and officers were not pleased with the decision. Black troops served in segregated regiments, which were always commanded by white officers. Frequently abused both physically and verbally, they were poorly equipped and paid less than white soldiers were. Most were initially assigned to menial labor details, but many blacks eventually saw significant combat, fighting in 449 engagements, including 39 major battles.

Confederate Response to Black Troops

Even though it, too, would authorize some use of black troops, the Confederate government was outraged by the presence of black soldiers in the Union forces used to fight in the South. On May 1, 1863,

Second Confiscation Act, 1862

Be it enacted by the Senate and House of Representatives of the United States of America in Congress assembled, That every person who shall hereafter commit the crime of treason against the United States, and shall be adjudged guilty thereof, shall suffer death, and all his slaves, if any, shall be declared and made free; or, at the discretion of the court, he shall be imprisoned for not less than five years and fined not less than ten thousand dollars, and all his slaves, if any, shall be declared and made free. . . .

SEC. 2. *And be it further enacted,* That if any person shall hereafter incite, set on foot, assist, or engage in any rebellion or insurrection against the authority of the United States, or the laws thereof, or shall give aid or comfort thereto, or shall engage in, or give aid and comfort to, any such existing rebellion or insurrection, and be convicted thereof, such person shall be punished by imprisonment for a period not exceeding ten years, or by a fine not exceeding ten thousand dollars, and by the liberation of all his slaves, if any he have; or by both of said punishments, at the discretion of the court. . . .

SEC. 9. *And be it further enacted,* That all slaves of persons who shall hereafter be engaged in rebellion against the government of the United States, or who shall in any way give aid or comfort thereto, escaping from such persons and taking refuge within the lines of the army; and all slaves captured from such persons or deserted by them and coming under the control of the government of the United States; and all slaves of such person found on [*or*] being within any place occupied by rebel forces and afterwards occupied by the forces of the United States, shall be deemed captives of war, and shall be forever free of their servitude, and not again held as slaves. . . .

SEC. 11. *And be it further enacted,* That the President of the United States is authorized to employ as many persons of African descent as he may deem necessary and proper for the suppression of this rebellion.

University of Maryland Department of History, Freedman and Southern Society Project, "Second Confiscation Act," in *Freedom: A Documentary History of Emancipation, 1861–1867,* www.history.umd.edu/Freedmen/conact2.htm.

the Confederate Congress authorized President Davis to "put to death or . . . otherwise [punish]" any black soldiers taken as prisoners of war. Among the alternative punishments was the enslavement of the prisoner. The act also authorized execution of white officers in command of black troops. President Lincoln responded with an executive order on July 30 warning that "for every soldier of the United States killed in violation of the laws of war, a Rebel soldier shall be executed; and for every one enslaved by the enemy or sold into Slavery, a Rebel soldier shall be placed at hard labor on public works."

Election of 1864

By 1864, the year in which Abraham Lincoln was to stand for reelection, the tide of the Civil War had been turned in favor of the Union; nevertheless, there was much war weariness in the North, and President Lincoln (along with his supporters and critics) was far from confident that he would be reelected. Clearly, the Confederates were losing the war, yet, just as clearly, they kept fighting—and both Southerners and Northerners kept dying. There was strong sentiment in much of the North for a negotiated peace with the Confederacy. Lincoln desperately wanted a major and unmistakably glorious military victory to rally support for the main plank in his reelection platform: total, unconditional triumph over the Confederacy and the restoration of the Union as a single nation without slavery. On August 5, 1864, Rear Admiral David Farragut gave the president a naval victory at the Battle of Mobile Bay, and it was indeed glorious.

Within his own party, Lincoln faced opposition from the most uncompromising of the Radical

Republicans. They wanted a hard-line abolitionist in the White House and pushed for the nomination of Major General John C. Frémont, whose Missouri emancipation order Lincoln had earlier countermanded. But, in the end, more moderate heads prevailed, and Lincoln was nominated for a second term. He chose a new running mate, replacing Vice President Hannibal Hamlin with Tennessee governor Andrew Johnson, a Democrat who had remained steadfastly loyal to the Union. Lincoln regarded his nomination as an important gesture signaling his desire to reconcile with the South—after it had surrendered unconditionally.

In August, even as the victory at Mobile Bay was unfolding, the Democratic Party convention in Chicago nominated George B. McClellan, the former commander in chief of the Army of the Potomac, whom Lincoln had dismissed because of his persistent lack of aggression. The Democratic Party platform included a pledge to make "efforts . . . for a cessation of hostilities," by which was clearly meant seeking a negotiated peace with the Confederacy rather than carrying the fight to unconditional surrender. Once nominated, however, McClellan was guided by his military sense, which saw the Confederacy as doomed, and he repudiated this plank of his party's platform. Lincoln, however, refused to let him off the hook. During his own campaign, he persisted in drawing a stark contrast between the Democrats (he did not single out McClellan) and himself: whereas the Democrats were willing to discard the enormous sacrifices that had been made in

this war, he would honor those sacrifices by continuing the fight to total victory.

The entry of Major General William Tecumseh Sherman into Atlanta on September 2, 1864, set the seal on Lincoln's prospects for reelection on November 8. He received 2,216,067 popular and 212 electoral votes to McClellan's 1,808,725 popular and 21 electoral votes. Most gratifying to the president was the fact that the soldiers of the U.S. Army had cast their ballots overwhelmingly for him.

Lincoln's Second Inaugural Address

Abraham Lincoln was a man of great intellect, great heart, and great eloquence. His two greatest speeches, the Gettysburg Address and the **Second Inaugural Address,** were also his briefest. The March 4, 1864, inaugural remarks made a simple statement about the progress of the war, what it had achieved, and what it had cost. It ended with a

This pro-McClellan campaign poster from the 1864 presidential election contrasts the candidates' positions on the Civil War and abolition.

Lincoln's Second Inaugural Address, 1864

On the occasion corresponding to this four years ago all thoughts were anxiously directed to an impending civil war. All dreaded it, all sought to avert it. While the inaugural address was being delivered from this place, devoted altogether to saving the Union without war, insurgent agents were in the city seeking to destroy it without war—seeking to dissolve the Union and divide effects by negotiation. Both parties deprecated war, but one of them would make war rather than let the nation survive, and the other would accept war rather than let it perish, and the war came.

One-eighth of the whole population were colored slaves, not distributed generally over the Union, but localized in the southern part of it. These slaves constituted a peculiar and powerful interest. All knew that this interest was somehow the cause of the war. To strengthen, perpetuate, and extend this interest was the object for which the insurgents would rend the Union even by war, while the Government claimed no right to do more than to restrict the territorial enlargement of it. Neither party expected for the war the magnitude or the duration which it has already attained. Neither anticipated that the cause of the conflict might cease with or even before the conflict itself should cease. Each looked for an easier triumph, and a result less fundamental and astounding. Both read the same Bible and pray to the same God, and each invokes His aid against the other. . . .

With malice toward none, with charity for all, with firmness in the right as God gives us to see the right, let us strive on to finish the work we are in, to bind up the nation's wounds, to care for him who shall have borne the battle and for his widow and his orphan, to do all which may achieve and cherish a just and lasting peace among ourselves and with all nations.

Excerpted from the Avalon Project at Yale Law School, "Second Inaugural Address of Abraham Lincoln," www.yale.edu/lawweb/avalon/presiden/inaug/lincoln2.htm.

moving and succinct statement of what Lincoln intended to be the healing policy of his second term, in which he intended to create a peace based on justice, compassion, and forgiveness.

Victory and Surrender

On April 2–4, 1865, the Union army marched into Richmond, Virginia, and a week later, Robert E. Lee surrendered the Army of Northern Virginia to Ulysses S. Grant at Appomattox Court House, Virginia. In practical military terms, this ended the Civil War, although fighting continued fitfully in the West until Confederate general Edmund Kirby Smith surrendered to Brigadier General E. R. S. Canby on May 26. (The very last Confederate commander to officially lay down arms was Stand Watie, on June 23, 1865, at Doakville, Indian Territory.)

No treaties were concluded between North and South because the Washington government did not recognize the Confederate States of America as a sovereign entity competent to conclude a treaty. Traditionally, historians have regarded the **Exchange of Letters at Appomattox** as the documents most dramatically signifying the end of the war. At 5:00 p.m. on April 7, 1865, Ulysses S. Grant sent a letter to Robert E. Lee, alluding to the "hopelessness of further resistance." He wrote: "I . . . regard it as my duty to shift from myself the responsibility for any further effusion of blood by asking of you the surrender of that portion of the C. S. Army known as the Army of Northern Virginia." Lee replied the same day. He disclaimed "the opinion you express of the hopelessness of further resistance," but continued, "I reciprocate your desire to avoid useless effusion of blood," and he asked for a proposal of surrender terms. On April 8, Grant replied that he lacked authority to state definitive terms, but simply stated that the "terms upon which peace can be had are well understood. By the South laying down their arms they will hasten that most desirable event." Grant closed, "Sincerely hoping that all our difficulties may be settled without the loss of another life, I subscribe myself, Very respectfully, your obedient servant, US GRANT, Lieutenant-General, U.S. Army." The two generals met at Wilmer McLean's farmhouse at Appomattox Court House on April 9 and drew up an exchange of letters.

The war was definitively ended by presidential proclamations issued on April 2 and August 20,

Exchange of Letters at Appomattox, 1865

Grant's Terms:

Headquarters Armies of the United States,
Appomattox Court-House, Va., April 9, 1865.

General R. E. Lee,
Commanding C. S. Army:

General:
In accordance with the substance of my letter to you of the 8th instant, I propose to receive the surrender of the Army of Northern Virginia on the following terms, to wit: Rolls of all the officers and men to be made in duplicate—one copy to be given to an officer to be designated by me, the other to be retained by such officer or officers as you may designate; the officers to give their individual paroles not to take up arms against the Government of the United States until properly exchanged, and each company or regimental commander sign a like parole for the men of their commands. The arms, artillery, and public property to be parked and stacked, and turned over to the officers appointed by me to receive them. This will not embrace the side-arms of the officers, nor their private horses or baggage. This done, each officer and man will be allowed to return to their homes, not to be disturbed by United States authority so long as they observe their paroles and the laws in force where they may reside.

Very respectfully,
U.S. GRANT, Lieutenant-General.

Lee's Response:

Headquarters Army of Northern Virginia,
Lieut. Gen. U.S. Grant,
Commanding Armies of the United States:

April 9, 1865.

General:
I have received your letter of this date containing the terms of surrender of the Army of Northern Virginia as proposed by you. As they are substantially the same as those expressed in your letter of the 8th instant, they are accepted. I will proceed to designate the proper officers to carry the stipulations into effect.

Very respectfully, your obedient servant,
R. E. LEE,
General.

Excerpted from Alan Axelrod, *American Treaties and Alliances* (Washington, D.C.: CQ Press, 2000), 75–76.

1866. More properly part of Reconstruction, these measures and documents are discussed in Chapter 18, along with presidential proclamations granting amnesty and pardon for the Confederate States and proclaiming provisional governments for those states.

BIBLIOGRAPHY

Boatner, Mark Mayo, III. *The Civil War Dictionary,* rev. ed. New York: David McKay, 1959.

Catton, Bruce. *The Coming Fury.* Garden City, N.Y.: Doubleday, 1961.

———. *Glory Road.* Reprint, New York: Anchor Books, 1990. First published 1952 by Doubleday.

———. *Mr. Lincoln's Army.* Reprint, New York: Anchor Books, 1990. First published 1951 by Doubleday.

———. *Never Call Retreat.* Garden City, N.Y.: Doubleday, 1965.

———. *A Stillness at Appomattox.* Reprint, New York: Anchor Books, 1990. First published 1953 by Doubleday.

———. *Terrible Swift Sword.* Garden City, N.Y.: Doubleday, 1963

———. *This Hallowed Ground.* Garden City, N.Y.: Doubleday, 1955.

Cornish, Dudley Taylor. *The Sable Arm: Black Troops in the Union Army, 1861–1865.* Lawrence: University of Kansas Press, 1987.

Current, Richard N., Paul D. Escott, Lawrence N. Powell, James I. Robertson Jr., and Emory M. Thomas, eds. *Encyclopedia of the Confederacy.* New York: Simon and Schuster, 1993.

Dupuy, R. Ernest, and Trevor N. Dupuy. *The Compact History of the Civil War.* New York: Warner Books, 1993.

Foote, Shelby. *The Civil War: A Narrative.* 4 vols. New York: Random House, 1958–1974. All reprinted 1986 by Vintage (New York).

CHAPTER 18

RECONSTRUCTION

(1865–1877)

At Issue

"Reconstruction" describes the twelve-year period following the Civil War during which the American government and people took legal, economic, and social action to solve the myriad problems associated with the readmission of the eleven former Confederate states to the Union.

Reconstruction Overview

Reconstruction proper began after the Civil War, but the administration of President Abraham Lincoln began preparing for the reintegration into the Union of the seceded Confederate states as early as 1862, the war's second year. At that time, Lincoln appointed provisional military governors for Louisiana, Tennessee, and North Carolina, states in which Union troops occupied at least some territory. In 1863 the administration began planning the reestablishment of popular local (nonmilitary) governments in Union-occupied Southern states to be put in place as soon as at least 10 percent of the state's voting population had taken the oath of allegiance prescribed by the U.S. government. The Radical Republicans—the congressional faction that favored harsh, even punitive treatment for the "states in rebellion" and sought to ensure good treatment of freed slaves at the hands of Southern governments—objected to Lincoln's initial plan on the grounds that it did not include provisions for the social and economic aspects of Reconstruction, that it was too lenient, and that it gave to the president too much jurisdic-

tional authority over Reconstruction policy and administration. In response, Congress passed the Wade-Davis Bill (discussed below) in 1864, which received a pocket veto from Lincoln (that is, the president did not sign the bill before Congress adjourned, so it did not become law).

Although Lincoln was uncompromising with regard to the military aspects of the Civil War—insisting on nothing less than total victory and the consequent unconditional restoration of the Union—it was clear from policy statements and speeches (especially his Second Inaugural Address; see Chapter 17) that he intended to take a healing or conciliatory approach to reuniting the North and the South once victory had been won. The assassination of President Lincoln on the evening of April 14, 1865 (he died the next morning) brought into office Tennessee Democrat Andrew Johnson, who was irascible, crude, blunt, and even uncouth, lacking Lincoln's dignity, charisma, judgment, eloquence, and general political savvy. His implementation of Lincoln's lenient Reconstruction policies alienated Congress, especially the Radical Republican wing, which wanted to punish the South. Eventually, this alienation would lead to Johnson's impeachment.

The Thirteenth Amendment, abolishing slavery in the United States, was passed by the Senate on April 8, 1864, and by the House (after a fight) on January 31, 1865, and was ratified by the states on December 18, 1865. The Fourteenth Amendment, which defined citizenship to include blacks, was passed by Congress in June 1866 and ratified on July 28, 1868—although most Southern states rejected it.

This rejection (along with a series of racist laws passed by Southern legislatures and violence perpetrated against blacks there) persuaded a majority of voters in the North that the South was incorrigible.

CHRONOLOGY OF RECONSTRUCTION

1862
- President Abraham Lincoln appoints provisional military governors for Louisiana, Tennessee, and North Carolina.

1863
- Lincoln proposes liberal Reconstruction program.

1864

July 2 The Wade-Davis Bill is passed; Lincoln exercises a pocket veto.

1865

Mar. 3 Congress passes the Freedmen's Bureau Act.

Apr. 14 Lincoln is assassinated. He dies on April 15 and is succeeded by Andrew Johnson.

May 29 President Johnson issues a Proclamation of Amnesty and Pardon for the Confederate States.

Dec. 18 The Thirteenth Amendment is ratified by the states.

1866

Apr. 9 Congress passes the Civil Rights Act of 1866.

July 24 Tennessee is readmitted to the Union.

1867

Mar. 2 Congress passes the Reconstruction Act of 1867 and overrides Johnson's veto of the Tenure of Office Act.

1868

May 16 and 26 Johnson is acquitted in his impeachment trial in both houses of Congress.

July 28 The Fourteenth Amendment is ratified by the states.

Dec. 7 The Fifteenth Amendment is passed.

1870

Feb. 3 The Fifteenth Amendment is ratified by the states.

1877
- The brokered election of Rutherford B. Hayes as president brings an end to Reconstruction.

Furthermore, Johnson's refusal to compromise with the Radical Republicans exacerbated the social and political gulf between North and South and tended to radicalize both Northerners and Southerners. The result was an overwhelming victory for the Radical Republicans in the congressional elections of 1868; this faction came to enjoy a majority in both houses, and the major era of congressionally controlled Reconstruction—called by historians "Radical Reconstruction"—began. It would last for a decade.

Tennessee, which had always had a substantial loyal minority, was readmitted to the Union on July 24, 1866. The Reconstruction Acts of 1867 (discussed below) divided the other ten former Confederate states into five military districts, and government was administered by military officers and enforced by U.S. troops. These states were readmitted to the Union between 1868 and 1870, after each accepted the Fourteenth Amendment. Those states readmitted after passage of the Fifteenth Amendment on December 7, 1868—an amendment guaranteeing the civil rights of the former slaves— also had to ratify that amendment as well.

As typically constituted under Radical Republican supervision, the civil governments of the restored states consisted of Republicans and included blacks (freed slaves, most of whom were uneducated and unprepared to administer or govern anything), "carpetbaggers" (Northerners who emigrated to the South to reap the political and material spoils of Restoration government), and "scalawags" (native Southerners who collaborated with blacks and carpetbaggers in government). These new civil governments were universally unpopular and were seen by Southern whites as tyrannically imposed upon them by the North.

Some of the greatest resentment and hostility was directed toward the Freedmen's Bureau, an agency created by Congress to feed, protect, and educate the freed slaves. The resentment drove the creation of white and white-supremacist organizations, including the Ku Klux Klan (KKK) and the similar Knights of the White Camelia (the spelling was idiosyncratic). These groups terrorized blacks (and whites who collaborated with blacks) as well as the carpetbaggers and scalawags. In many parts of the South, the KKK and similar organizations functioned as shadow governments.

Generally speaking, many Southerners employed terror, intimidation, and fraud to wrestle control of state governments back into the hands of conservatives, who sabotaged Radical Reconstruction measures. Reconstruction was ended suddenly in 1877 as a result of a backroom political deal that put Republican Rutherford B. Hayes into the White House in exchange for his pledge to withdraw from the South the last of the military governments and other paraphernalia of Reconstruction (see "The Decline and Fall of Reconstruction," below).

Although most American historians in the early twentieth century portrayed Reconstruction as both dictatorial and corrupt, more recent historians have emphasized the high-minded, well-intentioned, beneficial, and often successful aspects of Reconstruction. These historians admit that Reconstruction was plagued by corruption, but, they argue, the level of corruption was no worse in Reconstruction governments than it was throughout the nation during the notoriously corrupt administration of President Ulysses S. Grant. For all the bitterness generated by Reconstruction, most of the reforms it introduced, ranging from protections of civil rights to reform of taxation policies, have endured to this day.

Lincoln's Postwar Plan

As the Civil War came to its end, President Lincoln drew up plans to create, as rapidly as possible, loyal governments in the Southern states. Each former Confederate who took an oath of loyalty to the U.S. government would be granted a full and complete amnesty, and when 10 percent of voters in a state had taken the oath, the state would be readmitted to the Union. Lincoln believed that this leniency would ultimately lead to the strengthening of the nation as well as of the Republican Party in the South.

"Radical" members of the first South Carolina legislature after the Civil War.

Wade-Davis Bill

Even before the war was over—and before Lincoln was assassinated—federal and local authorities created new governments for Louisiana, Tennessee, and Arkansas. Congress, however, refused to recognize the new governments set up for the three states and offered instead the Wade-Davis Bill. Sponsored by Radical Republican senators Benjamin F. Wade and Henry W. Davis, the bill provided for the appointment of provisional military governors in the formerly seceded states. Only after a simple majority of a state's white citizens swore allegiance to the Union could the state call a constitutional convention, which would be a prerequisite to readmission to the Union. The Wade-Davis Bill required that each state constitution explicitly abolish slavery, repudiate secession, and bar all former Confederate officials from holding office or even voting. Moreover, to qualify for the right to vote, every citizen would be required to swear an oath (in addition to the loyalty oath) testifying that he had never voluntarily aided the Confederacy. Such an oath would automatically disenfranchise former Confederate soldiers as well as anyone who had in any tangible way supported the government of Jefferson Davis.

President Lincoln exercised a pocket veto of the Wade-Davis Bill. It is a peculiarity of the American federal system that if a bill is presented for presidential signature within ten days of congressional adjournment, the president may indirectly veto it simply by holding it, unsigned—in effect, putting it in his pocket—until after Congress adjourns.

Because President Lincoln was assassinated, the Wade-Davis Bill would have to be resubmitted to President Andrew Johnson when Congress reconvened. Johnson was eager to see the restoration of the states proceed rapidly. He took the bill in hand and modified it by insisting that the oath concerning

Andrew Johnson
(1808–1875)

Born in Raleigh, North Carolina, Andrew Johnson was one of two sons of a local constable, whose death when Johnson was three years old left the family in poverty. At age fourteen Johnson was apprenticed to a tailor; he was seventeen when he broke his indenture and moved with his mother and brother to Greeneville, Tennessee, where he opened a tailor shop. Johnson hired a man to read to him while he did his work, and thereby gained an education in history, oratory, and law—including the U.S. Constitution, which he committed to memory.

At eighteen Johnson married sixteen-year-old Eliza McCardle, who taught him to read and write with fluency (he was barely literate before this) and to do arithmetic. Gradually, his tailor shop became a gathering place for political discussion. Johnson, a natural orator, became popular and was elected to local offices. In 1843 he began a decade of service in the U.S. House of Representatives. He was elected governor of Tennessee in 1853, but resigned in 1857 to take his seat in the U.S. Senate.

As a Democratic senator, Johnson, who owned a small number of slaves, generally espoused the Southern view, opposing abolition and favoring low tariffs; however, he was an outspoken opponent of secession. When his state left the Union in June 1861, he became the only Southern senator who did not relinquish his seat, and he refused to join the Confederacy. Lincoln rewarded his loyalty in May 1862 by appointing him military governor of Tennessee, which was occupied and under federal control. Lincoln also saw in Johnson, a "War Democrat," an opportunity to broaden the base of the Republican Party and therefore chose him as his running mate in 1864.

Johnson lacked finesse as a public figure and was sometimes seen intoxicated in public. Some accounts report that he was drunk on the day he assumed the office of president. He certainly was faced with an appallingly difficult task: nothing less than the reconstruction of the Union. Johnson was determined to carry through a lenient Reconstruction program—as he believed President Lincoln would have wanted. Unfortunately, he lacked Lincoln's charisma, character, and political savvy, and his opposition to the Radical Republican Congress resulted in open warfare between the executive and legislative branches. This led inexorably to Johnson's impeachment and, save for the vote of a single senator, very nearly to his removal from office.

Although Johnson served out Lincoln's term, his power in government was virtually neutralized by Congress, and he did not seek renomination. He returned to Tennessee, where he ran unsuccessfully for the Senate in 1869 and for the House in 1872. He was reelected to the Senate in 1875, shortly before he died.

past conduct be dropped and that amnesty be granted to anyone who took an oath to be loyal to the Union from then on. He also did not want the creation of state governments to be contingent on the majority of the population taking the loyalty oath. However, Johnson did require the states to ratify the Thirteenth Amendment, which abolished slavery, and to forbid slavery in their constitutions; to repudiate debts incurred during the rebellion (so that the federal government would not be responsible for them); and to explicitly declare secession, in fact and in theory, null and void.

Johnson did not wait for Congress to approve his changes to the bill before he issued proclamations granting amnesty and defining the nature of provisional governments for each of the former Confederate states (discussed below). By the end of 1865, all of the former Confederate states had complied with the terms Johnson had promulgated, except for Texas, which delayed its compliance until 1866.

Congress, however, was not about to accept such high-handedness from the likes of Andrew Johnson, and his battle against Wade-Davis was doomed from the start. The fact was that a majority of the members of Congress genuinely feared and deeply resented restoring power to the people who had risen up against the government. Congress was also moved by very real outrage over the manner in which the former Confederate states, while ostensibly agreeing to free the slaves and abolish slavery, nevertheless kept black men and women in de facto bondage and subservience with laws that effectively denied them the vote and other rights. More pragmatically, the Republican majority in Congress had no desire to allow measures that would enable or promote the revival of the Democratic Party.

Andrew Johnson's Proclamations

Rather than bargain with the Radical Republicans in Congress, President Johnson issued a blanket **Proclamation of Amnesty and Pardon for the Confederate States** on May 29, 1865. Although Johnson claimed that his proclamation was being made in the spirit of Wade-Davis, it conditioned amnesty on very little indeed—principally the taking of a loyalty

---

Proclamation of Amnesty and Pardon for the Confederate States, 1865

To the end . . . that the authority of the government of the United States may be restored and that peace, order, and freedom may be established, I, Andrew Johnson, President of the United States, do proclaim and declare that I hereby grant to all persons who have, directly or indirectly, participated in the existing rebellion, except as hereinafter excepted, amnesty and pardon, with restoration of all rights of property, except as to slaves and except in cases where legal proceedings under the laws of the United States providing for the confiscation of property of persons engaged in rebellion have been instituted; but upon the condition, nevertheless, that every such person shall take and subscribe the following oath (or affirmation) and thenceforward keep, and maintain said oath inviolate, and which oath shall be registered for permanent preservation and shall be of the tenor and effect following, to wit:

I, _____ _____, do solemnly swear (or affirm), in presence of Almighty God, that I will henceforth faithfully support, protect, and defend the Constitution of the United States and the Union of the States thereunder, and that I will in like manner abide by and faithfully support all laws and proclamations which have been made during the existing rebellion with reference to the emancipation of slaves. So help me God.

Excerpted from "Andrew Johnson: Proclamation of Amnesty and Pardon for the Confederate States," in *Compilation of the Messages and Papers of the Presidents, 1789–1897,* ed. James D. Richardson, (Washington, D.C.: U.S. Government Printing Office, 1920), 6:310–312.

oath—whereas Wade-Davis required an oath not only pledging future loyalty, but also swearing virtual non-involvement in the rebellion that had just ended.

In addition to proclaiming a general amnesty on May 29, 1865, Johnson created by proclamation provisional governments for the states, which, while still military occupation governments, included more lenient terms than suited the Radical Republicans in Congress. The **Proclamation of Provisional Government for North Carolina** was typical. It emphasized that the military government was to be regarded as a strictly temporary measure, to be put in place only until a normal civil government could be installed. Indeed, the proclamations made clear that the military was to do nothing to impede the creation of civil government.

Johnson's proclamations did not succeed in sidestepping Congress but, rather, enflamed Congress, which protested that the president's Reconstruction conditions simply returned power to the very people who had tried to destroy the Union. Furthermore, noting that the president had done nothing to protect the rights of freed slaves, Congress passed the Freedmen's Bureau Act in 1865 and the Civil Rights Act in 1866, both of which Johnson vetoed, insisting that the former Confederate states were entitled immediately to representation in Congress.

Congress responded by refusing to recognize the legitimacy of the provisional governments Johnson had created and also overrode all of the president's vetoes. Further, Congress passed a Reconstruction Act on March 2, 1867, that put all of the South, save Tennessee, under military government and prescribed much more stringent preconditions for the removal of military government and each state's readmission to the Union (discussed below).

Freedmen's Bureau

On March 3, 1865, Congress passed "An Act to Establish a Bureau for the Relief of Freedmen and Refugees," popularly known as the Freedmen's Bureau Act, which established the U.S. Bureau of Refugees, Freedmen, and Abandoned Lands (better known as the Freedman's Bureau). The act was vetoed by President Johnson, but Congress easily overrode the veto.

The Freedmen's Bureau was intended to render practical aid to the approximately four million newly freed slaves. Its director was Major General Oliver O. Howard, a Civil War hero and abolitionist who would go on to become a founder of Howard University, the nation's foremost institution of higher learning for African Americans.

Proclamation of Provisional Government for North Carolina, 1865

[I]n obedience to the high and solemn duties imposed upon me by the Constitution of the United States and for the purpose of enabling the loyal people of said state to organize a state government whereby justice may be established, domestic tranquillity insured, and loyal citizens protected in all their rights of life, liberty, and property, I, Andrew Johnson, President of the United States and commander in chief of the Army and Navy of the United States, do hereby appoint William W. Holden provisional governor of the state of North Carolina, whose duty it shall be, at the earliest practicable period, to prescribe such rules and regulations as

may be necessary and proper for convening a convention composed of delegates to be chosen by that portion of the people of said state who are loyal to the United States, and no others, for the purpose of altering or amending the constitution thereof, and with authority to exercise within the limits of said state all the powers necessary and proper to enable such loyal people of the state of North Carolina to restore said state to its constitutional relations to the Federal government.

Excerpted from Donna L. Dickerson, *The Reconstruction Era: Primary Documents on Events from 1865 to 1877* (Westport, Conn.: Greenwood Press, 2004), 124.

The Freedmen's Bureau was, effectively, the first federal welfare agency. Under its auspices, hospitals were built and medical care provided to about one million former slaves. The bureau also distributed emergency food rations, not just to ex-slaves, but also to Southern whites left destitute by the war. The bureau created educational programs for former slaves (most of whom were illiterate), establishing more than 1,000 schools, including many black colleges.

A teacher and her pupils in front of a Freedmen's School in North Carolina (circa 1865–1872).

Although the Freedmen's Bureau was tasked with safeguarding the civil rights of freed slaves, it was given no significant enforcement authority and rarely even succeeded in trying cases in the courts. The bureau was also responsible for overseeing the redistribution of lands deemed to have been abandoned during the war; however, Johnson frequently intervened in these instances and saw to it that abandoned lands were summarily "restored" to pardoned white Southerners. This brought the bureau into direct conflict with the president, and although Howard appealed to Congress to enact explicit land redistribution legislation, Congress did not respond. In the end, most freed slaves subsisted as sharecroppers, tenants on white-owned lands. The practical features of their relationship to white landowners often differed very little from slavery. The existence of the Freedmen's Bureau was ended by Congress in July 1872.

Civil Rights Act of 1866

Another piece of legislation President Johnson vetoed (with Congress overriding the veto) was the first civil rights statute ever enacted by any nation: the **Civil Rights Act of 1866,** passed on April 9, 1866, was intended to enforce the Thirteenth Amendment, which abolished slavery in the United States. The act specifically declared all former slaves to be citizens of the United States—a measure subsequently codified in the Fourteenth Amendment.

Fourteenth Amendment

Both houses of Congress passed the **Fourteenth Amendment** (on June 8 and June 13, 1866), declaring freed slaves and other blacks to be citizens, prohibiting states from discriminating against any class of citizens, and barring former Confederate leaders from federal or state office until Congress should act to remove the disqualification.

The Reconstruction Acts of 1867

Most of the newly created Southern state governments refused to ratify the Fourteenth Amendment.

Civil Rights Act of 1866

An Act to protect all Persons in the United States in their Civil Rights, and furnish the Means of their Vindication.

Be it enacted by the Senate and House of Representatives of the United States of America in Congress assembled, That all persons born in the United States and not subject to any foreign power, excluding Indians not taxed, are hereby declared to be citizens of the United States; and such citizens, of every race and color, without regard to any previous condition of slavery or involuntary servitude, except as a punishment for crime whereof the party shall have been duly convicted, shall have the same right, in every State and Territory in the United States, to make and enforce contracts, to sue, be parties, and give evidence, to inherit, purchase, lease, sell, hold, and convey real and personal property, and to full and equal benefit of all laws and proceedings for the security of person and property, as is enjoyed by white citizens, and shall be subject to like punishment, pains, and penalties, and to none other, any law, statute, ordinance, regulation, or custom, to the contrary notwithstanding.

Excerpted from MultiEducator, History Central, "The Civil Rights Act," www.multied.com/documents/ civilrightsact.html.

Fourteenth Amendment, 1866

Section 1. All persons born or naturalized in the United States, and subject to the jurisdiction thereof, are citizens of the United States and of the state wherein they reside. No state shall make or enforce any law which shall abridge the privileges or immunities of citizens of the United States; nor shall any state deprive any person of life, liberty, or property, without due process of law; nor deny to any person within its jurisdiction the equal protection of the laws.

Excerpted from FindLaw, "U.S. Constitution: Fourteenth Amendment," http://caselaw.lp.findlaw.com/data/constitution/amendment14/.

In response, Congress in 1867 passed a series of Reconstruction Acts, which put the South under strict military occupation and effectively voided Johnson's earlier proclamations that had reinstated former Confederate states. Congress thereby took Reconstruction out of the president's hands and delivered it into those of Congress. The new regime was called Congressional Reconstruction or Radical Reconstruction, and it explicitly made the federal government responsible for the protection of ex-slaves.

The 1867 acts consisted of three separate measures, which introduced the following actions:

- Created five military districts in the seceded states (except Tennessee, which had ratified the

Fourteenth Amendment and had therefore been duly readmitted to the Union)
- Defined the authority of the military officials heading each military district (they were empowered to appoint and remove state officials)
- Required the registration of voters, to include all freedmen as well as white men who took the "extended" loyalty oath (both testifying to noninvolvement in the "rebellion" and pledging future loyalty to the United States)
- Called for state constitutional conventions, composed of elected delegates, to draft state constitutions that included guarantees of black male suffrage
- Required that states ratify the Fourteenth Amendment as a condition of readmission to the Union and restoration of civil state government

Impeachment

The Reconstruction Acts of 1867 were a major escalation of the war between Andrew Johnson and Congress. Knowing that a veto was hopeless, Johnson attempted to render the acts moot simply by refusing to enforce them. This created the political climate in which his impeachment became inevitable.

On March 2, 1867, Congress overrode President Johnson's veto of the Tenure of Office Act. This legislation—which barred the president from dismissing, without senatorial approval, any civil office holder who had been appointed with the advice and consent of the Senate—was deliberately provocative because it challenged the constitutionally mandated separation of powers between the executive and legislative branches of government. Although the act was an attempt by Congress to usurp as many executive prerogatives as possible, it was more immediately intended to prevent Johnson from removing Secretary of War Edwin Stanton, a powerful ally of the Radical Republicans. Johnson intended to challenge the law in the Supreme Court, so he defiantly dismissed Stanton in 1868. Interpreting this as a "high crime or misdemeanor," the House of Representatives voted to impeach the president.

Because the Tenure of Office Act was of such dubious constitutionality (indeed, the act was partially repealed in 1869, repealed in its entirety in 1887, and found by the U.S. Supreme Court in 1926 to have been unconstitutional), and President Johnson was obviously challenging it for the purpose of bringing it before the Supreme Court, the charges against Johnson were weak and transparently partisan. Even weaker were charges that he had deliberately attempted to ridicule and undermine Congress. Nevertheless, the House voted up the charges against Johnson, and the Senate duly held an impeachment trial during March–May 1868. In the end, the key votes on May 16 and 26, 1868, fell one short of the two-thirds majority required for conviction. Seven Republicans had voted with Johnson's Democratic supporters.

Although Johnson was acquitted, the conflict between the White House and Congress was so intense that, for all practical purposes, he remained president in name only. The Radical Republican Congress was left to administer a Reconstruction program that, while often high minded and intent on genuine reform, was tainted by sectional vindictiveness and a nakedly apparent political agenda: the suppression and ultimate destruction of the Democratic Party.

President Andrew Johnson challenged the Tenure of Office Act by dismissing Secretary of War Edwin Stanton (pictured here). Congress responded by attempting to impeach Johnson.

The Decline and Fall of Reconstruction

As Reconstruction became harsher and, as many white Southerners saw it, increasingly humiliating, a militant, ugly, and violent grassroots resistance movement grew up throughout the states of the former Confederacy. In 1866 a band of Confederate veterans formed what was ostensibly a social club in Pulaski, Tennessee. Like many other fraternities, it borrowed its name from classical Greek, in this case corrupting the Greek word for circle, *kyklos,* into *Ku Klux* and adding to the end of it the alliterative *Klan,* which may have been intended to appeal to the

[From the Independent Monitor, Tuscaloosa, Alabama, September 1, 1868.]
A PROSPECTIVE SCENE IN THE CITY OF OAKS, 4TH OF MARCH, 1869.

"Hang, curs, hang! * * * * * Their complexion is perfect gallows. Stand fast, good fate, to their hanging! * * * If they be not born to be hanged, our case is miserable."

The above cut represents the fate in store for those great pests of Southern society—the carpet-bagger and scalawag—if found in Dixie's land after the break of day on the 4th of March next.

A Facsimile put in Evidence before the Congressional Committee.

Reproduction of a Ku Klux Klan warning that was published September 1, 1868, in the Independent Monitor, *Tuscaloosa, Alabama. This facsimile was later introduced as evidence at a congressional investigation of the KKK during the Grant administration.*

region's many Scotch-Irish immigrants, who were familiar with Scottish clans. Soon, the Ku Klux Klan (KKK) and related organizations, including the Knights of the White Camelia, became the chief means by which Southerners resisted and subverted the workings and institutions of Radical Reconstruction. In many places, the KKK became a shadow government, enforcing its will by terrorizing blacks and supporters of Reconstruction with acts of intimidation, violence, and even murder.

On February 3, 1870 a majority of states ratified the Fifteenth Amendment, which prohibited the states from denying the vote to persons on the basis of "race, color, or previous condition of servitude." Ratification was a prerequisite for readmission to the union, and before the year was out, all of the former Confederate states had been readmitted; however, in response to the Fifteenth Amendment, the influence

of the KKK grew throughout much of the South. The organization's leader, former Confederate general Nathan Bedford Forrest, had already come to believe that KKK violence was out of control and, in 1869, had officially disbanded the Klan. But local branches (called "klaverns") refused to dissolve themselves and became increasingly lawless. In 1870 Congress passed the Force Act, authorizing the president to suppress Klan (and similar) activities by force, impose various penalties on terrorist organizations, and even, if necessary to restore order, suspend habeas corpus.

The troubled term of Andrew Johnson ended early in 1869 with the inauguration of Ulysses S. Grant. The corruption that had already beset the Reconstruction-era South now spread nationwide under the new administration. Grant himself was above reproach, but he proved incapable of policing his own administration, and just as he did little to curb the lawless ways of his political subordinates and associates, so he consistently declined to use the authority Congress had given him for dealing with the KKK. Only after violence, especially the lynching of blacks, had become a national scandal did Grant send federal troops into the areas of the most intense Klan activity. He also suspended habeas corpus in nine South Carolina counties and authorized certain arrests. Despite this, the KKK largely succeeded in its mission of terrorizing black Southerners into submission before it largely disappeared during the 1880s. The Klan would remain dormant until the early twentieth century.

By the mid-1870s, most white Southerners no longer saw a need for the white-robed, white-hooded secrecy of the KKK. A white supremacy movement steadily grew in influence, and many state laws were enacted to institutionalize the social, legal, and economic subjugation of blacks. These "Jim Crow laws" (named after a racially demeaning song and dance performed in the blackface minstrel shows popular at the time in the North as well as the South) made a mockery of federal Reconstruction legislation.

Advocates of Jim Crow laws were dubbed "Redeemers," and by 1876 their political clout had reached a national level. In that presidential election year, Democrat Samuel J. Tilden captured the vote of the "solid South" (as the Reconstruction-era Southern Democratic voting bloc was called), which gave him national returns that outpolled Republican presidential candidate Rutherford B. Hayes by a quarter-million votes. Rather than concede the election, however, Republicans used Reconstruction laws to override and reverse the popular electoral tally in three Southern states, on the grounds that blacks had been intimidated and thereby prevented from voting. The election was sent to the House of Representatives, which failed to resolve it. As Inauguration Day, March 4, approached, lawmakers discussed the possibility of authorizing the current secretary of state to serve as an interim chief executive until the election could be decided. Meanwhile, secession talk revived in some parts of the South.

Just two days before the inauguration deadline, Congress created a bipartisan Electoral Commission while legislators worked behind the scenes to hammer out a deal that would decide the election. Republicans and Southern Democrats ultimately agreed to admit Hayes into office, provided that he would immediately end Reconstruction and withdraw all U.S. troops from the states of the former Confederacy and that, furthermore, no Republican administration would ever again attempt to impose federal law on the Jim Crow South. Thus Hayes succeeded Grant as president—he was plagued by the mocking title of address "Your Fraudulency"—and Reconstruction came to an abrupt end.

BIBLIOGRAPHY

Cimbala, Paul A., and Randall M. Miller, eds. *The Freedmen's Bureau and Reconstruction: Reconsiderations.* New York: Fordham University Press, 1999.

Foner, Eric. *Reconstruction: America's Unfinished Revolution, 1863–1877.* New York: Harper Perennial Modern Classics, 2002.

Stampp, Kenneth M. *The Era of Reconstruction, 1865–1877.* New York: Vintage, 1967.

Vorenberg, Michael. *Final Freedom: The Civil War, the Abolition of Slavery, and the Thirteenth Amendment.* New York: Cambridge University Press, 2001.

CHAPTER 19

CHEYENNE-ARAPAHO WAR
(1864–1865)

At Issue

War erupted when Cheyenne and Arapaho Indians resisted the attempts of Governor John Evans of Colorado Territory to usurp mineral-rich tribal lands.

The Conflict

During the mid-1860s, Governor John Evans of Colorado Territory tried and failed to secure mineral-rich Cheyenne and Arapaho hunting grounds in exchange for the Indians' removal to reservation lands and the grant of a government annuity. After exhausting negotiation options, Evans asked Colorado militia colonel John M. Chivington, the military commander of the territory, to drive the Indians out.

The Cheyenne were generally peaceful during this period, but the actions of a militant faction of young warriors, known as the Hotamitainio (Dog Soldier Society), provided sufficient provocation for Chivington to declare war on all the Cheyenne. Attacks he launched in 1864 provoked Indian counterraids, which soon escalated matters to the level of territorial crisis. In response, Evans and Chivington formed the Third Colorado Cavalry, which, unprovoked, attacked the peaceful Cheyenne camp of Chief Black Kettle at Sand Creek, about forty miles northeast of Fort Lyon, on November 29, 1864. Two hundred Cheyenne were killed, two-thirds of them women and children. Nine chiefs died, but Black Kettle escaped. The "Sand Creek Massacre" united the Southern Sioux, Northern Arapaho, and Cheyenne Indians in a series of retaliatory raids

during late 1864 and early 1865, which the U.S. Army labeled the Cheyenne-Arapaho War.

On January 7, 1865, 1,000 Sioux and Cheyenne warriors raided and looted the tiny mining settlement of Julesburg, Colorado. Then raiding continued as the Indians worked their way north. On February 4–6 and 8, large numbers of Indians skirmished indecisively with much smaller army units near Forts Mitchell and Laramie. Fifty settlers were killed, and 1,500 head of cattle taken. Brigadier General Robert B. Mitchell worked feverishly to organize a military response, but his efforts were hampered by harsh winter weather. In the meantime, Mitchell's commanding officer, U.S. Army major general John C. Pope, planned a grand offensive against the Indians that called for the cavalry to make a series of strikes while infantry guarded the mail and emigration trails. Pope pressed into his infantry force so-called Galvanized Yankees, Confederate prisoners of war who had been granted parole on condition that they serve the Union armies in the West—fighting the Indians and not their former Confederate comrades. The campaign, however, proved abortive. While it floundered, negotiators began hammering out a peace with the Cheyenne, Arapaho, Kiowa, and Comanche tribes.

The negotiations notwithstanding, on July 26, 1865, 1,000–3,000 warriors massed to attack a cavalry unit guarding the North Platte River crossing of the Oregon-California Trail. Major Martin Anderson, commanding the Eleventh Kansas Cavalry and elements of two Ohio units at Upper Platte Bridge, 130 miles north of Fort Laramie, dispatched

Lieutenant Caspar W. Collins and 20 cavalry troopers to escort a wagon train. Ambushed by hundreds of warriors, this detachment fought with great valor: all but 5 of the troopers survived to make their way back to the stockade, having killed 60 of the attackers and wounded 130 more. Brigadier General Patrick E. Connor responded to the ambush by sending 3,000 troopers on a major sweep of Powder River country, where they destroyed one Arapaho village and engaged the Sioux. The early onset of severe winter weather put a stop to this campaign, and the Cheyenne-Arapaho War simply ended without a definitive military resolution.

Territorial Policy: Governor Evans

From a modern historical perspective, it is impossible to regard the actions of John Evans, territorial governor of Colorado, in a positive light. He conspired with Colonel John M. Chivington to provoke war with the Cheyenne for the sole purpose of moving the Indians off their hunting grounds so that the land could be opened to mining interests. Yet Evans hardly started out to be a cold-hearted exploiter, and, in fact, his background was typical of the idealistic and reform-minded men who often administered Indian policy. Typical, too, were the tragic results his policies produced.

Born in Waynesville, Ohio, in 1814, Evans graduated from medical school in Cincinnati in 1838 and practiced medicine in Indiana until 1845, when he was appointed the first superintendent of the state hospital for the insane. Three years later, he was appointed to a professorship at the Rush Medical School in Chicago, and then, in 1851, became one of the founders of Northwestern University in Evanston, Illinois—a town named in his honor.

President Abraham Lincoln appointed Evans governor of Colorado Territory in 1862 and, *ex officio*, territorial superintendent of Indian affairs. Like other high-minded reformers of the period, Evans favored the policy of severalty and the ultimate breakup of the reservations. However, he linked severalty with the opening of Indian lands to mining and development, and this objective, which he saw as essential to the prosperity of the territory, overrode his stewardship of Indian matters. His policy was, in effect, to develop the territorial economy, no matter the cost to Colorado's Indian population. Evans reasoned that the prosperity of the territory would ultimately benefit whites and Indians. Yet to reach this end, he was willing to use violent and unjust means.

Chivington, the "Fighting Parson"

Evans's partner in the crime committed against the Cheyenne and other Colorado tribes was John Milton Chivington. Like Evans, he was an Ohioan by birth. He was ordained a Methodist minister in 1844 and preached to white settlers as well as Indians along the frontiers of Kansas, Missouri, and Illinois before the Civil War. In 1860 he moved to Denver, Colorado Territory, where he preached to area miners. When Evans commissioned him a major of the Colorado volunteers in 1861, he was dubbed the "Fighting Parson."

Appointed to command the Colorado militia district in 1863, Chivington made war on the Cheyenne

---

CHRONOLOGY OF THE CHEYENNE-ARAPAHO WAR

1864

Nov. 29 Chivington's Third Colorado Cavalry perpetrates the "Sand Creek Massacre."

Late 1864–Early 1865

- Southern Sioux, Northern Arapaho, and Cheyenne Indians raid throughout the Colorado Territory in retaliation for Sand Creek.

1865

July 26 A large warrior force of 1,000–3,000 Indians attack a cavalry unit guarding the Oregon-California Trail's North Platte River crossing.

Summer–Fall General Patrick E. Connor sends 3,000 troops in a campaign against "hostiles" in the Powder River country. Unseasonably early snow storms cut the campaign short in September. The war ends without definitive military resolution.

and Arapaho tribes. Although he did so at the request of Governor Evans, he went into battle persuaded that there would be no "civilizing" of the Indians. His policy was genocidal, as he made clear in an 1864 speech given at Denver. There he called for the extermination of all Indians, including infants, observing, infamously, "Nits make lice!"

The Sand Creek Massacre

Having enticed, with Governor Evans, a large number of Cheyenne to an encampment at Sand Creek by promising to make peace on mutually agreeable terms, Colonel Chivington set them up for slaughter. Presumably acting on Chivington's

instructions, Major Scott J. Anthony cut the Indians' government rations and demanded the surrender of their weapons. When a group of unarmed and hungry Arapahos approached nearby Fort Lyon to trade buffalo hides for rations, Anthony fired on them, probably acting on orders aimed at deliberately provoking combat. As relations deteriorated and the Indians became hungrier, the Third Colorado Cavalry gathered at Fort Lyon.

On November 28, 1864, Chivington deployed his 700-man force, which included four howitzers, around Chief Black Kettle's followers, who had been gathering at Sand Creek over a period of several weeks. The next morning, unprovoked, Chivington and his men perpetrated the massacre. The "Sand

"The Battle of Sand Creek," 1864

Among the brilliant feats of arms in Indian warfare, the recent campaign of our Colorado volunteers will stand in history with few rivals, and none to exceed it in final results. We are not prepared to write its history, which can only be done by some one who accompanied the expedition, but we have gathered from those who participated in it and from others who were in that part of the country, some facts which will doubtless interest many of our readers.

The people of Colorado are well aware of the situation occupied by the third regiment during the great snow-storm which set in the last of October....

... As daylight dawned they came in sight of the Indian camp, after a forced midnight march of forty-two miles, in eight hours, across the rough, unbroken plain. But little time was required for preparation. The forces had been divided and arranged for battle on the march, and just as the sun rose they dashed upon the enemy with yells that would put a Comanche army to blush. Although utterly surprised, the savages were not unprepared, and for a time their defense told terribly against our ranks. Their main force rallied and formed in line of battle on the bluffs beyond the creek, where they were protected by rudely constructed rifle-pits, from which they main-

tained a steady fire until the shells from company C's (third regiment) howitzers began dropping among them, when they scattered and fought each for himself in genuine Indian fashion. As the battle progressed the field of carriage widened until it extended over not less than twelve miles of territory. The Indians who could escaped or secreted themselves, and by three o'clock in the afternoon the carnage had ceased. It was estimated that between three and four hundred of the savages got away with their lives. Of the balance there were neither wounded nor prisoners. Their strength at the beginning of the action was estimated at nine hundred....

Whether viewed as a march or as a battle, the exploit has few, if any, parallels. A march of 260 miles in but a fraction more than five days, with deep snow, scanty forage, and no road, is a remarkable feat, whilst the utter surprise of a large Indian village is unprecedented. In no single battle in North America, we believe, have so many Indians been slain.

Excerpt transcribed from the *Rocky Mountain News*, December 17, 1864, with permission from the Colorado Historical Society.

Creek Massacre" ignited a general war between whites and Indians throughout the Colorado Territory.

Congress Responds

In March 1865 Congress responded to the Sand Creek Massacre, sometimes referred to as the Chivington Massacre, by convening a joint congressional-military inquiry under the direction of Senator James Doolittle, a leading congressional voice for Indian policy reform. The joint committee censured Chivington, but the army refused to court-martial him. When his term of enlistment in the Colorado militia expired in January 1865, he left the service, thereby avoiding any future possibility of a military trial. Congress also acted against the regular army in Colorado by cutting off funding for General Pope's planned offensive in the Colorado Territory, which, delayed by inclement winter weather, never got under way.

Public Opinion and Indian Policy (1864–1865)

Senator Doolittle was zealous in his investigation of the Sand Creek Massacre and toured the tribal lands of the Great Plains to assess the situation for himself. This was the origin of the so-called Doolittle Committee Report, officially titled "Report on the Condition of the Indian Tribes" (see Chapter 14), published in 1867. The report was the foundation of the general Indian policy reform movement that followed the Civil War. More immediately, the massacre created substantial public outrage in the East, where it was seen as an egregious act of extermination. In the West, especially in Colorado, economic motives often outweighed moral outrage. **"The Battle of Sand Creek,"** an 1864 editorial in the *Rocky Mountain News* portrayed the Sand Creek affair as a heroic achievement: "Among the brilliant feats of arms in Indian warfare, the recent campaign

of our Colorado volunteers will stand in history with few rivals, and none to exceed it in final results."

It should also be noted that the Sand Creek Massacre came at a time when Coloradans were sharply divided on the issue of statehood. Evans and Chivington favored statehood, whereas some local politicians and many mining officials preferred to maintain the more freewheeling political and economic environment of territorial status. This group was eager to disseminate the story of Sand Creek as widely as possible, not with the humanitarian aim of drawing attention to the persecution of the Indians, but with the purpose of torpedoing the careers of Evans and Chivington.

BIBLIOGRAPHY

Axelrod, Alan. *Chronicle of the Indian Wars: From Colonial Times to Wounded Knee.* New York: Macmillan General Reference, 1993.

Debo, Angie. *A History of the Indians in the United States.* Norman: University of Oklahoma Press, 1977.

Grimell, George B. *The Fighting Cheyennes.* Norman: University of Oklahoma Press, 1982.

Hoig, Stan. *Sand Creek Massacre.* Norman: University of Oklahoma Press, 1974.

McDermott, John D. *A Guide to the Indian Wars of the West.* Lincoln: University of Nebraska Press, 1998.

Michno, Gregory F. *Encyclopedia of Indian Wars: Western Battles and Skirmishes 1850–1890.* Missoula, Mont: Mountain Press Publishing Company, 2003.

Phillips, Charles, and Alan Axelrod, eds. *The Encyclopedia of the American West.* 4 vols. New York: Macmillan General Reference, 1996.

Prucha, Francis P. *The Great Father: The United States Government and the American Indians.* Lincoln: University of Nebraska Press, 1984.

Utley, Robert M. *Indian Wars.* New York: Mariner Books, 2002.

CHAPTER 20

WAR FOR THE BOZEMAN TRAIL AND HANCOCK'S CAMPAIGN (1866–1868)

At Issue

The influential Oglala Sioux chief Red Cloud resisted the encroachment of westward-bound white emigrants who traversed the Bozeman Trail. Even as federal treaty commissioners negotiated with the Oglala and their Cheyenne allies, the army, in Hancock's Campaign, conducted a punitive expedition against the hostile tribes of the central and southern Great Plains.

The Conflicts

Chief Red Cloud of the Oglala Sioux refused to cede or sell to the federal government land traversed by the Bozeman Trail—an emigrant route that began at Julesburg, Colorado, and was the shortest way to the gold fields of Virginia City, Montana—and warned that he would allow no whites to pass over the trail. In response to this threat, Colonel Henry B. Carrington established three forts along the trail: Fort Reno at the forks of the Powder River and Fort Phil Kearny (to become his field headquarters) at the forks of Piney Creek, both in Wyoming, and Fort C. F. Smith near the Bighorn River, in Montana.

Red Cloud attacked the forts during the summer, before they were completed. Intent on finishing the forts, Carrington refused to take anything other than defensive action. This created a crisis of morale among his command, prompting Captain William J. Fetterman to boast that with eighty men he could "ride through the entire Sioux nation." When a war party attacked a wagon train hauling wood to the fort

on December 6, 1866, Carrington ordered Fetterman, Lieutenant Horatio S. Bingham, and thirty cavalrymen to drive the marauding Sioux west while he led twenty-five mounted infantry troops to cut the Indians off from behind. The action miscarried, Bingham was killed, and the troops retreated to Fort Phil Kearny. Emboldened, the Indians freely attacked wood trains and supply parties.

Red Cloud (Mahpiua Luta)
(1822–1909)

Red Cloud did not inherit his position among the Oglala Sioux, but rose to prominence on the strength of his leadership and bravery. During 1865–1868 he led a vigorous and effective opposition among the Sioux and the Cheyenne to the construction and fortification of the Bozeman Trail, forcing the abandonment of the trail. This achieved, Red Cloud agreed to the Treaty of Fort Laramie (1868) and settled on the Red Cloud Agency in Nebraska. Although he ceased making war, Red Cloud continued to speak out against U.S. Indian policy and became a respected spokesman who visited Washington, D.C., several times to make his views known.

On December 21, Carrington again dispatched Fetterman in a new attempt to drive the Indians away from the wood road. Fetterman deliberately exceeded his orders by staging a major attack against the Sioux, which resulted in his defeat and death, as well as the deaths of all seventy-nine men under his command, at the hands of Chief Crazy Horse, who led 1,500–2,000 warriors.

On August 1, 1867, the Sioux attacked another army detachment. In the so-called Hayfield Fight, they targeted a hay-cutting detail near Fort C. F. Smith but were repulsed. The next day, they hit a woodcutting party near Fort Phil Kearny in the battle known as the Wagon Box Fight (the soldiers took refuge behind a makeshift corral fashioned of wagon bodies, or wagon boxes). Again, the warriors were repulsed.

Even though they had been defeated in the Hayfield and Wagon Box fights, Red Cloud and the other war leaders refused to talk peace. This prompted General William T. Sherman, in command of the army's western district, to send General Winfield Scott Hancock on a punitive expedition against the Southern Cheyennes, the Southern Arapahos, the Kiowas, and the Oglala and Southern Brulé Sioux. Hancock's Campaign (sometimes called Hancock's War) began on April 8, 1867, when Hancock led a column to a Cheyenne and Sioux village for the purpose of impressing the Indians with the overwhelming might of the army. The women and children of the village fled at the approach of the troops. Hancock sent his senior field officer, Lieutenant Colonel George Armstrong Custer, commanding the Seventh Cavalry, to surround the village to prevent the men from following the women in flight. Nevertheless, by morning the village was entirely deserted. Hancock ordered Custer to hunt down the fleeing Cheyennes and Sioux.

Custer's sweep through the plains extended from April through July. Although hotly pursued, the warriors terrorized Kansas with raids and managed to outrun Custer and his command, which, exhausted, broke off the chase. Having thus lost the initiative, what had begun as an offensive campaign became an unsuccessful attempt to defend civilian settlements. Unable to eradicate the Indians, the government decided to reopen negotiations. In the end, two sets of treaties were concluded, one at Medicine Lodge Creek, Kansas, in 1867 and the other at Fort Laramie, Wyoming, the following year.

In the Wake of the Fetterman Massacre

The dispute over the Bozeman Trail took place even as construction of the first American transcontinental railroad was nearing completion. The federal government and the army understood that the railroad would render such trails obsolete. Had logic prevailed, the army would have withdrawn from the trail, peacefully leaving the Indians to control it. But the Fetterman Massacre removed the dispute from the realm of logic and reason. Sensational news stories created a public outcry, and General Sherman could not allow the authority and honor of the U.S. Army to be compromised or the loss of eighty

CHRONOLOGY OF THE WAR FOR THE BOZEMAN TRAIL AND HANCOCK'S CAMPAIGN

1866

June 17 Colonel Henry B. Carrington is dispatched to defend the Bozeman Trail against Red Cloud and others.

Summer Red Cloud repeatedly attacks the Bozeman Trail forts.

Dec. 6 An Oglala war party attacks a wagon train; Captain William J. Fetterman counterattacks, but is forced to retreat.

Dec. 21 The Fetterman Massacre occurs.

1867

Aug. 1 The Hayfield Fight occurs.

Aug. 2 The Wagon Box Fight occurs.

Apr. 8 Hancock's Campaign begins.

Apr.–July Under orders from Hancock, George A. Custer sweeps the plains, without success.

Oct. 21 and 28 The Treaty of Medicine Lodge is concluded.

1868

Apr. 29 The Treaty of Fort Laramie is concluded.

Oglala Sioux chief Red Cloud is pictured here (seated, center) leading an Indian delegation to Washington, D.C., in the early 1870s. Although he ceased making war after signing the Treaty of Fort Laramie in 1868, Red Cloud continued to be an outspoken opponent of U.S. Indian policy.

21). It was bloody incidents such as the Fetterman Massacre that made rational negotiation between the federal government and tribal representatives all but impossible.

The Peace Commission

The Fetterman Massacre also deepened the divide between the military and civilian components of U.S. Indian policy. The military high command responded punitively to the incident, whereas Congress heightened its "peace offensive" by passing,

soldiers to go unanswered. The objective of meting out punishment for the Fetterman Massacre drove Sherman to launch Hancock's Campaign as well as Sheridan's Campaign of 1868–1869 (see Chapter on July 20, 1867, **An Act to Establish Peace with Certain Hostile Indian Tribes.** The act created the Indian Peace Commission, made up of army officers and civilian authorities, which was to meet with the

An Act to Establish Peace with Certain Hostile Indian Tribes, 1867

Be it enacted . . . , That the President of the United States be, and he is hereby, authorized to appoint a commission to consist of three officers of the army not below the rank of brigadier general, who, together with N. G. Taylor, Commissioner of Indian Affairs, John B. Henderson, Chairman of the Committee of Indian Affairs of the Senate, S. F. Tappan, and John B. Sanborn, shall have power and authority to call together the chiefs and headmen of such bands or tribes of Indians as are now waging war against the United States or committing depredations upon

the people thereof, to ascertain the alleged reasons for their acts of hostility, and in their discretion, under the direction of the President, to make and conclude with said bands or tribes such treaty stipulations, subject to the action of the Senate, as may remove all just causes of complaint on their part.

Excerpted from Francis Paul Prucha, ed., *Documents of United States Indian Policy,* 2d ed. (Lincoln: University of Nebraska Press, 1990), 105.

Indians to determine the reasons for their acts and, based on that information, conclude treaties that would bring lasting peace.

Treaty of Medicine Lodge (1867)

The first major treaty negotiated by the Peace Commission was the **Treaty of Medicine Lodge,** which was actually a portfolio of three separate treaties. The first, signed on October 21, 1867, was concluded with the Kiowa and Comanche tribes. The second, signed on the same day, was concluded with the Kiowa-Apaches. The third, with the Cheyennes and Arapahos, was signed on October 28. The Medicine Lodge documents established reservations for these tribes, which brought them into close contact with the Sioux, Shoshones, Bannocks, and Navajos and, in the long run, created the basis for further conflict as demand increased for ever-dwindling resources on reservations.

Fort Laramie Treaty (1868)

The **Treaty of Fort Laramie,** signed on April 29, 1868, with Red Cloud and the Brulés, Oglalas, Miniconjous, Yanktonais, Hunkpapas, Blackfeet, Cutheads, Two Kettles, Sans Arcs, and Santees—all Sioux bands—as well as the Arapahos, was far more effective than the Medicine Lodge documents because it gave Red Cloud most of what he had fought for, including white abandonment of the Bozeman Trail forts. The treaty actually succeeded in bringing temporary peace to the portion of the northern plains controlled by these tribes.

The Treaty of Fort Laramie had four major parts. In the first part, both sides agreed to peace. The second part reserved the region west of the Missouri River and east of the Rockies for the "absolute and undisturbed use" of the Sioux. The third part provided a government reservation and subsidy agreement. The final part acknowledged the Bozeman Trail and the land adjacent to it as "unceded Indian territory," from which white settlement and military installations were barred.

Treaty of Medicine Lodge, 1867

ARTICLE 1.
The said Apache tribe of Indians agree to confederate and become incorporated with the said Kiowa and Comanche Indians, and to accept as their permanent home the reservation described in the aforesaid treaty with said Kiowa and Comanche tribes, concluded as aforesaid at this place, and they pledge themselves to make no permanent settlement at any place, nor on any lands, outside of said reservation.

ARTICLE 2.
The Kiowa and Comanche tribes, on their part, agree that all the benefits and advantages arising from the employment of physicians, teachers, carpenters, millers, engineers, farmers, and blacksmiths, agreed to be furnished under the provisions of their said treaty, together with all the advantages to be derived from the construction of agency buildings, warehouses, mills, and other structures, and also from the establishment of schools upon their said reservation, shall be jointly and equally shared and enjoyed by the said Apache Indians, as though they had been originally a part of said tribes; and they further agree that all other benefits arising from said treaty shall be jointly and equally shared as aforesaid.

ARTICLE 3.
The United States, on its part, agrees that clothing and other articles named in Article X. of said original treaty, together with all money or other annuities agreed to be furnished under any of the provisions of said treaty, to the Kiowa and Comanches, shall be shared equally by the Apaches.

Excerpted from the Avalon Project at Yale Law School, "Treaty with the Kiowa, Comanche, and Apache," www.yale.edu/lawweb/avalon/ntreaty/kicoap67.htm.

Red Cloud and other Indian leaders hailed the treaty as a major triumph because it effectively recognized Sioux power and authority in the Bighorn region. As federal negotiators viewed it, however, the

Treaty of Fort Laramie, 1868

ARTICLE I.

From this day forward all war between the parties to this agreement shall for ever cease. The government of the United States desires peace, and its honor is hereby pledged to keep it. The Indians desire peace, and they now pledge their honor to maintain it.

If bad men among the whites, or among other people subject to the authority of the United States, shall commit any wrong upon the person or property of the Indians, the United States will, upon proof made to the agent, and forwarded to the Commissioner of Indian Affairs at Washington city, proceed at once to cause the offender to be arrested and punished according to the laws of the United States, and also reimburse the injured person for the loss sustained.

If bad men among the Indians shall commit a wrong or depredation upon the person or property of nay one, white, black, or Indian, subject to the authority of the United States, and at peace therewith, the Indians herein named solemnly agree that they will, upon proof made to their agent, and notice by him, deliver up the wrongdoer to the United States, to be tried and punished according to its laws. . . .

ARTICLE VI.

If any individual belonging to said tribes of Indians, or legally incorporated with them, being the head of a family, shall desire to commence farming, he shall have the privilege to select, in the presence and with the assistance of the agent then in charge, a tract of land within said reservation, not exceeding three hundred and twenty acres in extent. . . .

ARTICLE VII.

In order to insure the civilization of the Indians entering into this treaty, the necessity of education is admitted, especially of such of them as are or may be settled on said agricultural reservations, and they, therefore, pledge themselves to compel their children, male and female, between the ages of six and sixteen years, to attend school. . . .

ARTICLE XI.

In consideration of the advantages and benefits conferred by this treaty and the many pledges of friendship by the United States, the tribes who are parties to this agreement hereby stipulate that they will relinquish all right to occupy permanently the territory outside their reservations as herein defined. . . . And they, the said Indians, further expressly agree:

  1st. That they will withdraw all opposition to the construction of the railroads now being built on the plains. . .

  3d. That they will not attack any persons at home, or travelling, nor molest or disturb any wagon trains, coaches, mules, or cattle belonging to the people of the United States, or to persons friendly therewith.

  4th. They will never capture, or carry off from the settlements, white women or children.

  5th. They will never kill or scalp white men, nor attempt to do them harm. . . .

ARTICLE XVI.

The United States hereby agrees and stipulates that the country north of the North Platte river and east of the summits of the Big Horn mountains shall be held and considered to be unceded Indian territory, and also stipulates and agrees that no white person or persons shall be permitted to settle upon or occupy any portion of the same.

Excerpted from the Avalon Project at Yale Law School, "Fort Laramie Treaty, 1868," www.yale.edu/lawweb/avalon/ntreaty/ nt001.htm.

concession of the Bozeman Trail was unimportant, since the transcontinental railroad was nearly finished, and the extensive provisions for government subsidy would surely entice the Sioux to settle on the reservation, where they would take up farming and undergo a metamorphosis from aggressive hunters to peaceful agrarians, an "evolution" long promoted in U.S. policies aimed at "civilizing" the Indians.

Federal Policy on "Indian Civilization": The Taylor Report

Encouraged in part by the apparent success of the Treaty of Fort Laramie, Commissioner of Indian Affairs Nathaniel G. Taylor issued an optimistic **Annual Report** for 1868, declaring that the Indians could "be elevated and enlightened to the proud stature of civilized manhood" provided that the "war policy" toward them was ended and a "new department of Indian affairs" was created, independent from both the War Department and the Department of the Interior. Taylor believed that the head of the new department would have to be given broad authority and power and be held "to a strict accountability."

Fragility of the Peace

Both the Medicine Lodge and Fort Laramie treaties pledged all parties to perpetual peace. In the case of the Medicine Lodge Treaty, however, the Cheyennes remained sharply divided between a peace faction and the militant Dog Soldier Society, a band of young, aggressive warriors who refused to accept confinement on any reservation. Throughout 1868, together with elements of the Brulé and Oglala Sioux, as well as Arapahos, the Dog Soldiers raided western Kansas and eastern Colorado, killing and wounding settlers and stealing stock.

As for the Kiowas and Comanches, in February 1868 Indian Agent Jesse Leavenworth arrived at their new reservation to find himself without the promised rations to distribute to the Indians, who were hungry after a hard winter. This situation provoked several thousand Kiowas and Comanches to raid various parts of Texas, and when raiders burned Leavenworth's own headquarters at the Wichita Agency, he summarily resigned. This incident, which illustrates the failure of the Indian Bureau to honor its promises and the demoralization of a well-meaning Indian agent, was typical of the fatally flawed execution of U.S. Indian policy.

With Leavenworth's resignation, the sole federal authority standing between the Indians and the citizens of Texas vanished. The southern plains erupted into renewed war. At the same time, the Cheyennes began to protest that they had not received the guns and ammunition pledged by the Medicine Lodge Treaty, and about 200 Cheyennes raided settlements along the Saline and Solomon rivers, destroying much property, killing fifteen white men, and allegedly raping five white women. The renewed terror moved the federal government to suddenly

---

Annual Report of the Commissioner of Indian Affairs, 1868

How can our Indian tribes be civilized?...

If might makes right, we are the strong and they the weak; and we would do no wrong to proceed by the cheapest and nearest route to the desired end, and could, therefore, justify ourselves in ignoring the natural as well as the conventional rights of the Indians. . . .

If, however, they have rights as well as we, then clearly it is our duty as well as sound policy to so solve the question of their future relations to us and each other, as to secure their rights and promote their highest interest, in the simplest, easiest, and most economical way possible.

But to assume they have no rights is to deny the fundamental principles of Christianity, as well as to contradict the whole theory upon which the government has uniformly acted towards them; we are therefore bound to respect their rights, and, if possible, make our interest harmonize with them. . . .

Excerpted from Francis Paul Prucha, ed., *Documents on United States Indian Policy*, 2d ed. (Lincoln: University of Nebraska Press, 1990), 123.

reverse its pacific policy, and General Sherman authorized Sheridan's Campaign of 1868–1869 (Chapter 21).

The Debate over Indian Policy Authority

Indian Commissioner Taylor was caught up in the intensifying debate over whether the Department of the Interior or the War Department should control Indian policy. His ultimate preference, as previously explained, was to create a new department independent of both existing departments; however, his immediate concern was to prevent Indian affairs from falling back into the hands of the War Department. He believed that the burden was too great for the secretary of war; that transferring the Indian Bureau to the War Department would necessitate the creation of a large standing army in the field and would be tantamount to a declaration of war against the Indians; that Indian policy as managed by the War Department had failed in the past; that military government would "destroy" and "demoralize" the Indian race; that the conduct of Indian affairs was "incompatible with the nature and objects of the military department"; and that moving the Indian Bureau to the War Department would offend the Indians.

In the end, the Indian Bureau was not returned to the War Department, but neither was a new department created. Instead, on April 10, 1869, President Ulysses S. Grant authorized a Board of Indian Commissioners, a group of unpaid philanthropists appointed to aid and advise the secretary of the interior on Indian affairs. It was a feeble compromise, which did little to improve the efficiency of the Indian Bureau within the Department of the Interior.

For its part, following the Fetterman Massacre, the military continued to pursue, independently from the Department of the Interior and at odds with it, an increasingly aggressive policy. Thus, yet again, federal policy toward the Indians was fragmented, confused, and set tragically at cross-purposes.

BIBLIOGRAPHY

Axelrod, Alan. *Chronicle of the Indian Wars: From Colonial Times to Wounded Knee.* New York: Macmillan General Reference, 1993.

Debo, Angie. *A History of the Indians in the United States.* Norman: University of Oklahoma Press, 1977.

Larson, Robert W. *Red Cloud: Warrior-Statesman of the Lakota Sioux.* Norman: University of Oklahoma Press, 1999.

McDermott, John D. *A Guide to the Indian Wars of the West.* Lincoln: University of Nebraska Press, 1998.

Michno, Gregory F. *Encyclopedia of Indian Wars: Western Battles and Skirmishes 1850–1890.* Missoula, Mont: Mountain Press Publishing Company, 2003.

Paul, R. Eli., ed. *Autobiography of Red Cloud: War Leader of the Oglalas.* Helena: Montana Historical Society Press, 1997.

Phillips, Charles, and Alan Axelrod, eds. *The Encyclopedia of the American West.* 4 vols. New York: Macmillan General Reference, 1996.

Prucha, Francis P. *The Great Father: The United States Government and the American Indians.* Lincoln: University of Nebraska Press, 1984.

Utley, Robert M. *Indian Wars.* New York: Mariner Books, 2002.

At Issue

The Snake Indians (Northern Paiutes) attacked miners in Oregon and Idaho Territory. In response, U.S. Army forces acted to confine them to reservations. Sheridan's Campaign had much the same purpose: to force recalcitrant Cheyenne (mainly "Dog Soldiers," aggressive Cheyenne warriors) onto reservations.

The Conflicts

During the Civil War, when the U.S. Army presence in southeastern Oregon and southwestern Idaho was greatly diminished, the Yahuskin and Walpapi bands of the Northern Paiutes, popularly known to whites as the Snakes, frequently harassed and raided miners in the mineral-rich region. Ad hoc volunteer forces from Oregon and Nevada made forays against the Snakes, but to no avail. After the Civil War, regular army forces were again available in the region, but initial operations against the Indians enjoyed little success. Under intense pressure from local whites, the army assigned Brevet Major General George Crook and his Twenty-third Infantry to campaign against the Snakes in an effort to force them onto a reservation. Between 1866 and 1868, Crook's forces engaged the Snakes at least forty-nine times during the Snake War, which was not so much a war as a series of guerrilla fights and running skirmishes, none of which was decisive. However, Crook kept the Snakes on the run, thereby creating a war of attrition.

By mid-1868 the Snakes had lost 329 warriors killed, 20 wounded, and 225 captured, but it was not until the war chief Pauline (or Paulina) fell in battle in January 1867 that the Snakes indicated a willingness to make peace. While most retired to a reservation, a militant minority remained at large under another chief, Old Weawea. On July 1, 1868, after peace talks, Old Weawea led most of the remaining Snakes to a reservation near Fort Harney. A small band of diehards refused to submit and eventually joined the Bannocks and Cayuses in the Bannock War of 1878 (Chapter 26).

No sooner had the Snake War concluded than Lieutenant General William Tecumseh Sherman and his principal field commander, Major General Philip Sheridan, decided to move against the Cheyenne and allied tribes, who had been raiding extensively in the region of the Saline and Solomon rivers in western Kansas and eastern Colorado. Understanding that the Indians were most vulnerable during the winter, Sheridan began his campaign, also known as the Southern Plains War, early in the fall of 1868 with the intention of continuing into winter.

Sheridan dispatched Major George A. Forsyth with fifty handpicked civilian plainsmen to patrol settlements and travel routes. On September 17, this small force encountered as many as 700 Dog Soldiers (militant young Cheyenne warriors) and Oglala Sioux in western Kansas. Forsyth quickly assumed a defensive position on an island in the nearly dry Arikara Fork of the Republican River. Although greatly outnumbered, Forsyth and his men had the advantage of carrying modern repeating carbines, which were capable of much more rapid fire than the Indians' older rifles. Twice, Forsyth was able to

Philip H. Sheridan

(1831–1888)

Born in Albany, New York, Philip Sheridan graduated from West Point in 1853 and served in Texas and Oregon, fighting Indians. Promoted to first lieutenant in March 1861, he rose to captain in May and fought in the Civil War (Chapter 17). His gallantry was such that he was eventually promoted to brigadier general of volunteers. He fought with great distinction and by April 1864 was commander of Cavalry Corps, Army of the Potomac, fighting directly under Ulysses S. Grant in the Battle of the Wilderness (May 5–6) and at Spotsylvania Court House (May 8–18). During this period he led several brilliant cavalry raids.

Assigned command of Union forces in the Shenandoah Valley in August, Sheridan conducted his finest campaign of the war through the valley in September 1864. Promoted to brigadier general of regulars in September, he was absent from his army when it was surprised at Cedar Creek on October 19. Sheridan galloped twenty miles to the battle—an action celebrated as "Sheridan's Ride"—and rallied his troops, who repulsed the enemy.

After he was promoted to major general of regulars in November, Sheridan received the thanks of Congress in February 1865, and then went on to raid Petersburg during February 27–March 24. He was instrumental in the culminating pursuit of Robert E. Lee's Army of Northern Virginia and Lee's defeat and surrender at Appomattox Court House on April 9, 1865.

In March 1867, after the war had ended, Sheridan was named military governor of the Reconstruction-era Fifth Military District (encompassing Louisiana and Texas), to which was added military command of the vast Department of the Missouri in September. He initiated a campaign against the Indian tribes of the Washita Valley, Oklahoma, during 1868–1869. In March 1869 Sheridan was promoted to lieutenant general with command of the Division of the Missouri. During 1876–1877, he had charge of the campaign against the Southern Plains Indians, then was named commander of the Military Divisions of the West and Southwest in 1878. In November 1883 he replaced his friend, mentor, and commanding officer William T. Sherman as general in chief of the U.S. Army and was promoted to general just two months before his death.

CHRONOLOGY OF THE SNAKE WAR AND SHERIDAN'S CAMPAIGN

1866–1868

- At least 49 engagements are fought between U.S. Army forces and the Snakes.

1867

Jan.   Chief Pauline (Paulina) is killed in battle; the Snakes make peace overtures.

1868

July 1   Old Weawea leads some 800 Snake Indians in surrender. The Snake War ends.

Early fall   Sheridan's Campaign begins.

Sept. 17   Major George A. Forsyth and his fifty men are attacked at Arikara Fork by 700 Cheyenne Dog Soldiers. The battle ends when Chief Roman Nose is killed, but Forsyth and his men endure an eight-day siege.

Nov. 27   Battle of Washita

Dec. 25   Battle of Soldier Spring

1869

Mar. 15   Custer takes hostages at Sweetwater Creek.

July 11   The Dog Soldiers are decisively defeated at the Battle of Summit Springs. Sheridan's Campaign ends.

repulse charges. When Roman Nose—probably the most capable war chief of the Cheyenne—was killed, the disheartened attackers temporarily withdrew. With half of his company dead or wounded, Forsyth slipped two messengers through the siege lines, who summoned reinforcements.

The next major action occurred in early winter, as Sheridan sent columns from Fort Bascom, New Mexico; Fort Lyon, Colorado; and, under Colonel George Armstrong Custer, from Fort Dodge, Kansas. The forces were to converge on the Indians' winter camps, which were known to be on the Canadian and Washita rivers, in Indian Territory. In the most famous—or infamous—battle of the campaign, on November 27, 1868, Custer led his Seventh Cavalry in an attack on Black Kettle's Cheyenne camp on the Washita River, even though the chief was a peace advocate. The attack provoked a counterattack, which was joined by warriors from other camps. Custer not only held his position, but also destroyed more than 900 Indian ponies and set Indian shelters ablaze. As night fell, Custer turned his men toward the Indian camps downstream, signaling his intention to target them next. Accordingly, the Indians broke off their counterattack in order to defend the other camps. Custer's maneuver had been a mere feint, however, and the attack did not materialize.

With the Indians now downstream, Custer and the Seventh Cavalry withdrew under cover of darkness from the Washita Valley. Casualties from the Battle of Washita included 103 Indians killed, among them 93 women, old men, and children—as well as the long-suffering Chief Black Kettle. Disheartened, the Cheyennes withdrew to the reservation.

After the battle, the Third Cavalry conducted raids that destroyed the Indians' winter provisions. With these supplies gone, some Kiowas sought refuge among the Kwahadi Comanches, a Comanche band that had yet to engage in the war. Most of the Kiowas surrendered, however, as did many Comanches.

Severe winter storms prevented Custer from beginning a new offensive against the Cheyennes until March 1869. By this time, the warriors had moved west into the Texas Panhandle. On March 15, 1869, at Sweetwater Creek, Custer came across the villages of Chiefs Medicine Arrow and Little Robe. He had been informed that the Indians were holding two white women hostage. Custer therefore restrained his forces and, instead of attacking, called for a parley. When a number of tribal chiefs agreed to talk, Custer seized three of them and then sent one back to the villages with surrender terms: release the hostages or the other two chiefs would be hanged.

Black Kettle (Moketavato, Motavato)

(ca. 1803–1868)

Even though Black Kettle was a "peace chief," he and his Cheyenne band were the victims of the 1864 Sand Creek Massacre (see Chapter 19). The chief had been a celebrated warrior in his youth, fighting rival tribes, including the Utes and Delawares. He favored friendship with the whites, signed a treaty pledging peace in Colorado and along the Santa Fe Trail, and in 1863 even had an audience with Abraham Lincoln in Washington, D.C.

Black Kettle stoutly resisted provocation to war during 1864 and managed to escape death in the attack on Sand Creek. Even after that outrage, he continued to counsel peace and agreed to accept relocation to reservations within Indian Territory, which white settlers soon invaded. The white incursions provoked renewed Indian hostility and led to Sheridan's Campaign of 1868–1869 in which Black Kettle was killed.

This contemporary wood engraving depicts prisoners captured by the Seventh Cavalry under Lieutenant Colonel George Armstrong Custer after his surprise attack on Black Kettle's Cheyenne village on the banks of the Washita River in present-day Oklahoma.

Like so much else relating to Indian policy, the label "Peace Policy" was inaccurate at best. The object of the Peace Policy was to enable the military conquest of hostile tribes, which, ultimately, would impose peace on the plains. The main strategy was to divide and conquer: By making reservations sufficiently attractive, complete with government-furnished refuge and sustenance, the Grant administration hoped to undermine the will of most Indians to make war. This would divide tribes and reduce the number of hostiles against which the army would have to contend. Even the generals agreed that it was cheaper to feed the Indians than fight them. As Francis A. Walker wrote in his **Annual Report of the Commissioner of Indian Affairs** for 1872, "By the reservation system and the feeding system combined, the occasions for collision are so reduced by lessening the points of contact, and the number of Indians available for hostile expeditions involving exposure, hardship, and danger is so diminished through the appeal made to their indolence and self-indulgence, that the Army in its present force is able to deal effectively with the few marauding bands which refuse to accept the terms of the Government."

The Cheyennes released the hostages and promised to follow Custer to Camp Supply, from which they would be marched to a reservation. But the Indians did not report as promised, and the Dog Soldiers, under Chief Tall Bull, joined forces with the Northern Cheyennes in the Powder River country.

On July 11, 1869, the Fifth Cavalry encountered the Dog Soldier camp at Summit Springs, Colorado. Some 250 troopers with about fifty Pawnee auxiliaries made a surprise attack, killing Tall Bull and many warriors. This proved to be a decisive defeat for the Dog Soldiers, forever ending their influence in western Kansas.

President Grant's "Peace Policy"

The Snake War and Sheridan's Campaign were prosecuted against the backdrop of what was popularly called Grant's "Peace Policy." President Grant personally formulated the policy with the intention of making the Great Plains safe for the passage of emigrants and for settlement.

War Department vs. Department of the Interior

One important motivation behind the Peace Policy had very little to do with white-Indian relations and everything to do with politics. Since 1849, when the

Bureau of Indian Affairs—and the authority to formulate Indian policy—was transferred from the War Department to the Department of the Interior, the two departments had wrangled bitterly over control of the Plains Indians. The Department of the Interior complained that the army's belligerence toward the tribes persistently undercut its attempts at instituting a humane policy and peaceful relations, whereas the War Department protested that Interior's policies made the federal government look weak in Indian eyes and, therefore, incited uprisings that exposed soldiers to constant danger.

President Grant hoped that his Peace Policy would be accepted as a viable compromise between the generals, who wanted jurisdiction over Indian affairs transferred back to the War Department, and Interior officials, who believed that peace and assimilation could—and should—be achieved without military force. The Peace Policy gave the army control over all Indians who refused to retire to reservations, while the Department of the Interior, typically acting through a variety of Protestant mission organizations, had authority over Indians who submitted to life on the reservations.

To his credit, Grant, who had come into office in favor of simply returning Indian affairs to the War Department, decided to test the Peace Policy in the Northern and Central Indian superintendencies, encompassing Nebraska, Kansas, and the Indian Territory, before applying it generally. He assigned the existing Indian agencies in the region to the management of the Society of Friends (the Quakers). Ultimately, removing Indian affairs from military control did not depend on the outcome of Grant's test of the Peace Policy. In 1870 Congress voted to bar military officers from holding civilian posts. The transition to civilian control having been mandated by Congress, Grant moved to expand the Peace Policy more rapidly than he had originally intended. He invited virtually all Christian denominations to participate in the administration of the Peace Policy, and he assigned the newly created Board of Indian Commissioners to undertake and oversee the assignment of agencies to the various churches that applied.

Annual Report of the Commissioner of Indian Affairs, 1872

The Indian policy, so called, of the Government, is a policy, and it is not a policy, or rather it consists of two policies, entirely distinct, seeming, indeed, to be mutually inconsistent and to reflect each upon the other: the one regulating the treatment of the tribes which are potentially hostile, that is, whose hostility is only repressed just so long as, and so far as, they are supported in idleness by the Government; the other regulating the treatment of those tribes which, from traditional friendship, from numerical weakness, or by the force of their location, are either indisposed toward, or incapable of, resistance to the demands of the Government. . . . It is, of course, hopelessly illogical that the expenditures of the Government should be proportioned not to the good but to the ill desert of the several tribes; that large bodies of Indians should be supported in entire indolence by the bounty of the Government simply because they are audacious and insolent, while well-disposed Indians are only assisted to self-maintenance, since it is known they will not fight. . . . And yet, for all this, the Government is right and its critics wrong; and the "Indian policy" is sound, sensible, and beneficent, because it reduces to the minimum the loss of life and property upon our frontier, and allows the freest development of our settlements and railways possible under the circumstances.

Excerpted from Francis Paul Prucha, ed., *Documents of United States Indian Policy,* 2d ed. (Lincoln: University of Nebraska Press, 1990), 137.

Secretary of the Interior Cox on Indian Policy (1869)

John D. Cox, Grant's first secretary of the interior, enthusiastically approved of the Peace Policy in his 1869 **Annual Report of the Secretary of the**

Annual Report of the Secretary of the Interior, 1869

The completion of one of the great lines of railway to the Pacific coast has totally changed the conditions under which the civilized population of the country come in contact with the wild tribes. Instead of a slowly advancing tide of migration, making its gradual inroads upon the circumference of the great interior wilderness, the very center of the desert has been pierced. Every station upon the railway has become a nucleus for a civilized settlement.... The range of the buffalo is being rapidly restricted, and the chase is becoming an uncertain reliance to the Indian for the sustenance of his family. If he is in want he will rob, as white men do in the like circumstances, and robbery is but the beginning of war, in which savage barbarities and retaliations soon cause a cry of extermination to be raised along the whole frontier.

It has long been the policy of the government to require of the tribes most nearly in contact with white settlements that they should fix their abode upon definite reservations....

A new policy is not so much needed as an enlarged and more enlightened application of the general principles of the old one. We are now in contact with all the aboriginal tribes within our borders, and can no longer assume that we may, even for a time, leave a large part of them out of the operation of our system.

I understand this policy to look to two objects: First, the location of the Indians upon fixed reservations, so that the pioneers and settlers may be freed from the terrors of wandering hostile tribes; and second, an earnest effort at their civilization, so that they may themselves be elevated in the scale of humanity, and our obligation to them as fellow-men be discharged.

Excerpted from Francis Paul Prucha, ed., *Documents of United States Indian Policy,* 2d ed. (Lincoln: University of Nebraska Press, 1990), 129.

Interior. He favored settlement of Indians on reservations with agencies run by the Quakers and overseen by the new Board of Indian Commissioners. Most significant, he expressed his belief that Grant's Peace Policy would both bring an improvement in white-Indian relations by pacifying the Indian tribes, and transform white attitudes toward the Indians. Until well into the 1870s, public opinion was mostly favorable, regarding the project of "civilizing"—that is, assimilating—the Indians with increased optimism.

Report of the Board of Indian Commissioners (1869)

Whereas Secretary of the Interior Cox expressed an almost blithe optimism in his 1869 report, the newly installed Indian commissioners took a very different tone in their **Report of the Board of Indian Commissioners,** issued on November 23, 1869. The document was stark and even shocking in its candor, presenting an indictment of "the history of the government connection with the Indians," which was described as "a shameful record of broken treaties and unfulfilled promises." The commissioners recommended abandoning the treaty system altogether, according the Indians the legal status of "wards of the government," and educating them "in industry, the arts of civilization, and the principles of Christianity," so that they might be elevated to "the rights of citizenship."

Congress acted on the recommendations of the Board of Indian Commissioners by passing, on March 3, 1871, legislation that abolished treaty making, abrogated all existing treaties, and universally reclassified Indians as federal wards.

The Fate of "Conquest through Kindness"

President Grant described his Peace Policy as a policy of "conquest through kindness." It was, really, the latest version of the old story of the Euro-American conquest of Native America: an assault by

Report of the Board of Indian Commissioners, 1869

Paradoxical as it may seem, the white man has been the chief obstacle in the way of Indian civilization. The benevolent measures attempted by the government for their advancement have been almost uniformly thwarted by the agencies employed to carry them out. The soldiers, sent for their protection, too often carried demoralization and disease into their midst. The agent, appointed to be their friend and counsellor, business manager, and the almoner of the government bounties, frequently went among them only to enrich himself in the shortest possible time, at the cost of the Indians. . . . The general interest of the trader was opposed to their enlightenment as tending to lessen his profits. Any increase of intelligence would render them less liable to his impositions; and, if occupied in agricultural pursuits, their product of furs would be proportionally decreased. The contractor's and transporter's interests were opposed to it, for the reason that the production of agricultural products on the spot would measurably cut off their profits in furnishing army supplies. The

interpreter knew that if they were taught, his occupation would be gone. The more submissive and patient the tribe, the greater the number of outlaws infesting their vicinity; and all these were the missionaries teaching them the most degrading vices of which humanity is capable. If in spite of these obstacles a tribe made some progress in agriculture, or their lands be came valuable from any cause, the process of civilization was summarily ended by driving them away from their homes with fire and sword, to undergo similar experiences in some new locality.

Whatever may have been the original character of the aborigines, many of them are now precisely what the course of treatment received from the whites must necessarily have made them—suspicious, revengeful, and cruel in their retaliation.

Excerpted from Francis Paul Prucha, ed., *Documents of United States Indian Policy,* 2d ed. (Lincoln: University of Nebraska Press, 1990), 132–133.

people who bore a sword in one hand and a Bible in the other. Kindness, of a sort, was indeed offered, but those Indians who chose to resist federal authority by refusing to accept this kindness found themselves at the mercy of a most unkind military. The Indians who did submit came immediately under the direct supervision of church-appointed Indian agents and were consigned to federal reservations. On these reservations, they were exposed to Christian teachers, whose job it was to persuade the Indians that it was in their best interest to abandon their own culture and become assimilated into the American mainstream. The Peace Policy, as it turned out, was but the harbinger of an increasingly coercive ethnocentric federal policy of compulsory assimilation, which would culminate in the 1880s and 1890s.

In the meantime, the Peace Policy was itself torn by growing rivalry among the various Christian denominations over assignment to the Indian agencies. While this squabbling was under way, a

growing number government officials as well as citizens questioned the constitutionality of the intimate association of church and state. While this argument simmered, the Catholic Church, through its Catholic Board of Indian Missions, steadily eroded the hegemony of the Protestants in the administration of Indian affairs. By the beginning of the 1880s, the Catholic Board of Indian Missions emerged as the largest holder of government contracts for Native American schools.

Before the end of the 1870s, Grant's Peace Policy was in precipitous decline, and church appointment of agents ended by 1883. "Conquest by kindness" was by no means a total failure, however. It was actually quite successful in pacifying most of the warlike tribes, so that by the late 1870s, only the Apaches of the Southwest continued to resist the military. The Peace Policy also proved effective in reforming the notoriously corrupt Indian agencies. Ethnocentric ideology notwithstanding, the religious administrators hired by the government were serious, committed, and almost always scrupulously honest. Nevertheless, in its most important dimension, "conquest by kindness" failed, for the policy made little progress in bringing about the assimilation of young Indians.

BIBLIOGRAPHY

Axelrod, Alan. *Chronicle of the Indian Wars: From Colonial Times to Wounded Knee.* New York: Macmillan General Reference, 1993.

Debo, Angie. *A History of the Indians in the United States.* Norman: University of Oklahoma Press, 1977.

McDermott, John D. *A Guide to the Indian Wars of the West.* Lincoln: University of Nebraska Press, 1998.

Michno, Gregory F. *Encyclopedia of Indian Wars: Western Battles and Skirmishes 1850–1890.* Missoula, Mont: Mountain Press Publishing Company, 2003.

Phillips, Charles, and Alan Axelrod, eds. *The Encyclopedia of the American West.* 4 vols. New York: Macmillan General Reference, 1996.

Prucha, Francis P. *The Great Father: The United States Government and the American Indians.* Lincoln: University of Nebraska Press, 1984.

Utley, Robert M. *Indian Wars.* New York: Mariner Books, 2002.

CHAPTER 22

MODOC WAR (1872–1873)

At Issue

The Modoc War was fought to dislodge the small Modoc tribe from the lava beds of northern California's Lost River country.

The Conflict

In contrast to the wide-ranging wars on the Great Plains, the Modoc War was fought in a concentrated area, the rugged Lost River Valley of northern California, against fewer than 200 members of a very small tribe numbering perhaps 400–500 individuals.

During the 1860s, the Modoc chief Kintpuash, known to whites as Captain Jack, brought his followers to Tule Lake on the Lost River. For seven years, they lived peacefully with their white neighbors by engaging in trade; however, as white settlement increased by the end of the decade, pressure mounted to relocate the Modocs to a reservation. Many Modocs retired peacefully to the reservation, but after three months, Captain Jack and sixty to seventy families returned to the Lost River. Even after their return, there was no real conflict with local whites; nevertheless, Thomas B. Odeneal, superintendent of Indian Affairs, recommended that the recalcitrant Modocs be removed by force.

On November 29, 1872, Captain James Jackson and Troop B, First Cavalry, numbering three officers and forty men, rode into Captain Jack's camp and set about disarming the Indians. The resulting exchange was called the Battle of Lost River. One Modoc was killed and another wounded, while the troopers suffered one killed and seven wounded (including one man wounded fatally).

While Jackson's troopers sparred with Captain Jack and his followers, a vigilante band of local ranchers attacked a smaller group of Modocs who followed a chief known to whites as Hooker Jim. After killing two of the ranchers and wounding a third, Hooker Jim's group rushed to join forces with Captain Jack, killing fourteen more whites along the way. Even united, Captain Jack and Hooker Jim mustered only about sixty warriors; however, they were masters of the terrain of the lava beds south of Tule Lake, a place the Indians called the Land of Burnt-Out Fires. This area became known to white residents as "Captain Jack's Stronghold."

On the night of January 16, 1873, Lieutenant Colonel Frank Wheaton led a force of 225 regular army troops supplemented by about 100 militia troops into Captain Jack's Stronghold. Wheaton directed a howitzer barrage against the Indians and then launched a dawn attack, in which 9 troopers were killed and 28 wounded. Indian casualties are unknown; there may not have been any.

With his army apparently unable to remove the Modoc holdouts by force, President Ulysses S. Grant appointed a peace commission to negotiate with Captain Jack and his followers. Talks commenced in March. On Good Friday, April 11, 1873, Captain Jack, under pressure from other warriors, assassinated the leader of the peace commission, Brigadier General E. R. S. Canby, and another negotiator. A third commissioner was wounded. After this, Jack and his band withdrew farther into the lava beds.

Edward R. S. Canby

(1817–1873)

Born in Boone County, Kentucky, E. R. S. Canby graduated at the bottom of the West Point class of 1839, but performed gallantly against the Seminoles (Chapter 8) and was among the officers in charge of the removal of the five Civilized Tribes from the Southeast to Indian Territory (Chapter 8). Canby saw action in the U.S.-Mexican War (Chapter 10) and earned brevet promotions to major and lieutenant colonel. He served well in the severely undermanned southwestern theater of the Civil War (Chapter 17) until he was recalled to the East to help quell the 1863 Draft Riots in New York City. In May 1864 Canby assumed command of the Military Division of Western Mississippi, participating in the Red River Campaign and coordinating ground forces with the navy in the capture of Mobile, Alabama.

After the Civil War, Canby served in various posts, was promoted to brigadier general in the regular army and, in 1870, was given command of the Department of the Columbia in the Far West. By 1872 he commanded the entire Division of the Pacific. In this capacity, he headed a peace commission to the recalcitrant Modocs and, ignoring warnings that he and his fellow commissioners were in danger, pushed Captain Jack to surrender. On Good Friday, April 11, 1873, Jack and other Modoc leaders responded by killing Canby and another commissioner and wounding a third.

Canby was the only general officer killed in the Indian Wars. His murder moved General in Chief William T. Sherman to send Colonel Alvin C. Gillem to capture or kill Captain Jack and his followers. Gillem pounded Modoc positions with howitzers and mortars during April 15–17, but the barrage had little effect. On April 26, Modoc warriors intercepted a reconnaissance party of five officers, fifty-nine enlisted men, and twelve Indian scouts under Captain Evan Thomas. With just twenty-two warriors, a Modoc called Scarface Charley ambushed the party, killing all of the officers and twenty of the enlisted men. Sixteen more were wounded.

Although the Modoc victories took their toll on army resources and morale, the Indians were not faring well either. As food and water dwindled by the

CHRONOLOGY OF THE MODOC WAR

1872

Nov. 29 Battle of Lost River

Dec. Vigilante ranchers clash with Modocs under Captain Jack, and the conflict widens. Captain Jack and other war leaders establish "Captain Jack's Stronghold" in the lava beds.

1873

Jan. 16 Battle of the Stronghold

Mar.–Apr. The Peace Commission negotiates fruitlessly with Captain Jack and his followers.

Apr. 11 Captain Jack and others murder two members of the Peace Commission and severely wound another.

Apr. 15–17 The infantry bombards Modoc positions with howitzers and mortars but fails to dislodge the Indians.

Apr. 26 Modoc warriors ambush a reconnaissance party under Captain Evan Thomas, killing twenty-five and wounding sixteen.

May 28–June 3 After a long pursuit, Captain Jack and others are captured. The Modoc War ends.

Brigadier General E. R. S. Canby, the only general who died in the Indian Wars, was killed by Modoc leader Captain Jack while conducting peace negotiations on April 11, 1873.

preceded the war. In response to pressure from reformers, a rider to the act abolished treaty making with the Indians and nullified all treaties in force. The status of the Indian tribes was unilaterally redefined from that of internal domestic nations to wards of the federal government. Doubtless, members of the House sincerely believed that the abrogation of the treaties (which were generally unenforceable) would bring about humanitarian reform and would ease the assimilation of the Indians into white civilization; however, another motive for inclusion of the rider was a growing sense that the Senate, responsible for ratifying the treaties, had too much power in managing Indian affairs.

Significantly, the Modoc War undermined two bedrock assumptions behind the abolition of treaty making and the reform movement from which it developed. First, the stubborn refusal of the Modocs to cede possession of the inhospitable lava beds and to accept life on a government-subsidized reserva-

middle of May, the Modocs dispersed. On May 28, guided by Hooker Jim, who had been captured earlier, a cavalry detachment located Captain Jack, his family, and a number of followers. A patrol cornered Jack and his family in a cave on June 3, thereby ending the Modoc War. Captain Jack and others identified as leaders of the "resistance"—Boston Charley, Black Jim, and Schonchin John—were tried, convicted, and hanged.

Abolition of Treaty Making (1871)

The Modoc War took place at the height of a humanitarian wave in the formulation of Indian policy. The March 3, 1871, passage of **An Act Making Appropriations for the Indian Department** immediately

An Act Making Appropriations for the Indian Department, 1871

Yankton Tribe of Sioux.— . . . For insurance and transportation of goods for the Yanktons, one thousand five hundred dollars: *Provided,* That hereafter no Indian nation or tribe within the territory of the United States shall be acknowledged or recognized as an independent nation, tribe, or power with whom the United States may contract by treaty: *Provided, further,* That nothing herein contained shall be construed to invalidate or impair the obligation of any treaty heretofore lawfully made and ratified with any such Indian nation or tribe.

Excerpted from Francis Paul Prucha, ed., *Documents of United States Indian Policy,* 2d ed. (Lincoln: University of Nebraska Press, 1990), 136.

tion should have brought into serious question the humanity, desirability, and, most of all, the viability of treating the Indians as wards of the federal government. Second, a cardinal assumption of the reformers was that the lifestyle of the Plains Indians—who required vast hunting grounds—was the main obstacle to assimilating the Indians into white civilization. The reformers believed that transforming Indians from hunters into farmers would inevitably assimilate them into the white mainstream. The Modocs were not hunters, however, but a sedentary tribe that had already established a peaceful trading relationship with white neighbors. According to reformist assumptions, they should have been well on their way to assimilation. Nevertheless, the Modocs waged war rather than submit to the reservation.

Indian Commissioner Walker on Indian Policy (1872)

Commissioner of Indian Affairs Francis Walker issued his Annual Report of the Commissioner of Indian Affairs on November 1, 1872 (see Chapter 21) on the eve of the Modoc War. The report was harshly critical of federal Indian policy, which, Walker wrote, actually consisted of two "mutually inconsistent" policies—one for hostile tribes, the other for docile tribes. He criticized federal policy for being abusive against uncooperative Indians while cultivating "indolence" and "idleness" among cooperative ones. Yet he concluded by pointing out that all of the Indians, one way or another, were doomed to domination by white civilization and that their only choice was to "yield or perish." This was a far cry from Grant's notion of "conquest by kindness"; however, Walker believed that "when the expansion and development of a civilized race involve the rapid destruction of the only means of subsistence possessed by members of a less fortunate race," the federal government incurred a moral obligation to "provide for the lower some substitute for the means of subsistence it has destroyed."

Walker cautioned that this "substitute" should not consist of "systematic gratuities of food and clothing," but of "directing these people to new pursuits which shall be consistent with the progress of civilization."

The Modoc War ultimately provided support for Walker's grim logic of "yield or perish," but it also suggested that a program of apparently rational humanitarian reform would not necessarily move all Indians to compliance.

The Peace Commission

After the army had repeatedly failed to dislodge the Modoc diehards from the lava beds of the Lost River, President Grant took the unusual step of appointing a peace commission to negotiate with Captain Jack. Grant empowered Brigadier General E. R. S. Canby, commander of the Department of the Columbia, to assemble the commission, which consisted of a Methodist minister named Eleaser Thomas (the Methodists were the religious group in charge of the Indian agencies and reservations in the region), former superintendent of Indian affairs Alfred B. Meacham, and former Indian affairs official L. S. Dyar.

Admitted into Captain Jack's camp in March 1873, Canby demanded unconditional surrender, to which the Indians replied that they wanted nothing more than the lava beds for their home—a place, they pointed out, so desolate that no white man would ever want to settle there. While true, it was, as Canby saw it, beside the point. Federal policy dictated that all Modocs be resettled on a reservation, so there was nothing to be negotiated. Captain Jack believed that, given sufficient time, he could persuade the peace commissioners to allow his group to remain in the lava beds, but the patience of his warriors wore thin, and he was pressured to end negotiations. On April 11, 1873, during yet another parley, Canby and Reverend Thomas were shot to death, Meacham was badly wounded, and Dyar fled for his life.

Response to the Assassination of General Canby

The murders immediately ended the search for a humane solution to Modoc resettlement. General John M. Schofield, Canby's immediate superior, received orders from General William T. Sherman: "Any measure of severity to the savages will be sustained."

While the army pressed its costly campaign against a handful of Modocs, the friction between the Department of the Interior and the War Department over Indian policy reached a crisis point. This time, the public was also outraged over the murder of a highly respected and very well-liked general officer; although the Grant Peace Policy was not officially ended by the Modoc affair, the army was subsequently given a freer hand to act more aggressively against the Kiowas (see Chapter 23) and the Apaches (see Chapter 24). In effect, the assassination of E. R. S. Canby marked the beginning of the main phase of what the army officially designated the Indian Wars.

The Modocs on Trial

Captain Jack and his family were captured in Langell's Valley on June 3, 1873, and General Jefferson C. Davis made preparations to execute Captain Jack and the other Modoc leaders without trial. Fearful of repercussions from the Department of the Interior, officials at the War Department intervened to prevent the executions and directed that the Indians be held for trial.

In a well-publicized trial, Captain Jack, Schonchin John, Black Jim, Boston Charley, Brancho (Barncho), and Slolux were convicted of murder and, on July 8, sentenced to hang. Persuaded that they were not directly responsible for the murders, President Grant commuted the sentences of Brancho and Slolux to imprisonment for life.

On October 3, 1873, Captain Jack, Schonchin John, Black Jim, and Boston Charley were hanged at Fort Klamath in Oregon. The rest of Jack's followers were sent as prisoners of war to the Quaw Paw Agency in Indian Territory.

A New Power for the President

As the killing of Canby raised the level of army aggressiveness in the Indian Wars, so the abolishment of treaty making removed any pretense of meaningful negotiation with the Indian tribes. The power to locate, define, and establish reservations lay exclusively with the president, who created them by means of executive order, typically acting on the recommendation of the Department of the Interior. Thus the tribes were denied even the most rudimentary input on their fate. The first major reservation created in this way was established for the Mescalero Apaches in New Mexico on May 29, 1873.

BIBLIOGRAPHY

Axelrod, Alan. *Chronicle of the Indian Wars: From Colonial Times to Wounded Knee.* New York: Macmillan General Reference, 1993.

Debo, Angie. *A History of the Indians in the United States.* Norman: University of Oklahoma Press, 1977.

McDermott, John D. *A Guide to the Indian Wars of the West.* Lincoln: University of Nebraska Press, 1998.

Michno, Gregory F. *Encyclopedia of Indian Wars: Western Battles and Skirmishes 1850–1890.* Missoula, Mont: Mountain Press Publishing Company, 2003.

Phillips, Charles, and Alan Axelrod, eds. *The Encyclopedia of the American West.* 4 vols. New York: Macmillan General Reference, 1996.

Prucha, Francis P. *The Great Father: The United States Government and the American Indians.* Lincoln: University of Nebraska Press, 1984.

Quinn, Arthur. *Hell with the Fire Out: A History of the Modoc War.* New York: Faber and Faber, 1997.

Riddle, Jeff C. *The Indian History of the Modoc War.* Mechanicsburg, Pa.: Stackpole Books, 2004.

Utley, Robert M. *Indian Wars.* New York: Mariner Books, 2002.

At Issue

Following the murder of Brigadier General E. R. S. Canby during the Modoc War (Chapter 22), the U.S. Army pursued an increasingly aggressive policy designed to force Indians onto reservations; the Kiowas, Comanches, and factions of the Cheyenne tribe resisted violently.

The Conflict

Although President Ulysses S. Grant's Peace Policy (see Chapter 21) officially remained in effect in the aftermath of the Modoc War (Chapter 22), humanitarian efforts were largely overshadowed by the U.S. Army's mission to round up recalcitrant Plains tribes and confine them to reservations. The first major Indian conflict after the Modoc War, sometimes called the Kiowa War, is more accurately termed the Red River War because it involved the Comanches and Cheyennes as well as the Kiowas.

From the Indians' point of view, the war was triggered by whites overhunting buffalo, nearly to the point of extermination. In spring 1874 Kiowa war chiefs Satanta and Big Tree led Comanche, Cheyenne, and Kiowa warriors in destructive raids throughout parts of Kansas and Texas, including an attack on Adobe Walls, Texas, on June 27, 1874. Seven hundred Indians descended on this buffalo hunters' camp, which, at the time, was occupied by only twenty-eight men and one woman. Remarkably, the defenders held off the attackers for five days until they were rescued by other hunters.

Grant's Peace Policy dictated that the army had responsibility for Indians who lived off the reservations, but the Department of the Interior (through Christian religious agencies) had authority over Indians on the reservations. Arguing that the raiders routinely used the reservations as refuges, General William T. Sherman secured President Grant's permission to invade the Comanche and Cheyenne reservations. He ordered generals John C. Pope (in command of forces in Kansas, New Mexico, parts of Colorado, and Indian Territory) and Christopher C. Augur (commanding Texas and parts of Indian Territory) to conduct simultaneous campaigns converging on the Staked Plains region of the Texas Panhandle. As 774 of Pope's men under Colonel Nelson A. Miles approached the Staked Plains escarpment on August 30, they encountered about 600 Cheyenne warriors. A running battle commenced that, twelve miles and five hours later, became a standoff at Tule Canyon, with all parties exhausted. Miles had insufficient supplies to press his attack and withdrew reluctantly, destroying one abandoned Indian village after another along the way.

As in other battles in the main phase of the Indian Wars, the Red River War involved climate and terrain that presented obstacles as formidable as any enemy. A drought in the region had left Miles short of water and other supplies, but on September 7, the drought suddenly gave way to torrential rains. Under these conditions, Miles rendezvoused with 225 troopers of the Eighth Cavalry under Major William R. Price. Reinforced, he slogged northward through

Satanta

(1830–1878)

Satanta, or White Bear, was the son of a medicine man. Although he was born on the northern plains, he migrated to the southern plains with his people. He took advantage of the withdrawal of army personnel during the Civil War to raid travelers along the Santa Fe Trail. In November 1864, after suffering defeat at the hands of Colonel Kit Carson (under the command of General James H. Carleton), the Kiowas signed a treaty ceding lands in New Mexico, Colorado, and Kansas. Satanta held out, however, and continued raiding Texas. After General Winfield Scott Hancock presented Satanta with a goodwill gift of a major general's dress uniform in April 1867, Satanta boldly wore it in a subsequent raid.

Satanta's boldness as a raider was matched by his reputation among whites as well as other warriors for eloquence. By the time he finally signed the Treaty of Medicine Lodge in October 1867 (Chapter 20), agreeing to settle on a reservation in Indian Territory, newspapers called him the "Orator of the Plains."

Satanta's compliance did not last long. In May 1871 he resumed raiding and was captured, tried, and sentenced to death. In response to humanitarian protests, his sentence was commuted to imprisonment at Huntsville, Texas. He was paroled in 1873 on the condition that he remain on the Kiowa reservation in Indian Territory (present-day Oklahoma). When Kiowa, Comanche, Cheyenne, and Arapaho war parties resumed raiding in 1874, Satanta voluntarily reported to officials to prove he was not participating in the raids. He was nevertheless arrested and returned to prison at Huntsville. Four years later, told that he would spend the rest of his life in prison, he committed suicide by jumping from the window of the prison hospital.

---

increasingly impassable mud in search of desperately needed supplies. On September 9, some 250 Comanche and Kiowa warriors under Lone Wolf, Satanta, and Big Tree attacked an army supply train and held it under siege for three days until Price's column approached, causing the attackers to flee. In the meantime, General Augur's most aggressive field officer, Colonel Ranald S. Mackenzie, in command of the Fourth Cavalry, approached from the southwest. During the night of September 26, the Fourth Cavalry camp was attacked by 250 Comanches near Tule Canyon. Mackenzie held through the night, then counterattacked in the morning, driving the attackers off then counterattacking at Palo Duro Canyon, where he destroyed a Kiowa-Comanche-Cheyenne village. Mackenzie appropriated 400 Indian ponies and slaughtered 1,424 more to deprive his enemy of them.

CHRONOLOGY OF THE RED RIVER (KIOWA) WAR

1874

Spring Satanta and Big Tree lead Comanche, Cheyenne, and Kiowa warriors in raids throughout the Texas and Kansas plains.

June 27 Comanches and Cheyennes attack Adobe Walls, Texas.

Aug. 30 Battle of the Staked Plains

Sept. 9–11 Comanche and Kiowa warriors attack an army supply train and hold it under siege for three days.

Sept. 26 Colonel Ranald S. Mackenzie's Fourth Cavalry repulses a Comanche attack at Tule Canyon.

Sept. 27 Battle of Palo Duro Canyon

Oct. 7 Satanta and other Kiowa war chiefs surrender at the Darlington Agency, bringing the war to an end.

Kiowa chief Satanta, shown here in 1870 wearing his prized medal sent by President James Buchanan, led raids throughout Texas and Kansas before surrendering at Darlington Agency in 1874.

Into early October, troopers under Colonel George P. Buell razed more villages, while Miles and Price pursued Gray Beard and his band of Cheyennes. Worse was to come for the Indians—what the army failed to destroy, the storms of a premature winter ravaged. During October, Kiowas and Cheyennes poured into Forts Sill and Darlington to accept settlement on reservations. Satanta, together with Woman's Heart and other Kiowa war chiefs, surrendered at the Darlington Agency on October 7, 1874.

Abandonment of Grant's Peace Policy

Through the 1870s and 1880s, the humanitarian impulses of the Peace Policy were overwhelmed as military domination, always a key part of the policy, usurped them. The increased scope and tempo of military operations in the West brought a great degree of success, as evident in the outcome of the Red River War. For the first time against the Indians, the army deployed significant numbers of troopers in coordinated offensive campaigns, converging from various military installations. These were not mere police actions, but full-scale strategic assaults. Bitter and destructive, the new style of making war proved quite effective.

Indian Commissioner Smith on Indian Citizenship (1874)

Even as the army was exercising greater aggression against the Plains tribes, Commissioner of Indian Affairs Edward P. Smith issued, in his 1874 Annual Report of the Commissioner of Indian Affairs, the first truly detailed proposal for assimilating the Indians into mainstream white American society. Declaring that the "fundamental failure" of "the management of Indian affairs" could be attributed to the "failure to recognize and treat the Indian as a man capable of civilization," Smith laid out a proposal for making Indians "a proper subject of the Government and amenable to its laws." Smith pointed out that the government sought to control Indians by installing them on reservations, yet persisted in withholding from them the government's most basic means of control: the law. The only way to resolve this paradox, Smith argued, was to promote the assimilation of the Indians by means of "qualified citizenship." Instead of relying on the military to control the Indians, the qualified citizenship status would extend to them coverage by civil law. Smith proposed that the secretary of the interior be given the authority to "prescribe for all tribes prepared, in his judgment, to adopt the same, an elective government, through which shall be administered all necessary police regulation of a reservation." In effect, qualified citizenship would entail an Indian government and, at least to some degree, an Indian police force. Neither would be based on traditional

Ranald Slidell Mackenzie

(1840–1889)

Born in New York City, Ranald Slidell Mackenzie was the son of prominent naval officer Alexander Slidell Mackenzie. He enrolled in Williams College, but left to accept an appointment to West Point, from which he graduated in 1862, first in his class. He saw distinguished action in the Civil War and was brevetted to lieutenant colonel for gallantry during the Petersburg campaign of June 13–18, 1864.

Promoted to colonel of volunteers, Mackenzie commanded the Second Connecticut Volunteers, which he led in combat in the Shenandoah Valley during July–October 1864. Wounded at Cedar Creek on October 19, he lost two fingers from his right hand—an injury that would later prompt Indians to call him Bad Hand. Brevetted to colonel in the regular army, he was also promoted to brigadier general of volunteers and given command of a cavalry division in the Army of the James. Mackenzie distinguished himself at Five Forks (April 1, 1865) and was brevetted yet again, to major general. After the war, however, he reverted to his permanent rank of captain.

After serving briefly in the Corps of Engineers, Mackenzie was named colonel of the Forty-first Infantry, a black unit, in 1867. Mackenzie fashioned his "Buffalo soldiers" into a superb force, which served with distinction along the Texas frontier. In 1869 the Forty-first and Thirty-eighth Infantry were consolidated as the Twenty-fourth Infantry, with Mackenzie as colonel of the new regiment.

In 1871 he transferred to command of the Fourth Cavalry at Fort Concho in San Angelo, Texas. As he had done with the black infantry units, he transformed this cavalry regiment into a crack outfit, which he took into action against Comanches and Kiowas raiding throughout southern Texas.

After defeating the Comanche war leader Mow-way in the summer of 1872, Mackenzie led his regiment west to fight Apaches raiding from bases deep within Mexico. During May 18–21, 1873, he led a lightning raid into Mexican territory to lay waste to three Apache villages near San Remolino (now El Remolino). He then fought in the Red River War, achieving a signal victory at Palo Duro Canyon, Texas, on September 28, 1874.

In 1876 Mackenzie, under General Philip Sheridan, fought the Sioux and northern Cheyennes, defeating Red Cloud and Red Leaf in Nebraska during October, then defeating Dull Knife at Crazy Woman Creek on November 25–26. These actions led to the defeat of the Sioux under Crazy Horse (Chapter 25).

In 1880 when the Utes domiciled at the White River Agency in northwestern Colorado threatened an uprising, Mackenzie quickly intervened, overseeing the peaceful transfer of 1,400 Utes to a new reservation in Utah in August 1881. In October, Mackenzie was named to command the District of New Mexico and quickly acted to extinguish raiding in the territory. Promoted to brigadier general, he was given command of the Department of Texas on October 30, 1883, but soon collapsed with a devastating physical and mental breakdown and was relieved of command. On March 24, 1884, he retired, suffering from the neurological effects of tertiary syphilis. He returned to the East an invalid and was nursed by his sister until his death five years later.

tribal patterns of leadership, but rather on a democratic model emulating the U.S. federal government. The Indian government would not be autonomous, for, in Smith's scheme, the federal government would also provide a "distinct territorial government, or United States court" to supervise the Indians' own elective government and would also furnish a force of federal marshals. Finally, the federal government would provide a specific "way into [full] citizenship for such as desire it." This entailed the transfer of land from joint tribal possession to "severalty by allotment"—that is, individual ownership.

General Sherman on the Transfer of the Indian Bureau

General William Tecumseh Sherman did not deign to address the subject of Indian citizenship, but instead lobbied for the transfer of the Indian Bureau to the War Department. His argument was decidedly non-ideological and appealed strictly to the federal government's desire for efficiency and economy (at least where Indian policy was concerned). **Sherman's Letter to the Chairman of the House Subcommittee on Indian Affairs,** dated January 19, 1876, explained that "as the military authorities are already charged with the duty of keeping the peace, I am sure they will be the better able to accomplish this end if intrusted with the issue of the annuities [due to reservation Indians], whether of money, food, or clothing." Sherman explained that army quartermaster facilities were ideal for such distribution. He

pointed out that the army was geographically well positioned to implement government policy while denying that it sought war with the Indians. He even preempted Department of the Interior claims concerning the civilizing of the Indian by suggesting how the Indians could be molded into society.

Commissioner Smith: The Principles of Indian Policy (1876)

The transfer of the Indian Bureau to the War Department did not come to pass, and on October 30, 1876, Commissioner Edward P. Smith issued his **Annual Report of the Commissioner of Indian Affairs,** in which he laid down the three principles he deemed essential for the welfare of the Indians and their progress toward full citizenship. The first was the concentration of all Indians on a few great reservations, which were to be consolidated from the many reservations in existence at the time. This, Smith asserted, would make controlling the Indians easier and would prevent conflict between Indians and their white neighbors. The second was the allotment of land in severalty—that is, the breakup of tribally

---

Sherman's Letter to the Chairman of the House Subcommittee on Indian Affairs, 1876

I firmly believe that the Army now occupies the positions and relations to the great mass of the Indian tribes that will better enable the Government to execute any line of policy it may deem wise and proper, than by any possible system that can be devised with civil agents. The Indians, more especially those who occupy the vast region west of the Mississippi, from the Rio Grande to the British line, are natural warriors, and have always looked to the military rather than to the civil agents of Government for protection or punishment. . . . The idea which prevails with some, that the Army wants war with the Indians, is not true. Such wars bring exposure, toil, risk, and privations, with no honor. There-

fore, it (the Army) naturally wants peace, and very often has prevented wars by its mere presence; and if intrusted with the exclusive management and control of the annuities and supplies, as well as force, I think Indian wars will cease, and the habits of the Indians will be gradually molded into a most necessary and useful branch of industry—the rearing of sheep, cattle, horses, &c. In some localities they may possibly be made farmers.

Excerpted from Francis Paul Prucha, ed., *Documents of United States Indian Policy,* 2d ed. (Lincoln: University of Nebraska Press, 1990), 147.

Annual Report of the Commissioner of Indian Affairs, 1876

ALLOTMENTS IN SEVERALTY.

It is doubtful whether any high degree of civilization is possible without individual ownership of land. The records of the past and the experience of the present testify that the soil should be made secure to the individual by all the guarantees which law can devise, and that nothing less will induce men to put forth their best exertions. . . .

I am not unaware that this proposition will meet with strenuous opposition from the Indians themselves. Like the whites, they have ambitious men, who will resist to the utmost of their power any change tending to reduce the authority which they have acquired by personal effort or by inheritance; but it is essential that these men and their claims should be pushed aside and that each individual should feel that his home is his own; that he owes no allegiance to any great man or to any faction; that he has a direct personal interest in the soil on which he lives, and that that interest will be faithfully protected for him and for his children by the Government.

Excerpted from Francis Paul Prucha, ed., *Documents of United States Indian Policy,* 2d ed. (Lincoln: University of Nebraska , 1990), 149.

held lands into parcels individually owned by the Indians and disposable by them as individuals. Finally, Smith repeated his earlier call for the extension of U.S. law over all of the Indians, so that they would come under civil rather than military control.

The consolidation of the reservations was never carried out, but Smith's other two proposals, severalty and the application of U.S. law to Indians, became important parts of U.S. Indian policy before the end of the century.

BIBLIOGRAPHY

Axelrod, Alan. *Chronicle of the Indian Wars: From Colonial Times to Wounded Knee.* New York: Macmillan General Reference, 1993.

Debo, Angie. *A History of the Indians in the United States.* Norman: University of Oklahoma Press, 1977.

Haley, James L. *The Buffalo War: The History of the Red River Indian Uprising of 1874.* Abilene, Texas: State House Press, 1998.

McDermott, John D. *A Guide to the Indian Wars of the West.* Lincoln: University of Nebraska Press, 1998.

Michno, Gregory F. *Encyclopedia of Indian Wars: Western Battles and Skirmishes 1850–1890.* Missoula, Mont: Mountain Press Publishing Company, 2003.

Phillips, Charles, and Alan Axelrod, eds. *The Encyclopedia of the American West.* 4 vols. New York: Macmillan General Reference, 1996.

Prucha, Francis P. *The Great Father: The United States Government and the American Indians.* Lincoln: University of Nebraska Press, 1984.

Utley, Robert M. *Indian Wars.* New York: Mariner Books, 2002.

CHAPTER 24

APACHE WAR

(1876–1886)

At Issue

Of all the Southwestern tribes, the Apaches, with their age-old warrior tradition, most violently resisted removal to reservations. Warfare was chronic during the period 1876–1886, as the U.S. Army sought to round up "outlaw" Apaches who refused removal.

The Conflict

In 1875 Commissioner of Indian Affairs Edward P. Smith issued a directive consolidating the four separate Apache reservations in Arizona and New Mexico into a single, large reservation at San Carlos, Arizona. In 1876 about half of the Chiricahua Apaches complied with the order, but the rest of the

Victorio (Bidu-ya)

(ca. 1825–1880)

Most likely born in what is now southern New Mexico, Victorio grew into young manhood and quickly established himself as a formidable warrior under Mimbreño Apache chief Mangas Coloradas. When Mangas Coloradas died in 1863, leadership of his band fell to Victorio, who acquired additional followers from among the Warm Springs proper, Mogollon, Copper Mine, Chiricahua, and Mescalero Apaches. With the Mimbreños, these bands, under Victorio, came to be known collectively as the Ojo Caliente, or Warm Springs Apaches. They acquired a much-feared reputation as ruthless raiders throughout New Mexico and Texas.

Victorio offered to end the raids in exchange for a permanent reservation at Warm Springs, but when negotiations broke down, he and his band were forced to settle in the much-hated San Carlos Reser-

vation of Arizona. On September 2, 1877, Victorio and 300 others left San Carlos. Although many soon surrendered to authorities, Victorio and 80 diehards holed up in the Mimbres Mountains, which they used as a headquarters to stage many raids.

Early in 1879, Victorio again attempted to settle at Warm Springs, but agreed to remove to the Mescalero Reservation at Tularosa, New Mexico. No sooner did he arrive than he was arrested and indicted on an old charge of murder and horse-stealing. He escaped on September 4, in company with a small band of trusted warriors as well as a large number of Mescalero Apaches. Once again, he led raids throughout the region, prompting the United States and Mexico to cooperate in his capture. He was killed by Mexican irregulars on October 15, 1880, while fleeing U.S. Army pursuers.

tribe scattered into Mexico. The Warm Springs (Ojo Caliente) Apaches were ordered to leave their reservation for the one at San Carlos in 1877. Some complied, but many dispersed. Those Apaches who complied with the move to San Carlos found that it was barren and disease ridden. From this squalor, two charismatic militants rose up: Victorio (a Warm Springs Apache chief) and Geronimo (a Chiricahua Apache warrior).

In a phase of the war often called Victorio's Resistance, Victorio led a breakout from San Carlos on September 2, 1877, taking with him more than 300 Warm Springs Apaches and a few Chiricahuas. Victorio and his followers evaded and fought with pur-

CHRONOLOGY OF THE APACHE WAR

1876–1877
- Factions of the Chiricahua and Warm Springs Apaches refuse orders to report to the San Carlos, Arizona, reservation.

1877
Sept. 2 Victorio's Resistance begins.
Oct. Victorio and his followers surrender at Fort Wingate, New Mexico, and are at first permitted to return to their homeland at Ojo Caliente, but then are returned to San Carlos.

1879
Sept. 4 Victorio leads raids throughout the Southwest and into Mexico.

1880
Oct. 15–16 Mexican forces defeat Victorio at the Battle of Tres Castillos, killing him and seventy-seven others. Victorio's Resistance ends. Following this, the influence of Geronimo and the Apache prophet Nakaidoklini rises.

1881
Aug. 30–
Sept. 4 Colonel Eugene A. Carr arrests Nakaidoklini. Carr's force is attacked and retreats to Fort Apache, which is held under siege.
Sept.–Oct. Apaches (including Geronimo) raid the Southwest as they make their way to Mexico.

1882
Apr. 19 An Apache war party rides into San Carlos, kills the reservation police chief, and forces Chief Loco and his faction of Warm Springs Apaches to return to Mexico with them. As they ride back, their raids kill thirty to fifty whites.
Apr. 23 Battle of Horseshoe Canyon
Apr. 30 U.S. Army forces, in pursuit of the Apaches in the Mexican state of Chihuahua, are ejected

from the country by Mexican colonel Lorenzo Garcia, who claims to have defeated a large Apache band.
July 6 White Mountain Apache warrior Natiotish leads an invasion of San Carlos and kills the new police chief, J. L. "Cibicu Charlie" Colvig, along with three of his deputies, then begins raiding throughout the Tonto Basin.
July 17 Battle of Big Dry Wash
July 29 Mexico and the United States conclude a reciprocal military treaty to address the Apache crisis.

1883
Mar. Geronimo and Chihuahua raid in Sonora, Mexico, while Apaches storm through Arizona and New Mexico.
May 15 After a pursuit into the Sierra Madre, U.S. Army scouts attack the encampment of Chato and Benito, prompting the Apaches, including Geronimo, to return to San Carlos.

1884
Mar. Geronimo and his followers reach San Carlos and immediately begin to stir rebellion.

1885
May Geronimo, Naiche, Chihuahua, Chief Nana, and 134 warriors break out of San Carlos and are pursued by the U.S. Army.
June 11 and
July 13 U.S. Army forces cross into Mexico, while 3,000 soldiers are deployed to seal the border.

1886
Mar. 25 Run to ground in Mexico, Geronimo and others surrender to General George Crook, but Geronimo makes a final escape.
Aug. Geronimo surrenders at Fort Bowie, Arizona, thereby ending the Apache War.

suing soldiers for about a month, but by the beginning of October they surrendered at Fort Wingate, New Mexico, and were permitted to return to their homeland at Ojo Caliente instead of San Carlos, pending a federal decision as to their placement. Before the year was out, they were ordered to return to San Carlos. About two years later, Victorio escaped the reservation. On September 4, 1879, believing he was about to be arrested, Victorio led 60 warriors in a raid against the Ninth Cavalry at Ojo Caliente, killing eight troopers. An influx of Mescalero Apaches brought Victorio's strength to about 150, and the augmented band raided extensively in the Mexican state of Chihuahua as well as parts of west Texas, southern New Mexico, and Arizona. Mexican and U.S. military forces cooperated in the pursuit of Victorio, who nevertheless remained at large for more than a year.

Mexican volunteers killed Victorio and seventy-seven other Apaches at the Battle of Tres Castillos on October 15–16, 1880. This ended "Victorio's Resistance," but survivors of the battle returned to New Mexico and joined Geronimo, who had emerged as the new leader of Apache resistance.

Geronimo (whose tribal name was Goyahkla) was one of several Apache leaders who used the Ojo Caliente Reservation in New Mexico as a staging area for raids beyond the reservation. When officials closed Ojo Caliente, Geronimo and sixteen others were forcibly removed to San Carlos on April 20, 1877. About one year later, Geronimo escaped to Mexico, but returned to San Carlos in 1880, having evaded Mexican troops.

It was during Geronimo's second confinement at San Carlos that Nakaidoklini became revered as a prophet among the Apaches. He foretold the resur-

Geronimo (Goyahkla)
(ca. 1823–1909)

Geronimo was born on the upper Gila River in present-day Arizona or New Mexico. He gained early and enduring renown as an Apache warrior and (as one Chiricahua admiringly described him) a "wild man." According to different sources, he was married seven or nine times—not always serially.

Following Chief Mangas Coloradas, young Geronimo and his family settled in Chihuahua, Mexico, where, on March 5, 1851, Mexican troops killed twenty-one Apaches, including Geronimo's mother, wife, and three children. Geronimo swore vengeance on all Mexicans and led raids along the U.S.-Mexican border region. When he was not engaged in a raid, he lived on the Ojo Caliente (New Mexico) reservation and, later, the San Carlos (Arizona) reservation. Except for brief intervals on these reservations, Geronimo lived as a fugitive from 1865 until his surrender in 1886.

Geronimo was in essence a guerrilla leader and possessed a tactical skill so great that he became the most famous Apache among whites during the 1880s. He was most intensely active during the late phase of the Apache War (1881–1886). He raided throughout the American Southwest and Mexico, repeatedly eluding large army task forces before he was compelled to surrender in August 1886, after leading his most recent pursuers on a 2,000-mile, four-month chase.

Geronimo and the other Chiricahua Apaches who surrendered with him were sent to prisons in the East. Geronimo was incarcerated in Florida and then in Alabama, before he was confined to a reservation adjacent to Fort Sill, Oklahoma. Even prior to his death, Geronimo was celebrated by Americans as a warrior of legendary proportions. In World War II, the U.S. Army honored him by adopting "Geronimo!" as the jump cry of its elite paratroops.

rection of the dead and a return to the days of Apache hegemony across the Southwest. Fearing an uprising, Colonel Eugene A. Carr, commandant of Fort Apache, Arizona, arrested Nakaidoklini on August 30, 1881. Carr's force was attacked by some 100 of Nakaidoklini's followers. In a panicked response, a cavalry sergeant shot and killed the prophet, and Carr's command barely escaped with their lives to Fort Apache, which came under attack. Reinforcements

Apache chief Geronimo (on left, mounted) was photographed in the Sierra Madre Mountains during negotiations with General George Crook in March 1886, prior to his final surrender in August.

were sent, and General William T. Sherman resolved that the army would put an end to what he called "this annual Apache stampede."

By the end of September 1881, Naiche (son of the Apache leader Cochise), the Nednhi Apache chief Juh, the Chiricahua Apache leader Chato, and Geronimo, with seventy-four braves, were off the reservation and bound for Mexico. They fought with army patrols, killed the San Carlos Reservation police chief on April 19, 1882, and forced Warm Springs Apache chief Loco and several hundred Indians to return to Mexico with them. En route to Mexico, the war party killed thirty to fifty whites. They repeatedly evaded army pursuers, who followed them into Mexico; the pursuit ended on April 30 when a Mexican infantry colonel ejected the American troops, ordering them to leave his country.

On July 6, 1882, a White Mountain Apache warrior named Natiotish led a small war party to the San Carlos Reservation, killed new police chief J. L. "Cibicu Charlie" Colvig and three of his deputies,

and then raided throughout Arizona's Tonto Basin until they were defeated in the July 17, 1882, Battle of Big Dry Wash.

After the Dry Wash fight, only the Chiricahua and Warm Springs Apaches, led principally by Geronimo, remained at large. Brigadier General George Crook, now in command of the Department of Arizona, used the authority of a new reciprocal military treaty between the United States and Mexico (signed July 29, 1882) to mount an ambitious campaign deep into Mexican territory. Following a major engagement on May 15, 1883 (in which nine warriors died and thirty lodges were destroyed), the Apaches emerged to negotiate with Crook. Geronimo and the others agreed to return to San Carlos, but did not arrive until March 1884. But no sooner had they returned than they began stirring rebellion. In May 1885, Geronimo, Naiche, Chihuahua, and the elderly chief Nana, together with 134 warriors, broke out of San Carlos and once again rode for Mexico. Crook responded by dispatching two troops of cavalry, with Apache scouts, into

Mexico on June 11 and July 13. Simultaneously, he deployed 3,000 soldiers to seal the border.

Geronimo eluded his pursuers in 1885, slipping through Crook's border forces into Arizona and New Mexico to terrorize the citizens. In October 1885 Crook sent another expedition into Mexico, which discovered the Apache camp on January 9, 1886, in Sonora, 200 miles south of the border. Although Geronimo fled, he sent a message indicating his willingness to discuss surrender. On March 25, Crook offered him and his warriors two alternatives: death in combat or two years of punitive exile in the East. The Apaches surrendered, but Geronimo bolted, taking only twenty men and thirteen women with him. General Philip Sheridan ordered Crook to retract the surrender conditions and accept only unconditional surrender. Frustrated and worn out, Crook resigned his command and was replaced by Brigadier General Nelson A. Miles, who dispatched a force under Captain Henry W. Lawton to capture Geronimo. By the end of August, Geronimo surrendered, thereby ending the Apache War.

Indian Commissioner Hayt on Indian Police (1877)

Geronimo and the resistant Apache factions were exceptions to the growing general trend of grudging Indian compliance with confinement to reservations.

Commissioner of Indian Affairs Ezra A. Hayt enthusiastically advocated in his 1877 **Annual Report of the Commissioner of Indian Affairs** the appointment of an Indian police force for each reservation. The idea caught on, and by 1879 Congress authorized a collective force of 800 privates, all Indians, with 100 white officers.

A Federal Court Rules in *Standing Bear v. Crook*

While the army struggled to control a small contingent of hostile Apaches, the military found itself also fighting a federal court. By its **Decision in *Standing Bear v. Crook*** (May 12, 1870), the U.S. Circuit Court for the District of Nebraska ruled against the army by releasing Standing Bear, a Ponca Indian, and others from detention. The Poncas had been held after fleeing Indian Territory for the reservation in Dakota Territory from which they had been ejected after the government inadvertently assigned it simultaneously to the Sioux. The language of the landmark decision concerning Indian affairs reflects an important shift in public opinion as the Indian tribes of the West slipped, ever faster, into ultimate decline. Sympathy for the Indians—whose plight would be chronicled in 1881 by reformer Helen Hunt Jackson in *A Century of Dishonor*—increased in proportion to the public's perception that their diminishing power

Annual Report of the Commissioner of Indian Affairs, 1877

The preservation of order is as necessary to the promotion of civilization as is the enactment of wise laws. Both are essential to the peace and happiness of any people. As a means of preserving order upon an Indian reservation, an Indian police has been found to be of prime importance. . . . I would recommend that the force be composed of Indians, properly officered and drilled by white men, and where capable Indians can be found, that they be promoted to command, as reward for faithful service. . . . I am thoroughly satisfied that the saving in life and property by the employment of such a force would be very large, and that it would materially aid in placing the entire Indian population of the country on the road to civilization.

Excerpted from Francis Paul Prucha, ed., *Documents of United States Indian Policy,* 2d ed. (Lincoln: University of Nebraska, 1990), 151.

Decision in Standing Bear v. Crook, *1870*

The reasoning advanced in support of my [Justice Elmer S. Dundy's] views, leads me to conclude:

1. That an Indian is a "person" within the meaning of the laws of the United States, and has, therefore, the right to sue out a writ of habeas corpus in a federal court. . . .
2. That General George Crook, the respondent, being commander of the military department of the Platte, has the custody of the relators, under color of authority of the United States, and in violation of the laws thereof. . . .
4. That the Indians possess the inherent right of expatriation, as well as the more fortunate white race, and have the inalienable right to "life, liberty, and the pursuit of happiness" . . . .
5. Being restrained of liberty under color of authority of the United States, and in violation of the laws thereof, the relators must be discharged from custody, and it is so ordered.

Excerpted from Francis Paul Prucha, ed., *Documents of United States Indian Policy,* 2d ed. (Lincoln: University of Nebraska, 1990), 153.

and dwindling numbers no longer made them a credible threat to the expansion of white settlement.

Secretary Schurz on Indian Policy (1880)

In Secretary of the Interior Carl Schurz, public sympathy for the Indians and their grievances found a strong and eloquent government advocate. He was a vigorous crusader against corruption, inefficiencies, and abuses in the Indian Office, and in his 1880 **Annual Report of the Secretary of the Interior** he reversed the policy that consolidated Indians onto a few large, central reservations. Like other reformers, he advocated an eventual end to the reservation system by allotting reservation lands in severalty to individual Indians—with the purpose of promoting their assimilation into the American mainstream.

Annual Report of the Secretary of the Interior, 1880

When I took charge of this department the opinion seemed to be generally prevailing that it were best for the Indians to be gathered together upon a few large reservations where they could be kept out of contact with the white population. . . . It was believed that this policy would be apt to keep the Indians out of hostile collision with their white neighbors, and in exclusive and congenial contact with their own kind, and thus prevent disturbances on the part of the Indians themselves and encroachments by the whites. . . .

More extensive observation and study of the matter gradually convinced me that this was a mistaken policy; that it would be vastly better for the Indians and more in accordance with justice as well as wise expediency to respect their home attachments, to leave them upon the lands they occupied, provided such lands were capable of yielding them a sustenance by agriculture or pastoral pursuits, and to begin and follow up the practice of introducing among them the habits and occupations of civilized life on the ground they inhabited.

Excerpted from Francis Paul Prucha, ed., *Documents of United States Indian Policy,* 2d ed. (Lincoln: University of Nebraska, 1990), 153–154.

Indian Commissioner Price on Civilizing the Indians (1881)

Although the Apache War was long, it involved a shrinking minority of the tribe and, by the 1880s, was identified in the public mind almost exclusively with Geronimo, who was seen as an outlaw—incorrigible or heroically colorful, depending on one's point of view. By the late 1870s, the public increasingly felt that the Indians presented little military threat. There was renewed public support for a federal effort to solve the "Indian problem" once and for all. In his **Annual Report of the Commissioner of Indian Affairs** issued on October 24, 1881, Hiram Price posited that the project of "civilizing" the Indians depended, first and foremost, on dismantling tribal lands and redistributing them in severalty to the ownership of individual Indians. Price argued that compelling Indians to support themselves on individual homesteads would bring them, of necessity, into the mainstream of American civilization.

Price proposed breaking up the lands and deeding them to individuals with titles that would be "inalienable for, say, twenty years"; that is, the Indian owners would be forbidden to sell their land for that period, which, Price believed, would be sufficient for them to become accustomed to working their land to the point of self-sufficiency. During this twenty-year period, Price proposed that the federal government supply the Indians with "teams, implements, and tools amply sufficient for farming purposes." They should also be furnished with "seed, food, and clothes for at least one year." Price concluded, "[I]n short, give [the Indian] every facility for making a comfortable living, and then *compel* him to depend upon his own exertions for a livelihood." Moreover, he advised, "let the laws that govern a white man govern the Indian." Price insisted that "if he expects to live and prosper in this

Annual Report of the Commissioner of Indian Affairs, 1881

It is claimed and admitted by all that the great object of the government is to civilize the Indians and render them such assistance in kind and degree as will make them self-supporting, and yet I think no one will deny that one part of our policy is calculated to produce the very opposite result. It must be apparent to the most casual observer that the system of gathering the Indians in bands or tribes on reservations and carrying to them victuals and clothes, thus relieving them of the necessity of labor, never will and never can civilize them. Labor is an essential element in producing civilization. If white men were treated as we treat the Indians the result would certainly be a race of worthless vagabonds. The greatest kindness the government can bestow upon the Indian is to teach him to labor for his own support, thus developing his true manhood, and, as a consequence, making him self-relying and self-supporting.

We are expending annually over one million dollars in feeding and clothing Indians where no treaty obligation exists for so doing. This is simply a gratuity. . . .

There is no one who has been a close observer of Indian history and the effect of contact of Indians with civilization, who is not well satisfied that one of two things must eventually take place, to wit, either civilization or extermination of the Indian. Savage and civilized life cannot live and prosper on the same ground. One of the two must die. If the Indians are to be civilized and become a happy and prosperous people, which is certainly the object and intention of our government, they must learn our language and adopt our modes of life. We are fifty millions of people, and they are only one-fourth of one million. The few must yield to the many.

Excerpted from Francis Paul Prucha, ed., *Documents of United States Indian Policy,* 2d ed. (Lincoln: University of Nebraska, 1990), 155–156.

country," the Indian "must learn the English language, and learn to *work.*"

Sherman: The End of the Army's Indian Problem (1883)

On October 27, 1883, General William T. Sherman retired from the U.S. Army as its general in chief and issued his **Final Report,** in which he declared that he regarded "the Indians as substantially eliminated from the problem of the Army." Sherman credited the actions of the army, the displacement of Indians by the march of white civilization, and the westward expansion of the railroad. The general made no mention of the future of the Indians themselves.

Courts of Indian Offenses

Reflecting a collective national sentiment that the "Indian problem" was indeed at an end, at least as far as military action was concerned, Secretary of the Interior Henry M. Teller approved the establishment on reservations of courts of Indian offenses for the purpose of eliminating "heathenish practices" among the tribes. As Teller explained in the **Annual Report of the Secretary of the Interior,** issued on November 1, 1883, the courts, as established at each agency, consisted of three Indians, preferably "the first three [Indian] officers in rank of the [reservation] police force." The commissioner of Indian affairs defined the offenses that constituted the courts' jurisdiction, and it was up to the Indian officers themselves both to prosecute and try "heathenish" offenders.

Ex Parte Crow Dog

The courts of Indian offenses, created by the Department of the Interior but ostensibly administered by Indian officials, reflected the ongoing ambiguity of Indian policy during this period. In effect, Indians were *segregated* on reservations for the ultimate purpose of *integrating* them into the white American mainstream. During this time, the position of the Indian with regard to federal laws was especially ambiguous, as demonstrated by the U.S. Supreme Court's 1883 decision in *Ex Parte Crow Dog.* The Brulé chief Crow Dog had been condemned to death by the First Judicial District Court of Dakota for the murder of another chief, Spotted Tail. In response, Crow Dog sued for his release on the grounds that the federal courts did not have jurisdiction over crimes committed in Indian country by one Indian against another. The Supreme Court agreed and

Sherman's Final Report, 1883

I now regard the Indians as substantially eliminated from the problem of the Army. There may be spasmodic and temporary alarms, but such Indian wars as have hitherto disturbed the public peace and tranquillity are not probable. The Army has been a large factor in producing this result, but it is not the only one. Immigration and the occupation by industrious farmers and miners of land vacated by the aborigines have been largely instrumental to that end, but the *railroad* which used to follow in the rear now goes forward with the picket-line in the great battle of civilization with barbarism, and has become the *greater* cause. I have in former reports, for the past fifteen years, treated of this matter, and now, on the eve of withdrawing from active participation in public affairs, I beg to emphasize much which I have spoken and written heretofore. The recent completion of the last of the four great transcontinental lines of railway has settled forever the Indian question, the Army question, and many others which have hitherto troubled the country.

Excerpted from Francis Paul Prucha, ed., *Documents of United States Indian Policy,* 2d ed. (Lincoln: University of Nebraska, 1990), 159.

Annual Report of the Secretary of the Interior, 1883

If it is the purpose of the Government to civilize the Indians, they must be compelled to desist from the savage and barbarous practices that are calculated to continue them in savagery, no matter what exterior influences are brought to bear on them. Very many of the progressive Indians have become fully alive to the pernicious influences of these heathenish practices indulged in by their people, and have sought to abolish them; in such efforts they have been aided by their missionaries, teachers, and agents, but this has been found impossible even with the aid thus given. The Government furnishes the teachers, and the charitable people contribute to the support of missionaries, and much time, labor, and money is yearly expended for their elevation, and yet a few non-progressive, degraded Indians are allowed to exhibit before the young and susceptible children all the debauchery, diabolism, and savagery of the worst state of the Indian race. Every man familiar with Indian life will bear witness to the pernicious influence of these savage rites and heathenish customs. . . .

. . . In accordance with the suggestions of this letter, the Commissioner of Indian Affairs established a tribunal at all agencies, except among the civilized Indians, consisting of three Indians, to be known as the court of Indian offenses.

Excerpted from Francis Paul Prucha, ed., *Documents of United States Indian Policy,* 2d ed. (Lincoln: University of Nebraska, 1990), 160–161.

Program of the Lake Mohonk Conference, 1884

WHAT IS NECESSARY TO SECURE INDIAN CITIZENSHIP

1st. *Resolved,* That the organization of the Indians in tribes is, and has been, one of the most serious hindrances to the advancement of the Indian toward civilization, and that every effort should be made to secure the disintegration of all tribal organizations; that to accomplish this result the Government should, except where it is clearly necessary either for the fulfillment of treaty stipulations or for some other binding reason, cease to recognize the Indians as political bodies or organized tribes.

2d. *Resolved,* That to all Indians who desire to hold their land in severalty allotments should be made without delay; and that to all other Indians like allotments should be made so soon as practicable.

3d. *Resolved,* That lands allotted and granted in severalty to Indians should be made inalienable for a period of not less than ten or more than twenty-five years.

4th. *Resolved,* That all adult male Indians should be admitted to the full privileges of citizenship by a process analogous to naturalization, upon evidence presented before the proper court of record of adequate intellectual and moral qualifications. . . .

5th. *Resolved,* That we earnestly and heartily approve of the Senate Bill No. 48, generally known as the Coke Bill, as the best practicable measure yet brought before Congress for the preservation of the Indian from aggression, for the disintegration of the tribal organizations, and for the ultimate breaking up of the reservation system; that we tender our hearty thanks and the thanks of the constituency which we represent to those members of the Senate who have framed this bill and secured its passage. We respectfully urge upon the House of Representatives the early adoption of this bill, that its beneficent provisions for rendering the Indian self-supporting and his land productive may be carried out with the least possible delay.

Excerpted from Francis Paul Prucha, ed., *Documents of United States Indian Policy,* 2d ed. (Lincoln: University of Nebraska, 1990), 163–164.

granted Crow Dog's petition. *Ex Parte Crow Dog* showed that the assertions of the military and the Department of the Interior notwithstanding, relations between Indians and the government were still fraught with a multitude of problems, misunderstandings, and a general absence of legal definitions.

The Lake Mohonk Conference

Recognizing the ongoing problems in white-Indian relations, philanthropic reformers in Indian affairs convened their second annual Lake Mohonk Conference, at Lake Mohonk, New York, in September 1884. The **Program of the Lake Mohonk Conference** addressed the issue of "What Is Necessary to Secure Indian Citizenship." The conference advocated "the disintegration of all tribal organizations" and urged the federal government to "cease to recognize the Indians as political bodies or organized tribes." It also advocated severalty and Indian citizenship "by a process analogous to naturalization."

The conference advocated not just legislation, but also education—for the Indians as well as white society. Indian education was to proceed along three tracks: industrial (that is, practical and vocational), intellectual, and moral and religious. In the meantime, the education of white society was to be aimed at increasingly shaping "public sentiment" in favor of Indian welfare and progress. Legislators frequently alluded to the Lake Mohonk Conference as they continued to grapple with the problems of for-mulating Indian policy, but the proceedings of the conference had little tangible effect.

BIBLIOGRAPHY

Aleshire, Peter. *Reaping the Whirlwind: The Apache Wars.* New York: Facts on File, 1998.

Axelrod, Alan. *Chronicle of the Indian Wars: From Colonial Times to Wounded Knee.* New York: Macmillan General Reference, 1993.

Debo, Angie. *A History of the Indians in the United States.* Norman: University of Oklahoma Press, 1977.

McDermott, John D. *A Guide to the Indian Wars of the West.* Lincoln: University of Nebraska Press, 1998.

Michno, Gregory F. *Encyclopedia of Indian Wars: Western Battles and Skirmishes 1850–1890.* Missoula, Mont: Mountain Press Publishing Company, 2003.

Phillips, Charles, and Alan Axelrod, eds. *The Encyclopedia of the American West.* 4 vols. New York: Macmillan General Reference, 1996.

Prucha, Francis P. *The Great Father: The United States Government and the American Indians.* Lincoln: University of Nebraska Press, 1984.

Roberts, David. *Once They Moved Like the Wind: Cochise, Geronimo, and the Apache Wars.* New York: Touchstone, 1994.

Utley, Robert M. *Indian Wars.* New York: Mariner Books, 2002.

CHAPTER 25

SIOUX WAR FOR THE BLACK HILLS (1876–1879)

At Issue

After gold was discovered in the Black Hills of Dakota Territory, the United States, claiming to act in defense of settlers, launched a war of aggression to remove the Sioux and Cheyenne Indians in the region and resettle them on reservations. The Indians considered the Black Hills sacred ground and fiercely resisted removal.

The Conflict

During a military patrol in the Black Hills in 1874, troopers under the command of Colonel George Armstrong Custer discovered gold. Within a year, news of their discovery had drawn thousands of prospectors, whose incursions violated the 1868 Treaty of Fort Laramie (see Chapter 20). The federal government, seeking to maintain the peace, offered to purchase or lease the Black Hills, but the Sioux, who believed the land sacred, refused to sell. In late 1875 the government ordered the Indians to report to a reservation by January 31, 1876, or they would be treated as hostiles. When the deadline passed, General Philip Sheridan attempted to launch a winter campaign. Harsh weather prevented all but General George Crook from mobilizing. He led 900 men out of Fort Fetterman, on the North Platte River in Wyoming, on March 1, 1876. During the last week of March, Crook sent Colonel Joseph J. Reynolds with about 300 cavalry troopers to attack a village on the Powder River. The Oglala Sioux and Cheyennes counterattacked, forcing Reynolds into retreat.

Crook's abortive foray galvanized Sioux unity under the inspired leadership of two extraordinary warriors, Crazy Horse and Sitting Bull.

Sheridan waited until late spring 1876 to mount a new campaign. His plan was for General Alfred Terry to lead a force from the east—including Custer and his famed Seventh Cavalry—while Colonel John Gibbon approached from the west and Crook marched out of Fort Fetterman. They were to converge on the Yellowstone River and intercept the Indians.

On the morning of June 17, 1876, Sitting Bull's Sioux and Cheyenne warriors attacked Crook's force at the Rosebud River in Montana Territory and forced it to retreat. Meanwhile, Terry's column had joined up with that of Gibbon at the mouth of the Rosebud, but neither commander was aware of the battle or Crook's retreat. Terry, Gibbon, and Custer convened to lay out the strategy for the rest of the campaign. The commanders believed the Sioux were encamped on a stream the white men called the Little Bighorn. The plan they developed called for Custer to lead the Seventh Cavalry across the Rosebud to the Little Bighorn from the south as Terry and Gibbon advanced to block the Indians from the north. This was intended to entrap Sitting Bull in a classic two-column flanking operation.

Launched on the morning of June 22, the plan assumed that Custer's highly mobile Seventh Cavalry would be the first to make contact, driving the Indians back against the larger forces of Gibbon and Terry. Custer, however, departed from the plan of crossing south of the Sioux position. Seeing that the

Indians' trail was much fresher than anticipated, he decided to attack directly and was so eager for a fight that he made no attempt to reconnoiter the strength of the enemy. Neither Custer nor his superiors had any idea of just how many Sioux warriors they faced. Historical estimates vary widely, from 1,500 to 6,000. Even if the lowest estimate is accurate, Custer, with a combined strength of 600, which he divided, was badly outnumbered.

Leading his men across the divide between the Rosebud and the Little Bighorn on June 25, Custer dispatched Captain Frederick W. Benteen and 125 men to the south to make sure that the Sioux had not moved into the upper valley of the Little Bighorn. As Custer approached the river, he spotted about forty warriors and sent Major Marcus A. Reno, with another contingent of 112 men, to attack them. When Reno was engulfed by masses of Sioux, Custer and his command rushed to join the fight, but warriors led by the Hunkpapa chief Gall rode across the Little Bighorn and readily pushed them back. As Gall advanced from the south, Crazy Horse moved in from the north, applying to Custer and his men the very tactic the army had planned to use against the Indians. The Battle of the Little Bighorn was over in an hour. Custer and all those under his immediate command were killed, but Benteen and the remnant of Reno's command were able to withdraw. Dug in along the bluffs, they successfully fought off a day-long siege. The next day, June 26, the siege resumed, but was lifted as Terry and Gibbon approached. Reno and Benteen sustained heavy casualties, but the

CHRONOLOGY OF THE SIOUX WAR FOR THE BLACK HILLS

1874
- Gold is discovered in the Black Hills in Dakota Territory.

1876
Jan. 31 The government-imposed deadline for Sioux evacuation from the Black Hills

Mar. 1 George Crook leads 900 soldiers out of Fort Fetterman, Wyoming, to begin the purge of the Sioux.

End of Mar. The Sioux force Crook to retreat from the Powder River.

June 17 The Battle of the Rosebud ends with Crook's second retreat.

June 25 Custer's command is annihilated at the Battle of the Little Bighorn.

Sept. 9 Battle of Slim Buttes

Nov. 25 Battle of Crazy Woman Creek; a delegation of Sioux solicits peace talks.

Dec. 16 Crow scouts (in army service) kill five members of a Sioux peace delegation, renewing violence along the Tongue River.

1877
Jan. 8 The Battle of Wolf Mountain ends the major phase of the Sioux War, dispersing some groups and sending Sitting Bull and his followers into Canada.

Early Apr. Large groups of Cheyennes surrender, and Crazy Horse surrenders with the Oglala

Sioux; however, fifty-one lodges of Miniconjou Sioux, led by Lame Deer, refuse to surrender.

May 7 Battle of Muddy Creek

Sept. 5 Crazy Horse is arrested on the reservation, then killed in a scuffle.

1878
Sept. 7 Dull Knife and Little Wolf break out of the reservation with 300 Northern Cheyenne; the army and citizen volunteers give chase.

Oct. 23 Fugitive Cheyennes, under Dull Knife, surrender at Camp Robinson; others, led by Little Wolf, remain at large.

1879
Jan. 9 Dull Knife breaks out from Camp Robinson after its commandant attempts to starve his people into marching to a reservation. Troops kill half of the fugitives, but public and political pressure allows the survivors to live with the Sioux at the Pine Ridge Reservation in southwestern Dakota Territory.

Mar. 29 Little Wolf and his faction finally surrender, ending the military phase of the war.

1881
July 19 Sitting Bull returns from Canada and surrenders at Fort Buford, Dakota Territory, bringing the war to its symbolic close.

George Armstrong Custer

(1839–1876)

Born in New Rumley, Ohio, George Armstrong Custer graduated from West Point at the bottom of his class on the eve of the Civil War, but soon proved himself a valiant field commander in combat. He was jumped from captain to brigadier general of volunteers and given command of the Michigan cavalry brigade. At twenty-three, he was (and remains) the youngest general officer in U.S. Army history. Custer was distinguished not only by his youth but also by his flamboyant appearance, which included long blond hair and a gaudy uniform of his own design. By the end of the war, he held the rank of major general, in command of a full division.

Custer returned to the postwar regular army as a lieutenant colonel and second in command of the newly authorized Seventh Cavalry Regiment. Because the unit's commanding colonel was frequently absent, Custer often acted as its commander, and the Seventh was molded in his dashing and flamboyant image. His first engagement in the Indian Wars came in Kansas, in 1867, and proved futile. He was court-martialed for taking leave without permission (to visit his wife)

and for "overmarching" his men. After a year's suspension, Custer returned to the field in 1868, eager to redeem himself. He attacked Chief Black Kettle's Cheyenne village (Chapter 21) on the Washita River in present-day Oklahoma. Although Black Kettle desired peace and posed to no danger, the army counted the Battle of Washita a great triumph, and Custer's reputation was rehabilitated.

During the Sioux War for the Black Hills, Custer's Seventh Cavalry participated in a campaign intended to drive the Sioux from the area. On June 25, 1876, Custer attacked the camp of Sitting Bull and Crazy Horse on Montana Territory's Little Bighorn River. The result of this attack was what the army called the "massacre" of Custer and five companies of the Seventh U.S. Cavalry.

Thanks in part to sympathetic journalists and the literary savvy of Custer's widow, Elizabeth ("Libbie"), Custer was transformed into a martyr in the struggle of "civilization" versus "savagery." He entered into American popular mythology and remains there despite many modern attempts to debunk the Custer image.

---

fate of Custer's command had been catastrophic: 200 mutilated corpses were strewn over the Little Bighorn battlefield.

After the "Little Bighorn Massacre," as the press called it, Congress authorized an increase in the army's strength and promptly turned over to the army complete control of the Sioux agencies. Nevertheless, except for the Battle of Slim Buttes, Dakota Territory, on September 9, the army avoided another fight until November 25, when the Fourth Cavalry under Ranald Mackenzie defeated a Cheyenne band led by Dull Knife and Little Wolf at the Battle of Crazy Woman Creek, Wyoming Territory. Following

the battle, a delegation of Cheyenne and Miniconjou and Sans Arc Sioux chiefs approached Colonel Nelson A. Miles to talk peace. As they neared his temporary quarters at Tongue River, Montana Territory, on December 16, they were attacked by the army's Crow scouts, who killed five of them. The incident provoked renewed attacks throughout December, to which Miles responded by marching about 350 men and two artillery pieces up the Tongue Valley. The Indians attempted an ambush, but hot-headed warriors attacked prematurely, revealing their position. On January 7, 1877, Miles's scouts captured a group of Cheyenne women and children. A war party of about 200 attempted to recover them, but failed and also alerted Miles to the presence of the even larger party of warriors waiting in ambush. With the element of surprise lost, the ambush became the Battle of Wolf Mountain on January 8.

Defeated along with Crazy Horse at Wolf Mountain, Sitting Bull led the Hunkpapa Sioux into Canada. The Cheyennes and the Miniconjou, Oglala, and Sans Arc Sioux dispersed widely. In early April large groups of Cheyennes surrendered, and Crazy Horse led the Oglala Sioux to the Red Cloud Agency and surrendered. But the Sioux War was not yet over.

Fifty-one lodges of Miniconjou Sioux, led by Lame Deer, refused to surrender and set out for the Rosebud to hunt buffalo. To engage them, Miles led a squadron of the Second Cavalry and six companies of infantry up the Tongue River. On May 7, he surprised Lame Deer's camp on a Rosebud tributary called Muddy Creek. A Miniconjou Sioux warrior named Hump, scouting for the army, persuaded Lame Deer and his chief lieutenant, Iron Star, to surrender. But when they approached Miles and his adjutant, shots were inadvertently exchanged, and both Lame Deer and Iron Star were killed. This touched off the

Sitting Bull (Tatanka Yotanka)

(ca. 1831–1890)

Sitting Bull was a member of the Hunkpapa tribe, a branch of the Teton Sioux. Born on the Grand River in present-day South Dakota, he was the son of a chief and, beginning in his early youth, acquired renown as a hunter and warrior. He rose to prominence in the elite Strong Heart warrior lodge by about 1856. His first major battle with white settlers came during the Santee Sioux Uprising of 1862–1863 (Chapter 16). On July 28, 1864, he fought General Alfred Sully at Killdeer Mountain, in modern North Dakota, but he was among those who agreed to the Treaty of Fort Laramie in 1868 (see Chapter 20).

When, in 1874, gold prospectors broke the peace established by the Treaty of Fort Laramie by invading the Black Hills, which were sacred to the Sioux, Sitting Bull became chief of the war council of combined Sioux, Cheyenne, and Arapaho Indians in Montana Territory. Although he was not present at the Battle of the Little Bighorn on June 25, 1876, he "made the medicine"—provided the spiritual power—that enabled the victory.

While Sitting Bull counted the Little Bighorn as a great triumph, he also believed that it would precipitate a major military campaign against the Sioux. In May 1877 he led most of the Hunkpapas

into Canada to avoid reprisals. The tribe fared poorly there, suffering from hunger and disease, and Sitting Bull finally led those who remained with him back to the United States. With 170 followers, he surrendered at Fort Buford, Dakota Territory, in July 1881.

Sitting Bull was held at Fort Randall, Dakota Territory, from 1881 to 1883, then was settled at Standing Rock Reservation, in present-day North Dakota. At this time, he became an advocate of traditional Sioux culture, which he struggled to maintain against the incursions and influence of the whites. Nevertheless, he befriended and profoundly respected one white man, William "Buffalo Bill" Cody, who recruited him as a performer in his Wild West Show during 1885–1886.

After leaving the Wild West Show, Sitting Bull returned to the reservation, where, during 1889–1890, he enthusiastically supported the religious revival the whites called the Ghost Dance. Fearing that the Ghost Dance, combined with Sitting Bull's presence, would foment a general uprising, the local Indian superintendent ordered Sitting Bull's preemptive arrest. On December 15, 1890, during the arrest attempt, Sitting Bull was slain with two of his sons.

Sioux chief Sitting Bull, one of the most influential Indian leaders of his time, is pictured here with "Buffalo Bill" Cody in Montreal, Canada, during an 1885 tour with Cody's Wild West Show.

brief Battle of Muddy Creek, which resulted in the deaths of fourteen Sioux and four cavalry troops. Following the battle, Miles burned a local Indian village and appropriated the Indians' ponies.

A series of skirmishes followed the Battle of Muddy Creek, but the Black Hills region was generally, if uneasily, peaceful. The biggest threat was Crazy Horse, who the army believed was intent on stirring a general revolt on the reservation. To forestall this, Crook ordered his arrest. While he was being taken into custody on September 5, 1877, he was stabbed to death in a scuffle involving soldiers and Indians.

In the meantime, the Northern Cheyennes reported to the Cheyenne and Arapaho Agency in Indian Territory by August 1877, but on September 7, 1878, Dull Knife and Little Wolf led 300 Northern Cheyennes in a break for the north. A combined force of army regulars and citizen volunteers followed in what came to be called the Pursuit of the Northern Cheyenne. Dull Knife and Little Wolf quarreled, dividing the fugitive band between them. Dull Knife's faction surrendered on October 23, 1878, while Little Wolf's continued northward. Dull Knife's group, although being held in the barracks at Camp Robinson, Nebraska, refused to return to Indian Territory. Hoping to force them out, the camp commandant, Captain Henry W. Wessells Jr., denied them all food and water. This provoked a breakout on the night of January 9, 1879. Pursuing soldiers gunned down about half of Dull Knife's people, then suddenly, in response to public and political pressure, allowed the survivors to live, as they requested, with the Sioux at the Pine Ridge Reservation in southwestern Dakota Territory.

Little Wolf's faction eluded the army throughout the winter, only to surrender, exhausted, on March 29, 1879, at the Little Missouri River. In the meantime, Sitting Bull remained in Canada with about 4,000 Hunkpapa, Oglala, Miniconjou, Sans Arc, and Blackfoot Sioux, as well as a handful of Nez Perces. Finally, on July 19, 1881, Sitting Bull and his band appeared at Fort Buford, in northwestern Dakota Territory, where he surrendered.

Federal Intervention in the Black Hills Dispute

The 1868 Treaty of Fort Laramie (see Chapter 20) guaranteed an end to white incursions into the Black Hills of Dakota Territory. The treaty held until the discovery of gold in the Black Hills during 1874. By this time, politicians and administrators alike had grown impatient with the Sioux, who accepted the government rations stipulated in the 1868 treaty but showed no inclination to become "civilized"—by assuming the sedentary lifestyle of yeoman farmers as the government wished. During the mid-1870s, the U.S. economy was assailed by one of the periodic financial panics that plagued a period of virtually unregulated financial speculation and manipulation. Although sympathetically inclined toward the

Indians in general, Congress—and much of the public—increasingly begrudged the funds devoted to Indian subsidies. Moreover, the prospect of a major gold strike, which would provide a desperately needed infusion of specie into an economy wobbling on inflated currency, was highly tempting. As a result, throughout Nebraska, Wyoming, Colorado, and the Dakota Territory, a public outcry began to swell: confine the Sioux to reservations once and for all, buy back the hunting rights guaranteed by the 1868 treaty—which encompassed the gold-rich Black Hills—and vigorously subdue all noncooperative, hostile Sioux.

When negotiations for the purchase of the Black Hills failed, the military was given leave to mount the campaign described

This part of an 1879 Northern Pacific Railroad timetable touts the protection of the U.S. military, apparently for white settlers and prospectors drawn by the discovery of gold in 1874, as the chief selling point on its route through the Black Hills. Settlers are also encouraged to take advantage of free and low-cost government and railroad land.

above. Simultaneously, government officials negotiating with the Sioux were ordered to offer a stark ultimatum: sell the hunting rights or starve. The army would burn villages, destroy crops and food stores, and appropriate or kill hunting ponies. The new policy was nothing less than a declaration of war.

In the Wake of the Little Bighorn

News of "Custer's Last Stand" at the Little Bighorn reached a public that had already been determined to settle the Sioux question with force. There was, initially, a collective national grief, which many compared to the sentiment that followed the Lincoln assassination in 1865. In the North, many grieved the fall of a Civil War hero, the celebrated "boy general" of the Union army. But the South also claimed George Armstrong Custer as one of its own. Typical was the response of the Richmond *Whig*, which wrote that Custer belonged "to all the Saxon race" and declared that he had perished in the furtherance of the "pride, the glory, and the grandeur of our imperishable race." Before the year was out, grief yielded to outrage and public calls for vengeance. In a phenomenon unprecedented during the Indian Wars, thousands of ordinary civilians volunteered to assist the army in hunting down the Sioux responsible for Custer's death.

The President and Congress Act

Following the Custer debacle, President Ulysses S. Grant at last gave the army what it had long asked for: an expansion of its jurisdiction, in the case of the Sioux, to cover not only those living outside the reservations, but also those within their borders. In effect, the president made friendly—or, at least, compliant—Indians prisoners of war. Congress was even more aggressive. Algernon Paddock, a senator from Nebraska, introduced a bill calling for the outright extermination of hostile Indians. The bill never left committee, but, in August 1876, Congress attached a rider to the Indian Appropriations Act of 1876, suspending all rations, including food, until the Sioux met certain conditions. A commission chaired by former commissioner of Indian affairs George Manypenny was sent to the Red Cloud Agency on September 7, 1876, to present the ultimatum to the Indians. The new agreement forced the cession of the Black Hills—7.3 million acres of the Great Sioux Reservation as established by the 1868 Treaty of Fort Laramie—as well as the renunciation of hunting rights to what, in 1868, had been unceded Indian territory. As a further concession, the Indians were to permit three new roads to traverse their reservation. In return, the government gave the Sioux 900,000 acres of additional grazing land on the north side of the reservation and guaranteed the resumption of annuity payments.

By law, the agreement was to be ratified by three-fourths of the adult male Sioux population; however, no attempt was made to gather enough signatures. After perhaps 10 percent of the Sioux had ratified the document, the commissioners took the agreement to President Grant who sent it to Congress for ratification. Congress enshrined in it law as the **Act of February 28, 1877.**

The Image of Sitting Bull

Even as the public demanded vengeance for the "murder" of Custer, demonizing the entire Sioux tribe, the American people could never bring themselves to condemn the greatest and most famous of

---

Act of February 28, 1877

Article 1. The said parties hereby agree that the northern and western boundaries of the reservation defined by article 2 of the treaty between the United States and different tribes of Sioux Indians, concluded April 29, 1868, and proclaimed February 24, 1869, shall be as follows. . . .

Article 2. The said Indians also agree and consent that wagon and other roads, not exceeding three in number, may be constructed and maintained, from convenient and accessible points on the Missouri river, through said reservation. . . .

Article 3. The said Indians also agree that they will hereafter receive all annuities provided by the said treaty of 1868. . . .

Article 4. The government of the United States and the said Indians, being mutually desirous that the latter shall be located in a country where they may eventually become self-supporting and acquire the arts of civilized life, it is therefore agreed that the said Indians shall select a delegation of five or more chiefs . . . [to] visit the Indian Territory under the guidance and protection of suitable persons . . . with a view to selecting therein a permanent home . . . where they may live like white men.

Excerpted from Cheyenne River Sioux Tribe, "Act of 1877," www.sioux.org/act_of_1877.html.

all Sioux leaders, Sitting Bull, who was generally regarded by whites as the noble leader of a tragic and doomed people. Among Indians, the adulation amounted to a quasi-religious reverence and was profoundly disturbing to the administrator of the Standing Rock Agency in Dakota Territory. He felt that Sitting Bull's immense popularity and influence could, at any time, incite an uprising. When William "Buffalo Bill" Cody recruited the chief for his famed touring Wild West Show in 1885, Sitting Bull was readily granted permission to leave the reservation. A figure of great dignity and charisma, Sitting Bull became an international celebrity as a result of his exposure in the Wild West Show. When he returned to Standing Rock after a season with Buffalo Bill, his reputation and image were more powerful than ever.

Shortly after his return, the Ghost Dance religious movement developed, which envisioned an Indian messiah who would sweep away the whites and restore the Indians to their former greatness. As the Ghost Dance grew in popularity and intensity, reservation officials decided to make a preemptive arrest of Sitting Bull in an effort to remove him from an already volatile situation. Arrested on December 15, 1890, Sitting Bull was killed in a skirmish as his faithful followers attempted to free him.

The Supreme Court Rules in *Elk v. Wilkins*

In the years following the Sioux War for the Black Hills, the federal government made steady inroads into Indian culture as well as Indian lands. Yet, although the often-stated goal of Grant's Peace Policy (see Chapter 21) was to assimilate the Indians, giving them a new identity as American citizens, there was great reluctance to actually take the steps necessary to achieve this goal, as illustrated by the November 3, 1884, **Supreme Court decision in *Elk v. Wilkins*.** John Elk, who had voluntarily

Supreme Court Decision in Elk v. Wilkins, *1884*

The question then is, whether an Indian, born a member of one of the Indian tribes within the United States, is, merely by reason of his birth within the United States, and of his afterwards voluntarily separating himself from his tribe and taking up his residence among white citizens, a citizen of the United States, within the meaning of the first section of the Fourteenth Amendment of the Constitution. . . .

Indians born within the territorial limits of the United States, members of, and owing immediate allegiance to, one of the Indian tribes (an alien, though dependent, power), although in a geographical sense born in the United States, are no more "born in the United States and subject to the jurisdiction thereof," within the meaning of the first section of the Fourteenth Amendment, than the children of subjects of any foreign government born within the domain of that government, or the children born within the United States, of ambassadors or other public ministers of foreign nations.

This view is confirmed by the second section of the Fourteenth Amendment, which provides that "representatives shall he apportioned among the several States according to their respective numbers, counting the whole number of persons in each State, excluding Indians not taxed." Slavery having been abolished, and the persons formerly held as slaves made citizens, this clause fixing the apportionment of representatives has abrogated so much of the corresponding clause of the original Constitution as counted only three-fifths of such persons. But Indians not taxed are still excluded from the count, for the reason that they are not citizens. . . .

The plaintiff, not being a citizen of the United States under the Fourteenth Amendment of the Constitution, has been deprived of no right secured by the Fifteenth Amendment, and cannot maintain this action.

Excerpted from Francis Paul Prucha, ed., *Documents of United States Indian Policy*, 2d ed. (Lincoln: University of Nebraska, 1990), 166–167.

separated from his tribe and lived among whites in Omaha, Nebraska, was a prime example of the assimilation that the government claimed to advocate. Yet when Elk attempted to vote, he was denied the right on the grounds that he was not a citizen. Basing his citizenship claim on the Fourteenth Amendment to the Constitution, Elk appealed through the courts. The Supreme Court denied his petition, holding that John Elk was not, in fact, a citizen. As a result, he was caught in legal as well as emotional limbo: he no longer identified with his tribe, yet was officially spurned by the white mainstream society. His fate was emblematic of the ambiguous status of the Indians after the Sioux War.

Indian Major Crimes Act of 1885

Even as the federal government declined to naturalize the Indians it ostensibly sought to assimilate, it took steps to extend the authority of federal law and federal courts over them. The **Indian Major Crimes Act,** passed on March 3, 1885, placed major crimes committed on Indian reservations by Indians under the jurisdiction of federal courts rather than tribal justice.

United States v. Kagama

On May 10, 1886, the Supreme Court handed down its decision in *United States v. Kagama,* which challenged the constitutionality of the Indian Major Crimes Act of 1885. When two Indians convicted of murder on the Hoopa Valley reservation in California challenged the law, the high court denied their petition and upheld their convictions. "The power of the General Government over these remnants of a race once powerful, now weak and diminished in numbers, is necessary to their protection," the Supreme Court declared.

BIBLIOGRAPHY

Axelrod, Alan. *Chronicle of the Indian Wars: From Colonial Times to Wounded Knee.* New York: Macmillan General Reference, 1993.

Debo, Angie. *A History of the Indians in the United States.* Norman: University of Oklahoma Press, 1977.

Lazarus, Edward. *Black Hills, White Justice: The Sioux Nation Versus the United States, 1775 to the Present.* New York: HarperCollins, 1991.

Indian Major Crimes Act of 1885

An Act making appropriations for the current and contingent expenses of the Indian Department.

SEC. 9. That immediately upon and after the date of the passage of this act all Indians, committing against the person or property of another Indian or other person any of the following crimes, namely, murder, manslaughter, rape, assault with intent to kill, arson, burglary, and larceny within any Territory of the United States, and either within or without an Indian reservation, shall be subject therefor to the laws of such Territory relating to said crimes, and shall be tried therefor in the same courts and the same penalties as are all other persons charged with the commission of said crimes, respectively; and the said courts are hereby given jurisdiction in all such cases; and all such Indians committing any of the above crimes against the person or property of another Indian or other person within the boundaries of any State of the United States, and within the limits of any Indian reservation, shall be subject to the same laws, tried in the same courts and in the same manner, and subject to the same penalties as are all other persons committing any of the above crimes within the exclusive jurisdiction of the United States.

Excerpted from Francis Paul Prucha, ed., *Documents of United States Indian Policy,* 2d ed. (Lincoln: University of Nebraska, 1990), 167–168.

McDermott, John D. *A Guide to the Indian Wars of the West.* Lincoln: University of Nebraska Press, 1998.

Michno, Gregory F. *Encyclopedia of Indian Wars: Western Battles and Skirmishes 1850–1890.* Missoula, Mont: Mountain Press Publishing Company, 2003.

Phillips, Charles, and Alan Axelrod, eds. *The Encyclopedia of the American West.* 4 vols. New York: Macmillan General Reference, 1996.

Prucha, Francis P. *The Great Father: The United States Government and the American Indians.* Lincoln: University of Nebraska Press, 1984.

Utley, Robert M. *Indian Wars.* New York: Mariner Books, 2002.

CHAPTER 26

NEZ PERCE, BANNOCK, SHEEPEATER, AND UTE WARS (1877–1879)

At Issue

Except for the Ute War, which was fought in Colorado, these conflicts took place principally in the rugged terrain of Idaho Territory and Oregon, with the Nez Perce War ranging into portions of the Washington and Montana territories as well. Of these conflicts, only the Nez Perce War had a genuine political dimension; the others were essentially police actions involving the pursuit of Indians who resisted removal from traditional lands for confinement to reservations.

The Conflicts

Nez Perce War (1877)

The Nez Perce lived in the Wallowa Valley of Oregon. After an 1863 gold rush made their land desirable for white settlement, federal commissioners negotiated a treaty that revised the boundaries of Nez Perce lands and created a division within the tribe between "treaty" and "nontreaty" factions. The treaty faction lived within the revised boundaries and was not displaced. The others refused to sign the treaty. Led by the venerable Chief Joseph the Elder, they continued to live in the Wallowa Valley, and, for more than a decade, the federal government did nothing. Indeed, in 1873, two years after Chief Joseph the Elder's death, President Ulysses S. Grant set aside part of the Wallowa Valley as a Nez Perce reservation. However, Oregon settlers began pressuring Grant to reopen all of the valley to white settlement. He therefore reversed his decision,

but Young Joseph, the son of Chief Joseph the Elder, refused to leave the disputed land.

In a meeting held during November 12–15, 1876, General O. O. Howard warned Young Joseph that his people had one month to vacate the reservation or be driven off by force. In consultation with other chiefs, Young Joseph decided that war would be hopeless and led his people to the reservation at Fort Lapwai, Idaho Territory. However, in the process of the relocation, a group of young warriors acted impulsively by killing four whites who were notorious for their abuse of Indians. This precipitate action incited rebellion among the diehard nontreaty Indians, some of whom fled south toward the Salmon River in Idaho Territory, killing fifteen more settlers along the way. Young Joseph had no choice but to lead his people in flight. His object was to join the revered Hunkpapa Sioux chief Sitting Bull in Canada, but to evade the army, he and his followers would take a torturous route during two months and over some 1,200 miles before fighting to a stand just forty miles south of the Canadian border.

In response to what were termed "Indian depredations," Howard sent 100 cavalrymen under Captain David Perry to confront Joseph. At dawn on June 17, 1877, Perry intercepted the Nez Perces at White Bird Canyon, Idaho Territory. Chief Joseph sent a peace delegation to Perry under a flag of truce. Not wanting to be caught shorthanded, Perry had recruited a handful of civilian volunteers to augment his force. Ignoring the white flag, these inexperienced and undisciplined men opened fire. In response, the Nez Perces counterattacked, routing

Perry's command and killing thirty-three men and one officer.

On June 22, Howard personally led about 400 troopers to White Bird Canyon with the purpose of bottling up the Indians there. Locals persuaded Howard that Chief Looking Glass—whose village was near the forks of the Clearwater River, a few miles north of the canyon—was intent on joining Joseph and the other hostiles. Howard sent troopers under Captain Stephen G. Whipple to surprise the village, but when Whipple learned that Looking Glass actually advocated neutrality, he decided to open talks with him instead of attacking. Once again,

however, the undisciplined civilian volunteers provoked a fight, which quickly swelled out of control on July 1, converting Looking Glass into a militant ally of Joseph's. For the next ten days, the army and the Nez Perces fought a running battle. On July 9–10, the Indians held a force of volunteers under siege at a place the volunteers later referred to as "Mount Misery."

The siege was hard on the volunteers, but it immobilized the Nez Perces long enough for Howard to bring up his main force to the rear of their position, and, on July 11, the two-day Battle of Clearwater began. The army drove the Indians from the

---

CHRONOLOGY OF THE NORTHWEST INDIAN WARS

NEZ PERCE WAR

1877

June 17 First Battle of White Bird Canyon

June 22 Second Battle of White Bird Canyon

July 9–10 Nez Perces lay siege to volunteers at "Mount Misery."

July 11–12 Battle of Clearwater

Aug. 9 Battle of Big Hole River

Aug. 19 Battle of the Camas Meadows

Sept. 13 After a battle at the site of present-day Billings, Montana, Chief Joseph decides to lead his people in flight to Canada.

Sept. 30–
Oct. 5 The Battle of Bear Paw Mountain results in the surrender of Chief Joseph and the end of the Nez Perce War.

BANNOCK WAR

1878

May 30 A Bannock shoots and wounds two white settlers, thereby triggering the war.

June 8 Bannock war leader Buffalo Horn is killed at the Battle of Silver City; the surviving Bannocks flee to Steens Mountain, Oregon, and join forces with a band of Northern Paiutes under medicine man Oytes and Chief Egan.

July 8 Battle of Birch Creek

July 13–15 In fighting at the Umatilla Reservation, Chief Egan is killed through Umatilla treachery.

Aug. 12 Oytes surrenders; most of the Bannocks follow him to a reservation within a month.

Sept. 12 Bannock diehards fight a final battle in Wyoming.

SHEEPEATER WAR

1879

May Sheepeaters (and/or Bannocks among them) kill five Chinese miners in a raid at Loon Creek. General O. O. Howard dispatches a small body of troops to hunt down the raiders in a police action that is soon called the Sheepeater War.

July 29 Battle of Big Creek Canyon

Aug. 19 Umatilla army scouts capture a deserted Sheepeater camp.

Aug. 20 Sheepeaters attack an army supply train. General Howard suspends the pursuit of the Sheepeaters.

Oct. 1–2 Fifty-one Sheepeaters and a handful of Bannocks surrender and are later settled on the Fort Hall Reservation in Idaho. The Sheepeater War ends.

UTE WAR

1879

Sept. 10 A scuffle between disgruntled Ute leaders and the inept White River Reservation Indian agent prompts a call for military aid.

Sept. 25–
Oct. 5 Battle of Milk Creek

Oct. 21 Officials negotiate the release of the Ute hostages. The war ends, and, the following year, the Utes retire to reservations.

Chief Joseph (Heinmot Tooyalaket)

(ca. 1840–1904)

Chief Joseph—also called Young Joseph or Joseph the Younger, to distinguish him from his father, Old Joseph or Joseph the Elder—was born into a period when conflict was developing between the government and the Nez Perce tribe. His father was among the tribal leaders who signed an 1855 treaty with Washington's territorial governor Isaac Stevens (see Chapter 13), ceding much of their land to the federal government in return for the guarantee of a large reservation in present-day Oregon and Idaho. The government, however, passively allowed settlers to violate the treaty by moving into the territory, and Old Joseph refused to sign the revised 1863 treaty to reduce the size of the reservation. When Old Joseph died in 1871, Young Joseph became chief of the nontreaty Nez Perces and carried on his father's policy of refusing to move from the Wallowa Valley.

Although Young Joseph was not a war chief, when homesteaders finally began to push into the Wallowa Valley, he gained great prestige by successfully protesting the incursion to the Indian Bureau, an action that resulted in President Ulysses S. Grant's 1873 proclamation establishing the Wallowa Valley as a reservation. The triumph was short lived, however.

During the Nez Perce War, Chief Joseph proved to be a skilled military commander, leading a band of 800 for three months in a trek over 1,700 miles of the most forbidding terrain on the continent. But the retreat took a terrible toll on the Nez Perces, ultimately persuading Joseph to surrender to Nelson A. Miles on October 5, 1877. His surrender speech, which was widely reported, is a monument to his dignity and the dignity of the Native American people.

Joseph and his followers were consigned to a reservation, first in eastern Kansas and then in Indian Territory (present-day Oklahoma). It was not until 1885 that Joseph and the other refugees were returned to the Pacific Northwest; half, including Joseph, were taken to a non–Nez Perce reservation in northern Washington Territory, the other half to a reservation in Idaho Territory. Joseph spent many years petitioning the government for permission to return to the Wallowa Valley, an effort in which he was aided by the military adversaries whose respect and admiration he had won: General O. O. Howard and Colonel Nelson A. Miles. About half of Joseph's followers were eventually resettled in the Wallowa Valley, but he remained on the Colville Reservation in Washington State, where he died in 1904.

---

field, but the troops were so exhausted that they could not pursue the fleeing bands. The army did not make contact with the Nez Perces again until August 9, when a force under Colonel John Gibbon surprised an Indian camp on the Big Hole River, Montana Territory. Losses were heavy on both sides, but Gibbon was forced to withdraw, permitting the Nez Perce survivors to flee more than 100 miles. Along the way, they killed nine whites, seized 250 horses, and raided a wagon train. They then entered the newly established Yellowstone National Park,

Wyoming Territory, where they created panic among the tourists.

Howard, along with Colonel Samuel D. Sturgis's Seventh Cavalry, attempted unsuccessfully to cut off the Indians' escape, but on August 19 the cavalry skirmished with Nez Perces on the Camas Meadows in southeastern Idaho Territory. This was followed on September 13 by a fight between the Seventh Cavalry and the Nez Perces at the site of present-day Billings, Montana. Following this, the Indians sought refuge among the Crows, but quickly learned

A wood engraving from a contemporary American newspaper depicts U.S. Army forces firing on Chief Joseph's camp at the Battle of Bear Paw Mountain shortly before his surrender in October 1877.

that Crow scouts had been fighting alongside Howard. The only course open to them, Joseph decided, was to flee to Canada, where they could join Sitting Bull of the Hunkpapa Sioux. En route, they rested just forty miles south of the Canadian border, at the northern edge of the Bear Paw Mountains, Idaho Territory. On September 30, leading 350–400 troops, Colonel Nelson A. Miles attacked them there, beginning the Battle of Bear Paw Mountain, which was fought through six snow-swept, freezing days. Finally, on October 5, Looking Glass was struck in the head by a stray bullet. This event prompted Joseph to surrender, and the war ended.

Bannock War (1878)

In the mid-1870s white settlement increasingly intruded into lands occupied by the Bannocks and was depleting game as well as destroying fields of native camas roots, a staple food the Bannocks and Northern Paiutes regularly dug on the Camas Prairie, about ninety miles southeast of modern Boise, Idaho. The Indians protested to the local Indian superintendent. When there was no response, an enraged Bannock took matters into his own hands by shooting and wounding two white settlers on May 30, 1878. Bannock chief Buffalo Horn, who had

served as an army scout during the Nez Perce War, was convinced that he and his people would be punished for this transgression, even if they apologized. Therefore, with about 200 warriors, including Northern Paiutes and Umatillas in addition to his Bannocks, he led a raid in southern Idaho Territory, killing ten whites. Buffalo Horn's rampage did not end until June 8, when armed civilians killed him near Silver City, southwest of Boise.

Leaderless, Buffalo Horn's warriors fled to Steens Mountain in Oregon, where they joined a band of Northern Paiutes, who, just days earlier, had followed a militant medicine man called Oytes and a chief called Egan in a breakout from the Malheur Reservation on June 5. The combined Bannock and Paiute forces mustered about 450 warriors. General O. O. Howard pursued this band relentlessly, but the Indians eluded the army—and continued terrorizing the region—until July 8, when Captain Reuben F. Bernard, leading seven troops of cavalry, discovered them on high bluffs along Birch Creek near Pilot Butte, Oregon. Bernard launched a risky uphill attack, but the Indians evaded him.

Following the Battle of Birch Creek, Oytes and Egan led the allied warriors south, presumably hoping to find refuge and reinforcement among the Nez Perces. Howard blocked them, whereupon the

Nelson A. Miles

(1839–1925)

Born near Westminster, Massachusetts, Nelson A. Miles attended school there and in Boston. During the Civil War (Chapter 17), he distinguished himself in combat, winning the Medal of Honor (conferred in 1892). Promoted to major general of volunteers after the war, he was given command of II Corps and also served as commandant of Fort Monroe, Virginia, where he was assigned as the jailer of former Confederate president Jefferson Davis, whom he treated so harshly that he was criticized by both Southerners and Northerners.

Miles was commissioned a colonel in the regular army and assigned in July 1866 to command the newly formed Fortieth Infantry, a black regiment. Displeased with his command, Miles continually lobbied for a change. In 1868 he made an advantageous marriage to Mary Sherman, niece of Senator John Sherman of Ohio and his brother, General William T. Sherman. Miles, much to his satisfaction, was given command of the Fifth Infantry in the West in March 1869. He was now an Indian fighter and earned renown for his aggressiveness and record of victories.

In 1880 Miles was promoted to brigadier general in the regular army and replaced George Crook as commander of U.S. forces in Arizona. Promoted to major general in 1890, Miles commanded the final operation of the Indian Wars, directing the suppression of the Ghost Dance uprising in 1890 (see Chapter 27). The massacre of Sioux at Wounded Knee Creek, perpetrated by the Seventh Cavalry under Colonel James W. Forsyth, had not been ordered by Miles, who bitterly condemned the action, relieved Forsyth of command, and convened a court of inquiry.

In 1895 Miles was commanding general of the army. He clashed with Secretary of War Russell A. Alger, who denied him a major role in the Spanish-American War (Chapter 29), although he did direct the conquest of Puerto Rico during that conflict.

Miles was promoted to lieutenant general in February 1901, but when he opposed Secretary of War Elihu Root's plans for wholesale army reform in 1903, he was forced into retirement. He volunteered for service during World War I, but was politely turned down by President Wilson. Miles died from a heart attack at age 85 while attending the circus with his grandchildren in Washington, D.C.

Indians turned north again, making for the Umatilla Reservation in Oregon. On July 12, Captain Evan Miles arrived at the reservation with a large force. A battle broke out on July 13 and was joined on July 15 by the Umatillas—on the side of the army. A party of Umatillas approached the Bannocks and Paiutes with an offer of alliance. They duped Chief Egan into coming away from his warriors, and then they killed him and presented his scalp to Miles as a trophy. This event scattered the Bannock-Paiute force, and Oytes surrendered on August 12. Many Bannocks followed him to a reservation within a month. A few diehards fought a final battle in Wyoming on September 12, 1878; the survivors finally withdrew to reservation life.

Sheepeater War (1879)

Even after the death of Egan and the surrender of Oytes, some Bannocks remained at large and found refuge among a group known as the Sheepeaters. This was a catchall name for renegade Shoshones and Bannocks who haunted the Salmon River Mountains of Idaho.

In May 1879 the Sheepeaters or their fugitive guests (or both) raided a mining camp on Loon

Creek and killed five Chinese miners. General Howard sent Captain Bernard with a troop of the First Cavalry and Lieutenant Henry Catley with fifty mounted soldiers of the Second Infantry, along with twenty Umatilla Indian scouts, to hunt down the raiders. This police action was called the Sheepeater War, and was fought on very small scale—the enemy consisted of no more than thirty-five warriors—but ranged over the extraordinarily difficult terrain of the Idaho mountains.

On July 29, Catley and his command were ambushed by fifteen warriors in Big Creek Canyon. Leaving behind all baggage and supplies, Catley escaped without casualty to his fifty men, but was relieved of command. On August 13, Bernard's cavalry joined what had been Catley's infantry, which was now commanded by Captain Albert G. Forse and augmented by an additional twenty-five troopers. The combined force went to the site of Catley's defeat in search of the Sheepeaters. On August 19, Umatilla scouts captured the contents of a Sheepeater camp, which included much of Catley's abandoned equipment and supplies. The Sheepeaters themselves were gone.

The Sheepeaters materialized on August 20, when they attacked an army supply train. Guards drove them off, but failed to give chase, and Howard temporarily ended the pursuit.

In September Lieutenant Edward S. Farrow set out with the Umatilla scouts on a foray into Sheepeater country. They captured two women and two children on September 21 and found an abandoned Sheepeater camp the following day. By interrogating one of the women, they learned that the warriors were exhausted and could not endure more pursuit. On October 1 and 2, fifty-one Sheepeaters, including warriors as well as women and children, and a handful of Bannocks surrendered to Farrow, ending the Sheepeater War.

Ute War (1879)

The Utes of western Colorado and the eastern Utah Territory lived south of the Bannocks and Northern Paiutes. Their country was invaded during the silver-mining boom of the late 1870s. As the miners became more numerous and influential in the region, they persuaded officials to close the Ute reservation and force the removal of the Utes to Indian Territory. In the meantime, Nathan C. Meeker, the Indian agent in charge of the White River Reservation in Colorado, hoping to force the Utes' transformation from hunters to farmers, ordered them to plow up their ponies' grazing land. On September 10, 1879, a Ute medicine man known to history only as Johnson protested to Meeker that plowing the lands would starve the horses. Meeker replied contemptuously that the Utes had too many ponies. At this, either Johnson or another leader, Chief Douglas, laid hands on Meeker and threw him out of his own front door. Alarmed, Meeker telegraphed military authorities for immediate aid.

Major Thomas T. "Tip" Thornburgh, commanding a mixed unit of 153 infantry and cavalrymen supplemented by 25 armed civilian volunteers, marched to Meeker's relief. Fearing that the arrival of a large body of troops would trigger an uprising, Meeker warned Thornburgh to halt his column and approach the agency with just five soldiers so that everyone could talk. Thornburgh agreed, but at the last minute moved 120 cavalrymen to the outskirts of the agency as a precaution. The Utes saw this as a gesture of bad faith and an outright prelude to attack. On September 25, the Utes and the soldiers faced one another. Suddenly, the major's adjutant waved his hat. Perhaps it was intended innocently as a greeting, but in the atmosphere that prevailed, someone—either an Indian or a soldier—took it for a signal. A shot was fired, and the Battle of Milk Creek began. Thornburgh fell almost immediately, and the troopers retreated across Milk Creek, where they took up defensive positions behind their circled wagon train. The battle became a week-long siege. Finally, on October 2, two of the defenders slipped through the Indian lines to summon reinforcements. Captain Francis Dodge arrived with a unit of black troopers ("Buffalo Soldiers") but failed to break the siege. On October 5, Colonel Wesley

Merritt arrived with a large contingent of cavalry and infantry, forcing the Utes to retreat. It was soon discovered that, during the battle and siege, Meeker and nine other agency employees had been killed. Meeker's wife and daughter, as well as another woman and her two children, were taken captive.

Generals Sherman and Sheridan wanted to launch an immediate punitive campaign, but Secretary of the Interior Carl Schurz intervened and, by October 21, negotiated the release of the hostages. At this point, the war simply ended, and the following year Chief Ouray led the Utes to reservations in eastern Utah Territory and southwestern Colorado.

Nez Perce Treaty Revision of 1863

On June 9, 1863, a new treaty between the United States and the Nez Perces was concluded, in which the tribe agreed "to relinquish ... to the United States the lands heretofore reserved for the use and occupation of the said tribe [by a treaty of June 11, 1855]." In return for the relinquishment, the United States paid the tribe $262,500 in addition to the annuities provided for in the 1855 treaty. The new treaty opened up a vast tract of Nez Perce land to white settlement and split the tribe into two factions. Those whose lands were preserved in the new treaty signed it; those whose lands were forfeit refused to sign and repudiated the treaty, which the government held as binding on all Nez Perces.

President Grant and the Wallowa Valley (1873)

When Chief Joseph the Elder refused to sign the 1863 treaty, he remained with his faction of the Nez Perce in the Wallowa Valley of Oregon. Although this was contrary to the treaty, the federal government chose to overlook the situation, and the Indians remained in this region for the next ten years. At last, on June 16, 1873, President Ulysses S. Grant signed an Executive Order Creating Wallowa Valley Reserve, which officially barred white settlement of the land on which the nontreaty faction of the tribe

had settled. Grant's order avoided war with the Indians, but the federal government soon reversed itself, opening the entire Wallowa Valley to white settlement in response to an outcry by local residents. This did not reflect a broad policy change; if anything, by this time, the mass of American public opinion favored humane and just treatment for the Indians. Nevertheless, the reversal of the executive order sent General Oliver O. Howard to evict the Nez Perces, and thus the Nez Perce War began.

Eloquence vs. Policy

By the 1870s, the American press and the American public often waxed sentimental about the "noble savage" and the "vanishing American," honoring the Indians even as their government continued to prosecute wars of conquest. Rarely were Indian warriors given much credit as military tacticians—although their bravery was often celebrated. In the case of the long pursuit of the Nez Perces, however, the press was generous in its praise, calling Chief Joseph the Younger "the Red Napoleon" because of the brilliance with which his followers continually eluded the army. The fact is that Joseph, who was not a war chief, probably played a minimal role in the military conduct of the long fighting flight toward Canada. Leadership of the warriors was mostly the responsibility of Looking Glass and Joseph's younger brother, Olikut. Nevertheless, even General William T. Sherman, never sentimental or generous where Indians were concerned, praised the conduct of the Nez Perces during their 1,700-mile retreat, noting that they had "displayed a courage and skill that elicited universal praise," fighting "with almost scientific skill, using advance and rear guards, skirmish lines, and field fortifications." Indeed, during the course of three months, about 800 Nez Perces (including no more than 200 warriors) successfully fought some 2,000 soldiers and army scouts. It is little wonder, then, that Joseph's eloquent speech, which accompanied his surrender at Bear Paw Mountain on October 5, 1877, was widely reported and reprinted:

I am tired of fighting. Our chiefs are killed. Looking Glass is dead. Toohoolhoolzote is dead. The old men are all dead. It is the young men who say, "Yes" or "No." He who led the young men [Olikut] is dead. It is cold, and we have no blankets. The little children are freezing to death. My people, some of them, have run away to the hills, and have no blankets, no food. No one knows where they are—perhaps freezing to death. I want to have time to look for my children, and see how many of them I can find. Maybe I shall find them among the dead. Hear me, my chiefs! I am tired. My heart is sick and sad. From where the sun now stands I will fight no more forever.

The Petition of Chief Joseph and the Generals

At the time of his surrender, Chief Joseph the Younger had earned considerable national fame. This encouraged him to believe that the principal condition under which he had surrendered—namely, that he and his band would be allowed to return to the Wallowa Valley—would be honored.

It was not. Despite his fame, Joseph and his people were transported to eastern Kansas and then to a reservation in Indian Territory. In this alien and—to them—highly uncongenial climate, many sickened and died.

With the earnest and remarkable support of his two former chief military adversaries, General O. O. Howard and Colonel Nelson A. Miles, Joseph suc-

cessfully petitioned for an audience with President Rutherford B. Hayes in 1879. He was warmly received and invited to plead his case, but it was not until 1885 that Joseph and his surviving followers were finally returned to the Pacific Northwest. Even then, they were not all returned to the Wallowa Valley. Instead, half of them, including Chief Joseph, were taken to the non–Nez Perce Colville Reservation, in northern Washington, while the others were settled in Idaho and in the Wallowa Valley. Joseph died in Colville in 1904.

BIBLIOGRAPHY

Axelrod, Alan. *Chronicle of the Indian Wars: From Colonial Times to Wounded Knee.* New York: Macmillan General Reference, 1993.

Beal, Merrill D. *"I Will Fight No More Forever": Chief Joseph and the Nez Perce War.* Seattle: University of Washington Press, 1963.

Hampton, Bruce. *Children of Grace: The Nez Perce War of 1877.* New York: Avon Books, 1995.

McDermott, John D. *A Guide to the Indian Wars of the West.* Lincoln: University of Nebraska Press, 1998.

Michno, Gregory F. *Encyclopedia of Indian Wars: Western Battles and Skirmishes 1850–1890.* Missoula, Mont: Mountain Press Publishing Company, 2003.

Phillips, Charles, and Alan Axelrod, eds. *The Encyclopedia of the American West.* 4 vols. New York: Macmillan General Reference, 1996.

Prucha, Francis P. *The Great Father: The United States Government and the American Indians.* Lincoln: University of Nebraska Press, 1984.

CHAPTER 27
SIOUX WAR OF 1890–1891

At Issue

This brief conflict concluded the so-called Indian Wars of the post–Civil War era and marked the final armed conflict in some 400 years of warfare between whites and Indians in America. The proximate cause was a brutal and inept effort by reservation officials and the army to suppress the Ghost Dance religion on Sioux reservations and thereby avert a feared Sioux uprising.

The Conflict

The final arrest of Geronimo ended the 1876–1886 Apache War (see Chapter 24) and the main phase of the "Indian Wars" of the post–Civil War era. As of 1886 nearly a quarter million Indians had been confined to reservations. Among this population were the Hunkpapa Sioux at the Standing Rock Reservation on the South Dakota–North Dakota border. Their chief, Sitting Bull, the most influential and revered

Wovoka (Jack Wilson)
(ca. 1856–1932)

Born along the Walker River in Mason Valley, Nevada, Wovoka is believed to have been the son of the Northern Paiute shaman Tavibo, whose teachings profoundly influenced him. In addition to imbibing Indian religion, Wovoka borrowed extensively from conventional Christianity, to which he was exposed when he worked on a ranch near present-day Yerrington, Nevada, living with a white family named Wilson.

Late in 1888, Wovoka fell ill with fever and remained ill during a total solar eclipse, which occurred on January 1, 1889. After recovering, Wovoka reported that he had been transported to heaven and had beheld the Creator, who charged him with spreading the message that the earth would soon be extinguished, to be reborn in a pure

state—entirely the realm of all Indians, including the dead. To propitiate this millennium, Wovoka introduced what whites called the "Ghost Dance" (see "The Ghost Dance," below).

Wovoka's new religion spread rapidly among the Shoshones, Arapahos, Cheyennes, and Sioux. Some deemed Wovoka nothing less than the messiah and called him the "Red Man's Christ." From the Ghost Dance, the so-called Ghost Dance Uprising developed as the culminating engagement of the Indian Wars. Wovoka was appalled by the blood shed ostensibly in the name of what he preached. He continued to counsel peace. After the Wounded Knee Massacre, the Ghost Dance rapidly died out. Wovoka lived on quietly with his wife and four children near Schurz, Nevada.

Indian leader of his time, was also well known to non-Indians. Although he remained peacefully on the reservation, Sitting Bull refused to cooperate with the local Indian agent and counseled his people generally to avoid contact with the white world. This defiance ran contrary to U.S. policy of "civilizing" Indians by dismantling the tribes in preparation for integrating them into mainstream, white society.

Late in the 1880s, a Paiute shaman's son named Wovoka became influential among the Indians of the western reservations. He preached a millennial religion composed of both Native and Christian traditions, promising the coming of a new, wholly Indian world. Wovoka gained status as a prophet and entreated his followers to hasten their deliverance by dancing the Ghost Dance (a homage to the spirit of ancestors) and by maintaining peaceful relations among themselves and with whites. Reservation authorities became alarmed as the Ghost Dance spread. Moreover, among the Teton Sioux Wovoka's admonition to peace was suppressed, and the Ghost Dance became a militant movement as the Teton chiefs Short Bull and Kicking Bear called for a violent uprising aimed at obliterating whites once and for all.

In response to the perceived unrest, army reinforcements arrived at the Pine Ridge and Rosebud reservations in South Dakota on November 20, 1890. Far from restoring order, the presence of the troops provoked about 3,000 Indians to move to a plateau at the northwest corner of the Pine Ridge Reservation. This position was dubbed the "Stronghold."

Wary of the incipient uprising at Pine Ridge, James McLaughlin, Indian agent at the nearby Standing Rock Reservation, sent forty-three reservation police officers on December 15, 1890, to arrest Sitting Bull, who lived on the reservation. The arrest became a fight, during which Sitting Bull was shot in the chest. A reservation police sergeant, Red Tomahawk, took it upon himself to administer the coup de grace by shooting Sitting Bull in the back of the head. This gave the Ghost Dance movement a martyr, and an uprising became all but inevitable.

As the situation became increasingly critical, General Miles decided to intercept another impor-

tant Ghost Dance leader, Miniconjou Sioux chief Big Foot, who was on his way to the Stronghold. What Miles did not know was that Big Foot had renounced the Ghost Dance religion and that Chief Red Cloud, a Pine Ridge leader friendly to the whites, had asked Big Foot to come to the reservation to attempt to persuade the Indians gathered at the Stronghold to surrender. Miles assumed that Big Foot's intention was to join the other hostiles at the Stronghold. On December 28, 1890, a squadron of the Seventh Cavalry located Big Foot and about 350 followers in a camp near a stream called Wounded Knee. By the morning of the following day, 500 cavalrymen under Colonel James W. Forsyth took up positions surrounding Big Foot's camp. They were equipped with four Hotchkiss guns—small, rapid-fire howitzers—which they trained on the camp from the surrounding hills. Thus covered, Forsyth planned

CHRONOLOGY OF THE SIOUX WAR

1890

Nov. 20 Alarmed over the spread of the Ghost Dance religion, large numbers of troops are sent to the Pine Ridge and Rosebud reservations in South Dakota; 3,000 Indians respond by taking up positions at the "Stronghold." A general uprising appears imminent.

Dec. 15 A botched attempt to arrest Sitting Bull at the Standing Rock Reservation on the North Dakota–South Dakota border triggers the feared uprising.

Dec. 28 A squadron of the Seventh Cavalry locates the Miniconjou Sioux chief Big Foot and about 350 followers in a camp at Wounded Knee, a stream in South Dakota.

Dec. 29 The Battle of Wounded Knee is fought.

Dec. 30 The Seventh Cavalry is ambushed near the Pine Ridge Agency, but is rescued by elements of the Ninth Cavalry. A large force surrounds the principal Sioux position at White Clay Creek, fifteen miles north of the Pine Ridge Agency.

1891

Jan. 15 The Sioux nation surrenders to Major General Nelson A. Miles, thereby ending the epoch of the Indian Wars.

Big Foot
(Si Tanka, Spotted Elk)
(ca. 1825–1890)

Big Foot earned renown not as a warrior, but as a diplomat who was frequently consulted throughout the Sioux nation to settle disputes. He inherited leadership of the Miniconjou Sioux from his father, Long Horn, who died in 1874.

In 1877 he led the Miniconjous in surrender at the conclusion of the Sioux War for the Black Hills (Chapter 25) and settled with them on the Cheyenne River Reservation in present-day South Dakota. Big Foot worked hard to encourage his people to make the best of life on the reservation. He encouraged the development of Indian agriculture and was an advocate of education for Indians. In the 1880s he represented his tribe as a delegate to Washington, D.C., where he lobbied for schools to be built on the reservation.

The Ghost Dance movement came to Big Foot's reservation in 1889, and Big Foot's band expanded as more and more Indians came to the reservation to join in the Ghost Dance. By the end of 1890, however, Big Foot decided that the Ghost Dance was futile and, once again, called for peace with the whites. He set out with a number of his followers for the Pine Ridge Reservation, at the invitation of Red Cloud, hoping to talk militant Sioux into making peace with the whites. En route, he fell ill with pneumonia. He and his band were intercepted by an army detachment at Wounded Knee Creek. On December 29, 1890, Big Foot and perhaps as many as 300 other Indians were killed in the Wounded Knee Massacre. Big Foot was not buried for three days. A photograph taken of his grotesquely contorted, frozen body has become a grim symbol of Wounded Knee.

to disarm the Indians and take them to the railroad, where they would board trains to remove them from what he designated the "zone of military operations." While disarming the Indians, the troopers encountered resistance, and shots were exchanged. As Indians began to flee, Forsyth ordered the deadly Hotchkiss guns to open fire. In less than an hour what the army designated as the Battle of Wounded Knee was over. Big Foot and 153 other Miniconjous—including women and children—lay dead, but many others limped or crawled away. To this day, the final toll has not been determined, although it is generally believed that 300 of the 350 who had been camped at Wounded Knee Creek were killed. The Seventh Cavalry suffered 25 killed and 39 wounded, virtually all of them victims of friendly fire.

The action at Wounded Knee provoked previously friendly Sioux factions to join the "hostiles" in an armed uprising. On December 30, warriors ambushed the Seventh Cavalry near the Pine Ridge Agency. Elements of the Ninth Cavalry rode to the rescue. This accomplished, Miles mobilized 3,500 troops—out of a total force of 5,000 in the area—to surround a mass of Sioux warriors gathered fifteen miles north of the Pine Ridge Agency along White Clay Creek in South Dakota. In contrast to his earlier rash actions, Miles exercised patient restraint, gradually contracting a ring of troopers around the Indians. This persuaded the Sioux that further resistance was futile, and on January 15, 1891, the Sioux nation surrendered. The Indian Wars had ended.

Dawes Severalty Act of 1887

The last bloody act of the Indian Wars played out against the culmination of a movement that had been gathering strength since the end of the Civil War, especially during the years of the "Peace Policy" promulgated by President Ulysses S. Grant (see Chapter 21). During this period, even as Indians were being more and more aggressively confined to reservations, reformers advocated their assimilation into the American mainstream. The reservations were to serve as a kind of halfway house, where the Indians would be educated and more or less forcibly acculturated. The object was to erase their tribal identity and affiliation as well as their tribal governments, replacing these, ultimately, with U.S. citizenship. Reformers disputed some of the details of the process, but all agreed that an essential step was to break up tribal lands into parcels that would be held "in severalty" by the individual Indians. Reformers believed that landowners could be readily transformed into citizens, whereas Indians who lived on tribal lands would naturally owe their allegiance to the tribe rather than to the United States. Moreover, as owners of individually and legally defined homesteads, the Indians would be obliged to abandon their wide-ranging hunting traditions and become sedentary yeoman farmers, a transformation that had long been envisioned as a prerequisite to assimilation.

At last, on February 8, 1887, Congress passed the General Allotment Act, better known as the Dawes Severalty Act (see Chapter 11), which gave the president authority to proceed with the division and subsequent allocation of tribal lands. Furthermore, the president was authorized to proclaim those Indians who received allotments citizens of the United States, thereby extending the authority of all federal and territorial laws to what had been reservation lands.

The Dawes Severalty Act was strongly supported by reformers, but it also received enthusiastic support from western whites, especially those living near the reservations. They understood that allotted lands, after the expiration of a certain period, could be sold by the Indian owners. In addition, once released from the subsidies provided by the reservation system, Indians were free to trade with whites. Many westerners believed that Indians would thus become so indebted that they would inevitably be forced to sell their lands. Indeed, this proved to be the case, and before the middle of the twentieth century, the Dawes Severalty Act was recognized as having accelerated the diminishment of the Indian people without having effected their just and productive assimilation into mainstream American society. The Dawes Severalty Act was finally replaced in 1934 by the Indian Reorganization Act (discussed below), which stopped the allotment process and permitted unsold surplus lands to be returned to tribal ownership.

Report of the Commissioner of Indian Affairs (1887): Use of English in Indian Schools

Along with severalty, education was regarded as key to the acculturation process. Commissioner of Indian Affairs J. D. C. Atkins argued in his **Annual Report of the Commissioner of Indian Affairs** for 1887 that English should be used exclusively in all Indian schools. Atkins believed that the use of English in the schools would soon bring about the extinction of tribal languages and, with that extinction, an end to tribal identity and affiliation.

An Act in Relation to Marriage between White Men and Indian Women (1888)

On August 9, 1888, Congress passed **An Act in Relation to Marriage between White Men and Indian Women,** which barred white men from acquiring tribal lands (or any other tribal privilege or interest) through marriage to an Indian woman, even though the woman may be entitled to land (or some other privilege or interest) by virtue of her membership in an Indian tribe. The act also provided for the automatic naturalization of any Indian woman who married any citizen of the United States. The effect of the law, like that of the other Indian-policy legislation of the period, was to further the dissolution of the tribes and of tribal identity in favor of identification with the United States and submission to its laws.

A System of Education for Indians (1889)

In 1889 Commissioner of Indian Affairs Thomas J. Morgan presented the most ambitious and detailed

Annual Report of the Commissioner of Indian Affairs, 1887

Longer and closer consideration of the subject has only deepened my conviction that it is a matter not only of importance, but of necessity that the Indians acquire the English language as rapidly as possible. The Government has entered upon the great work of educating and citizenizing the Indians and establishing them upon homesteads. The adults are expected to assume the role of citizens, and of course the rising generation will he expected and required more nearly to fill the measure of citizenship, and the main purpose of educating them is to enable them to read, write, and speak the English language and to transact business with English-speaking people. When they take upon themselves the responsibilities and privileges of citizenship their vernacular will be of no advantage. Only through the medium of the English tongue can they acquire a knowledge of the Constitution of the country and their rights and duties thereunder.

Every nation is jealous of its own language, and no nation ought to be more so than ours, which approaches nearer than any other nationality to the perfect protection of its people. True Americans all feel that the Constitution, laws, and institutions of the United States, in their adaptation to the wants and requirements of man, are superior to those of any other country; and they should understand that by the spread of the English language will these laws and institutions be more firmly established and widely disseminated. Nothing so surely and perfectly stamps upon an individual a national characteristic as language.... Only English has been allowed to be taught in the public schools in the territory acquired by this country from Spain, Mexico, and Russia, although the native populations spoke another tongue.... If the Indians were in Germany or France or any other civilized country, they should be instructed in the language there used. As they are in an English-speaking country, they must be taught the language which they must use in transacting business with the people of this country.

Excerpted from Francis Paul Prucha, ed., *Documents of United States Indian Policy,* 2d ed. (Lincoln: University of Nebraska, 1990), 174–175.

federal proposal for **A System of Education for Indians** developed to that time. The most significant feature of the system was that it made virtually no concessions to any special needs of the Indians, but rather was simply a wholesale adoption of the scheme then in operation in most public schools throughout the United States. In this, the commissioner recognized that an important purpose of American public schools was to disseminate the mainstream cultural values of citizenship—in short, to promote a uniformity of "Americanization" among schoolchildren. In an age of massive European immigration, the public schools were the prime American melting pot. Morgan sought to apply this same principle and function to schools for Indians.

The Ghost Dance

The Ghost Dance, which provoked much panic among reservation authorities, was a religious movement among some western tribes during 1889–1891 that was intended to restore the Native American way of life as it was before contact with white culture. Its leading exponent was Wovoka (also known as Jack Wilson), a Northern Paiute from the Mason and Smith valleys in western Nevada, who came to be widely regarded as a prophet. He was inspired by an earlier Ghost Dance movement, which had come into being about 1870 in western Nevada. This he conflated with Protestant Christianity and its work ethic, to which he was exposed when he lived on a white family's ranch.

An Act in Relation to Marriage between White Men and Indian Women, 1888

Be it enacted . . . , That no white man, not otherwise a member of any tribe of Indians, who may hereafter marry, an Indian woman, member of any Indian tribe in the United States, or any of its Territories except the five civilized tribes in the Indian territory, shall by such marriage hereafter acquire any right to any tribal property, privilege, or interest whatever to which any member of such tribe is entitled.

SEC. 2. That every Indian woman, member of any such tribe of Indians, who may hereafter be married to any citizen of the United States, is hereby declared to become by such marriage a citizen of the United States.

Excerpted from Francis Paul Prucha, ed., *Documents of United States Indian Policy,* 2d ed. (Lincoln: University of Nebraska, 1990), 176–177.

On New Year's Day 1889 Wovoka, who had been ill since late 1888, reportedly lapsed into a comatose state in which (he subsequently reported) he had died and entered heaven. There the Creator charged him with carrying a message to the Indian tribes, ordering them to be honest and hard working and to

A System of Education for Indians, 1889

The American Indians, not including the so-called Indians of Alaska, are supposed to number about 250,000, and to have a school population (six to sixteen years) of perhaps 50,000. If we exclude the five civilized tribes which provide for the education of their own children and the New York Indians, who are provided for by that State, the number of Indians of school age to be educated by the Government does not exceed 36,000, of whom 15,000 were enrolled in schools last year, leaving but 21,000 to be provided with school privileges.

These people are separated into numerous tribes, and differ very widely in their language, religion, native characteristics, and modes of life. Some are very ignorant and degraded, living an indolent and brutish sort of life, while others have attained to a high degree of civilization, scarcely inferior to that of their white neighbors. . . . Education is to be the medium through which the rising generation of Indians are to be brought into fraternal and harmonious relationship with their white fellow-citizens, and with them enjoy the sweets of refined homes, the

delight of social intercourse, the emoluments of commerce and trade, the advantages of travel, together with the pleasures that come from literature, science, and philosophy, and the solace and stimulus afforded by a true religion.

. . . It is no longer doubtful that, under a wise system of education, carefully administered, the condition of this whole people can be radically improved in a single generation.

. . . The task is not by any means an herculean one. The entire Indian school population is less than that of Rhode Island. The Government of the United States, now one of the richest on the face of the earth, with an overflowing Treasury, has at its command unlimited means, and can undertake and complete this work without feeling it to be in any degree a burden.

Excerpted from Francis Paul Prucha, ed., *Documents of United States Indian Policy,* 2d ed. (Lincoln: University of Nebraska, 1990), 178–179.

The Ghost Dance by the Ogallala [sic] Sioux at the Pine Ridge Agency, Dakota, *a drawing by Frederick Remington, based on sketches made on the spot. The Ghost Dance, which began as a peaceful homage to ancestors, was used among some Sioux as a call for an uprising against whites. Alarmed, the U.S. military suppressed the practice of the dance. These efforts resulted in the death of Sitting Bull and the massacre at Wounded Knee, which effectively ended the Indian Wars.*

to erode tribal identity. Wovoka's message came, then, at a most critical time, and the Ghost Dance found many enthusiastic adherents, some of whom (especially among the Teton Sioux) ignored the admonition to peace and transformed the Ghost Dance into a militant rebellion.

The Public Response to Wounded Knee

refrain from warfare among themselves or against the whites. The Creator also instructed Wovoka to enjoin the Indians to perform ritual dances, which would bring about a kind of millennium, the restoration of the world as it had been before the advent of the white man. The buffalo would be restored in their former numbers, and, indeed, there would be a general resurrection of deceased Indians. Wovoka reported to his followers that this rebirth would come early in 1891.

The promise of the Ghost Dance religion came at the nadir of fortune for the western tribes. By this time, the relentless execution of the government's reservation policy had greatly reduced the footprint of the Indian on the land, and the Dawes Severalty Act of 1887 was already decreasing the Indians' holdings even more drastically. In addition to the physical depletion of the Indian population, the inroads of white culture and religion were continuing

During much of the nineteenth century—after the Indian Removal Act of 1830 (Chapter 8)—many voices protested the unjust and even horrific fate of the western tribes. Nevertheless, public reaction to the Battle of Wounded Knee was generally favorable to the army—despite the fact that General Nelson A. Miles himself sought the court martial of Colonel James W. Forsyth for what Miles deemed his brutal mishandling of the Wounded Knee encounter. Over Miles's protests, Forsyth and his men were exonerated of all wrongdoing, and no fewer than twenty Medals of Honor were awarded to federal soldiers for action related to Wounded Knee.

To many who lived near the reservations, the Battle of Wounded Knee was part of a justified campaign against the members of a dangerous Indian religious cult, which sought nothing less than the destruction of all white people. L. Frank Baum (who would later earn lasting fame as the author of *The Wonderful Wizard of Oz*) was a frontier newspaper editor in the 1890s. His editorial in the January 3, 1891, issue of the *Aberdeen (S.D.) Saturday Pioneer* begins:

The peculiar policy of the government in employing so weak and vacillating a person as General Miles to look after the uneasy Indians, has resulted in a terrible loss of blood to our soldiers, and a battle which, at its best, is a disgrace to the war department. There has been plenty of time for prompt and decisive measures, the employment of which would have prevented this disaster.

It is difficult to determine from the editorial whether Baum considered Wounded Knee a "disgrace"

because of the death of the Indians or the soldiers; however, he continues:

The *Pioneer* has before declared that our only safety depends upon the total extirmination [sic] of the Indians. Having wronged them for centuries we had better, in order to protect our civilization, follow it up by one more wrong and wipe these untamed and untamable creatures from the face of the earth. In this lies future safety for our settlers and the soldiers who are under incompetent commands. Otherwise, we may expect future years to be as

Indian Reorganization Act, 1934

BE IT ENACTED by the Senate and House of Representatives of the United States of America in Congress assembled, That hereafter no land of any Indian reservation, created or set apart by treaty or agreement with the Indians, Act of Congress, Executive order, purchase, or otherwise, shall be allotted in severalty to any Indian. . . .

Sec. 3. The Secretary of the Interior, if he shall find it to be in the public interest, is hereby authorized to restore to tribal ownership the remaining surplus lands of any Indian reservation. . . .

Sec. 6. The Secretary of the Interior is directed to make rules and regulations for the operation and management of Indian forestry units on the principle of sustained-yield management. . . .

Sec. 10. There is hereby authorized to be appropriated, out of any funds in the Treasury not otherwise appropriated, the sum of $10,000,000 to be established as a revolving fund from which the Secretary of the Interior, under such rules and regulations as he may prescribe, may make loans to Indian chartered corporations for the purpose of promoting the economic development of such tribes and of their members. . . .

Sec. 11. There is hereby authorized to be appropriated, out of any funds in the United States Treasury not otherwise appropriated, a sum not to exceed $250,000 annually, together with any unexpended balances of previous appropriations made pursuant

to this section, for loans to Indians for the payment of tuition and other expenses in recognized vocational and trade schools. . . .

Sec. 12. The Secretary of the Interior is directed to establish standards of health, age, character, experience, knowledge, and ability for Indians who maybe appointed, without regard to civil-service laws, to the various positions maintained, now or hereafter, by the Indian Office, in the administration of functions or services affecting any Indian tribe. . . .

Sec. 16. Any Indian tribe, or tribes, residing on the same reservation, shall have the right to organize for its common welfare, and may adopt an appropriate constitution and bylaws, which shall become effective when ratified by a majority vote of the adult members of the tribe, or of the adult Indians residing on such reservation, as the case may be, at a special election authorized and called by the Secretary of the Interior under such rules and regulations as he may prescribe. . . .

Sec. 17. The Secretary of the Interior may, upon petition by at least one-third of the adult Indians, issue a charter of incorporation to such tribe.

Excerpted from Charles J. Kappler, ed., *Indian Affairs: Laws and Treaties,* vol. 5, *Laws* (Washington, D.C.: U.S. Government Printing Office, 1941), 378–383, from the Oklahoma State University Library, http://digital.library.okstate.edu/kappler/vol5/html_files/v5p0378.html.

full of trouble with the redskins as those have been in the past.

Baum's chilling words express the cold-hearted frustration some whites felt concerning relations with the Indians: having proved to be "untamable creatures," they could be dealt with only by genocide—one additional "wrong" to culminate centuries of wrongs—in order to preserve white civilization.

It was not until the last third of the twentieth century that the Battle of Wounded Knee came to be generally regarded as an atrocity committed against the Sioux.

Indian Policy after 1891

Despite the genocidal sentiment in some quarters of the American public, official Indian policy after the end of this, the final engagement of the Indian Wars, continued to emphasize assimilation and the attendant dissolution of the tribes and tribal land holdings. It was not until the 1930s that a new and very different wave of reform was ushered in with the general liberalization of the federal policy under President Franklin D. Roosevelt during the Great Depression. Federal administrators now sought to undo years of the government's attempts to erase Indian power and identity. In 1934, frankly admitting the abject failure of the policy of "total assimilation" codified in the Dawes Severalty Act of 1887, Congress passed the **Indian Reorganization Act,** which ended the practice of severalty allotments and returned unsold surplus lands to tribal ownership. The act also promoted tribal self-government by encouraging tribes to write constitutions and assume the management of their own affairs. Congress additionally created a loan program to aid tribal land purchases, educational efforts, and the development of tribal government. A major reversal of some seventy-five years of government policy, the 1934 act remains today the principal basis of federal Indian legislation.

BIBLIOGRAPHY

Axelrod, Alan. *Chronicle of the Indian Wars: From Colonial Times to Wounded Knee.* New York: Macmillan General Reference, 1993.

Debo, Angie. *A History of the Indians in the United States.* Norman: University of Oklahoma Press, 1977.

McDermott, John D. *A Guide to the Indian Wars of the West.* Lincoln: University of Nebraska Press, 1998.

Michno, Gregory F. *Encyclopedia of Indian Wars: Western Battles and Skirmishes 1850–1890.* Missoula, Mont: Mountain Press Publishing Company, 2003.

Mooney, James. *The Ghost-Dance Religion and the Sioux Outbreak of 1890.* Lincoln: University of Nebraska Press, 1991.

———. *The Ghost-Dance Religion and Wounded Knee.* New York: Dover, 1991.

Phillips, Charles, and Alan Axelrod, eds. *The Encyclopedia of the American West.* 4 vols. New York: Macmillan General Reference, 1996.

Prucha, Francis P. *The Great Father: The United States Government and the American Indians.* Lincoln: University of Nebraska Press, 1984.

Utley, Robert M. *Indian Wars.* New York: Mariner Books, 2002.

At Issue

Historians recognize two Philippine insurrections during this period. The first, a struggle during 1896–1897 for independence from Spain, did not involve the U.S. military directly; nevertheless, the conflict created conditions of great importance to the Spanish-American War (see Chapter 29). The second Philippine Insurrection, during 1898–1902, was a rebellion against the United States provoked by the U.S. annexation of the Philippines despite a Filipino declaration of independence.

The Conflicts

The Philippines had long been an oppressed Spanish colony. In 1896 colonial officials arrested, tried, and executed José Rizal, a charismatic poet considered a founding father of the independence movement. His execution made him a martyr, and on August 26, 1896, rebel leaders responded by calling Filipinos to arms against Spanish rule. The insurrection soon splintered into rival factions organized around Andres Bonifacio, leader of an earlier independence movement, and Emilio Aguinaldo, the mayor of the Luzon province of Cavite. Aguinaldo accused his rival of treason, and in April 1897 he arrested, tried, and executed Bonifacio. This consolidated leadership of the rebellion and focused the fighting in and around Cavite, over which Spanish colonial forces regained control by August 1897—but at a heavy cost. Eager to end the fighting, despite their victory, Spanish officials in December 1897 concluded with the rebels the Pact of Biak-na-bato, which spared the lives of Aguinaldo and other rebel leaders in exchange for their accepting voluntary exile in Hong Kong. Additionally, Spain gave each leader 400,000 pesos and pledged to introduce a schedule of liberal reforms into the government of the islands. Not surprisingly, the Spanish government failed to deliver the reforms.

Aguinaldo returned to the Philippines on May 19, 1898, after the U.S. Navy had destroyed the Spanish fleet in Manila Bay during the Spanish-American War. Eager for an ally in the Philippines, the United States backed Aguinaldo in organizing a Filipino army, which fought with American ground forces to defeat Spanish troops on the islands. This accomplished, Aguinaldo declared Philippine independence from Spain on June 12, 1898, but Spain nevertheless ceded the islands to the United States for $20,000,000 as a condition of the Treaty of Paris (December 10, 1898), by which the Spanish-American War was concluded.

Immediately following the fall of Manila to American forces in the Spanish-American War, Aguinaldo and his insurgents concluded an informal truce with the occupying U.S. Army. However, in January 1899, pursuant to the Treaty of Paris, the United States announced annexation of the Philippines. Aguinaldo responded by proclaiming a Philippine republic under the "Malolos Constitution," with himself as president. His truce with the Americans dissolved, and fighting broke out on February 4—the eve of U.S. Senate ratification of the Treaty of Paris. When Filipino forces attacked an American guard post near Manila, the 12,000 U.S. troops faced about 40,000 insurgents. Despite the odds, Major General Elwell S. Otis counterattacked, inflicting roughly 3,000 insurgent casualties. During February 22–24, Filipinos under General Antonio Luna attacked Manila, but were met by reinforced American troops under General Arthur MacArthur. By March 31, MacArthur had pushed Luna and his army back to Malolos, the insurgent capital and stronghold.

Deciding that he could not prevail against the American army in a conventional war, Aguinaldo disbanded the army and embarked instead on a guerrilla campaign. Additional U.S. forces soon arrived in the islands and carried the war into southern Luzon, the Visayan Islands, Mindanao, and Sulu. Filipino Scouts, native troops in the U.S. service and under the command of General Frederick Funston, captured Aguinaldo on March 23, 1901.

Aguinaldo was pressed into renouncing the independence movement, swearing allegiance to the United States, and issuing a proclamation calling for peace. But contrary to U.S. hopes, this decapitating blow did not end the insurgency, and for the next year, American forces were subject to sporadic attack. The response was a long and costly campaign to capture individual guerrilla leaders, the last of whom concluded a treaty with the United States on May 6, 1902. Although the major fighting had ended, armed outbreaks continued in various parts of the islands (see Chapter 30) until full independence was granted after World War II.

Yellow Journalism

During the Spanish-American War, "yellow journalism"—sensational reporting intended to sell papers—fueled popular American interest in the first Philippine Insurrection, against Spain. Yellow journalism produced some important stories exposing social injustice, corruption, and public fraud, but it

---

CHRONOLOGY OF THE PHILIPPINE INSURRECTIONS

FIRST PHILIPPINE INSURRECTION   1896–1897

1896

Aug. 26 Rebel call to arms against Spanish rule

1897

Aug. Luzon is retaken by the Spanish.

Dec. 15 The conclusion of the Pact of Biak-na-bato ends the insurrection.

SECOND PHILIPPINE INSURRECTION   1898–1902

1898

May 19 With U.S. backing, Emilio Aguinaldo returns to the Philippines.

June 12 Filipinos declare independence.

Dec 10 Treaty of Paris, which concludes the Spanish-American War, cedes the Philippines to the United States

1899

Jan. The United States annexes the Philippines.

Jan. 23 Filipinos proclaim a republic under the Malolos Constitution.

Feb. 4 Insurgents attack a U.S. guard post near Manila.

Feb. 22–24 Insurgents attack Manila.

Mar. 31 U.S. troops under General Arthur MacArthur, having pushed the insurgents out of Manila, bottle them up in their stronghold at Malolo.

1899–1901

- The insurrection becomes a guerrilla war after U.S. forces subdue all major conventional resistance.

1901

Mar. 23 Filipino Scouts under General Frederick Funston capture Aguinaldo, who swears allegiance to the United States.

1901–1902

- Despite Aguinaldo's capture, guerrilla fighting continues.

1902

May 6 The last guerrilla leaders sign a treaty with U.S. authorities.

July 4 President Theodore Roosevelt signs proclamation ending the second Philippine Insurrection and guaranteeing amnesty.

also drove publishers to find more sensational stories and, when necessary, to enhance those stories to make them more attractive to readers. Accordingly, in the mid-1890s, rival newspaper barons William Randolph Hearst and Joseph Pulitzer dispatched reporters to Cuba, where an independence movement was emerging. Reporters such as James Creelman and artists including the great painter of life in the American West, Frederic Remington, covered the developing story. Initially, Hearst and Pulitzer did not dispatch reporters to the remote Philippines, but stories on Cuba, which dramatized what today would be called human rights violations perpetrated by Spain, colored American popular opinion concerning the Philippines. The Spanish—personified by General Valeriano Weyler, sent in February 1896 to impose martial law on Cuba—were demonized. Hearst's paper branded the general "Butcher Weyler" after he incarcerated those identified as rebel sympathizers in what he called "reconcentration camps," squalid prison camps in which thousands were left to languish.

Although Weyler's actions only affected Cuba, the American public generally assumed that Spain treated its Philippine colony much as it treated Cuba: with brutal oppression. American popular sympathy for the first Philippine Insurrection ran high.

The Imperial Impulse

On July 12, 1893, University of Wisconsin history professor Frederick Jackson Turner delivered a paper at the World's Columbian Exposition in Chicago. In the paper, entitled **"The Significance of the Frontier in American History,"** Turner pointed out that, based on the 1890 U.S. census, it was no longer pos-

"The Significance of the Frontier in American History," 1893

In a recent bulletin of the Superintendent of the Census for 1890 appear these significant words: "Up to and including 1880 the country had a frontier of settlement, but at present the unsettled area has been so broken into by isolated bodies of settlement that there can hardly be said to be a frontier line. In the discussion of its extent, its westward movement, etc., it can not, therefore, any longer have a place in the census reports." This brief official statement marks the closing of a great historic movement. . . .

Behind institutions, behind constitutional forms and modifications, lie the vital forces that call these organs into life and shape them to meet changing conditions. The peculiarity of American institutions is the fact that they have been compelled to adapt themselves to the changes of an expanding people—to the changes involved in crossing a continent, in winning a wilderness, and in developing at each area of this progress out of the primitive economic and political conditions of the frontier into the complexity of city life. Said Calhoun in 1817, "We are great, and rapidly—I was about to say fearfully—growing!" So saying, he touched the distinguishing

feature of American life. All peoples show development; the germ theory of politics has been sufficiently emphasized. In the case of most nations, however, the development has occurred in a limited area, and if the nation has expanded, it has met other growing peoples whom it has conquered. But in the case of the United States we have a different phenomenon. . . . American development has exhibited not merely advance along a single line, but a return to primitive conditions on a continually advancing frontier line, and a new development for that area. American social development has been continually beginning over again on the frontier. . . . And now, four centuries from the discovery of America, at the end of a hundred years of life under the Constitution, the frontier has gone, and with its going has closed the first period of American history.

Excerpted from Frederick Jackson Turner, "The Significance of the Frontier in American History," in *The Frontier in American History* (New York: Henry Holt and Co., 1921), from American Studies at the University of Virginia, http://xroads.virginia.edu/~Hyper/TURNER/.

sible to designate a western frontier based on population. That meant, Turner concluded, the American frontier was now "closed." Turner argued that America's unique vital energy, which had driven the settlement of the frontier, would "continue to demand a wider field of exercise" elsewhere in the world. Without what Turner called the "safety valve" of the frontier, energetic Americans would surely undertake imperialist ventures overseas.

Most modern historians have discounted Turner's "Frontier Thesis," yet he had identified a growing imperial impulse in American foreign policy that would find expression in the Spanish-American War and the second Philippine Insurrection, which followed it.

Relations with Aguinaldo

Those Americans who were aware of Emilio Aguinaldo during the first Philippine Insurrection admired him as a hero of the people, if only because they considered Spain's administration of the Philippines tyrannical and barbaric. When Aguinaldo went into voluntary exile in Hong Kong pursuant to the 1897 Pact of Biak-na-Bato, he was largely forgotten in the United States; however, after the outbreak of the Spanish-American War, Aguinaldo contacted U.S. officials and made arrangements to return to the Philippines as an ally of the United States. He arrived in the islands on May 19, 1898.

On June 12, less than a month after Aguinaldo's return, the Filipinos declared independence from Spain and proclaimed a provisional republic, with Aguinaldo as president. In September, a revolutionary assembly ratified independence. On December 10, 1898, however, the Treaty of Paris, ending the Spanish-American War, ceded the Philippines to the United States. Aguinaldo continued to move his country toward independence, and his relations with the U.S. government rapidly deteriorated. On January 23, 1899, the revolutionary assembly approved the "Malolos Constitution," by which the provisional Philippines republic was proclaimed permanent. Aguinaldo was elected president.

A majority of the American public regarded the "rebellion" as an act of "ingratitude," and Aguinaldo, whom the American press had hailed as a hero, was now portrayed as a "savage" and a "beast" who had ordered nothing less than the extermination of all Americans in the islands. In fact, Aguinaldo had issued no such order.

In this American newspaper cartoon from April 1899, Emilio Aguinaldo (representing the Philippine insurgency that followed the U.S. annexation of the Philippines) resists being rescued by Uncle Sam, who regrets attempting to save him. The American public viewed the rebellion as an act of treachery and ingratitude.

President McKinley on the Acquisition of the Philippines

President William McKinley had reluctantly embarked upon the Spanish-American War, but with victory at hand, he was not about to relinquish the spoils of war, despite Aguinaldo's intransigence. As McKinley explained to a delegation of foreign ministers visiting the White House, he had three principal reasons for annexation:

1. He believed that to give the Philippines back to Spain would be cowardly and dishonorable.
2. He believed that allowing them to fall into the hands of a European power, such as Germany or France, would be a loss to American business interests.
3. He believed that recognizing Filipino independence would create anarchy, because the Filipinos were "not ready for self-government."

The only morally acceptable alternative, the president argued, was for the United States to assume the responsibility of government for the islands and set about "civilizing" the Filipinos in the spirit of democracy and Christian charity.

In the **Instructions to Peace Commissioners,** which McKinley composed on September 16, 1898, and sent to the commissioners negotiating the Treaty of Paris with Spain, the president was even more broadly ideological. He contrasted the situation of the Philippines with that of Cuba and Puerto Rico. The Caribbean, located at the doorstep of the United States, was vital to national security; a foreign presence could not be tolerated there.

American Empire: Pro and Con

While a substantial majority of Americans supported U.S. actions in Cuba and Puerto Rico during the Spanish-American War, they were less enthusiastic about the annexation of the Philippines. Most Americans were willing to accept the liberation (or conquest) of the Caribbean islands as necessary to the security of the United States. Many, however, were disturbed by the nakedly imperialist gesture of

Instructions to Peace Commissioners, 1898

Our aim in the adjustment of peace should be directed to lasting results and to the achievement of the common good under the demands of civilization, rather than to ambitious designs. The terms of the [peace] protocol were framed upon this consideration. The abandonment of the Western Hemisphere by Spain was an imperative necessity. . . .

The Philippines stand upon a different basis. It is nonetheless true, however, that without any original thought of complete or even partial acquisition, the presence and success of our arms at Manila imposes upon us obligations which we cannot disregard. The march of events rules and overrules human action. Avowing unreservedly the purpose which has animated all our effort, and still solicitous to adhere to it, we cannot be unmindful that, without any desire or design on our part, the war has brought us new duties and responsibilities which we must meet and discharge as becomes a great nation on whose growth and career from the beginning the ruler of nations has plainly written the high command and pledge of civilization.

Incidental to our tenure in the Philippines is the commercial opportunity to which American statesmanship cannot be indifferent. It is just to use every legitimate means for the enlargement of American trade; but we seek no advantages in the Orient which are not common to all. Asking only the open door for ourselves, we are ready to accord the open door to others.

Excerpted from "William McKinley: The Acquisition of the Philippines," in *Annals of America,* ed. Mortimer J. Adler and Charles Van Doren (Chicago: Encyclopaedia Britannica, 1976), 12:231–232.

taking the far-off Philippines. The opposing arguments were effectively expressed by Charles Denby, former American minister to China, and by Morrison I. Swift, a popular writer on political subjects.

Published in the pages of the magazine *Forum* in November 1898, Denby's **"Shall We Keep the Philippines?"** acknowledged the persuasive power of "Washington's Farewell Address, which is against the acquisition of foreign territory," but insisted that "the world has moved and circumstances are changed."

Swift attacked the conflation of commercial motives with a sense of divinely ordained mission. In

"Shall We Keep the Philippines?" 1898

If we give up the Philippines, we throw away the splendid opportunity to assert our influence in the Far East. We do this deliberately; and the world will laugh at us. Why did we take Manila? Why did we send 20,000 troops to Luzon? Did we do it to emulate the French king who marched his men up the hill and down again? There was no purpose in the conquest of Manila unless we intended to hold it.

The Philippines are a foothold for us in the Far East. Their possession gives us standing and influence. It gives us also valuable trade both in exports and imports. . . .

There is, perhaps, no such thing as manifest destiny; but there is an evident fitness in the happening of events and a logical result of human action. Dewey's victory is an epoch in the affairs of the Far East. We hold our heads higher. We are coming to our own. We are stretching out our hands for what nature meant should be ours. We are taking our proper rank among the nations of the world. We are after markets, the greatest markets now existing in the world. Along with these markets will go our beneficent institutions, and humanity will bless us.

Excerpted from Charles Denby, "Shall We Keep the Philippines?" in *Annals of America,* ed. Mortimer J. Adler and Charles Van Doren (Chicago: Encyclopaedia Britannica, 1976), 12:233–235.

Imperialism and Liberty, *1899*

The most momentous fact of the century is the *manner* of foisting imperialism upon us. To do it with our consent would have been one thing; to do it without our consent, as it has been done, is the greatest fourth-dimensional marvel of time. . . . The act of confiscating instead of liberating Spain's territory had to be painted as an act of humanity. It was easy enough to say that all the Spanish islands should be liberated from Spain, but the pinch came in showing the humanity of our keeping them, particularly on top of our biblical asseverations not to do so. Our rulers got over that by inventing that the islanders are not fit to govern themselves. . . .

Finally the evolution of imperialism reached a stage where the pretense of acting for humanity was an impediment. It prevented steps which were necessary if the juggernaut of progress was to murder on.

It was an impediment, yet so tasteful a bait to the pious that it could not be done without. A very daring experiment was tried, that of disclosing the true purpose, territorial conquest for wealth, and painting the stars and stripes of humanity upon it. This plan included the full confession that trade had become the *A* and *Z* of the whole matter, but asserting that Yankee trade never went anywhere without carrying a superior article of humanity and civilization in its pack.

If this atrocious humbug found lodgment in the American spleen, every conceivable things necessary for the world spread of American monopolies would be tolerated by the people.

Excerpted from Morrison I. Swift, "Without Consent of the American Governed," in *Imperialism and Liberty* (Los Angeles: The Ronbroke Press, 1899), 375–378.

his 1899 book, *Imperialism and Liberty,* he declared that apologists for annexation had merely "hammered" God into "greed" while permitting the result to retain "the image of God"—that is, they used a religious and moral crusade as cover for an imperialist policy really driven by commercial avarice.

Aguinaldo Co-opted

With Aguinaldo's capture on March 23, 1901, an arrangement was brokered similar to that between Spain and Aguinaldo at the end of the first Philippine Insurrection. Aguinaldo agreed to take an oath of allegiance to the United States and retire, in Manila, to private life in return for a generous pension from the U.S. government. The American agreement with Aguinaldo did not end the second insurrection, though, because individual guerrilla leaders continued to fight. It did, however, presage the ultimate end of the war.

Aguinaldo attempted a return to politics in 1935 in a run for the presidency when a commonwealth government was established for the Philippines in preparation for independence. He was defeated but reemerged during World War II when the Japanese occupiers of the Philippines coerced him into spouting anti-American propaganda. After the war, this resulted in Aguinaldo's arrest and brief imprisonment. Under a grant of amnesty, he was released and in 1950 joined the government of the Philippine republic as a member of the Council of State. Late in life, he worked to improve relations between the Philippines and the United States.

Governor Taft

On March 15, 1900, William Howard Taft resigned as a judge on the United States Sixth Circuit Court of Appeals to accept appointment by President McKinley as chairman of the Second Philippine

Proclamation Ending the Philippine-American War, 1902

Whereas during the course of the insurrection against the Kingdom of Spain and against the Government of the United States, persons engaged therein, or those in sympathy with and abetting them, committed many acts in violation of the laws of civilized warfare, but it is believed that such acts were generally committed in ignorance of those laws, and under orders issued by the civil or insurrectionary leaders; and

Whereas it is deemed to be wise and humane, in accordance with the beneficent purposes of the Government of the United States towards the Filipino people, and conducive to peace, order, and loyalty among them, that the doers of such acts who have not already suffered punishment shall not be held criminally responsible, but shall be relieved from punishment for participation in these insurrections, and for unlawful acts committed during the course thereof, by a general amnesty and pardon:

Now, therefore, be it known that I, Theodore Roosevelt, President of the United States of America, by virtue of the power and authority vested in me by the Constitution, do hereby proclaim and declare, without reservation or condition, except as hereinafter provided, a full and complete pardon and amnesty to all persons in the Philippine Archipelago. . . .

Provided further, That every person who shall seek to avail himself of this proclamation shall take and subscribe the following oath before any authority in the Philippine Archipelago authorized to administer oaths, namely:

"I, _____, solemnly swear (or affirm) that I recognize and accept the supreme authority of the United States of America in the Philippine Islands and will maintain true faith and allegiance thereto; that I impose upon myself this obligation voluntarily, without mental reservation or purpose of evasion. So help me God."

Alan Axelrod, *American Treaties and Alliances* (Washington, D.C.: CQ Press, 2000), 82.

Commission. His task was to create a civil government for the islands to replace the military administration, which had been put in place immediately after annexation. Universally praised for his efforts, Taft was appointed the first civilian governor of the Philippines in 1901. He was an enlightened administrator who developed an extraordinary rapport with the Filipinos and worked vigorously to advance the economic development of the chronically impoverished islands. Taft's tenure did much to repair relations between the majority of Filipinos and the government of the United States.

Proclamation of 1902

On July 4, 1902, President Theodore Roosevelt signed the **Proclamation Ending the Philippine-American War,** which declared the Philippine Insurrection to be ended and granted amnesty to all those involved—except those living in "the country inhabited by the Moro tribes," where resistance to the United States occupation and government persisted (see Chapter 30).

BIBLIOGRAPHY

Graff, Henry F., ed. *American Imperialism and the Philippine Insurrection: Testimony Taken from Hearings on Affairs in the Philippine Islands before the Senate Committee on the Philippines, 1902.* Boston: Little, Brown, 1969.

Taylor, John R. M. *The Philippine Insurrection against the United States: A Compilation of Documents with Notes and Introduction.* Pasay City, Philippines: Eugenio Lopez Foundation, 1971.

Walsh, John E. *The Philippine Insurrection, 1899–1902: America's Only Try for an Overseas Empire.* New York: Watts, 1973.

CHAPTER 29

SPANISH-AMERICAN WAR

(1898)

At Issue

The United States cited Spanish atrocities in Cuba and the explosion of the battleship USS *Maine* as reasons for launching a war against Spain to seize its possessions in the Caribbean and the Philippines.

The Conflict

Amid growing "war fever" in America, stimulated by "yellow journalism" recounting Spanish atrocities against Cubans and encouraged by certain American business interests, President William McKinley ordered the battleship USS *Maine* into Havana Harbor in January 1898 for the purpose of protecting American citizens and property in the Cuban capital. On February 9, American newspaper mogul William Randolph Hearst published a purloined letter in which the Spanish minister to the United States insulted President McKinley. Days later, on February 15, the *Maine,* at anchor in Havana Harbor, blew up, killing 266 crewmen. A naval court of inquiry speedily concluded that the ship had struck a mine, but could not determine who had placed it. In deliberate echo of the war cry of the Texas War of Independence (Chapter 9)—"Remember the Alamo!"—Americans exhorted their government to "Remember the *Maine* . . . to hell with Spain!" After some delay, President McKinley on April 11 asked Congress to authorize an invasion of Cuba. The legislators outdid him by voting a resolution to recognize Cuban independence from Spain. In reaction, Spain declared war on the United States on April 23,

1898, and the United States responded in kind two days later.

Much as it had done in the War of 1812 (Chapter 6), the United States plunged into the conflict with mostly unprepared forces. The navy had recently expanded and modernized, but the regular army of 1898 was miniscule, numbering just 26,000 officers and troops. Recruitment moved apace, but building the requisite numbers was only part of the problem. A strategy for mass deployment had not been formulated. Originally, planners devised a plan that called for committing ground troops to Cuba no sooner than October, the end of the disease-plagued rainy season. In the meantime, the navy would blockade the island. Most planners believed that the ground forces would never be needed because the blockade would, in time, deprive the enemy of resources. Once the Spanish troops had evacuated Cuba, an American occupation force could move in unopposed.

Politicians and the public alike objected to the blockade as too slow and insufficiently glorious, if not downright dishonorable. Yielding to the popular outcry, Secretary of War Russell M. Alger ordered regular infantry regiments to be transported to New Orleans, Louisiana, Tampa, Florida, and Mobile, Alabama, for transport to Cuba. However, a lack of troop transports and other logistical problems delayed deployment of the army.

In the meantime, the navy, far better prepared for a large-scale deployment, moved quickly. In addition to the blockade of Cuba, which began on April 22, naval strategy called for attacking and sinking whatever Spanish ships were harbored in the Philippines.

This accomplished, Manila was to be captured and a blockade of the Philippine ports instituted—thereby cutting off a critical source of Spanish revenue. Although the public's focus was on Cuba, war planners believed that U.S. possession of the Philippines would put negotiators in a powerful position to compel Spain to agree to Cuban liberation. Therefore, in January 1898, well before the army began planning for a war, Acting Secretary of the Navy Theodore Roosevelt had transmitted war-preparation instructions to naval commanders, including Commodore George Dewey, whose Asiatic Squadron (five cruisers and two gunboats) was ordered to assemble in Hong Kong and make ready to sail to the Philippines on a moment's notice.

Dewey received the attack order on April 24 and reached Manila Bay during the night of April 30. On May 1, he destroyed the Spanish fleet at Cavite in a matter of hours, inflicting 381 Spanish casualties, while suffering just eight wounded. Dewey then occupied Cavite and blockaded Manila, pending the arrival of land forces. On June 30, 10,000 U.S. troops under General Wesley Merritt disembarked at Manila Bay. Both Dewey and Merritt appealed to the Spanish government in Madrid for the bloodless surrender of Manila, but Spanish honor demanded at least a show of resistance. Therefore, on August 13, American troops, operating in concert with Filipino guerrillas, attacked, covered by naval bombardment. The Spanish garrison surrendered the next day.

While the war proceeded rapidly in the Philippines, Major General Nelson A. Miles prepared to lead army units from Tampa to Cuba, but uncertainty about the location of a Spanish fleet under Admiral Pascual Cervera y Topete prevented the invasion from launching. In late May, reconnaissance revealed that Cervera had slipped through the U.S. naval blockade of Cuba and had put in at the heavily fortified bay of Santiago de Cuba. Rear Admiral William T. Sampson decided to blockade the Spanish fleet in the harbor. Accomplishing this during May–July, he tried next to silence the Spanish forts with naval bombardment, but could not. Army land forces were called in to assault the batteries while the marines (who had landed on June 10) overran the Spanish defenders of Guantanamo Bay

CHRONOLOGY OF THE SPANISH-AMERICAN WAR

1898

Feb. 9 The letter of a Spanish diplomat, insulting President William McKinley, is published; Americans are outraged.

Feb. 15 The *Maine* explodes in Havana Harbor, Cuba.

Mar. 31 Spain rejects U.S. demands for Cuban independence.

Apr. 11 McKinley asks Congress for authorization to invade Cuba.

Apr. 16 The Teller Amendment passes in U.S. Congress, forbidding the U.S. annexation of Cuba.

Apr. 19 The U.S. Congress declares Cuba independent.

Apr. 22 The U.S. naval blockade of Cuba begins.

Apr. 23 Spain declares war on the United States.

Apr. 25 U.S. declaration of war becomes effective, retroactive to April 22.

May 1 Battle of Manila Bay, Philippine Islands

May 12 The U.S. Navy bombards San Juan, Puerto Rico, without warning

May 25 McKinley issues a call for volunteers; the first army expedition leaves San Francisco for Manila.

June 10 U.S. Marines land at Guantanamo Bay, Cuba.

June 21 Guam is taken peacefully by U.S. forces.

June 22 U.S Army forces land on Cuba.

June 24 Battle of Las Guasimas, Cuba

June 30 U.S. troops land at Manila Bay, Philippines.

July 1 Battles of El Caney and San Juan Heights, Cuba

July 3 Battle of Santiago, Cuba; the U.S. Navy destroys the Spanish fleet there

July 17 Spain's Santiago garrison surrenders.

July 25 The U.S. Army invades Puerto Rico.

Aug. 12 An armistice is concluded.

Aug. 14 Manila falls to U.S. forces.

Nov. 28 Spain agrees to cede the Philippines Islands to the United States.

Dec. 10 The Treaty of Paris is signed.

George Dewey

(1837–1917)

George Dewey was born in Montpelier, Vermont, and attended Norwich University before enrolling in the U.S. Naval Academy, from which he graduated in 1858. He served extensively in the Civil War. Rising steadily, he was promoted to commander in April 1872 and to captain in September 1884. In 1889 he was named chief of the Bureau of Equipment and in 1895 president of the Board of Inspection and Survey. These posts gave Dewey a thorough appreciation of the modern battleship, and he therefore became one of the principal architects of a technologically advanced U.S. Navy.

Promoted to commodore in February 1896, Dewey was, at his request, assigned to sea duty as commander of the Asiatic Squadron (beginning in November 1897). He and the squadron were in Hong Kong when the Spanish-American War broke out on April 25, 1898. Following orders, he sailed to the Philippines and attacked the Spanish squadron off Cavite in Manila Bay. He opened the engagement at 5:40 a.m. on May 1 with an order to his flag captain, Charles V. Gridley, that instantly became famous: "You may fire when ready, Gridley." By noon, all of the Spanish vessels had either been sunk or abandoned. Promoted to rear admiral on May 10, he provided the naval support to U.S. Army forces, which took Manila on August 14.

On March 3, 1899, Dewey was promoted to Admiral of the Navy, a rank specially created for him in recognition of his achievement. When he returned to the United States in September, he was given a hero's welcome and, exempted from mandatory retirement regulations, was named president of the Navy General Board, where he served until his death in 1917.

and established a base of operations that remains there today.

On June 14, the U.S. V Corps, under Major General William R. Shafter, left Tampa but did not arrive in Cuba, near Santiago, until June 20. Many of the troops became ill from confinement in overcrowded, unsanitary conditions aboard the transport ships. Shafter doubted that his troops, especially with so many ill, could fight immediately upon landing. Instead of attacking the forts at Santiago Bay as Sampson preferred, Shafter landed to the east at Daiquiri and disembarked his troops during June 22–25 amid great confusion, in which many cavalry mounts were lost. Spanish commanders failed to exploit the inept landing even though Spanish forces numbered 200,000 in Cuba, with 36,000 stationed in Santiago alone. U.S. forces plus some 5,000 Cuban insurgents numbered no more than 22,000.

Even before all disembarkation problems had been resolved, elements of V Corps advanced west toward the high ground of San Juan, a series of ridges east of Santiago. On June 23, Brigadier General Henry W. Lawton led the American vanguard along the coast from Daiquiri to Siboney, which he established as the principal U.S. base of operations. On June 24, Brigadier General Joseph Wheeler led his dismounted cavalry troops inland along the road to Santiago and captured Las Guasimas after briefly engaging a retreating Spanish force. V Corps units assumed positions five miles outside of San Juan Heights and awaited the arrival of Shafter's divisions. But Shafter, alarmed at how rapidly the tropical conditions were debilitating his troops, and fearing the arrival of severe weather, decided to make an immediate frontal attack against San Juan Heights. He assigned infantry under Brigadier General Jacob F. Kent to attack on the left and Wheeler's dismounted cavalry on the right. They were supported by 6,500 men, who would capture the village of El Caney, cutting off supplies to Santiago and blocking Spanish reinforcements. After securing El Caney, Lawton was to join the main assault against San Juan. As a diversionary feint, Shafter sent a freshly landed brigade to advance along the coast from Siboney.

The assault commenced at dawn on July 1, but rapidly threatened to disintegrate under the merciless tropical sun. Shafter himself was felled by heat stroke, and his troops, bottled up along the congested main trail to San Juan Heights, were cut down by Spanish gunfire. To make matters worse, Lawton encountered heavy resistance at El Caney, which delayed him. Despite the problems, Kent and Wheeler attacked San Juan Heights by midday. Par-

ticipating units included two African American cavalry regiments as well as a volunteer regiment dubbed the "Rough Riders," commanded by Theodore Roosevelt, who had resigned from the Navy Department to accept a volunteer lieutenant colonel's commission. These three unmounted cavalry regiments seized and occupied Kettle Hill, as Kent's infantry charged up San Juan Heights, and forced the defenders there into retreat.

Although Shafter achieved his initial objectives, casualties were higher than expected, and illness continued to take a heavy toll. Shafter notified Secretary of War Alger that he wanted to withdraw to higher ground where his forces would be more easily supplied, easier to defend, and probably healthier. Alger replied that any retreat would have a harmful effect on the morale of the country. Shafter therefore appealed to the navy to enter Santiago Bay immediately and launch an attack from the water. The navy demurred, and operations briefly stalled. However, at precisely this juncture, the Spanish defenders of Santiago, short of food, water, and ammunition, evacuated the city. This, in turn, prompted the Spanish navy under Cervera to attempt a run out of port on July 3. In a two-hour exchange, Commodore Winfield S. Schley destroyed Cervera's fleet, bringing the immediate surrender of about 23,500 Spanish troops in the area of Santiago and, on July 17, the surrender of the Santiago garrison itself.

Theodore Roosevelt (center, in suspenders) gave up his position as acting secretary of the navy to lead a volunteer regiment in Cuba known as the "Rough Riders." They are depicted here on top of the hill they captured at the Battle of San Juan in 1898.

On July 21, Miles led some 3,000 troops from Guantanamo Bay, Cuba, to

Theodore Roosevelt

(1858–1919)

Theodore Roosevelt was born into an old New York family on October 27, 1858. A sickly child, young Roosevelt was determined to build up his body and, with great willpower, subjected himself to a regimen of vigorous exercise, sports, and outdoor activity he later celebrated as "the strenuous life." His early career was varied, and he was by turns (and sometimes simultaneously) a popular author, rancher, and politician. Appointed assistant secretary of the navy in the administration of President McKinley in 1897, he was an enthusiastic advocate of preparation for war against Spain over its colonial policies in Cuba. He was also instrumental in preparing the navy for just such a war.

When the Spanish-American War broke out in 1898, Roosevelt stepped down from his Navy Department post and organized a volunteer cavalry unit, which was nicknamed the "Rough Riders." He served with it in Cuba as its dashing colonel—although, to his disappointment, his troops fought dismounted because their horses had failed to arrive on the island.

Roosevelt's brilliant, if brief, war record and his reputation as a zealous reformer propelled him to election as governor of New York in 1898. When Republican Party boss Thomas Collier Platt grew wary of his uncompromising reform policies, he engineered Roosevelt's nomination as McKinley's second-term vice presidential running mate in 1900. Roosevelt assumed that the vice presidency could well be a political dead end for him—certainly, that is what Platt had intended— but the assassination of President McKinley put Roosevelt in the White House, making him the youngest president in U.S. history.

"TR" immediately took aim at the big corporate trusts, wielding the Sherman Anti-Trust Act of 1890 as a club against them. The American people approved of his Progressive reforms, and he was elected in his own right, becoming even more zealous in his Progressivism. His administration gave government a principal role in regulating American industry in order to protect the public welfare. In foreign policy, Roosevelt was bold. When, in 1903, Colombia rejected a treaty giving the United States the right to dig a canal across the Isthmus of Panama, he sanctioned the revolution that created an independent Panama and immediately concluded a treaty with that new nation. This done, he personally supervised the planning and construction of the Panama Canal.

Roosevelt was an American imperialist, who advocated extending the nation's sphere of influence in the world, by force if necessary. Criticized by some as a warmonger, he nevertheless earned the Nobel Peace Prize for mediating an end to the Russo-Japanese War in 1905.

After leaving office in 1909, he embarked on a variety of adventures, including African big-game hunting. Then, bolting from the Republican Party, he collaborated with Wisconsin senator Robert M. La Follette to found the Progressive Party, which was popularly called the Bull Moose Party. As a third-party presidential candidate, Roosevelt outpolled Republican William Howard Taft in the 1912 elections, but lost to Democrat Woodrow Wilson.

Guanica on the southeastern coast of Puerto Rico. When he landed on July 25, he quickly advanced to the port town of Ponce, where he set up a base for 10,000 troops who arrived from the U.S. mainland during the first week of August. From Ponce, Miles led four columns toward San Juan, where he was warmly greeted by Puerto Ricans, who considered the arrival of American troops a liberation. The campaign was suspended on August 14, when news arrived that Spain had signed a peace protocol.

During the armistice, the Treaty of Paris was negotiated. Signed on December 10, 1898, it secured Spain's grant of independence for Cuba and the outright cession to the United States of Puerto Rico, Guam, and the Philippine Islands.

Presidents Cleveland and McKinley on the "Cuban Situation"

President Grover Cleveland delivered his **Final Address to Congress** on December 7, 1896, when the Cuban Revolution was well under way. The struggle in Cuba was hardly a major issue for most Americans, but political leaders recognized that the policies and activities of a colonial power approximately 90 miles from the United States would, sooner or later, affect the nation. Nevertheless, Cleveland advocated peaceful means to resolve the Cuban crisis. His position reflected the sentiments of a majority of Americans at the time.

A year later, President William McKinley delivered his **First Message to Congress** on December 6, 1897, in which he took an evenhanded and patient position that surprised and doubtless exasperated his fellow Republicans. In the twelve months since Cleveland's last address, the Cuban situation had become, in McKinley's estimation, the "most important problem with which this government is now called upon to deal."

Yellow Journalism and the Narrowing of Public Opinion

The end of the nineteenth century in the United States saw the rise of "yellow journalism," as newspapers competed for readers by offering increasingly

---

Cleveland's Final Address to Congress, 1896

The spectacle of the utter ruin of an adjoining country, by nature one of the most fertile and charming on the globe, would engage the serious attention of the government and people of the United States in any circumstances. In point of fact, they have a concern with it which is by no means of a wholly sentimental or philanthropic character. It lies so near to us as to be hardly separated from our territory. Our actual pecuniary interest in it is second to that of the people and government of Spain. It is reasonably estimated that at least from $30 million to $50 million of American capital are invested in plantations and in railroad, mining, and other business enterprises on the island. The volume of trade between the United States and Cuba, which in 1889 amounted to about $64 million, rose in 1893 to about $103 million, and in 1894, the year before the present insurrection broke out, amounted to nearly $96 million. . . .

These inevitable entanglements of the United States with the rebellion in Cuba, the large American property interests affected, and considerations of philanthropy and humanity in general, have led to a vehement demand in various quarters for some sort of positive intervention on the part of the United States. . . .

It is now also suggested that the United States should buy the island—a suggestion possibly worthy of consideration if there were any evidence of a desire or willingness on the part of Spain to entertain such a proposal. It is urged, finally, that, all other methods failing, the existing internecine strife in Cuba should be terminated by our intervention, even at the cost of a war between the United States and Spain—a war which its advocates confidently prophesy could be neither large in its proportions nor doubtful in its issue.

The correctness of this forecast need be neither affirmed nor denied. The United States has nevertheless a character to maintain as a nation, which plainly dictates that right and not might should be the rule of its conduct.

Excerpted from Grover Cleveland, "American Interests in the Cuban Revolution," in *Annals of America*, ed. Mortimer J. Adler and Charles Van Doren (Chicago: Encyclopaedia Britannica, 1976), 12:120–121.

McKinley's First Message to Congress, 1897

The instructions given to our new minister to Spain before his departure for his post directed him to impress upon that government the sincere wish of the United States to lend its aid toward the ending of the war in Cuba by reaching a peaceful and lasting result, just and honorable alike to Spain and to the Cuban people. . . .

No solution was proposed to which the slightest idea of humiliation to Spain could attach, and indeed precise proposals were withheld to avoid embarrassment to that government. All that was asked or expected was that some safe way might be speedily provided and permanent peace restored. . . .

In the absence of a declaration of the measures that [the U.S.] government proposes to take in carrying out its proffer of good offices, [the Spanish government] suggests that Spain be left free to conduct military operations and grant political reforms, while the United States for its part shall enforce its neutral obligations and cut off the assistance which it is asserted the insurgents receive from this country. . . .

The immediate amelioration of existing conditions under the new administration of Cuban affairs is predicted, and therewith the disturbance and all occasion for any change of attitude on the part of the United States.

Excerpted from William McKinley, "The Alternatives in Cuba," in *Annals of America,* ed. Mortimer J. Adler and Charles Van Doren (Chicago: Encyclopaedia Britannica, 1976), 12:162–163.

sensational stories. The situation in Cuba, in which Spain was portrayed as a villain, offered rich material for the likes of rival publishers Joseph Pulitzer and William Randolph Hearst.

What particularly moved American public opinion was the institution in Cuba of "reconcentration camps," stockades in which rebels and those identified as rebel sympathizers were confined after removal from their homes. Conditions ranged from poor to inhumane. As many American newspapers portrayed the situation, Spain was a barbaric (or "medieval") and incompetent nation incapable of administering Cuba rationally and humanely. This was not only a moral affront—on America's doorstep, no less—but a menace to U.S. business and financial interests in Cuba.

Under an almost unrelenting barrage of sensational news stories from the island, American public opinion was converted from an attitude of patient forbearance advocated by presidents Cleveland and McKinley to an increasing degree of war fever.

The Loss of the *Maine*

On January 25, 1898, the U.S. battleship *Maine* arrived in Havana Harbor, having been reluctantly dispatched by President McKinley to protect American interests threatened by violence on the island. On February 15, the ship suddenly exploded in the harbor. At the end of March, a U.S. Navy court of inquiry concluded that contact with a submarine mine had caused the explosion. The court did not assign responsibility for the placing of the mine, leaving open the question as to whether it had been placed by Spanish forces, by Spanish loyalists (without authorization from Spain), or by Cuban rebels, who hoped to provoke U.S. entry into the war. (Modern inquiries into the *Maine* disaster have all concluded that the explosion was an accident and almost certainly resulted from spontaneous combustion in the ship's powder magazine.) That the court assigned no blame hardly mattered to the majority of American newspapers, which printed (as Hearst's papers did) such headlines as "Maine Was Destroyed by Treachery!" and "The Whole Country Thrills with War Fever!" Representative of American popular response to the explosion of the *Maine* was an April 1898 article by journalist Albert Shaw entitled **"The Progress of the World,"** which presented the case for going to war.

The explosion of the USS Maine *in Havana, Cuba, triggered the Spanish-American War. Sensationalized reporting—such as this front-page headline from Joseph Pulitzer's* World *of February 17, 1898, which talks of a rumored "plot to blow up the ship"—helped feed America's "war fever."*

and, on April 9, 1898, the commander of Spanish forces in Cuba was instructed to grant an armistice to the rebels in preparation for peace talks. Despite these concessions to American demands, President McKinley, propelled by public, political, and commercial pressure, went before Congress on April 11 to ask for authorization to invade Cuba. Instead of focusing on Spain's most recent conciliatory measures, the president's **War Message** recounted events since 1896, claiming that the American people had patiently endured economic and general security hardships and calling the continued armed chaos in Cuba, so close to American shores, intolerable. McKinley concluded with the explosion of the *Maine.* Although he mentioned that the naval court of inquiry "did not assume to place the responsibility" for the explosion, the president nevertheless used it just as the press and a majority of the public were using it—as a pretext for war.

McKinley Temporizes

Even after the *Maine* explosion, President McKinley hoped to avoid war. On March 26, the U.S. Department of State sent a cable of **Instructions to Ambassador Stewart L. Woodford** in Spain. The following day, more specific instructions were cabled.

The War Message

Spain clearly wanted to avoid war with the United States. The Madrid government instructed Cuba's governor general to revoke the reconcentration policy

Resolution on Cuban Independence and the Teller Amendment

In response to President McKinley's request for a war resolution, Congress on April 19 voted a **Resolution on Cuban Independence,** recognizing the independence of Cuba and authorizing war with Spain with the object of forcing that country to a similar recognition. In tying the war resolution to the recognition of independence, Congress gave the president more than he had asked for. Nevertheless,

"The Progress of the World," 1898

It is not true that battleships are in the habit of blowing themselves up. . . .

It has been known perfectly well that Spanish hatred might at any time manifest itself by attempts upon the life of the American representative in Havana. . . . The Spaniards themselves . . . looked upon the sending of the *Maine* as a further aggravation of the long series of . . . grievances against the United States. They regarded the presence of the *Maine* at Havana as a menace to Spanish sovereignty in the island and as an encouragement to the insurgents. . . .

Quite regardless of the responsibilities for the *Maine* incident, it is apparently true that the great majority of the American people are hoping that President McKinley will promptly utilize the occasion to secure the complete pacification and independence of Cuba. There are a few people in the United States—we should not like to believe that more than 100 could be found out of a population of *75 million*—who believe that the United States ought to join hands with Spain in forcing the Cuban insurgents to lay down their arms and to accept Spanish sovereignty as a permanent condition under the promise of practical home rule. It needs no argument, of course, to convince the American people that such a proposal reaches the lowest depths of infamy. . . .

. . . The insurgents, with no outside help, have held their own for more than three years, and Spain is unable to conquer them. The people of the United States do not intend to help Spain hold Cuba. On the contrary, they are now ready, in one way or in another, to help the Cubans drive Spain out of the Western Hemisphere. If the occasion goes past and we allow this Cuban struggle to run on indefinitely, the American people will have lost several degrees of self-respect and will certainly not have gained anything in the opinion of mankind.

Excerpted from Albert Shaw, "The Progress of the World," in *Annals of America,* ed. Mortimer J. Adler and Charles Van Doren (Chicago: Encyclopaedia Britannica, 1976), 12:168, 172–173.

there was rancorous debate from a sizable minority who questioned the government's intentions in waging war. To placate anti-imperialist elements in Congress, Senator Henry M. Teller of Colorado drafted the Teller Amendment, which was passed by Congress on April 16 and became the fourth paragraph of the war resolution as enacted.

Apologies for War

The Spanish-American War was a war of choice rather than of necessity, and despite patriotic and economic zeal for the war in most quarters, there was a general uneasiness about the conflict, which prompted the war's apologists to spill a great deal of ink. In the *Louisville (Ky.) Courier-Journal* of April 20, 1898, editor Henry Watterson published **"The Right of Our Might,"** deliberately cutting through the commercial and political rationales for the war and translating its cause into nothing less than a holy crusade. In **"War with Spain, and After"** (June 1898), Walter Hines Page, editor of the *Atlantic Monthly,* defined the significance of the war as the United States' entry onto the world stage as a world power.

Logistical Problems

Lack of organization and efficiency in the ground-war logistics were major problems and gave rise to accusations of incompetence and corruption. In hindsight, there appears to have been little outright corruption—in contrast to supply operations during much of the Civil War—but there was a great deal of incompetence, resulting almost exclusively from inexperience in planning and executing overseas operations.

The Spanish-American War was the first American war fought overseas. Although shortly before the

Instructions to Ambassador Stewart L. Woodford, 1898

From the March 26, 1898, cable:

The President's desire is for peace. He cannot look upon the suffering and starvation in Cuba save with horror. The concentration of men, women, and children in the fortified towns and permitting them to starve is unbearable to a Christian nation geographically so close as ours to Cuba. All this has shocked and inflamed the American mind, as it has the civilized world, where its extent and character are known.

It was represented to him in November that the Blanco government would at once release the suffering and so modify the Weyler order as to permit those who were able to return to their homes and till the fields from which they had been driven. There has been no relief to the starving except such as the American people have supplied. The reconcentration order has not been practically superseded.

There is no hope of peace through Spanish arms. The Spanish government seems unable to conquer the insurgents. . . . The war has disturbed the peace and tranquility of our people.

We do not want the island. The President has . . . urged the government of Spain to secure [an honorable] peace. She still has the opportunity to do it. . . . Will she? Peace is the desired end.

For your own guidance, the President suggests that if Spain will revoke the reconcentration order and maintain the people until they can support themselves and offer to the Cubans full self-government, with reasonable indemnity, the President will gladly assist in its consummation. If Spain should invite the United States to mediate for peace and the insurgents would make like request, the President might undertake such office of friendship.

From the March 27, 1898, cable:

Believed the Maine report will be held in Congress for a short time without action. A feeling of deliberation prevails in both houses of Congress. See if the following can be done:

First, armistice until October 1. Negotiations meantime looking for peace between Spain and insurgents through friendly offices of President United States.

Second, immediate revocation of *reconcentrado* [reconcentration] order . . . .

Add, if possible, third, if terms of peace not satisfactorily settled by October 1, President of the United States to be final arbiter between Spain and insurgents.

If Spain agrees, President will use friendly offices to get insurgents to accept plan. Prompt action desirable.

Excerpted from "American Ultimatum to Spain," in *Annals of America,* ed. Mortimer J. Adler and Charles Van Doren (Chicago: Encyclopaedia Britannica, 1976), 12:167–168.

---

war the army's quartermaster general, Brigadier General Marshall I. Ludington, had begun investigating the feasibility of chartering commercial vessels as troop transports, this procedure was hampered by a law barring U.S. registry of foreign vessels.

For the Cuba expedition, therefore, the army could charter only U.S. vessels. By July 1, it had chartered forty-three transports, four water boats, three steam lighters, three decked barges, two ocean tugs to go to Cuba and another fourteen transports on the Pacific coast for the Philippines expedition; more were added in July and August. The army discovered that it could not charter enough vessels, so it purchased fourteen additional steamships. Nevertheless, by the time the Cuban expedition left Tampa, Florida, on June 14 aboard thirty-eight vessels, faulty estimates of carrying capacity meant that only 17,000 of a planned force of 25,000 troops could be transported. Worse, the transports had been fitted out to accommodate troops for the short run from Tampa to Havana, Cuba (the original destination), not for the much longer voyage to Santiago. Conditions on board were overcrowded and unhealthy. The absence of cooking facilities meant that soldiers had to eat

McKinley's War Message, 1898

In any event, the destruction of the *Maine,* by whatever exterior cause, is a patent and impressive proof of a state of things in Cuba that is intolerable. That condition is thus shown to be such that the Spanish government cannot assure safety and security to a vessel of the American Navy in the harbor of Havana on a mission of peace, and rightfully there.

The long trial has proved that the object for which Spain has waged the war cannot be attained. The fire of insurrection may flame or may smolder with varying seasons, but it has not been, and it is plain that it cannot be, extinguished by present methods. The only hope of relief and repose from a condition which can no longer be endured is the enforced pacification of Cuba. In the name of humanity, in the name of civilization, in behalf of endangered American interests which give us the right and the duty to speak and to act, the war in Cuba must stop.

In view of these facts and of these considerations, I ask the Congress to authorize and empower the President to take measures to secure a full and final termination of hostilities between the government of Spain and the people of Cuba, and to secure in the island the establishment of a stable government, capable of maintaining order and observing its international obligations, insuring peace and tranquillity and the security of its citizens as well as our own, and to use the military and naval forces of the United States as may be necessary for these purposes.

Excerpted from "McKinley's War Message," in *Annals of America,* ed. Mortimer J. Adler and Charles Van Doren (Chicago: Encyclopaedia Britannica, 1976), 12:178.

Resolution on Cuban Independence, 1898

JOINT Resolution for the recognition of the independence of the people of Cuba, demanding that the Government of Spain relinquish its authority and government in the Island of Cuba, and to withdraw its land and naval forces from Cuba and Cuban waters, and directing the President of the United States to use the land and naval forces of the United States to carry these resolutions into effect.

Whereas, the abhorrent conditions which have existed for more than three years in the Island of Cuba, so near our own borders, have shocked the moral sense of the people of the United States, have been a disgrace to Christian civilization, culminating, as they have, in the destruction of a United States battle-ship, with two hundred and sixty-six of its officers and crew, while on a friendly visit in the harbor of Havana, and can not longer be endured, as has been set forth by the President of the United States in his message to Congress of April eleventh, eighteen hundred and ninety-eight, upon which the action of Congress was invited: Therefore,

Resolved, by the Senate and House of Representatives of the United States of America in Congress assembled, First. That the people of the Island of Cuba are, and of right ought to be, free and independent.

Second. That it is the duty of the United States to demand, and the Government of the United States does hereby demand, that the Government of Spain at once relinquish its authority and government in the Island of Cuba, and withdraw its land and naval forces from Cuba and Cuban waters.

Third. That the President of the United States be, and he hereby is, directed and empowered to use the entire land and naval forces of the United States, and to call into the actual service of the United States, the militia of the several States, to such extent as may be necessary to carry these resolutions into effect.

Fourth. That the United States hereby disclaims any disposition or intention to exercise sovereignty, jurisdiction, or control over said Islands except for the pacification thereof, and asserts its determination, when that is accomplished, to leave the government and control of the Island to the people.

Excerpted from *American Historical Documents 1000–1904,* Vol. 43 *The Harvard Classics* (New York: P. F. Collier & Sons, 1909–1914), from Bartleby.com, 2001, www.bartleby.com/43/45.html.

"The Right of Our Might," 1898

[W]hether the war be long or short, it is a war into which this nation will go with a fervor, with a power, with a unanimity that would make it invincible if it were repelling not only the encroachments of Spain but the assaults of every monarch in Europe who profanes the name of divinity in the cause of kingcraft. . . .

. . . It is not a war of conquest. It is not a war of envy or enmity. It is not a war of pillage or gain. . . . We are not going to the musty records of title archives to find our warrant for this war.

We find it in the law supreme—the law high above the law of titles in lands, in chattels, in human bodies and human souls—the law of man, the law of God.

We find it in our own inspiration, our own destiny. We find it in the peals of the bell that rang out our sovereignty from Philadelphia; we find it in the blood of the patriots who won our independence at the cannon's mouth; we find it in the splendid structure of our national life, built up through over a hundred years of consecration to liberty and defiance to despotism. . . .

That is the right of our might; that is the sign in which we conquer.

Excerpted from Henry Watterson, "The Right of Our Might," in *Annals of America,* ed. Mortimer J. Adler and Charles Van Doren (Chicago: Encyclopaedia Britannica, 1976), 12:194.

"War with Spain, and After," 1898

The problems that seem likely to follow the war are graver than those that have led up to it; and if it be too late to ask whether we entered into it without sufficient deliberation, it is not too soon to make sure of every step that we now take. The inspiring unanimity of the people in following their leaders proves to be as earnest and strong as it ever was under any form of government; and this popular acquiescence in war puts a new responsibility on those leaders, and may put our institutions and our people themselves to a new test. A change in our national policy may change our very character; and we are now playing with the great forces that may shape the future of the world—almost before we know it.

Yesterday we were going about the prosaic tasks of peace, content with our own problems of administra-

tion and finance, a nation to ourselves—"commercials," as our enemies call us in derision. Today we are face to face with the sort of problems that have grown up in the management of world empires, and the policies of other nations are of intimate concern to us. Shall we still be content with peaceful industry, or does there yet lurk in us the adventurous spirit of our Anglo-Saxon forefathers? And have we come to a time when, no more great enterprises awaiting us at home, we shall be tempted to seek them abroad?

Excerpted from Walter Hines Page, "War with Spain, and After," in *Annals of America,* ed. Mortimer J. Adler and Charles Van Doren (Chicago: Encyclopaedia Britannica, 1976), 12:195.

canned beef almost exclusively, rations that, in all too many cases, proved to be spoiled or tainted. Cases of food poisoning—from minor to fatal—were plentiful.

Rations for troops in Cuba and the Philippines were adequate in terms of quantity, but often poor in

quality. Little thought had been given to problems of food spoilage in tropical climates and none to special rations suited for the climate. There was a similar problem with clothing. The regulars began the war in their traditional blue wool uniforms, which were hardly suited to the tropics. Only toward the end of the war were troops provided with more suitable lightweight uniforms—and only those troops bound for the Philippines. Further, medical supplies and expertise were insufficient, particularly in the Cuban theater of the war. Only 369 soldiers died in combat, whereas 2,565 succumbed to disease, including typhoid and yellow fever.

In response to public demand after the war, President McKinley appointed a special commission headed by former general and railroad magnate Grenville Dodge to investigate the army's handling of logistics, transportation, and medical care. While the Dodge Commission found no evidence of outright corruption or intentional neglect of duty, it did conclude that substantial improvements were called for, especially in supplying camps, avoiding congestion at ports of embarkation, and planning for seagoing transports. The experience of the Spanish-America War produced major reforms in the logistics service of the U.S. Army.

The Treaty of Paris

The United States and Spain concluded an armistice on August 12, 1898, and the formal and final **Treaty of Paris** was signed on December 10. Because the Teller Amendment barred U.S. annexation of Cuba, American treaty negotiators did not seek to acquire the island. Instead, Article I obliged Spain to grant and recognize the independence of Cuba. The Teller Amendment did not apply to other Spanish possessions, and President McKinley pressed his negotiators to obtain cession of Puerto Rico, Guam, and the Philippine Islands. For this reason, the treaty was controversial and the Senate fight over ratification was bitter: proponents argued that it was America's duty to serve the world as the agent of Christian civilization, whereas opponents decried American imperialism. Still others—mostly businessmen and merchants—pointed out that the acquisitions in the Pacific were economically essential to U.S. trade with China and the rest of Asia. In the end, the treaty was ratified by a margin of 57 to 27—just two votes more than the two-thirds majority required.

Secretary Hay on "A Splendid Little War"

Much of the controversy surrounding and following the Spanish-American War was outweighed by the

---

Treaty of Paris, 1898

Article I.
Spain relinquishes all claim of sovereignty over and title to Cuba. And as the island is, upon its evacuation by Spain, to be occupied by the United States, the United States will, so long as such occupation shall last, assume and discharge the obligations that may under international law result from the fact of its occupation, for the protection of life and property.

Article II.
Spain cedes to the United States the island of Porto Rico and other islands now under Spanish sovereignty in the West Indies, and the island of Guam in the Marianas or Ladrones.

Article III.
Spain cedes to the United States the archipelago known as the Philippine Islands, and comprehending the islands. . . .

Article IX.
Spanish subjects, natives of the Peninsula, residing in the territory over which Spain by the present treaty relinquishes or cedes her sovereignty, may remain in such territory or may remove therefrom, retaining in either event all their rights of property. . . .

The civil rights and political status of the native inhabitants of the territories hereby ceded to the United States shall be determined by the Congress.

Article X.
The inhabitants of the territories over which Spain relinquishes or cedes her sovereignty shall be secured in the free exercise of their religion.

Excerpted from the Avalon Project at Yale Law School, "Treaty of Peace between the United States and Spain," www.yale.edu/lawweb/avalon/diplomacy/spain/sp1898.htm.

successful demonstration of American arms. Secretary of State John Hay famously called the conflict "a splendid little war," because in less than one hundred days the American navy and army had liberated 13 million people living on 165,000 square miles of what had been Spanish colonial territory, acquiring in the process a considerable degree of control over Cuba, possession of Puerto Rico, and important territory in the Pacific. The United States was becoming a major player on the world stage—a significant power in the Far East and the dominant power in the Caribbean. Splendid or not, the brief Spanish-American War led to the four-year guerrilla insurrection against American dominion in the Philippines (see Chapters 28 and 30).

Platt Amendment

The United States maintained a military occupation force in Cuba for five years after the war. In 1900 a nominally independent Cuba drafted a constitution that lacked clauses defining Cuban-U.S. relations. Because the U.S. government wanted to maintain a high degree of control over Cuba, it conditioned military withdrawal on the insertion of such clauses.

Secretary of War Elihu Root drew up the desired provisions and attached them to the Army Appropriations Bill of 1901 as the "Platt Amendment," which was sponsored by Senator Orville H. Platt. The document, which was largely incorporated into the Cuban Constitution of 1902, effectively made Cuba a U.S. protectorate. The Platt Amendment limited Cuba's treaty-making capacity and its authority to contract public debt. It secured for the United States Cuban land for naval bases and coaling stations and reserved to the United States the authority to intervene in Cuban affairs to preserve Cuba's independence and maintain order.

BIBLIOGRAPHY

Bradford, James C., ed. *Crucible of Empire: The Spanish-American War and Its Aftermath.* Annapolis, Md.: Naval Institute Press, 1993.

Marrin, Albert. *The Spanish-American War.* New York: Atheneum, 1991.

Musicant, Ivan. *Empire by Default: The Spanish-American War and the Dawn of the American Century.* New York: Henry Holt, 1998.

CHAPTER 30

MORO WARS

(1901–1913)

The Conflicts

American influence in the Philippines (see Chapter 28), following the islands' annexation by the United States as a result of the Spanish-American War (Chapter 29), was primarily concentrated in the north, particularly on the large island of Luzon. The southern islands were, for the most part, neglected. There, resistance to U.S. annexation was less a matter of politics and government than of religion and culture, and the Americans were fairly slow to recognize the seriousness of the conflict in the southern region.

In August 1899 Brigadier General John C. Bates of the U.S. Army negotiated an agreement with the sultan of Sulu, nominal leader of the Moros, the Islamic people living mainly on the southern islands of Mindanao and the Sulu Archipelago. The sultan recognized U.S. sovereignty over the Moros in return for American military protection for the sultan's subjects. In addition, the sultan retained jurisdiction in Moro criminal cases, while the United States agreed to respect Islamic religious customs and to permit the continuation of slavery in the area. The agreement was weak, however, because the sultan's control over the Moros was far from absolute. Among many Moros, resistance to the Americans took on the intensity of a religious war.

In November 1901 Captain John J. Pershing persuaded Moros living on the north shore of Mindanao's Lake Lanao to make peace. The Moros on the southern shore, however, continued to clash with U.S. troops as well as with the American-trained and -equipped native Moro Constabulary.

Brigadier General George Davis, with 1,200 American troops, took the Moro stronghold at Pandapatan on southwestern Mindanao. There the army established Camp Vicars, with Pershing in command. From this base, between June 1902 and May 1903, Pershing launched a new diplomatic campaign followed by a series of contained but highly effective military expeditions. By the summer of 1903, when Pershing departed the Philippines, the worst of the Moro violence had been quelled, although sporadic local outbursts continued.

In 1903 Major General Leonard Wood arrived as military governor of the Moro region. In contrast to Pershing, Wood was determined simply to beat the Moros into submission. His hard-line approach touched off a guerrilla war, which the Moros fought from bases or strongholds they called *cottas*. In response, on October 22, 1905, Wood's command ambushed and killed Dato Ali, a major guerrilla leader.

It soon became apparent that Dato Ali's death had not ended the Moro resistance. As 1905 closed, a large contingent of Moros occupied Bud Dajo, a crater atop a 2,100-foot-high extinct volcano. It was a formidable natural fortress, which became a major embarrassment to U.S. forces because it enabled the Moros to successfully resist all efforts at conquest. On March 5, 1906, Colonel Joseph W. Duncan attacked Bud Dajo in force, and it fell on March 8.

The reduction of Bud Dajo brought a measure of peace to the Moro province for the next three years; however, the roots of resistance remained stubborn. In 1909 Pershing, now a brigadier general, became military commander of the Moro Province in Mindanao. He was distressed to find that, under Wood, the atmosphere had grown poisonous. Pershing set about rebuilding trust and establishing positive relationships. His goal was not merely to suppress an insurrection, but to bring enduring peace to the Moro province by disarming the tribe. He issued a disarmament order on September 8, 1911, setting a deadline of December 1. In October, however, the Moros reacted violently and, on December 3 and 5, Pershing dispatched troops to put down incipient rebellions. The Moros sent word that they wished to negotiate peace, but they used the ensuing armistice to retake Bud Dajo on December 14. Pershing responded quickly and the Moros withdrew on December 24. Once again, Moro violence diminished, although it did not completely end.

In January 1913 more than 5,000 Moros, including women and children, took armed refuge on Bud Bagsak, another extinct volcano. Pershing attempted to persuade them to evacuate. When they refused, he launched an amphibious assault on June 11, 1913. By this time, Moro guerrillas had established additional well-defended *cottas* at the villages of Langusan, Pujagan, Matunkup, Puyacabao, and Bunga. Nevertheless, one by one, each fell to Pershing's systematic assault. On June 15, Bud Bagsak was captured, and the Moro Wars came to an end.

Reflections on Professor Turner's Thesis

As discussed in Chapter 28, on July 12, 1893, University of Wisconsin history professor Frederick Jackson Turner delivered a provocative paper, entitled "The Significance of the Frontier in American History," in which he argued that, with the closure of the American continental frontier, the United States was destined to turn its expansionist energies outward, engaging in imperialist ventures. The Spanish-American War (Chapter 29) and the annexation of the Philippines (Chapter 28) seemed to bear this

---

CHRONOLOGY OF THE MORO WARS

1899

Aug. 20 Bates Treaty is concluded with the sultan of Sulu.

1901

Nov. Captain John J. Pershing negotiates peace with Moros living on the north shore of Lake Lanao. Brigadier General George Davis leads an expedition to neutralize the Moro stronghold of Pandapatan.

1902–1903

June–May By combining diplomacy and military operations, Pershing pacifies most of the Moros.

Summer Major General Leonard Wood replaces Pershing and institutes a more aggressive military policy, which incites a guerrilla war.

1905

Oct. 22 Moro guerrilla leader Datao Ali is killed.

1906

Mar. 8 The major Moro stronghold of Bud Dajo falls, bringing relative peace to the Moro region, although a low-level guerrilla war continues.

1909

• After his promotion to brigadier general, Pershing is appointed military commander of the Moro Province of the Philippines and vigorously combines diplomacy with military campaigning throughout Mindanao.

1911

Sept. 8 Pershing issues a Moro disarmament order.

Dec. 3 and 5 Pershing sends troops to put down an incipient Moro rebellion.

Dec. 14 The Moros reoccupy Bud Dajo.

Dec. 22 Pershing surrounds Bud Dajo.

Dec. 24 The Moros evacuate Bud Dajo, and the violence diminishes.

1913

Jan. Some 5,000 Moros take refuge on Bud Bagsak.

June 11 Pershing mounts an amphibious assault on Bud Bagsak.

June 15 Bud Bagsak falls, bringing the Moro Wars to an end.

theory out. Yet some apologists for these conflicts argued that that they were more economic than imperialist in nature: The annexation of the Philippines, in particular, was necessary to give the United States an advantageous position in trade with Asia. Without such an Asian outpost, American trade would be at the mercy of European powers, which already held various Asian colonial possessions.

Playing in counterpoint to the economic justification for these early overseas forays was a religious and cultural theme. Material gains aside, many insisted America was also duty-bound to sow democracy and Christian civilization. In the northern Philippines, Christianity had been firmly inculcated by centuries of Spanish rule (although, by "Christianity," most Americans meant *Protestant* Christianity rather than Spanish-imposed Roman Catholicism). But the southern Philippines had a large Muslim population—the Moros—for whom the American occupation was less a matter of economics than an imperialist intrusion. Whereas the Philippine Insurrections were political struggles, the Moro Wars were conflicts over religion and culture.

The Vastness of the Philippines

The Philippine Islands present a coastline of some 21,500 miles—an archipelago of 3,141 islands, of which 1,668 are inhabited and named. The terms of the annexation of the Philippines from Spain as a result of the Spanish-American War (Chapter 29) were vague. American negotiators simply assumed that all of the islands were part of the cession, even though Spain by no means controlled or claimed to possess all of them.

If the physical vastness of the Philippine Islands was not appreciated by the American government, even less understood was the ethnic and religious diversity of the islands. Although most Filipinos were Roman Catholic, Muslims formed a large minority and were in the south a majority. So diverse are the Filipino peoples that scholars have never accurately tallied the number of native languages and dialects spoken on the islands, but they believe

there to be about seventy of them. Official U.S. policy in the early twentieth century was wholly insensitive to this diversity, although a few enlightened military officers and administrators—notably John J. Pershing and William Howard Taft—made earnest efforts to understand and to respect the various religious and cultural needs of the people.

Culture Clash on Mindanao and the Sulu Archipelago

The Moros, representing about 5 percent of the Philippine population and occupying Mindanao, Palawan, the Sulu Archipelago, and other southern islands, never constituted a homogenous entity. Although the Moros were racially similar to other Filipinos, their adherence to Islam (introduced from Borneo and Malaya in the fourteenth century) differentiated them from the majority of the population. Although each Moro tribe tended to practice Islam differently, the faith served to unite them when they were threatened. The Americans were hardly the first outsiders to pose such a threat. The Spanish had been fighting the Moros, without success, since the sixteenth century.

Agreement with the Sultan of Sulu

Stumbling into the complexity of Philippine culture and ethnicity, the United States did in the southern Philippines much as it had done, repeatedly, with the Indian tribes of North America. Officials identified someone they deemed to be in charge and offered that person an agreement. Although it had never worked well with Indian treaties—because chiefs were not heads of state, and their agreements were not necessarily binding on their people—this same treaty model was applied in the case of the Moros. Brigadier General John C. Bates negotiated an agreement with the sultan of Sulu, who was deemed—unilaterally by the United States—to have sovereignty over the Moros. However, although he was influential, he had no sovereign power and was not a head of state.

Bates Treaty, 1899

Article I.
The sovereignty of the United States over the whole Archipelago of Jolo [Sulu], and its dependencies, is declared and acknowledged.

Article II.
The United States flag will be used in the Archipelago of Jolo, and its dependencies, on land and sea.

Article III.
The rights and dignities of His Highness the Sultan, and his Datos [administrative officials], shall be fully respected; the Moros are not to be interfered with on account of their religion; all religious customs are to be respected, and no one is to be persecuted on account of his religion. . . .

Article IX.
Where crimes and offenses are committed by Moros against Moros, the government of the Sultan will bring to trial and punishment the criminals and offenders, who will be delivered to the government of the Sultan by the United States authorities if in their possession. In all other cases persons charged with crimes or offenses will be delivered to the United States authorities for trial and punishment.

Article X.
Any slave in the Archipelago of Jolo shall have the right to purchase freedom by paying to the master the usual market value.

Article XI.
In case of any trouble with subjects of the Sultan, the American authorities in the islands will be instructed to make careful investigation before resorting to harsh measures, as in most cases serious trouble can thus be avoided. . . .

Article XIII.
The United States will give full protection to the Sultan and his subjects in case any foreign nation should attempt to impose upon them. . . .

Article XV.
The United States government will pay the following monthly salaries:

To the Sultan $250.00 (Mexican dollars) . . .

Excerpted from U.S. Congress, *U.S. Treaties at Large,* vol. 31, *56th Congress, 1899–1901* (Washington, D.C.: U.S. Government Printing Office, 1902), 1942.

The **Bates Treaty** was concluded on August 20, 1899. Its major points were these: the sultan agreed to recognize U.S. sovereignty over the Moros; the United States agreed to provide military protection for the sultan's "subjects" (a misnomer applied to the majority of the Moros); the United States conceded to the sultan jurisdiction in criminal cases; and the United States agreed to respect Islam as practiced among the Moros. Most controversially, Bates, on behalf of the U.S. government, agreed to permit the continuation of slavery among the Moros.

Although the Moro uprisings were suppressed, separatist efforts by the southern Muslims directed toward the U.S. administration and, after World War II, toward the Philippine government repeatedly reemerged during the twentieth century and continue today.

BIBLIOGRAPHY

Boot, Max. *The Savage Wars of Peace: Small Wars and the Rise of American Power.* New York: Basic Books, 2003.

Linn, Brian McAllister. *The U.S. Army and Counterinsurgency in the Philippine War, 1899–1902.* Chapel Hill: University of North Carolina Press, 1989

Walsh, John E. *Philippine Insurrection, 1899–1902.* New York: Scholastic, 1973.

At Issue

The Boxer Rebellion was the product of Chinese perceptions that foreign interests were causing the economic and political subjugation of China to the West. Militant radicals launched an uprising to expel all foreigners from the country.

The Conflict

In 1899 U.S. Secretary of State John Hay endorsed an "Open Door" policy toward China, which would give the United States, all European nations, and Japan equal access to Chinese trade. China, the subject of the policy, was not consulted.

During this period, China was wracked by political and social instability, and the government was held together tenuously by Cixi, the dowager empress. Radical Chinese factions organized a militant movement against foreign influence, and on January 11, 1900, the dowager empress issued a proclamation approving the uprising of a secret society called the Yihe Quang, loosely translated as the "righteous harmony of fists" and called by Westerners the "Boxers."

By the spring of 1900, Boxers were rampaging throughout the country, committing acts of vandalism in Peking (modern Beijing), sabotaging rail and telegraph lines, and menacing foreigners as well as Chinese Christians. To protect American nationals in China, two U.S. Navy vessels, the USS *Monocacy* and the USS *Newark,* were dispatched to the port of Taku, which defended Tientsin (present-day Tianjin),

about forty miles away. The *Newark* joined a number of European warships off Taku Bar on May 27. Two days later, 49 marines under Captain John T. Myers landed at Tientsin. Additional landing parties at Taku soon brought the U.S. military contingent to 150. Barred by Chinese authorities from traveling by rail, the troops moved by scow up the Pei-Ho River to Tientsin. The U.S. forces in Tientsin were quickly joined by a coalition of troops from England, France, Russia, Austria, Italy, and Japan.

On May 30, Chinese officials yielded to Western demands that coalition forces be permitted to travel from Tientsin by train to Peking, the capital, to reinforce the small contingent of embassy and legation guards. On May 31, Captain Myers and 55 marines joined more than 300 troops from the other coalition nations on the eighty-mile rail journey to the capital. Anticipating a siege, Myers ordered his men to discard their baggage and take extra ammunition instead. The coalition forces agreed that they would be commanded by Vice Admiral Sir Edward Seymour of the British Royal Navy.

By the time the troops advanced on Peking, Boxer riots had increased both in frequency and intensity. On June 6, the Boxers severed the railroad between Peking and Tientsin. On June 8, they cut the telegraph lines into the capital. At this point, the American consul in Tientsin, judging that the situation had become critical, threatened to take action with the forces he had available to break through instantly to Peking on his own authority. The threat pushed Admiral Seymour to authorize what came to be called the Seymour Expedition: four trains carrying about 2,000 coalition troops from Tientsin to Peking. The first train left on the morning of June 10, and the others followed at intervals during the rest of the day. Their progress was hindered by the sabotaged rail lines.

Shortly after the last of the four trains had pulled out of Tientsin, Chinese imperial forces supporting the Boxers began shelling the city's foreign sections. A mere 1,100 foreign troops, including a small contingent of U.S. Marines, remained in Tientsin with very little weaponry to defend themselves or the nationals of their countries. After Boxers severed the rail and telegraph lines between Tientsin and the coast, coalition commanders decided that the relief of Tientsin could be effected by taking forts at Taku, which defended the river passage to Tientsin, and the rail station at Tongku, where troops could embark for the city. Russian, German, British, Japanese, Italian, and Austrian officers demanded on June 16 that the Chinese commander of the forts surrender by the following day. In response, the forts fired on the warships at Taku Bar. The European ships returned fire for four hours, forcing the Chinese to abandon the forts, which were immediately occupied by landing parties. (The American vessels did not participate in the naval bombardment or the capture of the forts because the U.S. naval commanders interpreted their mandate strictly as the direct defense of U.S. nationals.)

The Chinese government—such as it was—deemed the shelling of Taku as the commencement of war and on June 18 declared war, ordering the imperial army to attack the Seymour Expedition. Chinese forces hit the first of the transport trains near Anting, twenty-five miles outside of Peking. They also cut rail lines behind the train, trapping it. Realizing that he was greatly outnumbered, Seymour ordered the train burned and the expedition to retreat, on foot, to Tientsin. The column reached Hsi Ku Arsenal, five miles from Tientsin, on June 22. The other three trains were halted, and the troops marched to the arsenal.

In the meantime, imperial troops had laid siege to the international quarter at Tientsin and to the diplomatic legations at Peking. Future U.S. president Herbert Hoover, at the time a young mining engineer working for a British firm, improvised fortifications and barricades to protect the entrances to the foreign enclave at Tientsin. When the Boxers attempted an invasion on June 18, they found the quarter heavily fortified and withdrew. But sporadic imperial artillery bombardment continued.

CHRONOLOGY OF THE BOXER REBELLION

1899

Sept. 6 U.S. Secretary of State John Hay sends the First Circular Letter, proposing the "Open Door" policy with regard to China.

1900

Jan. 11 The Chinese dowager empress officially sanctions the Boxer movement.

May 27 U.S. Navy ships arrive in Chinese waters to defend American nationals in China.

May 29 The first U.S. Marines land in China.

May 31 The first marine contingent heads for Peking (Beijing).

June 10 Chinese imperial forces shell the foreign quarter of Tientsin.

June 16 European ships bombard Taku.

June 18 Chinese imperial court declares war.

June 18–25 The 2,100 European, Japanese, and American troops of the "Seymour Expedition" fall under attack and siege.

June 20 Marines land at Taku.

June 25 Coalition troops relieve the besieged Seymour Expedition.

June–July The siege of Tientsin is lifted.

Aug. 4 A coalition army of 18,700 troops advances on Peking

Aug. 14 U.S. Marines capture a section of the Tartar Wall, enabling British troops to enter Peking.

Aug. 15 Marines shell the gates of the Forbidden City, prompting the Boxers to withdraw from Peking, thereby ending the major combat phase of the war, although low-level cleanup operations continue into 1901.

On June 20, U.S. Marines from the Philippines landed at Taku. They set off on foot for Tientsin, joining a Russian battalion en route. The combined force engaged Chinese troops on the morning of June 21. Outnumbered, they retired to a base at Chengliang Chang, where they were reinforced by British troops. This polyglot force resumed the advance on June 22, engaged Chinese forces several times, and arrived at Tientsin on June 24, then relieved the Seymour Expedition at Hsi-Ku Arsenal on June 25. (The coalition destroyed the arsenal to keep it out of Chinese hands.)

After helping suppress the Boxer Rebellion, the U.S. Fourteenth Infantry marches through the Forbidden City in Peking, China, in mid-August 1900.

The arrival of the coalition forces enabled the evacuation of foreigners from Tientsin, and over the next month, operations continued against Boxers and imperial troops in the Tientsin area. During this period, the United States and the other coalition powers sent reinforcements. The American contingent, designated the China Relief Expedition, was commanded by Major General Adna Chaffee. By August, international coalition forces numbered 18,700 troops. On August 4, the army began the 60-mile march from Tientsin to Peking. On August 5, imperial troops attacked. In a six-hour battle, Japanese and British troops routed the Chinese, pushing them out of Piet Sang. On August 6, the U.S. Marine contingent repulsed an attack and ejected the Boxers from the Yang-tsun area.

Acting on their own initiative, Russian troops on August 13 advanced prematurely into Peking, where they were quickly overwhelmed. Only the timely action of the other coalition troops saved them from being cut off. On August 14, elements of the U.S. Fourteenth Infantry and a detachment of marines captured a section of the Tartar Wall. From this position, they covered British troops, who entered the Outer City to relieve the besieged legations (a Japanese and a German diplomat had been killed during the siege). On August 15, marines cleared the barricades from Chien-mien (present-day Tiananmen) Gate outside the Forbidden City, established artillery positions there, and fired on the gates of the Forbidden City itself, destroying them. This, along with the relief of the legations, effectively ended the Boxer Rebellion.

Background: Sino-American Relations

Throughout the nineteenth century, the prevailing Western attitude toward China was one of racial superiority. The American **Chinese Exclusion Act** of 1882 was typical. Although Chinese constituted only .002 percent of the U.S. population at the time, Congress responded to demands by labor interests (which attributed falling wages and other economic ills to the presence of Chinese workers) by passing the nation's first significant law limiting immigration. The statute suspended Chinese immigration for ten years and declared the Chinese ineligible for naturalization as citizens. The act was renewed in 1892, and in 1902 Chinese immigration was made permanently illegal.

(The exclusion acts were not repealed until December 17, 1943, when the Seventy-Eighth Congress passed "An Act to Repeal the Chinese Exclusion Acts, to Establish Quotas, and for Other Purposes.")

Chinese Exclusion Act of 1882

Preamble. Whereas, in the opinion of the Government of the United States the coming of Chinese laborers to this country endangers the good order of certain localities within the territory thereof: Therefore,

Be it enacted by the Senate and House of Representatives of the United States of America in Congress assembled, That from and after the expiration of ninety days next after the passage of this act, and until the expiration of ten years next after the passage of this act, the coming of Chinese laborers to the United States be, and the same is hereby, suspended. . . .

SEC. 13. That this act shall not apply to diplomatic and other officers of the Chinese Government. . . .

SEC. 14. That hereafter no State court or court of the United States shall admit Chinese to citizenship; and all laws in conflict with this act are hereby repealed.

SEC. 15. That the words "Chinese laborers," whenever used in this act, shall be construed to mean both skilled and unskilled laborers and Chinese employed in mining.

Excerpted from Alan Axelrod, *Minority Rights in America* (Washington, D.C.: CQ Press, 2002), 342–343.

John Hay

(1838–1905)

A native of Salem, Indiana, Hay studied law in Springfield, Illinois, where he became acquainted with Abraham Lincoln. After Lincoln was elected president in 1860, Hay served as his private secretary from 1861 to 1865. Following Lincoln's assassination, Hay served in a number of diplomatic posts in Europe, before leaving government service for five years to work as a journalist for the *New York Tribune.* He then was appointed assistant secretary of state in 1879 and served until 1881.

President William McKinley appointed him ambassador to Britain in 1897, then elevated him to secretary of state the following year. Hay was a key participant in the Paris negotiations that ended the Spanish-American War (Chapter 29), and he was an effective advocate for the annexation of the Philippines. In effect, therefore, Hay presided over the creation of the United States as an imperialist power.

Hay's name is most closely associated with the promulgation of the "Open Door" policy toward China. His next important diplomatic achievement was the negotiation in 1901 of the second Hay-Pauncefote Treaty with Britain, which gave the United States exclusive rights to build a canal across the Isthmus of Panama. In 1903 Hay was instrumental in obtaining independence for Panama, which enabled canal construction to begin.

Hay was a man of remarkable energy and intellect. In addition to his work as a diplomat, he published a collection of verse, *Pike County Ballads and Other Pieces* (1871), and a novel, *The Bread-Winners* (1883). With John G. Nicolay, Hay wrote *Abraham Lincoln: A History* (1890) and edited *Lincoln's Complete Works* (1894).

Apart from barring Chinese immigration, the U.S. government showed little interest in China until the late 1800s, when it became increasingly clear that other Western powers—and Japan—were carving out significant trade niches with China, from which the United States was effectively excluded. By 1899 Chinese trade amounted to no more than 2 percent of all American trade, and U.S. government officials, backed by business interests, wanted more.

Secretary Hay Endorses the "Open Door" Policy toward China

John Hay, secretary of state in the cabinet of President William McKinley, operating in an era of American imperialism—which saw the Spanish-American War (Chapter 29) and the annexation of the Philippines (Chapters 28 and 30) and Hawaii—was eager to expand the American sphere of influence into Asia. He was, therefore, highly receptive to the "Open Door" trade policy advocated by British customs official Alfred E. Hippisley. Hippisley proposed guaranteeing all of the Western powers and Japan equal access to Chinese trade.

On September 6, 1899, Hay elaborated on Hippisley's idea in the First Circular Letter to Germany, England, France, Russia, Austria, Italy, and Japan. Hay stated that the policy of the United States would be to bring about permanent safety and peace to China, preserve Chinese territorial and administrative integrity, protect all rights guaranteed to friendly powers by treaty and international law, and safeguard the principle of equal and impartial trade with all parts of the Chinese empire. Hay sought "formal recognition by the various powers claiming 'spheres of interest' that they shall enjoy perfect equality of treatment for their commerce and navigation within such 'spheres.'"

The Shape of Public Opinion (1899–1901)

While American government and business interests were eager to expand trade into China, the public, initially indifferent to China and often blatantly hostile to the Chinese, was becoming increasingly sympathetic to the work of Western Christian missionaries operating in China.

To convert the Chinese, many Americans believed, would be to civilize them. However, Christian missionary activity was highly provocative in many parts of China, and it had the effect of increasing the popularity and influence of the Boxers. When the Boxers began attacking converts, missionaries, and churches, the American public became outraged. Popular magazines carried many stories of persecution and Boxer terrorism, including the **Account of Fei Ch'i-Hao,** a Chinese Christian who detailed Boxer depredations in Shansi.

Building a Coalition, Backing into a War

Despite public opinion favoring intervention in the Boxer situation, the United States did not immediately send a large force. Instead, it participated in an international coalition including troops from Russia, Japan, France, and Britain, all under the command of British vice admiral Sir Edward Seymour. During June 1900 fighting became intense, and the Boxers killed some 250 foreigners and untold numbers of Chinese Christians. On June 20, they laid siege to the Western embassies in Peking. The German minister, Baron Klemens von Ketteler, was among those murdered.

The ferocity of Boxer activity led to several reinforcements from the coalition nations, so that the final strength of the polyglot army in China was 18,700 by August. For a brief period, the suppression of the Boxer Rebellion amounted to a full-scale war.

The Boxer Protocol of 1901

The dispersal of the Boxers from Peking on August 15, 1900, marked the end of major combat, although coalition forces continued to sweep through northern China to suppress residual Boxer activity until early 1901.

Account of Fei Ch'i-Hao, 1903

Late in July a proclamation of the Governor was posted in the city in which occurred the words, "Exterminate foreigners, kill devils." Native Christians must leave the church or pay the penalty with their lives. . . .

Once across the river I reached a small inn outside the wall of P'ing Yao. I had walked twenty miles that day—the longest walk I had ever taken, and I threw myself down to sleep without eating anything.

Often I awoke with a start and turned my aching body, asking myself, "Where am I? How came I here? Are my Western friends indeed killed? I must be dreaming."

But I was so tired that sleep would soon overcome me again. The sun had risen when I opened my eyes in the morning. I forced myself to rise, washed my face, and asked for a little food, but could not get it down. Sitting down I heard loud talking and laughter among the guests. The topic of conversation was the massacre of foreigners the day before! One said:

"There were ten ocean men killed, three men, four women, and three little devils."

Another added, "Lij Cheng San yesterday morning came ahead with twenty soldiers and waited in the village. When the foreigners with their soldier escort arrived a gun was fired for a signal, and all the soldiers set to work at once."

Then one after another added gruesome details, how the cruel swords had slashed, how the baggage had been stolen, how the very clothing had been stripped from the poor bodies, and how they had then been flung into a wayside pit.

"Are there still foreigners in Fen Chou Fu?" I asked.

"No, they were all killed yesterday."

Excerpted from Luella Miner, *Two Heroes of Cathay* (New York: F. Revell, 1903), 89–90.

On July 3, 1900, while the war was still in its early phase, Secretary Hay issued a Second Circular Letter, in which he sought to affirm international adherence to the principles of the Open Door policy. Hay wrote that "the policy of the government of the United States is to seek a solution which may bring about permanent safety and peace to China, preserve Chinese territorial and administrative entity, protect all rights guaranteed to friendly powers by treaty and international law, and safeguard for the world the principle of equal and impartial trade with all parts of the Chinese Empire."

Despite the Open Door policy and its reaffirmation, after the withdrawal of the Boxers from Peking, in 1901 the coalition nations drew up the **Boxer Protocol,** a document that was anything but kind in its treatment of China. It levied an exorbitant $333,000,000 indemnity against the Chinese and compelled the nation's government to agree to the permanent stationing of U.S. and other troops in the country. The United States was to receive $24,500,000 of the indemnity; however, the American government unilaterally decided to reduce its share to $12,000,000, and in 1924 entirely forgave the unpaid balance on the reduced amount. The gesture was intended to demonstrate to the Chinese the U.S. government's good faith; nevertheless, the United States repeatedly acquiesced in violations of the Open Door policy.

Taft-Katsura Memorandum of 1905 and Lansing-Ishii Agreement of 1917

The **Taft-Katsura Memorandum** of 1905, between the United States and Japan, established a foundation for a Japanese protectorate in Korea, a political step that threatened Chinese sovereignty and gave Japan a significant degree of economic control over Chinese trade.

The **Lansing-Ishii Agreement** of 1917 was an acknowledgment by the United States of Japan's "special interests" in China and helped set the stage

Boxer Protocol, 1901

ARTICLE 1.

1) By an Imperial Edict of the 9th June last, . . . Prince of the First Rank, Chun, was appointed Ambassador of His Majesty the Emperor of China, and directed in that capacity to convey to His Majesty the German Emperor the expression of the regrets of His Majesty the Emperor of China and of the Chinese Government at the assassination of his Excellency the late Baron von Ketteler, German Minister. . . .

2) The Chinese Government has stated that it will erect on the spot of the assassination of his Excellency the late Baron von Ketteler, commemorative monument worthy of the rank of the deceased, and bearing an inscription in the Latin, German, and Chinese languages which shall express the regrets of His Majesty the Emperor of China for the murder committed. . . .

ARTICLE II.

1) Imperial Edicts of the 13th and 21st February, 1901, inflicted the following punishments on the principal authors of the attempts and of the crimes committed against the foreign Governments and their nationals [list of punishments follows]. . . .

ARTICLE III.

So as to make honourable reparation for the assassination of Mr. Sugiyama, Chancellor of the Japanese Legation, His Majesty the Emperor of China, by an Imperial Edict of the 18th June, 1901, appointed Na T'ung, Vice-President of the Board of Finances, to be his Envoy Extraordinary, and specially directed him to convey to His Majesty the Emperor of Japan the expression of the regrets of His Majesty the Emperor of China and of his Government at the assassination of Mr. Sugiyama.

ARTICLE IV.

The Chinese Government has agreed to erect an expiatory monument in each of the foreign or international cemeteries which were desecrated, and in which the tombs were destroyed. . . .

ARTICLE V.

China has agreed to prohibit the importation into its territory of arms and ammunition . . . for a term of two years. New Edicts may be issued subsequently extending this. . . .

ARTICLE VI.

By an Imperial Edict dated the 29th May, 1901, His Majesty the Emperor of China agreed to pay the Powers an indemnity of 450,000,000 of Haikwan taels. . . .

ARTICLE VII.

The Chinese Government has agreed that the quarter occupied by the Legations shall be considered as one specially reserved for their use and placed under their exclusive control, in which Chinese shall not have the right to reside, and which may be made defensible. . . .

ARTICLE VIII.

The Chinese Government has consented to raze the forts of Taku, and those which might impede free communication between Peking and the sea. Steps have been taken for carrying this out.

ARTICLE IX.

The Chinese Government conceded the right to the Powers in the Protocol annexed to the letter of the 16th January, 1901, to occupy certain points. . . .

ARTICLE X.

The Chinese Government has agreed to post and to have published during two years in all district cities the following Imperial Edicts:

1) Edict of the 1st February, 1901, prohibiting for ever under pain of death, membership in any anti-foreign society. . . .

4) Edicts of the 1st February, 1901, declaring all Governors General, Governors, and provincial or local officials responsible for order in their respective districts, and that in case of new anti-foreign troubles or other infractions of the Treaties which shall not be immediately repressed and the authors of which shall not have been punished, these officials shall be immediately dismissed.

Excerpted from the John Jay College of Criminal Justice, CUNY, "Boxer Protocol (Peking): Agreement between China and the Foreign Powers," http://web.jjay.cuny.edu/~jobrien/reference/ob26.html.

Taft-Katsura Memorandum, 1905

Count Katsura and [William Howard Taft, personal representative of President Theodore Roosevelt] had a long and confidential conversation on the morning of July 27 [1905]. Among other topics of conversation the following views were exchanged regarding . . . Korea and . . . the maintenance of general peace in the Far East.

. . . [I]n regard to the Korean question Count Katsura observed that . . . [i]f left to herself after the war, Korea will certainly draw back to her habit of improvidently entering into any agreements or treaties with other powers, thus resuscitating the same international complications as existed before the war. In view of the foregoing circumstances, Japan feels absolutely constrained to take some definite steps with a view to precluding the possibility of Korea falling back into her former condition and of placing [Japan] again under the necessity of entering upon another foreign war. [Taft] fully admitted the justness of the Count's observations and remarked to the effect that, in his person[al] opinion, the establishment by Japanese troops of a suzerainty over Korea to the extent of requiring that Korea enter into no foreign treaties without the consent of Japan was the logical result of the present war and would directly contribute to peace in the East.

Excerpted from Tyler Dennett, "President Roosevelt's Secret Pact with Japan," *Current History* (October 1924): 15–21.

Lansing-Ishii Agreement, 1917

DEPARTMENT OF STATE,
Washington, NOV. 2, 1917.

Excellency:
. . . The governments of the United States and Japan recognize that territorial propinquity creates special relations between countries, and, consequently, the government of the United States recognizes that Japan has special interests in China, particularly in the part to which her possessions are contiguous.

The territorial sovereignty of China, nevertheless, remains unimpaired, and the government of the United States has every confidence in the repeated assurances of the Imperial Japanese government that while geographical position gives Japan such special interests they have no desire to discriminate against the trade of other nations or to disregard the commercial rights heretofore granted by China in treaties with other powers.

The governments of the United States and Japan deny that they have any purpose to infringe in any way the independence or territorial integrity of China, and they declare, furthermore, that they always adhere to the principle of the so-called "open door" or equal opportunity for commerce and industry in China.

Excerpted from "The Lansing-Ishii Exchange of Notes," in Carnegie Endowment for International Peace, *The Imperial Japanese Mission 1917* (Washington, D.C.: Carnegie Endowment for International Peace, 1918), from the World War I Document Archive, Brigham Young University Library, www.lib.byu.edu/~rdh/wwi/comment/japanvisit/JapanA2.htm.

for the 1932 Japanese invasion of Manchuria, a prelude to World War II (Chapter 36).

Most immediately, the Boxer Protocol hastened the final collapse of the Qing, or Manchu, dynasty, which had ruled China since 1644. IIumiliated and weakened by the protocol, the Qing government fell easy prey to the Chinese Revolution of 1911.

BIBLIOGRAPHY

Boot, Max. *The Savage Wars of Peace: Small Wars and the Rise of American Power.* New York: Basic Books, 2003.

Harrington, Peter. *Peking 1900: The Boxer Rebellion.* London: Osprey, 2001.

Preston, Diana. *Boxer Rebellion.* New York: Berkeley, 2001.

At Issue in Panama

At the turn of the twentieth century, Panama was a province of Colombia. After the Colombian senate refused to ratify the Hay-Herrán Treaty, which would have given the United States the right to build a canal across the Isthmus of Panama, the United States supported a rebellion that created the independent republic of Panama. The new republic quickly concluded the Hay-Bunau-Varilla Treaty, which authorized the canal and the creation of a U.S.-controlled Panama Canal Zone.

The Conflict

In 1881 the Compagnie Universelle du Canal Interocéanique—the French Panama Canal company—began construction of the canal across the Isthmus of Panama. Despite the credentials and experience of the project's manager, Ferdinand de Lesseps (who had already built the Suez Canal in Egypt, which was completed in 1869), the French project suffered from poor logistical planning and irregularities in finance. Most of all, it was plagued by the tropical diseases, especially yellow fever, endemic to the isthmus.

After the French project collapsed in 1889 and a later attempt to reorganize the bankrupt company failed, the project's chief engineer, Philippe Bunau-Varilla, approached the United States with an offer to purchase the right to build the canal. President

Theodore Roosevelt commissioned him to negotiate a treaty with Colombia, of which Panama was then a province. This led to the Hay-Herrán Treaty (named for U.S. Secretary of State John Hay and Colombian foreign minister Tomás Herrán), signed on January 22, 1903, which provided for the United States to build and control the canal as well as a zone on either side of the canal. When the Colombian senate declined to ratify the treaty on August 12, 1903, Bunau-Varilla organized a revolt in Panama (where discontent with government was high) against Colombia, collaborating with railway workers, firefighters, and soldiers in an uprising and declaration of independence (November 3–4).

In support of the revolution, the United States dispatched warships to both sides of the Panamanian isthmus. On November 6, 1903, Roosevelt recog-

CHRONOLOGY OF THE PANAMANIAN REVOLUTION

1903

Aug. 12 Colombian senate declines to ratify the Hay-Herrán Treaty.

Nov. 3–4 Panamanian rebels declare independence from Colombia. U.S. warships are dispatched to both sides of the isthmus.

Nov. 6 President Theodore Roosevelt recognizes Panamanian independence.

Nov. 18 The Hay-Bunau-Varilla Treaty is concluded.

Philippe Jean Bunau-Varilla

(1859–1940)

Philippe Jean Bunau-Varilla graduated with a degree in civil engineering from Paris's École Nationale des Ponts et Chaussées (National School of Bridges and Roads). By 1884 he was the chief engineer for the Compagnie Universelle du Canal Interocéanique's Panama Canal project, and he became a major investor in the enterprise as well. After the company went bankrupt in 1889, Bunau-Varilla was a driving force behind its reorganization in 1894. With Bunau-Varilla at the helm, the new company assumed the rights to build a canal across the isthmus of Panama. When Bunau-Varilla was unable to obtain the necessary financial banking in France, he worked to sell to the United States the rights to build and operate the canal.

By 1901 Bunau-Varilla had persuaded Senator Mark Hanna and President Theodore Roosevelt to build the canal through Panama. When the senate of Colombia (of which Panama was a province) resisted, Bunau-Varilla became one of the leaders of a popular uprising to win Panamanian independence from Colombia. With the help of the American government, Bunau-Varilla got himself appointed "First Minister Plenipotentiary and Envoy Extraordinary of the Republic of Panama to Washington" and immediately concluded a canal treaty with U.S. secretary of state John Hay.

Bunau-Varilla emerged from the Panama Canal adventure a wealthy man. He continued his career as an engineer, however, and was responsible for developing a water chlorination process that was used to supply the besieged Verdun fortress during World War I.

nized Panamanian independence and immediately received Bunau-Varilla as minister from the new republic. Days later, on November 18, Secretary Hay concluded with Bunau-Varilla a treaty with even more generous terms than the treaty the Colombian senate had refused to ratify.

Panama Canal Background

The advantages of a canal cut somewhere across the isthmus of Central America were long obvious to anyone who looked at a world map. Here was a means of joining the planet's two great oceans. By the nineteenth century most speculators and planners had settled on two routes, one through Panama and the other through Nicaragua. As early as 1835, the U.S. Senate passed a resolution in favor of a canal and proposed a route through Nicaragua. However, the focus shifted to Panama during the course of the century as construction began on the Panama Rail-

road, designed to carry passengers and freight offloaded from ships on one coast to ships waiting on the other. The route of the railroad effectively marked the route for an adjacent canal.

Roosevelt and Hanna

In 1899 President William McKinley set up the Walker Commission to decide the best route for a canal, and in 1902 the commission issued a report favoring the Nicaraguan route. The feeling was that the French failure in Panama called for a fresh start elsewhere. The assassination of President McKinley in September 1901 brought Theodore Roosevelt into office. Roosevelt saw the canal as the means by which the United States could gain control over both of its coastal oceans and thereby become a true world power.

While the president, Congress, and the public were contemplating the military desirability of a

In this 1903 political cartoon, President Theodore Roosevelt buries the Colombian capital of Bogota in dirt being excavated to build the Panama Canal. When Colombia refused to ratify a treaty that would allow the United States to build the canal across Colombia's Panama province, the United States encouraged a rebellion that led to the creation of an independent Panama and the U.S.-controlled Panama Canal Zone.

amendment to the Senate version of the Hepburn Bill authorizing the president to acquire the French company's assets and concessions for $40,000,000. After a vigorous Senate debate the Panama route was chosen on June 19, 1902, by a margin of eight votes.

The Hay-Herrán Treaty

The Colombian chargé d'affaires, Dr. Tomas Herrán, and U.S. secretary of state John Hay negotiated the Hay-Herrán Treaty. Signed in Washington, D.C., on January 22, 1903, it affirmed the right of the Compagnie Nouvelle, which now held an option on the canal route, to sell its properties to the United States. It also included an agreement by Colombia to lease a strip of land to the United States for construction of a canal in exchange for a payment to Colombia of $10 million in cash and, beginning after nine years, an annuity of $250,000.

canal, Bunau-Varilla told the directors of Compagnie Nouvelle (the restructured Compagnie Universelle) that a U.S. decision to build the canal in Nicaragua would leave their stock worthless. He persuaded the directors to reduce the valuation of the company's Panama assets to just $40,000,000—precisely the cost ceiling set by the Walker Commission. Nevertheless, in 1902 the U.S. House of Representatives narrowly passed the Hepburn Bill favoring Nicaragua. At this point, President Roosevelt met with the Walker Commission and told them that he wanted to accept the French offer as the most practical and expedient means of securing the rights to build and operate the canal. He instructed the commission to prepare a supplementary report favoring the Panama route. Roosevelt submitted the supplementary report to Congress in January 1902, and Wisconsin Senator John Coit Spooner introduced an

The treaty fell somewhat short of what Roosevelt had wanted, which was an agreement that would give the United States total control over the proposed canal and a sovereign canal zone. Despite this shortcoming, Roosevelt approved and the U.S. Senate ratified the treaty on March 14, 1903. The Colombian senate, however, delayed ratification in the hope of increasing the price offered by the United States. Soon its position hardened even further, as Colombian popular opinion turned against "Yankee imperialism" and what was seen as an assault on national sovereignty.

A New Panama Policy: Recognition of Independence

After the Colombian senate declined to ratify the treaty on August 12, 1903, President Roosevelt abruptly terminated negotiations with Colombia and threw his support behind a Panamanian independence movement that the indefatigable Frenchman Bunau-Varilla was instrumental in organizing. Roosevelt sent warships to both sides of the isthmus to block the sea approaches. Marines were dispatched to protect the Panama railroad, and the cruiser USS *Nashville* interdicted a Colombian attempt to land troops.

Thanks to unofficial military assistance from the United States, the Panamanian revolution was both successful and virtually bloodless. The United States recognized Panamanian independence on November 6, 1903.

The Hay-Bunau-Varilla Treaty

Within days of Panamian independence, Philippe Bunau-Varilla was named the new republic's "First Minister Plenipotentiary and Envoy Extraordinary" fully authorized to negotiate a canal treaty with Secretary of State John Hay. The **Hay-Bunau-Varilla Treaty,** signed on November 18, 1903, gave President Roosevelt what the ill-fated Hay-Herrán Treaty had not: total control over the Panama Canal and a land grant to the United States, in perpetuity and as if sovereign, of a canal zone extending for five miles on either side of the canal itself. Since the United States was the de facto guarantor of Panamanian independence, the new Panamanian senate had little choice but to ratify the treaty, which it did on December 2, 1903. The United States Senate followed suit on February 23, 1904, and Panama was paid $10 million.

Hay-Bunau-Varilla Treaty, 1903

ARTICLE I
The United States guarantees and will maintain the independence of the Republic of Panama.

ARTICLE II
The Republic of Panama grants to the United States in perpetuity the use, occupation and control of a zone of land and land under water for the construction maintenance, operation, sanitation and protection of said Canal of the width of ten miles extending to the distance of five miles on each side of the center line of the route of the Canal to be constructed; the said zone beginning in the Caribbean Sea three marine miles from mean low water mark and extending to and across the Isthmus of Panama into the Pacific ocean to a distance of three marine miles from mean low water mark with the proviso that the cities of Panama and Colon and the harbors adjacent to said cities, which are included within the boundaries of the zone above described, shall not be included within this grant. . . .

ARTICLE III
The Republic of Panama grants to the United States all the rights, power and authority within the zone mentioned and described in Article II. . . .

ARTICLE IX
The United States agrees that the ports at either entrance of the Canal and the waters thereof, and the Republic of Panama agrees that the towns of Panama and Colon shall be free for all time. . . .

ARTICLE XIV
As the price or compensation for the rights, powers and privileges granted in this convention by the Republic of Panama to the United States, the Government of the United States agrees to pay to the Republic of Panama the sum of ten million dollars . . . and also an annual payment during the life of this convention of two hundred and fifty thousand dollars.

Excerpted from Alan Axelrod, *American Treaties and Alliances* (Washington, D.C.: CQ Press, 2000), 283–286.

At Issue in Nicaragua

The American-backed Conservative Party rebelled against the nationalist Liberal Party and its leader, the brutal dictator José Santos Zelaya.

The Conflict

Beginning on October 10, 1909, Juan J. Estrada, Adolfo Díaz, and Emiliano Chamorro Vargas organized the Conservative Party, consisting of powerful, influential, and prosperous Nicaraguans, in a rebellion against the leader of the Liberal Party, President José Santos Zelaya. Zelaya, who was both a nationalist and a brutal dictator, opposed the influence of American business interests in Nicaragua.

The rebellion began near the city of Bluefields, on Nicaragua's eastern coast, and gradually spread west. U.S. president William Howard Taft welcomed it because Zelaya's regime was repugnant to democratic principles, hostile toward U.S. business interests, and had mistreated U.S. diplomats. The greatest provocation came in October 1909 when Zelaya captured and executed two American citizens, Leonard Croce and Leroy Canon, who had volunteered for service as officers in Chamorro's revolutionary army. In response, U.S. secretary of state Philander Knox severed diplomatic relations with the Zelaya government on December 1, 1909, and President Taft ordered military action. The Nicaraguan Expeditionary Brigade of U.S. Marines arrived at Cristobal, in Panama's Canal Zone, on December 12 and then sailed for the port of Corinto, Nicaragua. Their arrival prompted Zelaya to relinquish the presidency on December 16 to José Madriz. Zelaya fled to Mexico. The marines returned to Panama on March 22, 1910.

Despite Zelaya's self-imposed exile, fighting broke out again near Bluefields, this time between rebels loyal to Juan J. Estrada and forces loyal to President Madriz. U.S. Navy commander William W. Gilmer, skipper of the USS *Paducah,* which was riding at anchor in the waters off Bluefields, issued a proclamation forbidding fighting within the city. Two hundred marines under Major Smedley D. Butler again arrived from the Canal Zone on May 30 to enforce the proclamation.

The principal dispute was over the disposition of the customs house at Bluefields. Estrada's rebels had seized it and used it as a source of finance. On May 27, Madriz's army retook it, even though Estrada's forces still occupied the city. Estrada demanded that customs duties be paid to his men in the city, whereas Madriz insisted that they be paid at the customs house he now controlled. U.S. authorities felt that Madriz was becoming dictatorial and dangerous, so they ordered that customs duties be paid to Estrada. This provided the financial support he needed to continue his revolt against Madriz. In the meantime, Butler's marines maintained civil order in Bluefields while Estrada, now well financed, captured the capital, Managua, on August 23. He was inaugurated as president on August 30, and on September 4, the marines returned to Panama.

Stability, however, proved elusive. Zelaya's followers were still active, and even many rebels who had supported Estrada were disappointed over the paltry share of power and spoils they had received. Some also protested the imperialism of the United States, to which the Estrada government was handing trade concessions and monopolies. When fighting broke out in Managua, Elliott Northcott, U.S. minister to Nicaragua, persuaded Estrada to resign in favor of his vice president, Adolfo Díaz. This brought a brief calm, but in 1912 General Luis Mena, who had been war minister under Estrada, took part of the army to Masaya and seized American-owned steamships on Lake Managua. In response, on August 4, 1912, 100 sailors from the USS *Annapolis* arrived in Managua, and 353 marines, under Butler, set off from Panama for Corinto. On August 14, the marines and 80 more sailors left Corinto by train for Managua, arriving on August 15. With this American military backing,

George F. Weitzel, who had replaced Northcott as minister in Managua, demanded that General Mena return the seized vessels. Mena refused, and more marines were called up.

On September 6, the first and second marine battalions of the First Provisional Regiment, commanded by Colonel Joseph H. Pendleton, joined Butler's small contingent in Managua. Pendleton, commanding the combined forces, set off to confront Mena. After falling ill in late September, Mena surrendered in return for a grant of political asylum in Panama.

The marines still had to reduce Mena ally General Benjamin Zeledon's stronghold in the Barranca-Coyatepe hills and neutralize the rebel positions in Masaya and León. On October 2, in concert with Nicaraguan government troops, the marines commenced an artillery bombardment. The following day, they stormed Zeledon's positions, which quickly yielded. The marines stepped aside as the Nicaraguan government troops ravaged and looted Masaya. The people of nearby León, anxious to avoid the fate of Masaya, quickly surrendered—to the U.S. Marines. The recapture of Masaya and León ended the revolt against the Díaz regime. During November 1913, the marines returned to Panama, save for a contingent of 100 legation guards stationed in Managua.

American Business in Nicaragua

The United States took little note of Nicaragua until the discovery of gold in California in 1848 made it a strategic location for travel between the Atlantic and Pacific oceans. American mogul Cornelius Vanderbilt saw an opportunity and threw his financial weight behind Nicaragua's Conservative Party. Thus he was able to purchase the concessions he needed to build a rail and shipping monopoly in Nicaragua. The colorful American filibusterer (adventurer) William Walker—who had attempted to create colonies in both Mexico and Nicaragua, and briefly became the president of Nicaragua— intervened on behalf of the Liberals. Vanderbilt used his money and influence to suppress Walker's

activities—with the diplomatic cooperation of the United States government.

From 1857, the year Walker fell from power, until 1893, Nicaragua was governed by the Conservative Party, whose leaders were supported by the United States and openly in the pay of U.S. business interests. This brought a measure of stability to Nicaragua but allowed neither freedom nor national self-determination; the outward quiet notwithstanding, the seeds of rebellion grew. The Liberal Party, led by José Santos Zelaya, displaced the Conservatives in 1893 and advocated an anti-U.S. nationalism. Zelaya, a brutal dictator, touted schemes for the unification of Central America, even as he denied U.S. businesses the wealth of concessions they had become accustomed to. He also resisted American attempts to negotiate rights to build a canal across Nicaragua. As during the

CHRONOLOGY OF THE NICARAGUAN CIVIL WAR

1909
Oct. 10 The Bluefields rebellion begins.
Dec. 1 The United States severs diplomatic relations with the Zelaya government.
Dec. 12 U.S. Marines depart for Nicaragua.
Dec. 16 Intimidated by the U.S. military presence, Zelaya resigns and goes into exile.

1910
Mar. 22 The marines leave Nicaragua; civil war resumes.
May 30 The marines return to Nicaragua.
Aug. 23 Juan J. Estrada, the U.S.-backed presidential contender, captures Managua.
Aug. 30 Estrada is inaugurated as the president of Nicaragua.
Sept. 4 The marines leave Nicaragua again; violence continues sporadically.

1912
Aug. 4–15 to Sept. 6 The marines return to Nicaragua.
Oct. 2–3 Marines and Nicaraguan government troops defeat rebel general Benjamin Zeledon. The civil war ends, and U.S.-backed Adolfo Díaz is restored to power.

Spanish-American War (Chapter 29), American business interests, especially transportation and fruit companies (and the American banks that financed them), clamored for U.S. intervention. When Zelaya displayed open hostility toward U.S. diplomats in the capital, Managua, and then executed two U.S. citizens (who were leading rebel forces against him), President Taft had reason enough for military intervention—and he had no trouble raising popular American support for it.

Dollar Diplomacy

Taft sent the navy and the marines to Nicaragua, but unlike his predecessor and mentor, Theodore Roosevelt, doing so went against his grain. Although he was willing to use the military to protect U.S. business interests in the Caribbean and Central America, Taft believed that those business interests, rather than the U.S. government, were responsible for creating stability in these and other volatile countries. In his December 1, 1912, **Message to Congress,** Taft explained that the "diplomacy of the present administration has sought to respond to modern ideas of commercial intercourse. This policy has been characterized as substituting dollars for bullets." Deriding Taft's policy as "dollar diplomacy," critics considered it a craven attempt to buy commerce-friendly political stability at the expense of local freedom and democracy. Taft saw the commercial solution as desirable—and far preferable to war, no matter how nobly motivated—but his successor,

Taft's Message to Congress, December 1, 1912

In Central America the aim [of U.S. foreign policy] has been to help such countries as Nicaragua and Honduras to help themselves. They are the immediate beneficiaries. The national benefit to the United States is twofold. First, it is obvious that the Monroe Doctrine is more vital in the neighborhood of the Panama Canal and the zone of the Caribbean than anywhere else. There, too, the maintenance of that doctrine falls most heavily upon the United States. It is therefore essential that the countries within that sphere shall be removed from the jeopardy involved by heavy foreign debt and chaotic national finances and from the ever present danger of international complications due to disorder at home. Hence, the United States has been glad to encourage and support American bankers who were willing to lend a helping hand to the financial rehabilitation of such countries because this financial rehabilitation and the protection of their customhouses from being the prey of would-be dictators would remove at one stroke the menace of foreign creditors and the menace of revolutionary disorder.

The second advantage to the United States is one affecting chiefly all the Southern and Gulf ports and the business and industry of the South. The republics of Central America and the Caribbean possess great natural wealth. They need only a measure of stability and the means of financial regeneration to enter upon an era of peace and prosperity, bringing profit and happiness to themselves and at the same time creating conditions sure to lead to a flourishing interchange of trade with this country.

I wish to call your especial attention to the recent occurrences in Nicaragua, for I believe the terrible events recorded there during the revolution of the past summer—the useless loss of life, the devastation of property, the bombardment of defenseless cities, the killing and wounding of women and children, the torturing of noncombatants to exact contributions, and the suffering of thousands of human beings—might have been averted had the Department of State, through approval of the loan convention by the Senate, been permitted to carry out its now well-developed policy of encouraging the extending of financial aid to weak Central American states.

Excerpted from "Dollar Diplomacy," in *Annals of America,* ed. Mortimer J. Adler and Charles Van Doren (Chicago: Encyclopaedia Britannica, 1976), 13:371–372.

Woodrow Wilson, would repudiate the policy early in his term, when he declined to support the Four Power Consortium, a four-nation bank pool that Taft had sponsored to promote railway construction in China.

Banana Republic: Growth of a Popular Image

The popular American short-story writer O. Henry (William Sydney Porter) included a story entitled "The Admiral" in his 1904 collection, *Cabbages and Kings*. It is a slight satire, a sketch of a Central American country whose government confiscates a sloop for nonpayment of customs duties and then decides, as a kind of joke, to proclaim this single vessel the nation's navy and to appoint a local half-wit named Don Felipe Carrera as fleet admiral. Carrera spends the rest of the brief story awaiting sailing orders that never come. O. Henry makes it clear that the fictional country he calls "Anchuria" is essentially owned by the "Vesuvius Fruit Company" and is, therefore, aptly described as a "small, maritime banana republic."

The American reading public of the time would have recognized "Anchuria" as Honduras—or just about any other Central American state—and the "Vesuvius Fruit Company" as a stand-in for the United Fruit Company or the Standard Fruit Company, giant American concerns. As for the phrase "banana republic," it caught on with the public and politicians alike to describe Honduras, Nicaragua, and other Caribbean and Central American countries that were essentially controlled by U.S. interests. The word "republic" was understood early in the twentieth century as something of a euphemism for a dictatorship, and "banana" suggested that the "republic" was largely a creation of the fruit companies that pulled the strings of government. Soon, "banana republic" came to describe any country "bought" by means of "dollar diplomacy."

As the twentieth century wore on, the phrase "banana republic" remained, but its original connotation changed. The phrase came to describe any Latin American dictatorship whose economy depended on peasant agriculture (for example, the cultivation of bananas) and that was corrupt, brutal, backward, and unstable, its dictatorial government maintained through fraud and corruption. Despite the broadened connotation, there remained in the American popular mind an impression that the government of the United States often supported banana republics. By the 1930s many Americans thought of the banana republics as de facto United States colonies.

Minority Report: Major Smedley Butler

In contrast to the widespread patriotic feelings that had been associated with the Spanish-American War and the resulting annexations, the U.S. intervention in Nicaragua left many Americans uneasy. Whereas the Taft administration generally regarded the intervention as a fine example of "substituting dollars for bullets," Smedley Butler, the marine major who had led operations on the ground in Nicaragua and who would go on to earn two Medals of Honor for extraordinary gallantry in the capture of Veracruz, Mexico (1914; see Chapter 33), published a startling little book in 1935 entitled *War Is a Racket*. In the book, Butler argued that the wars in which he had fought had been driven not by patriotism but by the profit motive and had benefited no more than a handful of entrepreneurs and capitalists at the expense of great public suffering and financial cost. Although the 1935 volume did not mention Nicaragua, a speech Butler had made in 1933, also entitled **"War Is a Racket,"** did: "I helped purify Nicaragua for the international banking house of Brown Brothers in 1909–1912," he declared.

Butler's point of view, which he disseminated widely—during one speaking tour, he delivered some 1,200 speeches in more than 700 U.S. cities—was an extreme expression of the disillusionment that swept the nation following the interventions of the early twentieth century, including America's participation

"War Is a Racket" Speech, 1933

War is just a racket. A racket is best described, I believe, as something that is not what it seems to the majority of people. Only a small inside group knows what it is about. It is conducted for the benefit of the very few at the expense of the masses. . . .

I wouldn't go to war again as I have done to protect some lousy investment of the bankers. There are only two things we should fight for. One is the defense of our homes and the other is the Bill of Rights. War for any other reason is simply a racket. . . .

. . . I spent thirty-three years and four months in active military service as a member of this country's most agile military force, the Marine Corps. I served in all commissioned ranks from Second Lieutenant to Major-General. And during that period, I spent most of my time being a high class muscle-man for Big Business, for Wall Street and for the Bankers. In short, I was a racketeer, a gangster for capitalism. . . .

I helped make Mexico, especially Tampico, safe for American oil interests in 1914. I helped make Haiti and Cuba a decent place for the National City Bank boys to collect revenues in. I helped in the raping of half a dozen Central American republics for the benefits of Wall Street. The record of racketeering is long. I helped purify Nicaragua for the international banking house of Brown Brothers in 1909–1912 (where have I heard that name before?). I brought light to the Dominican Republic for American sugar interests in 1916. In China I helped to see to it that Standard Oil went its way unmolested.

During those years, I had, as the boys in the back room would say, a swell racket. Looking back on it, I feel that I could have given Al Capone a few hints. The best he could do was to operate his racket in three districts. I operated on three continents.

Excerpted from Federation of American Scientists, Military Analysis Network, "Smedley Butler on Interventionism," www.fas.org/man/smedley.htm.

in World War I (Chapter 34). Butler's cynicism was the product of an era of "dollar diplomacy."

BIBLIOGRAPHY

Anderson, Thomas P. *Politics in Central America: Guatemala, El Salvador, Honduras, and Nicaragua.* New York: Praeger, 1988.

Barton, Jonathan R. *Political Geography of Latin America.* New York: Routledge, 1997.

Crawley, Eduardo. *Nicaragua in Perspective.* New York: St. Martin's Press, 1984.

Espino, Ovido Diaz. *How Wall Street Created a Nation: J. P. Morgan, Teddy Roosevelt, and the Panama Canal.* New York: Four Walls Eight Windows Press, 2001.

LaFeber, Walter. *Panama Canal.* New York: Oxford University Press, 1993.

McCullough, David. *The Path between the Seas: The Creation of the Panama Canal, 1870–1914.* New York: Simon and Schuster, 1999.

Walker, Thomas W. *Nicaragua: Living in the Shadow of the Eagle,* 4th ed. Boulder, Colo.: Westview Press, 2003.

CHAPTER 33

PUNITIVE EXPEDITION AGAINST PANCHO VILLA (1916–1917)

At Issue

The Mexican revolutionary and social bandit Pancho Villa, presumably seeking to enhance his political power in Mexico by challenging the United States, raided the southern New Mexico town of Columbus. President Woodrow Wilson responded by launching a military offensive to capture or kill Villa and his men.

The Conflict

The 1913 assassination of Mexican president Francisco Madero created a power vacuum, which several candidates rushed to fill. The right-wing dictator Victoriano Huerta usurped the office by force of arms. On April 21, with the approval of the U.S. Congress, President Woodrow Wilson sent a small amphibious force to seize control of the port of Veracruz to prevent the landing there of arms and other equipment being transported to Huerta aboard a German ship. The landing party met stiff resistance, whereupon Wilson ordered a larger assault to occupy the city, which brought about the collapse of the Huerta government on July 15. Huerta was replaced in 1915 by the more moderate Venustiano Carranza, whom Wilson favored.

The installation of Carranza did not end revolutionary activity. One of the most colorful and charismatic of the Mexican revolutionaries was Doroteo Arango, who later called himself Francisco Villa but became best known as Pancho Villa. Breaking with Carranza because of the president's failure to commit to social reform, Villa took to the mountains of the

north toward the end of 1915. There, for unknown reasons, he executed seventeen American citizens in the Mexican town of Santa Isabel during January 1916. Next, on March 9, he and some 500 "Villistas" crossed the border and raided Columbus, New Mexico. Ten American civilians and fourteen U.S. soldiers were killed, as were at least 100 of Villa's men.

Villa's executions and raid outraged Americans, prompting President Wilson to send a "Punitive Expedition" into Mexico. On March 14, 1916, Brigadier General John J. Pershing assumed command of two cavalry brigades and a brigade of infantry, about 15,000 troops total. Pershing's orders were to locate, pursue, and destroy Villa's forces. Although President Carranza consented to allow the Punitive Expedition to advance into Mexico on

CHRONOLOGY OF THE PUNITIVE EXPEDITION
1916
Mar. 9 Pancho Villa raids Columbus, New Mexico.
Mar. 15 Brigadier General John J. Pershing's Punitive Expedition advances into Mexico.
Mar. 29 "Battle" of Guerrero
Apr. 1 "Battle" of Aguas Calientas
Apr. 12–13 Standoff at Parral
Apr. 22 "Battle" of Tomochic
May 5 "Battle" of Ojos Azulas
Late June A bloody exchange in Carrizal brings about negotiations between Pershing and the Carranzistas.
1917
Feb. Pershing's Punitive Expedition leaves Mexico.

Venustiano Carranza

(1859–1920)

Born in Cuatro Ciénegas, Mexico, the son of a landowner, Carranza became governor of Coahuila in 1910 and joined the rebellion led by Francisco Madero against Porfirio Díaz. After the fall of Díaz, Carranza led forces opposed to Victoriano Huerta in 1913. Menaced by pro-Carranza U.S. forces, Huerta fled in 1914. But Carranza's so-called Constitutionalist Army also began to fragment, and Pancho Villa and Emiliano Zapata rose to prominence in opposition to Carranza's provisional government. Despite this opposition, Carranza prevailed after his force, commanded by General Alvaro Obregón, defeated Villa at Celaya in April 1915.

Carranza was a political rather than a social reformer. Although he acceded to the provisions of the 1917 constitution that created reforms in land ownership and labor, when he was elevated to constitutional president on May 1, 1917, he did almost nothing to implement the reforms. This encouraged Villa and Zapata to continue their rebellion, and Mexico remained highly unstable.

Mexico's precarious position was aggravated by Carranza's intense nationalism, which put him at odds with the United States. As he approached the constitutionally mandated end of his term in 1920, Carranza lobbied for the election of his handpicked successor, Ignacio Bonillas. This provoked a rebellion by radical generals in April 1920, and Carranza fled Mexico City by train. Carrying government records and treasure, he was bound for Veracruz when his train was attacked on April 8, 1920. Carranza took to horseback and made for the mountains in Tlaxcalantongo, where, on the night of May 20–21, he was assassinated.

March 15, during the eleven months that it remained in the country, the expedition wore out its welcome. Pershing found himself contending not only with Villistas but also Carranzistas.

The Punitive Expedition located and killed most of Villa's top lieutenants and a number of his supporters. Pancho Villa himself, however, eluded capture, and by May 1916 relations between the United States and the Carranza government had deteriorated so badly that Carranzistas began to make hit-and-run raids across the border. President Wilson mobilized large numbers of the National Guard, and U.S. troop strength along the border reached 158,000 men. Wishing to stabilize relations with the Carranza government and persuaded that Villa, although still at large, no longer posed a threat to the United States, President Wilson accordingly ordered the withdrawal of the Punitive Expedition in early 1917. The last of the troops withdrew on February 5, 1917. Villa never raided the United States again.

U.S.-Mexican Relations and American Business Interests

After the U.S.-Mexican War of 1846–1848 (Chapter 10), the United States began doing business with conservative elements in Mexico; transactions included the Gadsden Purchase of 1853, through which the United States acquired the territory that is now southern Arizona and southern New Mexico. In 1855, when Benito Juárez overthrew the brutal Santa Anna regime, American popular sentiment favored Juárez and the democratic reforms he promised, but the U.S. government was nevertheless quick to recognize Santa Anna's conservative regime when it again seized power in 1857. American business interests and the government were far more comfortable dealing with authoritarian regimes than with liberal revolutionary ones. When conservative and dictatorial Porfirio Díaz assumed the Mexican presidency (he would rule from 1877 to

Pancho Villa
(1878–1923)

Born to a farmhand, Pancho Villa (born Doroteo Arango) was orphaned in early childhood. After his sister was raped by one of the owners of the estate on which he worked, Villa killed the man and fled to the mountains, where he grew to young adulthood as a bandit and a fugitive.

Villa joined Francisco Madero's uprising against Porfirio Díaz in 1909 and soon emerged as a naturally charismatic leader and guerrilla fighter of great skill. His life in the mountains had given him intimate knowledge of the Mexican back-country, and he brought into Madero's service the equivalent of an entire division of guerillas.

Madero leagued with the brutal Victoriano Huerta, and in 1912, fearing Villa's popularity, Huerta ordered him executed. Madero intervened and commuted the sentence to a prison term. Villa escaped in November 1912 and found refuge in the United States. When Madero fell to an assassin in 1913, Villa returned to Mexico and quickly assembled a new paramilitary force of several thousand men: the División del Norte. He joined forces with Venustiano Carranza, Huerta's rival and, after winning a number of victories against Huerta, was rewarded by Carranza with an appointment as governor of the state of Chihuahua in December 1913. After Carranza and Villa achieved their final triumph over Huerta in June 1914, the two rode triumphantly together into Mexico City.

The Villa-Carranza partnership did not last long. The men soon fell into conflict, and Villa fled Mexico City in company with revolutionary leader Emiliano Zapata in December 1914. Carranza repeatedly defeated Villa, forcing him and Zapata to take refuge in Mexico's northern mountains. It was during this period that Villa executed seventeen Americans at Santa Isabel (January 1916) and raided Columbus, New Mexico (March 1916), provoking President Wilson to launch the Punitive Expedition against him.

The combination of Villa's guerrilla skill, his familiarity with the countryside, and the intense loyalty he commanded among the Mexican peasantry made him an elusive target. Pershing and his force never ran Villa to ground—although they did badly maul his army, especially his top officer corps.

Following the overthrow of the Carranza government in 1920, Villa was pardoned by the new Mexican government upon his pledge to withdraw from politics forever. Although he complied, he was assassinated in 1923. His killers have never been identified.

1880 and again from 1884 to 1911), U.S. government and business alike welcomed the increased stability of the Mexican government and its economy. American funding was poured into Mexico as Díaz made many guarantees aimed at protecting investors. Thanks to U.S. investment, Mexico modernized its railroad system and public works, but many Mexicans feared that the infrastructure improvements masked a widening gap between Mexico's rich and poor and caused overdependence on the United States. Many nationalists felt their country's sovereignty was rapidly eroding.

Despite a period of relative prosperity, the growing social discontent in Mexico erupted into the Mexican Revolution of 1910, a watershed event in U.S.-Mexican relations. Wishing to protect U.S. financial interests in Mexico, President Wilson sent the military south of the border twice: to Veracruz in 1914 (discussed below) and on the Punitive Expedition in 1916–1917.

These interventions did little to help American business interests in Mexico. Mexico's reform constitution of 1917 gave the state the right to expropriate property owned by foreign nations and nationals—provided that the seizure was judged useful for improving social conditions. In February 1918 President Carranza revoked all foreign-held titles to Mexican oil wells, but exempted many U.S.-held properties and claims to Mexican natural resources. After Carranza was assassinated in 1920, President Wilson chose not to recognize the new president, Alvaro Obregón, who Wilson feared would extend the ownership prohibitions and apply them retroactively to all U.S. holdings. Withholding recognition of the new government bought sufficient time for the administration of President Warren G. Harding, who succeeded Wilson, to negotiate the Bucareli Agreements of August 1923, in which Mexico promised to honor foreign ownership rights that existed before 1917. Harding's successor, Calvin Coolidge, responded to this concession by reestablishing diplomatic relations with Mexico.

The Veracruz Decision (1914)

By 1914 Victoriano Huerta was struggling to ward off threats from radical Emiliano Zapata in the south and moderate Venustiano Carranza in the north. Carranza and his forces were about ten miles outside Tampico, Tamaulipas, on March 26, 1914. Held by the Huerta government, this town was home to many U.S. citizens who worked in the oil industry. To protect these interests, a number of U.S. Navy warships, under Rear Admiral Henry T. Mayo, rode at anchor off Tampico. When Carranza laid siege to Tampico, the navy vessels launched their whaleboats to evacuate U.S. nationals. With fuel running low, the commander of the gunboat USS *Dolphin* arranged to pick up oil from a warehouse on April 9. The warehouse was located near Iturbide Bridge, which was heavily defended by Huerta's forces. When nine U.S. sailors approached the warehouse in a whaleboat, Huerta's troops confronted them. Neither side spoke the other's language, and, at gunpoint, the Mexican troops marched the sailors to their regimental headquarters.

The sailors were soon released, but Admiral Mayo demanded a formal apology. The local Mexican commander complied, but failed to follow Mayo's further demand that he hoist the U.S. flag on Mexican soil and render a twenty-one-gun salute. Seeing an occasion to demonstrate the resolve of the United States to protect its financial interests in the area, President Wilson on April 20 addressed Congress on the **Tampico Affair** and secured approval for an armed

Wilson on the Tampico Affair, 1914

Subsequent explanations and formal apologies did not and could not alter the popular impression, which it is possible it had been the object of the Huertista authorities to create, that the government of the United States was being singled out, and might be singled out with impunity, for slights and affronts in retaliation for its refusal to recognize the pretensions of General Huerta to be regarded as the constitutional provisional president of the Republic of Mexico. The manifest danger of such a situation was that such offenses might grow from bad to worse until something happened of so gross and intolerable a sort as to lead directly and inevitably to armed conflict. It was necessary that the apologies of General Huerta and his representatives should go much fur-

ther, that they should be such to attract the attention of the whole population to their significance, and such as to impress upon General Huerta himself the necessity of seeing to it that no further occasion for explanations and professed regret should arise.

I, therefore, felt it my duty to sustain Admiral Mayo . . . and to insist that the flag of the United States should be saluted in such a way as to indicate a new spirit and attitude on the part of the Huertistas. Such a salute General Huerta has refused, and I have come to ask your approval and support in the course I now purpose to pursue.

Excerpted from "The Tampico Affair," in *Annals of America*, ed. Mortimer J. Adler and Charles Van Doren (Chicago: Encyclopaedia Britannica, 1976), 13:469.

invasion. Troops under Major General Frederick Funston occupied Veracruz for the next seven months, creating among the Mexican people much resentment toward the United States.

Villa's Reasons for the Raid on Columbus, New Mexico

Villa's reasons for raiding the United States are difficult to determine with certainty. Many historians believe that Villa decided to execute seventeen U.S. citizens in the Mexican town of Santa Isabel in January 1916 in a desperate attempt to demonstrate that Carranza did not control northern Mexico. This explanation, however, does not adequately account for why,

Brigadier General John J. Pershing (pictured in the foreground) and Lieutenant James Collins cross the Santa Maria River in Mexico in pursuit of Pancho Villa in 1916.

two months later, he crossed the border into Columbus, New Mexico, and fought with civilians and soldiers from the nearby Thirteenth Cavalry. Certainly he must have known that the March 9 raid would not go unanswered. Some historians argue that he wanted to exact personal revenge against a country that had failed to support him. Others theorize that he intended to provoke an American intervention in Mexican affairs that would make Carranza look weak and subservient to the United States. Yet others maintain that Villa had a master plan to provoke a war between Mexico and the United States that would destabilize and ultimately unseat the Carranza government.

The Punitive Expedition

Following the Columbus raid, President Wilson had little choice but to authorize an expedition to hunt down Pancho Villa. While Villa had been fighting Huerta, whose corruption and cruelty reminded

many Americans of the Spanish misrule of Cuba that helped ignite the Spanish-American War (Chapter 29), Villa had emerged as a Robin Hood figure, popular on both sides of the border. But his raid on Columbus brought universal condemnation throughout the United States, even as many in Mexico saw him as an avenger of decades of *yanqui* oppression.

The Punitive Expedition lasted eleven months and significantly damaged the already precarious relations between Mexico and the United States. During that time, Pershing and his 15,000 infantrymen and cavalrymen failed even to catch sight of Villa himself. As a tired and frustrated Pershing telegraphed to Washington, "Villa is everywhere, but Villa is nowhere."

Yet the expedition was not a military failure. Villa's army was badly mauled, and his top commanders killed. Whatever else Pershing failed to accomplish, Pancho Villa never attempted another raid into the United States. At the time, however, many Mexicans pointed to Villa with pride as the only military leader since the War of 1812 to invade the continental United States.

BIBLIOGRAPHY

Eisenhower, John S. D. *Intervention! The United States and the Mexican Revolution, 1913–1917.* New York: W. W. Norton, 1995.

Stout, Joseph A. *Border Conflict: Villistas, Carranzistas and the Punitive Expedition, 1915–1920.* Fort Worth: Texas Christian University Press, 1999.

Tompkins, Frank. *Chasing Villa: The Last Campaign of the U.S. Cavalry.* Silver City, N.M.: High Lonesome Books, 1996.

CHAPTER 34

WORLD WAR I

(U.S. PARTICIPATION, 1917–1918)

At Issue

World War I—then known as the Great War—had been under way for three years when the United States joined the fight on April 6, 1917. The war was triggered by the assassination of Austrian archduke Franz Ferdinand and his wife, Grand Duchess Sophie, in Sarajevo, the capital of Bosnia-Herzegovina, on June 28, 1914. Serbia, which was blamed for the assassination, rebuffed Austria-Hungary's immoderate "July Ultimatum," starting a chain reaction of treaty obligations among most European nations. The European nations fought either with the Allies (leading members were France, Britain, Russia, and—later—Italy) or the Central Powers (leading members were Germany, Austria-Hungary, and Turkey). The United States, after several violations of its rights as a neutral, declared war on the Central Powers ostensibly to defend its neutrality rights but also, according to President Woodrow Wilson, to participate in a crusade to make the world "safe for democracy."

The Conflict

Although the United States did not enter World War I until April 6, 1917, it is important to understand the course of the war before then.

The European War

At the beginning of the twentieth century, Europe was tensely bound by two hostile systems of alliance: the Triple Alliance of Germany, Austria-Hungary, and Italy versus the Triple Entente of France, Russia, and Britain. These two major alliances were supplemented by a host of lesser (often secret) agreements, which effectively committed the major signatories to aid various smaller nations should they become involved in war. The system of alliances did not produce a more secure Europe as intended; rather it virtually ensured that a relatively minor incident would eventually trigger a major war.

The requisite incident was the June 28, 1914, assassination of Archduke Franz Ferdinand and his wife, Grand Duchess Sophie, of Austria-Hungary in Sarajevo, the capital of Bosnia-Herzegovina. The assassin, student Gavrilo Princip, had ties to a Serbian-based secret society (the "Black Hand"), which advocated the liberation of the small Slavic states (including Bosnia-Herzegovina) from the Austro-Hungarian Empire. Although there was no evidence of official Serbian complicity in the assassination, Count Leopold von Berchtold, Austria-Hungary's foreign minister, seized the opportunity to punish Serbia (recently independent from the Austro-Hungarian Empire), with the intent of crushing the nationalist movement that was sweeping the Balkans. Berchtold presented an ultimatum to Serbia that would have effectively ended that nation's sovereignty. When Serbia balked, Austria-Hungary declared war on July 29, 1914, triggering a domino effect of alliances and treaties. By early August Britain, France, Belgium, and Russia (the Allies) were pitted against Germany and Austria-Hungary (the Central Powers). Later, Italy would side with the Allies, while Turkey and some lesser states would side with the Central Powers.

Nearly surrounded by enemies, Germany and Austria-Hungary fought a two-front war, facing Russia in the east and France and Britain in the west. In the opening weeks of the war, Austria-Hungary faltered on the Eastern Front, but Germany devastated the Russian armies. Meanwhile, Germany advanced deep into France, coming within thirty miles of Paris. After the war's first month, with supply lines stretched thin, the Germans halted their westward advance, and the Western Front soon hardened into a complex of opposing trenches that extended from the Belgian coast in the north to the Swiss border in the south. For the next four years the war on the Western Front remained strategically deadlocked. New weapons like the machine gun led to unprecedented casualties as the opposing armies repeatedly proved incapable of taking their opponents' territory.

American Involvement Begins

By April 1917 every major Allied offensive had failed, and the Central Powers were in possession of huge tracts of Allied territory. The war was still deadlocked, but the Allies were clearly weakening. The United States declared war on Germany on April 6, 1917, but the U.S. entry did not bring immediate relief. Building up, training, and mobilizing U.S. forces required many months, during which the commander in charge of the American Expeditionary Force (AEF), General John J. Pershing, resisted French and British demands to commit his forces to battle piecemeal and under foreign command.

Allied Desperation

In late 1917 only 175,000 U.S. troops were in Europe, even as Germany launched a series of offensives against the Western Front. Complicating matters was the outbreak of the Russian revolutions of 1917, bringing to power the Bolshevik (Communist)

CHRONOLOGY OF U.S. PARTICIPATION IN WORLD WAR I

1915

May 7 A German U-boat sinks the British liner *Lusitania*. The loss of American lives creates a U.S.-German diplomatic crisis.

1917

Feb. 1 Germany resumes unrestricted submarine warfare.

Feb. 3 The United States severs diplomatic relations with Germany.

Mar. 1 The Zimmermann Telegram, a German proposal of an alliance with Mexico against the United States, is revealed to the public.

Apr. 6 The United States declares war on Germany.

May 12 General John J. Pershing is named commander of the American Expeditionary Force.

1918

Jan. 8 President Woodrow Wilson makes his "Fourteen Points" speech.

May 28 U.S. troops win their first major action, the Battle of Cantigny.

May 30–
June 26 The Battles of Château-Thierry and Belleau Woods are fought.

July 18–
Aug. 5 Franco-American forces push back the Marne salient during the Aisne-Marne Offensive.

Sept. 12–13 U.S. troops drive the Germans out of the Saint-Mihiel salient.

Sept. 26–
Nov. 11 The Meuse-Argonne Offensive is fought; it is the final Franco-American offensive of the war.

Oct. 6 In a message to President Wilson, Prince Max of Baden, Germany's new chancellor, requests an armistice.

Nov. 11 The Armistice is declared; fighting ends at 11:00 a.m.

1919

Jan. 18–
June 28 President Woodrow Wilson leads negotiation over the Treaty of Versailles, which, ultimately, falls far short of his aspirations.

John J. Pershing

(1860–1948)

John Joseph Pershing was born in Laclede, Missouri, where he grew up on a farm. From 1878 to 1882, he taught school and then obtained an appointment to West Point. Upon graduating in 1886, he was commissioned a second lieutenant in the Sixth Cavalry, and he served in the American West during the late phase of the Indian Wars.

From 1891 to 1895, he taught at the University of Nebraska as commandant of cadets. He was promoted to first lieutenant in 1892 and was permitted extended leave to earn a law degree, which was awarded in June 1893. Pershing next saw service during October 1895–October 1896 with the Tenth Cavalry, an African American regiment of "Buffalo Soldiers," which, like all such segregated units, was commanded by white officers. As a result of this assignment, Pershing earned the nickname "Black Jack." He left the Tenth Cavalry when General Nelson A. Miles selected him as his aide.

After stints as a tactics instructor on the West Point faculty (1897) and as quartermaster of the Tenth Cavalry (April 1898), Pershing fought at El Caney–San Juan Hill (July 1–3, 1898) in the Spanish-American War, but fell ill with malaria and was sent back to the United States for convalescence; he was assigned "quiet duty" at the War Department in August 1898.

In 1899 Pershing requested a posting to the Philippines, where he was engaged in the pacification of the Moros (Chapter 30). He returned to Washington, D.C., and staff duty shortly before his marriage to Helen Francis Warren on January 25, 1905. From March 1905 to September 1906, he was posted to Japan as a military attaché and observer in the Russo-Japanese War (see Chapter 39). This assignment brought him into contact with President Theodore Roosevelt, who, impressed with Captain Pershing, ordered his promotion—in a single step—to brigadier general on September 20, 1906.

Pershing returned to the Philippines to command a brigade at Fort McKinley, near Manila, in December 1906. After briefly visiting his home in the United States, Pershing accepted an appointment as military commander of Moro Province in November 1909. He served in this post until early 1914.

Pershing returned to the United States in April 1914 to take command of the Eighth Brigade in San Francisco, but was almost immediately dispatched to the Texas-Mexico border region as the disorder and violence of civil war in Mexico spilled into the United States. On August 27, 1915, while Pershing was serving in Texas, a fire swept through his family's quarters in the Presidio at San Francisco, killing his wife and three of their daughters.

On March 9, 1916, the revolutionary bandit Pancho Villa raided Columbus, New Mexico, killing ten civilians and fourteen soldiers. This prompted President Woodrow Wilson to send Pershing on a "Punitive Expedition" to invade Mexico in pursuit of Villa (Chapter 33). Although Pershing failed to capture Villa, the expedition killed his chief lieutenants and suppressed all of Villa's activities north of the border before the mission ended on January 27, 1917.

On May 12, 1917, Pershing was named commander-in-charge of the American Expeditionary Force (AEF), which was to be sent to Europe to fight in World War I. He created a U.S. Army of unprecedented scale and prepared it for combat on an extraordinary scale. After leading U.S. forces throughout the war, he was greeted on his return to the United States in 1919 as a hero. He was promoted to a rank created specifically for him— General of the Armies, which outranks five-star generals and has been held only by Pershing and (posthumously) by George Washington. He turned down many entreaties to enter politics and remained in the military as army chief of staff (appointed July 21, 1921), serving in this post until he retired on September 13, 1924. With the assistance of a young lieutenant colonel Dwight Eisenhower, Pershing wrote his memoirs in 1931.

regime, which withdrew Russia from the war on December 15, 1917, leaving Germany free to send virtually all of its troops to the Western Front. The German generalissimo, Erich Ludendorff, intended to destroy the British army and thereby force the French to negotiate a peace favorable to Germany. The first two Ludendorff offensives—on the Somme (March 21–April 5, 1918) and the Lys River (April 9–29)—resulted in nearly one million casualties. In the third, on the Aisne River (May 27–June 6), the Germans broke through the Allied forward defenses, advancing to Château-Thierry on the Marne River, just fifty miles outside Paris.

U.S. Forces Join the Fight

U.S. troops played a small role in resisting the second Ludendorff offensive in spring 1918, but the first significant U.S. military action occurred on April 20, 1918, in France near Seicheprey along the Saint-Mihiel salient where German troops easily overran American positions. Undaunted by this initial failure, Pershing rushed to reinforce the French along the Marne River. In the meantime, Major General Robert Lee Bullard launched the first American offensive of the war, against a heavily fortified German position in the village of Cantigny. On May 28, the U.S. First Division drove the Germans out. Over the next two days, the Americans repulsed German counterattacks, winning a victory that boosted Allied morale and made up for the defeat at Seicheprey.

Château-Thierry

When the third Ludendorff offensive reached Château-Thierry, the U.S. Second and Third Divisions prevented the Germans from crossing the Marne on June 1, then, with the French, counterattacked with great success.

Belleau Wood

While the U.S. Army distinguished itself at Cantigny and Château-Thierry, the U.S. Marine Corps performed spectacularly in taking Belleau Wood, a critical approach to Paris. Moving in advance of the army's Second Division, the marines marched across a wheat field swept by machine gun fire to take Belleau Wood. The casualties suffered on June 6, 1918, were the heaviest single-day losses in Marine Corps history until the marines took the Japanese-held island of Tarawa in World War II (Chapter 36). The battle, which started on June 1, did not end until June 26, when Ludendorff's advance was stopped cold.

Major Phase of U.S. Participation

Ludendorff's fourth offensive came at Noyon and Montdidier, just southeast of Cantigny and northwest of Château-Thierry. A Franco-American counterattack halted the advance of the German Eighteenth Army by June 11. On June 12, the Franco-American force repulsed an attack by the German Seventh Army.

By this time, more than a quarter million Americans were arriving in France each month, and by June 1918 seven of the twenty-five U.S. divisions in France were in action at the front. In desperation, Ludendorff mounted his fifth offensive in five months. His principal objective was to destroy the British army in Flanders, Belgium, but he launched a preliminary offensive against the French and Americans, focusing on the fortified city of Reims, France. The French halted their attackers during the night of July 14–15, but west of Reims the Germans crossed the Marne River with fourteen divisions. The Americans blocked the advance, earning the U.S. Third Division the nickname "Rock of the Marne."

Second Battle of the Marne

Ludendorff's five offensives cost more Allied than German lives, but had nonetheless failed in their objectives. On July 17, 1918, the French commander, Ferdinand Foch, observed that Ludendorff was pulling troops out of the Marne sector—which threatened Paris—to send them north, against the British forces of Sir Douglas Haig. Foch knew that such a massive movement made the Germans vulnerable, and he exploited the opportunity. Foch concentrated his available forces to attack after Ludendorff had withdrawn some troops, but before he could gather enough of them in the north to overwhelm Haig.

The high-stakes counteroffensive was launched on July 18, 1918, with four French armies and eight U.S. divisions. Ludendorff, who had already withdrawn some troops from the sector, began a general withdrawal on the night of July 18. The Allies advanced against his withdrawing forces through August 5, thereby gaining victory in the Second Battle of the Marne and triumphantly ending the Aisne-Marne Offensive.

Amiens Offensive

Soon after, Field Marshal Sir Douglas Haig mounted an Anglo-French attack east of Amiens in northwestern France, along the Somme River. The Allies rolled over the Germans, taking more than 15,000 prisoners on August 8, 1918. By August 22, the German positions crumbled, and Ludendorff was forced to withdraw to the Hindenburg Line, his last-ditch defensive position, which was located twenty-five miles east of what had been the main system of German trenches.

Saint-Mihiel Salient

The U.S. First Army, with the French II Colonial Corps attached to it, was dispatched to the Saint-Mihiel sector on August 30, 1918, to drive out the German forces that had held it since 1915. General Pershing learned that Ludendorff had ordered withdrawal from the salient, to begin on September 11. Although this would relinquish Saint-Mihiel to the Allies, it would also preserve the German army intact. Pershing, therefore, was determined to attack. On the morning of September 12, sixteen U.S. divisions attacked, supported by French artillery and tanks as

well as American, French, Italian, and Portuguese pilots flying airplanes under the command of U.S. military air pioneer Colonel William "Billy" Mitchell.

After a spectacular thirty-six-hour battle, the Germans surrendered en masse. The reduction of the Saint-Mihiel salient involved a half million American troops and was the biggest U.S. military operation since the Civil War (Chapter 17).

Meuse-Argonne Offensive

The Saint-Mihiel sector secured, Pershing, without pausing to rest and refit, moved the entire First Army sixty miles north to the Verdun sector to take part in the Meuse-Argonne Offensive, which spanned September 26 through the Armistice, November 11. Marshal Ferdinand Foch, the French supreme commander of the Allied forces, proposed sending the Franco-American force in a drive that would gain control of German supply lines along the Western Front.

Working with his young aide, Colonel George C. Marshall (who would go on to become U.S. Army chief of staff in World War II), Pershing transferred an entire 500,000-troop army, by night, into position for the surprise attack that would initiate the offensive. It began on the morning of September 26 against heavily fortified German defenses. The drive slowed by early October as the dense Argonne Forest offered no room for maneuver, but by the end of the month, the final German line broke.

Toward the Armistice

After taking the Argonne Forest, U.S. forces raced through German positions in the Meuse Valley during the first eleven days of November. The U.S. First Division was about to take Sedan on November 6, when Pershing's headquarters ordered a halt so that the honor of conquering that city would go to the French. On November 10, the Second U.S Army launched a drive toward the village of Montmédy, breaking it off the next day at 11:00 a.m. sharp, the hour of Armistice.

"He Kept Us Out of War": The Wilson Platform of 1916

Woodrow Wilson won the presidential election of 1912, easily beating third-party candidate and former president Theodore Roosevelt and Republican incumbent William Howard Taft. Wilson's impressive plurality was propelled by his promise to reform American government, which he did to a remarkable degree—possibly too well, because by the end of his first term, many Americans were clearly tired of the idealistic rigors of Wilsonian

Woodrow Wilson

(1856–1924)

Thomas Woodrow Wilson—he would rarely use his first name—was born in Staunton, Virginia, the son of a Presbyterian minister. He was educated at Princeton University (then called the College of New Jersey) and the University of Virginia Law School. After briefly practicing law in Atlanta, Georgia, he embarked on graduate study in political science, earning his doctorate at Johns Hopkins University and beginning an academic career. Wilson rose to particular prominence on the faculty of his alma mater, Princeton, and became that institution's president in 1902. He introduced sweeping academic reforms, which raised the sleepy college to the status of a world-class university. This garnered national attention, and in 1910 the Democratic Party tapped him as their candidate for New Jersey governor. Wilson brought to corrupt New Jersey politics the same reforming zeal he had brought to Princeton. He asserted independence from the party conservatives as well as from the party machine and ran on a Progressive platform, very much in the mold of Theodore Roosevelt.

The nation took notice. Nominated for president at the 1912 Democratic convention, Wilson campaigned on a program he called the "New Freedom," which stressed individualism, states' rights, and Progressive reform. From the White House, he quickly shepherded through Congress three landmark pieces of legislation: the Underwood Act, which dramatically reduced tariffs; a graduated federal income tax, which required a constitutional amendment; and the Federal Reserve Act, which provided the simultaneously more stable and more elastic money supply sorely needed by the national economy.

Although he ran for reelection with the slogan "He kept us out of war," within months of beginning his second term, Wilson began to steer the nation toward war, finally asking Congress on April 2, 1917, for a declaration. During the war, Wilson worked to mobilize a major American effort, which introduced into American life distinctively non-Wilsonian measures designed to promote the war and suppress dissent. Yet Wilson also maintained a high degree of idealism; he presented his famous "Fourteen Points" to Congress in January 1918. When the Armistice came on November 11, 1918, Wilson took a leading role in crafting the Treaty of Versailles and the League of Nations.

Wilson was hailed in Europe—though the Treaty of Versailles fell far short of the just and magnanimous document he had hoped for—but he was far less successful in his own country after the war. The midterm elections of 1918 had shifted the balance in Congress to the Republicans, and the U.S. Senate rejected both the Treaty of Versailles and the League of Nations. Unwilling to compromise, Wilson embarked on a national tour to mobilize public opinion in favor of the treaty and the League. While delivering a speech in Pueblo, Colorado, the exhausted Wilson collapsed. He was rushed back to Washington, where he suffered a stroke and served out the remainder of his second term as a semi-invalid. The League of Nations never won acceptance, and Wilson, sick and embittered, died in 1924, three years after leaving the White House to Warren G. Harding.

reform. The 1916 election brought no landslide. Wilson narrowly edged out Republican candidate Charles Evans Hughes by just twenty-three electoral votes and somewhat more than half a million popular votes. Most pundits agreed that Wilson had eked out this victory largely on the strength of his campaign slogan: "He kept us out of war."

On that first Tuesday of November 1916, when they went to the polls, most Americans saw the "Great War" not as a profound ideological crusade, but as a peculiarly European contagion, spread by a tangle of Old World tyrannies and corrupt, interlocking treaties. Americans were happy to have no part in the struggle.

U.S. Neutrality

During his first term, President Wilson publicly insisted on maintaining American neutrality in the "European War." This was not only politically prudent, it was profitable: as a neutral power, the United States was entitled (indeed, obliged by international law and custom) to trade impartially with all of the belligerents.

President Wilson sought to bolster the legal and political dimensions of neutrality. He had repeatedly offered his services as a mediator to negotiate an end to the war (see "Mediation Attempts," below), and he redoubled these efforts following his 1916 reelec-

tion. What the American government sought to bring about, he explained in the ideological manifesto he presented to the Senate on January 22, 1917, was **Peace without Victory.** He declared that the United States must persuade the belligerents to end the deadlocked war in a manner that would be beneficial for all parties and, indeed, for all humanity.

The Proportion of Trade Shifts

Impartial neutrality was more easily proclaimed than actually achieved. The actions of the Central Powers, particularly Germany, made it increasingly difficult to avoid taking sides. Germany's declarations of war on France and Russia, entirely unprovoked, were impossible to justify. Germany's violation of Belgian neutrality was brutal and infamous—and its brutality, real as it was, was greatly magnified by British propaganda.

The flow of trade from the United States increasingly turned away from the Central Powers and toward the Allies. Partly, this was motivated by a growing American revulsion against the actions of "the Hun," but, even more, it was the product of a collective business decision among U.S. manufacturers and financial institutions. High demand, an ample supply of gold, favorable shipping, and the realities of geography made dealing with the Allies far more reliable and profitable than doing business

Wilson's "Peace without Victory" Speech, 1917

Is the present war a struggle for a just and secure peace, or only for a new balance of power? If it be only a struggle for a new balance of power, who will guarantee, who can guarantee the stable equilibrium of the new arrangement? Only a tranquil Europe can be a stable Europe. There must be, not a balance of power but a community of power; not organized rivalries but an organized, common peace. . . .

I am proposing that all nations henceforth avoid entangling alliances which would draw them into competitions of power, catch them in a net of intrigue

and selfish rivalry, and disturb their own affairs with influences intruded from without. There is no entangling alliance in a concert of power. When all unite to act in the same sense and with the same purpose, all act in the common interest and are free to live their own lives under a common protection.

Excerpted from "Woodrow Wilson: Peace without Victory," in *Annals of America,* ed. Mortimer J. Adler and Charles Van Doren (Chicago: Encyclopaedia Britannica, 1976), 14: 65–69.

with Germany and the other Central Powers. More-over, financial and business interests increasingly believed that the Allies would win, which made them a far better credit risk than the Central Powers. By 1917 American firms had done some $2 billion in business with the Allies, and U.S. banks had made $2.5 billion in loans to them. In contrast, American banks had loaned a mere $45 million to Germany. Inexorably, the American economy was becoming wedded to the Allied cause.

For its part, Germany's conduct of the war offered nothing to discourage the shift. At every turn, Germany seemed to violate some rule of "civilized" warfare—bombing British civilians, using poison gas at Ypres, and, of most concern to American business, unleashing unrestricted submarine (U-boat) warfare against commercial shipping.

President Wilson was not immune to the growing favoritism. While he responded to every German violation of American neutrality rights, he consistently overlooked British and French violations, the most egregious of which were the blockade of Germany and the mining of the North Sea. By the end of 1916, American "neutrality" was by no means impartial; the United States claimed the rights of a neutral, but increasingly favored the Allies.

Public Opinion in a Nation of Immigrants

The Anglo-Franco bias that characterized American industrialists, financiers, and the Wilson administration was not reflected in the masses of the American people. The nation's very large German American community was, of course, pro-German. It raised significant charitable funds for the Fatherland, and even agitated for U.S. entry into the war on the side of the kaiser. The even larger Irish American community tended to side with any nation that fought the hated English. To most other Americans—those who did not run a bank, a steel mill, or a munitions plant—it made little difference who won this "Great War," just as long as the United States stayed out of it. Such public opinion prevailed at least until the end of 1916.

Loss of the *Lusitania*

Throughout American history, the foundation of U.S. sovereignty and the nation's rights as a neutral had been the principle of freedom of the seas. The War of 1812 (Chapter 6) had been fought (ostensibly, at least) over this very issue. To continue doing business with the European powers, freedom of the seas was essential. Thus, Germany's policy of unrestricted submarine warfare was a great concern. Not surprisingly, therefore, the first major challenge to Wilson's neutrality policy was the May 7, 1915, sinking of the British liner *Lusitania* by a German U-boat, with the loss of 1,198 lives, including 124 Americans.

The *Lusitania* incident heightened anti-German sentiment in the United States. President Wilson steered a careful course, writing a stern note of diplomatic protest to the Germans. War hawks, such as Theodore Roosevelt, condemned the note as a weak response, whereas pacifists, most prominently Wilson's secretary of state, Williams Jennings Bryan, thought the note blatantly provocative. After Wilson penned a second note, Bryan resigned in protest.

Wilson's notes brought no immediate result. In August another passenger ship, the *Arabic,* was sunk. But after this, finally anxious to avert U.S. entry into the war, Germany's Kaiser Wilhelm II ordered an end to unrestricted submarine warfare—meaning that U-boats were required to surface, give warning, and allow passengers to abandon ship before opening fire.

Mediation Attempts

If Secretary of State Bryan resigned because he sincerely believed Wilson wanted to enter the Great War, he was mistaken—at least at the time of his resignation. In 1915–1916 what the president wanted was the United States to shape a peace that would influence the world.

Colonel Edward M. House, a Texas politician and highly influential adviser to the president, frequently served as the Wilson's quasi-official personal envoy. At the outbreak of the Great War, House became the

In Three Parts—24 Pages.
PART I—TELEGRAPH SHEET—10 PAGES

The Los Angeles Times

1781 1915

Liberty Under Law—Equal Rights—True Industrial Freedom

SATURDAY MORNING,   MAY 8, 1915

PRICE 2½ CENTS

OVER A THOUSAND LIVES PROBABLY LOST
WHEN THE GERMANS SANK THE LUSITANIA.

"Strict Accountability."
SUSPEND JUDGMENT, SAYS PRESIDENT WILSON.

Executive Faces Necessity of Making Good War Zone Protest to Germany.

United States Authorities will Make a Thorough Inquiry into the Number of Americans Lost on the Lusitania and will Include in Whatever Representations are Made Some Other Grievance.

Two Views of Ship that Was.

Retribution.
FIVE TO SIX HUNDRED SURVIVORS LANDED ALONG THE IRISH COAST.

Two Torpedoes Fired, Without a Note of Warning, into the Steel Sides of the Huge Cunarder.

Passengers at Luncheon, Confident that the Swift Atlantic Liner Could Elude Any War Craft Afloat, Taken Completely by Surprise — England's Fastest Merchant Vessel Submerged in Fifteen Minutes.

[BY ATLANTIC CABLE AND A.P.]

QUEENSTOWN, May 8, 4:24 a.m.—Survivors of the Lusitania who have arrived here estimate that only about 650 of those aboard the steamer were saved and only a small proportion of those rescued were saloon passengers.

LONDON, May 8.—Only a few of the first-class passengers on board the Lusitania, sunk today by a German submarine, were saved. Most of them remained on board, thinking the great ship would stay afloat. Trawlers arriving at Queenstown have about one hundred bodies on board.

WASHINGTON, May 8.—A dispatch to the State Department early today from American Consul Frost at Queenstown stated that the total number of survivors of the Lusitania was about 700. The Consul's dispatch gave a partial list of American survivors, but did not say definitely whether any Americans had been lost.

LONDON, May 8, 5:58 a.m.—Signals have been received at Queenstown that an armed trawler believed to be the Heron and two fishing trawlers are bringing in 100 more bodies. The Cunard line agent states that the total number of persons aboard the Lusitania was 2160.

LONDON, May 8, 4:42 a.m.—The Times' Queenstown correspondent says that some of the survivors who have arrived there report that Alfred Vanderbilt was drowned. Inquiry failed to develop any trace of Charles Frohman, who is believed lost.

The front page of the Los Angeles Times *on May 8, 1915, announces that a German submarine sank the* Lusitania *the previous day and features an image of the British liner. The practice of unrestricted submarine warfare by Germany in World War I challenged President Wilson's neutrality policy and edged the United States closer to entering the war on the side of the Allies.*

administration's expert on the conflict. Early in 1916 Wilson sent House to London and Paris to sound out Allied leaders on the prospect of U.S. mediation between the belligerents. Most historians now believe that House was not up to the task. Although he was earnest, he was unsophisticated in the ways of European diplomacy. Almost certainly, Wilson would have better served the nation and the world by making a more formal effort at mediation. As it was, House's talks with British foreign secretary Sir Edward Grey produced the **House-Grey Memorandum** (composed by Grey) of February 22, 1916, which embodied Grey's understanding that the

United States might enter the war if Germany rejected Wilson's mediation, but that the right to initiate U.S. mediation rested with Britain. That is, Grey put the emphasis on the possibility of U.S. entry rather than on Wilson's offer to mediate.

House's ambiguous proposal to Grey was a genuine effort at initiating binding mediation, yet on another level, it marked the first step toward U.S. entry into the war. As the presidential elections of 1916 approached, Wilson pulled back, fearing that American mediation could set off a controversy that would seem to contradict his he-kept-us-out-of-war reelection platform.

The House-Grey Memorandum, 1916

(Confidential)
Colonel House told me that President Wilson was ready, on hearing from France and England that the moment was opportune, to propose that a Conference should be summoned to put an end to the war. Should the Allies accept this proposal, and should Germany refuse it, the United States would probably enter the war against Germany. Colonel House expressed the opinion that, if such a Conference met, it would secure peace on terms not unfavourable to the Allies; and, if it failed to secure peace, the United States would [probably] leave the Conference as a belligerent on the side of the Allies, if Germany was unreasonable.

Excerpted from "October 1915–February 1916: The House-Grey Memorandum," in the World War I Document Archive, Brigham Young University Library, www.lib.byu.edu/~rdh/wwi/1916/housgrey.html.

Even after his reelection, Wilson delayed resumption of his mediation efforts. Then, on December 12, 1916, bolstered by a German victory over Romania, German chancellor Theobald von Bethmann Hollweg proposed his own peace terms. They were, in a word, outrageous. Bethmann proposed the German annexation of Belgium as well as the occupied portion of northeastern France— approximately 10 percent of that nation. The unreasonableness of the proposal moved Wilson to intervene on December 18. He invited the combatants to state their war aims unambiguously. This seemed a reasonable first step toward "peace without victory," yet Secretary of State Robert Lansing secretly encouraged the Allies to propose "war aims" that were as extreme as those enunciated by Germany. Thus, the Germans rightly suspected collusion between the Wilson administration and the Allies. Although Germany agreed to negotiate, the German government refused to budge from its December 12 statement, and by mid-January 1917, hopes for peace evaporated.

Lansing's behind-the-scenes manipulations suggest that Wilson was less interested in creating peace than he had claimed. Some historians believe that he was instead already preparing a case for American entry into the war, by setting up Germany to reject a "legitimate" attempt at a negotiated peace.

Preparedness

On January 9, 1917, Kaiser Wilhelm II ordered the resumption of unrestricted submarine warfare effective February 1. President Wilson severed diplomatic relations with Germany on February 3, 1917, after a U.S. warship, the *Housatonic,* was torpedoed and sunk. On February 26, he asked Congress for the authority to arm U.S.-flagged merchant vessels and to take other military measures to protect American commerce. Wilson branded the new policy "armed neutrality."

This was the first official step in what was already an ongoing preparedness movement. The president had previously met calls for a formal program of military preparedness with the response that America was and would remain the "champion of peace." But as early as August 1914, "interventionists"—including former president Theodore Roosevelt, financier J. P. Morgan, and Senator Henry Cabot Lodge—had called for the United States to begin planning for entry into the conflict. Although the sinking of the *Lusitania* had prompted no more than a stern diplomatic note from President Wilson, it had moved U.S. Army Chief of Staff Leonard Wood to establish at Plattsburg, New York, the first of the "businessmen's military training camps." By the summer of 1916, well before U.S. entry into the war in April 1917 and the signing of the Selective Draft Act the following month, 40,000 men had been put through basic training as part of the "Plattsburg Movement." Even though the training was "unofficial," it was conducted by officers and noncommissioned officers of the U.S. Army, and the program was promoted by an advertising campaign financed by the government.

Wilson did not officially sanction the preparedness movement, but he did encourage American industry to assume a war footing. Even before the declaration of war, Wilson created several emergency federal agencies, including the Council of National Defense, the Civilian Advisory Committee, and the Shipping Board, to facilitate the shift to a war economy.

The "Punitive Expedition" Wilson authorized in 1916–1917 against Mexican revolutionary Francisco "Pancho" Villa (Chapter 33) prompted Congress to pass the sweeping National Defense Act of 1916. This legislation appropriated funds for the enlargement of the regular army, the creation of a federal National Guard (until then, this force had been strictly organized on the state level, like a militia), and an ambitious expansion of the navy. While it is true that the United States entered World War I in April 1917 largely unprepared, the Defense Act of 1916 had at least laid the foundation for mobilization, as had the various unofficial preparedness initiatives.

Catalyst for War:
The Zimmermann Telegram

Shortly after President Wilson severed diplomatic relations with Germany in February 1917, British intelligence authorities turned over a telegram they had intercepted between German foreign minister Alfred Zimmermann and the German ambassador to Mexico. Transmitted on January 16, 1917, the **Zimmermann Telegram** authorized the ambassador to propose a German-Mexican alliance to Mexican president Venustiano Carranza. In return for a declaration of war against the United States, Mexico would receive German support in a military campaign to recover its "lost territory in New Mexico, Texas, and Arizona." Zimmermann also wanted Carranza to invite Japan to join the anti-American alliance.

It was an explosive discovery. Although no evidence suggests that Carranza seriously considered the proposal, President Wilson made the Zimmermann Telegram public on March 1. The document stirred patriotic outrage and sufficient anti-German sentiment to move Wilson to ask Congress for a dec-

Zimmermann Telegram, 1917

Berlin, January 19, 1917

On the first of February we intend to begin submarine warfare unrestricted. In spite of this, it is our intention to endeavor to keep neutral the United States of America.

If this attempt is not successful, we propose an alliance on the following basis with Mexico: That we shall make war together and together make peace. We shall give general financial support, and it is understood that Mexico is to reconquer the lost territory in New Mexico, Texas, and Arizona. The details are left to you for settlement. . . .

You are instructed to inform the President of Mexico of the above in the greatest confidence as soon as it is certain that there will be an outbreak of war with the United States and suggest that the President of Mexico, on his own initiative, should communicate with Japan suggesting adherence at once to this plan; at the same time, offer to mediate between Germany and Japan.

Please call to the attention of the President of Mexico that the employment of ruthless submarine warfare now promises to compel England to make peace in a few months.

Zimmermann
(Secretary of State)

Excerpted from "19 January 1917: The Zimmermann Note to the German Minister to Mexico," in the World War I Document Archive, Brigham Young University Library, www.lib.byu.edu/~rdh/wwi/1917/zimmerman.html.

laration of war on April 2, 1917. Unlike President William McKinley in the Spanish-American War, Wilson did not bow to popular sentiment so much as he *used* it. By April 1917 he had decided that the United States stood to gain political, ideological, and moral advantages as a world power if it contributed to the Great War. The Zimmerman Telegram gave him the leverage he needed to recruit popular support for what was, ultimately, a political and ideological decision.

Declaration of War

Some historians believe that even as he delivered his thirty-two-minute **War Message to Congress** on the evening of April 2, 1917, Woodrow Wilson hoped that he would not actually have to send troops to Europe and that the mere threat of doing so would be sufficient to end the war. Be this as it may, Wilson's war message was filled with high-minded idealism: "There is one choice we can not make, we are incapable of making: we will not choose the path of submission and suffer the most sacred rights of our nation and our people to be ignored or violated." Most famously, he spoke of fighting a war "for the ultimate peace of the world and the liberation of its peoples,

the German peoples included." It would be, he said, a war to make the "world . . . safe for democracy."

Propaganda Campaign

Less than six months after his reelection, the president who "kept us out of war" asked Congress for a declaration of war. Wilson knew that the Zimmermann Telegram and other German outrages had infuriated America, but he needed to sustain public sentiment in favor of the war. To consult on press relations, Wilson summoned George Creel, a crusading journalist who had worked on both of his presidential campaigns. Even in a war to defend democratic ideals, Wilson wanted to exercise abso-

Wilson's War Message to Congress, 1917

The present German submarine warfare against commerce is a warfare against mankind. It is a war against all nations. American ships have been sunk, American lives taken. . . . Our motive will not be revenge or the victorious assertion of the physical might of the nation, but only the vindication of right, of human right, of which we are only a single champion.

. . . There is one choice we can not make, we are incapable of making: we will not choose the path of submission and suffer the most sacred rights of our nation and our people to be ignored or violated. The wrongs against which we now array ourselves are no common wrongs; they cut to the very roots of human life.

. . . Our object . . . is to vindicate the principles of peace and justice in the life of the world as against selfish and autocratic power and to set up amongst the really free and self-governed peoples of the world such a concert of purpose and of action as will henceforth ensure the observance of those principles. Neutrality is no longer feasible or desirable where the peace of the world is involved and the freedom of its peoples, and the menace to that peace and freedom lies in the existence of autocratic governments backed by organized force which is controlled wholly by their will, not by the will of their people.

We have seen the last of neutrality in such circumstances. . . .

We have no quarrel with the German people. We have no feeling towards them but one of sympathy and friendship. It was not upon their impulse that their Government acted in entering this war. It was not with their previous knowledge or approval. It was a war determined upon as wars used to be determined upon in the old, unhappy days when peoples were nowhere consulted by their rulers and wars were provoked and waged in the interest of dynasties or of little groups of ambitious men who were accustomed to use their fellow men as pawns and tools. . . .

A steadfast concert for peace can never be maintained except by a partnership of democratic nations. No autocratic government could be trusted to keep faith within it or observe its covenants. . . .

. . . We are glad, now that we see the facts with no veil of false pretense about them, to fight thus for the ultimate peace of the world and for the liberation of its peoples, the German peoples included. . . . The world must be made safe for democracy.

Excerpted from "2 April 1917: President Woodrow Wilson's War Message," in the World War I Document Archive, Brigham Young University Library, www.lib.byu.edu/~rdh/wwi/1917/wilswarm.html.

lute government control over the dissemination of information. Creel persuaded him, however, that an executive order censoring the media would do more harm than good and proposed instead enticing the press into "voluntary" self-censorship in exchange for a steady supply of news and images of the war. Then, with input from Wilson's cabinet, Creel proposed, and Wilson approved, the creation of a "Committee on Public Information," the first official U.S. agency responsible for producing propaganda.

As chairman, Creel's primary job was furnishing the nation with war news, but he quickly expanded his portfolio into outright propaganda or "opinion management," an enterprise that made President Wilson's idealistic political theories known in every American village and crossroads and throughout the world. Rarely consulting Wilson's cabinet, Creel extensively privatized the committee. Few of the 150,000 committee staffers and volunteers were government employees. At the top levels, they were the movers and shakers of the nation's popular entertainment and information media, the advertising industry, and the emerging field of public relations. The "Creel Committee," as it became known, was not above sensationalism, purposeful distortion, and outright fictionalization, but it also promoted highly accurate accounts of battle, especially on the Western Front. Creel enjoyed a substantial reputation for credibility among editors.

In addition to supplying the press with news stories, the Creel Committee administered a cadre of "Four-Minute Men," an allusion to the Minuteman militia of the American Revolution. These men delivered informative and persuasive speeches on war-related topics in no more than four minutes, the time it took a professional projectionist to change feature-length reels in the movie houses of the day. By Armistice Day 1918 there were 75,000 Four-Minute Men organized into 7,629 formally established branches.

Creel believed that the public's perception of reality is created primarily through language; however, he was also aware of the power of images, and he dedicated extensive resources to producing and disseminating war photographs, posters, and motion pictures. Probably the best-remembered committee bureau was the Division of Pictorial Publicity. To head it, Creel recruited the most famous popular illustrator of the day, Charles Dana Gibson, creator of the celebrated "Gibson Girl." Under Gibson's direction, this unit produced graphically distinguished and often quite striking patriotic war posters and illustrated ads. Today, the posters are prized by collectors.

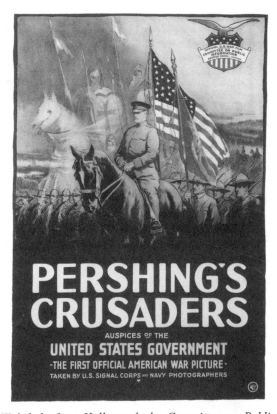

With help from Hollywood, the Committee on Public Information, the first official U.S. propaganda agency, churned out popular films with lurid titles such as The Claws of the Hun *and* The Prussian Cur. *Less sensational was the 1918 documentary* Pershing's Crusaders, *which was billed as the first official American war movie. The film's title and poster liken American troops to the crusading knights shown in the background, promoting U.S. involvement in the war as a noble cause.*

Creel also enlisted educators to work directly in the nation's classrooms. The Division of Civic and Educational Cooperatives created entire curriculums for every educational level, intended to produce citizens who understood America's war aims and war effort just the way President Wilson hoped they would. During its roughly two years of operation, the division put out more than 75 million pieces of literature, ranging from 4-page leaflets to a 321-page *War Cyclopedia.* The division also published an illustrated newspaper distributed to schoolchildren of all ages and intended to be shared with their parents. By this means, Creel believed his propaganda and information reached directly into 20 million homes on a monthly basis.

This 1918 World War I recruiting poster for the U.S. Navy appeals to individuals' patriotism and at the same time anticipates a greater American presence on the world stage. The artist, James Montgomery Flagg, created the famous Uncle Sam "I Want You" recruiting poster in 1916.

During 1917–1918 the population of the United States was approximately 100 million, of which 14.5 million had been born in other countries and 17.5 million were first-generation natives. "Hyphenated Americans" they were called during the war years, and Creel was determined to tailor committee programs to them so that these disparate immigrant groups would *want* to help the war effort. Creel had to combat opposition from many quarters of the government, which saw the hyphenated Americans not as potential patriots, but as possible spies and saboteurs. Even as Creel authorized a host of foreign-language programs, many states were enacting legislation forbidding German to be spoken in public. Several states extended the ban to *any* foreign language.

Key to President Wilson's concept of the war was that America's participation had to be seen as an expression of the will of the people, and it became an important part of the Creel Committee's work to shape the perception of the war accordingly. The committee sought to counter the position of various "radical" groups, especially the Socialists and the International Workers of the World (IWW), that this war was just one in an endless line of imperialist engagements fought by workers in the service of capitalist profiteers. To do so, the committee created a Division of Industrial Relations, which worked directly with employers to disseminate information to employees (the innovative "pay-envelope program" delivered a key war message with each paycheck) and to ensure high levels of productivity and the speedy resolution of any grievances that might lead to interruptions in war-related production.

While the primary task facing the Creel Committee was transforming an ambivalent and traditionally isolationist America into a nation of ideologically motivated warriors, the committee also soon turned its attention to the rest of the world. The international mission of the committee was extensive:

1. The committee produced propaganda for both covert and overt distribution to Germany and the other Central Powers. This mission involved a campaign of disinformation, intended to disrupt

and mislead the enemy, and outright espionage, designed to gauge the state of the enemy's morale.

2. The committee distributed propaganda to neutral nations in a mostly successful effort to win a measure of moral support for the Allies.

3. In perhaps its most controversial international mission, the committee waged a public relations campaign among the Allied nations, especially Britain, France, and Italy. Largely managed by American public relations pioneer Edward Bernays, the campaign aimed to ensure that people would be receptive to President Wilson's war aims and his idealistic program for the postwar world.

4. Creel gave special committee envoys the forlorn task of wading into the chaos of revolutionary Russia in the hope of salvaging that nation for the Allies. It was a mission at once hazardous and desperate, and ultimately quite hopeless.

5. Closer to home, the committee sent propaganda materials and agents into Mexico, whose relations with the United States had deteriorated precipitously. The committee attempted to prevent Mexico from being exploited by German agents as an avenue of infiltration or as a listening post.

Selective Service Act of 1917

In April 1916 Newton D. Baker, the former mayor of Cleveland, Ohio, who possessed no military experience whatsoever, became U.S. secretary of war. In this same year, the National Defense Act was passed, authorizing the expansion of the U.S. Army from 133,000 to 175,000–286,000 troops, but only in the event of war.

During the month the United States entered the war, April 1917, the French lost approximately the same number of men as constituted the entire regular U.S. Army. President Wilson realized that military conscription, a draft, would be necessary to build up the strength of the army rapidly—not just to 286,000 men, but to millions.

Secretary Baker directed General Enoch H. Crowder, a military officer who was personally opposed to the draft, to draw up a Selective Service Act. Crowder completed his assignment within twenty-four hours of Baker's order. On May 18, the Selective Service Act of 1917 was signed into law; 23.9 million men were registered for the draft over the next two years, and 2.8 million, most between the ages of twenty-one and thirty, were actually drafted.

The Espionage Act of 1917 and the Sedition Act of 1918

On June 15, 1917, President Wilson signed into law the **Espionage Act of 1917,** and little less than a year later, on May 16, 1918, the so-called **Sedition Act of 1918** (actually an amendment to the 1917 act).

The Espionage Act broadly defined *espionage* as obtaining or attempting to obtain "information respecting the national defence with intent or reason to believe that the information to be obtained is to be used to the injury of the United States, or to the advantage of any foreign nation." It also encompassed such acts as entering, flying over, or otherwise obtaining information "concerning any vessel, aircraft, work of defence, navy yard, naval station, submarine base, coaling station, fort, battery, torpedo station, dockyard, canal, railroad, arsenal, camp, factory, mine, telegraph, telephone, wireless, or signal station, building, office, or other place connected with the national defence." Punishment for such offenses was set at a fine of no more than $10,000, imprisonment for no more than twenty years, or both. Broad as it was, all of this was fairly standard wartime anti-espionage legislation. Less standard—and more open to political or judicial abuse—was the act's prohibition against disseminating false information "with intent to interfere with the operation or success of the military or naval forces of the United States or to promote the success of its enemies and whoever when the United States is at war" and the provisions concerning conspiracy and harboring. These gave the government extensive power of arrest and prosecution.

Far more controversial was the amendment to the 1917 act, popularly called the Sedition Act of 1918.

Espionage Act of 1917

Section 3

Whoever, when the United States is at war, shall willfully make or convey false reports or false statements with intent to interfere with the operation or success of the military or naval forces of the United States or to promote the success of its enemies and whoever when the United States is at war, shall willfully cause or attempt to cause insubordination, disloyalty, mutiny, refusal of duty, in the military or naval forces of the United States, or shall willfully obstruct the recruiting or enlistment service of the United States, to the injury of the service or of the United States, shall be punished by a fine of not more than $10,000 or imprisonment for not more than twenty years, or both.

Section 4

If two or more persons conspire to violate the provisions of section two or three of this title, and one or more of such persons does any act to effect the object of the conspiracy, each of the parties to such conspiracy shall be punished.

Excerpted from First World War.com, "Primary Documents: U.S. Espionage Act, 15 June 1917, " www. firstworldwar.com/source/espionageact.htm.

This legislation made it a crime to say, print, write, or publish anything that might be deemed "disloyal" regarding the U.S. government, flag, or military uniform. For example, it was illegal to speak out against the purchase of war bonds or any other war-related effort.

Before the end of the war, more than 2,000 people were jailed under these acts, and even more were rounded up under similar (typically even broader) state statutes enacted during this period.

Patriots and Slackers

Despite the patriotic fervor of the majority of Americans, a vocal minority opposed America's role in the war. In 1917 the Senate vote approving the resolutions to declare war was 82-6 and the House vote was 373-50—overwhelming pro-war majorities, to be sure, but not unanimous.

There was sufficient protest against the draft to cause anxiety that the nation might see a repetition of the bloody Draft Riots of the Civil War. No such protests materialized, however. There were legal challenges to the draft, but the Supreme Court upheld the constitutionality of the Selective Service Act. Although organized anti-draft protest was rare, draft evasion was common. The government estimated that as many as 3 million young men successfully avoided draft registration. Most evaders were neither identified nor prosecuted. Of those who were called up, 338,000 (12 percent of draftees) failed to report for induction or deserted shortly after their arrival at training facilities.

Individuals who evaded the draft were popularly condemned as "slackers" and were sometimes rounded up by police or even citizen posses in "slacker raids" of dubious constitutionality. It was routine for military and civilian law enforcement to randomly challenge young men and demand to see their draft-registration cards. About half of the 338,000 delinquents were apprehended in this fashion.

Some young men who opposed the war claimed conscientious objector (CO) status and sought exemption from service on religious, political, or philosophical grounds. Of 64,693 draft registrants who identified themselves as conscientious objectors, 20,000 were drafted, and 80 percent of these were persuaded to serve as regular combat soldiers. Of the 4,000 or so who persisted in refusing to bear arms, 1,300 accepted unarmed service in the medical corps or in other noncombatant roles. Most others were "furloughed" as agricultural laborers—an activity deemed essential to the war effort. A small minority, 540 individuals, were court-martialed and imprisoned.

The "slacker" label was applied not only to draft dodgers, but to anyone deemed to show insufficient patriotic zeal for the war and especially those who failed to purchase Liberty Bonds or War Stamps (see

Sedition Act of 1918

Section 3.

Whoever, when the United States is at war, shall willfully make or convey false reports or false statements with intent to interfere with the operation or success of the military or naval forces of the United States, or to promote the success of its enemies, or shall willfully make or convey false reports, or false statements, . . . or incite insubordination, disloyalty, mutiny, or refusal of duty, in the military or naval forces of the United States, or shall willfully obstruct . . . the recruiting or enlistment service of the United States, or . . . shall willfully utter, print, write, or publish any disloyal, profane, scurrilous, or abusive language about the form of government of the United States, or the Constitution of the United States, or the military or naval forces of the United States . . . or shall willfully display the flag of any foreign enemy, or shall willfully . . . urge, incite, or advocate any curtailment of production . . . or advocate, teach, defend, or suggest the doing of any of the acts or things in this section enumerated and whoever shall by word or act support or favor the cause of any country with which the United States is at war or by word or act oppose the cause of the United States therein, shall be punished by a fine of not more than $10,000 or imprisonment for not more than twenty years, or both.

Excerpted from "16 May 1918: The U.S. Sedition Act," in the World War I Document Archive, Brigham Young University Library, www.lib.byu.edu/~rdh/wwi/1918/usspy.html.

"Liberty Loans," below). The social pressure exerted against those identified as slackers could be intense, ranging from the loss of employment to intimidation and even outright acts of violence. However, the primary victims of discrimination, intimidation, and violence were German Americans and any apparently "foreign" persons perceived as somehow related to the enemy. This was especially true in the Midwest, where anti-German sentiment typically ran high. Mass emotion sometimes spawned vandalism and boycotting of German-owned shops, and lynching, though rare, was not unheard of.

Liberty Loans

Prosecuting the Great War cost the United States approximately $30 billion. Part of the cost was funded by the new graduated federal income tax, enacted in 1916, but most of the money—about two-thirds—was provided through the voluntary purchase of war bonds in a program of Liberty Loans. The First Liberty Loan, authorized by Congress, was approved by President Wilson on April 24, 1917. The bond drives were endorsed by celebrities, including such Hollywood movie stars as Douglas Fairbanks

and Mary Pickford, and the purchase of bonds, while voluntary, was considered a patriotic duty. Those who were perceived as having failed to buy their fair share of bonds were generally branded as slackers. In all the loan campaigns combined, the U.S. Treasury offered the public a total of $18.5 billion in interest-bearing bonds. Americans oversubscribed this offering by $5 billion. All of the loans were duly repaid, with redemption dates beginning in the late 1920s and extending into the 1940s, when the longest-term bonds reached full maturity.

Wilson's Fourteen Points

On January 8, 1918, President Wilson addressed Congress on the subject of America's war aims. He enumerated fourteen conditions as comprising "the only possible program" for world peace. The **Fourteen Points** were Wilson's idealistic justification for the enormous sacrifices of the Great War, and included the following:

- Point 1: "[O]pen covenants, openly arrived at," mandating an end to the kind of secret treaties and alliances that had dragged Europe into war

Wilson's "Fourteen Points" Speech, 1918

Gentlemen of the Congress,
. . . The day of conquest and aggrandizement is gone by; so is also the day of secret covenants. . . . We entered this war because violations of right had occurred which touched us to the quick and made the life of our own people impossible. . . . What we demand in this war, therefore, is nothing peculiar to ourselves. It is that the world be made fit and safe to live in; and particularly that it be made safe for every peace-loving nation which, like our own, wishes to live its own life, determine its own institutions, be assured of justice and fair dealing by the other peo-

ples of the world as against force and selfish aggression. All the peoples of the world are in effect partners in this interest, and for our own part we see very clearly that unless justice be done to others it will not be done to us. The program of the world's peace, therefore, is our program; and that program, the only possible program, as we see it, is this. . . . [President Wilson enumerates his "Fourteen Points."]

Excerpted from "8 January 1918: President Woodrow Wilson's Fourteen Points," in the World War I Document Archive, Brigham Young University Library, www.lib.byu. edu/~rdh/wwi/1918/14points.html.

- Point 2: Freedom of the seas
- Point 3: Removal of economic barriers to international trade
- Point 4: Radical international reduction of armaments to the lowest point consistent with domestic security
- Point 5: Modification of all colonial claims on the basis of the selfdetermination of peoples

Eight additional points addressed specific postwar territorial settlements, and the fourteenth point—for Wilson, the most important of all—called for the creation of a "league of nations," an international body that would guarantee political independence and territorial integrity for all nations and would provide a forum for the peaceful resolution of conflict. The league would be the world's chief alternative to war for the settlement of all disputes.

Wilson and the Treaty of Versailles

The Armistice at the eleventh hour of the eleventh day of the eleventh month of 1918 ended the shooting in World War I. A peace conference among the Allies—but deliberately excluding the Central Powers (German, Austria-Hungary, and their allies)—was convened at Paris on January 18, 1919. Ostensibly, twenty-seven Allied nations had a hand

in creating the Treaty of Versailles, which formally ended the war, but it was really only the four major Allied powers—Britain, France, Italy, and the United States—that substantively shaped the document.

Believing that the United States' decisive contribution to the war earned the nation a leading place among the "Big Four" (as the major Allied powers were known), President Wilson planned to ensure that the treaty conformed to his Fourteen Points. This meant that the peace would have to be conciliatory rather than punitive, bringing not a mere change in the balance of power among the belligerents, but a permanent change in the nature of global politics and the relations among nations. Opposed to Wilson's approach was French premier Georges Clemenceau, who intended to secure France against future German attack by destroying Germany's ability ever to make war again. He sought a thoroughly punitive treaty. The two other constituents of the Big Four, British prime minister David Lloyd George and Italian premier Vittorio Orlando, also had agendas. Personally, Lloyd George favored the moderate approach proposed by Wilson; however, he had been elected in large measure on his promise that Germany would not only be defeated, but punished. He was also deeply concerned that Wilson's Fourteen Points would interfere with Britain's imperial colonial policy. As for Orlando, his focus was narrow. He simply wanted to ensure that Italy received the territories it had been promised in 1915 as an inducement to join the Allied cause.

In the end, the Treaty of Versailles was both punitive and humiliating to Germany and the other Central Powers. Its chief provisions included:

- The return of Alsace and Lorraine to France
- The placement of the Saarland (a German state bordering France) under the supervision of the League of Nations until 1935
- The cession to Belgium of three small northern areas of Germany
- Pursuant to a plebiscite (a popular referendum vote) in Schleswig, the cession of northern Schleswig to Denmark
- The creation of a new Poland, which would incorporate most of what had been German West Prussia and Poznén (Posen), as well as a "corridor" to the Baltic Sea
- Pursuant to a plebiscite, the Polish annexation of part of Upper Silesia
- The loss of the port of Danzig (Gdansk), which was declared a free city, independent of any state
- The loss of Germany's overseas colonies in China, the Pacific, and Africa (which were taken over by Britain, France, Japan, and other Allied nations)
- German endorsement of a "war-guilt clause," admitting fault in having caused the war

The Treaty of Versailles accused the German emperor, Kaiser Wilhelm II, of war crimes. The treaty guaranteed him a fair trial and reserved the right to bring unspecified others before war crimes tribunals. (Despite this, neither Wilhelm nor anyone else was tried.) Among the most damaging provisions of the treaty was a call for Germany to pay reparations. These were not computed until 1921, when they were fixed at $33 billion. All of the Allied powers understood that this staggering sum (in 1920s dollars) would destroy the German economy, but they insisted upon payment nevertheless.

The treaty sought to eliminate Germany as a military threat; therefore, its army was limited to 100,000 troops and its general staff abolished. Additionally, munitions production was drastically limited. Germany west of the Rhine and up to thirty miles east of that river was declared a demilitarized zone, and Allied occupation of the Rhineland was set to continue for at least fifteen years, perhaps longer.

President Wilson was disappointed by the punitive nature of the treaty, but he consoled himself with three things. First, the forced disarmament of Germany might spark voluntary disarmament by other nations. Second, the Treaty of Versailles did include the Covenant of the League of Nations, which, pursuant to his fourteenth point, created an international body intended chiefly for the peaceful arbitration of international disputes. Third, Wilson believed that the many injustices of the treaty would ultimately be corrected by the League of Nations.

The Treaty of Versailles proved to be one of the tragic documents of modern history. Its punitive terms created the political, economic, and emotional climate that enabled the rise of Adolf Hitler and Nazism. Instead of preventing future wars, it made a second world war virtually inevitable.

Losing the Peace: The Senate Rebels and the People Follow

Woodrow Wilson returned to the United States, presenting the Treaty of Versailles as the best compromise obtainable. Yet while Wilson had been in Europe for six months, he had lost touch with the changing mood in the United States. The American electorate had put a Republican majority in both the House of Representatives and the Senate, and Wilson had high handedly refused to consult with any Republicans concerning the treaty or the League of Nations. This political lapse proved fatal as Wilson's longtime nemesis, Senator Henry Cabot Lodge, led Republican opposition to the League of Nations. Since ratification of the Treaty of Versailles required acceptance of the League of Nations, the Senate indicated that it would reject both.

Even in the face of the Senate's refusal to ratify the Treaty of Versailles, thereby preventing the

United States from joining the League of Nations, President Wilson declined to mend political fences. Declaring the League to be above politics, he refused to negotiate and instead decided to bring popular pressure on the Senate by taking his case directly to the people. Wilson embarked on a grueling 9,500-mile transcontinental whistle-stop speaking tour. On September 25, 1919, exhausted by his labors, Wilson collapsed after a speech in Pueblo, Colorado. He was rushed back to Washington, where, a week later, he suffered a massive stroke, which left him unable to carry on the fight for the League of Nations and barely able to serve out the rest of his term. Wilson instructed his followers to make no compromise on the question of the League, and the Republican majority accordingly rejected both the Treaty of Versailles and the League of Nations. The United States concluded separate, simple peace treaties with Germany, Hungary, and Austria in 1921.

"Return to Normalcy"

In the presidential election of 1920, the nation overwhelmingly rejected the Democratic ticket of James M. Cox and Franklin D. Roosevelt, who pledged to support the League of Nations, and elected instead Warren G. Harding, a conservative Republican. In sharp contrast with Wilson, Harding was neither an intellectual nor an idealist. His chief campaign promise had been to bring about a national "return to normalcy," by which he meant a return to the isolationism that had marked the period following the Spanish-American War. In his very first address to Congress, he disavowed any part "in directing the destinies of the world," and he declared that the League of Nations was "not for us."

BIBLIOGRAPHY

Coffman, Edward M. *The War to End All Wars: The American Military Experience in World War I.* Madison: University of Wisconsin Press, 1986.

Gilbert, Martin. *The First World War: A Complete History.* New York: Henry Holt, 1994.

Golberg, George. *The Peace to End Peace: The Paris Peace Conference of 1919.* New York: Harcourt, 1969.

Keegan, John. *The First World War.* New York: Knopf, 1999.

Kennedy, David M. *Over Here: The First World War and American Society.* New York: Oxford University Press, 1982.

Venzon, Anne Cipriano, ed. *The United States in the First World War: An Encyclopedia.* New York and London: Garland, 1995.

At Issue

After the collapse of a U.S.-backed Liberal-Conservative coalition government (see Chapter 32) and the withdrawal of U.S. forces, Liberal and Conservative factions descended into civil war.

The Conflict

From the end of the Nicaraguan Civil War of 1909–1912 (Chapter 32) until 1925, when the United States backed a coalition government formed between Conservative president Carlos Solórzano and Liberal vice president Bautista Sacasa, a small force of no more than 100 U.S. Marines policed and kept order in Nicaragua. However, on October 25, 1925, shortly after the marines left, General Emiliano Chamorro Vargas and Adolfo Díaz, both Conservatives, mounted a coup d'état against the Liberal portion of the coalition, driving Sacasa and others out of office. This prompted Solórzano to resign in January 1926, making way for Chamorro to be inaugurated as president.

The government of the United States refused to recognize the new government. In the meantime, charismatic general Augusto César Sandino led the

Augusto César Sandino

(1893–1934)

Guerrilla leader Augusto Sandino came to prominence in 1926 when he organized armed support to back up the claim of the Liberal nationalist Juan Bautista Sacasa to the presidency. Following the U.S. Marine intervention in support of the Conservative government of Adolfo Díaz, Sandino led a long guerrilla campaign that targeted the marines and the U.S.-supported Nicaraguan National Guard. Whereas the U.S. government viewed Sandino as an anti-American leftist, most Latin Americans viewed him as a popular hero fighting for the national sovereignty of a long-suffering Latin American nation. It was in large measure due to this collective attitude among the Latin American republics that U.S.

presidents Herbert Hoover and Franklin D. Roosevelt would reverse the policy of earlier administrations (beginning with Theodore Roosevelt and culminating in Calvin Coolidge) to use military intervention in Central and South America.

Sandino was instrumental in prompting the final withdrawal of the U.S. Marines in January 1933. However, even though he was promised safe conduct from his exile in Mexico to meet with the newly elected president, he was abducted and assassinated by Anastasio Somoza García's National Guard. This succeeded only in making Sandino a popular martyr, from whom the leftist revolutionary Sandinistas of the 1970s took their name (Chapter 41).

Liberals and other nationalists in a revolt against Chamorro. Although the United States did not support Chamorro, the Sandinistas (as the liberal rebels were called) alienated American interests by seizing and nationalizing U.S. property in Nicaragua. The United States responded by dispatching gunboats and marines, whose arrival prompted a truce and provoked the ouster of Chamorro, who fled the country.

In October 1926 the Nicaraguan congress elected the Conservative Díaz president. Meanwhile, Sacasa returned to Nicaragua from exile in Mexico and, with Mexican support, set up a rival Liberal government on the east coast of Nicaragua. This renewed the civil war, as Sacasa's followers—including a rebel army under General José María Moncada—fought Díaz's government forces.

Díaz called on U.S. president Calvin Coolidge for military assistance. In 1927 the American presi-

dent authorized the dispatch of several warships and a contingent of 2,000 marines. Once again, the marines' arrival was sufficient to restore order. Coolidge further authorized aid to the Díaz government in the form of weapons and other war materiel.

Sandino, a committed nationalist who had long resented U.S. intervention in Central American affairs, was moved to join the fight by what he deemed U.S. imperialism. He transformed the civil war into a guerrilla conflict and led a military campaign against the Americans that attracted a wide and loyal following.

Sandino publicly vowed to expel the marines from Nicaragua. They, in turn, were determined to capture or kill him. As for Coolidge, he hoped to negotiate an end to the conflict. He named former secretary of war Henry L. Stimson "special commissioner" to Nicaragua and assigned him to mediate

---

CHRONOLOGY OF THE NICARAGUAN CIVIL WAR OF 1925–1933

1925

Oct. 25 In a coup d'état, General Emiliano Chamorro Vargas and Adolfo Díaz drive Nicaraguan Liberals from office.

1926

Jan. Chamorro becomes president.

Jan.–Oct. General Augusto César Sandino leads a nationalist and Liberal revolt against Chamorro, in the process seizing and nationalizing U.S. property in Nicaragua, which prompts the United States to dispatch gunboats and marines. During the ensuing truce, Chamorro leaves office and flees the country.

Oct. The Nicaraguan congress elects the Conservative Díaz president. Former Liberal vice president Bautista Sacasa returns to Nicaragua from exile in Mexico and sets up a rival Liberal government on the east coast of Nicaragua. Civil war resumes. Díaz asks for U.S. military aid.

1927

April U.S. warships and 2,000 marines arrive in Nicaragua. Order is temporarily restored, but Sandino inaugurates a guerilla civil war.

1928

Nov. 4 Under U.S. supervision, José María Moncada, a Liberal, is elected president. Deeming the result to be tainted by American intervention, Sandino refuses to accept the result and continues guerilla warfare against the marines, which continues until 1933, although Sandino flees to Mexico.

1932

Dec. Sacasa is elected president and opens negotiations with Sandino (still in Mexico), who agrees to end the guerrilla war when the U.S. Marines withdraw.

1933

Jan. The marines withdraw; Sacasa grants Sandino amnesty, and he returns to Nicaragua.

1934

Feb. 21 In violation of a pledge of safe conduct, Nicaraguan National Guard chief Anastasio Somoza García orders the assassination of Sandino, clearing the way for Somoza's rise to political power.

between the rival leaders Díaz and Moncada. Stimson persuaded them to disarm and to allow the United States to supervise the upcoming election. On November 4, 1928, Moncada, the Liberal candidate, was elected; Sandino, however, insisted the result had been tainted by U.S. intervention. His guerrillas continued to clash with the marines, yet managed to evade a showdown battle.

A standoff developed. Sandino could not oust the marines, but neither could the marines suppress his guerrilla war. With the ground war bogged down, the United States bombed the mountain regions known to harbor Sandinista guerrillas. These air attacks sent Sandino fleeing to Mexico, but, from there, he continued to direct guerrilla activities in Nicaragua.

In 1932 Sacasa was elected president and opened negotiations with Sandino, who agreed to break off hostilities as soon as the U.S. Marines withdrew. They did so in January 1933, and Sacasa granted Sandino amnesty. Sandino returned to Nicaragua, where he was assassinated in 1934 by soldiers of the U.S.-equipped Nicaraguan National Guard, which was under the control of Conservative Anastasio Somoza García, the powerful son of a wealthy coffee planter, who had been educated in the United States as well as Nicaragua. This was the origin of the Somoza family's forty-four-year, U.S.-backed regime in Nicaragua. It also gave the combined Liberal and nationalist causes a compelling martyr in the slain Sandino, around whom an enduring resistance movement developed, which resulted in renewed civil war in the 1970s and 1980s (see Chapter 41), in which the United States again became involved.

Background of U.S. Intervention

Many Americans consider their nation to be the embodiment and champion of liberal democracy. In practice, however, this was not the case in U.S. policy toward the emerging nations of Central America. From 1838, the year in which Nicaragua became independent, Liberal and Conservative partisans clashed violently over control of the govern-

ment. As discussed in Chapter 32, the Conservative faction became increasingly aligned with U.S. business interests, most notably the Central American transportation empire of Cornelius Vanderbilt and the great American fruit companies. A succession of U.S. presidential administrations collaborated with American business to support Conservative regimes, willing to run Nicaragua essentially as a U.S. client state. American military intervention was sometimes necessary to bolster the Conservative governments, which were largely unpopular, corrupt, and brutal. American support of these governments—together with the oppressive presence of fruit and other big companies, which wielded great power over local governments—provoked the rise of an enduring and militant opposition, which was liberal, nationalistic, and vehemently anti–North American.

Despite U.S. support of the Conservative Party, the Liberal Party regained power in 1893, but was forced to yield once again to the Conservatives in the Civil War of 1909–1912 (Chapter 32). Following this conflict, a small U.S. Marine contingent (a single company, about 100 men) was maintained in Nicaragua, and the United States engineered an uneasy coalition between a Conservative president (Carlos Solórzano) and a Liberal vice president (Bautista Sacasa) in 1925. With this government in place, U.S. president Calvin Coolidge withdrew the marines, whereupon the coalition almost immediately collapsed (see the events summarized in "The Conflict," above).

Policy during the Coolidge Administration

President Calvin Coolidge explained his **Rationale for Military Intervention in Nicaragua** in a speech to Congress on January 10, 1927. He made no secret of the motive of protecting American financial interests in the country and regarded the restoration and maintenance of a Conservative government, friendly to U.S. business, as justification for intervention in the internal affairs of a sovereign nation.

Rationale for Military Intervention in Nicaragua, 1927

There is no question that if the revolution continues, American investments and business interests in Nicaragua will be very seriously affected, if not destroyed. The currency, which is now at par, will be inflated. American as well as foreign bondholders will undoubtedly look to the United States for the protection of their interests. It is true that the United States did not establish the financial plan by any treaty, but it nevertheless did aid through diplomatic channels and advise in the negotiation and establishment of this plan for the financial rehabilitation of Nicaragua.

Manifestly, the relation of this government to the Nicaraguan situation and its policy in the existing emergency are determined by the facts which I have described. The proprietary rights of the United States in the Nicaraguan canal route, with the necessary implications growing out of it affecting the Panama Canal, together with the obligations flowing from the investments of all classes of our citizens in Nicaragua, place us in a position of peculiar respon-

sibility. I am sure it is not the desire of the United States to intervene in the internal affairs of Nicaragua or of any other Central American republic. Nevertheless, it must be said that we have a very definite and special interest in the maintenance of order and good government in Nicaragua at the present time, that the stability, prosperity, and independence of all Central American countries can never be a matter of indifference to us.

The United States cannot, therefore, fail to view with deep concern any serious threat to stability and constitutional government in Nicaragua tending toward anarchy and jeopardizing American interests. . . .

Consequently, I have deemed it my duty to use the powers committed to me to ensure the adequate protection of all American interests in Nicaragua.

Excerpted from Calvin Coolidge, "Message to Congress, January 10, 1927," in *Annals of America,* ed. Mortimer J. Adler and Charles Van Doren (Chicago: Encyclopaedia Britannica, 1976), 14:522–523.

Policy during the Hoover Administration

Between the end of the Spanish-American War (Chapter 29) and the onset of the Great Depression in 1929, the U.S. military intervened in Latin American civil insurrections—including those in Nicaragua—a total of thirty-two times. As a condition for the withdrawal of U.S. Marines from Nicaragua in 1925, President Coolidge insisted on the establishment of a Nicaraguan National Guard, equipped by the United States and trained by the marines. The Coolidge administration approved—some would say handpicked—Anastasio Somoza García as a principal commander of the guard, which greatly facilitated his later rise to political power.

Shortly after Herbert Hoover took office as president in 1929, he sent Secretary of State Henry L. Stimson to report on conditions in Nicaragua. Stimson was impressed by Somoza, who assumed

increasing control of the guard during the early 1930s and positioned himself to take over the Nicaraguan government (which he would do on January 1, 1937). Stimson returned from Nicaragua persuaded that direct U.S. military intervention was no longer a necessary or viable policy in Nicaragua and other Latin American countries. Instead, economic support (in the form of military equipment) could be used to bolster governments that were friendly to U.S. business interests and that would bring stability to the region. In **"The United States and the Other Republics,"** a speech delivered to the Council of Foreign Relations in New York on February 6, 1931, Stimson articulated the policy of the Hoover administration. It was a repudiation of the Monroe Doctrine used by Theodore Roosevelt and Coolidge to justify military intervention in Latin America, and a reinterpretation of that doctrine as a mandate for the United States to respect the autonomy and independence of the Latin American republics. This change in interpretation laid the foundation for the "Good Neighbor Policy" of Hoover's successor, Franklin Roosevelt.

Roosevelt on Somoza: ". . . But He's *Our* Son of a Bitch"

Anastasio Somoza García was neither an experienced nor especially talented military commander, but he had been educated in the United States, spoke fluent English, and was willing to cooperate with American interests in Nicaragua. Accordingly, U.S. officials under Hoover and then Franklin D. Roosevelt supported him, and when the last U.S. Marines evacuated Nicaragua in January 1933, the American ambassador successfully urged Somoza's appointment as commander in chief of the National Guard. This put Somoza in position to order the assassination of Sandino on February 21, 1934, followed by the assassination of many former Sandino supporters.

"The United States and the Other Republics," 1931

From the beginning we have made the preservation of individual independence of [the Latin American] nations correspond with our own interest. This was announced in the Monroe Doctrine and has been maintained ever since. That doctrine, far from being an assertion of suzerainty over our sister republics, was an assertion of their individual rights as independent nations. It declared to the world that this independence was so vital to our own safety that we could be willing to fight for it against an aggressive Europe. The Monroe Doctrine was a declaration of the United States versus Europe—not of the United States versus Latin America.

Excerpted from Henry L. Stimson, "The United States and the Other Republics," in *Annals of America,* ed. Mortimer J. Adler and Charles Van Doren (Chicago: Encyclopaedia Britannica, 1976), 15:72–73.

Anastasio Somoza García
(1896–1956)

Born in San Marcos, Nicaragua, to the family of a wealthy coffee planter, Anastasio Somoza García was educated in Nicaragua and in Philadelphia, at the Pierce Business School. After returning to Nicaragua in the early 1920s, he married into the prominent Debayle family, whose members were active in the Nicaraguan Liberal Party (PLN). In 1926 he and other PLN members successfully engineered the ouster of President Adolfo Díaz, and Somoza assumed the title of general. He served President José María Moncada as under secretary for foreign affairs while also acting as a translator for the U.S. Marines in Nicaragua. This put Somoza in position to rise in the newly created, U.S.-supported Nicaraguan National Guard, over which he ultimately assumed total control.

Using his position in the National Guard, Somoza overthrew his wife's uncle, President Juan Bautista Sacasa, in 1936 and achieved election to the presidency. Despite his ostensibly liberal pedigree, Somoza instituted a repressive regime that was friendly to the United States and U.S. business interests, but that was rife with corruption that added enormously to the Somoza family's wealth. Somoza not only ruled as a dictator, but also established a dynasty that continued until the Nicaraguan Civil War of 1978 (Chapter 41). Somoza's own presidency was ended on September 21, 1956, when he was shot by nationalist poet Rigoberto Lopez Perez. He was flown to a U.S. military hospital in the Panama Canal Zone, where he died a week later. He was succeeded by his son Luis Somoza Debayle.

In June 1936 Somoza forced Sacasa to resign and installed in his place a series of puppets who held office until December, when elections ushered Somoza into the presidency by a landslide. He was inaugurated on January 1, 1937.

In the meantime, President Roosevelt, who had broken with Herbert Hoover on many policies, deliberately continued Hoover's policy of noninterference in the internal affairs of Latin America by announcing the **Good Neighbor Policy** in a speech at Chautauqua, New York, on August 14, 1936.

Both Hoover's initiative and Roosevelt's Good Neighbor Policy were more pragmatic than idealistic. Although both presidents rejected outright military intervention in places like Nicaragua, they nevertheless supported friendly regimes, which generally meant regimes run by strongmen or, as in the case of Somoza, dictators. Such regimes were thought to be preferable to what were in effect U.S. military governments on the one hand and indigenous revolutionary Communist regimes on the other. As Roosevelt famously put it, "Somoza may be a son of a bitch, but he's our son of a bitch."

BIBLIOGRAPHY

Pastor, Robert A. *Not Condemned to Repetition: The United States and Nicaragua,* 2d ed. Denver: Westview Press, 2002.

Sklar, Holly. *Washington's War on Nicaragua.* Boston: South End Press, 1988.

Walker, Thomas W. *Nicaragua: Living in the Shadow of the Eagle,* 4th ed. Boulder, Colo.: Westview Press, 2003.

Good Neighbor Policy, 1936

[O]n the 4th of March, 1933, I made the following declaration:

> In the field of world policy I would dedicate this nation to the policy of the good neighbor—the neighbor who resolutely respects himself and, because he does so, respects the rights of others—the neighbor who respects his obligations and respects the sanctity of his agreements in and with a world of neighbors.

This declaration represents my purpose; but it represents more than a purpose, for it stands for a practice. . . .

Throughout the Americas the spirit of the good neighbor is a practical and living fact. The twenty-one American republics are not only living together in friendship and in peace—they are united in the determination so to remain.

. . . But peace in the Western world is not all that we seek.

It is our hope that knowledge of the practical application of the good-neighbor policy in this hemisphere will be borne home to our neighbors across the seas.

Excerpted from Franklin D. Roosevelt, "The Good Neighbor Policy," in *Annals of America,* ed. Mortimer J. Adler and Charles Van Doren (Chicago: Encyclopaedia Britannica, 1976), 15:352–353.

CHAPTER 36

WORLD WAR II
(U.S. PARTICIPATION, 1941–1945)

At Issue

World War II pitted the rapacious Axis powers—Germany, Italy, and Japan—against the Western democracies and the Soviet Union (the Allies) in a struggle over ideology, territory, and (given the racist, genocidal doctrine of German and Japanese leaders) the very right of certain peoples to exist. The United States, already sympathetic to the Allied cause, was drawn into the war when it was directly attacked by Japan.

The Conflict

Adolf Hitler, Germany's absolute dictator, began World War II by invading Poland on September 1, 1939, in search of what he called "*Lebensraum*," "living space" (a term he borrowed and distorted from the work of Friedrich Ratzel, a German geographer and ethnographer) for his Third Reich, the German government under the militant Nazi regime. The invasion was the culmination of a program of aggressive German expansion in Europe, beginning with the remilitarization of the Rhineland in violation of the Treaty of Versailles on March 7, 1936, followed by the *Anschluss* (annexation) of Austria on March 13, 1938, and the annexation of the Czech Sudetenland pursuant to the Munich Conference of September 29–30, 1938 (see "U.S. Policy on Appeasement," below). Poland crumbled rapidly in the September 1939 invasion that began the war. After an interval of relative quiet (often called the "Phony War"), Hitler turned against Belgium, Holland, and France, all of

which were occupied by June 1940. Italy joined its ally Germany on July 10, 1940, declaring war on prostrate France. Britain prepared to defend itself against an invasion it believed inevitable. The situation in Europe became even darker when, on June 22, 1941, Hitler abrogated his nonaggression pact with Joseph Stalin and invaded the Soviet Union, initially rolling over the stunned Red Army.

Although the administration of President Franklin D. Roosevelt was sympathetic to the Allies (the nations opposing the Axis powers of Germany, Italy, and Japan), the United States remained neutral at first. But as U.S. relations with Japan deteriorated (see "Toward Pearl Harbor," below), Japan made a devastating surprise raid on the U.S. Navy and Army installation at Pearl Harbor, Hawaii Territory, on December 7, 1941, bringing the United States into the war.

President Franklin D. Roosevelt declared war against Japan on December 8; this was followed on December 11 by declarations against the United States from Japan's allies, Germany and Italy, which were reciprocated on the same day by the United States.

Early Japanese Triumphs

After Pearl Harbor, the Japanese attacked U.S.-held Wake Island, taking it on December 23. Another U.S. Pacific possession, Guam, fell on December 10. In Asia, Japanese forces invaded Kowloon, Hong Kong, during December, forcing the British (the Americans' chief ally) to withdraw to Hong Kong

CHRONOLOGY OF U.S. PARTICIPATION IN WORLD WAR II

1941

Dec. 7–8 The Japanese attack Pearl Harbor, Midway Island, Wake Island, Guam, the Philippines, British Malaya, Hong Kong, and Thailand.

Dec. 8 The United States declares war on Japan.

Dec. 11 Germany and Italy declare war on the United States, which reciprocates.

Dec. 23 Wake Island falls to Japan.

1942

Mar. 17 General Douglas MacArthur assumes command of Allied forces in the Southwest Pacific.

Apr. 9 Bataan, Philippines, falls to Japan; the "Bataan Death March" begins.

Apr. 18 The Doolittle Raid

May 7–8 Battle of the Coral Sea

May 6 Corregidor, the last U.S. bastion in the Philippines, falls to Japan.

June 3–6 Battle of Midway

Aug. 7 The U.S. Marines land on Guadalcanal and Tulagi.

Nov. 8 U.S forces land in North Africa.

Nov. 12–13 Naval Battle of Guadalcanal

1943

Feb. 8 Guadalcanal falls to U.S. forces.

May 13 Allied victory in North Africa

July 9–10 The Allies invade Sicily.

Aug. 17 Sicily falls to the Allies.

Sept. 3 The Allies invade mainland Italy.

Sept. 8 Italy surrenders, but the Germans continue to fight fiercely.

Sept. 9 U.S. forces land at Salerno.

Nov. 1 The United States invades Bougainville, which falls by December.

Nov. 20 The United States invades the Gilbert Islands.

Nov. 20–24 Battles take place on Tarawa and the other Gilbert Islands; the islands fall to the United States.

1944

Jan. 4 Allied assault on Monte Cassino, Italy, begins.

Jan. 22 The Allies land at Anzio, Italy.

Feb. 22 Eniwetok in the Marshall Islands falls to U.S. forces.

Mar. 7 U.S. troops land in Burma.

Mar. 20 The Admiralty Islands fall to U.S. forces.

Apr. 3 Bikini and other Marshall atolls fall to U.S. forces

May 18 Monte Cassino, Italy, falls to the Allies.

June 4 The Fifth U.S. Army enters Rome.

June 6 D-Day invasion at Normandy

June 15 The United States invades Saipan, Mariana Islands.

June 16 U.S. air raids commence against mainland Japan.

June 19–20 Battle of the Philippine Sea

June 25–July 1 U.S. forces take Cherbourg, France

July 21 The United States invades Guam.

July 24 The U.S. Marines land on Tinian.

Aug. 25 U.S. forces enter Paris.

Sept. 15 The U.S. Marines invade Peleliu.

Oct. 20 The Sixth U.S. Army lands on Leyte, beginning the major phase of Philippine liberation.

Oct. 21 Aachen is the first German city to fall to Allied forces (First U.S. Army).

Oct. 23–26 Battle of Leyte Gulf

Dec. 16 The Battle of the Bulge begins.

1945

Jan. 16 Battle of the Bulge ends; last major German resistance collapses.

Feb. 4 U.S. forces enter Manila.

Feb. 15–16 U.S. forces land on Bataan and Corregidor.

Mar. 16 Iwo Jima falls to the United States, but sporadic fighting continues through March 24.

Apr. 1–4 U.S. forces land on Okinawa.

Apr. 12 President Franklin D. Roosevelt dies; Harry S. Truman becomes president.

May 7–8 Germany surrenders.

June 21 Okinawa falls to the United States.

July 5 MacArthur declares the Philippines liberated.

July 16 Successful atomic bomb test in New Mexico

Aug. 6 Atomic bomb dropped on Hiroshima

Aug. 9 Atomic bomb dropped on Nagasaki

Aug. 14–15 Japan accepts Allied surrender terms, and a cease-fire is declared.

Sept. 2 Japan signs surrender instrument aboard the USS *Missouri*, Tokyo Bay.

Island, which fell on Christmas day. On December 8, northern Malaya was invaded, and by December 31, the British forces had fallen back on Singapore.

On the Philippine Islands, a U.S. commonwealth, General Douglas MacArthur commanded some 144,400 troops, including 22,400 U.S. regulars and the Philippine Army's 107,000 men, most of whom were not trained, organized, or armed. Additionally, MacArthur commanded the U.S. Far East Air Force, which included thirty-five B-17 bombers and about ninety other combat aircraft. The U.S. Navy had four destroyers, twenty-eight submarines, and smaller surface craft in the Philippines. MacArthur's plan was to deploy most of his ground forces north of the capital city of Manila to resist an invasion via Lingayen Gulf and to use the B-17s to hit Formosa (Taiwan) in counterattack. He hoped to hold out long enough to receive reinforcements.

But on December 8, the Japanese made a surprise attack that destroyed more than half of the B-17s. On December 10, Japanese bombers demolished the naval base at Cavite, while Japanese troops landed at Luzon. By December 22, the inadequate Philippine Army collapsed before the onslaught. U.S. units made an orderly retreat. MacArthur was forced to abandon Manila and withdrew to the Bataan peninsula, where he set up a stubborn defense. In mid-March 1942, President Roosevelt ordered MacArthur to evacuate to Australia, from where he made a broadcast to the islands, pledging, "I shall return." Major General Jonathan M. Wainwright was left to defend Bataan as best he could, but on April 9, 1942, with the situation hopeless, he surrendered. The Japanese forced some 70,000 U.S. and Filipino troops under the command of Wainwright's subordinate Major General Edward P. King Jr. to make a horrific sixty-mile march through the jungle from Bataan to a prison camp. About 10,000 men died during the "Bataan Death March," which became an infamous symbol of Japanese brutality. (After the war, on April 3, 1946, Japanese general Masaharu Homma was executed for this war crime.) The remaining U.S. and Filipino forces, which had taken refuge at Corregidor, a natural fortress, surrendered on May 6.

More Allied Losses in Asia and the Pacific

January 1942 brought British defeat on the Malay peninsula, followed during February by the Japanese conquest of Singapore. Thailand and Burma were invaded during January–March. With the aid of Chinese forces, the Allies reorganized, but they were forced to retreat from Mandalay and Burma, leaving China isolated. Air power became the principal means of Allied resistance as Colonel Claire Chennault deployed his "Flying Tigers"—officially, the American Volunteer Group (AVG)—to intercept Japanese bomber attacks and defend Rangoon. Major General Joseph "Vinegar Joe" Stilwell organized a continuous airlift to supply Kunming, China, after the fall of Burma, flying "the Hump," as airmen called the treacherous route from Indian bases to China over the eastern Himalayas. These desperate measures retarded Japanese progress in China, but hardly stopped it.

The Japanese Plan

Early in 1942 the Japanese formulated a plan to seize Tulagi, in the Solomon Islands, and Port Moresby, New Guinea, which would render Australia vulnerable to invasion. Simultaneously, the Japanese Imperial Combined Fleet intended to capture Midway Island in the central Pacific and, in the process, destroy the portion of the American Pacific fleet that had survived Pearl Harbor. If Japan could seize Midway, it would be able to create an unbroken defensive chain of islands from the Aleutians in the north, through Midway, Wake Island, and the Marshalls and Gilberts. Once in possession of these, New Caledonia, the Fijis, and Samoa could be invaded, completely isolating Australia.

The Doolittle Raid

U.S. planners were desperate to make a counterstrike against Japan. U.S. Army Air Force lieutenant colonel James "Jimmy" Doolittle was assigned to carry out a daring and unconventional bombing raid on Tokyo and other Japanese cities using sixteen B-25 "Mitchell" medium bombers flown from the deck of the aircraft

Douglas MacArthur

(1880–1964)

The son of General Arthur MacArthur (who became the army's senior ranking officer), Douglas MacArthur was born at Little Rock Barracks, Arkansas, and graduated from West Point first in the class of 1903. He served in the Philippines and in Asia and, in 1906–1907, as aide to President Theodore Roosevelt. He served on the general staff from September 1913 to 1917, participating in the Vera Cruz expedition during April–November 1914 (see Chapter 33).

With U.S. entry into World War I (Chapter 34), MacArthur was instrumental in creating the Forty-Second "Rainbow" Division and served as its chief of staff when it was sent to France in October 1917. MacArthur fought at Aisne-Marne (July 25–August 2), then commanded a brigade during the assault on the Saint-Mihiel salient from September 12 to September 17. He led a brigade at Meuse Argonne (October 4–November 11, 1918) and commanded the entire Forty-Second in the "race to Sedan" at the end of the war (November 6–11).

After serving with occupation forces in Germany, MacArthur returned to the United States in April 1919 and became superintendent of West Point until 1922, when he accepted a command in the Philippines, where he remained until January 1925. He went back to the Philippines again in 1928, when he was named commander of the Department of the Philippines. In 1930 he returned to the United States as chief of staff of the U.S. Army.

In October 1935 MacArthur went back to the Philippines to organize its defenses in preparation for granting it independence from the United States. The new Philippine government appointed MacArthur field marshal in August 1936, and he resigned his commission in the U.S. Army to accept the appointment. He accepted recall to American service on the eve of war with Japan (July 26, 1941).

The Japanese attacked the Philippines on December 8, 1941, and MacArthur led a gallant defense. When no reinforcements were sent, on orders from President Franklin D. Roosevelt, MacArthur was evacuated to Australia on March 11, 1942. Decorated with the Medal of Honor (an award his father had also won), MacArthur was made supreme commander of the Allied forces in the Southwest Pacific Area. Always intent on liberating the Philippines, MacArthur insisted (against considerable opposition) that this be a key part of U.S. strategy in the Pacific.

In April 1945 MacArthur was named commander of U.S. ground forces in the Pacific and was to lead the anticipated Allied invasion of Japan. The dropping of atomic bombs on Hiroshima and Nagasaki in August, however, brought Japanese surrender before the invasion was launched. Promoted to General of the Army, MacArthur was given the honor of accepting the formal Japanese surrender on September 2, 1945. He served as supreme commander of Allied occupation forces in Japan, governing the devastated nation with a strong hand tempered by benevolence and introducing democracy to the nation.

When, on June 25, 1950, Communist North Korean troops invaded South Korea, MacArthur was named supreme commander of the United Nations forces and directed the defense of the Pusan perimeter during August 5–September 15. On September 15, he launched the most brilliant military operation of his career, landing a force at Inchon, enveloping the North Koreans, and driving them out of South Korea (Chapter 37). However, during November 25–26, Communist Chinese forces entered the war, forcing MacArthur into retreat. MacArthur publicly advocated bombing targets in China itself, which President Harry S. Truman and others feared would trigger a nuclear world war. MacArthur persisted, prompting Truman to relieve him of command on April 11, 1951.

MacArthur returned to the United States, where he was hailed as a national hero. On April 19, 1951, he delivered a stirring valedictory address to Congress, declaring that "old soldiers never die, they just fade away." With that he retired from public life.

carrier *Hornet,* the only platform that could come within striking range of the targets. Launched on April 18, 1942, the raid inflicted slight physical damage on Japan, but its psychological effect was profound. It gave American morale a substantial boost even as it shocked the Japanese, who were forced to allocate more of their fighter aircraft for home defense.

As for the American bombers involved in the raid, they lacked sufficient range to return to an American base and were too big to land on the *Hornet.* Some managed to land safely in China, while others were abandoned in the air as their crews bailed out. Almost miraculously, Doolittle and seventy other mission members eventually found their way back home. One airman was killed in parachuting from his plane. Eight were captured by the Japanese; three of them were executed and one died in prison.

Battle of the Coral Sea

Before the Doolittle Raid, many Japanese opposed Admiral Isoroku Yamamoto's high-risk proposal to lure the American fleet to defeat at Midway to help position the Japanese fleet for an invasion of Australia. After the raid, the opposition dissolved, and Japanese forces sailed to Tulagi, in the Solomon Islands, and Port Moresby, New Guinea, in May 1942. Tulagi fell without opposition, but the larger force sailing to New Guinea was intercepted on May 7, 1942, by aircraft launched from the *Lexington* and *Yorktown* carriers. This began the Battle of the Coral Sea, as the Japanese carrier *Shoho* was sunk, forcing the Japanese fleet's now-undefended troop transports to turn back. On May 8, the battle became a duel between carrier-launched aircraft. Coral Sea was a tactical victory for Japan (which shot down more planes and sank more ships), but also a strategic defeat, because, for the first time, a Japanese advance had been stopped. Port Moresby was saved from invasion, and the Japanese fleet was driven out of the Coral Sea.

Battle of Midway

Despite the strategic setback of the Coral Sea, Admiral Yamamoto remained intent on taking Midway Island. He sent a diversionary force to Alaska's Aleutian Islands—a U.S. territory—while Admiral Chuichi Nagumo (commander of the Pearl Harbor attack) took a four-carrier strike force followed by an eighty-eight-ship invasion fleet to Midway. U.S. admiral Chester A. Nimitz brought together two task forces east of Midway. He then launched aircraft from fields on Midway against elements of the Japanese fleet on June 3. The air attack failed, and, on June 4, 108 Japanese aircraft bombed Midway, inflicting severe damage. U.S. forces made three more failed air attacks against the Japanese fleet, resulting in heavy American losses. A fourth attack on June 4, however, sank three Japanese aircraft carriers in the space of five minutes. A fourth Japanese carrier, *Hiryu,* was sunk in a separate attack later in the day, but not before *Hiryu's* planes had delivered a fatal blow against the USS *Yorktown.*

Japanese forces began withdrawing on June 5, 1942. On June 6, U.S. forces sank a Japanese cruiser, but the American fleet was too depleted to give chase. Still, the hard-won victory was decisive. For the loss of 307 men, 150 planes, a destroyer, and the *Yorktown,* the Americans had destroyed 275 Japanese planes, four carriers, and a cruiser, and had killed about 4,800 Japanese sailors and airmen. The initiative in the Pacific had passed irreversibly to the United States.

Battle of Guadalcanal

Defeat at Midway forced the Japanese to turn their attention instead to the Southwest Pacific. When the Japanese began to build an airfield on Guadalcanal in the Solomon chain, U.S. Marines assaulted Tulagi and Guadalcanal on August 7, 1942. For the next four months, the marines resisted Japanese counterattack. At last, on the night of November 12–13, an outnumbered U.S. cruiser force under Admiral William "Bull" Halsey rescued the marines by forcing a Japanese troop convoy into the open, where its ships fell prey to air attack. With the flow of Japanese reinforcements to Guadalcanal cut off, more marines were landed, and, by early February 1943, the Japanese evacuated the island. As Midway had turned the tide of the naval war in the Pacific, so Guadalcanal altered the course of the land war by demonstrating that the "invincible" Imperial Japanese Army could be defeated.

In the meantime, on New Guinea, combined U.S. and Australian forces defeated the Japanese attack on Port Moresby and Buna-Gona.

Europe (1942)

For the United States, World War II was a two-front war. Throughout 1942 the United States served as the "arsenal of democracy," rushing munitions and other supplies to Britain and Russia via hazardous convoy routes. U.S. planners wanted to use England as a staging area from which they would invade Nazi-held Europe via the English Channel. The British, however, believed that such an attack was premature and favored an alternative invasion via what British prime minister Winston Churchill called the "soft underbelly of Europe." Churchill proposed defeating the Axis powers (principally Germany and Italy in Europe) and Vichy France (the government of Nazi-occupied France, ostensibly cooperating with the Axis) in North Africa, then invading Sicily, and finally advancing up the Italian mainland into Europe. Once the Allies had established a serious threat in southern Europe, Churchill believed, the cross-Channel invasion could be mounted, especially in view of developments on the Eastern Front.

There, in a sudden abrogation of his non-aggression pact with Joseph Stalin, Adolf Hitler had invaded the Soviet Union on June 22, 1941. Initially, the Red Army had crumbled before the German onslaught, but at the Battle of Stalingrad (August 21, 1942–February 2, 1943), the tide began to turn. Not only was the German invasion halted, it was—slowly and at great cost—turned back, and Hitler's armies were forced into a desperate fighting retreat. Churchill, with President Roosevelt's concurrence, believed that an Anglo-American attack from the south would aid the Soviets by drawing off German forces from the Eastern Front and ultimately set up

Germany for envelopment: the Soviet forces pressing from the east and the Anglo-American forces from the south. Once the Mediterranean front had been established in North Africa and Italy, another Anglo-American invasion could be mounted across the English Channel to squeeze the Germans from the west.

North African Campaign

Field Marshal Sir Bernard Law Montgomery led the Eighth British Army to a hard-fought victory against German-Italian Panzer (armored) units at the second Battle of El Alamein, in Egypt, during October–November 1942. On November 13, Tobruk fell, followed by Tripoli on January 23, 1943. Montgomery then pursued the enemy across the Tunisian frontier during February.

In the meantime, on November 8, 1942, U.S. forces landed in North Africa (Operation Torch), securing bases in Vichy-occupied Morocco and Algeria, from which operations would be launched eastward against Tunisia, into which Montgomery was pushing the Axis forces. Unfortunately, in the first major engagement with the Germans, at Kasserine Pass during February 14–22, 1943, the U.S. II Corps suffered a humiliating defeat. Under Major General George S. Patton Jr., however, the Americans began working in concert with the British against the combined German-Italian army. On May 13, 1943, the Italian First Army surrendered to Montgomery, signaling the collapse of the Axis position in North Africa and setting the stage for the Allied invasion of Europe.

Battle of the Atlantic

While war raged on land and sea in the Pacific and on land in Europe and North Africa, German U-boats took a devastating toll on Allied troop and cargo transports in the Atlantic Ocean. U.S. Navy "hunter-killer" groups coordinated antisubmarine attacks using surface vessels and aircraft and gradually transformed the U-boats from the hunters to the hunted. The Battle of the Atlantic did not end until Germany surrendered in May 1945.

Air War in Europe (1943)

As the North African, Sicilian, and mainland Italian campaigns unfolded during 1942–1943, U.S. ground forces were building up in England, preparing for the cross-Channel invasion. Meanwhile, the Eighth U.S. Air Force arrived in England and, in coordination with Britain's Royal Air Force (RAF), began on August 17, 1942, a relentless campaign of round-the-clock air raids against Germany.

Sicily Invasion

Operation Husky, the invasion of Sicily from North Africa, was launched on the night of July 9–10, 1943. The Allies easily achieved air supremacy, and beachheads were quickly secured. Field Marshal Montgomery's British Eighth Army captured Syracuse on July 12, followed by Augusta on July 14. While the British advance was halted at Catania by Axis defenders, Lieutenant General Patton led the Seventh U.S. Army in capturing the port of Licata and then beat back a counterattack at Gela. The U.S. II Corps, now under Major General Omar Bradley, drove up the center of Sicily, taking San Stefano. Patton next took Palermo (July 22) and Messina (August 17), which ended the thirty-eight-day battle for Sicily.

Upon Sicily's fall on August 17, Italian dictator Benito Mussolini was forced out of office and replaced by Marshal Pietro Badoglio, who secretly sought peace with the Allies. This raised Allied hopes for the rapid conquest of Italy; however, Hitler committed many German forces to its defense, and the campaign proved costly, continuing until the end of the war in Europe and resulting in 312,000 Allied casualties.

South Pacific "Island-Hopping" Campaign

As operations in North Africa made inroads, Allied victories on Guadalcanal and New Guinea began to erode Japan's defensive perimeter. The Allies—primarily the Americans under General Douglas MacArthur (land forces) and Admiral Chester A. Nimitz (naval forces)—engaged in an "island-hopping" campaign, selectively invading one island, then hopping over others to invade another island, leaving the enemy cut off and neutralized in between. This strategy made for rapid progress toward the Japanese mainland.

The first major objective of the island-hopping campaign was the reduction of Rabaul, the main Japanese base in the South Pacific. Overall command of the South Pacific Area was given to MacArthur, who directed a two-pronged offensive in the region: Admiral William "Bull" Halsey drove the Third Fleet northwestward through the Solomon Islands, while General Walter Krueger led the Sixth Army through New Guinea and New Britain toward Rabaul. By October 2, 1942, southeastern New Guinea had been secured to use as a staging area for an assault on New Britain Island. By the end of the year a firm beachhead had been established on that island.

Simultaneously, U.S. land and naval forces set off to take the central and northern Solomon Islands. By December 1943 Bougainville, the last Japanese bastion in the Solomons, fell and became a major Allied base.

U.S. operations in the South Pacific during 1943 were masterpieces of coordination among land, air, and naval forces. While the U.S. Seventh Fleet worked to control the waters around New Guinea, elements of the Third Fleet supported island-hopping operations throughout the Solomons, culminating in carrier strikes against Rabaul on November 5 and 11.

Air operations throughout this period were principally a contest for air superiority, which the Australian-American Fifth Air Force achieved by May 1943. Another high point in the South Pacific air war came at the Battle of the Bismarck Sea, during March 2–4, 1943, when U.S. aircraft sank seven Japanese troop transports, curtailing Japanese efforts to reinforce and supply New Guinea.

Although Japanese air strength had suffered devastating attrition by early 1943, Admiral Yamamoto sent most of his depleted air squadrons to counterattack newly established Allied bases in New Guinea and the Solomons during April 7–12. In the end, the attacks proved more costly to the Japanese than to the Allied defenders. Thanks to intercepted radio traffic, Allied fighters were able to shoot down two Japanese bombers, one of which was transporting Yamamoto. The Imperial Japanese Navy never recovered from the loss of their brilliant admiral.

The Central Pacific Campaign (1943)

During much of 1943, the Fifth U.S. Fleet, the Fifth Amphibious Force, and the V Amphibious Corps (Marines) assembled in Hawaii, the Fijis, and the New Hebrides. It was the largest naval force the United States had ever mustered. The Fifth Fleet sailed west across the Pacific and further coordinated operations with the Seventh U.S. Army Air Force and elements of the Third Fleet. During November 13–20, 1943, USAAF (U.S.-Australian Air Force) bombers strafed Tarawa and Makin in the Gilbert Islands preparatory to an amphibious assault. The assault commenced November 20 against Tarawa and Makin, which fell to the marines within three days. By the 24th, the marines had taken Tarawa and the other Gilbert Islands objectives. Because of an especially fierce Japanese defense, Tarawa proved to be one of the most formidable objectives of the entire war, but its capture put Admiral Nimitz in position to attack the Marshalls and then to destroy the major Japanese naval base at Truk (see "Continuation of the Island-Hopping Campaign," below).

Italian Campaign (1943)

On September 3, 1943, the British Eighth Army invaded at Calabria on the toe of the Italian boot. On September 9, the day after the Allies concluded an armistice with Italy's Marshal Badoglio, the Fifth U.S. Army (under Lieutenant General Mark Clark) landed at Salerno, where it was met with fierce German resistance. It was not until September 18 that British and American operations were sufficiently coordinated to enable the Fifth Army to secure the Salerno beachhead. Through early October the Fifth U.S. and the British Eighth armies advanced northward, but they slowed to a bloody halt at the Volturno River (October 12–November 14), beyond which German commander Albert Kesselring had established the Winter Line (also called the Gustav Line), a formidable series of defenses stretching from the Gulf of Gaeta to the Adriatic Sea. The end of 1943 found the Allied advance stalled here, southeast of the Rapido River. Nevertheless, the Italian campaign was forcing the Germans to commit troops who otherwise would be fighting the Soviets on the Eastern Front. As the Allies and Germans slugged it out in Italy during 1943, the war turned sharply against the Germans in the Soviet Union, whose Red Army was beginning to push the Nazi invaders westward.

Continuation of the Island-Hopping Campaign (1944)

By early 1944 the Solomons had been secured, and Rabaul was completely cut off. West of the Solomons, Saidor, the Admiralties, and New Britain all came under Allied control early in the year. During March and April, combined U.S. and Australian forces encircled the Japanese at Hollandia, New Guinea, inflicting extremely heavy casualties. After this, the Allies took or neutralized the islands of Wakde (May 17), Biak (May 27–June 29), Wewak and Aitape (June 28–August 5), Noemfoor (July 2–7), and Sansapor (July 30).

Island hopping continued in the Central Pacific as Nimitz targeted the Marshall Islands, followed by the Marianas. U.S. forces landed on Kwajalein Island, in the Marshalls, on January 29, 1944, securing the island by February 7. Truk, a major Japanese naval base, next fell under heavy attack even as U.S. Marines and Army troops captured Engebi, Eniwetok, and Parry islands before the massive V Amphibious Force of U.S. Marines landed on Saipan, in the Mariana Islands, beginning on June 15. The conquest of this island was among the bloodiest campaigns of the Central Pacific war.

Battle of the Philippine Sea

The invasion of Saipan and the Mariana Islands forced the Japanese fleet out into the open for the first time since the battles of Midway and Guadalcanal. Admiral Soemu Toyoda, determined to destroy the American fleet, ordered an attack on ships supporting the Saipan landings. Admiral Raymond Spruance responded by sending Task Force 58, under Admiral Marc Mitscher, to intercept the Japanese fleet. The result, beginning on the morning of June 19, was the Battle of the Philippine Sea, between the Marianas and the Philippines. After eight hours of continuous aerial combat, 330 of the 430 aircraft the Japanese committed to battle had been lost. Of 450 U.S. aircraft, only 30 were downed. American pilots called this single most decisive aerial battle of the war the "Marianas Turkey Shoot."

During the air battle, U.S. submarines sank two Japanese carriers, and by nightfall the Japanese fleet was in retreat. Mitscher pursued on June 20, launching 209 planes, which sank the carrier *Hiyo* and shot down forty of the seventy-five Japanese aircraft defending against the attack. In addition to planes and ships, the Japanese lost irreplaceable veteran pilots. The U.S. Saipan landings, which had begun on June 15, continued unimpeded.

Philippines Campaign

The Saipan landings and the Battle of the Philippine Sea put American forces in position to begin the liberation of the Philippines. During October 13–16, Admiral Halsey's Third Fleet attacked Formosa, Okinawa, and Luzon. On October 20, landings at Leyte commenced, and on the 22nd, MacArthur himself waded ashore, mounted a radio truck, and broadcast: "People of the Philippines: I have returned! By the grace of Almighty God our forces stand again on Philippine soil—soil consecrated in the blood of our two people. Rally to me!"

Retaking the Philippines was a long and arduous struggle, and it was not until July 5, 1945, that MacArthur declared the Philippines liberated.

Italy (1944)

In Italy, the campaign was slow and costly. During January 1944 the Fifth U.S. Army and British Eighth Army advanced to the Rapido River, but could progress no farther. On January 22, an Anglo-American force of 50,000 landed at Anzio, where they were virtually unopposed. However, a delay allowed the Germans to reinforce and counterattack during February 16–29. The situation at Anzio hardened into a costly stalemate. In the meantime, other U.S. forces hammered away with three assaults against Monte Cassino, a major German redoubt (strong point) blocking the advance to Rome. The first two battles of Monte Cassino (January 4 and February 15–18) resulted in Allied repulses. The Third Battle of Monte Cassino (March 15–23, 1944), covered by massive air support, also failed to produce a breakthrough. Finally, a massive frontal assault during May 11–25, coordinated with Allied air force interdiction of German supply lines, produced a breakthrough toward Rome. Even that, however, came at a high price. In order to take Rome, General Mark Clark had to shift his Fifth Army, thereby sparing the German Tenth Army from envelopment. In this way, Rome, essentially a political and psychological objective, was gained at the expense of a more pressing military objective. Once Rome fell on June 4, the Allied advance to the Arno River was rapid, but 1944 ended with the Italian campaign still from finished.

Overlord

After months of planning, Allied forces in England prepared to cross the English Channel and invade German-occupied France via the beaches of Normandy. While the Allies used tactics ranging from fake radio messages to inflatable rubber decoy tanks to deceive the Germans into thinking that Lieutenant General George S. Patton Jr. was preparing an invasion force to land at the Pas de Calais (the most geographically likely place for an invasion), five Normandy beaches were actually targeted. The westernmost beach was designated Utah, with Omaha Beach just to the east of it. At these two points, Lieutenant General Omar Bradley's First U.S. Army would land, his force divided by an impassable estuary. This was risky; however, a landing at Utah Beach was necessary to take Cherbourg, a port critical to logistical support of the ongoing operation. Airborne troops were to parachute in before the main landing to clear resistance so that the two forces could be linked up farther inland. To the east were beaches designated Gold, Juno, and Sword. The British Second Army (with a Canadian corps) would land on these. Overall command of the landing, designated Operation Overlord, was given to General Dwight D. Eisenhower, supreme Allied commander.

The force, two-thirds American, consisted of about a million combat troops, supported by another million logistical troops. The invaders faced Hitler's formidable "Atlantic Wall" of fortifications, which was manned by ten Panzer (armored) divisions, fifteen infantry divisions, and thirty-three coast-defense divisions.

Dwight D. Eisenhower
(1890–1969)

Born in Denison, Texas, "Ike" Eisenhower was raised in Abilene, Kansas. Although he graduated from West Point in 1915, he did not see combat in World War I, but was assigned to a series of training missions in the United States. However, his strategic and administrative skills were recognized, and in 1924–1926 he attended Command and General Staff School, graduating at the top his class. In 1928 he graduated from the Army War College.

From 1933 to 1935 Eisenhower served as Douglas MacArthur's chief of staff, serving with him in the Philippines until 1939. On U.S. entry into World War II, Eisenhower was appointed assistant chief of the Army War Plans Division (December 1941–June 1942). Promoted to major general in April 1942, he was named to command the European Theater of Operations (which included North Africa) on June 25. He served as Allied commander for Operation Torch, the invasion of French North Africa, and then directed the invasion and conquest of Tunisia during November 17, 1942–May 13, 1943. He oversaw the conquest of Sicily, during July 9–August 17, 1943, and the first phase of the invasion of mainland Italy, beginning on September 3.

In October 1942 Eisenhower was sent to London to plan the Normandy invasion ("D-Day"). Named supreme commander of the Allied Expeditionary Force in December, he directed Operation Overlord, the Allied assault on Normandy (June 6–July 24, 1944) and then commanded the advance across France into Germany. Following the Allied victory in Germany on May 7–8, 1945, he commanded occupation forces until November, when he returned to the United States a hero.

From November 1945 to February 1948 Eisenhower served as army chief of staff. Upon retiring, he became president of Columbia University until President Harry S. Truman recalled him to military service in December 1950 as Supreme Allied Commander Europe (SACEUR) and commander of the newly created NATO forces. Two years later, Eisenhower again retired to run for president on the Republican ticket. After a landslide victory, he served two terms (1953–1961), presiding over a period of international turbulence as well as U.S. economic prosperity. After the inauguration of John F. Kennedy in January 1961, Ike Eisenhower entered a quiet retirement.

The greatest amphibious operation in military history, Operation Overlord commenced on "D-Day," June 6, 1944. By nightfall, five divisions were ashore, and beachheads were firmly established everywhere except on Omaha Beach, where German resistance was heaviest. The defenders occupied positions on high cliffs, which were taken only by the initiative and courage of individual commanders and troops. By the evening of June 6, the Americans had penetrated a little over a mile and had lost some 3,000 killed or wounded—fifteen times more men than at Utah beach. During June 7–18, the Allied invasion expanded inland while the battle for the key port of Cherbourg dragged on until June 30. On July 5, Operation Overlord gave way to Operation Cobra, the breakout from the Norman hedgerow country. This was the start of a phenomenal drive through France and into Germany, chiefly spearheaded by Patton and the Third U.S. Army.

On August 25, 1944, U.S. and Free French troops liberated Paris while Operation Anvil-Dragoon (which had begun on August 15) brought the Seventh U.S. Army into the south of France. Meanwhile, the British concentrated on the north, pursuing the retreating Germans into the Low Countries.

At the German Frontier

Despite a shortage of fuel and supplies, the Allies steadily approached the German border. British field marshal Montgomery put into motion Operation Market-Garden, a plan to secure Rhine river crossings for the Allied drive into Germany. Market-Garden failed to take all of the planned bridges, especially the key crossing at Arnhem; however, Montgomery did manage to secure Antwerp, a port the Allies badly needed.

To the south, Bradley pressed against the Siegfried Line (also known as the Western Wall), a system of pillboxes and strong points built along Germany's western frontier. The first breach in the line was punched through at Aachen, which the First U.S. Army captured on October 21. Throughout November the Allies attacked German forces west of the Rhine. During November 16–December 15, the Roer River–Hürtgen Forest region was heavily contested. South of this, Patton's Third Army swept through the Lorraine, near the French border with Germany, while Allied forces conducted operations that liberated the Alsatian towns of Mulhouse and Strasbourg.

Battle of the Bulge

Despite the disappointment of Operation Market-Garden, by December 1944 the Allied advance seemed unstoppable. The Allies, perhaps growing complacent, were stunned by a heavy German counteroffensive in Luxembourg and Belgium beginning on December 16, 1944. Popularly called the Battle of the Bulge, the Ardennes Offensive was a massive assault by twenty German divisions that drove a great salient (or bulge) into the First U.S. Army line. Aware that Bastogne was the key to the entire Ardennes region and that to lose it would allow the Germans to split the Allied forces, Lieutenant General Omar Bradley ordered the U.S. 101st Airborne to join the Tenth Armored Division to hold the position. Enveloped, these units fought desperately until January 16, when Patton's Third Army not only rescued the Bastogne defenders, but transformed a near disaster into a victory that broke the back of the German army. There was minor action in Alsace and Lorraine during January 1945, but Ardennes was the last genuine German offensive of the war.

Main Advance across the Rhine

After repulsing the Ardennes Offensive, the Allies advanced rapidly in the north of France and in Belgium and Luxembourg. On March 7, a task force of the U.S. Ninth Armored Division secured a bridgehead at Remagen, which greatly accelerated the Allied advance across the Rhine. On March 22, Patton crossed the Rhine at Oppenheim with virtually no resistance. Within two days, the Third Army began rolling into Germany en masse. Just behind Patton was British commander Montgomery, who crossed his forces to the north above the Ruhr. Additional crossings followed before the end of the month.

Victory in Italy

In April 1945 Montgomery's British Eighth Army struck the German Tenth Army southeast of Bologna. This was followed by the breakthrough of the Fifth U.S. Army into the Po Valley. From this point through the end of the war in Europe, the Fifth U.S. and British Eighth armies pursued the retreating Germans far into northern Italy.

Japan Endgame (1945)

By 1945 it was apparent that Japan had been defeated. Yet the nation's militarists refused to surrender territories they had held since the beginning of the Pacific war, which even now included much of Burma and southern Asia as well as a large part of China. Strategic bombing of the Japanese mainland, which began June 16, 1944, although physically devastating, had done little to break the militarists' will to fight.

Battle of Iwo Jima

Possession of Iwo Jima, eight square miles of rock in the Bonin Islands, was vital to establish a forward base in the U.S. advance against the Japanese mainland. On February 19, 1945, the Fifth U.S. Fleet landed the V Amphibious Corps of marines on the southeastern end of the island. Fighting was fierce, and it was February 23 before the high ground, Mount Suribachi, was captured. The Iwo Jima battle continued through March 24 and cost 6,891 marines killed and 18,070 wounded. Of the Japanese garrison of 22,000, only 212 lived to surrender.

Okinawa Campaign

In March 1945 U.S. forces began the conquest of the Ryukyu, the southernmost island of Japan itself. The Fifth Fleet spearheaded a massive amphibious action that landed the Tenth Army, XXIV Corps, and III Marine Amphibious Corps on Okinawa, where they faced formidable opposition from 130,000 Japanese troops. While the land forces fought, the Japanese unleashed a new tactic first used to a limited degree at the Battle of Iwo Jima—the *kamikaze,* a suicide flight in which a Japanese pilot crashed his explosive-laden aircraft into an American ship. At Okinawa, the carriers *Franklin, Yorktown,* and *Wasp* were severely damaged by kamikazes. The attacks, however, did not deter the landings, which took place during April 1–4.

While a great naval battle raged, U.S. land forces made slow but steady progress that culminated on June 21 when the Japanese headquarters on the island was overrun. Japanese casualties totaled 107,500 dead, and American casualties were in excess of 12,000 killed and 37,000 wounded. The fall of Okinawa destroyed what remained of Japan's navy and air force.

Victory in Europe

Leaving the capture of Berlin to the Soviet Red Army, Supreme Allied Commander Dwight D. Eisenhower ordered the U.S. Twelfth Army Group east through central Germany, to advance on Leipzig. The Americans and British next encircled the Ruhr, trapping some 300,000 survivors of German Army Group B. To the north, German Army Group H was being defeated in Holland and northwestern Germany. British and Canadian forces defeated the last German resistance in Holland and the northwestern Rhineland while the Twelfth Army Group swept around to the east, as far as Czechoslovakia and, on April 25, made contact with the advancing Soviets at Torgau. The U.S. Sixth Army Group advanced through southern Germany and Austria. At the Brenner Pass, in the Tyrol at the Italian-Austrian border, the Seventh U.S. Army made contact with the Fifth U.S. Army, which had completed its tortured advance through Italy.

His defeat clear, Adolf Hitler committed suicide on April 30, having appointed Admiral Karl Dönitz to succeed him as head of state. Dönitz surrendered all German forces during May 7–8, ending World War II in Europe.

Japan Surrenders

At Alamogordo, New Mexico, on July 16, 1945, the United States successfully tested the world's first atomic bomb, the product of the secret Manhattan Project. The following month, on August 6, 1945, a lone B-29 bomber dropped "Little Boy" on Hiroshima, instantly killing nearly 80,000 people. On August 9, "Fat Man" was dropped on Nagasaki, destroying about half the city and instantly killing some 40,000 people. In both cities, more civilians succumbed to injuries and radiation poisoning later.

On August 14, Emperor Hirohito accepted the Allied peace terms, and a cease-fire was declared on August 15. On September 2, 1945, General MacArthur presided over the Japanese signing of the formal surrender document on the deck of the U.S. battleship *Missouri,* anchored in Tokyo Bay. World War II was over.

Butcher's Bill

On September 2, 1945, the Allies achieved victory in a war that had become nothing less than a crusade for the survival of civilization. Yet much of Europe and most of Japan lay in ruins. The Axis powers had mobilized as many as 21.7 million soldiers, of whom 7.1 million were killed. The Allies had mustered some 51.2 million men and women, of whom 13.2 million had died (U.S. combat deaths were 407,318 out of 16.4 million troops mobilized). Civilian deaths can only be estimated. Among the Allies, the Soviet Union lost at least 12 million killed (although many recent British and Russian historians believe the figure was much higher). Poland lost 6.8 million; Yugoslavia, 1.2 million; France, 350,000; Greece, 325,000; Czechoslovakia, 91,000; Belgium, 76,000; Norway, 7,000; and the United States, 6,000. Among the Axis nations, Germany lost more than 1.2 million civilians; Hungary, 290,000; Romania, 200,000; Austria, 170,000; Italy, 152,941; Bulgaria, 10,000;

and Finland, 2,000. Japanese civilian deaths amounted to at least 658,595. About 12 million of the total number of civilians killed were murdered in German concentration camps, either directly or through various forms of privation; of this number, half—6 million—were Jewish victims of what Hitler called the "Final Solution" and the rest of the world came to call the Holocaust.

The Four Neutrality Acts of 1935–1939

In 1935, as another "European war" loomed on the horizon, the U.S. Congress passed the first of four Neutrality Acts. The act of August 1935 was motivated by Italy's May 1935 invasion of Ethiopia and empowered the president to embargo arms shipments to belligerents but placed no limit on such strategic materials as oil, steel, and copper.

In response to the Spanish Civil War, which began in 1936, Congress passed a second Neutrality Act (May 1, 1937), which specified civil wars among the conflicts to which the neutrality restrictions applied. The president was also empowered to add strategic materials to the list of embargoed goods and to forbid travel by U.S. citizens on vessels belonging to the belligerents. The 1937 legislation additionally prohibited the arming of American merchant vessels.

On November 4, 1939, President Franklin D. Roosevelt signed into law the Neutrality Act of 1939, which replaced the act of 1937. Passed after the outbreak of World War II in Europe, the new law permitted the sale of arms and strategic materials to belligerents, except as might be prohibited by presidential proclamation. All sales were to be on a cash-and-carry basis only, so that the United States could not be drawn into war by holding the debt of a belligerent country or by violating a blockade in order to deliver goods. Additionally, the 1939 act gave the president the authority to designate "combat areas," through which travel by U.S. nationals and vessels would be prohibited.

As passed, the 1939 act retained the earlier prohibition against the arming of merchant vessels;

Franklin D. Roosevelt

(1882–1945)

Franklin Delano Roosevelt was born to genteel privilege at Hyde Park, New York, and educated at Groton Preparatory School (Groton, Massachusetts) and Harvard University. During his college years, Roosevelt was influenced by the Progressive political philosophy of President Theodore Roosevelt, his fifth cousin, and also fell in love with Teddy's niece, Eleanor Roosevelt, who was a passionate advocate for the poor. They married on March 17, 1905.

Roosevelt attended Columbia University Law School but did not graduate, although he passed the New York bar and entered a Wall Street law firm. In 1910 he won election to the New York State senate and was reelected in 1912. He became assistant secretary of the navy under President Woodrow Wilson, and after the outbreak of World War I, he became an advocate of U.S. military preparedness.

In 1920 Roosevelt, nominated as running mate to Democratic presidential candidate James M. Cox, vigorously campaigned for U.S. entry into the League of Nations. His ticket lost in the Republican landslide that put Warren G. Harding and Calvin Coolidge into office. Roosevelt then pursued a business career as he awaited his next political opportunity. He was struck with polio in August 1921, which left him paralyzed from the waist down. With the encouragement of his wife and other close associates, Roosevelt remained active in politics, and his appearances at the 1924 and 1928 Democratic conventions kept him before the public.

Roosevelt won his bid for governor of New York in 1928. During his two terms, he introduced significant social reforms and, after the onset of the Great Depression, bold relief legislation. His performance as governor catapulted him to the Democratic presidential nomination in 1932.

In the depths of the Depression, Roosevelt brought forth his sweeping New Deal program of social and economic legislation. Although the New Deal by no means ended the Depression, it did offer relief to millions and renewed faith in democracy during an era when, in Europe, many nations were turning into Fascist (Italy and Germany) or Communist (the Soviet Union) dictatorships.

Roosevelt was reelected to an unprecedented third term in 1940. As war erupted in Europe and Asia, he aligned American neutrality to favor the Allies. He created a partnership with Britain that stopped just short of a formal military alliance. Roosevelt pledged to make the United States the "arsenal of democracy"—and ushered in the nation's first peacetime military draft. When the United States finally entered the war after the Japanese attack on Pearl Harbor (December 7, 1941), it did so better prepared for war than ever before in its history.

Like Winston Churchill in Britain, Roosevelt took a hands-on role in leading the nation through World War II. Elected to a fourth term in 1944, he served until April 12, 1945, when he was felled by a cerebral hemorrhage less than a month before victory came in Europe.

however, on November 17, 1941, during what amounted to an undeclared naval war with Germany on the Atlantic, Congress amended the act to permit the arming of merchant vessels and also to permit those vessels to carry cargoes into belligerent ports. This amendment was so significant that historians generally consider this legislation the fourth of the U.S. Neutrality Acts. The acts trace the evolution from neutrality to alliance.

U.S. Policy on Appeasement

In May 1937 Neville Chamberlain replaced the retiring Stanley Baldwin as prime minister of

Britain. The Baldwin government had maintained a pacifist policy with regard to preparedness for war, yet had bound Britain to a number of military treaties, chiefly with France, Czechoslovakia, and Poland, which could easily draw Britain into war if any of those nations were attacked. Chamberlain hoped to avoid conflict and therefore proposed a policy of "active appeasement" with regard to Germany. He intended to ascertain precisely what Adolf Hitler wanted and then, if possible, to give it to him. This, Chamberlain hoped, would conserve British military resources to fight Italy and Japan, which he judged to pose greater threats than Germany.

When Hitler announced his intention to annex the Sudentenland, a German-speaking region of Czechoslovakia, Chamberlain warned him to negotiate with the Czechs. In response, Hitler blustered, and Chamberlain caved in. He flew to Berchtesgaden, Hitler's Bavarian mountain retreat, and agreed to the immediate cession of part of a country that he did not represent, asking only that Hitler delay an invasion until he could persuade Paris and Prague to go along with the plan.

Like Britain, France was bound by treaty to defend Czech sovereignty. Appalled by Chamberlain's proposal, the French government appealed to President Roosevelt to somehow aid in the defense of Czech rights. Roosevelt, however, knew that he would be unable to persuade Congress to intervene. Unwilling to stand alone, the French government acquiesced. Chamberlain then organized the Munich Conference on September 29–30, 1938, which formalized the betrayal of the Czechs, ceding the Sudetenland to Germany in return for Hitler's pledge that he would make no more territorial demands in Europe.

Roosevelt understood that the shift after World War I from Woodrow Wilson's internationalism to Warren G. Harding's isolationism had endured. He was well aware that this policy of disengagement led Hitler to dismiss the United States as of no military concern. When Hitler almost immediately violated his Munich pledge, effectively seized the remainder

of Czechoslovakia, and then set his sights on Poland, Roosevelt sadly concluded that had the United States engaged with Britain and France, appeasement would have been defeated and Hitler quite possibly stopped in his tracks. Although he withheld public comment, Roosevelt believed that America's disengagement had helped make a new world war inevitable. He increasingly urged the United States to prepare for a war he was certain would come.

Budgeting for War

Popular mythology depicts America as wholly unprepared for war at the time of the Japanese attack on Pearl Harbor on December 7, 1941. In fact, thanks to Roosevelt's advocacy of rearmament, the United States entered World War II better prepared than for any previous war in its history.

On January 3, 1940, with the war in Europe under way, President Roosevelt asked Congress to provide $1.8 billion for national defense, including a program to produce an unprecedented 50,000 aircraft. On May 16, with the Battle of France clearly being won by the Nazis, Roosevelt asked Congress for an additional $2.5 billion to expand the army and the navy. This was followed on May 31 by the introduction of the Accelerated U.S. Defense Plan, in which the president requested an additional $1.3 billion to accelerate the fulfillment of military and naval requirements.

On June 22, 1940, Congress passed the National Defense Act, designed to generate $994 million annually for the American war effort. To accommodate anticipated wartime expenditures, Congress raised the national debt limit by what was then an astounding $4 billion, to $49 billion.

On July 20, 1940, President Roosevelt signed the so-called Two-Ocean Navy Act, in anticipation of fighting a two-front war, against Germany in the Atlantic and Japan in the Pacific. More than $5.2 billion was expended to increase the size of naval forces by 70 percent. The act called for the construction of 201 new warships, including 7 battleships.

Peacetime Draft

Added to the spectacular increases in military budget was legislation to reactivate the Selective Service, which had conscripted men into the army during World War I. The Burke-Wadsworth Bill—drafted by Grenville Clark, leader of a World War I veterans association called the Military Training Camps Association—was brought before Congress on June 20, 1940. Passed as the Selective Training and Service Act of 1940 on September 16, 1940, it authorized the first peacetime draft in U.S. history, requiring men between the ages of twenty-one and thirty to register with local draft boards.

The act provided for selection of conscripts by lottery. Each man drafted was to serve for one year in the Western Hemisphere or in U.S. possessions or territories in other parts of the world. No more than 900,000 men were to be in training at any one time, so that 1.2 million regular army soldiers and 800,000 reservists would be available in any twelve-month period. By October 16, 1940, 16.4 million American men had registered for the draft; the lottery was conducted for the first time on October 29. Specifically exempted from combat service were conscientious objectors, men "who, by reason of religious training and belief, [are] conscientiously opposed to participation in war in any form." In contrast to policy in World War I, which gave the military jurisdiction over conscientious objectors, the 1940 Selective Service Act assigned oversight to civilian draft boards. If a local draft board sustained a conscientious objection, the objector was to "be assigned to noncombatant service as defined by the President, or shall if he is found to be conscientiously opposed to participation in such noncombatant service, in lieu of such induction, be assigned to work of national importance under civilian direction." As a result, conscientious objectors received better treatment, and they were given the opportunity to render genuinely useful service in noncombat roles.

Early in the summer of 1941, President Roosevelt asked Congress to extend the term of duty for the conscripts beyond twelve months. The request was controversial, and the House of Representatives approved it by just one vote, the Senate by a wider margin. Understandably, the extension created significant discontent among draftees, many of whom threatened to desert after their original twelve months of service had elapsed. Actual desertion rates, however, were low. Once the United States entered the war on December 8, 1941, a new act expanded the liability for service to men between the ages of eighteen and forty-five, and required registration by all men between the ages of eighteen and sixty-five. The term of service was defined as the duration of the war plus six months. Between 1940 and 1947 (the year in which the wartime Selective Service Act expired, after a series of extensions by Congress), more than 10 million men had been inducted.

The Lend-Lease Concept and the Lend-Lease Act

Shortly after the war began in Europe in September 1939, Winston Churchill, who joined the British War Cabinet as first lord of the Admiralty under Prime Minister Neville Chamberlain, appealed to President Roosevelt for military aid. Roosevelt could not act contrary to U.S. neutrality laws, but he made it clear that his sympathies lay with Britain. Over the course of a few months, Roosevelt and Churchill formed a kind of personal alliance that preceded an actual political and military alliance.

On June 3, 1940, Churchill made an urgent appeal for weapons and equipment following the evacuation from Dunkirk, in France, during which the British army had to abandon much of its hardware in order to rescue the soldiers. Britain was now vulnerable to invasion by the Germans. At Roosevelt's direction, the U.S. War Department immediately shipped large numbers of obsolescent but serviceable rifles, machine guns, field artillery pieces, and ammunition to Britain.

On June 16, Congress passed the Pittman Act, which authorized the sale of munitions to any North, Central, or South American republic. The act was

This 1941 British cartoon, entitled "The Way of a Stork," depicts gratitude at the "birth" of the Lend-Lease Act, which allowed President Roosevelt to accomodate U.S. neutrality law while providing an embattled Britain with war materiel. The Lend-Lease concept was a major step in a developing Anglo-American alliance.

extended on September 26, authorizing the U.S. Export-Import Bank to lend such states up to $500 million and to permit any of them to acquire munitions up to a total value of $400 million.

On August 18, President Roosevelt met with Canadian prime minister Mackenzie King and agreed to create a Joint Board of Defense for the coordination of U.S. and Canadian defensive measures. The following month, on September 2, 1940, the U.S. and British governments concluded a significant defense agreement by which the U.S. Navy transferred fifty World War I–era destroyers to the Royal Navy in exchange for ninety-nine-year leases on British naval and air stations in Antigua, the Bahamas, Bermuda, British Guiana, Jamaica, Newfoundland, St. Lucia, and Trinidad.

The "Destroyers-for-Bases Deal" clearly marked the end of U.S. neutrality in spirit if not in official declaration. The next step came on November 20, 1940, with the Stimson-Layton Agreement, in which U.S. secretary of war Henry Stimson and British minister of supply Sir Walter Layton agreed to a significant partial standardization of British and American weapons and military equipment. Most important, the agreement generally pooled U.S. and British technical knowledge, including patents on weapons production.

These various measures led up to An Act to Promote the Defense of the United States, popularly called the **Lend-Lease Act,** which was signed into law on March 11, 1941. As early as the summer of 1940, British prime minister Winston Churchill had warned the United States that his nation would soon be unable to acquire war materiel from the United States on the cash-and-carry basis decreed by the U.S. neutrality law. On December 8, 1940, therefore, President Roosevelt suggested the concept of lend-lease as an alternative to cash for arms. The legislation that resulted gave the president the authority to aid any nation whose defense he deemed critical to the United States; it further authorized the government to accept payment "in kind or property, or any other direct or indirect benefit which the President deems satisfactory."

By the end of the war, more than forty nations had participated in the Lend-Lease program, to a total of aid valued at $49.1 billion.

The Atlantic Charter

The Lend-Lease Act was a major step toward a formal Anglo-American alliance. The next step was taken during August 9–12, 1941, when President Roosevelt and Prime Minister Churchill met aboard their nations' naval vessels in Placentia Bay, off the coast of Newfoundland, Canada, and drew up the **Atlantic Charter,** which stated eight American and British aims in war as well as peace.

Lend-Lease Act, 1941

Section 3.

(a) Notwithstanding the provisions of any other law, the President may, from time to time, when he deems it in the interest of national defense, authorize the Secretary of War, the Secretary of the Navy, or the head of any other department or agency of the Government

(1) To manufacture in arsenals, factories, and ship-yards under their jurisdiction, or otherwise procure, to the extent to which funds are made available therefor, or contracts are authorized from time to time by the Congress, or both, any defense article for the government of any country whose defense the President deems vital to the defense of the United States.

(2) To sell, transfer title to, exchange, lease, lend, or otherwise dispose of, to any such government any defense article, but no defense article not manufactured or procured under paragraph (1) shall in any way be disposed of under this paragraph, except after consultation with the Chief of Staff of the Army or the Chief of Naval Operations of the Navy, or both. The value of defense articles disposed of in any way under authority of this paragraph, and procured from funds heretofore appropriated, shall not exceed $1,300,000,000. The value of such defense articles shall be determined by the head of the department or agency concerned or such other department, agency or officer as shall be designated in the manner provided in the rules and regulations issued hereunder. Defense articles procured from funds hereafter appropriated to any department or agency of the Government, other than from funds authorized to be appropriated under this Act, shall not be disposed of in any way under authority of this paragraph except to the extent hereafter authorized by the Congress in the Acts appropriating such funds or otherwise.

Excerpted from the Avalon Project at Yale Law School, "Master Lend-Lease Agreement," www.yale.edu/lawweb/avalon/decade/decade04.htm.

Period of Undeclared War

Even as the United States increasingly aligned itself with Britain (and the other Allies) while maintaining an official policy of neutrality, it also issued jointly with twenty-one Latin American countries the Declaration of Panama (October 3, 1939), creating in the waters of the Americas a 300-mile "neutrality zone" off limits to all belligerents. U.S. Navy ships were assigned the mission of "neutrality patrol" in these waters. Early in 1941 the neutrality patrol was pushed out to a distance of 2,000 miles from the U.S. coast, and in August, after the conclusion of the Atlantic Charter, American warships began escorting fast convoys partway to Britain. The escort operations resulted in an undeclared naval war between the United States and Germany. On September 4, 1941, the destroyer USS *Greer* was attacked by a German submarine. On October 15, the USS *Kearny* was attacked, and on October 31, the USS *Reuben James* was sunk. It was the sinking of the *Reuben James* and other armed exchanges that prompted Congress, on November 17, 1941, to amend the latest Neutrality Act to permit the arming of merchant vessels and to allow merchant vessels to carry cargoes into belligerent ports.

Toward Pearl Harbor

After the Japanese bombed Pearl Harbor on December 7, 1941, the Roosevelt administration portrayed the attack as a complete surprise and utterly unprovoked. However, Japanese expansion into China in the Sino-Japanese War (1937–1941) and into Southeast Asia had damaged Japanese-American relations. Under Roosevelt, the United States sought to curb Japanese aggression not by military action, but by economic sanctions. Intended as an alternative to war, the sanctions ultimately provoked war.

On January 26, 1940, the U.S.-Japanese Trade Treaty of 1911 expired. In response, Secretary of

Atlantic Charter, 1941

The President of the United States of America and the Prime Minister, Mr. Churchill, representing His Majesty's Government in the United Kingdom, . . . deem it right to make known certain common principles in the national policies of their respective countries on which they base their hopes for a better future for the world.

First, their countries seek no aggrandizement, territorial or other;

Second, they desire to see no territorial changes that do not accord with the freely expressed wishes of the peoples concerned;

Third, they respect the right of all peoples to choose the form of government under which they will live; and they wish to see sovereign rights and self government restored to those who have been forcibly deprived of them;

Fourth, they will endeavor, with due respect for their existing obligations, to further the enjoyment by all States, great or small, victor or vanquished, of access, on equal terms, to the trade and to the raw materials of the world which are needed for their economic prosperity;

Fifth, they desire to bring about the fullest collaboration between all nations in the economic field with the object of securing, for all, improved labor standards, economic advancement and social security;

Sixth, after the final destruction of the Nazi tyranny, they hope to see established a peace which will afford to all nations the means of dwelling in safety within their own boundaries, and which will afford assurance that all the men in all lands may live out their lives in freedom from fear and want;

Seventh, such a peace should enable all men to traverse the high seas and oceans without hindrance;

Eighth, they believe that all of the nations of the world, for realistic as well as spiritual reasons must come to the abandonment of the use of force. Since no future peace can be maintained if land, sea or air armaments continue to be employed by nations which threaten, or may threaten, aggression outside of their frontiers, they believe, pending the establishment of a wider and permanent system of general security, that the disarmament of such nations is essential. They will likewise aid and encourage all other practicable measure which will lighten for peace-loving peoples the crushing burden of armaments.

Franklin D. Roosevelt
Winston S. Churchill

Excerpted from the Avalon Project at Yale Law School, "Atlantic Charter, August 14, 1941," www.yale.edu/lawweb/avalon/wwii/atlantic.htm.

State Cordell Hull informed the Japanese government that trade would continue strictly on a day-to-day basis. On April 17, 1940, Hull issued a warning to Japan that the United States would oppose any forcible change in the status quo of the Netherlands East Indies, which Japan wanted to incorporate into what it called its "Asian Co-prosperity Sphere." Despite this warning, when France fell to Germany, the Japanese government dispatched warships to French Indochinese ports on June 25, 1940. The following month, on July 16, the Japanese government took a major step toward militaristic totalitarianism along German lines by forming a new ministry under Prince Fumumaro Konoye.

At about this time, the Roosevelt administration began to threaten an embargo on oil exports to Japan. On September 12, 1940, U.S. ambassador to Tokyo Joseph Grew warned Hull that Japan might retaliate. On September 22, 1940, Japanese forces began to occupy French Indochina and subsequently advanced into China. This provoked, on September 26, an embargo on the exportation of scrap iron and steel from the United States to countries outside the Western Hemisphere (with the exception of Britain), effective October 16. The Japanese declared the policy an "unfriendly act" on October 8. In the meantime, they had concluded with Germany and Italy the Three-Power, or Axis, Pact on September

27, 1940. This alliance called for military as well as economic cooperation among the three signatories for ten years. Italy, Germany, and Japan mutually pledged assistance in the event that any of them became involved in a war with a power not then a belligerent— meaning the Soviet Union and the United States.

On July 26, 1941, President Roosevelt issued an executive order freezing all Japanese credit in the United States in response to the Japanese occupation of French Indochina, thereby bringing American-Japanese trade to a complete stop. The president placed all armed forces in the Philippines under U.S. control and warned Japanese ambassador Admiral Kichisaburo Nomura that additional attempts to expand Japanese military control in the Far East would necessitate America's taking steps to protect its

rights and interests. On August 17, Roosevelt repeated and intensified the warning, and on August 24, Britain pledged military aid to the United States should the United States became involved in a war with the Japanese. Japan became an outright military dictatorship on October 17, 1941, when Prince Konoye was replaced by General Hideki Tojo as prime minister. Tojo, who was completely committed to the Axis, also served as minister of war.

Between November 20 and December 7, 1941, Japanese delegates met with U.S. State Department officials in Washington, D.C., ostensibly in an effort to avert war. On November 29, Secretary of State Hull informed the British ambassador to the United States that the talks had all but collapsed. On December 7, Ambassador Nomura and special envoy

Roosevelt's War Message, 1941

Yesterday, December 7, 1941—a date which will live in infamy—the United States of America was suddenly and deliberately attacked by naval and air forces of the Empire of Japan.

The United States was at peace with that nation and, at the solicitation of Japan, was still in conversation with its Government and its Emperor looking toward the maintenance of peace in the Pacific. Indeed, one hour after Japanese air squadrons had commenced bombing in the American Island of Oahu, the Japanese Ambassador to the United States and his colleague delivered to our Secretary of State a formal reply to a recent American message. And while this reply stated that it seemed useless to continue the existing diplomatic negotiations, it contained no threat or hint of war or of armed attack.

It will be recorded that the distance of Hawaii from Japan makes it obvious that the attack was deliberately planned many days or even weeks ago. During the intervening time the Japanese Government has deliberately sought to deceive the United States by false statements and expressions of hope for continued peace.

The attack yesterday on the Hawaiian Islands has caused severe damage to American naval and military forces. I regret to tell you that very many Amer-

ican lives have been lost. In addition American ships have been reported torpedoed on the high seas between San Francisco and Honolulu.

Yesterday the Japanese Government also launched an attack against Malaya.

Last night Japanese forces attacked Hong Kong.

Last night Japanese forces attacked Guam.

Last night Japanese forces attacked the Philippine Islands.

Last night the Japanese attacked Wake Island. And this morning the Japanese attacked Midway Island. . . .

But always will our Whole Nation remember the character of the onslaught against us.

No matter how long it may take us to overcome this premeditated invasion, the American people in their righteous might will win through to absolute victory. . . .

With confidence in our armed forces—with the unbounding determination of our people—we will gain the inevitable triumph—so help us God.

Excerpted from Franklin D. Roosevelt, "Address to Congress Requesting a Declaration of War with Japan," December 8, 1941, in *Public Papers of the Presidents of the United States: Franklin D., Roosevelt, 1933–1945,* from the American Presidency Project, University of California, Santa Barbara, www.presidency.ucsb.edu.

Saburo Kurusu met with Hull to inform the U.S. government that the Japanese empire had severed diplomatic relations; however, the complexity of the instructions sent to the envoys and the time consumed in deciphering encrypted diplomatic communications unintentionally delayed this meeting until after the attack on Pearl Harbor had already taken place. In effect, then, the attack, during a time of peace, was technically "unprovoked" and in violation of international law.

Policy: Pacific vs. Atlantic

The "sneak attack" on Pearl Harbor instantly rallied the nation for war, and President Roosevelt's **War Message** on December 8, 1941, resulted in an all-but-unanimous vote for a declaration of war in Congress. (Only Montana representative Jeannette Rankin, who had in 1917 voted against U.S. entry into World War I, voted against the declaration.)

American popular opinion craved instant vengeance against "the Japs"; however, Roosevelt and his top military advisers agreed that the European war had to be the first priority, because, despite Pearl Harbor, Hitler represented the more immediate threat to the United States.

Bad News and Bold Heroes

Although the president considered the war in Europe to be the biggest threat, it was in the Pacific that the United States initially suffered one defeat after another at the hands of the Japanese. President Roosevelt addressed these reversals frankly in speeches to Congress and in his periodic radio addresses to the American people, which were popularly called "Fireside Chats." His **Fireside Chat of February 23, 1942,** was typical. Roosevelt asked the American people to listen to his broadcast while looking at a world map. He explained the scope of the war and the consequences of defeat: "Until our flow of supplies gives us clear superiority we must keep on striking our enemies wherever and whenever we can meet them, even if, for a while, we have to yield ground."

But the Roosevelt administration realized that eloquence alone was not sufficient to sustain American public morale during the early phases of the

Roosevelt's Fireside Chat of February 23, 1942

Your Government has unmistakable confidence in your ability to hear the worst, without flinching or losing heart. You must, in turn, have complete confidence that your Government is keeping nothing from you except information that will help the enemy in his attempt to destroy us. In a democracy there is always a solemn pact of truth between government and the people, but there must also always be a full use of discretion, and that word "discretion" applies to the critics of government as well. . . .

Germany, Italy and Japan are very close to their maximum output of planes, guns, tanks and ships. The United Nations are not—especially the United States of America.

Our first job then is to build up production—uninterrupted production—so that the United Nations can maintain control of the seas and attain control of the air—not merely a slight superiority, but an overwhelming superiority. . . .

This generation of Americans has come to realize, with a present and personal realization, that there is something larger and more important than the life of any individual or of any individual group—something for which a man will sacrifice, and gladly sacrifice, not only his pleasures, not only his goods, not only his associations with those he loves, but his life itself. In time of crisis when the future is in the balance, we come to understand, with full recognition and devotion, what this nation is and what we owe to it. . . .

The task that we Americans now face will test us to the uttermost. Never before have we been called upon for such a prodigious effort. Never before have we had so little time in which to do so much.

Excerpted from John Grafton, ed., *Franklin Delano Roosevelt: Great Speeches* (Mineola, N.Y.: Dover, 1999), 117–125.

war. Roosevelt asked the army and navy to propose and plan strikes against Japan as early as possible; this request led to the bold Doolittle Raid on April 18, 1942, which boosted American morale.

Japanese Internment

Even before U.S. entry into the war, Congress passed the Smith Act (U.S. Alien Registration Act) on June 28, 1940, which made it unlawful to advocate the overthrow or destruction of the U.S. government by force or violence or to be a member of a group that advocated such goals. It further required the registration of aliens resident in the United States. After December 7, 1941, some German and Italian aliens in the United States were subject to arrest and deten-

tion, even for extended periods. However, suspicion, fear, and outright hatred of the Japanese was far more intense and widespread, and it applied not just to resident aliens, but also to American citizens of Japanese descent.

At the time of Pearl Harbor, about 120,000 persons of immediate Japanese descent were resident in the United States. Of these, some 80,000 had been born in the country and were U.S. citizens. Within four days after the Pearl Harbor attack, the Federal Bureau of Investigation (FBI) had arrested and detained 1,370 Japanese Americans as "dangerous enemy aliens," despite their American citizenship. On December 22, the Agriculture Committee of the Los Angeles Chamber of Commerce called for all Japanese and Japanese Americans to be put under federal control. (For many years, Japanese American farmers had been successfully farming in California, Oregon, and Washington, offering stiff competition to the white farmers who controlled the Agriculture Committee.) On January 5, 1942, all U.S. draft boards automatically classified Japanese American selective service registrants as enemy aliens, and many Japanese Americans who were already serving were discharged or restricted to menial labor duties. On January 6, Leland Ford, the member of Congress representing the California district encompassing Los Angeles, sent a telegram to Secretary of State Cordell Hull, asking that all Japanese Americans be physically relocated away from the West Coast. Before the end of the month, the California State Personnel Board voted to bar from civil service positions all "descendants of natives with whom the United States [is] at war." As

This February 1942 photograph from the U.S. War Relocation Authority shows an Oakland, Calif., newsstand. The San Francisco Examiner *trumpets impending plans to relocate all Japanese Americans residing within 200 miles of the Pacific coast of the United States. More than 100,000 Japanese Americans were sent to internment camps across the United States, where they remained until the end of the war.*

worded, the ban included descendants of Germans and Italians, but it was only put into practice against Japanese Americans.

On January 29, U.S. attorney general Francis Biddle established "prohibited zones," areas forbidden to all enemy aliens. Accordingly German and Italian as well as Japanese aliens were ordered to leave San Francisco waterfront areas. The next day California attorney general Earl Warren (who would in the 1950s become nationally known as the civil libertarian chief justice of the U.S. Supreme Court) called for immediate preemptive action to prevent a repetition of Pearl Harbor. In response, the U.S. Army designated twelve "restricted areas" along the Pacific coast. In these areas, enemy aliens were subject to a curfew from 9:00 p.m. to 6:00 a.m. and were permitted to travel only to and from work, never going more than five miles from their homes.

On February 6, 1942, an American Legion post in Portland, Oregon, published an appeal for the removal of Japanese Americans from the West Coast. This was followed a week later by an appeal from the entire West Coast congressional delegation to President Roosevelt, asking for an executive order. On February 16, the California Joint Immigration Committee urged that all Japanese Americans be removed from the Pacific Coast and other vital areas of the state.

By February 19, the FBI had in custody 2,192 Japanese Americans, and on that day, President Roosevelt signed **Executive Order 9066,** authorizing the secretary of war to define military areas "from which any or all persons may be excluded as deemed necessary or desirable." As interpreted and executed by Secretary of War Henry Stimson and the man he put in charge of the operations, Lieutenant General John DeWitt, this meant that all Japanese—both U.S. citizens (*Nisei*) and noncitizens (*Issei*)—living within 200 miles of the Pacific Coast were to be "evacuated." Pursuant to this order, more than 100,000 persons were moved to internment camps in California, Idaho, Utah, Arizona, Wyoming, Colorado, and Arkansas.

The only significant opposition to internment came from Quaker activists and the American Civil Liberties Union. The ACLU funded lawsuits brought

Executive Order 9066, 1942

Whereas, the successful prosecution of the war requires every possible protection against espionage and against sabotage to national-defense material, national-defense premises and national defense utilities . . . :

Now therefore, by virtue of the authority vested in me as President of the United States, and Commander in Chief of the Army and Navy, I hereby authorize and direct the Secretary of War, and the Military Commanders whom he may from time to time designate . . . to prescribe military areas in such places and of such extent as he or the appropriate Military Commander may determine, from which any or all persons may be excluded, and with respect to which, the right of any persons to enter, remain in, or leave shall be subject to whatever restriction the Secretary of War or the appropriate Military Commander may impose in his discretion.

The Secretary of War is hereby authorized to provide for residents of any such area who are excluded therefrom, such transportation, food, shelter, and other accommodations as may be necessary, in the judgment of the Secretary of War or the said Military Commander, and until other arrangements are made, to accomplish the purpose of this order.

Excerpted from Franklin D. Roosevelt, "Executive Order 9066—Authorizing the Secretary of War to Prescribe Military Areas," February 19, 1942, in *Public Papers of the Presidents of the United States: Franklin D. Roosevelt, 1933–1945,* from the American Presidency Project, University of California, Santa Barbara, www.presidency.ucsb.edu.

before the U.S. Supreme Court—most notably *Hirabayashi v. United States* (320 U.S. 81 [1943], decided June 21, 1943) and *Korematsu v. United States* (323 U.S. 214 [1944], decided December 18, 1944)—but in all cases, the Court upheld the constitutionality of the executive order in a time of war.

On December 17, 1944, Major General Henry C. Pratt issued Public Proclamation No. 21, which, effective January 2, 1945, permitted the evacuees to return to their homes, thereby ending the Japanese internment policy and program.

Congress subsequently passed the Japanese American Evacuation Claims Act of 1948, which paid out approximately $31 million in compensation to former internees. It represented a small fraction of the actual financial losses incurred; nevertheless, all subsequent individual suits seeking compensation from the government failed until 1968, when a new act of Congress reimbursed some who had lost property because of their relocation. Twenty years later, in 1988, Congress appropriated more funds to pay a lump sum of $20,000 to each of the 60,000 surviving Japanese American internees.

Propaganda and Public Relations

In contrast to the massive, centralized propaganda machine created by George Creel during World War I (see Chapter 34), propaganda and public relations efforts in World War II were more diffuse. Given the nature of the war—a response to a Japanese attack on American territory and a crusade against enemies whose actions and declarations were manifestly evil—there was little need to "sell" the effort to the American people. War correspondents were given much greater freedom to report the war than was the case in World War I, and the major public relations effort was directed toward achieving four goals:

1. To exhort all Americans to make sacrifices and accept sacrifices: to serve in the armed forces, to achieve maximum production in war-related industries, and to contribute financially through the purchase of war bonds
2. To control information by preventing destructive rumors and the dissemination of secret information
3. To portray the solidarity of the great wartime alliances, especially with Britain
4. To rehabilitate the image of the Soviet Union, transforming the popular American conception of the nation as a Communist enemy into a perception of the Soviet Union as a gallant ally in a war against a common foe

Censorship was not nearly as heavy handed as it had been during World War I, and most newspaper editors and the producers of popular entertainment cooperated enthusiastically. The American public readily identified with the leading personalities of the war: the "monsters" of the Axis—Adolf Hitler of Germany, Benito Mussolini of Italy, and Hideki Tojo of Japan; and the "heroic leaders" of the Allies—especially Britain's prime minister Winston Churchill and American president Franklin D. Roosevelt, already considered a hero by many Americans for his leadership during the Great Depression. Americans also learned to idolize Douglas MacArthur and Dwight D. Eisenhower of the U.S. Army and Chester A. Nimitz and William "Bull" Halsey of the U.S. Navy, among many others. But more than anything, they perceived World War II as a soldier's war in which the "GI" or "dogface," as the enlisted man was called, became the collective hero. He was typically seen as both streetwise and spirited, a man whose wisecracking cynicism ended where his devotion to protecting his loved ones at home began.

World War II involved and made demands on the American home front to a greater degree than any previous conflict, save the Civil War (Chapter 17). Americans quickly adopted Winston Churchill's trademark two-finger "V for Victory" sign. Civilians eagerly bought war bonds, and they scratched out Victory Gardens in their backyards for the purpose of growing vegetables to help conserve food for "our boys." They readily submitted to a complex rationing system for food, fuel, clothing, and other commodities—although black-market activity was not uncommon. Women, who had played an important part in war production during World War I, served even more extensively in the second war. "Rosie the Riveter," a female factory worker clad in denim overalls and brandishing a rivet gun, became a universal icon of the war effort.

As in World War I, posters were used in World War II to promote bond drives. The government employed such notable artists as James Montgomery Flagg, whose popular version of the traditional Uncle Sam figure reappeared with great frequency.

Leading magazine illustrator Norman Rockwell concentrated on home-front images, including most famously his "Four Freedoms" series—"Freedom from Fear," "Freedom from Want," "Freedom of Speech," and "Freedom of Worship"—themes Franklin D. Roosevelt had enumerated in his 1942 State of the Union Address. These images illustrated what the United States was fighting for: practical, everyday issues that affected all Americans.

Many World War II posters depicted American servicemen—handsome and determined soldiers, sailors, and marines doing their duty and relying on the public's wholehearted support. For the first time in any war, glamorous women were depicted in the special uniforms of their own auxiliary service branches—the U.S. Navy's WAVES (Women Accepted for Voluntary Emergency Service) and the U.S. Army's WACs (Women's Auxiliary Corps) as well as the uniforms of the services' Nurse Corps—rather than dressed, as in the earlier war, in their brothers' or boyfriends' uniforms, or as Miss Liberty.

Hollywood films assumed an even greater propaganda role in World War II than they had in World War I. A highly active and influential government agency, the Office of War Information (OWI), was created to monitor and advise producers in all the mass media, but its efforts were the most vigorous with regard to the film industry. OWI wielded a strong moral authority, reviewing scripts as well as finished films and always putting to them a single overriding question: *How will this help win the war?* While OWI did not have *direct* censorship authority, it did communicate with the Office of Censorship, which could prevent the release of a movie to the foreign markets that were so vital to Hollywood's bottom line.

Congressional Oversight: The Truman Committee

Senator Harry S. Truman of Missouri initially took an interest in defense contracting to remedy his state's failure to get its fair share of defense contracts. This parochial objective, however, was soon eclipsed by Truman's growing concern over reports of inefficiency and outright corruption in the defense production program. In 1941 Truman was named to chair what was officially called the Senate War Investigating Committee, but became far better known as the Truman Committee.

The Truman Committee was ruthless in holding military officers, civil administrators, and especially defense contractors to the highest standards of efficiency, performance, and value for money. Truman uncovered widespread waste and fraud, but he was less interested in punishing poor performers and wrongdoers than in motivating them to deliver what they had promised. Accordingly, the committee made it a practice to issue draft reports of its findings to the corporations, unions, and government agencies under investigation, thereby inviting voluntary correction of abuses before prosecution commenced. The Truman Committee was launched on a budget of only $15,000 but probably saved the United States more than $15 billion. Less readily calculated are the positive effects of the increased production the committee made possible and the advances in the safety and reliability of certain equipment and weapons systems—most famously of the faulty Martin B-26 medium bomber, which the Truman Committee succeeded in getting redesigned. Truman's leadership resulted in his selection as Roosevelt's running mate in the president's fourth-term campaign of 1944.

Wartime Race Relations

During World War I, despite intense racial tensions in the United States, urgent demands spurred the enlistment or conscription of approximately 380,000 African Americans; however, 89 percent of these men were assigned to labor units, and only 11 percent were committed to combat. After World War I, African American army troops dwindled to 5,000 (2 percent of the service), with just five black officers. World War II saw a spectacular rise in black membership in the army—900,000 troops by war's end. Again, all served in segregated units, and most were in support roles.

One major African American labor leader, A. Philip Randolph, founder (in 1925) of the Brotherhood of Sleeping Car Porters, made a significant assault on racial discrimination in the months prior to the United States' entry into the war. Randolph warned President Franklin D. Roosevelt that he would lead a protest march on Washington, D.C., if racial discrimination in defense industries and federal agencies did not end. In response, on June 25, 1941, Roosevelt issued Executive Order 8802, which prohibited discrimination in all defense plants and federal bureaus. The order also established the Fair Employment Practices Committee to resolve grievances. During the war itself, Randolph refrained from pressing to integrate the armed forces, fearing such a campaign would be perceived as harmful to the war effort. Immediately after the war ended, however, he founded the League for Nonviolent Civil Disobedience against Military Segregation, an organization that was instrumental in President Harry S. Truman's decision to issue Executive Order 9981 on July 26, 1948, effectively ordering the integration of the armed forces.

As early as October 25, 1940, President Roosevelt had promoted Colonel Benjamin O. Davis Sr. to the temporary rank of brigadier general, making him the first African American to hold general officer rank. Davis retired on July 31, 1941, but was recalled to active duty with the permanent rank of brigadier general the following day. He was sent to Europe in September 1942 as an "Advisor on Negro Problems," assigned to manage the difficulties inherent in a segregated army.

In June 1941 Roosevelt also directed that the U.S. Army Air Forces be opened—albeit in a limited way—to black pilots. One of these men was Brigadier General Davis's son, Captain Benjamin O. Davis Jr., who was among the first of the so-called "Tuskegee Airmen," a unit of African American pilots trained at the all-black Tuskegee Institute in Alabama. (Davis was promoted to colonel during the war and retired from the air force in 1970 as a lieutenant general.) The Tuskegee Airmen served with great distinction as fighter pilots in the North African

and Italian theaters—typically escorting white-crewed heavy bombers—but their units remained segregated throughout the war.

Race relations in the U.S. Marine Corps were more restrictive than in the army. Prior to World War II, the Corps accepted no black enlistments. Just before the war, pursuant to directives from President Roosevelt, the commandant of the Marine Corps appointed a commission to study how black marines could best be used, but actual enlistments were not accepted until after the Japanese attack on Pearl Harbor. A segregated training facility, Camp Johnson, was established outside the central marine facility, Camp Lejeune, South Carolina, and the first recruits arrived in August 1942 to make up the Fifty-first Defense Battalion. Initially, all drill instructors were white, but they were replaced by black instructors as soon as they became available. The black marines were used almost exclusively as stewards and laborers, not as combat troops. In all, 19,000 African Americans served in the Marine Corps during World War II. Most had been drafted, and no black marine was commissioned an officer during the war.

Before the late nineteenth-century transition from sail to steam, the U.S. Navy enrolled many black sailors, whose labor was necessary to haul and set sails. As steam reduced the need for "hands," recruitment of African Americans declined, and those blacks who did join the navy were mainly assigned to service positions, typically as "mess boys," stewards, and orderlies serving white officers. After the United States gained control of the Philippines, black naval personnel were increasingly replaced by Filipinos, so that by America's entry into World War I, Filipinos outnumbered African Americans in the navy.

Beginning about 1932, African American enlistment rose; however, black personnel were still confined to service positions, and segregation was enforced aboard ships as well as in shore accommodations. In 1940 Walter White of the National Association for the Advancement of Colored People (NAACP), together with A. Phillip Randolph and another activist, T. Arnold Hill, wrote a letter to

President Roosevelt protesting the restrictions on black employment in the navy. Roosevelt responded by approving a plan to promote "fair treatment," but the navy pointedly failed to implement it, arguing that morale would suffer. After the United States entered World War II, the NAACP made a new appeal, this time to Secretary of the Navy Frank Knox, to accept African Americans in expanded roles. When Knox declined to act, the NAACP again appealed directly to the president, who in June 1942 personally prevailed upon the naval leadership to adopt an expanded assignment policy. The new guidelines admitted African American sailors to service in construction battalions, supply depots, air stations, shore stations, section bases, and yard craft. Although they were no longer restricted to mess duty, the new positions were still labor assignments rather than combat postings.

In December 1942 President Roosevelt issued an executive order calling for African Americans to make up 10 percent of all personnel drafted for all of the services. This created an especially dramatic increase in the naval enlistment of blacks—by July 1943, 12,000 were being inducted monthly. As of December 1943, 101,573 African Americans had enlisted in the navy. Of this number, 37,981 (37 percent) served in the Stewards Branch as "mess boys." The others served primarily in land-based support roles and as Shore Patrol (police security) personnel. Few black sailors were assigned sea duty.

Late in 1943, in an effort to improve morale among African American sailors, the navy commissioned a small number of black officers. The men selected were divided into line and staff officers. In January 1944 the line officers began segregated ten-week training courses at the Great Lakes Naval Training Center, and from this program twelve commissioned officers and one warrant officer emerged, the first African American officers in U.S. Navy history. They were assigned to recruit-training programs and small patrol craft and tugs. The officer candidates selected for commissioning as staff officers received their training in the summer of 1944 and graduated as ensigns or lieutenants junior grade

and were assigned to the Chaplain Corps, the Dental Corps, the Civil Engineer Corps, the Medical Corps, and the Supply Corps. During all of World War II, just 58 of 160,000 African American sailors were commissioned as officers.

Among enlisted personnel, genuine reform began in 1944, after Secretary of War Knox died and was replaced by James Forrestal. A political liberal and a civil rights activist, Forrestal launched a trial program in which black personnel were assigned to general sea-duty positions. To discourage segregation, the African American sailors were placed exclusively on large auxiliary vessels (such as cargo craft and tankers) and constituted no more than 10 percent of the crew of any one ship. Twenty-five ships were thus integrated, and none reported significant race-relation problems. The success of the pilot program prompted Forrestal to assign African American general service personnel to all auxiliary ships of the fleet. Perhaps more significant, the special training program for African American recruits was terminated, and they were assigned to the same training centers as whites. Thus it was in the U.S. Navy that the most important advances in military race relations were made during World War II.

The GI Bill

In contrast to the modest advances in race relations, World War II brought sweeping social change in the form of the Servicemen's Readjustment Act, better known as the "GI Bill of Rights" or the "GI Bill," signed by President Roosevelt on June 22, 1944.

The GI Bill provided federal aid to help veterans adjust to civilian life in the areas of hospitalization, purchase of homes and businesses, and, most importantly, education. The bill enabled former servicemen to receive a stipend of $20 per week for fifty-two weeks while they looked for work. It also provided them with low-interest home loans, which encouraged the growth of suburbs after the war, as many American families moved out of urban apartments. This contributed to a postwar democratization of housing in America, even as the GI Bill's provision of tuition, subsistence, books and supplies, equipment, and counseling services enabled veterans to receive the kind of college education previously reserved mainly for the children of the affluent. During the seven years following the end of World War II, some 8 million veterans received educational benefits. Of that number, approximately 2.3 million attended colleges and universities, 3.5 million received vocational school training, and 3.4 million received on-the-job training.

Atomic Weapons: Public Policy and Public Opinion

World War I had elevated the United States to the status of a major world power, but after the Republican Congress rejected U.S. membership in the League of Nations, the nation largely withdrew from international affairs. When Roosevelt took office, he began a policy of reengagement, and World War II thrust America into the very forefront of global politics. At the end of the war, the United States emerged as the most powerful nation in the world, its military supremacy ensured in large measure by its possession of the "ultimate weapon"—the atomic bomb.

The product of the massive Manhattan Project, a top-secret Anglo-American program that had begun even before U.S. entry into the war, the atomic bomb was successfully tested at Alamagordo, New Mexico, on July 16, 1945. Roosevelt's death on April 12, 1945, put Harry S. Truman into office, leaving him with the decision of whether, where, and when to use the new weapon, which was of unprecedented destructive potential. Some of the scientists who had worked on the project petitioned Truman and other leaders either to refrain altogether from using a weapon they considered immoral or, at minimum, to demonstrate the bomb to Japanese observers prior to dropping it on a Japanese target.

Truman clearly appreciated the moral dimension of using the atomic bomb, but he saw it as an alternative to a bloody invasion of the land of an enemy who, thus far, had defended each of its outlying possessions to the death. Military planners predicted that as many as a million Allied casualties would result from an invasion of Japan, which would also cost the lives of many more millions of Japanese. Accordingly, Truman believed he had no choice other than to order the atomic bomb to be used. It was, accordingly, dropped on Hiroshima on August 6, 1945, and on Nagasaki on August 9. On August 14, the Japanese accepted the Allied terms of surrender.

For the rest of his life, Harry S. Truman was questioned about the "difficulty" of his decision to use the atomic bomb against Japan. Every time he was asked, Truman denied that it had been a difficult decision and asserted that, under the circumstances, he had regarded "the bomb" as merely another military weapon—one so powerful that it might, at long last, end the war. After the war, however, he took the important step of ushering through Congress the Atomic Energy Act, which he signed on August 1, 1946, creating a civilian Atomic Energy Commission, thereby removing from military control the development and production of nuclear weapons and mandating research and development of peaceful uses of nuclear energy.

Yalta and Potsdam Conferences

The conduct of World War II had been punctuated by a series of major conferences among the Allies, the most important of which were those held at Washington, D.C. (December 22, 1941–January 14, 1942; June 20–25, 1942; and May 12–27, 1943); Casablanca, Morocco (January 14–24, 1943); Quebec, Canada (August 17–24, 1943, and September 12–16, 1944); Cairo, Egypt (November 23–26, 1943); Tehran, Iran (November 28–December 1, 1943); and Yalta, Crimea, in the Soviet Union (February 4–11, 1945)—the last conference an ailing Roosevelt attended. With Churchill and Stalin, Roosevelt formulated plans for dealing with a defeated Germany and attempted to hammer out a policy for postwar Europe. Also on the table was an agreement for the creation of the United Nations and, concluded in secret, a definition of the terms on which the Soviets would enter the war against Japan.

Roosevelt's successor, Harry S. Truman, represented the United States at the next Allied conference with Stalin and Churchill (who was replaced by Clement Attlee after the British election). This meeting, held during July 17–August 2, 1945, at the Berlin suburb of Potsdam, Germany, was the last of the Allied conferences of World War II. It was while he attended this conference that Truman learned of the successful test of the atomic bomb and announced to Stalin the development of "the most powerful explosive ever made." Truman was puzzled that the Soviet leader seemed unimpressed by the news and assumed that Stalin simply did not understand the magnitude of the revelation—especially since Truman had carefully avoided revealing that the new explosive was an atomic bomb. In fact, and quite unknown to Truman, Stalin had a mole at the Los Alamos Laboratory, Klaus Fuchs, and was already aware of the existence of the Manhattan Project and the bomb.

In addition to the news concerning the atomic bomb, other major issues discussed were the European peace settlements; the immediate postwar administration of a defeated Germany; the determination of Poland's boundaries; the terms of the occupation of Austria; the Soviet role in eastern Europe; Axis war reparations; and the strategy for bringing the Pacific war to a conclusion. At the very end of this list was the subject of Korea. The nation had been occupied by Japan since the beginning of World War II, and the Allies agreed that the Soviets would clear remaining Japanese resistance and accept the surrender of Japanese troops north of the 38th parallel and U.S. forces would do the same south of that line. Little discussion and less thought was given to this division, which the Western allies considered no more than an administrative convenience for the

The "Big Three"—Prime Minister Winston Churchill, President Franklin Roosevelt, and Marshal Joseph Stalin—meet at Yalta in 1945. Representing the major Allied powers, the leaders of the "Grand Alliance" came to the summit with their own plans for European postwar reorganization. Many historians believe that Roosevelt, who would only live several months longer, made too many concessions to Stalin, setting the stage for the Cold War.

immediate period of the postwar occupation. It would, in fact, lead to the Korean War (Chapter 37).

Selling the Marshall Plan

At the end of the war, the Truman administration was determined not to repeat the tragic error of World War I, which imposed on a defeated Germany the ruinous terms of the Treaty of Versailles—terms that had created such economic devastation and national humiliation that they fomented the rise of Adolf Hitler and the Nazi Party and, Truman and many others believed, led to World War II. Even more pressing at the end of World War II was the threat posed by the Communist Soviet Union. The Soviets had entered the war in league with Germany. After being betrayed by Hitler's invasion on June 22, 1941, however, the nation was transformed into what Churchill and Roosevelt called a "gallant ally."

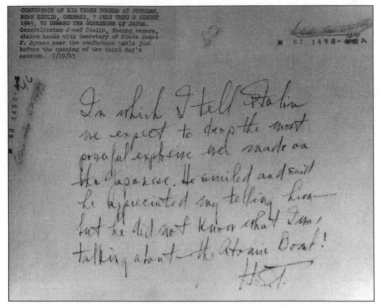

CONFERENCE OF BIG THREE POWERS AT POTSDAM, NEAR BERLIN, GERMANY, 7 JULY THRU 2 AUGUST 1945, TO DEMAND THE SURRENDER OF JAPAN. Generalissimo Josef Stalin, facing camera, shakes hands with Secretary of State James F. Byrnes near the conference table just before the opening of the third day's session. 7/19/45

In which I tell Stalin we expect to drop the most powerful explosive ever made on the Japanese. He smiled and said he appreciated my telling him — but he did not know what I was talking about — the Atomic Bomb!

HST.

President Harry S. Truman's handwritten note on the back of a photograph taken at the Potsdam Conference on July 19, 1945—the last meeting of the "Big Three" powers that defeated Germany—describes how he told Joseph Stalin about the atomic bomb. Truman's assertion that Stalin did not know about the bomb proved wrong, as the Soviets were working on their own atomic project that in 1949 resulted in the first successful Soviet atomic test and helped fuel the fire of the emerging Cold War.

Throughout the rest of the war, anti-Communist hostility was suspended in the United States and Britain, but no sooner was Germany defeated than the Soviet Union positioned itself to assume control over as much of Europe as it could possibly take into its powerful embrace.

With Europe devastated, the United States had begun to send aid and relief well before the war had ended; this aid amounted to some $9 billion by early 1947. The war had shattered lives as well as infrastructure, and it had also disrupted the basics of trade. Farmers could still produce food, but city dwellers had no way to pay for it. Industrial plants could be rebuilt, but neither urbanites nor farmers could pay for the goods produced. This level of economic paralysis made the ground fertile for the Communist "solution" the Soviets offered.

There were several plans to restart the European economy on Truman's desk. Secretary of State James F. Byrnes proposed an aid plan in a speech at the Stuttgart Opera House in Germany on September 6, 1946, and General Lucius D. Clay laid out a program for the reindustrialization of Germany. At about this time, Undersecretary of State Dean Acheson and Vice President Alben W. Barkley formulated their own relief plans. All of these men worked against an opposing plan, introduced by Secretary of the Treasury Henry Morgenthau Jr. In the "Morgenthau Plan," Germany would pay for most of the rebuilding of Europe through massive war reparations, which (by design) would also prevent Germany from ever being rebuilt as an industrial power. Morgenthau wanted the nation reduced to a pre-industrial agricultural state. President Roosevelt had endorsed the Morgenthau Plan, but Truman saw in it the repetition of Versailles. He did not want to have won the war only to lose the peace—as had happened following World War I.

George Catlett Marshall, who as U.S. Army chief of staff during the war had been one of the architects of the Allied military victory, replaced Byrnes as secretary of state in January 1947. He saw economic aid to Europe as a necessary humanitarian measure and also as a means of countering Soviet expansionism. With his staff, Marshall prepared a European Recovery Program, which he announced in a speech at Harvard University on June 5, 1947. Momentous as it was, the speech contained no details concerning the plan and offered not a single number or dollar figure. Instead, Marshall simply called on Europeans to create their own plan for European recovery, which the United States would fund. It was the launch of an aid program unprecedented in the history of the United States or, for that matter, the world.

Truman and Marshall assumed that the aid plan would be unpopular among Americans. For that reason, no American journalists were invited to attend the Harvard speech. Indeed, Truman even called a Washington press conference that day, precisely to draw attention away from Cambridge. In contrast, Undersecretary of State Dean Acheson was assigned to contact European journalists, so that the speech would get full coverage in Europe. Truman wanted the U.S. government to make a promise that American politicians would be too embarrassed to withdraw. Once the plan was announced, however, Marshall toured the country to promote it and found that American taxpayers accepted it.

As for Europe, Marshall made it clear that European cooperation—not selfish nationalism—was a precondition for receiving aid. The Committee for European Economic Cooperation, made up of delegates from sixteen nations, requested and received $22.4 billion from the United States.

The Marshall Plan proved a great humanitarian and political success—perhaps the greatest positive legacy of America's participation in World War II. It not only provided emergency aid to millions, but it also gave Europe the tools with which it built its own economic recovery. This was a more formidable bulwark against the spread of Soviet Communism than any Western military deterrent. (The Soviet Union and Soviet-bloc nations were invited to participate in the benefits of the plan, but pointedly declined.) Winston Churchill characterized the Marshall Plan as the "most unsordid act in modern history."

BIBLIOGRAPHY

Atkinson, Richard. *An Army at Dawn: The War in North Africa, 1942–1943.* New York: Henry Holt, 2002.

Botjer, George F. *Sideshow War: The Italian Campaign, 1943–1945.* College Station: Texas A&M University Press, 1996.

Keegan, John. *The Second World War.* New York: Viking, 1989.

Morison, Samuel Eliot. *The Two-Ocean War.* New York: Galahad, 1997.

Spector, Ronald H. *Eagle against the Sun: The American War against Japan.* New York: Free Press, 1985.

Taylor, A. J. P. *The Origins of the Second World War.* New York: Atheneum, 1983.

———, ed. *History of World War II.* London: Octopus, 1974.

Weigley, Russell Frank. *Eisenhower's Lieutenants: The Campaign for France and Germany, 1944–1945.* Bloomington: Indiana University Press, 1981.

CHAPTER 37

KOREAN WAR (1950–1953)

At Issue

In May 1948, Korea was split along the 38th parallel into a Communist, pro-Soviet North Korea (the People's Democratic Republic of Korea) and a capitalist, pro-West South Korea (Republic of Korea). On June 25, 1950, the North Korean People's Army invaded South Korea, prompting the United Nations—led militarily by the United States—to come to the aid of the South Koreans.

The Conflict

As World War II ended (Chapter 36), the United States occupied the southern portion of the Korean peninsula and the Soviet Union the northern portion. The United States acquiesced in the north-south partition of Korea, which had been occupied by Japan during the war, as a temporary expedient pending Korea's restoration to peacetime conditions. The Soviets, however, seized on the partition to bring northern Korea into the Communist sphere and built fortifications along the 38th parallel. In September 1947 the United States requested that the United Nations intervene to bring about Korean unification. Over Soviet objections, the UN voted to establish a unified government for Korea following a general election. With Soviet backing, North Korean Communists barred the UN commission from holding elections north of the 38th parallel. The elections proceeded south of the parallel on May 10, 1948, however, creating the Republic of Korea (ROK) under President Syngman Rhee. When the UN twice affirmed the ROK as the lawful government of Korea, the Soviets supported the establishment of a rival government in North Korea, sponsoring the May 25, 1948, elections that created the People's Democratic Republic of Korea (DRK), under the leadership of Kim Il-Sung, a Soviet-trained Korean Communist.

After the DRK was established, the Soviets announced that they would withdraw Red Army troops from the country by January 1, 1949. The United States also withdrew its troops, but resolved to train and equip a security force for South Korea and to provide economic development aid while continuing to press the UN for the reunification of Korea. The United States limited its military aid proposal to training and equipping an ROK army of no more than 65,000, a coast guard of 4,000, and a police force of 35,000. Tanks, artillery, and an air force would not be funded. President Rhee argued for much larger forces and, on his own, created an air force. The United States completed a military withdrawal from Korea on June 29, 1949, leaving behind a 472-troop U.S. Korean Military Advisory Group (KMAG).

The Soviets supplied military equipment to North Korea and initially encouraged low-level guerrilla warfare. Kim Il-Sung, however, persuaded Soviet premier Joseph Stalin to support a full-scale invasion of the south, which began at 4:00 a.m. on June 25, 1950, as North Korean People's Army (NKPA) units crossed the 38th parallel, easily overrunning inferior South Korean forces. The main NKPA force captured Seoul, the South Korean capital, about thirty-five miles below the parallel, while smaller forces moved down the center of the Korean peninsula and along the east coast. U.S. president Harry S. Truman ordered General Douglas MacArthur, commander of the U.S. Far East Command, to send the ROK army equipment and ammunition to replace all that it had abandoned in retreat.

In truth, there was little more that the United States could do quickly. The rush to demobilize after World War II had left U.S. forces understaffed and underequipped. Moreover, while President Truman wanted to contain Communist aggression in Korea, he did not want to trigger a major war involving the Soviets and quite possibly the Communist Chinese, who were on the verge of victory over the Chinese Nationalists in the civil war engulfing China.

Truman ordered the Seventh U.S. Fleet to proceed toward Korea, but then redeployed most of it to Formosa (Taiwan), in an effort to discourage Chinese Communists from attacking the Chinese Nationalists' island stronghold. Truman also ordered MacArthur to make air and naval strikes against North Korean positions below the 38th parallel. Finally, on June 30, 1950, he authorized MacArthur to use all available U.S. forces. The key word was "available." All that were ready to fight were some understrength units of the Eighth Army, the Twenty-ninth Regimental Combat Team, and the modestly sized Far East Air Force. In the meantime—on June 25—Truman had secured a UN resolution authorizing military action against North Korea. Truman named MacArthur commander of U.S. and UN forces; several UN member nations participated in the Korean War, but the United States contributed by far the greatest numbers of troops and equipment.

Despite the resolution, UN military objectives were unclear. Left undecided was whether UN forces would be permitted to operate north of the 38th parallel or would simply remain on the defensive in the South. Nevertheless, U.S. ground forces began arriving in Korea on June 30, by which time the NKPA had crossed the Han River *south* of Seoul and was still on the move. By July 3, Kimpo Airfield, near Seoul, and the port of Inchon, on South Korea's

west coast, were in Communist hands. Without time to consolidate his forces, MacArthur decided to act immediately. Grasping that the North Koreans intended to take the port of Pusan, a large city on South Korea's east coast, MacArthur deployed "Task Force Smith" just above Pusan on July 5. Outgunned, the task force retreated, and the NKPA pushed ROK and U.S. forces to Taejon, in south central South Korea, by July 13.

CHRONOLOGY OF THE KOREAN WAR

1950

June 25 North Korean troops invade South Korea. The United Nations authorizes U.S. (and U.S.-directed coalition) action in Korea.

July 5 U.S. "Task Force Smith" is defeated above Pusan.

Aug. 7 The United States begins a counterattack from Pusan.

Sept. 15 General Douglas MacArthur leads the Inchon landing.

Oct. 1 U.S.-supplied South Korean forces cross the 38th parallel into North Korea.

Oct. 9 The U.S. Eighth Army crosses the 38th parallel into North Korea.

Nov. 25 300,000 Chinese troops cross the Yalu River into North Korea.

Dec. 15 U.S.-led UN and South Korean forces, having withdrawn to South Korea, establish a defensive line at the 38th parallel.

Dec. 25 The Chinese are stopped at 38th parallel.

1951

Jan. 4 Seoul falls to North Korean troops.

Jan. 25 U.S. "meat grinder" operation commences.

Apr. 11 Truman relieves MacArthur for insubordination; Matthew Ridgway assumes command of the UN coalition.

Apr. 22 A Chinese "Spring Offensive" drives Ridgway back to Seoul.

June 1 Ridgway pushes the Chinese north of the 38th parallel.

July 10 Peace talks begin at Kaesong. Guerrilla-style war continues without major gains for either side.

1953

July 27 U.S. and North Korean representatives sign an armistice.

During these desperate delaying actions, MacArthur built up forces in Japan. On July 18, two divisions were moved to South Korea to reinforce Taejon, but the city was captured by the NKPA on July 20. As humiliating as these defeats were, MacArthur saw that the NKPA had stretched its lines of communication and supply to the breaking point; while U.S. ground troops were outnumbered, the U.S. Air Force was able to interdict NKPA supply lines. Simultaneously, a naval blockade was proving highly effective in cutting off NKPA supplies by sea.

At last, on the ground, Lieutenant General Walton H. Walker, commander of the Eighth U.S. Army, decided to make a stand along a line north of Pusan—the 140-mile-long "Pusan perimeter"—which extended in an arc from the Korea Strait to the Sea of Japan. Despite being outnumbered, Walker's troops enjoyed efficient communication and could be shifted rapidly to meet attacks wherever they might occur. The Pusan defense therefore bought MacArthur the time he needed to build up forces sufficient for a counterattack, which began on August 7.

MacArthur wanted to exploit the NKPA's supply problems by creating a pincers attack, trapping the North Koreans between the Eighth Army on the south and another force attacking from the north. To position a large force north of the NKPA, MacArthur decided on a high-risk amphibious assault at Inchon. Although this position was ideally suited from a strategic point of view, Inchon's variable tides created great hazards for landing craft, and the approach to the harbor lay through a narrow and treacherous channel. Furthermore, the troops, once landed, would have to scale a high seawall, then fight through a thickly populated area. Nevertheless, MacArthur committed all of his forces to the Inchon assault, leaving nothing in reserve.

The Inchon operation was launched on September 15, 1950, and proved a spectacular success. Within two weeks, Seoul was liberated. During September 16–23, Walker's Eighth Army began its counterattack. After first offering stiff resistance, the NKPA began a rapid withdrawal. The Eighth Army pursued, linking up with the Inchon landing force on September 26. By this time, the NKPA had recrossed the 38th parallel. This left UN planners to decide whether to invade North Korea or to remain in a defensive position south of the parallel. Although both Communist China and the Soviet Union had stated their intention to defend against such an invasion, President Truman decided to take the gamble. On September 27, he ordered General MacArthur to pursue the NKPA across the 38th parallel, cautioning that he was to press the advance only in the absence of Chinese or Soviet intervention. Truman further warned MacArthur that once UN forces neared the Yalu River (the border with Manchuria) and the Tumen River (the border with the Soviet Union), he was to use South Korean (ROK) troops exclusively.

Two ROK corps crossed the 38th parallel on October 1, and, on October 9, Walker led the Eighth Army's I Corps across. By October 19, I Corps had cleared Pyongyang, the North Korean capital, and by October 24 was just fifty miles outside Manchuria. ROK forces were also now positioned close to the Chinese border.

At this point, China threatened to intervene, and Truman called a conference with MacArthur on Wake Island in the north Pacific, about 2,300 miles west of Hawaii. After the general assured him that the Chinese were bluffing and would not invade, Truman authorized the advance to continue. The troops met with increasingly strong resistance, and, on October 26, MacArthur determined that Communist Chinese troops were strengthening the North Korean lines. By November, it became clear that five Chinese divisions had joined the fight. Although this was a significant force, MacArthur believed that a truly massive Chinese commitment would not be made. He was wrong. During the night of November 25, 1950, waves of Chinese troops hit the Eighth Army hard on its center and right. Two days later, yet more powerful Chinese attacks overran units of X Corps on its left flank. By November 28, all UN positions were caving in against the onslaught of some 300,000 Chinese troops.

Walker withdrew the Eighth Army and UN troops as quickly as he could to prevent envelopment. Even

UN air superiority evaporated as Soviet-built Chinese MiG-15 jet fighters outperformed U.S. piston-driven craft. By December 15, with severe losses, UN forces had withdrawn to the 38th parallel, where they began to establish a defensive line across the width of the Korean peninsula. Simultaneously, a combined air and sealift evacuated X Corps from North Korea. In the course of the evacuation, Walker was killed in an automobile accident, and Lieutenant General Matthew B. Ridgway replaced him as commander of the Eighth Army.

MacArthur responded to Chinese intervention by lobbying for permission to attack China, especially the airfields in Manchuria. Wanting to avoid a new world war, Truman and the Joint Chiefs of Staff ordered MacArthur to limit the war, keeping it within Korea. MacArthur protested.

In the meantime, Seoul fell to the Communists on January 4, 1951; however, the Chinese did not pursue the Eighth Army south of the capital, and within weeks U.S. and UN forces had halted all Chinese advances. Ridgway believed that by fighting a war of attrition, the Communists, over time, could be defeated. MacArthur, however, continued to assert that victory was possible only by attacking China. Nevertheless, the Joint Chiefs of Staff and Truman restricted MacArthur to defending his positions in Korea in a manner that inflicted as many casualties on the enemy as possible. Thus, on January 25, 1951, Ridgway began a slow and excruciating offensive that frontline soldiers dubbed the "meat grinder" because, without making any dramatic breakthroughs, it relentlessly ground away at the enemy. By mid-March, Seoul had been liberated, and by March 21, U.S.-led UN troops were back at the 38th parallel.

And it was at the 38th parallel that the U.S-led UN troops halted. The UN had decided that securing

Refugees from Pyongyang, North Korea, on December 4, 1950, flee south across the Taedong River to escape advancing Chinese Communist troops, who entered the war in support of North Korea. (This photograph by Max Desfor won a Pulitzer Prize in 1951.)

South Korea below the 38th parallel was an acceptable outcome of the war. MacArthur was informed that President Truman intended to initiate negotiations with the Chinese and North Koreans on the basis of current positions. Outraged, MacArthur preempted Truman's announcement by making an unauthorized announcement of his own, declaring that if the UN would expand the conflict to North Korea's coastal areas and interior strongholds, the Chinese would certainly back down. This announcement forced Truman to postpone his peace initiative. On April 5, 1951, MacArthur forced the issue further.

On that date, Representative Joseph W. Martin read into the *Congressional Record* a letter from MacArthur stating the necessity of opening up a second front against China itself, allying with Nationalist Chinese troops. It was an act of gross insubordination, and, on April 11, Truman relieved MacArthur as UN commander.

Matthew Ridgway, appointed to replace MacArthur, turned over the 80,000 men of the Eighth Army to Lieutenant General James A. Van Fleet. On April 22, a new massive offensive, consisting of twenty-one Chinese and nine North Korean divisions, descended on the U.S.-led UN forces. Although the first phase of this "Spring Offensive" inflicted some 7,000 casualties on the Eighth Army, the Communists lost ten times that number. They unleashed a second phase of the offensive on May 14, attacking the right flank of X Corps with twenty divisions, only to discover that Van Fleet had anticipated this attack and had bolstered his front lines. The offensive was blunted, and the Communists absorbed some 90,000 casualties.

At this point, the character of the war radically changed. The Communists abandoned the mass offensive and began making stealthy hit-and-run attacks using small units. The rest of the war consisted of these guerrilla tactics. Van Fleet assumed the offensive, advancing on May 22, 1951, but was ordered to halt the next month—having pushed the Chinese north of the 38th parallel on June 1—lest the Soviets be provoked to enter the war.

Peace talks, initially brokered by the Soviet ambassador to the UN, Yakov A. Malik, began on July 10, 1951, at Kaesong and dragged on for two years, during which grim guerrilla combat continued. It was finally agreed that an armistice would require accord on a demarcation line and demilitarized zone, impartial supervision of the truce, and arrangements for return of prisoners of war. The disposition of prisoners proved to be the most difficult issue. UN negotiators wanted prisoners to decide for themselves whether they would return home; the Communists, fearful of mass defection, held out for mandatory repatriation. Hoping to break the dead-

lock, General Mark Clark, who succeeded Ridgway as UN commander in May 1952, intensified bombing raids on North Korea. But it was not until April 1953 that the issue was resolved by a compromise that permitted freed prisoners to choose sides, under the supervision of a neutral commission.

At this point, South Korean president Syngman Rhee, who wanted nothing short of Korean unification (under his leadership) and wholly voluntary repatriation, sabotaged the peace process by ordering the release of 25,000 North Korean prisoners who wanted to live in the South. In order to regain Rhee's cooperation, the United States pledged a mutual security agreement and long-term economic aid; however, the armistice of July 27, 1953, went unsigned by Rhee. It did not matter. The armistice held, and the shooting war was over. No formal treaty was ever signed.

Potsdam Conference

As discussed in Chapter 36, this July 17–August 2, 1945, meeting among the leaders of the United States, the Soviet Union, and Britain included a decision to for the temporary division of Korea, which had been occupied by Japan since the beginning of World War II, between Soviet and American administration. While the Soviets would clear remaining Japanese resistance and accept the surrender of Japanese troops north of the 38th parallel, U.S. forces would do the same south of that line. The Americans assumed a Soviet understanding and agreement that the division would end after a sovereign, unified government had been created in Korea. President Truman glossed over the fact that President Franklin Roosevelt had failed to get a definitive response from Joseph Stalin at the Yalta Conference in February 1945 when he proposed establishing an international trusteeship for Korea to prepare it for independence after the final defeat of Japan. Stalin had not objected at that time, but neither had he agreed. At Potsdam Stalin accepted the division of responsibility in Korea, but did not comment on its temporary nature.

Harry S. Truman

(1884–1972)

Born in Lamar, Missouri, and raised in Independence, Harry Truman was the son of a farmer. After high school, he worked as a bank clerk in Kansas City, then returned to the family farm near Grandview in 1906. When the United States entered World War I in 1917, thirty-three-year-old Truman volunteered and served in France as the captain of a field artillery battery. He returned to the United States in 1919, married his childhood sweetheart, Elizabeth ("Bess") Wallace, and started a haberdashery. The business went bankrupt, and in 1922, supported by the powerful machine of Thomas Pendergast, the Democratic boss of Kansas City, Truman was elected to a county judgeship (in Missouri, this was the equivalent of a county commissioner). Although he failed to gain reelection in 1924, he was elected presiding judge of the county court in 1926 and served two four-year terms, building a reputation for honesty and efficiency. This made Truman popular, but it alarmed Pendergast, who was fearful that he could not control his protégé. Nevertheless, after others declined Pendergast's offer of support for U.S. Senate candidacy, Truman accepted—and won.

Truman entered the Senate in 1935. During his second term, he created the Special Committee Investigating National Defense (known as the Truman Committee) and earned national recognition for its investigations of graft, fraud, and deficiencies in war production. In 1944 President Franklin Roosevelt chose Truman as his running mate in his fourth-term candidacy. After serving eighty-two days as vice president, Truman was sworn in as thirty-third president of the United States following Roosevelt's sudden death on April 12, 1945. Not since Andrew Johnson had followed the assassinated Abraham Lincoln into office had a vice president been required to meet so formidable a challenge. Although the war in Europe was near victory, the war against Japan was far from over. Truman saw the nation through the rest of World War II, deciding to use atomic weapons against Japan and handling the difficult negotiations with the Soviets at the end of the war.

In the postwar environment, Truman became the architect of America's Cold War strategy of the "containment" of communism. He implemented this policy in aid to Greece and Turkey, both of which were threatened by Communist insurgencies in 1947, and through the Marshall Plan, which undercut the appeal of communism in Europe by aiding economic recovery. In 1948 Truman stood for reelection to his own term and, contrary to all predictions, defeated Republican candidate Thomas E. Dewey. During his second term, Truman introduced an extension of Roosevelt's New Deal, called the Fair Deal, which included ambitious social welfare programs—most of which were defeated or diluted. Truman scored a new Cold War victory in 1948 with his circumvention of the Soviet blockade of West Berlin by means of the Berlin Airlift, and he led the United States in the creation of the North Atlantic Treaty Organization (NATO), a military coalition with other Western democracies to resist Communist aggression.

The most severe test of the "Truman Doctrine," as the containment policy was called, came in June 1950, with the start of the Korean War, in which the president walked a thin line between the objectives of defeating the Communists and avoiding a third world war. Truman's conduct of the war, especially his relief of General Douglas MacArthur as supreme commander of U.S. and UN forces in Korea, caused his popularity to plummet, and he chose not to run for a second term in his own right. In retirement, Truman wrote two memoirs and devoted much of his time to his favorite pursuit, reading history. He lived long enough to see himself regarded by many as a great American president.

The "Containment" Concept and Policy

From May 1944 to April 1946 George F. Kennan headed the U.S. diplomatic mission to the Soviet Union. Shortly before he left this post, he transmitted to Secretary of State James Byrnes an 8,000-word document that became known to history as the **"Long Telegram."** In it, he outlined a strategy for conducting postwar diplomatic relations with the Soviet Union. He explained his impression that the Soviet leadership had a "neurotic view of world affairs," characterized by intense insecurity, which would drive the Soviets to expand their sphere of influence and control, even to the point of war. The critical problem for the United States would be checking this expansion without triggering World War III. Kennan proposed that the United States take steps to "contain"—that was his word—the spread of Soviet influence in areas of vital strategic importance to the nation. The "containment of communism"—not its annihilation, which would have entailed a major war—became the policy of the Truman administration and was America's basis for prosecuting the half-century Cold War against the Soviet Union and Communist China.

The first test of containment came during a civil war in Greece. Democratic elections in March 1946 had returned King George II to the Greek throne, and when he died just six months later, his brother, Paul, succeeded him. During the transition, the Greek Communist Party created what it called the Democratic Army, which sought to overthrow King Paul. The Greek Communists were a small minority, but they had the backing of the Soviet Union, which stood to gain control of Greece if the Communists won the civil war. On March 12, 1947, Truman addressed a joint session of Congress, calling for the United States to confront and contain the Communists in Greece by sending direct aid to the elected majority government. He put this call in a larger context by proclaiming as the policy of the United States support for "free peoples" everywhere in their fight against Communist subversion. The press called this the "Truman Doctrine," echoing the "Monroe Doctrine"—President James Monroe's defiant 1823 warning to European powers not to interfere in the affairs of the Western Hemisphere.

Thanks to U.S. aid, King Paul's government defeated the Communist Party in Greece. In the meantime, Kennan reworked the Long Telegram into

Kennan's "Long Telegram," 1946

In [Soviet communism], we have . . . a political force committed fanatically to the belief that with US there can be no permanent *modus vivendi* that it is desirable and necessary that the internal harmony of our society be disrupted, our traditional way of life be destroyed, the international authority of our state be broken, if Soviet power is to be secure. This political force has complete power of disposition over energies of one of world's greatest peoples and resources of world's richest national territory, and is borne along by deep and powerful currents of Russian nationalism. In addition, it has an elaborate and far flung apparatus for exertion of its influence in other countries, an apparatus of amazing flexibility and versatility, managed by people whose experience and skill in underground methods are presumably without parallel in history. . . . Problem of how to cope with this force [is] undoubtedly greatest task our diplomacy has ever faced and probably greatest it will ever have to face. . . . I would like to record my conviction that problem is within our power to solve—and that without recourse to any general military conflict.

Excerpted from the National Security Archive, George Washington University, "George Kennan's 'Long Telegram' (Moscow to Washington, February 22, 1946)," in Cold War Documents, www.gwu.edu/~nsarchiv/coldwar/documents/episode-1/kennan.htm.

an article entitled "The Sources of Soviet Conduct," which was published in the July 1974 issue of *Foreign Affairs* under the pseudonym "X." The "X Article" became the ideological basis for further elaboration of the Truman Doctrine, which mandated (in the words of Kennan's article) the "long-term, patient but firm and vigilant containment of Russian expansive tendencies . . . [by the] adroit and vigilant application of counter-force at a series of constantly shifting geographical and political points, corresponding to the shifts and maneuvers of Soviet policy."

Truman's response to the next Soviet-triggered crisis, the Soviet blockade of Berlin in June 1948, flowed directly from the containment concept. The Berlin Airlift, which spanned June 26, 1948, to September 30, 1949, defied the blockade without provoking a world war. It was one of the great early triumphs of the Cold War, forcing the Soviets to lift the blockade and thereby tacitly admit the right of West Berlin to exist in the very midst of East Germany.

Thus, when Soviet-backed North Korean forces invaded South Korea on June 24, 1950, President Truman believed he had a proven approach to Communist aggression. He would do what he had done before: take steps to *contain* communism. In this case, there was no alternative to war—the North Koreans had invaded, and they were shooting—but there was an alternative to a world war. Truman would lead something new in international politics: a *limited* war.

Korean Aid Package

The Communist victory in the Chinese Civil War, combined with the first Soviet tests of atomic weapons in 1949, prompted the creation of a policy designated NSC (National Security Council) 48/2, which implemented "containment" in Asia. The policy specified that the effort would be predominantly nonmilitary, consisting mainly of a program of economic aid given to non-Communist regimes in Asia.

When the 40,000-troop U.S. garrison withdrew from South Korea (except for 472 military advisers) after World War II, the nation was left with light weapons only—and the rudiments of an air force. The situation was made worse when, on January 12, 1950, Secretary of State Dean Acheson delivered a speech to the National Press Club in which he explained that America's Pacific defense perimeter was made up of the Aleutian Islands, the Ryukyu Islands (of Japan), and the Philippines. By failing to mention South Korea—an apparently unintentional omission—Acheson seemed to imply that the United States would not defend South Korea and effectively encouraged North Korean aggression.

Security Council Resolution of June 27, 1950

The June 25, 1950, invasion of South Korea triggered a week of meetings in the Truman White House as the president and his cabinet sought to determine the most effective and viable course of action. On the morning of June 27, President Truman met with congressional leaders to report on the developments in Korea. That afternoon, acting on the president's instructions, Secretary of State Dean Acheson called for a meeting of the UN Security Council to put before it a resolution calling on all member nations to assist South Korea. Prepared by the State Department, the resolution had been ready in the morning, but was not introduced until the late afternoon because the Indian delegation had been awaiting instructions from its government. In the hostile ideological climate of the times, even this minor delay gave the Soviet delegation propaganda ammunition, allowing them to suggest that the United States was attempting to coerce members into action they were actually unwilling to take. At 3:00 p.m. the **Security Council Resolution of June 27, 1950,** was introduced and adopted, the Soviets having boycotted the Security Council meeting. It would be the first major test of the world deliberative body, which had been created during the final days of World War II.

Security Council Resolution of June 27, 1950

The Security Council,

Having determined that the armed attack upon the Republic of Korea by forces from North Korea constitutes a breach of the peace,

Having called for an immediate cessation of hostilities, and

Having called upon the authorities of North Korea to withdraw forthwith their armed forces to the 38th parallel, and

Having noted from the report of the United Nations Commission for Korea that the authorities in North Korea have neither ceased hostilities nor withdrawn their armed forces to the 38th parallel and that urgent military measures are required to restore international peace and security, and

Having noted the appeal from the Republic of Korea to the United Nations for immediate and effective steps to secure peace and security,

Recommends that the Members of the United Nations furnish such assistance to the Republic of Korea as may be necessary to repel the armed attack and to restore international peace and security in the area.

Excerpted from the Truman Presidential Library and Museum, "Resolution Dated June 27, 1950 . . . ," in the Papers of Eben A. Ayers, www.trumanlibrary.org/whistlestop /study_collections/korea/large/week1/ayer_1_1.htm.

"Police Action"

Immediately following the Security Council vote approving aid to South Korea, President Truman issued to the press a **statement** explaining that he had "ordered United States air and sea forces to give the Korean Government troops aid and support" pursuant to the Security Council resolution. Truman was careful, first and foremost, to present the mobilization order as part of a UN operation, not as the exclusive decision of the United States government. He also took care to define the support as "air and sea forces," leaving out, for the present, mention of ground forces. Truman was well aware of the wariness with which the American public viewed the deployment of soldiers on the ground. Finally, Truman included an ideological justification for intervention in Korea that was in line with the Truman Doctrine and the policy of containment of Communist aggression not only in Korea, but potentially in Formosa (Taiwan), the refuge of the anti-Communist Nationalist Chinese.

In his 1956 *Memoirs,* Truman carefully explained the thinking behind his policy of limited warfare in Korea:

Statement by President Harry S. Truman, June 27, 1950

The attack upon Korea makes it plain beyond all doubt that Communism has passed beyond the use of subversion to conquer independent nations and will now use armed invasion and war. It has defied the orders of the Security Council of the United Nations issued to preserve international peace and security. In these circumstances the occupation of Formosa [Taiwan] by Communist forces would be a direct threat to the security of the Pacific area and to United States forces performing their lawful and necessary functions in that area.

Excerpted from the Truman Presidential Library and Museum, "Statement, dated June 27, 1950 . . . ," in the Papers of George M. Elsey, www.trumanlibrary.org/ whistlestop/study_collections/korea/large/week1/kw_ 27_1.htm.

In Korea, the Communists challenged us, but they were capable of challenging us in a similar way in many places and, what was even more serious, they could, if they chose, plunge us and the world into another and far more terrible war. Every decision I made in connection with the Korean conflict had this one aim in mind: to prevent a third world war and the terrible destruction it would bring to the civilized world. This meant that we should not do anything that would provide the excuse to the Soviets and plunge the free nations into full-scale all-out war.

But it was not easy to sell this concept of limited warfare to the American people, who had recently come through an all-out world war in which the United States had triumphed. The Korean conflict was in every respect dangerous: to those charged with commanding and fighting a "limited war," to the freedom of nations, to the survival of the "civilized world," and to the political careers of Truman and those associated with him.

The difficulty of even speaking about this new kind of conflict, which redefined the parameters of combat as well as the meaning of victory, was made apparent during a presidential press conference on June 29, 1950—Truman's first since the crisis had begun. Truman told reporters, "We are not at war." He was asked if he could be quoted. "Yes," he replied. "We are not at war." A reporter then asked if it would therefore be correct to call the American intervention in Korea a "police action under the United Nations." Truman replied: "Yes. That is exactly what it amounts to." Although the phrase "police action" was accurate as far as Truman's intentions for the war were concerned, the term tended to frustrate military leaders, soldiers, and the public alike, leading to a sharp and accelerating decline in Truman's popularity throughout the entire conflict and setting the stage for a dramatic confrontation between the president and his chief commander on the ground, General Douglas MacArthur.

Racial Integration of the Armed Forces

As the Korean War forced politicians, the military, and the public to rethink the meaning and nature of warfare in the nuclear age, it also compelled changes in thought and attitude in another sociopolitical arena. Many commentators have noted that World War II advanced the integration of the races in the United States by introducing large numbers of white soldiers to large numbers of black soldiers in a manner unknown to peacetime American society. To a degree, this observation is accurate; however, the armed forces of World War II were themselves segregated and remained so throughout the war. In the army, for example, African American troops served in all-black units (though usually commanded by white officers), and the overwhelming majority of black troops were assigned to supply and labor units, not to combat outfits. In the navy, segregation was also the rule, although, toward the end of the war, steps were taken to integrate ships' crews to a limited degree. As in the army, black naval personnel were almost exclusively assigned to noncombat roles, such as food service, stevedore (loading and unloading) functions, and construction work.

The Korean War saw a far greater degree of desegregation of the American armed forces. The foundation of this racial integration predated the conflict. On July 26, 1948, President Truman issued **Executive Order 9981,** directing that "all persons in the Armed Services" were to receive "equality of treatment and opportunity . . . without regard to race." The order did not specifically mention integration, but when a reporter asked the president if "integration" was what the order meant, he responded with a simple "Yes."

It is significant that President Truman chose to take the first major postwar step toward racial integration by means of an executive order rather than legislation, which would have led to a long and divisive fight in Congress and could quite possibly have been defeated. Yet while the executive order was a bold statement of presidential policy, it did not result in the rapid integration of the armed forces. The catalyst for integration was the Korean War, which made such heavy demands on military resources that the army high command had little choice but to integrate black and white soldiers in the same combat units. The Korean War was the first American conflict since the War of 1812 (Chapter 6) in which black and white troops served side by side.

Relief of MacArthur

In 1951 no American military figure, except perhaps for Dwight D. Eisenhower, was more popular than Douglas MacArthur. Most Americans agreed that it was a good thing he was in charge in Korea. Even after Chinese troops entered the war, overwhelming the U.S.-led UN coalition positions and prompting a massive retreat, most of the public continued to support MacArthur, including his proclamation that

---

Executive Order 9981, 1948

Establishing the President's Committee on Equality of Treatment and Opportunity in the Armed Forces.

WHEREAS it is essential that there be maintained in the armed services of the United States the highest standards of democracy, with equality of treatment and opportunity for all those who serve in our country's defense:

NOW THEREFORE . . .

1. It is hereby declared to be the policy of the President that there shall be equality of treatment and opportunity for all persons in the armed services without regard to race, color, religion or national origin. This policy shall be put into effect as rapidly as possible, having due regard to the time required to effectuate any necessary changes without impairing efficiency or morale.

2. There shall be created in the National Military Establishment an advisory committee to be known as the President's Committee on Equality of Treatment and Opportunity in the Armed Services, which shall be composed of seven members to be designated by the President.

3. The Committee is authorized on behalf of the President to examine into the rules, procedures and practices of the Armed Services in order to determine in what respect such rules, procedures and practices may be altered or improved with a view to carrying out the policy of this order.

Excerpted from Harry S. Truman, "Executive Order 9981," Truman Presidential Library and Museum, www.trumanlibrary.org/9981a.htm.

This 1951 American cartoon by L. J. Roche shows President Harry S. Truman, Secretary of State Dean Acheson, and the Pentagon taking the heat for Truman's decision to remove General Douglas MacArthur from his post as supreme commander of UN forces in Korea. This decision, made in the face of MacArthur's open insubordination of the commander in chief's orders, was very unpopular with the American public.

there was "no substitute for victory" and his advocacy of vastly expanding the war, if necessary into Manchuria. Through a **Joint Chiefs of Staff Communication to MacArthur,** President Truman issued orders severely limiting the response to the invasion, directing MacArthur to defend his forces as best as possible, while inflicting as many casualties on the enemy as he could, but to evacuate the Korean peninsula if the UN position became untenable. In his **Reply,** MacArthur called for recognition that a state of war now existed between the United States (and other UN nations) and China, and he requested authorization to extend the war into China.

The president was persuaded that expanding the war into China would touch off World War III. MacArthur, however, did not limit his disagreement with the president's policy to his reply to the Joint Chiefs. He also sent a letter to Republican House minority leader Joe Martin advocating expansion. After Martin read the letter into the *Congressional Record,* Truman noted in his diary on April 6, 1951: "This looks like the last straw. Rank insubordination.

... I call in Gen. [George S.] Marshall, Dean Acheson, Mr. [Averell] Harriman and Gen. [Omar] Bradley before Cabinet to discuss situation." Truman continued, "I've come to the conclusion that our Big General in the Far East must be recalled." Bradley, the Cabinet, and the Joint Chiefs agreed that MacArthur's insubordination called for his relief as supreme commander in Korea. Truman approved recall orders on April 9, 1951.

Truman's decision was enormously unpopular and raised a public outcry, which MacArthur sought to heighten when he returned to the United States to a tumultuous hero's welcome. In his famous **Farewell Address** delivered to a joint session of Congress on April 19, 1951, he asserted that "there is no substitute for victory" in war.

Revised War Aims

General MacArthur was replaced by Lieutenant General Matthew Ridgway, who, in contrast to MacArthur, interpreted the Joint Chiefs' directive—

Joint Chiefs of Staff Communication and MacArthur's Reply, 1951

Joint Chiefs of Staff Communication, December 10, 1951:

Not considered practicable to obtain at this time significant additional forces from other United Nations. Therefore, in light of present situation, your basic directive, to furnish to ROK [Republic of Korea] assistance as necessary to repel armed attack and restore to the area security and peace, is modified. Your directive now is to defend in successive positions, subject to safety of your troops as your primary consideration, inflicting as much damage to hostile forces in Korea as possible.

MacArthur's Reply, December 12, 1951:

Should a policy determination be reached by our government or through it by the United Nations to recognize the state of war which has been forced upon us by the Chinese authorities and to take retaliatory measures within our capabilities, we could: (1) blockade the coast of China; (2) destroy through naval gunfire and air bombardment China's industrial capacity to wage war; (3) secure reinforcements from the Nationalist [Chinese] garrison in Formosa [Taiwan] to strengthen our position in Korea if we decided to continue the fight for that peninsula; and (4) release existing restrictions upon the Formosan garrison for diversionary action (possibly leading to counterinvasion) against vulnerable areas of the Chinese mainland.

I believe that by the foregoing measures we could severely cripple and largely neutralize China's capability to wage aggressive war and thus save Asia from the engulfment otherwise facing it.

Excerpted from "The Issue of Limited War in Korea," in *Annals of America,* ed. Mortimer J. Adler and Charles Van Doren (Chicago: Encyclopaedia Britannica, 1976), 17:50–51.

MacArthur's Farewell Address, 1951

While I was not consulted prior to the President's decision to intervene in support of the Republic of Korea, that decision from a military standpoint, proved a sound one, as we hurled back the invader and decimated his forces. Our victory was complete, and our objectives within reach, when Red China intervened with numerically superior ground forces.

This created a new war and an entirely new situation . . . which called for new decisions in the diplomatic sphere to permit the realistic adjustment of military strategy.

Such decisions have not been forthcoming.

While no man in his right mind would advocate sending our ground forces into continental China, and such was never given a thought, the new situation did urgently demand a drastic revision of strategic planning if our political aim was to defeat this new enemy as we had defeated the old.

. . . I felt that military necessity in the conduct of the war made necessary: first the intensification of our economic blockade against China; two the imposition of a naval blockade against the China coast; three removal of restrictions on air reconnaissance of China's coastal areas and of Manchuria; four removal of restrictions on the forces of the Republic of China on Formosa, with logistical support to contribute to their effective operations against the common enemy. . . .

. . . [O]nce war is forced upon us, there is no other alternative than to apply every available means to bring it to a swift end.

War's very object is victory, not prolonged indecision.

In war there is no substitute for victory.

Excerpted from Douglas MacArthur, "Farewell Address to Congress," in *Annals of America*, ed. Mortimer J. Adler and Charles Van Doren (Chicago: Encyclopaedia Britannica, 1976), 17:79–84.

to defend U.N. positions, inflicting as many casualties as possible—as a viable prescription for victory in a *limited* war. In the operation informally dubbed the "meat grinder," Ridgway transformed what had been a war of invasion and counterinvasion into a war of attrition, which slowly forced the North Korean and Chinese troops into retreat above the 38th parallel. Once this was achieved, both the United Nations and the U.S. government revised their war aims. No longer was the objective the establishment of a unified Korea based on the popular will, but rather, in the strictest sense, the containment of communism within North Korea. For their part, the Communists also revised their war goals, transforming the war of invasion (involving masses of troops) into a guerrilla war, intended to create exhaustion on the side of the UN forces and thereby compel a settlement favorable to the Communists. The effect of this new war was to prolong peace talks over two years.

The Forgotten War

The Korean War was never officially ended. The armistice concluded on June 27, 1953, divided the nation at the 38th parallel, and endures as a ceasefire rather than a peace. As of 2006, some 30,000 U.S. troops remain stationed in South Korea as, in effect, a garrison along a hostile border.

Many Americans saw the Korean War as an American defeat, made all the more bitter by the fact that it followed so closely on the hard-won victory in World War II. Others saw the armistice as the fortunate avoidance of another world war. Still others—among them President Truman and his advisers—interpreted the outcome in Korea as the very definition of "victory" in the nuclear age. The resolution of the war had successfully contained communism. In this way, it fulfilled the prescription of the Truman Doctrine, just as the Marshall Plan, the Berlin Airlift, and military aid to Greece had. Most important, the resolution of the Korean War had accomplished containment without weakening the U.S. military's position in the world's other hot spots (including contested West Germany and West Berlin) or touching off a new and more devastating world conflagration.

BIBLIOGRAPHY

Cumings, Bruce. *The Origins of the Korean War.* 2 vols. Princeton, N.J.: Princeton University Press, 1981–1990.

Fehrenbach, T. R. *This Kind of War: A Study in Unpreparedness.* New York: Macmillan, 1963.

Ferrell, Robert H., ed.. *Off the Record: The Private Papers of Harry S. Truman.* Columbia: University of Missouri Press, 1980.

Hastings, Max. *The Korean War.* London: M. Joseph, 1987.

McCullough, David. *Truman.* New York: Simon and Schuster, 1992.

Truman, Harry S. *Memoirs.* Vol. 2, *Years of Trial and Hope.* Garden City, N.Y.: Doubleday, 1956.

Varhola, Michael J. *Fire and Ice: The Korean War, 1950–1953.* New York: Da Capo Press, 2000.

At Issue

The Vietnam War, like the Korean War (Chapter 37), reflected an effort by the United States to "contain" communism. From the perspective of the Vietnamese people, the conflict was a civil war.

The Conflict

During World War II, after France surrendered to Germany in June 1940, Germany's Japanese allies permitted French colonial officials to remain nominally in control of French Indochina (including Vietnam). After France was liberated in 1945, the Japanese seized full control of Vietnam, ejecting the French authorities that had kept indigenous nationalist groups in check. The largest and most powerful of these groups was the Viet Minh, which, under the leadership of Soviet-trained Ho Chi Minh, launched a guerrilla war against the Japanese occupation forces and, aided by U.S. Office of Strategic Services (OSS) military teams, took control of Vietnam's north. When World War II ended, Ho refused to relinquish power to returning French colonialists, and a chronic state of guerrilla war developed. Although American president Harry S. Truman was an anti-imperialist, he felt that an independent Vietnam would become a Communist Vietnam. When the Communists emerged victorious in China in 1949, Truman reluctantly accepted French rule in Vietnam. On February 7, 1950, the United States recognized Vietnam as constituted by the French under their puppet, the former emperor Bao Dai.

Within two weeks, the French threatened to abandon the nation to Ho Chi Minh if U.S. economic and military aid were not forthcoming. Some $75 million was appropriated immediately. Shortly afterward, on June 25, 1950, Communist forces from North Korea invaded South Korea (Chapter 37), and Truman stepped up aid to the French in Vietnam.

On August 3, 1950, the first contingent of U.S. military advisers—the U.S. Military Assistance Advisory Group (MAAG)—arrived in Saigon to work with the French forces. By 1952 the United States was financing one-third of the French military effort in Vietnam, which culminated during March 13–May 7, 1954, in the Battle of Dien Bien Phu. Despite U.S. logistical support, the French lost to Communist forces. President Eisenhower, who pledged support to the government of Ngo Dinh Diem on October 24, 1954, contemplated direct U.S. military intervention, but lacking a French commitment to train and employ indigenous troops and ultimately to grant Vietnam its independence, he did not act.

The fall of Dien Bien Phu was followed by additional Viet Minh victories. In July the French and the Viet Minh concluded the Geneva Accord, calling a cease-fire and dividing Vietnam along the 17th parallel. While Ho Chi Minh set up a government in the North, the United States worked with French and South Vietnamese authorities to build a South Vietnamese government and military. Gradually, the French withdrew, leaving the country—and its problems—to the South Vietnamese and, increasingly, to the United States, which the Eisenhower administration had committed to a long-term advisory role.

Fearing that a plebiscite (a popular referendum) mandated by the Geneva Accord would reunify Vietnam under Ho Chi Minh, South Vietnam president Ngo Dinh Diem rejected the accord in 1956 and refused to hold a vote in the South. In September 1959 Diem's refusal prompted the Viet Cong (a Communist guerrilla group that succeeded and absorbed elements of the Viet Minh) to begin outright guerrilla warfare against the South. In 1960 the United States expanded its MAAG advisers to 685 men, including Special Forces teams assigned to train Vietnamese Rangers. Despite the decreasing stability of the Diem government, Eisenhower's successor, John F. Kennedy, authorized increased numbers of military advisers to combat a Viet Cong insurgency that had swelled to 14,000 guerrillas in South Vietnam. In October 1961 Kennedy sent General Maxwell Taylor and White House adviser Walt Rostow to Vietnam to make recommendations. Although they advised against committing substantial U.S. ground forces,

CHRONOLOGY OF THE VIETNAM WAR

1954
May 7 The French are defeated at Dien Bien Phu by Communist forces.

July 20 The Republic of Vietnam is organized.

Oct. 24 President Eisenhower pledges support to the government of Ngo Dinh Diem.

1955
Nov. 1 Eisenhower deploys the Military Assistance Advisory Group to train the South Vietnamese army.

1959
July 8 Two U.S. servicemen are killed—the first Americans killed in action in Vietnam.

1963
Nov. 2 South Vietnamese President Ngo Dinh Diem is assassinated.

1964
Aug. 2 and 4 Gulf of Tonkin Incident

Aug. 7 Congress approves the Gulf of Tonkin Resolution.

1965
Mar. 2 Operation Rolling Thunder begins; the bombing campaign continues through May 11.

Mar. 8–9 First American combat ground troops (not advisers) arrive in Vietnam.

Apr. 7 President Johnson offers North Vietnam economic aid in exchange for peace; the offer is rejected.

Apr. 17 First major anti-war rally is held in Washington, D.C.

1967
Oct. 21–23 50,000 people demonstrate against the war in Washington, D.C.

1968
Jan. 21 The three-month Battle of Khe Sanh begins.

Jan. 30 The Tet Offensive begins.

Mar. 16 My Lai massacre

May 10 Peace talks begin in Paris.

1969
June 8 President Nixon announces the first troop withdrawals from South Vietnam.

Nov. 15 250,000 people demonstrate against the war in Washington, D.C.

1970
Apr. 30 U.S. and South Vietnamese forces invade Cambodia.

May 4 Kent State Massacre

May 9 150,000 protestors converge on Washington, D.C.

1971
Feb. South Vietnamese and U.S. forces invade Laos.

1972
Dec. Hanoi is bombed.

1973
Jan. 27 The Paris Peace Accords are signed.

Mar. 29 The last U.S. combat troops leave Vietnam.

1974
Aug. 9 President Nixon announces his resignation.

Sept. 16 President Ford offers clemency to draft evaders and military deserters.

1975
Apr. 21 South Vietnamese president Thieu resigns.

Apr. 29–30 Saigon falls. U.S. personnel and South Vietnamese refugees are evacuated. South Vietnamese president Duong Van Minh surrenders.

Apr. 30 Vietnam is reunified under Communist regime.

Taylor and Rostow recommended that the air force transition from a logistical and training role to some involvement in combat. Kennedy's approval on November 3, 1961, marked a shift to a "limited partnership and working collaboration."

In the fall of 1961 the Kennedy administration authorized joint U.S.–South Vietnamese naval patrols south of the 17th parallel, and by June 30, 1962, there were 6,419 American soldiers and airmen in South Vietnam. By mid-August, the number jumped to 11,412, and—thanks to U.S.-supplied equipment, training, and funding—the Army of the Republic of Vietnam (ARVN) reached 300,000, surpassing the 280,000 troops of the North Vietnam Army (NVA). By early 1963, ARVN numbers approached 400,000, yet Viet Cong attacks increased, and in the Mekong Delta, the war escalated from guerrilla engagements to full-scale field operations. By the end of the year, the Viet Cong were clearly gaining ground. With the war claiming about 2,000 lives each week, popular support for Diem's notoriously corrupt South Vietnamese government rapidly eroded. Concerned that the South was nearing collapse, the Kennedy administration acquiesced in a CIA-backed military coup resulting in Diem's assassination on November 2, 1963. A military junta set up a provisional government, which the United States recognized on November 8. Taking advantage of the chaos, the Viet Cong stepped up their attacks, and American forces heightened their response.

On November 22, 1963, President John F. Kennedy was assassinated, and Vice President Lyndon Johnson took office. The Joint Chiefs of Staff advised expanding the war with decisive action against North Vietnam, including the bombing of Hanoi. Still pondering whether to expand the war, President Johnson did not authorize the strikes.

On August 7, 1964, following reports of the Tonkin Gulf Incident (purported North Vietnamese attacks on U.S. destroyers on August 2 and 4), the U.S. Senate passed the Tonkin Gulf Resolution (see "Johnson and the Tonkin Gulf Resolution," below), giving the president virtually unlimited discretionary

powers to conduct the war. In the meantime, Viet Cong attacks had roughly doubled. On November 1, 1964, Viet Cong penetrated the perimeter of the Bien Hoa air base, killing 4 U.S. Air Force personnel and wounding 72. The Joint Chiefs recommended severe reprisals, but President Johnson, on the eve of reelection, declined to act until after his landslide electoral victory, when he authorized restricted air strikes on neighboring Laos, through which North Vietnamese insurgents were entering the South (Operation Barrel Roll).

On December 27, Viet Cong raided the hamlet of Binh Gia, and then, on December 31, inflicted heavy casualties on the U.S. Fourth Marine Battalion, which had marched to Binh Gia's relief. This, combined with an earlier Viet Cong attack on Saigon's Brink Hotel, housing U.S. officers and advisers, prompted Maxwell Taylor, U.S. ambassador to South Vietnam, to recommend immediate bombing of North Vietnam.

Taylor's recommendation came during a time of heightened instability in South Vietnam, which had had no fewer than eleven governments since the fall of Diem. President Johnson pondered whether to commit U.S. forces directly or to disengage, allowing the government of Vietnam to take whatever form it might. Then, on February 7, 1965, Viet Cong mortar squads and demolition teams attacked U.S. advisory forces near Pleiku, killing 9 Americans and wounding 108. In response, Johnson authorized Operation Flaming Dart, an air strike against NVA barracks near Dong Hoi, North Vietnam, on February 9. An NVA counterstrike came the next day against an American barracks at Qui Nhon, followed by a U.S. reprisal on the 11th. These exchanges definitively marked the end of the U.S. advisory phase in the Vietnam War and the beginning of active combat.

On March 2, 1965, Operation Rolling Thunder, a long series of air strikes against North Vietnam, commenced. During March 8–9, the first American ground troops—combat soldiers, not advisers—arrived. Even as he committed troops, President Johnson continued to look for a way out. On April 7,

Lyndon B. Johnson

(1908–1973)

Lyndon Baines Johnson was born near Johnson City in the Texas midlands, into a politically active but financially strained family. He worked his way through Southwest Texas State Teachers College (now Texas State University–San Marcos); after graduation, he taught in impoverished rural Texas. The experience stirred his social consciousness, and in 1937 he ran for and won a seat in the House of Representatives, campaigning on a strong New Deal platform.

With the outbreak of World War II, Johnson became the first member of Congress to leave the House in order to serve overseas. He attained the naval rank of lieutenant commander, served in the South Pacific, and was awarded a Silver Star. He returned to the House before the war ended, served a total of six terms, and was elected to the Senate in 1948.

Johnson was regarded as a skillful politician who was especially effective in managing contentious relations between the Democratic Party's southern and northern factions. He became, in 1953, the youngest minority leader in Senate history and, in 1954, when the Democrats gained a majority, majority leader. He worked effectively in a bipartisan manner and engineered passage of important initiatives of the Republican Eisenhower administration, including early civil rights legislation. Chosen as John F. Kennedy's running mate in 1960, he became vice president and was instrumental in promoting the nation's fledgling space program. Johnson assumed the presidency on November 22, 1963, after Kennedy was assassinated.

Johnson energetically exploited the memory of the "martyred president" to achieve enactment of the welfare and civil rights measures Kennedy had been unable to gain passage for. Johnson offered America a vision of what he called the "Great Society," built on equal opportunity for all citizens. The first fruit was passage of the sweeping Civil Rights Act of 1964 and a tax cut intended to aid disadvantaged and middle-class Americans.

Voters elected Johnson in his own right in 1964 by 15 million votes, the widest popular margin in American history. Claiming a mandate, Johnson presented to Congress an agenda, including aid to education, Medicare and Medicaid, urban renewal, beautification, conservation, economic development of depressed regions, a "War on Poverty," and the Voting Rights Act of 1965. He also championed the opening phases of Project Apollo, the exploration of the moon.

The Vietnam War increasingly occupied Johnson, ultimately drawing off funding from Great Society programs. Johnson brought U.S. involvement in the war to its highest level of troop commitment, and he presided over a nation deeply divided by the war. Recognizing that he had become a divisive figure, he withdrew as a candidate for reelection in 1968. Peace talks with the North Vietnamese were initiated before he left office, but Johnson died of a heart attack at his Texas ranch on January 22, 1973, before the Paris Peace Accords were signed.

---

he offered the North Vietnamese economic aid in exchange for peace, but his offer was spurned. Rolling Thunder continued through May 11, when the air strikes were suspended as the United States again sought peace talks unsuccessfully. The operation resumed on May 18 and continued through 1968.

As the war escalated, President Johnson and his military advisers struggled to establish objectives. The original goal of reunifying Vietnam was discarded, and aims were restricted to keeping South Vietnam independent. Johnson hoped to wage primarily an air war that would prevent North Vietnamese infiltration into the South, inflict heavy casualties on the NVA and Viet Cong, and raise the morale of the ARVN and the South Vietnamese people. General William Westmoreland, commanding U.S. forces in Vietnam, argued that bombing alone was insufficient and called for infantry to block the major route by which the North Vietnamese infiltrated the South. Johnson objected, but approved the use of "air cavalry," a helicopter-borne infantry force well suited to combat in undeveloped areas. The First Cavalry Division (Airmobile) was first deployed in the campaign for the Central Highlands during late 1965 and early 1966. There were also major conventional ground operations. The first of these was launched in Bien Hoa Province, just twenty miles northeast of Saigon, on June 28, 1965, and met with mixed success. Operation Star-Light, undertaken during August 18–21, 1965, pitted more than 5,000 marines against the Viet Cong First Regiment and was a major victory, destroying a large Viet Cong base. The Central Highlands campaign culminated in the Battle of the Ia Drang Valley during October 23–November 20, 1965, in which the First Cavalry Division thwarted a North Vietnamese attempt to seize Pleiku, which would have cut South Vietnam in half.

Early 1966 began with Operation Marauder (January 1–8), the first foray of an American unit into the Mekong Delta. This was followed during January 19–February 21 by Operation Van Buren, by which U.S. and ARVN forces secured Phu Yen Province in the central coastal region. This operation set the pattern for the "search-and-destroy" actions that would become typical of the war. They were generally successful in securing contested territory for a limited time, but the Viet Cong usually returned. Although North Vietnamese losses consistently exceeded those of U.S. and ARVN forces, the North Vietnamese proved willing to make enormous sacrifices in what became a protracted war of attrition.

Between March and the late fall of 1966, U.S. Marines continually engaged the enemy in the northern provinces of South Vietnam. Ground movement was coordinated with the massive bombing of North Vietnamese infiltration routes near the border of North Vietnam and Laos. By the summer, the Central Highlands once more became a critical hot spot. Elsewhere, the 101st Airborne fought in Kontum Province, and, in June and July, the First Division, in concert with the Fifth ARVN Division, became heavily engaged in Binh Long Province, seventy miles north of Saigon. All of these operations were typical of what the military called the "main force" war: an attempt simply to crush the insurgents wherever they surfaced. The objective was to meet force with overwhelming force.

By 1967 the main force concept was increasingly augmented by ground operations aimed at destroying Viet Cong sources of food and supply. While the U.S. military took on the principal burden of both the main force and interdiction operations, the ARVN developed a "pacification program," which was intended to win the "hearts and minds" of the South Vietnamese peasantry and turn them against the Communist insurgents. Pacification included military components, but also education, land reform, communications, agriculture, and other civil programs. The idea was to root out the Viet Cong infrastructure, village by village, and develop in each village a self-defense capability. By mid-1967, the program was producing measurable results, especially evident in increased desertion rates among South Vietnamese Communist units. However, the American public became increasingly concerned about an aspect of the pacification effort known as the Phoenix Program, which used ARVN "intelligence-action teams" to capture or kill South Vietnamese civilians who supplied and sheltered Viet Cong.

Controversy also swirled around the intensified U.S. bombing of North Vietnamese targets during 1966–1967, which caused many civilian casualties and provoked antiaircraft defense from North Vietnamese surface-to-air missiles that downed many U.S. aircraft. Some in the Johnson administration advocated bombing as essential in a war of attrition and a practice that would eventually drive the Communists to the negotiating table. Critics, both inside and outside the government, argued that the bombing only hardened the will of the Hanoi government. Eight times in 1967, President Johnson called temporary halts to the bombing in an effort to facilitate peace talks. Each time, the talks failed to materialize.

Beginning on January 30, 1968—the Vietnamese lunar holiday called "Tet"—North Vietnam staged a series of massive offensives, first along the border, or Demilitarized Zone (DMZ) at the 17th parallel, then deep into South Vietnam. Communist forces attacked major cities and military bases throughout the South. Even the newly constructed U.S. embassy in Saigon was targeted, as was the large Tan Son Nhut Air Base. Farther north, the Marine outpost at Khe Sanh—where fighting had begun on January 21—was cut off and held under heavy siege until mid-March. Of an estimated 84,000 Communist attackers, 45,000 were killed. U.S. casualties were 1,536 dead, 7,764 wounded, and 11 missing; The ARVN suffered 2,788 dead, 8,299 wounded, and 587 missing. By any military measure, the U.S.-ARVN defense against Tet was a triumph.

Nevertheless, by 1968 a large anti-war movement had developed in the United States (see "Emergence of the Anti-war Movement," below). Among the American public, the three-week Tet Offensive was widely perceived as a devastating Communist victory. It persuaded many Americans, including politicians and policymakers, that the war was unwinnable. By the middle of March, public opinion polls revealed that 70 percent of the American people favored a phased withdrawal of U.S. forces from Vietnam, which would reach their highest point—536,000—by the end of 1968. President Johnson responded to the rising tide of anti-war sentiment with two surprise television announcements on March 31, 1968. He declared that he would restrict bombing above the 20th parallel, thereby opening the door to a negotiated settlement of the war, and he announced that he would not seek another term as president.

Cease-fire negotiations began in Paris in May, only to stall over Hanoi's demands for a complete bombing halt and the presence of the Viet Cong's political parent organization, the National Liberation Front, at the peace table. In November Johnson agreed, but despite this "light at the end of the tunnel" (a phrase often repeated during the war), the presidential campaign of Democrat Hubert Humphrey faltered, and Republican Richard M. Nixon, who claimed to have a "secret plan" to end the war, won a narrow victory.

Nixon had campaigned on vague promises to end the war, but once he entered the White House, he promptly expanded the war into neighboring Laos and Cambodia. As he widened the conflict, however, Nixon instituted a policy of "Vietnamization," a transition of responsibility for the war from U.S. to ARVN forces. The American military services instituted rush training programs for South Vietnamese ground and air forces, and in May 1969 the withdrawal of U.S. Army ground units from Vietnam began while the Paris peace talks, which had begun under Johnson in 1968, wore on fruitlessly. Despite U.S. training and material aid, ARVN performance proved consistently disappointing. The performance of U.S. troops also deteriorated as many in the ranks became convinced that the war was a lost cause. Whereas units in the mid-1960s engaged in bold "search-and-destroy" missions, troops in the 1970s mockingly referred to such patrols as "search-and-avoid" missions.

Despite problems of morale and performance, Vietnamization unquestionably reduced U.S. casualties. Yet even as he pulled troops out of Vietnam, President Nixon sent ground forces to attack Communist supply and staging areas in the neighboring country of Cambodia, an incursion that triggered violent protests in the United States (see "The Kent State Massacre," below). Yielding to protests and political pressure, Nixon soon withdrew all ground forces from Cambodia, but simultaneously intensified bombing raids of that country. When Communist infiltration continued unabated, the United States supplied air support for an ARVN invasion of Laos in February 1971.

By late 1971, withdrawals had reduced U.S. troop strength to 175,000 in Vietnam. In March 1972 Communist forces of the National Liberation Front exploited the reduced U.S. presence with the so-called Easter Offensive into South Vietnam, which routed ARVN troops until President Nixon redoubled air attacks, mined Haiphong harbor, and established a naval blockade of the North. These acts were sufficient to prompt U.S. negotiator Henry Kissinger and North Vietnamese representative Le Duc Tho to formulate an agreement governing the withdrawal of U.S. troops, the return of prisoners of war, and a political settlement through the establishment of a special council of reconciliation. South Vietnamese president Nguyen Van Thieu rejected the peace terms, however, because they permitted Viet Cong forces to remain in the South. Nevertheless, the Kissinger-Tho breakthrough enabled President Nixon to announce that "peace is at hand" and assured him reelection in 1972. But once he had been reelected, Nixon threw his support behind Thieu, repudiating the peace terms Kissinger had negotiated. Next, in a bid to bring the North Vietnamese back to negotiations, Nixon ordered eleven consecutive days of intensive "Christmas bombing" of North Vietnamese cities (Operation Linebacker II) during December 18–29. The massive raids, including the bombing of Hanoi, prompted the North Vietnamese to resume negotiations on January 8, 1973. The Paris Peace Accords were signed on January 27 (see "The Paris Peace Talks and Accords," below).

The accords did not bring an end to the fighting, nor did the massive bombing program bring victory. The U.S. withdrawal continued, however, and on March 29, 1973, the last American combat troops departed Vietnam, leaving behind about 8,500 U.S. civilian "technicians." Despite a new cease-fire agreement concluded on June 13, 1973, both the North and South routinely violated the Paris Accords. The United States continued to send military and economic aid to the Thieu government, resumed bombing Cambodia, and menaced North Vietnam with reconnaissance overflights, but a war-weary U.S. Congress had turned against President Nixon (who was mired in the Watergate Scandal that would soon force his resignation) and passed the War Powers Act in November 1973, greatly diminishing

the president's authority to conduct undeclared wars. President Gerald Ford, who succeeded Nixon in August 1974, requested $300 million in "supplemental aid" to South Vietnam, only to be turned down flat by Congress.

Starting in early 1975, the demoralized South Vietnamese suffered one military defeat after another, culminating on April 30, 1975, with the surrender to the North by the last president of South Vietnam, Lieutenant General Duong Van Minh. (Thieu had resigned on April 21.) During April 29–30, U.S. Navy helicopters conducted a frenzied evacuation of remaining Americans and select South Vietnamese from the roof of the U.S. embassy in Saigon.

In all, 58,193 Americans died in Vietnam and approximately 149,000 were wounded. The ARVN counted 197,000 killed and 502,000 wounded. North Vietnamese military losses were 731,000 killed and an unknown number wounded. An estimated 587,000 civilian noncombatants, in North and South Vietnam, were also killed.

Policy under Truman: Reluctant Support of French Colonialism

As discussed in Chapter 37, the Truman administration developed a so-called containment policy, which employed economic, diplomatic, and military means to "contain" aggressive Communist expansion wherever it occurred. In Asia, this policy led to the Korean War as well as to economic and military aid for the faltering French colonial regime that returned to Vietnam after World War II. While President Truman was opposed to colonialism, he believed that North Vietnamese leader Ho Chi Minh would inevitably align a unified Vietnam with Soviet or Chinese communism, creating yet another Communist satellite state. To counter the threat, he was willing to compromise democratic principles; therefore in 1950, after the outbreak of the Korean War, Truman authorized $10 million to aid the French in Vietnam, and he sent 123 noncombat logistical support troops to help in the fight against the Viet Minh. The following year, Truman authorized $150 million in military aid to the French.

The Eisenhower Era: Domino Theory

Despite U.S. aid, the French hold on Vietnam rapidly eroded, culminating in the disastrous military defeat at Dien Bien Phu during March 13–May 7, 1954. While the battle was still being fought, President Dwight D. Eisenhower, who had dealt with Vietnam even more gingerly than his predecessor Harry S. Truman had, presented a rationale for fighting communism in Vietnam at a **News Conference** on April 7, 1954. "You have a row of dominoes set up," he explained, "you knock over the first one, and what will happen to the last one is the certainty that it will go over very quickly." This awkward sentence was transformed by the press into the so-called domino theory, which offered the American public a simple metaphor that justified a U.S. commitment to a far-off and obscure country more persuasively than any abstract political discussion could have. For the next two decades, the "domino theory" would be invoked as the rationale for ever-deepening involvement in Vietnam.

Indeed, there was growing evidence to support the domino theory during the Eisenhower administration. In 1954 Ho Chi Minh formed Group 100 to

Eisenhower's News Conference, April 7, 1954

Q. Robert Richards, Copley Press: Mr. President, would you mind commenting on the strategic importance of Indochina to the free world? I think there has been, across the country, some lack of understanding on just what it means to us.

THE PRESIDENT. You have, of course, both the specific and the general when you talk about such things.

First of all, you have the specific value of a locality in its production of materials that the world needs.

Then you have the possibility that many human beings pass under a dictatorship that is inimical to the free world.

Finally, you have broader considerations that might follow what you would call the "falling domino" principle. You have a row of dominoes set up, you knock over the first one, and what will happen to the last one is the certainty that it will go over very quickly. So you could have a beginning of a disintegration that would have the most profound influences.

Now, with respect to the first one, two of the items from this particular area that the world uses are tin and tungsten. They are very important. There are others, of course, the rubber plantations and so on.

Then with respect to more people passing under this domination, Asia, after all, has already lost some 450 million of its peoples to the Communist dictatorship, and we simply can't afford greater losses.

But when we come to the possible sequence of events, the loss of Indochina, of Burma, of Thailand, of the Peninsula, and Indonesia following, now you begin to talk about areas that not only multiply the disadvantages that you would suffer through loss of materials, sources of materials, but now you are talking really about millions and millions and millions of people.

Finally, the geographical position achieved thereby does many things. It turns the so-called island defensive chain of Japan, Formosa, of the Philippines and to the southward; it moves in to threaten Australia and New Zealand.

It takes away, in its economic aspects, that region that Japan must have as a trading area or Japan, in turn, will have only one place in the world to go—that is, toward the Communist areas in order to live.

So, the possible consequences of the loss are just incalculable to the free world.

Excerpted from "The President's News Conference of April 7, 1954," in *Public Papers of the Presidents of the United States: Dwight D. Eisenhower, 1953–1961,* from the American Presidency Project, University of California, Santa Barbara, www.presidency.ucsb.edu.

direct, organize, train, and supply the Pathet Lao, Communist guerrillas struggling to gain control of Vietnam's neighbor, Laos. The following year, Ho Chi Minh launched the "Anti-Landlord Movement" in North Vietnam, sending armed cadres into villages to eliminate political opponents in order to achieve land reform. These events persuaded Eisenhower to deploy, on November 1, 1955, the Military Assistance Advisory Group (MAAG) to train the South Vietnam Army. To the American public, Eisenhower stressed that the military personnel being sent into Vietnam were strictly advisers and would not be involved in combat. However, the last French troops left Vietnam in April 1956, North Vietnamese forces invaded Laos in December 1958, and on July 8, 1959, two members of MAAG, Charles Ovnand and Dale R. Buis, became the first and second Americans killed in action in Vietnam.

Policy during the Kennedy Era

As John F. Kennedy succeeded Eisenhower in January 1961, Soviet premier Nikita Khrushchev announced his intention to support what he called "wars of national liberation" wherever they might be fought throughout the world. This declaration served to confirm Kennedy's ongoing pursuit of America's developing policy of containment. Kennedy increased American involvement in Vietnam in May 1961 by sending 400 "Green Berets" as "special advisers" to train South Vietnamese soldiers. Although Kennedy insisted that these troops were to serve in an advisory capacity only, it was significant that, as Special Forces soldiers, they were the U.S. Army's elite. Their presence betokened an elevated military commitment.

In June 1961 Kennedy and Khrushchev met at the Vienna Summit. It was a contentious meeting, in which the American president protested North Vietnam's aggression in Laos and warned Khrushchev that the United States supported the neutrality of that nation. Although Khrushchev agreed to endorse a neutral Laos, President Kennedy left the summit persuaded that the Soviets were committed to

the Communist domination of Laos. He believed that the Soviets intended to challenge America's will to maintain its containment policy. "Now we have a problem in making our power credible," he commented, "and Vietnam looks like the place."

Increasingly, the superpowers—the United States and the Soviet Union—fought one another in proxy wars in places like Vietnam, thereby avoiding the potentially cataclysmic risks (such as World War III) of direct confrontation. During his election campaign, Kennedy had stressed his intention to maintain a strong strategic (nuclear) deterrent force and to achieve long-range missile parity with the Soviets. Once in office, however, he placed more emphasis on proxy wars—"brushfire wars," as they were popularly called—and he pushed for the development of Special Forces (such as the Green Berets) to fight them effectively. As originally conceived, Special Forces were to be used behind enemy lines in the event of a conventional Soviet invasion of Europe; however, Kennedy decided to deploy them in Vietnam, a war that seemed perfectly suited to their use. He was especially anxious to succeed in Vietnam, having failed in the April 1961 Bay of Pigs invasion intended to overthrow Cuba's Fidel Castro, having been powerless to prevent the construction of the Berlin Wall, and having exerted little influence in negotiating a settlement between the pro-Western and Communist factions in Laos. In part, Kennedy feared for the prestige of his administration, but he was even more concerned that the United States was losing credibility as a deterrent force in the eyes of the Soviets and the rest of the world.

In October 1961 the Viet Cong upped the ante in Vietnam with a series of successful attacks on the South. Kennedy's secretary of defense, Robert McNamara, recommended immediate escalation by sending six divisions (200,000 troops) to Vietnam. Kennedy, however, decided to move much more cautiously. On August 1, 1962, the president signed the **Foreign Assistance Act of 1962,** which provided for "military assistance to countries which are on the rim of the Communist world and under direct attack," and by the end of his presidency in

November 1963, he had expanded U.S. involvement to a role combining advisory and combat functions. But the total troop commitment was still no more than 16,000. The Viet Cong continued to score military successes, most notably their January 3, 1963 victory over ARVN forces in the Battle of Ap Bac. In May 1963 Arizona senator Barry Goldwater, who would receive the Republican nomination for the presidency in 1964, suggested using atomic bombs in Vietnam. Kennedy was far from considering such an option.

From the standpoint of containment, the prowess of the Viet Cong was not Kennedy's only concern. The South Vietnamese government under President Ngo Dinh Diem was corrupt, inefficient, and unpopular. The most immediate problem was the Catholic Diem's persecution of Vietnam's Buddhist majority, which provoked in May 1963 a Buddhist riot over the display of religious flags during the celebration of Buddha's birthday. When Diem cracked down on the protests, several Buddhist monks publicly set themselves on fire. Most infamously, on June 11, 1963, Thích Quảng Đức doused himself with gasoline and set himself ablaze in the middle of a busy Saigon intersection. The horrific event received worldwide press coverage, which was embarrassing to Diem's patron, the United States, and was exploited by Communist agents operating in the South to increase instability. When Diem refused U.S. demands that he moderate his policies toward the Buddhist majority, the White House became at least passively complicit in a CIA-supported South Vietnamese military coup d'état that overthrew Diem on November 1, 1963, and then murdered him the following day.

To the limited extent that the American public paid attention to Vietnam in 1963, it had a generally unfavorable opinion of Diem; however, his murder was a shock. Although few Americans thought the United States should support South Vietnam's government, many agreed that it was important to block Communist expansion.

The overthrow of Diem's government served only to make the South less stable. The military junta that assumed the reins of government was politically

Foreign Assistance Act of 1962

Sec. 502

Defense articles and defense services to any country shall be furnished solely for internal security ... for legitimate self-defense, to permit the recipient country to participate in regional or collective arrangements or measures consistent with the Charter of the United Nations, or otherwise to permit the recipient country to participate in collective measures requested by the United Nations for the purpose of maintaining or restoring international peace and security, or for the purpose of assisting foreign military forces in less developed friendly countries.

Excerpted from Committee on International Relations and Committee on Foreign Relations, *Legislation on Foreign Relations through 2002,* vol. I-A (Washington: U.S. Government Printing Office, 2003), 228.

inexperienced and generally inept. Coups and countercoups followed, so that seven governments rose and fell in 1964 alone. Whereas Diem had spurned the advice of the United States, each of the new governments was compliant with U.S. direction, yet was incapable of commanding the loyalty of a majority of the South Vietnamese. If the conflict between the North and the South was viewed as a civil war by the Vietnamese, the multiple conflicts within the South constituted a civil war within the civil war and created a power vacuum that the Communists continually attempted to exploit.

President Kennedy was assassinated on November 22, 1963, in Dallas, Texas. Most current historians believe that Kennedy, who had already authorized the withdrawal of 1,000 troops in October 1963, probably intended to disengage from Vietnam, but was keeping his plans under wraps to avoid political attacks from the American right wing before his reelection run in 1964. Perhaps the most compelling evidence that Kennedy intended to withdraw was his refusal to accept the advice of his secretary of defense to raise troop numbers exponentially.

Johnson and the Tonkin Gulf Resolution (1964)

Kennedy was succeeded by Lyndon Baines Johnson, under whom U.S. involvement in the Vietnam War would expand from 16,000 troops at the end of 1963 to more than 500,000 by the end of 1968. After Johnson's attempts at peace talks were rebuffed by Hanoi, the president took the advice of the Joint Chiefs of Staff, who advised him to expand the war and take decisive action against North Vietnam, which Kennedy had not done.

In June 1964 Johnson appointed General William Westmoreland, an advocate of expanding the ground war, to take command of the army in Vietnam. On July 27, 1964, 5,000 additional "advisers" were ordered to South Vietnam, bringing the total to 21,000. Four days later, the destroyer USS *Maddox* set out on a reconnaissance mission in the Tonkin Gulf. On August 2, it reported itself under attack—in international waters—by five North Vietnamese patrol boats. After incurring inconsequential damage by a single machine gun bullet, the *Maddox* withdrew to South Vietnamese waters and was joined by the destroyer USS *C. Turner Joy.*

On August 4, American patrol boats detected what they interpreted as signals indicating another attack by the North Vietnamese. This prompted the *Maddox* and *C. Turner Joy* to direct fire against the radar targets for some two hours. Although the destroyer crews sincerely believed they were under attack, current military historians and even some former crew members have concluded that the radar signals were false targets and that no attack was taking place.

Responding to the reported attacks, President Johnson ordered retaliatory strikes and appeared on national television on the evening of August 4 to describe the attacks and the retaliation. The *Maddox* had been providing intelligence in direct support of South Vietnamese attacks against the North, but

Secretary of Defense Robert McNamara characterized the North Vietnamese attacks as unprovoked. He testified to Congress that there was "unequivocal proof" of the "unprovoked" second attack—an assertion that in 1995 he admitted was untrue. After **Senate Debate** following the secretary's testimony and President Johnson's August 5 message to Congress on the situation in Southeast Asia, Congress on August 7 passed a joint **Tonkin Gulf Resolution**, which authorized President Johnson "to take all necessary steps, including the use of armed force, to assist any member or protocol state of the Southeast Asia Collective Defense Treaty requesting assistance in defense of its freedom." The Tonkin Gulf incident and the congressional resolution that followed it massively escalated U.S. involvement in the Vietnam War.

During and after the Vietnam War, evidence was presented discrediting the Tonkin Gulf Incident. This culminated on November 30, 2005, when the National Security Agency (NSA) declassified and released documents, the most disturbing of which was a 2001 article in which an NSA historian, Robert J. Hanyok, asserted that NSA intelligence officers had "deliberately skewed" the evidence that was passed on to policymakers as well as the public in order to indicate that North Vietnamese ships had attacked American destroyers on August 4, 1964.

Johnson and His Advisers

On November 27, 1965, the Pentagon formally reported to President Johnson that major operations intended to neutralize Viet Cong forces in 1966 required an increase of troops from 120,000 to 400,000. Although Johnson authorized an increase to 184,000 troops by the end of 1965, he did not act on the Pentagon's recommendation until he met in February 1966 with General William Westmoreland in Honolulu. In an argument that Johnson found persuasive, Westmoreland held that the current U.S. strength had prevented the defeat of South Vietnam, but was insufficient to mount a decisive offensive. Westmoreland asserted that the increase to 400,000

Senate Debate on the Tonkin Gulf Resolution, 1964

MR. NELSON [Gaylord Nelson, D-Wis.]: ... Am I to understand that it is the sense of Congress that we are saying to the executive branch: "If it becomes necessary to prevent further aggression, we agree now, in advance, that you may land as many divisions as deemed necessary, and engage in a direct military assault on North Vietnam if it becomes the judgment of the Executive, the Commander in Chief, that this is the only way to prevent further aggression"?

MR. FULBRIGHT [William Fulbright, D-Ark.]: As I stated, Section I is intended to deal primarily with aggression against our forces. ... I do not know what the limits are. I do not think this resolution can be determinative of that fact. I think it would indicate that he [the president] would take reasonable means first to prevent any further aggression, or repel further aggression against our own forces. ... I do not know how to answer the Senator's question and give him an absolute assurance that large numbers of troops would not be put ashore. I would deplore it. ...

MR. NELSON: ... My concern is that we in Congress could give the impression to the public that we are prepared at this time to change our mission and substantially expand our commitment. If that is what the sense of Congress is, I am opposed to the resolution. I therefore ask the distinguished Senator from Arkansas if he would consent to accept an amendment [that explicitly says Congress wants no extension of the present military conflict and no U.S. direct military involvement].

MR. FULBRIGHT: ... The Senator has put into his amendment a statement of policy that is unobjectionable. However, I cannot accept the amendment under the circumstances. I do not believe it is contrary to the joint resolution, but it is an enlargement. I am informed that the House is now voting on this reso-lution. The House joint resolution is about to be presented to us. I cannot accept the amendment and go to conference with it, and thus take responsibility for delaying matters.

MR. GRUENING [Ernest Gruening, D-Alaska]: ... Regrettably, I find myself in disagreement with the President's Southeast Asian policy. ... The serious events of the past few days, the attack by North Vietnamese vessels on American warships and our reprisal, strikes me as the inevitable and foreseeable concomitant and consequence of U.S. unilateral military aggressive policy in Southeast Asia. ... We now are about to authorize the President if he sees fit to move our Armed Forces ... not only into South Vietnam, but also into North Vietnam, Laos, Cambodia, Thailand, and of course the authorization includes all the rest of the SEATO [Southeast Asian Treaty Organization] nations. That means sending our American boys into combat in a war in which we have no business, which is not our war, into which we have been misguidedly drawn, which is steadily being escalated. This resolution is a further authorization for escalation unlimited. I am opposed to sacrificing a single American boy in this venture. We have lost far too many already. ...

MR. MORSE [Wayne Morse, D-Ore.]: ... I believe that history will record that we have made a great mistake in subverting and circumventing the Constitution of the United States. ... I believe this resolution to be a historic mistake. I believe that within the next century, future generations will look with dismay and great disappointment upon a Congress which is now about to make such a historic mistake.

Excerpted from *Congressional Record,* 88th Cong., 2d sess., 1964, 110, 18458–18459 and 18470–18471.

troops would by early 1967 create what he called the "crossover point," the high point at which Viet Cong and NVA casualties would finally be unacceptable to the North Vietnamese. Accordingly, Johnson authorized an increase to 429,000 troops by August 1966.

Westmoreland used his greatly increased forces to mount many search-and-destroy missions, which did indeed inflict massive North Vietnamese casualties. The crossover point, however, remained elusive. Worse, the "pacification" phase of the offensive—

Tonkin Gulf Resolution, 1964

Resolved by the Senate and House of Representatives of the United States of America in Congress assembled,

That the Congress approves and supports the determination of the President, as Commander in Chief, to take all necessary measures to repel any armed attack against the forces of the United States and to prevent further aggression.

Section 2. The United States regards as vital to its national interest and to world peace the maintenance of international peace and security in southeast Asia. Consonant with the Constitution of the United States and the Charter of the United Nations and in accordance with its obligations under the Southeast Asia Collective Defense Treaty, the United States is, there-

fore, prepared, as the President determines, to take all necessary steps, including the use of armed force, to assist any member or protocol state of the Southeast Asia Collective Defense Treaty requesting assistance in defense of its freedom.

Section 3. This resolution shall expire when the President shall determine that the peace and security of the area is reasonably assured by international conditions created by action of the United Nations or otherwise, except that it may be terminated earlier by concurrent resolution of the Congress.

Excerpted from the Avalon Project at Yale Law School, "The Tonkin Gulf Incident, 1964," www.yale.edu/lawweb/avalon/tonkin-g.htm.

---

village-level operations intended to root out Viet Cong and Viet Cong sympathizers and also to "win the hearts and minds" of the South Vietnamese—floundered. While U.S. forces carried out the "main force" operations of the war—the major battles—the ARVN forces charged with pacification proved corrupt, incompetent, demoralized, and generally incapable of accomplishing their mission.

Emergence of the Anti-war Movement (1967)

As the increased commitment of troops—during a time when virtually all young men between the ages of eighteen and twenty-five were liable to the military draft—failed to bring the war tangibly closer to victory, an increasing number of Americans, politicians and citizens alike, began to voice their opposition to the war. The year 1967 may be identified as the turning point in the American popular attitude. In 1965 polls gave President Johnson an 80 percent approval rating. By the end of 1967, approval was only at 40 percent. Respondents identified the Vietnam War as the reason for their disapproval.

Johnson's "Media Offensive"

To counter the growing anti-war movement, the Johnson administration launched a "media offensive," which was fronted by General Westmoreland, who was brought home to present U.S. military achievements in the war. Westmoreland argued that the U.S. and ARVN effort was inflicting losses that outpaced enemy recruitment and reinforcement. He and other administration officials also defended the much-maligned pacification program. Officials estimated that 800,000–1,000,000 South Vietnamese villagers had been "liberated" from Communist control in 1966. In 1965 Communist insurgents had closed 70 percent of South Vietnam's roadways and waterways; by the beginning of 1967, Westmoreland and others pointed out, 60 percent were open.

In one sense, the media offensive was successful: few challenged the accuracy of Westmoreland's data. Yet the data hardly mattered. The disparity between the statistics and the lack of movement toward peace suggested to a growing number of Americans that the war was at a stalemate. President Johnson continued to assure television viewers that there was "light at the end of the tunnel," but the mounting number of U.S. casualties created what the press dubbed a "credibility gap" between what the administration claimed and what the public believed.

Increasingly, Americans became divided between those who opposed the war and those who continued to support it. In Congress, this translated into a division between "doves" (opponents of the war) and "hawks" (the war's supporters). With each passing month, the ranks of the doves rose, as did the volume of their voices. When Congress formally proposed to the administration a vigorous peace initiative in the autumn of 1967, Secretary of State Dean Rusk called a news conference on October 12, claiming that such initiatives were futile because North Vietnam would not entertain them. This response did nothing to quell anti-war sentiment, and all Johnson and Westmoreland could do was to assert that progress was being made. On November 21, Westmoreland declared to reporters: "I am absolutely certain that whereas in 1965 the enemy was winning, today he is certainly losing."

On the face of it, both Johnson and Westmoreland were correct. Military progress was being made. Militarily, the North was suffering more casualties than the combined U.S. and ARVN forces. Yet neither the president nor the commander in charge seemed willing to acknowledge that these truths were beside the point, which was that the North Vietnamese had a seemingly limitless capacity for absorbing losses. They were simply willing to die for their cause, and to die in numbers much greater than those who opposed them.

The Television War

Johnson's "media war" made extensive use of television, the very medium that was providing the American public with extensive news coverage of the war. Whereas the Korean War (Chapter 37) had taken place during the medium's infancy and was therefore reported mainly by newspapers, Vietnam exploded during the first great heyday of televised news. By the middle of 1965, all of the major networks opened Saigon bureaus, which grew into the third largest they maintained, behind only New York and Washington, D.C.

Historians of television and popular culture often remark that television coverage of Vietnam helped to create the anti-war movement by bringing into the nation's living rooms graphic images of the horrors of war. In August 1965 CBS aired a report showing U.S. Marines igniting the thatched roofs of the village of Cam Ne with Zippo lighters. During the Tet Offensive (see "The Tet Crisis" below) in 1968, NBC viewers saw Colonel Nguyen Ngoc Loan blow out the brains of his captive in a Saigon street—an image also widely published in American newspapers and magazines. For the most part, however, television reporting studiously *avoided* scenes of atrocity or bloodshed, at least until the end of the 1960s. Coverage up to the period of the Tet Offensive was mostly upbeat and relayed to viewers what military spokespeople had provided to reporters in daily press briefings. Most of this coverage was rather abstract; the reports were read by the news anchors and illustrated not with combat footage, but by battle maps. Although casualty figures were reported, generally on a weekly basis, the U.S. casualty count was always accompanied by the enemy "body count," which greatly exceeded the losses incurred by American forces. To a sports-minded public accustomed to keeping score, it must have appeared for some time that America was winning.

After the Tet Offensive and then as U.S. troop withdrawals began in 1969, the television coverage changed, reflecting the growing skepticism among journalists concerning government claims of progress and the "light at the end of the tunnel." This skepticism reflected changing American public opinion at least as much as it led or shaped that opinion. Even so, such reflection tended to crystallize or validate anti-war sentiment. Indeed, by the 1970s, more and more Vietnam reporting juxtaposed events overseas with coverage of the anti-war movement at home. What little television coverage the anti-war movement had received early in the war had tended to portray it as fringe protest or even as a

Communist-inspired effort to undermine the war effort. But by the late 1960s and early 1970s, it was being covered as a legitimate, even mainstream, political movement.

The Tet Crisis (1968)

The massive Communist offensive launched on January 30, 1968, to coincide with the Vietnamese lunar holiday Tet, ended about two months later. Militarily, the U.S.-ARVN response to Tet was an overwhelming tactical victory. But it was hard for the American public to see it that way: American casualties had risen from 780 per month during 1967 to 2,000 in February 1968. The media and anti-war politicians compared Tet—especially the long siege of Khe Sanh—to Dien Bien Phu, the humiliating 1954 defeat that ended French involvement in Vietnam. The comparison was not analogous, but Tet nevertheless hardened public opposition to the war and sharply divided legislators. When a somewhat distorted news story broke in March, announcing that General Westmoreland wanted an additional 200,000 men committed to the war, a wave of outrage swept the American public. Anti-war demonstrations became bigger, angrier, and more numerous. By the middle of March, public opinion polls revealed that 70 percent of Americans favored a phased withdrawal of U.S. forces from Vietnam, and, at the end of the month, President Johnson initiated a process designed to withdraw the United States from the war. Although Westmoreland never received the number of troops he wanted, American forces peaked at 536,000 by the end of 1968.

From Protest to Resistance

By 1968 it had become commonplace for newspaper and television news commentators to write or speak of "the war in Vietnam" and the parallel "war at home." The anti-war movement encompassed a wide range of Americans; however, leftist radicals were always part of the movement, and their presence was symptomatic of a growing dissatisfaction with a war

variously condemned as unjust, immoral, or just plain futile. Moreover, many saw the Vietnam War as the product of an unholy alliance between the government and big business—what President Dwight Eisenhower (certainly no radical) had called the "military industrial complex" in his January 17, 1961, farewell address, and what many Americans now referred to as "the Establishment." Vietnam radicalized many in the middle class. It divided the nation. Many feared—and some hoped—it would bring a genuine social and political revolution.

One of the principal drivers of the anti-war movement was the military draft. Young men were liable to fight, kill, and quite possibly die in a war that fewer and fewer Americans supported. Moreover, as during the Civil War (Chapter 17)—but not World War I (Chapter 34) or World War II (Chapter 36)—there was a perception of social injustice in the draft. Although the selective service law did not allow for commutation fees or the purchase of substitutes (as during the Civil War), it did provide various deferments, including those for college students. Many believed that this was, in effect, a pass for the children of the white middle class, because fewer African American or Hispanic young men attended college. Therefore, anti-war activists commonly asserted that the Vietnam War was being fought disproportionately by members of racial and ethnic minorities.

Popular perceptions aside, the army preferred to deploy volunteers in the belief that they made better combat soldiers than did draftees. Two-thirds of the army personnel who fought in Vietnam were voluntary enlistees. Most draftees remained in the United States or were assigned to noncombat roles. Further, minorities did not bear a disproportionate burden in the war. Of those killed in the conflict, 86 percent were white, 12.5 percent were black, and 1.2 percent were members of other races. These percentages accurately reflected the racial makeup of the nation at the time.

It is nevertheless true that draftees fought and died, and many young men actively protested this situation. During the war, approximately 100,000 "draft dodgers" fled the country. It is believed that 50,000–90,000 crossed into Canada, where they were treated as immigrants, because draft evasion was not a criminal offense under Canadian law. Untold others became fugitives within the United States.

The war also induced substantial numbers of soldiers to desert. These individuals had a more difficult time escaping the law, because Canada provided no convenient haven. Under Canadian law, military desertion was a crime, and the Canadian military opposed the government's turning a blind eye to it. It is estimated that no more than 1,000 deserters found refuge north of the border, and while the Canadian government reserved the right to prosecute deserters, not a single case was brought to trial.

Draft evasion and desertion were bitter issues throughout the war. Even many who objected to the war condemned both practices. Fleeing to Canada was effectively a form of exile; those who returned were often prosecuted. It was not until 1977, after the war, that President Jimmy Carter issued a general amnesty to draft evaders in an effort to heal the national cultural wounds inflicted by the war. Even so, an estimated 50,000 men chose to remain permanently in Canada.

Even some Americans who were not subject to the draft found active means of protesting the war. By 1972 federal officials estimated that 200,000–500,000 persons refused to pay the federal excise tax on their telephone bills in a mostly symbolic gesture to withhold funding for the war. A much smaller number, about 20,000, refused to pay part or all of their income tax bills; few of these individuals were criminally prosecuted.

Johnson Steps Down

Perhaps no figure associated with the Vietnam War was more tragic than President Lyndon Baines Johnson. He had entered office determined to create a legacy of social welfare and justice legislation unequaled since Franklin Roosevelt's New Deal. Medicare, Medicaid, the Civil Rights Act of 1964, and the Voting Rights Act of 1965 were highlights of the policy program Johnson called the "Great Society." Yet Johnson increasingly became associated with the Vietnam War, which drained the funding from many social programs.

In the wake of the Tet crisis and facing increasing anti-war protests, President Johnson recognized that he had become the most divisive American president of modern times. He also came to believe that peace negotiations could never succeed as long as he was in the White House. Thus, he announced, in a televised **Presidential Address** of March 31, 1968, his decision not to run for a second full term.

Showing the strain caused by dealing with the Vietnam conflict, President Lyndon Johnson works on a speech in the White House Cabinet Room on March 30, 1968. In a televised address the following day, Johnson announced that he would not seek or accept his party's nomination for reelection.

Johnson's Presidential Address, March 31, 1968

Throughout this entire, long period, I have been sustained by a single principle: that what we are doing now, in Vietnam, is vital not only to the security of Southeast Asia, but it is vital to the security of every American. . . .

. . . Tonight I have offered the first in what I hope will be a series of mutual moves toward peace. I pray that it will not be rejected by the leaders of North Vietnam. . . .

. . . The ultimate strength of our country and our cause will lie not in powerful weapons or infinite resources or boundless wealth, but will lie in the unity of our people.

This I believe very deeply.

Throughout my entire public career I have followed the personal philosophy that I am a free man, an American, a public servant, and a member of my party, in that order always and only.

For 37 years in the service of our Nation, first as a Congressman, as a Senator, and as Vice President, and now as your President, I have put the unity of the people first. I have put it ahead of any divisive partisanship.

And in these times as in times before, it is true that a house divided against itself by the spirit of faction, of party, of region, of religion, of race, is a house that cannot stand.

There is division in the American house now. There is divisiveness among us all tonight. And holding the trust that is mine, as President of all the people, I cannot disregard the peril to the progress of the American people and the hope and the prospect of peace for all peoples.

So, I would ask all Americans, whatever their personal interests or concern, to guard against divisiveness and all its ugly consequences. . . .

. . . I have concluded that I should not permit the Presidency to become involved in the partisan divisions that are developing in this political year.

With America's sons in the fields far away, with America's future under challenge right here at home, with our hopes and the world's hopes for peace in the balance every day, I do not believe that I should devote an hour or a day of my time to any personal partisan causes or to any duties other than the awesome duties of this office—the Presidency of your country.

Accordingly, I shall not seek, and I will not accept, the nomination of my party for another term as your President.

Excerpted from Lyndon Baines Johnson Library and Museum, "President Lyndon B. Johnson's Address to the Nation Announcing Steps to Limit the War in Vietnam and Reporting His Decision Not to Seek Reelection, March 31,1968," www.lbjlib.utexas.edu/johnson/archives.hom/speeches.hom/680331.asp.

The 1968 Presidential Election

President Johnson's withdrawal from the 1968 presidential election left open the very real possibility that the Democrats might nominate an anti-war candidate. The first of these to emerge was Senator Eugene McCarthy of Minnesota, whose strong showing in the Democratic primary in New Hampshire encouraged another anti-war candidate, Robert F. Kennedy, Massachusetts senator and former attorney general, to throw his hat into the ring. After winning the Indiana and Nebraska primaries, Kennedy headed to California, where, after declaring victory in that primary on June 6, 1968, he was gunned down by assassin Sirhan Sirhan.

Robert Kennedy's death gave the "mainstream" Democratic candidate, Vice President Hubert H. Humphrey, a commanding lead for the nomination. McCarthy managed to garner just 23 percent of the delegates at the Democratic National Convention held in Chicago during August 26–29, 1968. Nevertheless, the party was hardly unified around Humphrey, who intended, he said, to prosecute the war to its conclusion. Some 10,000 anti-war and civil rights protestors descended on Chicago during the convention, appropriating the city's Grant and

Lincoln parks as campgrounds. These protestors disrupted the convention in protest of Humphrey's nomination, and a violent clash broke out between the protestors and the Chicago police, which reporters and other eyewitnesses described as a "police riot."

In contrast to the disarray among the Democrats, the Republicans united behind their candidate: Richard M. Nixon, the former vice president under Dwight D. Eisenhower. Nixon also vowed to continue the war—but to achieve "peace with honor." Nixon won the election by a narrow margin, with 43.4 percent of the vote to Humphrey's 42.7 percent. Third-party candidate George Wallace (who ran on a conservative segregationist platform) captured 13.5 percent.

The closeness of the race left people to wonder how Robert Kennedy would have fared, had he achieved his party's nomination. Pitting an anti-war candidate against a pro-war candidate likely would have transformed the 1968 elections into a referendum on the war and might have changed the course of history.

Policy and Strategy under Nixon and Kissinger

As many had predicted, Nixon's "secret plan to end the war" failed to materialize after the new president took office. "Tricky Dick," an enduring epithet bestowed on him in 1950 by a small southern Cali-

Henry A. Kissinger

(1923–)

Born in Germany, Henry Kissinger moved with his family to the United States in 1938 to escape the Nazi persecution of Jews. He was naturalized in 1943 and, after studying accounting at City College, New York, served in the U.S. Army during World War II. He remained in the army after the war as part of the U.S. military government of occupation. After returning to the United States, he received a Ph.D. in 1954 from Harvard, then joined the faculty there. From 1959 to 1969, he was director of Harvard's Defense Studies Program and during this period worked as a security consultant to several U.S. agencies. He earned a national reputation as an expert on American strategic policy and a persuasive advocate of building a strong nuclear deterrent.

In December 1968 President Nixon appointed Kissinger assistant for national security affairs. He subsequently served as head of the U.S. National Security Council (1969–1975) and as secretary of state (September 1973–January 20, 1977). He was instrumental in engineering with Nixon the policy of détente with the Soviet Union and normalized relations with China. He was

instrumental in the SALT I arms-limitation agreement with the Soviet Union (1972).

Kissinger was initially a hardliner in the Vietnam War and urged Nixon to bomb Cambodia during 1969–1970, but he was also instrumental in the implementation of Nixon's Vietnamization policy and was the chief U.S. negotiator with the North Vietnamese during the Paris Peace Talks, which produced the Paris Peace Accords of January 23, 1973. In 1973 Kissinger shared the Nobel Prize for Peace with his North Vietnamese counterpart, Le Duc Tho—who declined to accept the prize.

Kissinger played a key role in mediating peace in the Arab-Israeli War of 1973 (Chapter 39) and reestablished diplomatic relations between Egypt and the United States, which had been severed in 1967. Kissinger remained in office as secretary of state after Nixon's resignation, serving through the term of President Ford. He then entered the private sector as a consultant, writer, and lecturer. In 1983 he was appointed by President Ronald Reagan as head of a national commission on Central American affairs.

fornia newspaper, had an unsavory reputation. Nixon's detractors—and there were many—regarded him as a devious Machiavellian figure. Nevertheless, with his foreign policy adviser, a brilliant former Harvard political scientist named Henry Kissinger, Nixon evolved a global strategy that called for improving relations with the Soviets (through expanded trade and an arms-limitation agreement) with the objective of disengaging Moscow from Hanoi, thereby isolating North Vietnam. In addition, Nixon wanted to normalize relations with the People's Republic of China, another source of support for the North Vietnamese. Once accomplished, this would dramatically alter the international political landscape, reducing Vietnam's political value to the Communists. Cut loose, the North Vietnamese would finally negotiate a peace the United States could justly call honorable.

In the shorter term, however, the war still had to be fought. Nixon and Kissinger formulated a new "two-track" approach. One consisted of uninterrupted military operations, while the other simultaneously offered the North Vietnamese diplomatic initiatives emphasizing the mutual benefits of a negotiated resolution. Although it was a plausible approach, it unfolded in the presence of what might be called a third track: the "Vietnamization" of the war. As he explained in his November 3, 1969, **Speech on Vietnamization,** President Nixon was committed to the reduction of U.S. ground forces by training and equipping ARVN troops to shoulder an ever-increasing share of combat. The North Vietnamese interpreted Vietnamization as proof that the United States had lost its resolve to win the war. This encouraged North Vietnamese negotiators to assume an aggressive and unyielding posture in peace talks, which accordingly became protracted and frustrating.

The My Lai Massacre Court Martial

Just as there was a popular impression that the war was being fought disproportionately by America's ethnic and racial minorities, so there was a general belief that many, if not most, soldiers returned from Vietnam emotionally shattered, in some cases having been transformed into drug addicts or even criminals. Although drug use among soldiers in Vietnam was widespread, the rate of addiction was no greater among returning veterans than among the general population in an era when the use of illegal drugs was common. Movies, television, and popular fiction frequently portrayed burned-out veterans whom the war had rendered unfit for civilian life; some were depicted as hopelessly psychopathic, having acquired in Vietnam a taste for killing. It was also not uncommon for anti-war protesters to call American soldiers "baby killers," a reference to the high rate of casualties inflicted on civilians in a war that involved so many irregular troops (virtually indistinguishable from civilians) and civilian collaborators. There is, however, no statistical evidence to suggest a higher rate of criminal behavior among Vietnam veterans than among the general population.

Nixon's Speech on Vietnamization, 1969

We have adopted a plan which we have worked out in cooperation with the South Vietnamese for the complete withdrawal of all U.S. combat ground forces, and their replacement by South Vietnamese forces on an orderly scheduled timetable. This withdrawal will be made from strength and not from weakness. As South Vietnamese forces become stronger, the rate of American withdrawal can become greater. . . .

Let us be united for peace. Let us also be united against defeat. Because let us understand: North Vietnam cannot defeat or humiliate the United States. Only Americans can do that.

Excerpted from Richard M. Nixon, "Address to the Nation on the War in Vietnam," November 3, 1969, in *Public Papers of the Presidents of the United States: Richard M. Nixon, 1969–1974,* from the American Presidency Project, University of California, Santa Barbara, www.presidency.ucsb.edu.

The tendency to demonize the soldier was brought to a head by the My Lai Massacre, which came to light on November 12, 1969, when investigative journalist Seymour Hersh reported the incident and its subsequent official cover-up. This was followed by the publication (initially in the Cleveland *Plain Dealer*) of horrific photographs of dead villagers who had been killed in the South Vietnamese hamlet of My Lai.

On March 16, 1968, apparently acting on orders from company commander Captain Ernest Medina, a U.S. infantry platoon marched into My Lai, allegedly a Viet Cong sanctuary and stronghold. Although no Viet Cong insurgents were found, Lieutenant William Calley directed the massacre of 347 unarmed civilians, including women, old men, and children, some of whom were herded into ditches, where they were shot. Some were tortured and raped before their execution. The grisly scenes were recorded by army photographers.

The army covered up the "My Lai Incident" until Ronald Ridenhour, a Vietnam veteran, sent letters to President Nixon and other officials. Hersh broke the story after conversations with Ridenhour, and the army finally began an investigation followed by court-martial proceedings against several soldiers, of whom only Calley was convicted on March 29, 1971.

For many Americans, My Lai symbolized the senseless brutality of the Vietnam War, a conflict in which the supposed defenders of democracy were seen slaughtering innocent women and children. Some condemned Calley, but others also regarded him as a victim, thrust into a war without firm rules or objectives and in which everyone was a potential enemy. Calley was sentenced to life imprisonment, but was released in September 1974 when a federal court overturned the conviction.

Invasion of Cambodia

As the Paris Peace talks faltered in the face of Vietnamization, President Nixon resorted to strikes at Communist supply and staging areas in Cambodia. His problem was to maintain the pace of staged troop withdrawals without weakening America's hand in the negotiations. In his April 30, 1970, **Speech on Cambodia,** the president tried to reconcile the American people to what most of them found a highly distasteful, even outrageous step: the invasion, by a great democratic power, of a neutral Buddhist nation. Although President Nixon claimed that Cambodia was a victim of Communist infiltration and that it had appealed to the United States and other nations for aid in ejecting the Communists, few Americans believed that the Cambodians intended to invite war on their territory.

The "Kent State Massacre" (May 4, 1970)

Troop withdrawals quieted anti-war protest for a time, but the invasion of Cambodia renewed protests with a vengeance, especially on college campuses, where demonstrations were often militant and resulted in major acts of vandalism—including, in some cases, arson directed against campus buildings associated with the Reserve Officer Training Corps (ROTC). On May 4, 1970, on the campus of Kent State University in Ohio, National Guardsmen sent to restore order on the campus fired on unarmed students, killing four and wounding nine. *Life* magazine published a devastating photograph of a young woman kneeling beside the body of a slain student, helplessly appealing for aid. It looked uncannily like an image from Vietnam itself. The photograph assumed iconic status, suggesting that the horrors of war had come to the home front.

The "Kent State Massacre" proved to be a watershed event in the anti-war movement. The shootings touched off the largest strike in American history, as more than 100 college campuses closed for the remainder of the school week after the incident. An estimated 5 million American students joined the strike. By mid-May some 500 colleges and universities had closed, and by the end of the month, more than 900 had shut their doors. Protests swept eight out of ten U.S. campuses, and 35,000 National Guardsmen were called up in sixteen states. At least

Nixon's Speech on Cambodia, 1970

Ten days ago, in my report to the Nation on Vietnam, I announced a decision to withdraw an additional 150,000 Americans from Vietnam over the next year. I said then that I was making that decision despite our concern over increased enemy activity in Laos, in Cambodia, and in South Vietnam.

At that time, I warned that if I concluded that increased enemy activity in any of these areas endangered the lives of Americans remaining in Vietnam, I would not hesitate to take strong and effective measures to deal with that situation.

Despite that warning, North Vietnam has increased its military aggression in all these areas, and particularly in Cambodia. . . .

To protect our men who are in Vietnam and to guarantee the continued success of our withdrawal and Vietnamization programs, I have concluded that the time has come for action. . . .

In cooperation with the armed forces of South Vietnam, attacks are being launched this week to clean out major enemy sanctuaries on the Cambodian-Vietnam border.

A major responsibility for the ground operations is being assumed by South Vietnamese forces. . . .

This is not an invasion of Cambodia. The areas in which these attacks will be launched are completely occupied and controlled by North Vietnamese forces. Our purpose is not to occupy the areas. Once enemy forces are driven out of these sanctuaries and once their military supplies are destroyed, we will withdraw. . . .

We take this action not for the purpose of expanding the war into Cambodia but for the purpose of ending the war in Vietnam and winning the just peace we all desire. We have made—we will continue to make every possible effort to end this war through negotiation at the conference table rather than through more fighting on the battlefield.

Excerpted from Richard M. Nixon, "Address to the Nation on the Situation in Southeast Asia," April 30, 1970, in *Public Papers of the Presidents of the United States: Richard M. Nixon, 1969–1974,* from the American Presidency Project, University of California, Santa Barbara, www.presidency.ucsb.edu.

---

thirty ROTC buildings were burned or bombed in the immediate aftermath of the Kent State shootings; at the University of Wisconsin—one of the nation's most radical campuses—twenty-seven fire bombings were reported. During May 1970 law enforcement authorities reported more arsons than in any month on record.

On May 9, 1970, more than 150,000 protesters converged on Washington, D.C., which assumed the character of a city under siege. No less a figure than former Supreme Court chief justice Earl Warren pronounced the aftermath of Kent State the worst crisis in American history since the Civil War.

The military also suffered a crisis. During May, more than 500 soldiers deserted each day, and mutinous conditions prevailed as some troops refused orders to cross into Cambodia. Some soldiers donned black armbands—a token of mourning for the slain students—and announced their intention to refuse to fight any longer in Vietnam. Most significant, within days of the shootings, President Nixon limited incursions into Cambodia to thirty-five kilometers inside the country and the duration to a maximum of two months. After that time elapsed, U.S. forces did withdraw. Soon after, Congress formally rescinded the Tonkin Gulf Resolution.

During the turmoil that followed Kent State, President Nixon began to take the kind of extreme—and even illegal—measures that would later figure in the Watergate scandal that erupted in 1972. In May 1970 he started compiling what he called an "enemies list," consisting chiefly of prominent anti-war activists. During the following month he began formulating strategies to monitor and discredit anti-war activists as well as members of Congress and other public figures who opposed the war.

Withdrawal and the End of Selective Service

Under President Nixon's secretary of defense, Melvin R. Laird, the gradual, phased disengagement of U.S. combat forces—or "Vietnamization"—progressed. During 1969, authorized troop strength in Vietnam was reduced to 484,000. By May 1, 1972, there were only 69,000 U.S. soldiers still in Vietnam. This coincided with a 95 percent reduction (from January 1969 to May 1972) in U.S. combat deaths compared with the peak reached in 1968. Despite increased funding to ARVN, monetary expenditures on Vietnam fell by about two-thirds between 1969 and 1972. This was indeed an achievement, although Laird's rosy assessment of Vietnamization in his 1973 final report as secretary of defense proved to be unfounded. He declared that Vietnamization had made the South Vietnamese people fully capable of providing for their own security against the North Vietnamese.

In terms of numbers of troops withdrawn, Vietnamization might be judged to have been a success; however, U.S. involvement in Vietnam remained extensive during the Nixon years, including the invasion of Cambodia, the renewed bombing of North Vietnam, the mining of Haiphong Harbor in the spring of 1972, and more bombing of the North in December 1972. Although Laird publicly supported these measures, he privately opposed them.

Even as he directed the withdrawal of ground forces from Vietnam, Laird planned to take the momentous step of ending the draft, setting June 30, 1973, as a target date. His goal was to create an All Volunteer Force (AVF). Laird and Nixon both believed that the draft had been the main fuel of the anti-war movement, and they reasoned that the AVF would give the president and Congress a freer hand in future decisions relating to war. Indeed, during Laird's tenure, from 1969 to 1973, draft call-ups fell precipitously: from 300,000 in 1969 to 200,000 in 1970, to 100,000 in 1971, and finally to 50,000 in 1972. On January 27, 1973, after the Paris Peace Accords were signed, Laird suspended the draft, fully five months ahead of his schedule.

The Pentagon Papers

President Nixon took major steps to disengage the United States from the Vietnam War, but his simultaneous expansion of aspects of the war—the Cambodian invasion and the bombing campaigns—created perhaps even more domestic turmoil during his administration than there had been during Johnson's.

John Kerry, a twenty-seven-year-old former navy lieutenant and head of the Vietnam Veterans Against the War (VVAW), testifies before the Senate Foreign Relations Committee on April 22, 1971. Kerry would later represent Massachusetts in the U.S. Senate and run as the Democratic nominee in the 2004 presidential election. Kerry's Vietnam record became campaign fodder in a race he lost to incumbent president George W. Bush.

When in June 1971 the *New York Times* published excerpts from a top-secret government study officially titled *The History of the U.S. Decision Making Process in Vietnam*—and called by *Times* editors "The Pentagon Papers"—Nixon initially believed he had been given a great political gift.

The Pentagon Papers material had been commissioned between 1967 and 1969 by Secretary of Defense Robert S. McNamara. Consisting of 3,000 pages of narrative by Defense Department analysts and 4,000 pages of original documents, the study chronicled the deepening of U.S. involvement in Vietnam from the Truman administration through the Johnson administration. The study illustrated how the Kennedy administration had transformed a policy of very limited involvement into a "broad commitment," which included the CIA-aided overthrow and assassination of South Vietnamese president Ngo Dinh Diem, a longtime U.S. ally. The study also revealed that the Tonkin Gulf Resolution had been drafted months before the purported North Vietnamese attacks on the American destroyers *Maddox* and *C. Turner Joy.* According to the study, Johnson had ordered the bombing of North Vietnam in 1965 despite the consensus of the U.S. intelligence community that even massive air raids would not discourage or prevent North Vietnam from continuing its support of the Viet Cong insurgency in South Vietnam.

Although the Pentagon Papers did cover the Eisenhower years, by far the most embarrassing and shocking revelations concerned Democratic administrations. Nixon at first believed that this would put his own efforts in a far more favorable light. But he soon decided that he could not let the leaking of classified documents go unchallenged, and he ordered Attorney General John Mitchell to threaten the *Times* with criminal charges of espionage. When this attempt at intimidation failed, the Department of Justice secured a temporary injunction that forced the suspension of publication of the Pentagon Papers series. On June 30, 1971, however, the U.S. Supreme Court ruled 6-3 to overturn the injunction on First Amendment (freedom of the press) grounds, and the *Times* continued to publish the Papers.

Nixon's response converted something that might have raised his stock with the American public into the beginning of what the press characterized as the "bunker mentality" of the Nixon White House. The president launched a series of covert—and often illegal—operations to stop further leaks and to discredit the principal Pentagon Papers whistleblower, Daniel Ellsberg, a former Defense Department analyst who had worked on the original study and, after turning against the war, systematically leaked the study's contents. Nixon set up a covert operations unit, reporting directly to the White House, dubbed "the Plumbers," because its mission was to find and stop leaks. The Plumbers' first mission was to burglarize the office of Ellsberg's psychiatrist in the hope of finding embarrassing material concerning his patient. Also discussed was a plan to physically assault Ellsberg in order to intimidate him into silence. Eventually the Plumbers were sent to Democratic National Headquarters in Washington's Watergate complex, where police apprehended them as they were in the process of bugging and burglarizing the offices to gather material that might help ensure President Nixon's reelection in 1972. In this way, the Vietnam War would claim another casualty: the presidency of Richard Nixon.

The Paris Peace Talks and Accords

The Paris Peace Talks had been initiated on May 10, 1968, under President Johnson. Like the Korean War peace talks (Chapter 37), they dragged on, faltered, collapsed, and were fitfully revived. As discussed in "The Conflict" (above), Nixon's foreign affairs adviser, Henry Kissinger, reached a tentative accord with his North Vietnamese counterpart in October 1972, which allowed President Nixon to declare to voters that "peace was at hand" in Vietnam. However, once he had achieved reelection, Nixon repudiated the terms of the tentative agreement and ordered intensive bombing operations in the North during December to bring the Communists back to the conference table. Negotiations resumed on January 8, 1973, and the Paris Peace Accords were agreed to on January 23, 1973, and signed on January 27. President Nixon made the momentous **Announcement of the Paris Peace Accords** on January 23. Critics of the president pointed out that the terms of the 1973 accords were virtually identical to those rejected in 1972.

Nixon's Decline and Fall

The Paris Peace Accords did remarkably little to stop the shooting war, which continued against the backdrop of President Nixon's downfall in the Watergate Scandal. Shortly after Nixon embarked upon his second term, revelations pointed to his having conspired to sabotage Democratic challengers and engaged in a conspiracy to impede the Watergate investigation itself. A swelling public outcry forced President Nixon to appoint in May 1973 a special prosecutor, who subpoenaed secret tape recordings of White House meetings. Nixon refused to yield these, and in October 1973 he ordered Attorney General Eliott Richardson to fire the special prosecutor, Archibald Cox. Richardson resigned rather than carry out the order, and Richardson's second-in-command, William Ruckelshaus, also refused. Nixon then fired Ruckelshaus. Nixon's solicitor general, Robert H. Bork, finally did the president's bidding, but public indignation over the firing of Cox, the resignation of Richardson, and the dismissal of Ruckelshaus (these events were dubbed the "Saturday Night Massacre") forced the president to appoint a new special prosecutor, Leon Jaworski.

The fight over the White House tapes continued, and in July 1974 Jaworski's grand jury named the president of the United States as an unindicted co-conspirator in an obstruction of justice. Shortly after this, the Supreme Court rejected Nixon's claim of executive privilege as the basis for refusing to produce the tapes. Some of the tapes were eventually released—minus a suspicious eighteen-and-a-half-minute gap—and on July 30, 1974, the House Judiciary Committee recommended the impeachment of Richard Nixon on three counts: obstruction of justice, abuse of presidential powers, and attempting to impede the impeachment process itself by refusing to release all of the evidence demanded. On August 5, the president released the remaining tapes, which clearly revealed the steps he had taken to block the FBI's investigation of the Watergate burglary. Just four days later, on August 9, 1974, Richard M. Nixon announced to the American people—and the world—his resignation from office.

Announcement of the Paris Peace Accords, 1973

Good evening:

I have asked for this radio and television time tonight for the purpose of announcing that we today have concluded an agreement to end the war and bring peace with honor in Vietnam and in Southeast Asia. . . .

. . . Throughout the years of negotiations, we have insisted on peace with honor. In my addresses to the Nation from this room of January 25 and May 8 [1972], I set forth the goals that we considered essential for peace with honor.

In the settlement that has now been agreed to, all the conditions that I laid down then have been met. . . .

The people of South Vietnam have been guaranteed the right to determine their own future, without outside interference. . . .

We shall continue to aid South Vietnam within the terms of the agreement, and we shall support efforts by the people of South Vietnam to settle their problems peacefully among themselves.

Excerpted from Richard M. Nixon, "Address to the Nation Announcing Conclusion of an Agreement on Ending the War and Restoring Peace in Vietnam," January 23, 1973, in *Public Papers of the Presidents of the United States: Richard M. Nixon, 1969–1974,* from the American Presidency Project, University of California, Santa Barbara, www.presidency.ucsb.edu.

An Exit without Strategy:
The Fall of Saigon

The downfall of Richard Nixon coincided with the inevitable collapse of the South Vietnamese government. Three American presidents—Kennedy, Johnson, and Nixon—had desperately sought to formulate an "exit strategy" from Vietnam. Johnson had once called his objective "victory," but the best Nixon could muster was "peace with honor." In the end, neither objective was achieved, and the exit—a frenzied evacuation of the last U.S. personnel remaining in Saigon, which was overrun by the forces of North Vietnam on April 29–30, 1975—was without strategy or plan. This ignominious end to so long a struggle brought to some Americans a number of cause of relief, but to many others it seemed a tragedy both for Vietnam and for the United States.

BIBLIOGRAPHY

Hanyok, Robert J. "Skunks, Bogies, and the Flying Fish: The Gulf of ? 4 August 1964." Cryptologic Quarterly no. 4/1 (2000/2001): 1–55

Manning, Robert, ed. The Vietnam Experience. vols. Boston: Boston Publishing 1981–1987.

Morrison, Wilbur H. The Elephant and the Tiger: The Full Story of the Vietnam War. Hippocrene Books, 1990.

Sigler, David B. Vietnam Battle Chronology: Army and Marine Corps Combat Units, 1960–1973. Jefferson, N.C., McFarland, 1

agreed to on January 23, 1973, and signed on January 27. President Nixon made the momentous **Announcement of the Paris Peace Accords** on January 23. Critics of the president pointed out that the terms of the 1973 accords were virtually identical to those rejected in 1972.

Nixon's Decline and Fall

The Paris Peace Accords did remarkably little to stop the shooting war, which continued against the backdrop of President Nixon's downfall in the Watergate Scandal. Shortly after Nixon embarked upon his second term, revelations pointed to his having conspired to sabotage Democratic challengers and engaged in a conspiracy to impede the Watergate investigation itself. A swelling public outcry forced President Nixon to appoint in May 1973 a special prosecutor, who subpoenaed secret tape recordings of White House meetings. Nixon refused to yield these, and in October 1973 he ordered Attorney General Eliott Richardson to fire the special prosecutor, Archibald Cox. Richardson resigned rather than carry out the order, and Richardson's second-in-command, William Ruckelshaus, also refused. Nixon then fired Ruckelshaus. Nixon's solicitor general, Robert H. Bork, finally did the president's bidding, but public indignation over the firing of Cox, the resignation of Richardson, and the dismissal of Ruckelshaus (these events were dubbed the "Saturday Night Massacre") forced the president to appoint a new special prosecutor, Leon Jaworski.

The fight over the White House tapes continued, and in July 1974 Jaworski's grand jury named the president of the United States as an unindicted co-conspirator in an obstruction of justice. Shortly after this, the Supreme Court rejected Nixon's claim of executive privilege as the basis for refusing to produce the tapes. Some of the tapes were eventually released—minus a suspicious eighteen-and-a-half-minute gap—and on July 30, 1974, the House Judiciary Committee recommended the impeachment of Richard Nixon on three counts: obstruction of justice, abuse of presidential powers, and attempting to impede the impeachment process itself by refusing to release all of the evidence demanded. On August 5, the president released the remaining tapes, which clearly revealed the steps he had taken to block the FBI's investigation of the Watergate burglary. Just four days later, on August 9, 1974, Richard M. Nixon announced to the American people—and the world—his resignation from office.

Announcement of the Paris Peace Accords, 1973

Good evening:

I have asked for this radio and television time tonight for the purpose of announcing that we today have concluded an agreement to end the war and bring peace with honor in Vietnam and in Southeast Asia. . . .

. . . Throughout the years of negotiations, we have insisted on peace with honor. In my addresses to the Nation from this room of January 25 and May 8 [1972], I set forth the goals that we considered essential for peace with honor.

In the settlement that has now been agreed to, all the conditions that I laid down then have been met. . . .

The people of South Vietnam have been guaranteed the right to determine their own future, without outside interference. . . .

We shall continue to aid South Vietnam within the terms of the agreement, and we shall support efforts by the people of South Vietnam to settle their problems peacefully among themselves.

Excerpted from Richard M. Nixon, "Address to the Nation Announcing Conclusion of an Agreement on Ending the War and Restoring Peace in Vietnam," January 23, 1973, in *Public Papers of the Presidents of the United States: Richard M. Nixon, 1969–1974,* from the American Presidency Project, University of California, Santa Barbara, www.presidency.ucsb.edu.

An Exit without Strategy: The Fall of Saigon

The downfall of Richard Nixon coincided with the inexorable collapse of the South Vietnamese government. Three American presidents—Kennedy, Johnson, and Nixon—had desperately sought to formulate an "exit strategy" from Vietnam. Johnson had once called his objective "victory," but the best Nixon could muster was "peace with honor." In the end, neither objective was achieved, and the exit—a frenzied evacuation of the last U.S. personnel remaining in Saigon, which was overrun by the forces of North Vietnam on April 29–30, 1975—was without strategy or plan. This ignominious end to so long a struggle brought to some Americans a numbed sense of relief, but to many others it seemed a tragedy both for Vietnam and for the United States.

BIBLIOGRAPHY

Haynok, Robert J. "Skunks, Bogies, Silent Hounds, and the Flying Fish: The Gulf of Tonkin Mystery, 2–4 August 1964," *Cryptologic Quarterly* 19/20, no. 4/1 (2000/2001): 1–55.

Manning, Robert, ed. *The Vietnam Experience,* 16 vols. Boston: Boston Publishing Company, 1981–1987.

Morrison, Wilbur H. *The Elephant and the Tiger: The Full Story of the Vietnam War.* New York: Hippcrene Books, 1990.

Sigler, David B. *Vietnam Battle Chronology: U.S. Army and Marine Corps Combat Operations, 1965–1973.* Jefferson, N.C.: McFarland, 1992.

CHAPTER 39

THE UNITED STATES
AS PEACEMAKER

Overview

The Spanish-American War of 1898 (Chapter 29) and the U.S. intervention in the Boxer Rebellion of 1899–1901 (Chapter 31) are typically viewed as turning points marking America's abandonment of the policy of isolationism and its bold entry onto the international stage as a bidder for world power. While the twentieth century saw intervals of renewed isolationist sentiment, especially after World War I (Chapter 34) and the exit of Woodrow Wilson, these wars on the cusp of the new century ushered in an era in which the United States played an increasingly dominant role in world affairs. That role was not always defined by military action or even economic intervention, but was frequently diplomatic.

The first grand instance of American diplomacy was the 1905 intervention in the Russo-Japanese War. Theodore Roosevelt, perhaps the nation's first frankly imperialist president, brought Russia and Japan together to negotiate an end to a conflict that—in light of Japan's own imperial ambitions—threatened world stability as well as U.S. interests in Asia. In the quiet New England town of Portsmouth, New Hampshire, the belligerents hammered out the Treaty of Portsmouth (1905). The president's role in this negotiation earned him a Nobel Peace Prize.

President Woodrow Wilson used America's participation in World War I as the basis for conceiving the League of Nations and what he hoped would be an enduring world peace. This hope proved forlorn, and the United States was compelled to fight a second world war just two decades after the first. The next epoch of American diplomatic peacemaking did

not come until the 1970s, when President Jimmy Carter helped to reconcile two apparently implacable enemies, Egypt and Israel, by bringing together Egyptian president Muhammad Anwar al-Sadat and Israeli prime minister Menachem Begin at Camp David, the presidential retreat in Maryland. The peace that was concluded in 1978 (and followed by subsequent agreements in 1979 and 1981) was backed by U.S. security guarantees. While general peace in the Middle East has proved elusive, Egypt and Israel have coexisted without violence since the end of the 1970s.

The next era of American peacemaking came in the 1990s, when President Bill Clinton helped broker a series of treaties and accords between Israel and the Palestine Liberation Organization (PLO), including Israel-PLO Recognition (1993), the PLO-Israel Accord (1993), the Agreement on Preparatory Transfer of Powers and Responsibilities (1994), Israeli-Palestinian Interim Agreement on the West Bank and the Gaza Strip (1995), and the Wye River Memorandum (1998). The Clinton administration also helped negotiate the Israel-Jordan Common Agenda (1993), the Washington Declaration (of Israel, Jordan, and the United States; 1994), and the Israel-Jordan Peace Treaty (1994). In 1996 the United States participated in the formulation of the Israel-Lebanon Ceasefire Understanding.

Although the administration of George W. Bush initially distanced itself from high-level involvement in Middle East affairs, the president announced on June 24, 2002, a "road map" for peace in the Middle East, calling for the creation of an independent

Palestinian state to exist side by side with Israel. The "road map" was the product of discussions among the United States, the European Union, Russia, and the United Nations.

The Middle East was not the only political hot spot during the 1980s and 1990s. The rapid decline and fall of communism, both in the Soviet Union and throughout the former Soviet satellite countries of Eastern Europe, brought what President George H. W. Bush called a "new world order" and a breathtaking measure of democracy, but also, in some instances, violent instability. The Balkan states that had been forcibly united under Communist Yugoslavia quickly fell into internecine warfare based on conflicting national and religious affiliations as well as quasi-racial, quasi-tribal allegiances. The Dayton Peace Accords, negotiated among the Republic of Bosnia and Herzegovina, the Republic of Croatia, and the Federal Republic of Yugoslavia in a series of meetings at Wright-Patterson Air Force Base, outside of Dayton, Ohio, ended war in Bosnia and Herzegovina in 1995, and the Kosovo Military

CHRONOLOGY OF AMERICAN PEACEMAKING

1904–1905
- Russo-Japanese War

1948–1949
- Arab-Israeli War

1967
- Arab-Israeli War ("Six-Day War")

1973
- Arab-Israeli War ("Yom Kippur War")

1975–1992
- Lebanese Civil War

1987–1992
- The "intifada" (PLO/Palestinian rebellion against Israel); continues sporadically

1992–1995
- War in Bosnia and Herzegovina

1998–1999
- War in Kosovo

Technical Agreement and the Rambouillet Accords (Interim Agreement for Peace and Self-Government in Kosovo) were concluded with U.S. mediation in 1999, after NATO (led by the United States) militarily intervened to end a civil war between the province of Kosovo and the Federal Republic of Yugoslavia and the Federal Republic of Serbia.

The Russo-Japanese War (1904–1905)

Although overshadowed by the subsequent great wars of the twentieth century, the Russo-Japanese War was horrific. Of approximately 1.4 million men fielded by Russia, 71,453 were killed and 141,800 wounded; of Japan's forces numbering 1.2 million, 80,378 died and 153,673 were wounded. At issue were the competing imperialist ambitions of Japan and Russia, specifically the question of which nation would control Manchuria and Korea. Fighting began on February 8, 1904, with a Japanese attack upon and blockade of the Russian fleet anchored at Port Arthur (present-day Lushun, China) following the refusal of Tsar Nicholas II to withdraw Russian troops occupying Manchuria. Those troops had marched into Manchuria during the Boxer Rebellion (Chapter 31), and the Russian government was unwilling to relinquish its toehold in the region. In response to the attack, Russia declared war on Japan.

The war saw the first use of modern warships as well as automatic weapons, but although Japan incurred higher casualties, it was Russia that suffered strategic and political disaster. It lost Port Arthur (January 1905), was crushed at the Battle of Mukden (February–March 1905), and lost most of its Baltic fleet at the Battle of Tsushima (May 27–28, 1905). At this point, U.S. president Theodore Roosevelt offered his services to mediate a peace.

Treaty of Portsmouth (1905)

Both Russia and Japan accepted Roosevelt's offer, and a peace conference was held at Portsmouth, New Hampshire, from August 9 to September 5, 1905. In

The front page of the August 29, 1905, issue of the Portsmouth *(N.H.)* Herald *proclaims peace and announces that "Russia and Japan have agreed upon terms and the war will end." Pictured are photographs of the four "men who solved the problem," Under Secretary of State Herbert H. D. Peirce, and the building in which the newspaper expected the treaty to be signed.*

the resulting **Treaty of Portsmouth,** Russia ceded control of Korea and also transferred to Japan its lease of Port Arthur and the Liaodong (Liaotung) Peninsula. Additionally, Russia ceded to Japan Sakhalin Island south of the 50th parallel; the Japanese renamed it Karafuto. The treaty laid down the terms under which the two nations were to conduct commerce in Manchuria and stipulated that railroads built by Japan and Russia in Manchuria could not be used for military purposes, but were to be reserved exclusively for commerce.

The Treaty of Portsmouth enhanced the international diplomatic prestige of the United States. It also humiliated Russia, a European nation, at the hands of Japan, an Asian state, which shocked many in the West. For Tsar Nicholas II, the war proved destructive. The Russian Revolution of 1905 followed within two months and was a prelude to the Russian revolutions of 1917, which brought an end to Nicholas II and the Romanov dynasty.

Israel and the Arab World

Since May 14, 1948, when President Harry S. Truman officially recognized the provisional Jewish government as the de facto authority of the new Jewish state, the policy of the United States has been pro-Israel. From the beginning, the American government has recognized Israel as the only true democracy in the Middle East and has supported it as an ally, giving it financial and military aid to assist in its frequent armed conflicts with its Arab neighbors.

Under Jimmy Carter, the policy of the U.S. government changed slightly but significantly. While still resolutely pro-Israel, the Carter administration resolved to bring about peaceful coexistence between Israel and Egypt. Thus, the United States was transformed from an ally of Israel to a good-faith mediator. The situation was helped by Egypt's president, Anwar al-Sadat, who wanted an alliance with the United States. In 1972 he summarily expelled from Egypt thousands of Soviet technicians and advisers who were the legacy of Sadat's pro-Soviet predecessor, Gamal Abdel Nasser. Sadat's purpose was to avoid what he saw as inevitable Soviet domination. In October 1973 he fought alongside Syria in the "Yom Kippur War" against Israel, but soon indicated a willingness to make peace. By doing so, he sought to realign his nation with America. By the end of 1973 Sadat had

Treaty of Portsmouth, 1905

The Emperor of Japan on the one part, and the Emperor of all the Russias, on the other part, animated by a desire to restore the blessings of peace, have resolved to conclude a treaty of peace. . . .

ARTICLE I.

There shall henceforth be peace and amity between their Majesties the Emperor of Japan and the Emperor of all the Russias, and between their respective States and subjects.

ARTICLE II.

The Imperial Russian Government, acknowledging that Japan possesses in Korea paramount political, military and economical interests engages neither to obstruct nor interfere with measures for guidance, protection and control which the Imperial Government of Japan may find necessary to take in Korea. . . . It is also agreed that, in order to avoid causes of misunderstanding, the two high contracting parties will abstain on the Russian-Korean frontier from taking any military measure which may menace the security of Russian or Korean territory.

ARTICLE III.

Japan and Russia mutually engage:

First.—To evacuate completely and simultaneously Manchuria, except the territory affected by the lease of the Liaotung Peninsula. . . .

Second.—To restore entirely and completely to the exclusive administration of China all portions of Manchuria now in occupation, or under the control of the Japanese or Russian troops, with the exception of the territory above mentioned.

The Imperial Government of Russia declares that it has not in Manchuria any territorial advantages or preferential or exclusive concessions in the impairment of Chinese sovereignty, or inconsistent with the principle of equal opportunity. . . .

ARTICLE V.

The Imperial Russian Government transfers and assigns to the Imperial Government of Japan, with the consent of the Government of China, the lease of Port Arthur, Talien and the adjacent territorial waters. . . .

ARTICLE VI.

The Imperial Russian Government engages to transfer and assign to the Imperial Government of Japan, without compensation and with the consent of the Chinese Government, the railway between Changchunfu and Kuanchangtsu and Port Arthur. . . .

ARTICLE VII.

Japan and Russia engage to exploit their respective railways in Manchuria exclusively for commercial and industrial purposes and nowise for strategic purposes. It is understood that this restriction does not apply to the railway in the territory affected by the lease of the Liaotung Peninsula. . . .

ARTICLE IX.

The Imperial Russian Government cedes to the Imperial Government of Japan in perpetuity and full sovereignty the southern portion of the Island of Saghalin [Sakhalin] and all the islands adjacent thereto.

Excerpted from the Japan-American Society of New Hampshire, "Treaty of Portsmouth," in *Portsmouth Peace Treaty 1905–2005*, http://process.portsmouthpeacetreaty.org/process/peace/TreatyText.pdf.

---

begun to forge a positive relationship with the United States via peace feelers toward Israel.

The Camp David Accords (1978)

In many ways, Egyptian president Anwar al-Sadat and his Israeli counterpart, Prime Minister Menachem Begin, had much in common. Both were fierce nationalists who had fought against British domination in the 1940s. Both feared and despised the Soviet Union. Both sought approval from the international community. In particular, both valued the United States as an ally. Yet Sadat and Begin, as leaders of their nations, embodied the seemingly eternal opposition of their nations. Years of conflict had led to the assumption that the survival of one

Jimmy Carter

(1924–)

James Earl Carter Jr., who always called himself "Jimmy," was born in the peanut-farming town of Plains, Georgia. He graduated in 1946 from the U.S. Naval Academy and married Rosalynn Smith, with whom he would have three sons and a daughter. During his seven-year naval career, Carter worked closely with Admiral Hyman Rickover in developing nuclear submarine technology.

Returning to Plains after leaving the navy, he served in the Georgia legislature and in 1970 was elected governor of Georgia. He drew national attention by his emphasis on such issues as ecology, creating efficient and compassionate government, and furthering the cause of civil rights and equal opportunity. Nominated as Democratic presidential candidate in 1976, he defeated Gerald R. Ford, who had succeeded Richard Nixon after his resignation in 1974.

Carter entered office during a period of much national discontent—he once referred to it as a "national malaise"—and economic crisis in the form of "stagflation," a combination of inflation, high unemployment, and stagnant growth. He also faced an energy crisis. Although Carter worked to improve employment, decrease the national budget deficit, and establish a national energy policy, a recession ensued, which led to broad voter discontent.

In foreign policy, human rights and diplomacy were at the center of Carter's administration. He brokered the Camp David agreement of 1978, which brought peace between Egypt and Israel. He obtained ratification of the Panama Canal treaties, and, building on the pioneering breakthroughs of Richard Nixon, he established full diplomatic relations with the People's Republic of China. However, the Soviet invasion of Afghanistan prompted him to suspend ratification of SALT II (Strategic Arms Limitation Treaty), and the Iran hostage crisis dominated his last fourteen months in office.

Carter's inability to resolve the hostage crisis, coupled with the woes of economic recession, contributed to the defeat of his bid for reelection in 1980. After he left the White House, Carter went on to earn renown as an advocate of human rights, an international mediator, and a prolific author. He was awarded the Nobel Prize for Peace in 2002.

---

nation excluded the survival of the other. What changed in the perception of both men was the realization that survival and prosperity were largely dependent on strong positive relations with the United States. The administrations of Richard Nixon and Jimmy Carter made it clear to Sadat and Begin that the United States would not choose between Egypt and Israel; therefore, good relations with America became the common ground on which the two Middle Eastern leaders met. It is highly unlikely that they would have been able to create peace with each other directly, but they found they could do so for the sake of relations with America.

Both men had to face down extreme opposition from within their own governments. Sadat made the first bold move when, on November 9, 1977, he abruptly departed from the written text of a speech to the Egyptian parliament and announced his intention to "go to the ends of the earth" to reach an accommodation with Israel. By this, he meant that he would travel to Israel to present his proposal for a peace settlement—provided that he was invited. Prime Minister Begin picked up the diplomatic hint and prompted the Israeli parliament (the Knesset) to present an invitation via a U.S. diplomat, Hermann Eilts. In response, on the evening of November 19, 1977, Anwar al-Sadat flew to Israel, landing at Ben-Gurion Airport outside Tel-Aviv.

Sadat's address to the Knesset created both great hope and great uncertainty—and a kind of diplo-

Anwar al-Sadat

(1918–1981)

Born December 25, 1918, in the Nile delta village of Mit Abul Kom, Sadat moved with his family to Cairo in 1925. There he grew to manhood under oppressive British imperialism. He dreamed of the liberation of Egypt. He graduated from the Cairo Military Academy in 1938 and during World War II collaborated with the Germans to force the British out of the country. British authorities arrested and imprisoned him in 1942, but he subsequently escaped and continued his anti-British activities. After the war, in 1950, Sadat joined Gamal Abdel Nasser's Free Officers group, which in 1952 staged a military coup against the Egyptian monarchy. Sadat supported Nasser's election to the presidency in 1956, held various posts in the Nasser government, and served as vice president during 1964–1966 and 1969–1970.

On Nasser's death, September 28, 1970, Sadat became acting president of Egypt and was confirmed as president by a plebiscite (popular referendum) two weeks later. Unlike Nasser, he distrusted the Soviets, who had a strong economic and military presence in Egypt. He expelled thousands of Soviet technicians and advisers from the country in 1972. After invading Israel in the Yom Kippur War of October 1973, in an apparent about-face, he began to work toward peace in the Middle East. This effort reached a dramatic climax during his visit to Israel in November 1977, when he presented a peace proposal before the Knesset (Israeli parliament). Sadat's overture led to the Camp David Accords (September 17, 1978) between Sadat and Israeli prime minister Menachem Begin that were mediated by President Jimmy Carter. Sadat and Begin were jointly awarded the Nobel Prize for Peace in 1978 and the following year concluded a formal peace treaty.

Sadat paid a high price for his visionary actions. His popularity fell in Egypt, and he was assassinated by members of al-Gamma al-Islamiyya, a militant Egyptian Islamic movement, on October 6, 1981, in Cairo, while reviewing a military parade commemorating the Arab-Israeli war of October 1973.

matic gridlock in both Egypt and Israel. To resolve it, U.S. president Jimmy Carter invited the two men to a summit at Camp David beginning on September 5, 1978. For the next dozen days, President Carter kept the leaders talking. They ultimately issued the **Camp David Accords.** These consisted of two agreements: a broad framework for achieving peace in the Middle East, and a more specific blueprint for a peace treaty between Egypt and Israel. The first document called for Israel to gradually grant self-government to the Palestinians in the Israeli-occupied West Bank and Gaza Strip and to partially withdraw its forces from these areas as a prelude to negotiations on their final status. The second document called for a phased withdrawal of Israeli forces from the Sinai Peninsula, which Israel captured during the Six-Day War of 1967, and the return of that region to Egypt within three years of the signing of a peace treaty. In addition to guaranteeing the right of passage for Israeli ships through the Egyptian-controlled Suez Canal, the Camp David Accords included a concession both Nasser and Sadat had repeatedly sworn that Egypt would never make. The documents affirmed Israel's right to exist.

Egyptian-Israeli Peace Treaty (1979)

On March 26, 1979, at the White House, Egyptian president Anwar al-Sadat and Israeli prime minister Menachem Begin signed a formal **Egyptian-Israeli Peace Treaty,** which came into force on April 25, 1979. The U.S.-brokered treaty ended the continuous state of war that had existed between Egypt and Israel since the founding of Israel in 1948.

Menachem Begin

(1913–1992)

Menachem Begin was born in Brest-Litovsk, Russia (now Belarus), and was educated at the University of Warsaw, graduating in 1935. An ardent Zionist during the 1930s, by 1938 he led the Polish branch of Betar, an organization of youth dedicated to creating a Jewish state on both sides of the Jordan River. With the Nazi invasion of Poland in September 1939, Begin fled to Vilnius, Lithuania. His parents and a brother were killed in concentration camps, and the Soviet authorities who controlled Vilnius deported Begin to Siberia in 1940. He was released in 1941 and fought in the Polish-army-in-exile, traveling with it to Palestine in 1942.

Once in Palestine, Begin joined the Irgun Zvai Leumi, a paramilitary force dedicated to establishing an independent Israel. He assumed command of the Irgun from 1943 to 1948 and was instrumental in establishing the state of Israel. The Irgun gave rise to the Herut ("Freedom") Party after independence, and Begin became the party's leader. In this capacity he was also leader of the opposition in the Knesset (Israeli parliament) until 1967, when he joined the National Unity government (1967–1970) as minister without portfolio—in effect, a government adviser. In 1970 Begin was named joint chairman of the Likud ("Unity") political coalition.

The Likud Party was victorious in the elections of May 17, 1977, and Begin, as prime minister, formed a government. He came into office adamant on the issue of holding the West Bank and the Gaza Strip, which had been occupied by Israel during the Arab-Israeli War of 1967. Yet he soon responded to the overtures of President Jimmy Carter and opened the negotiations with President Anwar al-Sadat of Egypt that resulted in the Camp David Accords of September 17, 1978. In 1978, with Sadat, Begin accepted the Nobel Peace Prize.

Following the elections of 1980, Begin formed a new coalition government. Although he had agreed to return the Sinai Peninsula to Egypt, he opposed the creation of a Palestinian state on the West Bank and the Gaza Strip. In June 1982 he backed an invasion of Lebanon intended to root out the Palestine Liberation Organization, which was based there. The raid was successful, but the large number of civilian casualties cost Israel support in the world community. This turn of events ultimately led to Begin's resignation from office in October 1983.

The United States government guaranteed that, in the event of actual or threatened violation of the treaty, it would, at the request of one or both signatories, "take such . . . action as it may deem appropriate and helpful to achieve compliance with the treaty." A Memorandum of Understanding of March 26, 1979, between the United States and Israel, stipulated that the United States would "provide support it deems appropriate for proper actions taken by Israel in response to . . . demonstrated violations of the treaty of peace." In an effort to divorce the memorandum from the treaty, the Egyptian government refused to recognize the binding legality of this document.

Finally, in connection with the treaty, the United States pledged financial assistance to Israel totaling $3 billion and to Egypt in the amount of $1.5 billion.

The Multinational Force and Air Surveillance (1981)

In the Egyptian-Israeli Peace Treaty, Israel agreed to return the entire Sinai Peninsula to Egypt in exchange for recognition of Israel's right to exist. The treaty stipulated a schedule for Israeli withdrawal from the Sinai, with the United States agreeing to provide aerial surveillance to certify

The Camp David Accords, 1978

The Framework for Peace in the Middle East

Framework

[T]his framework, as appropriate, is intended by [the parties] to constitute a basis for peace not only between Egypt and Israel, but also between Israel and each of its other neighbors which is prepared to negotiate peace with Israel on this basis. With that objective in mind, they have agreed to proceed as follows:

West Bank and Gaza

Egypt, Israel, Jordan and the representatives of the Palestinian people should participate in negotiations on the resolution of the Palestinian problem in all its aspects. To achieve that objective, negotiations relating to the West Bank and Gaza should proceed in three stages:

Egypt and Israel agree that, in order to ensure a peaceful and orderly transfer of authority, and taking into account the security concerns of all the parties, there should be transitional arrangements for the West Bank and Gaza for a period not exceeding five years. . . .

Egypt-Israel undertake not to resort to the threat or the use of force to settle disputes. Any disputes shall be settled by peaceful means. . . .

Egypt and Israel state that the principles and provisions described below should apply to peace treaties between Israel and each of its neighbors—Egypt, Jordan, Syria and Lebanon. Signatories shall establish among themselves relationships normal to states at peace with one another. To this end, they should undertake to abide by all the provisions of the U.N. Charter. Steps to be taken in this respect include:

full recognition;

abolishing economic boycotts;

guaranteeing that under their jurisdiction the citizens of the other parties shall enjoy the protection of the due process of law. . . .

Framework for the Conclusion of a Peace Treaty between Egypt and Israel

In order to achieve peace between them, Israel and Egypt agree to negotiate in good faith with a goal of concluding within three months of the signing of this framework a peace treaty between them. . . .

The following matters are agreed between the parties:

the full exercise of Egyptian sovereignty up to the internationally recognized border between Egypt and mandated Palestine;

the withdrawal of Israeli armed forces from the Sinai;

the use of airfields left by the Israelis near al-Arish, Rafah, Ras en-Naqb, and Sharm el-Sheikh for civilian purposes only. . . .

After a peace treaty is signed, and after the interim withdrawal is complete, normal relations will be established between Egypt and Israel, including full recognition, including diplomatic, economic and cultural relations; termination of economic boycotts and barriers to the free movement of goods and people; and mutual protection of citizens by the due process of law.

Excerpted from the Avalon Project at Yale Law School, "The Camp David Accords," www.yale.edu/lawweb/avalon/mideast/campdav.htm.

Israeli compliance with the withdrawal provisions and to ensure that Egypt would not build up military forces in the ceded region. An Exchange of Notes Constituting an Agreement Concerning Air Surveillance Flights Provided by the United States of America was signed by Egypt, Israel, and the United States on July 23 and 25, 1981, at Cairo and on July 23 and 31, 1981, at Tel Aviv. It came into force on July 31, 1981.

The air surveillance agreement was additional to an agreement specifying monitoring of the region by the United Nations' multinational force.

Egyptian president Anwar al-Sadat, U.S. president Jimmy Carter, and Israeli prime minister Menachem Begin (pictured left to right) clasp hands on the north lawn of the White House after signing the Egyptian-Israeli Peace Treaty on March 26, 1979.

Egyptian-Israeli Peace Treaty, 1979

The Government of the Arab Republic of Egypt and the Government of the State of Israel;

PREAMBLE
Convinced of the urgent necessity of the establishment of a just, comprehensive and lasting peace in the Middle East . . . ;

Reaffirming their adherence to the "Framework for Peace in the Middle East Agreed at Camp David," dated September 17, 1978;

Noting that the aforementioned Framework as appropriate is intended to constitute a basis for peace not only between Egypt and Israel but also between Israel and each of its other Arab neighbors which is prepared to negotiate peace with it on this basis; . . .

Agree to the following provisions in the free exercise of their sovereignty, in order to implement the "Framework for the Conclusion of a Peace Treaty Between Egypt and Israel";

Article I
The state of war between the Parties will be terminated and peace will be established between them upon the exchange of instruments of ratification of this Treaty. . . .

Article II
The permanent boundary between Egypt and Israel is the recognized international boundary between Egypt and the former mandated territory of Palestine. . . .

Article III
The Parties will apply between them the provisions of the Charter of the United Nations and the principles of international law governing relations among states in times of peace. In particular: They recognize and will respect each other's sovereignty, territorial integrity and political independence.

Excerpted from the Avalon Project at Yale Law School, "Treaty Between Israel and Egypt," www.yale.edu/lawweb/avalon/mideast/isregypt.htm.

Israel and Palestine (1993–1998)

The creation of Israel in 1948 left Palestinians and their descendants landless. In 1964 the Palestine Liberation Organization (PLO) consolidated leadership of various nationalist groups with the declared goal of creating a "democratic and secular" Palestinian state. Following the defeat of the Arabs in the Six-Day War against Israel in 1967, the PLO garnered universal recognition among Arab nations and interests as representative of the Palestinian cause, and from that point on, a state of war existed between the PLO and Israel. There seemed no possibility for negotiation, let alone reconciliation.

In April 1993 Yasir Arafat, who had led the PLO since 1969, and Israeli prime minister Yitzhak Rabin entered into secret negotiations, which had been brokered by the administration of President Bill Clinton. The first product of these talks was an exchange of letters by which Israel acknowledged the right of the people of Palestine to create a sovereign state and by which the PLO acknowledged the legitimacy of the Israeli state. This **Israel-PLO Recognition,** between

Israel-PLO Recognition, 1993

From Yasir Arafat to Yitzhak Rabin:

September 9, 1993
Mr. Prime Minister,

The signing of the Declaration of Principles marks a new era in the history of the Middle East. In firm conviction thereof, I would like to confirm the following PLO commitments:

The PLO recognizes the right of the State of Israel to exist in peace and security.

The PLO accepts United Nations Security Council Resolutions 242 and 338 [laying down principles for ultimate Palestinian self-government].

The PLO commits itself to the Middle East peace process, and to a peaceful resolution of the conflict between the two sides and declares that all outstanding issues relating to permanent status will be resolved through negotiations.

The PLO considers that the signing of the Declaration of Principles constitutes a historic event, inaugurating a new epoch of peaceful coexistence, free from violence and all other acts which endanger peace and stability. Accordingly, the PLO renounces the use of terrorism and other acts of violence and will assume responsibility over all PLO elements and personnel in order to assure their compliance, prevent violations and discipline violators.

In view of the promise of a new era and the signing of the Declaration of Principles and based on Palestinian acceptance of Security Council Resolu-

tions 242 and 338, the PLO affirms that those articles of the Palestinian Covenant which deny Israel's right to exist, and the provisions of the Covenant which are inconsistent with the commitments of this letter are now inoperative and no longer valid. Consequently, the PLO undertakes to submit to the Palestinian National Council for formal approval the necessary changes in regard to the Palestinian Covenant.

Sincerely,
Yasir Arafat
Chairman The Palestine Liberation Organization

From Yitzhak Rabin to Yasir Arafat:

September 9, 1993
Mr. Chairman,

In response to your letter of September 9, 1993, I wish to confirm to you that, in light of the PLO commitments included in your letter, the Government of Israel has decided to recognize the PLO as the representative of the Palestinian people and commence negotiations with the PLO within the Middle East peace process.

Yitzhak Rabin
Prime Minister of Israel

Excerpted from Alan Axelrod, *American Treaties and Alliances* (Washington, D.C.: CQ Press, 2000), 251.

two implacable enemies, seemed nothing less than miraculous. The letters were exchanged and came into effect on September 9, 1993.

On September 13, 1993, just days after the exchange of letters between Arafat and Rabin, a "Declaration of Principles on Interim Self-Government Arrangements"—the **PLO-Israel Accord**—was publicly signed in Washington, D.C., as President Clinton looked on.

Pursuant to the PLO-Israel Accord and in preparation for another U.S.-brokered agreement, the Israeli-Palestinian Interim Agreement on the West Bank and the Gaza Strip, Israel and the PLO concluded an Agreement on Preparatory Transfer of Powers and Responsibilities. Signed on August 29, 1994, at Erez, Israel, the agreement specified that "Israel shall transfer and the Palestinian Authority shall assume powers and responsibilities from the Israeli military government and its Civil Administration in the West Bank in the following spheres: education and culture, health, social welfare, tourism, direct taxation and Value Added Tax on local production. . . ." Jerusalem was excluded from the transfer. Additionally, the agreement defined the nature and scope of the governing entity called the "Palestinian Authority," placing special emphasis on procedures for administering civil laws and promoting a "process of reconciliation" between Israel and the Palestinians. The agreement addressed in detail budgetary issues, as well as issues relating to education and culture, health, social welfare, tourism, and taxation.

The Israeli-Palestinian Interim Agreement on the West Bank and the Gaza Strip, signed on September 28, 1995, was the culminating document intended to normalize relations between the PLO and Israel. The agreement officially transferred control of the West Bank and the Gaza Strip from Israel to a "Palestinian Authority" (also referred to as "the Council"). In addition to detailing the constitution of the Council and calling for popular elections, the agreement specified the establishment of an open government for the Palestinians, judicial review authority for Palestinian courts, the staged withdrawal of Israeli

PLO-Israel Accord, 1993

Article 1
The aim of the Israeli-Palestinian negotiations within the current Middle East peace process is, among other things, to establish a Palestinian Interim Self-Government Authority, the elected Council (the "Council"), for the Palestinian people in the West Bank and the Gaza Strip, for a transitional period not exceeding five years, leading to a permanent settlement. . . .

Article 3
In order that the Palestinian people in the West Bank and Gaza Strip may govern themselves according to democratic principles, direct, free and general political elections will be held for the Council under agreed supervision and international observation, while the Palestinian police will ensure public order. . . .

Article 8
In order to guarantee public order and internal security for the Palestinians of the West Bank and the Gaza Strip, the Council will establish a strong police force, while Israel will continue to carry the responsibility for defending against external threats, as well as the responsibility for overall security of Israelis for the purpose of safeguarding their internal security and public order. . . .

Article 14
[Mandates the withdrawal of Israel from the Gaza Strip and Jericho area]

Excerpted from Alan Axelrod, *American Treaties and Alliances* (Washington, DC: CQ Press, 2000), 252–253.

forces from the West Bank and the Gaza Strip, and a definition of the territory to be transferred. Additionally, the agreement called for the creation of a Palestinian police force, measures to prevent terrorism and build confidence, and a pledge to protect human rights. Economic issues were addressed, including a definition of economic relations between Israel and the Palestinians.

In October 1998 President Clinton hosted a summit of Israeli and Palestinian leaders at Wye River, Maryland, with the object of getting them to formulate precise steps for the implementation of the Interim Agreement on the West Bank and Gaza Strip. The result of the summit was the Wye River Memorandum, signed in Washington, D.C., with President Clinton as witness, on October 28, 1998. The memorandum specified the transfer by Israel to the Palestinians of certain specified percentages of the West Bank and Gaza Strip in exchange for various security guarantees, including a guarantee of zero tolerance for terror and violence against both sides.

The American "Road Map" (2002–)

After taking office in 2001, the administration of George W. Bush initially distanced itself from the ambitious Middle East initiatives of the Clinton administration, but on June 24, 2002, the president announced a "road map" for peace. It was a plan formulated jointly by the United States, the European Union, Russia, and the United Nations (the so-called "quartet") to resolve the Israeli-Palestinian conflict. The road map called for an independent Palestinian state to be created adjacent to, and to coexist peacefully with, Israel. Thus President Bush became the first American president to call for the creation of a Palestinian state.

In endorsing statehood for the Palestinians, the road map required the Palestinian Authority to make democratic reforms and to renounce violence. Israel was required to accept a reformed Palestinian government and to end Israeli settlement of the Gaza Strip and West Bank in stages as the Palestinian Authority demonstrated the removal of the threat of violence. On April 30, 2003, the U.S. Department of State issued a statement redefining the road map as a Performance-Based Road Map to a Permanent Two-State Solution to the Israeli-Palestinian Conflict. The new document laid out three phases in progress toward the permanent solution. Phase I addressed steps to end violence, normalize Palestinian life, and build Palestinian institutions. Phase II established a transition, during which "efforts are focused on the option of creating an independent Palestinian state with provisional borders and attributes of sovereignty." These would be shaped by a new constitution and were to serve "as a way station to a permanent status settlement." Finally, Phase III would bring a permanent status agreement and an end to the Israeli-Palestinian conflict by consolidating reforms, stabilizing Palestinian institutions, and achieving "effective Palestinian security performance."

In August 2005 the Israelis began disengaging from the Gaza Strip and a small portion of the West Bank. Nevertheless, the "peace" created by the U.S.-brokered agreements has proven fragile and elusive.

Israel and Jordan (1993–1994)

From 1948 until the end of the 1950s, relations between Jordan and Israel were hostile, but, in contrast to Israeli relations with the other Arab nations, they were not violent. By the mid-1960s, however, Jordan was regularly being used as a staging area for PLO raids into Israel. Israel responded by raiding the Jordanian-controlled West Bank.

Jordan's King Hussein had been attempting to improve relations with Israel and had not sanctioned the extremists operating within his kingdom. At one point, he even severed diplomatic relations with Syria, the chief sponsor of the raids. Then, early in 1967, as tensions rose between Israel and Egypt and Syria, Hussein abruptly reversed his position. On May 30, he signed a mutual defense pact with Egypt. During the Arab-Israeli War of 1967 (the "Six-Day War"), Jordan, fighting alongside Egypt, lost the West Bank to Israel.

After the 1967 war, Hussein resumed secret talks with Israel and demonstrated his good faith by refusing to participate in the 1973 Arab-Israeli "Yom Kippur War." Despite this demonstration, the ascension of the right-wing Likud Party in the Israeli elections of 1977 brought an announcement by Prime Minister Menachem Begin that he would formally annex all of the West Bank. From the end of 1977 until 1984, Jordan suspended all contact with Israel. During the 1980s, however, Hussein worked toward the creation of a Jordanian-Palestinian-Israeli joint administration of the West Bank, intended to make that territory independent of the PLO while enabling Jordan to reach a settlement with Israel. The 1987 intifada, a Palestinian uprising on the West Bank, suddenly moved King Hussein to renounce Jordanian claims to sovereignty of the West Bank in favor of the PLO.

In 1993 Israel and the PLO reached accord. Immediately after Begin and Arafat signed their initial agreements, the Clinton administration brokered the **Israel-Jordan Common Agenda,** which was signed in Washington on September 14, 1993. It called for the two nations to search for steps to arrive at a state of peace based on Security Council Resolutions 242 and 338. Resolution 242 mandated withdrawal of Israeli armed forces from occupied territories, and the "termination of all claims or states of belligerency and respect for and acknowledgment of the sovereignty, territorial integrity and political independence of every State in the area and their right to live in peace within secure and recognized boundaries free from threats or acts of force." Resolution 338 called for "negotiations . . . between the parties concerned under appropriate auspices aimed at establishing a just and durable peace in the Middle East."

Working from the Israel-Jordan Common Agenda, President Clinton, Jordan's Crown Prince Hassan, and Israeli foreign minister Shimon Peres formed the Trilateral United States-Jordan-Israel Economic Committee in Washington on October 1, 1993. While the committee worked to establish lasting peace between Jordan and Israel, King Hussein and Prime Minister Rabin continued personal negotiations. In the summer of 1994, President Clinton invited the two leaders to Washington for a culminating conference. The result was the Washington Declaration, which affirmed the determination of "His Majesty

Israel-Jordan Common Agenda, 1993

Components of Israel-Jordan Peace Negotiations:

1. Searching for steps to arrive at a state of peace based on Security Council Resolutions 242 and 338. . . .
2. Security:
   Refraining from actions or activities by either side that may adversely affect the security of the other or may prejudge the final outcome of negotiations.
3. Threats to security resulting from all kinds of terrorism:
   Mutual commitment not to threaten each other by any use of force and not to use weapons by one side against the other including conventional and non-conventional mass destruction weapons.
4. Mutual commitment, as a matter of priority and as soon as possible, to work towards a Middle East free from weapons of mass destruction, conventional and non-conventional weapons; this goal is to be achieved in the context of a comprehensive, lasting and stable peace characterized by the renunciation of the use of force, reconciliation and openness. . . .
   Mutually agreed upon security arrangements and security confidence building measures.
5. Water. . . .
6. Refugees and Displaced Persons. . . .
7. Borders and Territorial Matters. . . .
8. Exploring the potentials of future bilateral cooperation, within a regional context where appropriate, in the following:
   Natural Resources . . .
   Human Resources . . .
   Infrastructure . . .
   Economic areas including tourism.

. . . It is anticipated that the above endeavor will ultimately, following the attainment of mutually satisfactory solutions to the elements of this agenda, culminate in a peace treaty.

Excerpted from Alan Axelrod, *American Treaties and Alliances* (Washington, D.C.: CQ Press, 2000), 253–254.

King Hussein and Prime Minister Yitzhak Rabin . . . to bring an end to bloodshed and sorrow," to work together to achieve a "just, lasting and comprehensive peace between Israel and its neighbours," and to conclude a treaty of peace between Jordan and Israel.

The Israel-Jordan Peace Treaty, signed on October 26, 1994, on the Israel-Jordan border (and attested to by the U.S. government in the capacity of witness), laid down ten major terms:

1. The establishment of full diplomatic relations between Israel and Jordan
2. An agreement on the international boundary
3. An agreement to end belligerency immediately
4. An agreement to cooperate in the prevention of terrorism
5. An agreement on allocations of water and the mutual development of new water resources
6. An agreement on freedom of access to all religious sites
7. The recognition of the special role of the Hashemite Kingdom (Jordan) over Muslim holy shrines in Jerusalem
8. An agreement to permit full freedom of passage by land, sea, and air
9. An agreement to cooperate in such areas as the economy, transportation, telecommunications, tourism, environment, energy, health, agriculture, and the war against crime and drugs
10. A commitment to resolve the problem of refugees and displaced persons

In addition to these major terms, five annexes stipulated details concerning the international boundary between Israel and Jordan, water policy, crime and drug policy, environmental policy, and interim measures to be taken on an immediate basis pending the conclusion of various definitive agreements pursuant to the treaty.

Israel and Lebanon (1996)

During the 1970s, the government of Lebanon disintegrated as the nation became the scene of Syrian-backed violence primarily directed against Israel. On July 17, 1981, the Israeli air force bombed PLO headquarters in West Beirut, inflicting collateral damage that included the deaths of some 300 civilians. Hoping to defuse the situation, the United States brokered a cease-fire between the Israelis and the PLO. Nevertheless, on June 6, 1982, a force of 60,000 Israeli troops invaded Lebanon. The Israeli leadership justified this action as necessary to halt PLO raids into Israeli territory, but it was apparent that the goal was more ambitious: to destroy the PLO in its principal bases and to establish a Lebanese government that would conclude a peace treaty with Israel along the lines of the Egyptian-Israeli Peace Treaty of 1979.

Israel and Lebanon signed a treaty on May 17, 1983, which called for the withdrawal of Israeli forces, the creation of a special security zone in the south, and the establishment of bilateral relations. The agreement, however, incited various renegade Lebanese factions to launch new attacks on Israel. As the Israeli withdrawal proceeded, these attacks turned against the international peacekeeping force stationed in Lebanon. Under fire, that force left Beirut in February 1984, whereupon Syria and Lebanese extremists forced the Lebanese government to denounce the 1983 Lebanon-Israel treaty. A full decade elapsed before the U.S. government, under President Bill Clinton, took an active role in Middle Eastern affairs and Israel and Lebanon resumed negotiations. These talks broke down in February 1994, whereupon Israel finally renounced claims to Lebanese land or resources, but stated its determination to ensure the security of its northern border. Israel proposed four terms of a permanent settlement of the Israeli-Lebanese crisis:

1. The deployment of the Lebanese Army north of a security zone for a period of six months to prevent any terror activities against the security zone and Israel
2. The conclusion of a peace agreement with Lebanon three months after the beginning of this deployment

3. The deployment of Israeli forces on the Lebanese front until such time as Israel became confident that all extremist groups operating out of Lebanon were disbanding their military branches

4. Guarantees that no harm would be inflicted upon Lebanese citizens and Southern Lebanese Army (a Christian militia with close ties to Israel) personnel residing in the security zone at the time and that these people would be absorbed in the governmental and societal fabric of Lebanon

Lebanon did not accept this offer and continued to serve as a staging area for PLO raids of Israeli. In April 1996 Israel launched Operation Grapes of Wrath, a military incursion into Lebanon. Soon thereafter, the Clinton administration helped negotiate an Israel-Lebanon Ceasefire Understanding which ended the Israeli incursion and effectively lowered the level of Lebanese attacks.

Serbia, Bosnia and Herzegovina, and Kosovo

As Communist governments were dissolving throughout Eastern Europe early in the 1990s, Slovenia and Croatia declared their secession from the Yugoslav federation on June 25, 1991. Macedonia broke away on December 19, and during February–March 1992, Bosnian Croats and Muslims also voted to secede. Serbia and Montenegro, the principal remaining constituents of Yugoslavia, created a new federation, adopting a new constitution on April 27, 1992.

Although the Bosnian Croats and Bosnian Muslims had approved referenda calling for the creation of an independent, multinational republic of Bosnia and Herzegovina, Bosnian Serbs refused to secede from the new Serbian-dominated Yugoslav federation. This refusal sparked a bitter civil war in Bosnia and Herzegovina beginning in 1992 (see Chapter 44). The Bosnian Serbs seized much of the north and east, "ethnically cleansing" these regions of non-Serb populations and creating more than two million refugees. The Croats gained control of the west,

while the Muslims struggled to maintain their hold on cities in the central and northwestern regions.

Dayton Peace Accords (1995)

The Bosnian Civil War was a humanitarian nightmare. The Clinton administration sought to broker a peace late in 1995. The result of the U.S. intervention was the Dayton Accords, the product of conferences held at Wright-Patterson Air Force Base, outside of Dayton, Ohio. Signed on November 21, 1995, by representatives of the Republic of Bosnia and Herzegovina, Republic of Croatia, and the Federal Republic of Yugoslavia, the Dayton Accords created a federalized Bosnia and Herzegovina, which was divided between a Bosnian Muslim and Bosnian Croat federation and a Bosnian Serb republic.

The accords specified that Bosnia and Herzegovina would be preserved as a single state within its present borders, but would consist of two parts: the Bosnian Croat Federation and the Bosnian Serb Republic; that the capital city of Sarajevo would remain united as the seat of a central government, to include a national parliament, the presidency, and a constitutional court with responsibility for foreign policy, foreign trade, monetary policy, citizenship, immigration and other important functions; and that the president and parliament would be chosen through free, democratic elections held under international supervision. The accords also guaranteed that refugees would be allowed to return to their homes, that everyone would be permitted to move freely throughout Bosnia and Herzegovina, that human rights would be monitored by an independent commission and an internationally trained civilian police force, and that individuals found guilty of war crimes would be excluded from political life. The accords provided for a strong international force to help keep the peace and to build the confidence of all parties.

Rambouillet Accords (1999)

Although the Dayton Accords ended the civil war in Bosnia and Herzegovina, they did not bring an end to all troubles in the Balkans. As constituted after

World War II, Yugoslavia consisted of six *republics:* Serbia; Croatia; Bosnia and Herzegovina; Macedonia; Slovenia; and Montenegro. In addition, two *provinces* were attached to Yugoslavia, Kosovo and Vojvodina. Josip Broz Tito, the benevolent dictator of post–World War II Yugoslavia, almost single-handedly willed Yugoslavia's diverse and jarring ethnic factions to remain together as a nation. With his death in 1980, however, the nation began to fall apart, a process that was accelerated by the fall of communism at the end of the decade. Slovenia and Croatia each declared independence, followed by Macedonia and then Bosnia and Herzegovina. Serbia and Montenegro joined to form the Federal Republic of Yugoslavia, under the leadership of Slobodan Milošević. The two provinces, Kosovo and Vojvodina, remained part of the new federal republic.

Less than a year after peace had been established in Bosnia and Herzegovina, violence erupted in Kosovo as the Kosovo Liberation Army (KLA) launched guerrilla attacks on Serbian police forces. Early in 1998 Yugoslav president Slobodan Milošević sent troops to Kosovo to crush the independence movement there. This triggered full-scale civil war. NATO (North Atlantic Treaty Organization) and the United Nations repeatedly attempted to broker a peace through talks held in Rambouillet, France.

Opened for signature on February 23, 1999, the Rambouillet Accords were signed only by the Kosovo Liberation Army, with witness signatures by the European Union, Russia, and the United States. The Federal Republic of Yugoslavia and Federal Republic of Serbia did not sign this three-year interim agreement intended to end conflict between Yugoslavia and Serbia, on one side, and Kosovo, on the other, as a step toward permanent peace.

With the talks in collapse, on March 24, NATO—led by the United States—launched air strikes on Serbian Yugoslavia in an effort to force compliance with the Rambouillet Accords (see Chapter 46). On June 10, 1999, the Milošević government finally agreed to a military withdrawal from Kosovo by

signing the Kosovo Military Technical Agreement, and Kosovo became a UN-administered region. By late 2006, although Kosovo was essentially peaceful, the Rambouillet Accords had still not come into force. Their chief provisions included:

- The provision of democratic self-government for Kosovo
- A security guarantee by international troops and local police (representative of all national communities in Kosovo) to provide routine law enforcement; all other forces were to leave Kosovo
- A mechanism for final settlement to be determined by an international meeting and based on the will of the people.

BIBLIOGRAPHY

Bildt, Carl. *Peace Journey: The Struggle for Peace in Bosnia.* New York: Orion, 1999.

Burg, Steven L., and Paul S. Shoup. *The War in Bosnia-Herzegovina: Ethnic Conflict and International Intervention.* Armonk, N.Y.: M. E. Sharpe, 1999.

Esthus, Raymond A. *Double Eagle and Rising Sun: The Russians and Japanese at Portsmouth in 1905.* Durham, N.C.: Duke University Press, 1995.

Holbrooke, Richard. *To End a War.* New York: Modern Library, 1999.

Malcolm, Noel. *Kosovo: A Short History.* New York: New York University Press, 1998.

Moore, John Norton. *The Arab-Israeli Conflict: The Difficult Search for Peace (1975–1988).* Princeton, N.J.: Princeton University Press, 1992.

Nish, Ian Hill. *The Origins of the Russo-Japanese War.* New York: Addison-Wesley, 1986.

Quandt, William B. *Camp David: Peacemaking and Politics.* Washington, D.C.: Brookings Institution, 1986.

Segev, Samuel. *Crossing the Jordan: Israel's Hard Road to Peace.* New York: St. Martin's Press, 1998.

At Issue

The Lebanese Civil War of 1958 was touched off when Camille Chamoun, the Maronite Christian president of Lebanon, established close ties with the West (especially the United States), thereby alienating Lebanon's Shiite Muslims, who favored an alliance with the Arab world.

The 1975–1992 conflict was the product of endemic religious strife between Lebanon's politically and economically dominant Christian minority and the economically disadvantaged Muslims, who had become the majority by the 1970s. The war began when the Maronite government made reprisals in response to the attempted assassination of President Chamoun.

The Conflicts

Civil War of 1958

Camille Chamoun, candidate of the Maronite (Christian) Party, was elected president of Lebanon in 1952. He established close ties with the West, particularly the United States, a policy that alienated Lebanon's Muslims, who at the time made up about half of the nation's population. They wanted Lebanon to identify with its Arab neighbors, many of which were openly hostile to the West. During May 9–13, 1958, Muslims, whose numbers and militancy had grown, staged several violent demonstrations against Chamoun. Riots erupted in the Lebanese capital, Beirut, as well as in Tripoli, Libya, appar-

ently organized and supported by the United Arab Republic (the union of Egypt and Syria that was created in January 1958). The UAR endorsed the militant Kamal Jumblatt, a Druse (a monotheistic Middle Eastern religious sect combining Jewish, Christian, Gnostic, Neoplatonic, and Iranian elements) chieftain who had already led successful confrontations against the Lebanese army.

When the rioting Lebanese Muslims called for Chamoun's immediate resignation, he appealed to U.S. president Dwight D. Eisenhower for military aid. On July 15, 1958, U.S. Marines began amphibious landings at Khalde Beach in Lebanon. On the following day, these forces were joined by airlifted marines, and on July 19 U.S. Army troops arrived. The peak U.S. military presence was 14,000 soldiers and marines.

The American forces marching into Beirut met with a mixed response, but no substantial resistance. U.S. and Lebanese government forces coordinated to patrol the most explosive areas of Beirut.

The U.S. presence enabled a tenuous cease-fire, during which U.S. deputy undersecretary of state Robert Murphy negotiated an agreement for a new election. That resulted in the election of another Maronite, General Faud Chehab. After his September 23, 1958, inauguration, U.S. troops withdrew.

Lebanese Civil War of 1975–1992

Lebanon's equivalent of a modern constitution, the National Pact of 1943, established a dominant political role for the Maronite Christian Social Democratic Party—popularly known as the Phalange Party. This became a frequent source of violence between Muslims and Christians. By the 1970s, the presence of Palestinian refugees and bases in Lebanon, from which the Palestine Liberation Organization (PLO) operated against Israel, aggravated the long-standing Christian-Muslim conflict and cre-

ated a powder-keg political environment. On April 13, 1975, four Phalangists were shot down during an attempt on the life of Phalange leader Pierre Jumayyil. Incorrectly assuming that the failed assassins were Palestinian, Phalangist forces retaliated the next day by attacking a bus carrying Palestinians through a Christian neighborhood. Twenty-six pas-

CHRONOLOGY OF INTERVENTIONS IN LEBANON

1958

May 9–13 Lebanese Muslims riot to protest the policies of President Camille Chamoun, a Maronite Christian.

July 15–19 U.S. forces arrive in Lebanon.

Sept. 23 U.S. military withdraws after new Lebanese elections, leaving the country in a tenuous peace.

1970s

• Palestine Liberation Organiztion (PLO) establishes bases in Lebanon.

1975

Apr. 13–14 Assassination attempt against Phalange leader Pierre Jumayyil; Phalange Christians retaliate against Palestinians, sparking civil war.

1976

Feb. 14 Syrians broker a settlement in the civil war.

Mar. Mutiny sweeps the Lebanese Army; many troops join the Muslim anti-Christian Lebanese National Movement.

Oct. 16 After a Syrian invasion of Lebanon, a peace conference convened in Riyadh, Saudi Arabia, formally ends the civil war.

1978

Mar. Israel invades southern Lebanon in retaliation for a March 11 Lebanese-based PLO attack near Tel Aviv, Israel.

1982

June 6 Israel invades Lebanon again, in retaliation for the attempted assassination of the Israeli ambassador to Britain.

Aug. After Syrian troops and PLO fighters agree to evacuate from Beirut, the Multi-National Force (MNF), including U.S. Marines, arrives.

Sept. 10 The MNF (including U.S. Marines) departs.

Sept. 14 Lebanese president Bachir Gemayel is assassinated.

Sept. 15 Israeli troops reenter Beirut.

Sept. 15–17 Lebanese militiamen raid Palestinian refugee camps.

Sept. 29 MNF troops (including U.S. Marines) return to Lebanon.

1983

Apr. 18 The U.S. embassy in Beirut is bombed.

May 17 Israel agrees to withdraw from Lebanon; Syria refuses to withdraw.

Sept. Druse and Christian forces clash.

Sept. 26 The United States and Saudi Arabia broker a cease-fire between Druse and Christian militias.

Oct. 23 U.S. and French MNF headquarters is bombed; 298 lives (mostly U.S. Marines) are lost.

Dec. 4 The U.S. Marines and Navy defend Beirut International Airport.

1984

Jan. 13 and 15 The Beirut International Airport is again under attack.

Feb. 6 Druse and Muslim militiamen seize most of Beirut.

Feb. 8 The USS *New Jersey* bombards Druse and Syrian guns positions in Beirut.

Feb. 10–11 The U.S. Navy evacuates U.S. and other foreign nationals from Beirut.

Feb. 21–26 The U.S. Marines withdraw to Sixth Fleet ships, ending U.S. intervention in Lebanon.

1990–1992

• Fighting continues in the civil war.

1991

May Warring militias (except for Hizballah) are dissolved.

1992

May Islamic extremists release Western hostages (held since mid-1980). Fighting ends.

sengers died, and before the end of the day, disorganized fighting spread throughout Lebanon. The government failed to respond effectively to the violence, and over the next several months a bloody pattern of violence developed among rival militia groups. The retaliations grew into outright civil war, not only between Christians and Muslims but also within various Christian and Muslim factions. Generally speaking, however, those in favor of upholding the government gathered under the umbrella of the Lebanese Front, while those opposed allied with the Lebanese National Movement, loosely led by Kamal Jumblatt.

By the end of 1975, the first year of the war, no side had made decisive gains, but it was apparent that the Lebanese Front had performed poorly against the Lebanese National Movement, disorganized as it was. The main force of the PLO—the Palestine Liberation Army (PLA)—exploited the general disarray to establish a strong political and military presence in Lebanon. Syria also intervened and, on February 14, 1976, was instrumental in hammering out a seventeen-point reform program called the "Constitutional Document." Hopes for peace were dashed, however, in March 1976 when a mutiny swept the Lebanese Army and many troops deserted to join the Lebanese National Movement. They formed the Lebanese Arab Army, which penetrated Christian-controlled Beirut, then attacked the presidential palace, forcing President Franjiyah to flee.

After the Lebanese National Movement made further gains, Syrian president Hafiz al-Assad authorized an invasion of Lebanon, which forced all sides to meet at a peace conference in Riyadh, Saudi Arabia, on October 16, 1976. This brought a formal end to the civil war, only to give rise to warfare between the Syrian occupying force and the Lebanese Arab Army. The situation was complicated further by a March 1978 invasion of southern Lebanon by the Israel Defense Forces (IDF) in retaliation for a March 11, 1978, Lebanese-based PLO guerrilla attack on an Israeli bus near Tel Aviv. In response to a U.S.-endorsed United Nations call, Israel withdrew after several months as a UN force

moved in. As years passed, conditions in Lebanon continued to deteriorate, and on June 6, 1982, Israel again invaded Lebanon, this time in retaliation for an assassination attempt on the Israeli ambassador to Britain. Israel's objective in this second invasion was to force the removal of PLO forces from the country. In August an agreement was reached for the evacuation of Syrian troops as well as PLO fighters from Beirut and the subsequent deployment of a three-nation Multinational Force (MNF) during the period of the evacuation.

By late August, the MNF, consisting of U.S. Marines as well as French and Italian military units, arrived in Beirut. When the evacuation ended, the MNF withdrew, and the U.S. Marines departed on September 10, 1982. On September 14, Bachir Gemayel, who had been elected president in August, was assassinated, and on September 15, Israeli troops again entered west Beirut. During the next three days, Lebanese Maronite militiamen, sent by the Israeli occupiers (with whom the militia cooperated) to root out PLO members, massacred hundreds of Palestinian civilians in the Sabra and Shatila refugee camps in west Beirut.

Bachir Gemayel's brother, Amine, was elected president by a unanimous vote of the parliament and took office on September 23, 1982. The U.S., French, and Italian troops of the MNF returned to Beirut at the end of the month to support the new government (a small British contingent would join them in February 1983). Soon after taking office, President Gemayel called for the withdrawal of Israeli, Syrian, and Palestinian forces from Lebanon; in late 1982, Lebanese-Israeli negotiations commenced with U.S. participation. On May 17, 1983, an agreement was concluded, providing for Israeli withdrawal, but Syria declined even to discuss the withdrawal of its troops.

In the meantime, Druse and Christian forces had clashed during 1982–1983, and when Israeli forces withdrew from the Shuf region at the beginning of September 1983, the Druse, backed by Syria, attacked the Christian Lebanese Forces militia as well as the Lebanese Army. The United States and

Saudi Arabia brokered a cease-fire on September 26, 1983, which left the Druse in control of most of the Shuf region.

While negotiations stalled between the Syrians and the Lebanese over Syrian troop withdrawal, a series of attacks during 1983 and 1984 were aimed at American interests in Lebanon. On April 18, 1983, the U.S. embassy in west Beirut was bombed, with the loss of 63 lives. On October 23, 1983, the United States and French MNF headquarters in Beirut was attacked, resulting in the loss of 298 lives, the majority of whom were U.S. Marines. On November 2, U.S. secretary of defense Caspar Weinberger announced that the suicide attack had been carried out by Iranians with the "sponsorship, knowledge, and authority of the Syrian government." U.S. Marines came under attack again on December 4, at Beirut International Airport, where they were fired upon from gun positions in Syrian-held territory. Eight marines were killed and two were wounded. U.S. Navy ships fired on the Syrian positions in retal-

iation, and twenty-nine U.S. Navy aircraft raided Syrian antiaircraft positions in the mountains east of Beirut. After two aircraft were downed in these attacks, the battleship USS *New Jersey* delivered a massive artillery bombardment against the antiaircraft positions.

On January 13, 1984, U.S. Marines patrolling the area of the Beirut International Airport were engaged in a half-hour battle by gunmen firing from a building east of their perimeter. Two days later, Druse gunners attacked the airport, drawing a response from the marines and from the USS *New Jersey* as well as the destroyer USS *Tattnall.* There were no American casualties.

February 1984 saw heavy fighting in the suburbs of Beirut between the Lebanese Arab Army and Shiite militiamen, and on February 6, Druse and Muslim militiamen seized much of Beirut, demanding the resignation of President Gemayel. The next day, President Ronald Reagan announced his decision to redeploy troops from Beirut International Airport to ships offshore, leaving behind a contingent of fewer than 100 marines to protect the U.S. embassy and other American interests. On February 8, the *New Jersey* bombarded Druse and Syrian gun positions, and during February 10–11, the navy evacuated American civilians and other foreign nationals from Beirut by helicopter. During February 21–26, the marines withdrew to ships of the Sixth Fleet, which remained offshore. This ended the U.S. mili-

President Ronald Reagan and Mrs. Reagan honor the victims of the bombing of the U.S. Embassy in Beirut at Andrews Air Force Base, Maryland, on April 23, 1983. The president then consoled the victims' families.

tary intervention in the Lebanese Civil War. The war, however, continued with considerable intensity through most of 1990 and was sporadic during 1991 and 1992, as the government gradually reasserted its control over Lebanese territory. All of the warring militias, save for Hizballah, were dissolved in May 1991, and government forces began mopping up armed Palestinian elements in Sidon during July 1991. In May 1992 various Western hostages, held since the mid-1980s by Hizballah extremists, were released.

Promulgation of the "Eisenhower Doctrine"

In a message to Congress on January 5, 1957, President Eisenhower promulgated what became known as the **Eisenhower Doctrine,** which stated that the United States would deploy its armed forces in response to threatened, imminent, or actual aggression, and that countries opposed to Communism would be given economic and military aid in their struggles. The doctrine was the rationale for U.S. intervention in Lebanon in 1958, and its broader context was a response to the Soviet Union's attempt to use the conflict over control of the Suez Canal as a pretext for entering Egypt (ostensibly to help Egyptian president Gamal Abdel Nasser preserve his nation's sovereignty against invasion by Israel and intervention by Britain and the United States). The Eisenhower Doctrine was born of a conviction that the independence of the nations of the Middle East was vital to U.S. interests and to the peace of the world. The Soviet threat to enter Egypt and Soviet backing of the UAR jeopardized the security of Jordan, Turkey, and Iraq, as well as Lebanon—all nations friendly to the West in the 1950s. In 1957 Iraqi army officers who were allied with the UAR overthrew Iraq's King Faisal, prompting Soviet-influenced Egypt to act with the new leaders of Iraq to destabilize Jordan and Lebanon by arming and supporting rebels in these nations. The Eisenhower Doctrine was a stand against incipient instability.

The Eisenhower Doctrine, 1957

The Middle East has abruptly reached a new and critical stage in its long and important history. . . . [S]ince the First World War there has been a steady evolution toward self-government and independence. This development the United States has welcomed and has encouraged. Our country supports without reservation the full sovereignty and independence of each and every nation of the Middle East.

The evolution to independence has in the main been a peaceful process. But the area has been often troubled. . . . [I]nstability has been heightened and, at times, manipulated by International Communism. . . .

The reason for Russia's interest in the Middle East is solely that of power politics. Considering her announced purpose of Communizing the world, it is easy to understand her hope of dominating the Middle East. . . .

The action which I propose would have the following features.

It would, first of all, authorize the United States to cooperate with and assist any nation or group of nations in the general area of the Middle East in the development of economic strength dedicated to the maintenance of national independence.

It would, in the second place, authorize the Executive to undertake in the same region programs of military assistance and cooperation with any nation or group of nations which desires such aid.

It would, in the third place, authorize such assistance and cooperation to include the employment of the armed forces of the United States to secure and protect the territorial integrity and political independence of such nations, requesting such aid, against overt armed aggression from any nation controlled by International Communism.

Excerpted from the Internet Modern History Sourcebook, "President Eisenhower: The Eisenhower Doctrine on the Middle East, A Message to Congress, January 5, 1957," www.fordham.edu/halsall/mod/1957eisenhowerdoctrine.html.

The Murphy Mission (1958)

On July 15, 1958, when the first contingent of marines landed, President Eisenhower called on the United Nations to intervene in Lebanon with a multinational peacekeeping force. When the Soviet Union vetoed the resolution of intervention, Eisenhower sent Deputy Undersecretary of State Robert D. Murphy to mediate among the warring Lebanese factions. In the meantime, the U.S. presence had enabled a tenuous cease-fire. Despite minor incidents, the U.S. Marines worked with Lebanese government forces to create a twenty-mile defensive perimeter around Beirut to prevent Syrian forces from attacking the capital and forcefully ousting President Chamoun. The American military intervention also bought time for Murphy to negotiate an agreement to hold a new election, which resulted in victory for another Maronite Christian, General Faud Chehab. Following his inauguration on September 23, 1958, the marines withdrew.

The New War: Period of U.S. Spectatorship

From the withdrawal of the U.S. Marines in 1958 through the mid-1970s, Lebanon presented a paradox. It was torn by internal religious tensions compounded by the increasing presence of Palestinian refugees and militant PLO fighters, yet the Republic of Lebanon, which had neither an absolute monarch nor a military dictator, was politically more democratic than any other Arab country. Largely for this reason, the United States remained a spectator in Lebanese internal affairs. Violence increased during the 1970s due in large measure to demographic changes in the country. The prosperous Maronite Christians, previously the largest religious community in Lebanon, became less numerous than the relatively impoverished Shiite Muslims. Despite their numbers, the Shiites in the 1970s had little political voice. This created the climate in which full-scale civil war erupted in 1975. Yet this civil war was no simple conflict between Muslims and Christians. To

the degree that it had any cohesion, the Muslim side was represented by the Lebanese National Movement (LNM). By the end of 1975, armed PLO factions, based in Palestinian refugee camps throughout western Lebanon, joined forces with the LNM. In response, some pro-Western elements of the Lebanese government invited Syrian military forces to enter the country to prevent an LNM victory. The United States quietly approved of this intervention.

When Israel invaded Lebanon in March 1978, the United States voted with the rest of the UN Security Council in favor of Security Council Resolution 425, which called upon Israel to withdraw immediately. President Jimmy Carter even threatened to suspend some U.S. aid to Israel. Israeli forces pulled back to a "security zone" along Lebanon's northern border with Israel but over the next several years defied nine more UN Security Council resolutions demanding a complete withdrawal. In the belief that a limited Israeli presence was necessary to prevent the complete collapse of Lebanon—and its takeover by the PLO—the United States repeatedly blocked the Security Council from enforcing its resolutions calling for total withdrawal.

President Reagan's Lebanon Policy

After Israel again invaded Lebanon on June 6, 1982, President Ronald Reagan intervened, and U.S. negotiators brokered an agreement in August whereby the PLO would evacuate its fighters and political offices from Beirut to Tunis, capital of the North African country of Tunisia. In return, Israel pledged not to overrun Beirut. As part of the agreement, the United States led a UN peacekeeping force to oversee the evacuation and to guarantee the safety of the Palestinian refugee population. As evidence of the apparently newfound stability of the government, on August 23 Bachir Gemayel, a Phalangist, became Lebanon's new president, and within two weeks U.S. forces withdrew from Lebanon, occasioning President Reagan's prematurely optimistic **Address to the Nation on United States Policy for Peace in the Middle East** (September 1, 1982).

Ronald Reagan

(1911–2004)

Ronald Wilson Reagan was born into the family of a small store owner in Tampico, Illinois, and worked his way through nearby Eureka College, where he studied economics and sociology. In college he also became interested in amateur theatrics and sports. By the mid-1930s, he fulfilled his first ambition, to become a radio sports announcer, and in 1937, after a screen test in Hollywood, he became an actor. Although he never attained the first ranks of this profession, he was successful, making fifty-three movies in his career. Reagan married actress Jane Wyman, with whom he had two children. After a divorce, he married another actress, Nancy Davis, with whom he also had two children.

A liberal Democrat as a young man, Reagan was elected president of the Screen Actors Guild during a period when Hollywood was under attack by right-wing politicians as a hotbed of Communism. By the late 1950s, when his film career ended, he had become increasingly conservative, and he changed his affiliation to the Republican Party. He continued to appear on television as the host of the *Death Valley Days* series and *General Electric Theater* and was increasingly sought after as a spokesman for conservatism. He ran successfully for governor of California in 1966 and was reelected in 1970.

After coming close to defeating Gerald Ford in the 1976 Republican primaries, Reagan ran for president in 1980 with a promise to restore the United States to economic prosperity and international prestige. He won a landslide victory over incumbent Jimmy Carter. On March 30, 1981, sixty-nine days after taking office, he was shot in the chest by John Hinckley, a deranged man, but despite his age and the seriousness of the wound, Reagan recovered quickly and demonstrated through the ordeal graceful wit and calm courage.

Reagan introduced sweeping changes to economic policy—dubbed "Reaganomics"—and spent unprecedented funds on defense, even as he cut taxes. The result was a massive deficit, but also the longest peacetime economic expansion in American history and a renewal of national self-confidence that propelled him to second-term landslide victory in 1984. Reagan was praised as "the great communicator," for his extraordinary rapport with many American voters. A hardliner where the Soviet Union was concerned, he negotiated with the Soviets a landmark treaty to eliminate intermediate-range ballistic missiles (IRBMs). In 1987 he stood before the Berlin Wall and challenged Soviet general secretary Gorbachev to "tear down this wall." His policies are widely credited with contributing to the collapse of the Soviet Union and Eastern European Communism and helping to end the Cold War. Far more controversial were his abortive intervention in Lebanon and his support of the anti-Communist "Contras" in Nicaragua.

Three days after the marines left Lebanon, President-elect Gemayel was assassinated in a bombing that may have been the work of Syrian intelligence operatives. Israel used the assassination as a justification for occupying Beirut, an action that drew only a mild rebuke from President Reagan. After the Israeli occupation, Phalangists killed more than a thousand Palestinian civilians in refugee camps, which had been left defenseless after the U.S. withdrawal.

At the end of September, Reagan sent the marines (as part of the MNF) back to Beirut as Israeli forces withdrew to positions just south of the Lebanese capital. The president intended to pressure the Lebanese government into negotiating a permanent peace agreement with Israel in return for an Israeli withdrawal. Additionally, the U.S. government wanted to force the withdrawal of Syrian forces and armed Palestinian groups. Although the U.S. presence in

Reagan's Address to the Nation on United States Policy for Peace in the Middle East, 1982

Today has been a day that should make us proud. It marked the end of the successful evacuation of PLO from Beirut, Lebanon. This peaceful step could never have been taken without the good offices of the United States and especially the truly heroic work of a great American diplomat, Ambassador Philip Habib.

Thanks to his efforts, I'm happy to announce that the U.S. Marine contingent helping to supervise the evacuation has accomplished its mission. Our young men should be out of Lebanon within 2 weeks. They, too, have served the cause of peace with distinction, and we can all be very proud of them. . . .

The evacuation of the PLO from Beirut is now complete, and we can now help the Lebanese to rebuild their war-torn country. We owe it to ourselves and to posterity to move quickly to build upon this achievement. A stable and revived Lebanon is essential to all our hopes for peace in the region. The people of Lebanon deserve the best efforts of the international community to turn the nightmares of the past several years into a new dawn of hope. But the opportunities for peace in the Middle East do not begin and end in Lebanon. As we help Lebanon rebuild, we must also move to resolve the root causes of conflict between Arabs and Israelis.

Excerpted from Ronald Reagan, "Address to the Nation on United States Policy for Peace in the Middle East," September 1, 1982, in *Public Papers of the Presidents of the United States: Ronald Reagan, 1981–1989,* from the American Presidency Project, University of California, Santa Barbara, www.presidency.ucsb.edu.

Lebanon triggered a violent backlash, including the April 1983 suicide bombing of the U.S. Embassy in Beirut, the Phalangist-led Lebanese government signed a peace treaty with Israel in May. It remained, however, unratified and was later canceled. The treaty failure prompted more U.S. military action, including fire from the guns of the battleship *New Jersey* against Syrian positions, which caused many collateral civilian casualties.

America Withdraws from Lebanon

Fighting between U.S. forces and the Syrian-supported Lebanese resistance continued into the fall of 1983, culminating on October 23 with the suicide bombing of the U.S. and French MNF headquarters. Combat escalated in the winter, as U.S. aircraft bombed Syrian positions in eastern Lebanon. In the face of growing antiwar sentiment in the United States, Reagan administration officials argued that a withdrawal of American forces would threaten the stability of the entire region and would be inter-preted as victory for terrorists. Nevertheless, by early 1984 the president and his advisers concluded that the American presence was attracting more extremist violence than it was suppressing. Accordingly, in February 1984 U.S. Navy helicopters evacuated U.S. and other foreign nationals from Beirut and the marines withdrew to ships off the Lebanese coast, thereby ending the U.S. intervention.

Despite the withdrawal, Muslim radicals continued in a course of anti-Western violence. Many of the Lebanese guerrillas joined together to form Hizballah (Party of God), a Muslim extremist organization, which contributed to the ongoing instability in the Middle East that the U.S. interventions in Lebanon had attempted to prevent. In September 1984 the rebuilt U.S. embassy was blown up again, killing 54 people, and a number of Americans still living in Lebanon were murdered or abducted. The Reagan administration made a covert effort to obtain Iranian influence to force the Lebanese abductors to release their American hostages, resulting in the infamous Iran-Contra scandal (Chapter 41).

BIBLIOGRAPHY

Fisk, Robert. *Pity the Nation: The Abduction of Lebanon,* 4th ed. New York: Nation Books, 2002.

Khazen, Farid el-. *The Breakdown of the State in Lebanon, 1967–1976.* Cambridge, Mass.: Harvard University Press, 2000.

Picard, Elizabeth. *Lebanon: A Shattered Country: Myths and Realities of the Wars in Lebanon,* rev. ed. Teaneck, N.J.: Holmes & Meier, 2002.

Rabinovich, Itamar. *The War for Lebanon, 1970–1985.* Ithaca, N.Y.: Cornell University Press, 1985.

Salibi, Kamal. *A House of Many Mansions: The History of Lebanon Reconsidered.* Berkeley: University of California Press, 1990.

At Issue

The Nicaraguan Civil War of 1978–1979, also called the Sandinista Revolution, was a Marxist rebellion against the brutal and corrupt Somoza regime, which had come to power with American support during the Nicaraguan Civil War of 1925–1933 (Chapter 35). The subsequent Nicaraguan Civil War of 1982–1990 was a counterrevolution by right-wing remnants of the Somoza-era National Guard. Aided by the United States, the "Contras" (as the counter-revolutionary rebels were called) fought fiercely, but were contained. Nevertheless, the Sandinistas were defeated in the 1990 elections.

The Honduran Civil War of 1981–1990 was a rebellion of leftist guerrillas (supported by the Sandinistas of Nicaragua) against the right-wing Honduran government (supported by the United States). The Honduran government, in turn, supported anti-Sandinista Contra forces in Nicaragua as well as in El Salvador.

The Conflicts

Nicaraguan Civil War of 1978–1979

Since the Nicaraguan Civil War of 1925–1933 (Chapter 35), the United States had supported the political regime of the Somoza family, which, although brutal and corrupt, was friendly to American political and business interests. In 1978 opposition to the Somozas—and to Nicaraguan president

Anastasio Somoza Debayle—became concentrated in the leftist Sandinista National Liberation Front (named in honor of Augusto César Sandino, a leading figure of the 1925–1933 civil war who was assassinated at the behest of Somoza Debayle's father, Anastasio Somoza García). The Sandinista rebellion developed in a context of weakening U.S. support for the Somoza government, which the U.S. State Department accused of human rights violations.

On January 10, 1978, the Somoza government instigated the assassination of anti-Somoza publisher Pedro Joaquin Chamorro. This triggered widespread riots, culminating in August 1978, when the Sandinistas stormed the National Palace in Managua. Taking 1,500 hostages, the Sandinistas demanded the release of 59 political prisoners along with their safe conduct out of Nicaragua. The prisoners were released, and the hostages in turn were freed. The "Sandinista Revolution" gained additional momentum when Costa Rican–based Sandinistas invaded Nicaragua on May 29, 1979, and fought the U.S.-equipped and -trained Nicaraguan National Guard over the next seven weeks. The United States declined to continue its support for the National Guard, which lost ground against the Sandinistas. Anastasio Somoza Debayle fled to the United States on July 17, 1979. Finding no welcome, he sought refuge in Paraguay, where he was assassinated in September 1980.

The new provisional Sandinista government, a five-member junta, was resolutely Marxist and anti-American, a situation that set the stage for more civil war.

Nicaraguan Civil War of 1982–1990

By the late 1970s, neither the brutal right-wing Somoza dictatorship nor the anti-American Marxist Sandinista dictatorship that replaced it met with U.S. approval. From the Sandinista point of view, the United States was a longtime enemy of the Nicaraguan people because of its support of the repressive Somozas. When in 1980 Congress delayed promised financial aid to Nicaragua, the Sandinista government turned to Fidel Castro's Communist Cuba for economic aid as well as military advisers. In one of his last acts before leaving

---

CHRONOLOGY OF THE CIVIL WARS IN NICARAGUA AND HONDURAS

NICARAGUAN CIVIL WAR
1978–1979

1978

Jan. 10 Anti-Somoza publisher Pedro Joaquin Chamorro is assassinated; many Nicaraguans riot.

Aug. Sandinistas occupy the National Palace and take 1,500 hostages, demanding the release of 59 political prisoners held by the Somoza government.

1979

May 29 Sandinistas invade Nicaragua from bases in Costa Rica, sparking a seven-week revolution.

July 17 Anastasio Somoza Debayle resigns as Nicaragua's president and flees. The civil war ends.

NICARAGUAN CIVIL WAR
1982–1990

1980

- The U.S. Congress delays promised financial aid to Nicaragua, prompting the Sandinista government to turn to Castro's Cuba for economic aid and military advisers.

1981

Jan. President Carter suspends all aid to Nicaragua, citing the Sandinistas' aid to leftist guerrillas in El Salvador.

November The Reagan administration authorizes $19 million to fund a CIA program to train the anti-Sandinista "Contras."

1982

Jan. Sandinista forces invade Miskito Indian settlements in Honduras, prompting the Miskitos to join the Contras.

1983–1984

- Contras invade Nicaragua from bases in Honduras in an effort to destabilize the government.

1985–1986

- The Sandinista army attacks the Nicaraguan Democratic Force (FDN), the largest of the Contra military groups, in combat that takes place in Honduras.

1987

Aug. 7 The Arias Treaty brings a degree of peace.

1990

Feb. 25 In peaceful elections, Violeta Barros de Chamorro defeats Daniel Ortega and becomes Nicaraguan president.

Nov. 13 A cease-fire is concluded; most fighting stops.

1991

Oct. 1 A treaty signed in Managua formally ends the war.

HONDURAN CIVIL WAR
1981–1990

1981

- Sporadic guerrilla war begins between anti-government leftists and the Honduran government. Contras as well as Sandinistas use Honduras as a base for guerrillas who periodically invade Nicaragua.

1982

- The U.S.-trained Battalion 316 becomes active in Honduras and commits increasingly notorious human rights abuses in an effort to suppress leftist guerrilla activity.

1982–1984

- The Honduran army (and Battalion 316) brutally suppresses the small Honduran guerrilla movement.

1990

- The war in Honduras rapidly winds down after the defeat of the Sandinistas in presidential elections.

office in January 1981, U.S. president Jimmy Carter suspended aid altogether, citing the Sandinistas' alliance with leftist guerrillas in El Salvador (which was torn by its own savage civil war).

Carter's successor, Ronald Reagan, entered office resolutely determined to remove the Sandinistas. In November 1981 the Reagan administration authorized $19 million to fund a Central Intelligence Agency (CIA) program to train a counterrevolutionary army, composed of mostly former Nicaraguan National Guardsmen, who called themselves the "Contras." By 1986 about 15,000 Contras had been trained, financed, and equipped by the United States. They operated mostly from bases in Honduras and Costa Rica—neighbors of Nicaragua—and were aided by Miskito Indians, who had left Nicaragua for Honduras after the Sandinista government tried forcibly to resettle them. In January 1982 Sandinista forces invaded the Miskito settlements in Honduras, killing more than 100 Indians. Other groups formed their own Contra forces, the most important of which were the Democratic Revolutionary Alliance (ARDE) and the Nicaraguan Democratic Force (FDN).

During 1983–1984 the Contras invaded Nicaragua from Honduras, attacking oil storage facilities, bridges, and other infrastructure installations in an effort to destabilize the government. In 1985–1986 the Sandinista army attacked the FDN in combat that took place in Honduras. Despite internal dissension within the FDN and a dispute between the FDN and ARDE, the Contras fought fiercely, inflicting heavy casualties on the Sandinistas, who were acutely underequipped because of a U.S. trade embargo. Although Congress had barred direct U.S. military aid to the Contras, officials within the Reagan administration devised a complex circumvention of the law, which became known as the Iran-Contra Affair (discussed below).

Despite U.S. aid, including the covert funding the Reagan administration had engineered, the Contras failed to overthrow the Sandinista government. A peace plan brokered by Costa Rican president Oscar Arias Sánchez called for an end to outside aid for the

Contras and resulted in a treaty signed on August 7, 1987. Fighting continued sporadically until new elections unseated Sandinista president Daniel Ortega Saavedra and replaced him and Sandinista legislators with an anti-Sandinista coalition, which concluded a peace accord with all parties involved in the civil war.

An estimated 30,000 people died in the course of the conflict, and the loss of U.S. aid and imposition of embargos reduced the nation to near economic ruin.

Honduran Civil War of 1981–1990

The Nicaraguan Civil War of 1982–1990 and the Salvadoran Civil War of 1977–1992 created a refugee crisis, with many fleeing to Honduras. This influx alarmed Honduran officials, who believed (quite correctly) that it would expose Honduras to attack from Nicaraguan and Salvadoran government and rebel forces.

Some of the Nicaraguan refugees in Honduras formed the anti-Sandinista Nicaraguan Democratic Force (FDN) and established bases from which to infiltrate and attack Nicaragua. Nicaraguan Sandinistas responded by invading Honduras to raid the FDN bases. This provoked the United States to provide helicopters and pilots to carry Honduran troops to the border regions to repel the invaders. In addition, 3,200 U.S. combat troops were sent to assist the anti-Sandinista Contras. The action touched off violent demonstrations by Hondurans who objected to a U.S. military presence in their country.

In fact, the 3,200 troops were only the public face of U.S. military involvement in Honduras. Strategically located between El Salvador and Nicaragua—both of which had anti-American leftist movements—Honduras was the base for all U.S. operations in Central America. From Honduras, the CIA supported covert operations, including the U.S.-trained Battalion 316, a secret Honduran army intelligence unit formed in 1982, which became notorious for human rights abuses. U.S. support also enabled the Honduran army to suppress the Honduran guerrilla movement between 1980 and 1984, often using imprisonment, torture, and murder as tools of oppression.

The Honduran Civil War rapidly petered out after the Sandinistas were defeated in the Nicaraguan elections of 1990, but violence continued as peasants seeking land reforms were attacked and killed during 1991 when they began farming idle privately held land.

School of the Americas

In 1947 the American government opened the U.S. Army School of the Americas (SOA) as part of a Cold War effort to train soldiers from Latin American countries whose governments were struggling against Communist or Marxist insurgencies, rebellions, and other movements. Between 1947 and January 2001, more than 60,000 Latin American troops were trained. (SOA was replaced in 2001 by the Western Hemisphere Institute for Security Cooperation.)

Among SOA's students were 4,318 Nicaraguans. According to critics, both within the U.S. government and in Nicaragua, the SOA-trained National Guard soldiers engaged in egregious human rights violations, including the use of electric shock, beatings, and rape. All National Guard troops specifically identified as having employed such methods had been trained at the SOA or at other U.S. facilities, including the Army Infantry and Ranger School, the Command and General Staff College, and the International Police Academy. In 1977 Amnesty International reported that seven of ten prisoners captured by the Somoza regime had been subjected to torture. The same report also revealed that peasants were routinely tortured and raped by National Guard patrols.

President Carter's Central American Policy

In his **Address to the United Nations General Assembly** on March 17, 1977, President Jimmy Carter announced that the promotion and protection of human rights would be at the forefront of American foreign policy. Carter authorized the systematic monitoring of human rights, and human rights

Carter's Address to the United Nations General Assembly, 1977

It is now 8 weeks since I became President. I have brought to office a firm commitment to a more open foreign policy. . . .

I see a hopeful world, a world dominated by increasing demands for basic freedoms, for fundamental rights, for higher standards of human existence. We are eager to take part in the shaping of that world. . . .

We will put our relations with Latin America on a more constructive footing, recognizing the global character of the region's problems. . . .

The basic thrust of human affairs points toward a more universal demand for fundamental human rights. The United States has a historical birthright to be associated with this process.

We in the United States accept this responsibility in the fullest and the most constructive sense. Ours is a commitment, and not just a political posture. I know perhaps as well as anyone that our own ideals in the area of human rights have not always been attained in the United States, but the American people have an abiding commitment to the full realization of these ideals. And we are determined, therefore, to deal with our deficiencies quickly and openly. We have nothing to conceal.

Excerpted from Jimmy Carter, "United Nations—Address Before the General Assembly," March 17, 1977, in *Public Papers of the Presidents of the United States: Jimmy Carter, 1977–1981*, from the American Presidency Project, University of California, Santa Barbara, www.presidency.ucsb.edu.

became the subject of a series of congressional hearings. As early as 1974, two amendments were made to the Foreign Assistance Act of 1961, which provided the foundation for human rights monitoring as a requisite for foreign assistance. In 1979 another amendment allowed the president to certify improvement in the human rights record to justify renewal or continuation of U.S. aid.

In 1977 the State Department published to Congress, as required by President Carter, its first annual report on human rights. By 1980 the annual report was formalized as *Country Reports on Human Rights Practices,* an ongoing series in which each presidential administration puts on the record its assessment of the human rights practices of countries to which military and other aid is given.

During the Carter years, the principal human rights focus was on Central and South America, especially Nicaragua, Guatemala, and El Salvador. The title of the State Department officer responsible for human rights was upgraded from coordinator to assistant secretary for human rights and humanitarian affairs. In addition, the State Department created in 1977 an independent Bureau of Human Rights and Humanitarian Affairs. The president also required the appointment of human rights officers in each overseas mission and made significant efforts to require greater accountability on the part of the CIA, specifying that intelligence operations were to be conducted—without exception—within Constitutional limits. Carter explicitly restated the prohibition on political assassinations first enacted during the Nixon administration.

By 1978, the Carter administration, citing human rights violations, began sharply curtailing security assistance to the Somoza dynasty; however, as the United States reduced its assistance, Israel and Argentina stepped in to fill the gap with military advisers, weapons, and even aircraft. There is still considerable controversy over the degree to which President Carter and his administration were aware of this flow of arms. Most experts insist that it could not have taken place without covert approval from the Pentagon and the CIA.

President Reagan's Central American Policy

Ronald Reagan, who took office in January 1981, by no means repudiated the human rights stance of the Carter administration, but he shifted the focus of Central American policy to the Cold War policy of containment (see Chapter 38). The Reagan administration opposed the Marxist Sandinista regime in Nicaragua, hoping to prevent the Sandinistas from exporting their Marxist revolution to neighboring nations. U.S. conservatives applauded the economic sanctions against the Sandinista government and economic aid to the "Contras," whom President Reagan called "freedom fighters" in the struggle against communism. Congressional Democrats and liberals generally opposed aid to the Contras, who were closely tied to the discredited Somoza regime.

During the Reagan administration, the CIA reemerged from its somewhat suppressed status during the Carter years to begin training a number of anti-Sandinista groups—all collectively referred to as Contras—and produced two published manuals, *Freedom Fighters Manual* and *Psychological Operations in Guerrilla Warfare.* The content of these manuals echoed the pre-Carter days of the SOA, and when human rights activists made the content known to the public, there was an outcry in the United States.

In December 1982 Congress passed the **Boland Amendment to the War Powers Act of 1973,** which barred the CIA or the Defense Department from covertly using funds to overthrow the Nicaraguan government. In 1984 a second Boland Amendment was passed in response to the CIA's mining of harbors on Nicaragua's Atlantic and Pacific coasts. In 1986 Congress, with a new Republican majority, appropriated $70 million in aid for the Contras.

Economic Warfare

The Reagan administration did not resort to military means alone in its effort to topple the Sandinista regime. The November 1984 election that made the

Boland Amendment to the War Powers Act of 1973, 1982

1. H.AMDT.461 to H.R.2968 An amendment to prohibit covert assistance for military operations in Nicaragua and to authorize overt interdiction assistance. The overt interdiction assistance consists of assistance furnished by the President on terms he may dictate to any friendly country in Central America to enable that country to prevent the use of its territory for the transfer of military equipment from or through Cuba or Nicaragua or any other country. The assistance must be overt. For this overt aid $30,000,000 is provided for FY'83 and $50,000,000 is provided for FY'84.

Excerpted from Library of Congress, " 'Thomas' Summary of Amendment 461 to HR 2968," http://thomas.loc.gov/cgi-bin/bdquery/z?d098:HR02968:@@@L&summ2=m&.

Sandinista candidate, Daniel Ortega Saavedra, president of Nicaragua was certified as fair and proper by international observers, including former president Carter. President Reagan nevertheless denounced it as fraudulent and intensified the economic warfare he had commenced against the Sandinistas in 1982, when he had used U.S. leverage in the World Bank and the Inter-American Development Bank to block loans to Nicaragua. In 1985 the president declared a full embargo against Nicaragua. This pushed an already fragile economy, drained by civil war, toward collapse. By 1988 inflation in Nicaragua reached 30,000 percent, prompting Ortega to slash government health, education, housing, and nutrition programs. These harsh measures sharply eroded Ortega's popularity among the suffering Nicaraguan population.

The Iran-Contra Affair

Even as Congress appropriated overt funds to aid the Contras, President Reagan, in a **Press Conference of November 15, 1986,** confirmed reports that the United States government had covertly sold arms to its implacable enemy, Iran. With this confirmation, the Iran-Contra Affair came to light, revealing the administration's efforts to back the Contras in violation of the Boland Amendment and

Reagan's Press Conference of November 15, 1986

Last Friday, after becoming concerned whether my national security apparatus had provided me with a security, or a complete factual record with respect to the implementation of my policy toward Iran, I directed the Attorney General to undertake a review of this matter over the weekend and report to me on Monday.

And yesterday, Secretary Meese provided me and the White House chief of staff with a report on his preliminary findings. And this report led me to conclude that I was not fully informed on the nature of one of the activities undertaken in connection with this initiative. . . .

I am deeply troubled that the implementation of a policy aimed at resolving a truly tragic situation in the Middle East has resulted in such controversy.

Excerpted from "Arms to Iran, Money to the Contras," in *Annals of America,* ed. Mortimer J. Adler and Charles Van Doren (Chicago: Encyclopaedia Britannica, 1976), 21:664–665.

well beyond what Congress had authorized.

At the time that he confirmed the reports of the arms sale, President Reagan denied that the purpose of the sale was to obtain the release of U.S. hostages still held by terrorists in Lebanon (see Chapter 40), but, in a televised address on March 4, 1987, he admitted an arms-for-hostages swap: "A few months ago I told the American people I did not trade arms for hostages. My heart and my best intentions tell me that's true, but the facts and evidence tell me it is not."

Then the plot thickened. Attorney General Edwin Meese announced that a portion of the revenue raised by the arms sales had been diverted to finance—illegally—the Contras. An extensive investigation revealed that in 1985 a cabal of Israelis had approached National Security Adviser Robert MacFarlane with a scheme in which Iran would use its influence to free the U.S. hostages held in Lebanon in exchange for arms. Secretary of State George Schultz and Secretary of Defense Caspar Weinberger had objected to the plan, but (MacFarlane testified) President Reagan had agreed to it. According to MacFarlane, U.S. Marine lieutenant colonel Oliver ("Ollie") North modified the scheme in order to funnel profits from the arms sales to the Contras, thereby killing the proverbial two birds with a single stone: freeing the hostages *and* financing a counterrevolution in Nicaragua.

Further investigation implicated senior administration officials including national security advisers John Poindexter and MacFarlane, CIA director William J. Casey (who died of a stroke in May 1987), and Weinberger. The president was not implicated, but many people believed he had known about and supported the scheme.

There were dire predictions that the Iran-Contra scandal would be the popular president's Water-

Oliver North is sworn in on July 7, 1987, prior to his testimony before the Iran Contra Committee. North testified that he "never personally discussed" with President Reagan the diversion of Iranian arms sales profits to Contra rebels.

gate—it was widely referred to as "Iran-Gate"—and would lead to his impeachment. But Reagan publicly admitted the wrongdoing of his administration and accepted responsibility for what had happened "on my watch." While some in the public and the press censured him, no official action was taken.

In testimony before Congress, Oliver North accepted most of the responsibility for the Iran-Contra Affair and denied that President Reagan was involved. He testified that he understood his actions were illegal but that aiding the Contras had been worth bending the law. Indicted in 1989, North was tried and convicted of accepting an illegal gratuity, aiding and abetting in the obstruction of a congressional inquiry (he had admitted lying to Congress), and destroying documents. He was sentenced to a three-year suspended prison term, two years probation, $150,000 in fines, and 1,200 hours community service, but his conviction was overturned in 1990 on appeal. Poindexter was convicted on five counts of deceiving Congress, but his convictions were also set aside. CIA administrator Clair E. George was indicted for perjury, but his trial ended in mistrial. Weinberger was indicted on five counts of lying to Congress but was not tried. All of those charged were ultimately pardoned by President Reagan's successor, former vice president George H. W. Bush. Although the 1994 report of special prosecutor Lawrence E. Walsh was strong in its criticism of both Reagan and Bush, neither was ever charged with criminal wrongdoing.

The Defeat of Ortega

Nicaraguan elections were held in 1990, in the wake of Ortega's draconian economic austerity program. The elections were subjected to intense international scrutiny and marred by Contra violence. In the end, the National Opposition Union Party, which was backed by the United States, emerged victorious. Its presidential candidate, Violeta Barros de Chamorro, had bona-fide anti-Somoza credentials—she was the widow of the crusading newspaper publisher slain by Somoza's National Guard—yet she was not hostile to the United States. She seemed to mollify, if not satisfy, everyone. The transition from Ortega to Chamorro was peaceful, and the Contras immediately agreed to a cease-fire. Within a short time, even the hardliners on both sides laid down their arms. The civil war ended.

BIBLIOGRAPHY

Anderson, Thomas P. *Politics in Central America: Guatemala, El Salvador, Honduras, and Nicaragua.* New York: Praeger, 1988.

Barton, Jonathan R. *Political Geography of Latin America.* New York: Routledge, 1997.

Busby, Robert. *Reagan and the Iran-Contra Affair.* New York: St. Martin's Press, 1987.

Crawley, Eduardo. *Nicaragua in Perspective.* New York: St. Martin's Press, 1984.

Hodges, Donald Clark. *Intellectual Foundations of the Nicaraguan Revolution.* Austin: University of Texas Press, 1986.

Schulz, Donald E., and Deborah Sundloff Schulz. *The United States, Honduras, and the Crisis in Central America.* Boulder, Colo.: Westview Press, 1994.

Walker, Thomas W. *Nicaragua,* 4th ed. Boulder, Colo.: Westview Press, 2003.

CHAPTER **42**

U.S. INVASIONS OF GRENADA (1983) AND PANAMA (1989)

At Issue in Grenada

The Reagan administration wanted to remove a Cuban Communist military contingent that had seized power in a coup d'état and to evacuate approximately 1,000 U.S. nationals believed to be in danger in this small West Indian island nation (population 110,000).

The Conflict

At the behest of Grenada's anti-American government, Fidel Castro sent Cuban troops to Grenada shortly after Maurice Bishop's Marxist-Leninist New Jewel movement overthrew the existing government in a 1979 coup d'état. Particularly alarming to President Ronald Reagan's military advisers was surveillance revealing that the regime was building, with the aid of Cuban military personnel, a 9,800-foot airstrip, which was far longer than warranted by local commercial or tourist service and obviously intended for high-performance military aircraft.

On October 19, 1983, a new coup resulted in the death of Bishop and put Deputy Prime Minister Bernard Coard and General Hudson Austin, both radical Marxists, at the head of the government. Sir Paul Scoon, Grenada's governor general (Grenada was legally part of the British Commonwealth of Nations), communicated secretly with the Organization of Eastern Caribbean States (OECS), appealing for aid to restore order. OECS in turn requested U.S.

military aid, which the United States provided quickly.

The administration's stated goals for the American intervention in Grenada were to "restore order and democracy" to the nation while preventing the spread of communism and rescuing the approximately 1,000 U.S. nationals—primarily medical students—believed to be in danger. On October 24, President Reagan briefed House and Senate leaders on his intention to invade Grenada.

The American invasion, codenamed Operation Urgent Fury, included a naval battle group from the aircraft carrier *Independence* as well as the helicopter carrier *Guam,* two U.S. Marine amphibious units, two Army Ranger battalions, a brigade of the

---

CHRONOLOGY OF THE INVASION OF GRENADA

1983

Oct. 19 Grenadian prime minister Maurice Bishop is killed in a coup; radical Marxists Bernard Coard and General Hudson Austin assume power.

Oct. 25 President Reagan authorizes Operation Urgent Fury, the invasion of Grenada, which is launched this day.

Oct. 28 The U.S. military declares Grenada secure.

Dec. 15 Having toppled the Marxist regime, U.S. forces withdraw, and a new government is appointed by the governor general.

Eighty-second Airborne Division, and various special operations units. These forces landed on Grenada on October 25, 1983. Opposing them were 500–600 Grenadian regulars, 2,000–2,500 ill-equipped militia troops, and about 800 Cuban military construction personnel. The invasion force seized the airport and destroyed Radio Free Grenada, the Coard government's principal broadcast facility. The U.S. nationals were evacuated without casualty; however, 18 U.S. military personnel were killed in the assault, and 116 were wounded. Grenadian forces lost 25 dead and 59 wounded, while Cuban casualties were 45 dead and 350 wounded. Grenada was under U.S. military control and declared secure by October 28.

President Ronald Reagan and Mrs. Reagan attend the memorial services for the U.S. Marines killed in Lebanon and the service members who died in the Grenada invasion at Camp Lejeune, North Carolina, on November 4, 1983. The president wrote in his diary that day, "It was a dreary day with constant rain which somehow seemed appropriate."

Democrats Connect Beirut and Grenada

In September 1983 Democratic Speaker of the House Thomas "Tip" O'Neill sent a congressional delegation to Lebanon to report on conditions there, particularly on the role of the U.S. Marines functioning as peacekeepers. Representative John Murtha (D-Pa.) issued a report on behalf of the delegation, warning of the dangerous vulnerability of the marine detachment in Beirut. He recommended the dispersal of the marines over a wider area rather than their concentration at the U.S. and French Multinational Force (MNF) peacekeeping headquarters, a location that the delegation found to be vulnerable to terrorism.

On October 23, 1983, soon after the report was released, a suicide bomber drove a truck loaded with TNT into the MNF headquarters in Beirut, killing 298 people, most of them U.S. Marines (see Chapter 40). The tragic attack exposed the Reagan administration to a firestorm of criticism for its military policy in Lebanon.

The criticism was blunted two days later when President Reagan authorized an invasion of Grenada after briefing House and Senate leaders on the plan. Although Congress did not object to the mission, congressional Democrats argued that the operation was intended, at least in part, to draw attention away from the tragedy in Beirut by providing an easy military triumph.

Reagan Connects Flight 007, Beirut, and Grenada

On August 31, 1983, Korean Airlines Flight 007 violated Soviet airspace, presumably by accident, and was shot down by overzealous Soviet air defense personnel. At the time of the incident, President Reagan referred to it as the "Korean airline massacre," a "crime against humanity," and an "act of barbarism . . . [of] inhuman brutality."

Two months later, in his televised October 27, 1983, **Address on Beirut and Grenada,** the president presented the invasion of Grenada as a stand against international terrorism and implied that the

Reagan's Address on Beirut and Grenada, 1983

Some 2 months ago we were shocked by the brutal massacre of 269 men, women, and children, more than 60 of them Americans, in the shooting down of a Korean airliner. Now, in these past several days, violence has erupted again, in Lebanon and Grenada.

In Lebanon, we have some 1,600 Marines, part of a multinational force that's trying to help the people of Lebanon restore order and stability to that troubled land. . . .

More than 200 . . . sleeping [marines] were killed in . . . one hideous, insane attack [on the MNF headquarters in Beirut]. Many others suffered injury and are hospitalized here or in Europe. . . .

. . . And now many of you are asking: Why should our young men be dying in Lebanon? Why is Lebanon important to us?

Well, it's true, Lebanon is a small country, more than five-and-a-half thousand miles from our shores on the edge of what we call the Middle East. . . . The area is key to the economic and political life of the West. Its strategic importance, its energy resources, the Suez Canal, and the well-being of the nearly 200 million people living there—all are vital to us and to world peace. . . .

Now, I know another part of the world is very much on our minds, a place much closer to our shores: Grenada. . . .

In 1979 trouble came to Grenada. Maurice Bishop, a protégé of Fidel Castro, staged a military coup. . . . He sought the help of Cuba in building an airport, which he claimed was for tourist trade, but which looked suspiciously suitable for military aircraft, including Soviet-built long-range bombers. . . . On October 12th, a small group in his militia seized him and put him under arrest. They were, if anything, more radical and more devoted to Castro's Cuba than he had been. . . . Bishop . . . and several members of his cabinet were subsequently executed. . . . Grenada was without a government, its only authority exercised by a self-proclaimed band of military men.

There were then about 1,000 of our citizens on Grenada, 800 of them students in St. George's University Medical School. Concerned that they'd be harmed or held as hostages, I ordered a flotilla of ships, then on its way to Lebanon with Marines, part of our regular rotation program, to circle south on a course that would put them somewhere in the vicinity of Grenada in case there should be a need to evacuate our people.

Last weekend, I was awakened in the early morning hours and told that six members of the Organization of Eastern Caribbean States, joined by Jamaica and Barbados, had sent an urgent request that we join them in a military operation to restore order and democracy to Grenada. . . .

. . . The legitimacy of their request, plus my own concern for our citizens, dictated my decision. . . . The nightmare of our hostages in Iran must never be repeated.

Two hours ago we released the first photos from Grenada. They included pictures of a warehouse of military equipment. . . . This warehouse contained weapons and ammunition stacked almost to the ceiling, enough to supply thousands of terrorists. Grenada, we were told, was a friendly island paradise for tourism. Well, it wasn't. It was a Soviet-Cuban colony, being readied as a major military bastion to export terror and undermine democracy. We got there just in time. . . .

The events in Lebanon and Grenada, though oceans apart, are closely related. Not only has Moscow assisted and encouraged the violence in both countries, but it provides direct support through a network of surrogates and terrorists. It is no coincidence that when the thugs tried to wrest control over Grenada, there were 30 Soviet advisers and hundreds of Cuban military and paramilitary forces on the island.

Excerpted from Ronald Reagan, "Address to the Nation on Events in Lebanon and Grenada," October 27, 1983, in *Public Papers of the Presidents of the United States: Ronald Reagan, 1981–1989,* from the American Presidency Project, University of California, Santa Barbara, www.presidency.ucsb.edu.

downing of Flight 007 was the first in a series of Soviet-supported terrorist acts. The attack on the marines in Beirut was the second. Grenada was being invaded to halt Communist preparations to use the nation as a base for future acts "to export terror and undermine democracy." Although critics argued that three different actors were involved—the Soviets, Muslim extremists, and Cuban-supported Communists—and that only the Beirut bombing was unambiguously a terrorist act, President Reagan justified the invasion of Grenada as a preemptive strike against terrorism.

The Reagan Containment Policy

Although the level of threat represented by the Marxist-Leninist regime in Grenada has been debated, the invasion was of a piece with the hard line Reagan took against Soviet-supported Communist aggression. The operation was intended to send a strong message to Cuba that no amount of foreign-supported Communist expansion would be permitted in the Americas. Viewed from a broad historical perspective, the invasion was in the spirit of the containment policy first enunciated by President Harry S. Truman in 1948 (see Chapter 37) and perhaps the Monroe Doctrine of 1823, which warned the empires of the Old World not to meddle in the New. As President Reagan saw it, Cuba was a proxy for the Soviet Union—insofar as all movements in aid of international communism were supported by the Soviet Union, either directly or ideologically— and Cuba's military activities in Grenada represented—at least symbolically—an attempt by the Soviet Union to extend its influence into the Western Hemisphere.

Information Management

The Reagan administration made efforts to ensure that the Grenada invasion would be interpreted as a stand against terrorism and the spread of communism. Fearing a liberal bias among the media—which some in the Reagan administration blamed for the failure of the Vietnam War (Chapter 38)—reporters were barred from landing with the troops. There were, therefore, no live reports on the invasion and no firsthand reports from Grenada until about sixty hours after the operation was launched.

Feeling that they had been deliberately excluded, the members of the media protested and did, in fact, tend to highlight the significant failures within a mission that, in an overall military sense, had been successful. The media gave after-the-fact coverage of the chief intelligence failure of the mission—that the invasion force did not have good information on the whereabouts of the American medical students, who were not centrally located but actually spread out over three sites—and especially the fiasco of poor military communications. The invading forces lacked an integrated, interoperable communications system. Uncoordinated radio frequencies prevented radio communications between U.S. Marines and Army Rangers, and it was even reported that one member of the invasion force had to place a commercial long-distance telephone call to Fort Bragg, North Carolina, to obtain C-130 gunship support for his unit, which was under fire.

Instead of achieving the "spin" the administration desired—a triumphal mission to foil terrorism—the media blackout created a backlash that tended to portray Operation Urgent Fury as a cakewalk against a pushover target that was nevertheless rife with errors.

INVASION OF PANAMA

At Issue in Panama

As U.S.-Panamanian relations deteriorated during the regime of Panama's strongman Manuel Antonio Noriega, the administration of U.S. president George H. W. Bush supported an alternative Panamanian government and invaded the country to arrest Noriega on drug-trafficking charges.

The Conflict

With the possible exception of the Punitive Expedition against Pancho Villa (Chapter 33), the 1989 invasion of Panama was unique in U.S. military history as an act of war committed for the purpose of apprehending a single person—in this case, a head of state, President Manuel Noriega of Panama.

In 1988 Noriega was indicted by a U.S. federal grand jury on charges of drug trafficking. Acting on this indictment, the administrations of Ronald Reagan and George H. W. Bush employed economic and diplomatic sanctions to pressure the dictator to resign. When these efforts succeeded only in hastening the deterioration of relations between Panama and the United States, additional military forces were deployed during the spring of 1989 to long-standing U.S. installations in Panama. In May Noriega vacated the presidential elections held on the 7th and installed

CHRONOLOGY OF THE INVASION OF PANAMA

1988

Feb. 5 Manuel Antonio Noriega is indicted on federal drug charges.

1989

May 7 Guillermo Endara wins the Panamanian election; Noriega vacates the result three days later.

Oct. 3 A coup attempt against Noriega fails.

Dec. 15 The Panama National Assembly bestows the title of "Maximum Leader" on Noriega, who accepts with a speech that the U.S. government interprets as a declaration of war against the United States.

Dec. 19 At a U.S. military base, Endara is sworn in as Panamanian president.

Dec. 20 Operation Just Cause is launched.

1990

Jan. 3 Noriega surrenders to American forces.

1992

July 10 Noriega is sentenced to forty years in a federal prison for eight counts of drug smuggling, conspiracy, and racketeering.

a puppet regime. This triggered a military coup d'état, which was crushed on October 3 by troops still loyal to Noriega. The coup and its defeat were followed by several incidents of harassment against U.S. citizens and then, on December 15, 1989, by a provocative pronouncement from Noriega. On that day Panama's National Assembly bestowed on him the title of "Maximum Leader." In his acceptance speech, Noriega declared that "the North American scheme, through constant psychological and military harassment, has created a state of war in Panama."

The Bush administration interpreted this as a declaration of war against the United States. A short time later, Panamanian soldiers killed an off-duty U.S. Army officer, whereupon, on December 19, 1989, the United States sanctioned the creation of a new government for Panama, led by President Guillermo Endara, who was sworn into office at a U.S. military base by a Panamanian judge. Early the next morning, Operation Just Cause was launched with an attack by F-117 Stealth fighters against the Panamanian Defense Force (PDF) barracks. On December 20, President Bush delivered a televised **Address on the Panama Invasion** to explain the operation to the American public.

After the air attack came ground assaults by some 24,000 American military personnel, including U.S. Army infantry and Rangers, U.S. Marines, and U.S. Navy SEALs. Marines were deployed to guard the entrances to the Panama Canal and other U.S. defense sites located in the Canal Zone. Rangers and other special task force personnel were airlifted by Apache attack helicopters to key points in the Canal Zone. Troops in M-113 armored personnel carriers rode out from Fort Sherman to engage PDF units encountered in Panama City. Rangers, reinforced by marines, advanced against the central Canal Zone, attacking along the way the Commandancia, headquarters of Noriega and the PDF. Other units captured Torrijos International Airport, the Bridge of the Americas, and Rio Hato airfield, 90 miles south of Panama City. Still more detachments took responsibility for force security on all U.S. military bases and set out to free prisoners taken by the PDF.

Bush's Address on the Panama Invasion, 1989

For nearly 2 years, the United States, nations of Latin America and the Caribbean have worked together to resolve the crisis in Panama. The goals of the United States have been to safeguard the lives of Americans, to defend democracy in Panama, to combat drug trafficking, and to protect the integrity of the Panama Canal treaty. Many attempts have been made to resolve this crisis through diplomacy and negotiations. All were rejected by the dictator of Panama, General Manuel Noriega, an indicted drug trafficker.

Last Friday, Noriega declared his military dictatorship to be in a state of war with the United States and publicly threatened the lives of Americans in Panama. The very next day, forces under his command shot and killed an unarmed American serviceman; wounded another; arrested and brutally beat a third American serviceman; and then brutally interrogated his wife, threatening her with sexual abuse. That was enough.

General Noriega's reckless threats and attacks upon Americans in Panama created an imminent danger to the 35,000 American citizens in Panama.

As President, I have no higher obligation than to safeguard the lives of American citizens. And that is why I directed our Armed Forces to protect the lives of American citizens in Panama and to bring General Noriega to justice in the United States. . . .

At this moment, U.S. forces, including forces deployed from the United States last night, are engaged in action in Panama. . . .

. . . [T]he United States today recognizes the democratically elected government of President Endara. . . .

Key military objectives have been achieved. Most organized resistance has been eliminated, but the operation is not over yet: General Noriega is in hiding. And nevertheless, yesterday a dictator ruled Panama, and today constitutionally elected leaders govern.

Excerpted from George Bush, "Address to the Nation Announcing United States Military Action in Panama," December 20, 1989, in *Public Papers of the Presidents of the United States: George Bush, 1989–1993,* from the American Presidency Project, University of California, Santa Barbara, www.presidency.ucsb.edu.

For the first time in its history, the Panama Canal was closed; it would reopen on December 21. Combat, mostly in Panama City, spanned five days, as marines conducted a manhunt for Noriega as well as PDF troops. A civil-affairs Ranger unit supported President Endara's effort to reestablish order and also created a new police force, the Panama Public Force, to take over after U.S. troops withdrew.

Noriega took refuge in the Vatican embassy (papal nunciature) in Panama City. Beginning on Christmas Day, U.S. forces surrounded the building and blasted it with rock music for ten days, until Noriega surrendered on January 3, 1990. He was then transported to the United States for trial.

Casualties were 314 PDF soldiers killed, 124 wounded, and 5,313 taken prisoner. Nineteen American soldiers were killed and 303 were wounded. Estimates of civilian casualties range from 200 to 4,000 killed.

Noriega as a U.S. Ally

Manuel Noriega had served as an intelligence officer under Panamanian dictator General Omar Torrijos during 1968–1978 and earned a reputation for brutality and corruption. It was long known that he was deeply involved in the smuggling of drugs and weapons. Nevertheless, he was considered an American ally, and he cooperated with the Drug Enforcement Administration (DEA), the U.S. military establishment, and the Central Intelligence Agency (CIA). He was an important intelligence source on Cuba's dictator, Fidel Castro, and routinely served as a back channel for communications between the U.S. government and Castro. During the civil war in Nicaragua (Chapter 41), he served U.S. interests similarly as a communications conduit to the Contras.

Because of his perceived value to the U.S. government, a succession of administrations, including

Manuel Antonio Noriega Morena

(1938–)

Manuel Noriega was born in Panama City into an impoverished family of Colombian origin. A bright child, he excelled in high school and earned a scholarship to the Chorrillos Military School in Lima, Peru. When he returned to Panama, he was commissioned a sublieutenant in the National Guard and quickly rose through the ranks, entering into the inner circle of Captain Omar Torrijos. With Torrijos, he participated in the 1968 military coup d'état that toppled the government of Arnulfo Arias and enabled Torrijos's rise as a powerful dictator. Throughout this rise, Noriega showed intense loyalty to Torrijos and was instrumental in suppressing a coup attempt against him. For this, Torrijos promoted Noriega to lieutenant colonel and chief of military intelligence.

After Torrijos died in a mysterious plane crash in 1981—some believed that Noriega had planted a bomb on board—Noriega jockeyed for power, becoming commander of the National Guard in 1983 and consolidating the armed forces into the Panamanian Defense Forces (PDF), with himself as general. This put him in position to control the civilian government and, despite the existence of an elected president, hold sway as military dictator of Panama.

Throughout the 1980s, charges accumulated against Noriega, including the brutal intimidation and even murder of critics and political rivals, general corruption, and criminal activities such as money laundering and drug trafficking. Relations between the United States and Noriega rapidly decayed, leading to the invasion of Panama and his arrest.

In 1992, after being convicted in a Miami, Florida, courtroom on eight counts of cocaine trafficking, racketeering, and money laundering, Noriega was sentenced to forty years in prison. In 1999 he was granted a ten-year reduction in his prison sentence after successfully arguing that he deserved credit for aiding the United States in furthering its Latin American interests. This made him eligible for release from prison in 2007.

---

those of Presidents Carter, Reagan, and George H. W. Bush, often looked the other way when Noriega's various abuses came to light. As commander of the PDF from 1983 to 1989, Noriega ruled Panama as the real power behind the elected president. When the clearly fraudulent elections of 1984 put Noriega's handpicked candidate, Nicolas Barlctta, into office, the Reagan administration raised no objection.

Noriega's Transition from Ally to Enemy

By the mid-1980s, it became increasingly difficult for Washington to continue to overlook Noriega's abuses. In September 1985 Dr. Hugo Spadafora, a popular Panamanian political activist, announced that he was about to expose Noriega's drug-trafficking and arms-smuggling activities. Spadafora was promptly captured, tortured, and murdered. The Panamanian media and opposition leaders demanded an investigation, but when President Barletta agreed, Noriega forced his resignation. In an effort to pressure Noriega to permit an investigation and to yield to civilian authority, the U.S. State Department diverted $14 million in aid intended for Panama to Guatemala—yet continued to assure Noriega that he still had the support of the U.S. government.

In June 1987 Colonel Roberto Diaz Herrera, an embittered Noriega deputy, publicly accused Noriega of Spadafora's murder and of fixing the 1984 elections. He also said that Noriega had been responsible for the death of Torrijos in 1981, claiming that

Noriega had planted a bomb on Torrijos's plane. The Herrera charges triggered widespread antigovernment protests and demands for Noriega's resignation. Noriega responded by charging Herrera with treason and by cracking down on the protestors.

On June 26, 1987, the U.S. Senate overwhelmingly approved a nonbinding resolution calling on Noriega to step down pending a "public accounting" of the Herrera charges. Noriega responded by sending government workers to riot near the U.S. embassy, virtually laying it under siege. This prompted the Reagan administration to suspend military aid to Panama, and the CIA summarily removed Noriega from its payroll. Other steps were taken to persuade Noriega to resign, but these came to nothing.

Drug-Trafficking Indictments

In February 1988 two U.S. federal grand juries in Miami and Tampa, Florida, indicted Manuel Noriega on multiple counts of racketeering, drug trafficking, and money laundering. The most important indictments accused Noriega of aiding the Colombian Medellin narcotics cartel to transport more than two tons of cocaine to the United States via Panama in return for a $4.5 million payment.

The indictments were handed down at the instigation of the Justice Department, which had consulted neither the White House nor the State Department. In effect, Justice handled the affair as if it were an ordinary domestic drug case. This created an embarrassing crisis within the Reagan administration, as the American public—weary of drug-related crime—began to demand action against Noriega.

In Panama, President Eric Arturo Delvalle (elected September 28, 1985) relieved Noriega as head of the PDF on February 25, 1988. Noriega responded by placing Delvalle under house arrest and cutting off his means of communication. Noriega thus retained command of the PDF, which largely remained loyal to him. Buckling to Noriega's pressure, the National Assembly then ousted Delvalle and replaced him.

Throughout the rest of 1988, the Reagan administration alternately encouraged the PDF to stage a coup against Noriega and attempted to entice Noriega to resign. Publicly, the administration imposed economic sanctions on Panama and reinforced the military presence on U.S. bases in the country.

Toward a Military Option

The Reagan administration internally debated outright military intervention in Panama, with the State Department in favor and the Defense Department opposed. State proposed a commando-style raid to capture Noriega and bring him to trial in the United States, but Defense and the Joint Chiefs of Staff raised legal, moral, and logistical objections.

On May 11, 1988, a new deal was publicly offered to Noriega in an effort to remove him from power quietly: retirement in exchange for a U.S. agreement to drop the federal indictments. Congress and Vice President George H. W. Bush strongly objected to the deal, and on May 17 the U.S. Senate passed a nonbinding amendment to the 1989 Defense Authorization Bill barring negotiations that "would involve the dropping of the drug-related indictments against" Noriega. President Reagan continued to push the deal, even as he froze Panamanian assets in the United States, suspended canal payments to the Panamanian government, revoked Panama's most-favored-nation trade status, and banned all payments to Panama from American individuals and companies. On April 6, 1988, more U.S. troops were sent to Panamanian bases, and a number of covert plans were launched to destabilize the Noriega regime, including attempts by a U.S.-supported group known as the "Hard Chargers" to foment a coup.

The Bush Policy

President George H. W. Bush entered office in 1989 apparently determined to remove Noriega. He hoped Noriega would be defeated in the May 1989 Panamanian elections and authorized covert operations to support the opposition. He also encouraged various election monitoring groups—including one led by former president Jimmy Carter—to observe the voting, which put Noriega's candidate, Carlos Duque, into office by a two-to-one margin. Evidence of fraud was blatant, as exit polls revealed a substantial majority for the opposition. Noriega responded to international criticism of the elections by nullifying them and simply appointing a crony as provisional president. This triggered mass protests, which were violently suppressed.

On May 11, 1989, President Bush announced a plan to remove Noriega by combining threats and incentives. The plan included cooperating with initiatives taken by members of the Organization of American States to address the Panama crisis; recalling the U.S. ambassador, Arthur Davis, from Panama; relocating U.S. government employees and their dependents; advising U.S. businesspeople in Panama to send their dependents back to the United States; continuing all economic sanctions; affirming U.S. obligations and rights under the Panama Canal treaties; and instituting military actions, to include sending a brigade (1,700–2,000 troops) to reinforce forces already in Panama.

On October 3, 1989, U.S. forces supported a peaceful coup attempt by Moises Giroldi, a member of Noriega's inner circle, but stood aside when PDF loyalists rescued Noriega, who was being held by Giroldi's men. Giroldi was tortured and killed, along with others who had supported the coup. At this point, Noriega's PDF began harassing not only Panamanian dissidents but Americans as well.

In the United States, the White House was criticized for its failure to support the Giroldi coup adequately. President Bush had been widely ridiculed as a "wimp" after a 1987 issue of *Newsweek* featured a cover story about the president entitled "The Wimp Factor." The epithet resurfaced after the coup, and it was in this atmosphere that the administration resolved to launch Operation Just Cause.

The Noriega Trial

Operation Just Cause (see "The Conflict," above) concluded with the capture of Manuel Noriega and his transportation to Miami, where during the fall of 1991 he stood trial for cocaine trafficking, racketeering, and money laundering. A parade of witnesses testified that he had laundered Colombian drug money in Panama and had used his country as a clearinghouse for cocaine bound for the United States. On April 10, 1992, a jury convicted Noriega on eight counts relating to all of the charges, and he was subsequently sentenced to forty years' imprisonment. It was the first time in history that the U.S. government had indicted, apprehended, tried, convicted, and punished a head of state for criminal acts.

Noriega's sentence was later reduced on appeal to thirty years. Further reductions—based on his record as a model prisoner—resulted in a projected release date (as of 2006) of September 2007.

BIBLIOGRAPHY

Donnelly, Thomas. *Operation Just Cause: The Storming of Panama.* New York: Lexington Books, 1991.

Gilmore, William C. *Grenada Intervention: Analysis and Documentation.* New York: Facts on File, 1985.

Hutchausen, Peter A. *America's Splendid Little Wars: A Short History of U.S. Military Engagements: 1975–2000.* New York: Viking, 2003.

McConnell, Malcolm. *Just Cause: The Real Story of America's High-Tech Invasion of Panama.* New York: St. Martin's Press, 1991.

Payne, Anthony J., Paul Sutton, and Tony Thorndike. *Grenada: Revolution and Invasion.* New York: St. Martin's Press, 1986.

CHAPTER 43

PERSIAN GULF WAR (1991)

At Issue

When Iraq invaded Kuwait, a UN-sanctioned coalition led by the United States fought to liberate the country and to protect key Middle Eastern oil supplies, especially in Saudi Arabia.

The Conflict

On August 2, 1990, the Iraqi army invaded Kuwait, and Iraq's president, Saddam Hussein, declared its annexation six days later. The United States and other nations feared that Iraq would next attack southward into Saudi Arabia, a major source of oil.

The administration of George H. W. Bush responded to the invasion by freezing Iraqi assets in American banks, imposing an embargo on trade with Iraq, and securing UN resolutions condemning the invasion and supporting military action. President Bush and Secretary of State James Baker assembled a coalition of forty-eight nations, of which thirty provided military forces (the United States making the largest contribution) and eighteen furnished economic, humanitarian, and other noncombat assistance. Saudi Arabia and other Arab states near Iraq made ports, airfields, and military staging areas available for a buildup of forces that began on August 7, 1990. This buildup phase, intended to defend Saudi Arabia against invasion, was called Operation Desert Shield and included a naval blockade of Iraq. On August 8, U.S. Air Force fighters began to arrive at Saudi air bases, and lead elements of the U.S. Army contingent arrived on

August 9. By August 12, the naval blockade was in place. By the end of October, 210,000 U.S. Army trooops and Marines had been deployed, in addition to 65,000 troops from other coalition nations.

On November 29, the United Nations passed a resolution authorizing military force to expel Iraq from Kuwait and setting a withdrawal deadline of January 15, 1991. As the deadline approached, 450,000 coalition troops were on the ground, ready to oppose a larger Iraqi force—about 530,000 troops—in Kuwait. (Coalition forces would ultimately number 660,000 by mid-February.) In addition to personnel, the coalition had 2,200 combat aircraft and 170 ships in the area, including six aircraft carriers and two battleships.

The deadline passed, and Saddam Hussein kept his troops in Kuwait. Operation Desert Shield became Operation Desert Storm as a massive air campaign was unleashed against Iraq and Iraqi positions in Kuwait on January 16. Over the next five weeks, coalition pilots flew more than 88,000 missions with losses of only twenty-two U.S. aircraft and nine planes from other coalition countries. The Iraqi air force offered almost no resistance, but Iraqi ground forces fired outdated Soviet-made "Scud" surface-to-surface missiles against targets in Israel and Saudi Arabia. Saddam hoped to goad Israel into joining the war, thereby alienating the Arab members of the coalition. Through deft diplomacy, the United States kept Israel out of the conflict, and the Scuds ultimately did little damage.

The air campaign was designed to prepare for the ground campaign, which was led chiefly by U.S.

general H. Norman Schwarzkopf. The overwhelming air supremacy of the coalition kept Iraqi reconnaissance aircraft at bay, and the ground offensive was launched at 4:00 a.m. on February 24, 1991. The army's XVIII Airborne Corps was positioned on the coalition's left flank. This unit was to move into Iraq on the far west and, striking deep within the country, cut off the Iraqi army in Kuwait, isolating it from support and reinforcement from the north. The French Sixth Light Armored Division would cover the XVIII Airborne Corp's left flank during this operation. The center of the ground force consisted of the U.S. VII Corps, the U.S. Second Armored Cavalry, and the British First Armored Division. These units were assigned to the main attack, in which they would move north into Iraq after the left and right flanks had been secured, then make a sharp right turn to advance into Kuwait from the west to attack Iraqi units there, including the elite Republican Guard. The right flank of the attack—mainly composed of U.S. Marines—was tasked with breaching Iraqi lines in Kuwait.

CHRONOLOGY OF THE PERSIAN GULF WAR

1990

Aug. 2 Iraq invades Kuwait and seizes Kuwaiti oil fields.

Aug. 6 The United Nations imposes a trade embargo on Iraq.

Aug. 7 Saudi Arabia requests U.S. troops to defend against a possible Iraqi invasion.

Aug. 8 Saddam Hussein annexes Kuwait.

Aug. 8 Operation Desert Shield begins as the first U.S. military forces arrive in Saudi Arabia.

Aug. 12 The United States imposes a naval blockade of Iraq.

Nov. 29 The UN Security Council passes a resolution setting the deadline for Iraqi withdrawal as January 15, 1991.

1991

Jan. 12 Congress authorizes war against Iraq.

Jan. 16 Operation Desert Storm commences with air attacks.

Jan. 25 Iraq perpetrates environmental terrorism by pumping millions of gallons of crude oil into the Persian Gulf.

Jan. 30 First important ground battle at Khafji, Saudi Arabia

Feb. 24 The major phase of the coalition's ground campaign begins.

Feb. 26 Saddam Hussein announces Iraq's withdrawal from Kuwait.

Feb. 27 Coalition forces enter Kuwait City. President George H. W. Bush declares Kuwait liberated.

H. Norman Schwarzkopf
(1934–)

As commander in chief, U.S. Central Command, Schwarzkopf was in charge of operations Desert Shield and Desert Storm and was—for the American people especially—the public face of the war.

He was born in Trenton, New Jersey. His father was a World War I army officer who headed the New Jersey State Police from 1921 to 1936 before returning to the U.S. Army during World War II. Young Schwarzkopf graduated from West Point in 1956 and held numerous staff strategic and personnel assignments before serving two tours of duty in Vietnam. He was an adviser to the Vietnamese Airborne during 1965–1966 and then a battalion commander, Americal Division, during 1969–1970. In 1974 he accepted a brigade command in Alaska in preference to another staff position, because he wanted to command in the field rather than from behind a desk.

Schwarzkopf was deputy commander of U.S. forces in the 1983 invasion of Grenada (Chapter 42) and was commander in charge during all phases of the Persian Gulf War. He exuded a combination of professionalism, common sense, warmth, and a passion for command. After the war, he was widely regarded as a national hero. He retired shortly after the conclusion of Operation Desert Storm.

The attacks on the first day were intended, in part, to screen the main attack and to deceive the Iraqis into thinking that the principal assault would come on the coast of Kuwait. Iraqi defenses were well developed, but only light resistance was offered, and coalition forces took many Iraqi prisoners. By the second day of the ground war, French troops had secured the left flank of the coalition advance, and U.S.

A destroyed Iraqi tank rests near a series of oil well fires in northern Kuwait during the Gulf War on March 9, 1991.

forces had cut off all avenues of Iraqi retreat and reinforcement. The U.S. Army's Twenty-fourth Division ended its advance in the southern city of Basra, Iraq, which sealed the remaining avenue of escape from Kuwait.

With the Iraqis in Kuwait occupied on their right flank, the U.S. VIII Airborne Corps made a surprise attack on the left flank, in the west. By nightfall of February 25, the VIII Airborne Corps was turning east into Kuwait. When the corps encountered units of the Republican Guard, this vaunted Iraqi unit broke and ran. By February 27, however, the Republican Guard was bottled up in U.S.-occupied Basra, and its Hammurabi Division attempted to engage the VIII Airborne Corps in a delaying action to allow the remainder of the Republican Guard to escape. The Hammurabi Division was destroyed, and the rest of the Republican Guard was captured or simply dissolved.

On February 26, Saddam Hussein announced that he would withdraw all forces from Kuwait. Coalition forces entered Kuwait City on February 27, and President Bush declared Kuwait liberated. A ceasefire was officially declared at 8:00 a.m. on February 28, after Iraq formally capitulated on U.S. terms. The

ground war had lasted just 100 hours. Kuwait was liberated at the cost to the coalition of 95 killed, 368 wounded, and 20 missing in action. Iraqi casualties were perhaps as many as 50,000 killed, 50,000 wounded, and 60,000 taken prisoner. Both Iraq and Kuwait suffered extensive destruction of infrastructure, and the environmental damage caused by Saddam's acts of destruction throughout the Kuwaiti oil fields, including the deliberate setting of oil fires and the dumping of crude oil into the Persian Gulf, would take many months to repair.

The Evolution of U.S. Policy on Iraq

During the administrations of Presidents Jimmy Carter and Ronald Reagan, the United States developed and maintained an alliance with Iraq, in large part because it was an enemy of Iran. In 1979 Iran's then-new radical Islamic government had seized the U.S. embassy and held Americans hostage for more than a year. Hoping to recruit Iraq as an ally and to increase pressure on Iran to release the hostages, President Carter quietly approved Saddam Hussein's invasion of Iran, which commenced on September 22, 1980. This was the beginning of a decade-long war that killed some one million people. Variously during the conflict, the United States supplied Iraq with funds, loans, military intelligence, advice, and weapons, often through third parties, including Jordan, Saudi Arabia, Kuwait, and Egypt. This assistance continued even after it was reported that Iraq was using chemical weapons and nerve gas against minority Kurds in its own country and in its war against Iran.

By 1985 the Central Intelligence Agency (CIA) had established direct intelligence links with Baghdad and was sharing U.S. satellite reconnaissance photography with the Iraqi military. From then virtually until the commencement of Operation Desert Shield, the U.S. Commerce Department routinely approved the sale of computers and other high-tech equipment to Iraq's weapons industry. Both the

Reagan and George H. W. Bush administrations approved the sale of various biological cultures to Iraq. As late as 1989 the Bush administration, in National Security Directive 26, issued a $1 billion loan guarantee to Iraq for weapons development, and in 1990 between July 18 and August 1—the day before the invasion of Kuwait—the Bush administration approved some $4.8 million in advanced technology sales to the Iraqi weapons ministry.

In July 1990, just days before the invasion, U.S. ambassador April Glaspie told Saddam Hussein that "we have no opinion on the Arab-Arab conflicts, like your border disagreement with Kuwait." Some contemporary analysts and recent historians believe that Saddam took this as tacit approval of the Kuwait invasion; if so, it was a diplomatic blunder. But when Iraq invaded Kuwait and threatened Saudi Arabia—

Saddam (Takriti) Hussein

(1937–)

Orphaned at nine months of age, Saddam Hussein was raised by an uncle, Khairallah Talfah, who led an unsuccessful coup d'état and bid for independence from Britain in 1941. Because he lacked family connections, Saddam was refused enrollment in the Baghdad Military Academy and turned instead to membership in the radical Ba'ath (Arab Socialist Renaissance) Party, which initially supported Abdul Karim Kassim's overthrow of the Iraqi monarchy in 1958, only to turn against Kassim. Saddam, who had already assassinated a Communist politician who ran against his uncle in a parliamentary election, volunteered in 1959 to assassinate Kassim. After the attempt failed, the wounded Saddam fled to Syria, then immigrated to Cairo, where he studied law.

After a three-year exile, Saddam sought to mislead Iraqi secret police by dropping the name Takriti (by which he was known at the time) and taking as his last name his father's first, Hussein. He then returned to Baghdad and organized a covert Ba'ath militia, which in February 1963

deposed and killed Kassim. One of Saddam's relatives, Ahmed Hassan Bakr, was named premier. On July 17, 1968, Bakr overthrew President Aref (the man who had installed him), and in July 1979 Bakir himself stepped down in favor of Saddam Hussein.

Saddam instituted a regime of police-state terror, much of it directed at the rebellious Kurds, against whom he would use nerve gas on March 16, 1988. In September 1980 he began an eight-year war against Iran, which proved so costly that it nearly led to a military coup against him. In 1990 he invaded and annexed Kuwait, only to be overwhelmingly defeated in the Persian Gulf War.

Saddam retained power after the war and, accused by the administration of George W. Bush of supporting anti-American terrorism and harboring weapons of mass destruction, became the target of Operation Iraqi Freedom (Chapter 48), which began in 2003. He was captured by U.S. forces and put on trial by an Iraqi court for war crimes and atrocities.

both close U.S. allies, trading partners, and key sources of oil—the U.S. attitude toward Iraq shifted abruptly.

The Vietnam Syndrome

By the time of the Persian Gulf War, Saddam Hussein had earned a reputation as a ruthless dictator possessed of a great willingness to kill and an equally great willingness to accept casualties among his own people and forces. The press and politicians alike frequently compared him to Adolf Hitler and Joseph Stalin. Moreover, Saddam possessed numerically the fifth-largest standing army in the world. There was anxiety among the American people that tangling with this man could be costly, and the confidence of the public was undermined by what the media described as the "Vietnam syndrome," the long-lingering specter of failure in a war that became a military quagmire, a political disaster, and a national nightmare. It was against the background of the Vietnam syndrome that George H. W. Bush had to build American confidence in the armed forces and rally popular support for the war that was about to begin.

Building a Coalition

The Bush administration sought to avoid "another Vietnam" by ensuring that the United States would not stand alone against Iraq. Hours after the invasion, the Kuwaiti and U.S. delegations called for a meeting of the UN Security Council, which passed Resolution 660 condemning the invasion and demanding a withdrawal of Iraqi troops. On August 3, the Arab League did the same, but called for the Arab League to resolve the conflict and warned against foreign intervention. On August 6, the Security Council passed Resolution 661 placing economic sanctions on Iraq.

Most of the Arab world recognized Saddam Hussein as a threat to the region. Much of the rest of the world also recognized the threat Iraq posed to energy resources, including the great Hama oil fields of Saudi Arabia. No one wanted Saddam Hussein to have a monopolistic control of extensive sources of oil.

Operation Desert Shield was launched on August 8 by the United States, President Bush declared, as a "wholly defensive" mission to prevent Iraq from invading Saudi Arabia. As this mission got under way, Saddam defiantly declared portions of Kuwait to be extensions of the Iraqi province of Basra and the rest of the country to be the nineteenth province of Iraq. In the meantime, the UN Security Council continued to pass resolutions, including the November 29, 1990, **Resolution 678,** which set January 15, 1991, as the deadline for Iraq's withdrawal from Kuwait and authorized "all necessary means to uphold and implement Resolution 660."

As the United Nations Security Council process continued, President Bush and Secretary of State James Baker assembled a coalition against Iraq consisting of 48 nations, of which 30 provided direct military support. The most important coalition members were—in addition to the United States—Australia, Canada, France, Germany, Saudi Arabia, the United Arab Emirates, the United Kingdom, and Kuwait itself. U.S. forces would constitute 74 percent of what would eventually be 660,000 coalition military personnel in the theater.

Opposition and Justification

Initially, some Americans were opposed to war in the Middle East. They objected that the United States should not exchange "blood for oil." Indeed, "No Blood For Oil" became a slogan of the relatively small but vocal antiwar movement that quickly developed. The Bush administration soon shifted its justification for war by taking the focus off of Saudi Arabia and citing instead Iraq's history of human rights abuses under Saddam Hussein as well as the potential that Iraq could develop nuclear weapons and other weapons of mass destruction. Most of all, President Bush repeatedly asserted that "naked aggression will not stand" and that history had taught the folly of appeasing tyrants.

Resolution 678, 1990

Adopted by the Security Council at its 2963rd meeting on 29 November 1990

The Security Council,

Recalling and reaffirming its resolutions . . . ,

Noting that, despite all efforts by the United Nations, Iraq refuses to comply with its obligation to implement resolution 660 (1990) and the above-mentioned subsequent relevant resolutions, in flagrant contempt of the Security Council,

Mindful of its duties and responsibilities under the Charter of the United Nations for the maintenance and preservation of international peace and security,

Determined to secure full compliance with its decisions,

Acting under Chapter VII of the Charter,

1. *Demands* that Iraq comply fully with resolution 660 (1990) and all subsequent relevant resolutions, and decides, while maintaining all its decisions, to allow Iraq one final opportunity, as a pause of good-will, to do so;

2. *Authorizes* Member States co-operating with the Government of Kuwait, unless Iraq on or before 15 January 1991 fully implements, as set forth in paragraph 1 above, the above-mentioned resolutions, to use all necessary means to uphold and implement resolution 660 (1990) and all subsequent relevant resolutions and to restore international peace and security in the area;

3. *Requests* all States to provide appropriate support for the actions undertaken in pursuance of paragraph 2 above;

4. *Requests* the States concerned to keep the Security Council regularly informed on the progress of actions undertaken pursuant to paragraphs 2 and 3 above;

5. *Decides* to remain seized of the matter.

Excerpted from United Nations Security Council, "Resolution 678: Iraq-Kuwait (29 November)," in Security Council Resolutions—1990, www.un.org/Docs/scres/1990/scres90.htm.

The Kuwaiti government went so far as to hire American public relations firm Hill and Knowlton to create a campaign dramatizing Iraq's human rights abuses, particularly the atrocities Iraq was committing in occupied Kuwait. Most notorious was a story that portrayed Iraqi soldiers as pulling babies out of incubators in Kuwaiti hospitals and leaving them to die on the floor. This was later revealed as a fabrication; nevertheless, there can be no doubt that the Iraqi invasion and occupation were brutal.

Diplomacy Fails

The United States demanded Iraq's immediate and complete withdrawal from Kuwait. Iraq responded by offering to withdraw only if there were simultaneous withdrawals of Syrian troops from Lebanon and Israeli troops from the West Bank, Gaza Strip, the Golan Heights, and southern Lebanon. Although Morocco and Jordan approved this proposal, Syria,

Israel, and the entire U.S.-led anti-Iraq coalition rejected it, arguing that there was no legitimate connection between these issues and the illegal occupation of Kuwait.

As the UN Security Council's January 15 deadline for Iraqi withdrawal approached, the U.S. Congress on January 12 authorized the use of military force to drive Iraq out of Kuwait. The war—Operation Desert Storm—began the day after the deadline passed. On the evening of January 16, 1991, President Bush delivered a televised **Address on the Persian Gulf War.**

Media Coverage of Operation Desert Storm

In contrast to the virtual media blackout imposed during the invasion of Grenada (Chapter 42), reporters—especially television's emerging twenty-four-hour news outlets, such as CNN—were given easy access to military commanders, and on-location coverage of the war was extensive. However, in the aftermath of the conflict, television coverage (and, to a lesser extent, that of other media) was condemned by liberal critics as biased, even jingoist reporting. Whether this bias—insofar as it existed—reflected the influence of politicians and the military, the perceived commercial interests of the media outlets themselves, or simply popular prejudices is difficult to determine. Moreover, during the war—as in any other war—the media relied on the military for access to events. For example, the U.S. Marines tended to receive disproportionate coverage because the Marine Corps provided more access than did the U.S. Army.

Highly controversial was the access broadcast television was given to closed-circuit video images produced by high-tech weaponry. Television viewers saw few images of gritty ground combat but were offered images from video cameras mounted on aircraft, missiles, and "smart bombs," showing the destruction of various targets (usually anonymous buildings) from the point-of-view of the inbound projectiles themselves. This led to criticism that the war was depicted as a kind of video game rather than the bloody business it really was.

Evaluating an Unfinished War

The Persian Gulf War was an overwhelming tactical triumph for the coalition—and particularly for the United States. It ended quietly, with peace conferences held in coalition-occupied Iraqi territory and the surrender of Iraqi forces.

As part of the surrender agreement, the Iraqis secured approval of the use of armed helicopters on their side of a temporary border, to be used, ostensibly, for government transport because the civilian transportation network had been largely destroyed. Many of these helicopters, however, were actually employed to put down a Shiite uprising against Saddam Hussein in the south of Iraq. In the meantime, in the north, Kurdish leaders—long at violent odds with the Saddam government—were encouraged to rebel by U.S. statements of support for an uprising. They began what they hoped would

Bush's Address on the Persian Gulf War, 1991

Tonight, 28 nations—countries from 5 continents, Europe and Asia, Africa, and the Arab League—have forces in the Gulf area standing shoulder to shoulder against Saddam Hussein. These countries had hoped the use of force could be avoided. Regrettably, we now believe that only force will make him leave.

Prior to ordering our forces into battle, I instructed our military commanders to take every necessary step to prevail as quickly as possible, and with the greatest degree of protection possible for American and allied service men and women. I've told the American people before that this will not be another Vietnam, and I repeat this here tonight. Our troops will have the best possible support in the entire world, and they will not be asked to fight with one hand tied behind their back. I'm hopeful that this fighting will not go on for long and that casualties will be held to an absolute minimum.

This is an historic moment. We have in this past year made great progress in ending the long era of conflict and cold war. We have before us the opportunity to forge for ourselves and for future generations a new world order—a world where the rule of law, not the law of the jungle, governs the conduct of nations. When we are successful—and we will be—we have a real chance at this new world order, an order in which a credible United Nations can use its peacekeeping role to fulfill the promise and vision of the U.N.'s founders.

Excerpted from George Bush, "Address to the Nation Announcing Allied Military Action in the Persian Gulf," January 16, 1991, in *Public Papers of the Presidents of the United States: George Bush, 1989–1993,* from the American Presidency Project, University of California, Santa Barbara, www.presidency.ucsb.edu.

develop into a coup d'état, but the implied American support failed to materialize, the Kurdish rebels were crushed, and millions of Kurdish refugees fled to Turkey and Iran.

Although the prevailing sentiment among Americans was that a significant victory had been won—and won with little cost—the Bush administration came under increasing criticism for its decision to allow Saddam Hussein to remain in power, rather than continuing the war, capturing Baghdad, and overthrowing the government. The administration responded to its critics by explaining that toppling the Saddam regime would have destroyed the cohesion of the coalition and would have left the United States alone in the war.

BIBLIOGRAPHY

Atkinson, Rick. *Crusade: The Untold Story of the Persian Gulf War.* New York: Houghton Mifflin, 1993.

Friedman, Lawrence, and Efrain Karsh. *The Gulf Conflict, 1990–1991: Diplomacy and War in the New World Order.* Princeton, N.J.: Princeton University Press, 1993.

Goodman, A. Sue. *Persian Gulf War, 1990–1991: Desert Shield/Desert Storm.* Maxwell AFB, Ala.: Air University Library, 1991.

Hallion, Richard P. *Storm over Iraq: Air Power and the Gulf War.* Washington, D.C.: Smithsonian Institution Press, 1992.

At Issue

Civil war began in Bosnia and Herzegovina after Croatia left the Yugoslav federation in 1991. Bosnian Catholic Croats and Muslim Slavs approved a February 29, 1992, referendum to create an independent multinational republic of Bosnia and Herzegovina, but Bosnian Orthodox Serbs refused to secede from Yugoslavia (dominated by Serbia). The United States intervened as part of a United Nations and NATO (North Atlantic Treaty Organisation) peacekeeping force.

The Conflict

The Balkans in the twentieth century were frequently torn by nationalist, ethnic, and religious conflict, which was held in check for much of the post–World War II period by Josep Broz Tito, the Communist dictator of a Yugoslavia that consisted of six "republics": Serbia, Croatia, Bosnia and Herzegovina, Macedonia, Slovenia, and Montenegro, plus two "provinces," Kosovo and Vojvodina. After Tito's death in 1980, violent factionalism tore the republics apart. Slovenia and Croatia each declared independence, followed by Macedonia and then Bosnia and Herzegovina. During 1989–1990, in the general collapse of communism throughout Eastern Europe, Bosnia and Herzegovina's Catholic Croats and Muslim Slavs approved a referendum on February 29, 1992, calling for an independent, multinational republic. The Bosnian Orthodox Serbs refused to secede from Yugoslavia, which was dominated by

Serbia, and civil war began. The flames were fanned by Serbian president Slobodan Milošević, who, claiming a duty to protect the Serb minority in Bosnia and Herzegovina, armed and financed the ethnic Serb-dominated Bosnian federal army. When the army shelled the Croat and Muslim areas of the Bosnian capital of Sarajevo, the international community responded by imposing a variety of economic sanctions against Serbia in an effort to impede its ability to supply Bosnian Serbs with weapons and other materiel. The sanctions suppressed the army but failed to prevent Bosnian Serb guerrillas from carrying out brutal campaigns of "ethnic cleansing" against Muslims and Croats. These campaigns were intended to clear certain areas for exclusive occupation by Bosnian Serbs. By July 1992 millions of Croatian and Muslim Bosnians had become refugees. In response, Bosnian Croats and Muslims carried out brutal retaliatory raids, including the ethnic cleansing of areas they controlled.

Other than the overall estimate that the war created some 2 million refugees, it is difficult to find precise assessments of the extent of the ethnic cleansing and other violence on both sides. The UN high commissioner for refugees listed Bosnian refugee populations resulting from ethnic cleansing as comprising 36 percent Serbs, 20 percent Croats, and 44 percent Muslims. This suggests that the Serbs were responsible for about 64 percent of the ethnic cleansing during the war.

In July 1992 NATO ships began to monitor and enforce UN arms embargos against Serbia, and in April 1993 NATO aircraft began to enforce UN

Security Council Resolution 816 (adopted March 31, 1993), which created a no-fly zone over Bosnia and Herzegovina. When Serb forces attempted to block UN humanitarian aid during July and August, U.S.

CHRONOLOGY OF THE WAR IN BOSNIA AND HERZEGOVINA

1992

Feb. 29 Bosnian Catholic Croats and Muslim Slavs approve a referendum to create an independent Bosnia and Herzegovina, but Bosnian Orthodox Serbs refuse to secede from Yugoslavia. Civil war begins between the Croats and Slavs one side and the Bosnian Serbs on the other.

May Western nations recognize Bosnia and Herzegovina as an independent state. The United Nations imposes sanctions on Serb-led Yugoslavia.

July NATO begins monitoring enforcement of arms embargos against Serbia.

July–Aug. Reports of "ethnic cleansing" and other atrocities become widespread. UN humanitarian aid is blocked by Serb forces. President Clinton orders humanitarian airlifts.

1992–1993

- A series of cease-fires are concluded among the combatants and are broken almost immediately.

1993

Apr. 12 NATO's Operation Deny Flight begins to enforce a no-fly zone over Bosnia and Herzegovina.

1994

April The United States leads NATO air strikes against Serb positions.

July Seventy percent of Bosnia and Herzegovina is under Serb control.

1995

Nov. 21 Bosnian Slav and Croatian leaders agree to the Dayton Peace Accords.

Nov. 27 President Clinton authorizes 20,000 U.S. ground troops to help enforce the accords.

Dec. 14 Bosnian Serb leaders sign the Dayton Peace Accords.

president Bill Clinton ordered humanitarian airlifts. By December 1995 some 100,000 sorties had been flown, most of them by U.S. aircraft. The Americans shot down intruders into the no-fly zone and provided close air support for UN ground forces, which had been assigned in 1992 to protect the Sarajevo International Airport and to provide security for humanitarian aid workers. By 1993 UN ground forces were also protecting designated Muslim Slav "safe havens" around various towns, including Sarajevo, Goražde, and Srebrenica. Substantial U.S. ground forces were not deployed until after the conclusion of the Dayton Accords, when they were used to help enforce an uneasy peace.

Early in 1994 Bosnian Muslims and Croats made peace and formed a confederation to oppose the Serbs. In August this confederation agreed to a plan formulated by the United States, Russia, Britain, France, and Germany, by which Bosnian territory would be divided nearly in half: 51 percent would go to the confederation and 49 percent to the Serbs. The Serbs, however, kept fighting the Muslims and Croats and during 1994 and 1995 perpetrated mass murders in the safe havens of Sarajevo, Srebrenica, and other, smaller towns.

After the manifest failure of an arms embargo imposed by the United States and western European powers, NATO, with the United States in the lead, launched air strikes against the Serb positions beginning in April 1994. Despite this, the Bosnian Serbs fought on, even intercepting and detaining a 24,000-troop UN peacekeeping mission. The economic measures and the air strikes did aid the military efforts of the Muslim-Croat alliance, which by September 1995 had reduced Serb-held territory in Bosnia and Herzegovina to less than half of the country, precisely the percentage specified in the peace plan endorsed by the Muslims and Croats. This finally persuaded the Bosnian Serbs to negotiate, and on December 14, 1995, with Bosnian Muslim and Croatian leaders, Bosnian Serb leaders signed the Dayton Peace Accords, brokered by the United States. The United States pledged participation in an international force to supervise the separa-

Slobodan Milošević

(1941–2006)

As president of Serbia from 1989–1997, Slobodan Milošević was a fierce nationalist who helped bring about the dissolution of the socialist Yugoslav federation. He then served as president of the Serb-dominated Federal Republic of Yugoslavia from 1997 to 2000.

Born in Serbia, Milošević joined the Communist Party of Yugoslavia as a young man and graduated from the University of Belgrade with a degree in law in 1964. He headed the state-owned gas company, was president of a Belgrade bank, and then entered politics in 1984, rising to the leadership of the League of Communists of Serbia (LCS) in December 1987. In 1989 Milošević became president of Serbia and resisted the anti-socialist, anti-Communist reforms then sweeping Eastern Europe. After Croatia and Slovenia left the Yugoslav federation, Milošević transformed the LCS into the Socialist Party of Serbia and was twice reelected to the Serbian presidency. As more of the federation dissolved, Milošević threw his support behind Serbian militias fighting to force Bosnia and Herzegovina and Croatia to remain united with Serbia. This gave rise to the civil war in Bosnia and Herzegovina.

Pressured militarily by the United States and western Europe and reeling under UN-imposed economic sanctions, Milošević agreed on behalf of the Bosnian Serbs to peace in November 1995; however, in 1998 the long-simmering conflict between Serbia and the ethnic Albanians of Kosovo erupted into full-scale warfare (see Chapter 46). After Serbs launched a major offensive in the spring of 1999, U.S.-led NATO forces retaliated with bombing strikes against Yugoslavia. Milošević stood firm and launched a campaign of ethnic cleansing of the Kosovar Albanians, creating a massive refugee crisis before he finally agreed to a peace accord in June.

In May 1999 the UN International Criminal Tribunal for the Former Yugoslavia, meeting at The Hague, indicted Milošević for war crimes. Defeated in the 2000 presidential elections by opposition leader Vojislav Koštunica, Milošević was arrested by the Yugoslav government in 2001 and remanded to The Hague to be tried for genocide, crimes against humanity, and war crimes. He died in prison on March 12, 2006, before the trial concluded.

tion of military groups within Bosnia and Herzegovina and to enforce the accords.

Struggle toward a U.S. Policy on Bosnia and Herzegovina

By any measure, the Bosnian war was a humanitarian crisis, and the media broadcast to the United States and the world images and stories of brutality and suffering. The media also tended to portray this complex civil war—which involved a tangle of nationalist, ethnic, and religious differences that could be traced back to the Middle Ages—as a straightforward contest of good versus evil, with Slobodan Milošević as a precise analogue to Adolf Hitler. Many Americans and western Europeans demanded aggressive intervention, and the administration of President Bill Clinton was often criticized—by the right as well as the left—for failing to make a major military commitment early in the conflict. Even after Clinton authorized extensive air strikes and humanitarian airlifts during 1993–1994, there were many who believed that only the presence of American ground troops would prove effective in ending a war that was being fought village by village and street by street. These critics were concerned that the reliance on air strikes would create excessive "collateral damage"—that is, a high rate of civilian casualties.

President Bill Clinton is escorted by General William Nash, U.S. Army, while walking past American soldiers saluting them following the president's arrival at the air base in Tuzla in northwest Bosnia and Herzegovina on January 13, 1996. During his front-line visit, the president told the peacekeeping troops they were carrying out a mission of heroes.

Clinton struggled to formulate a U.S. policy in the crisis. He saw U.S. leadership as necessary to end the crisis (and, conversely, the continuation of the crisis as an indictment of U.S. leadership), yet he viewed the crisis as essentially a European problem. During his election campaign in 1992, candidate Clinton had assailed President George H. W. Bush for doing too little to end the Bosnian bloodshed, only to vacillate when he himself entered office. After two-and-a-half years in office, he sent 20,000 American troops (as part of a 60,000-troop NATO force) to Bosnia and Herzegovina in 1995, because he believed that the United States would at some point be compelled to extricate UN peacekeepers or to enforce a peace.

Peace Plans

The Clinton administration formulated its policy against the background of three different peace plans that had been proposed for Bosnia and Herzegovina.

British foreign secretary Lord Carrington and Portugal's ambassador to the European Community (EC), Jorge Cutileiro, formulated the Carrington-Cutileiro plan in September 1991 as an attempt to head off war. The principal ethnic groups in Bosnia and Herzegovina would share power administratively, and the central government would be progressively devolved, until all government would be administered by the local ethnic communities. All of Bosnia and Herzegovina would be divided into Muslim, Serbian, and Croatian districts. Initially the plan was accepted by all three factions, but the Bosnian Muslims withdrew, and the plan collapsed.

In early January 1993 UN special envoy Cyrus Vance and EC representative Lord David Owen proposed the Vance-Owen peace plan, which divided Bosnia and Herzegovina into ten semi-autonomous regions along ethnic and religious lines. Although it was backed by the UN, the Clinton administration was wary of it (fearing that it effectively ratified ethnic cleansing). The Bosnian Serb assembly rejected it on May 5.

Cyrus Vance resigned as UN special envoy on April 1 and was replaced by Norwegian foreign minister Thorvald Stoltenberg on May 1. On August 20, Stoltenberg and Lord Owen proposed partitioning Bosnia into three ethnic states, in which Bosnian Serb forces would be given 52 percent of Bosnia and Herzegovina's territory, Bosnian Muslims would be allotted 30 percent, and Bosnian Croats would receive 18 percent. The Bosnian Muslims rejected the plan on August 29, 1993.

Toward U.S. Ground Intervention

In May 1993 U.S. secretary of state Warren Christopher proposed another plan: exempt the Muslim-dominated Bosnian government from the UN arms embargo to give it an advantage over the Serbs and, if necessary, provide precision air strikes by NATO forces to support the Bosnian government troops. Western European leaders rejected this proposal even as the killing continued in Bosnia and Herzegovina, and the world perceived the United States as hesitant to act.

In June 1995 western European leaders, headed by French president Jacques Chirac—whose nation had the most NATO troops in Bosnia and Herzegovina—pressed for a more aggressive policy against the Serbs. In the meantime, a Croatian offensive in August managed to expel the Serbs from Krajina, Croatia, prompting Milošević to send out peace feelers, even as a Bosnian Serb attack on Sarajevo triggered new NATO air attacks against the Serbs. The U.S. Congress took the initiative by voting to require the Clinton administration to lift the arms embargo on Bosnia and Herzegovina. President Clinton believed that lifting the embargo would prompt the western European NATO members to withdraw their troops unless the United States also made a ground forces commitment. On November 21 and December 14, 1995, the Dayton Peace Accords were signed, creating a federalized Bosnia and Herzegovina divided between a Bosnian Muslim and Croat federation and a Bosnian Serb republic. With the accords in hand, President Clinton felt more comfortable about finally contributing ground forces to the NATO mission. On November 27, he delivered an **Address on Bosnia and Herzegovina,** in which he announced his decision to authorize 20,000 U.S.

Clinton's Address on Bosnia and Herzegovina, 1995

Last week, the warring factions in Bosnia reached a peace agreement as a result of our efforts in Dayton, Ohio, and the support of our European and Russian partners. Tonight I want to speak with you about implementing the Bosnian peace agreement and why our values and interests as Americans require that we participate.

Let me say at the outset America's role will not be about fighting a war. It will be about helping the people of Bosnia to secure their own peace agreement. Our mission will be limited, focused, and under the command of an American general.

In fulfilling this mission, we will have the chance to help stop the killing of innocent civilians, especially children, and at the same time, to bring stability to central Europe, a region of the world that is vital to our national interests. It is the right thing to do.

... [T]he United States led NATO's heavy and continuous air strikes, many of them flown by skilled and brave American pilots. Those air strikes, together with the renewed determination of our European partners, and the Bosnian and Croat gains on the battlefield, convinced the Serbs, finally, to start thinking about making peace. . . .

... [J]ust three weeks ago, the Muslims, Croats and Serbs came to Dayton, Ohio, in America's heartland, to negotiate a settlement. There, exhausted by war, they made a commitment to peace. . . . And they asked for America's help as they implement this peace agreement.

America has a responsibility to answer that request, to help to turn this moment of hope into an enduring reality. To do that, troops from our country and around the world would go into Bosnia to give them the confidence and support they need to implement their peace plan.

Excerpted from William J. Clinton, "Address to the Nation on Implementation of the Peace Agreement in Bosnia-Herzegovina," November 27, 1995, in *Public Papers of the Presidents of the United States: William J. Clinton, 1993–2001,* from the American Presidency Project, University of California, Santa Barbara, www.presidency.ucsb.edu.

ground troops as part of a 60,000-troop NATO army to enforce the accords.

In the end, the Clinton administration justified the commitment of U.S. troops for two reasons in addition to the humanitarian basis. Clinton asserted that the U.S.-led NATO mission was necessary to prevent a possible wider European war and that a NATO failure would weaken the credibility of the alliance and encourage other aggressors to act.

America as Peace Broker: Dayton Accords

Before committing U.S. troops to Bosnia and Herzegovina, the United States brokered the Dayton Peace Accords in a series of conferences held at Wright-Patterson Air Force Base, outside Dayton, Ohio. This process is discussed in the "Serbia, Bosnia and Herzegovina, and Kosovo" section of Chapter 39, "The United States as Peacemaker."

BIBLIOGRAPHY

Burg, Steven L., and Paul S. Shoup. *The War in Bosnia-Herzegovina: Ethnic Conflict and International Intervention.* Armonk, N.Y.: M. E. Sharpe, 2000.

Malcolm, Hoel. *Bosnia: A Short History.* New York: New York University Press, 1996.

At Issue

The civil war in Somalia was (and, at press time, continues to be) a struggle among rival warlords in the context of political anarchy. The United States became involved in the struggle as part of a UN-sanctioned effort to bring humanitarian aid to the stricken country and, in the process, restore order.

The Conflict

Somalia, on the horn of Africa, became independent in 1960; control of the country had been contested by Britain, France, and Italy. Like many former colonial possessions, it has led a chaotic and violent existence since gaining its independence. Its first president, Cabdirashiid Cali Sherma'arke, was assassinated in 1969 in a military coup d'état led by Major General Maxamed Siyaad Barre, who replaced the parliamentary government with a dictatorial Supreme Revolutionary Council. Barre aligned himself with the Soviet Union and invaded Ethiopia in an attempt to annex the Ogaden region. The Soviets, however, shifted their support to Ethiopia. Barre's invasion was defeated, and the Barre government progressively disintegrated, leaving no central authority in its place. By the spring of 1988, Somalia was in anarchy, torn between feuding clans led by warlords. At this time, the Somali National Movement (SNM) began seizing towns and military facilities in the north of the country, killing thousands of civilians and also creating many thousands of refugees, who fled to Ethiopia.

Although much of the country came under the control of the SNM, Mogadishu, the Somali capital, remained in Barre's hands. In March 1989 government troops belonging to the Ogadeni clan mutinied against Barre in Kismayo. That rebellion was not suppressed until July, by which time the SNM had seized even more of the country. Amid intense violence, UN and other aid workers were evacuated in May 1989.

On July 9, 1989, the Catholic bishop of Mogadishu was assassinated, and violence swept the capital. In an effort to preserve power, Barre announced multiparty elections. Various rebel factions thwarted the voting, then staged a coup against Barre. Although he was effectively without a country, Barre nevertheless clung to his title as 1990 came to a close. At this point, the renewed promise of free elections was sufficient to bring a fleeting intermission in the civil war; however, the rival clans soon began the fighting anew.

By late 1990 the major warlord rivals were General Mohamed Farrah Aidid, of the Hawiye clan and leader of the Somali National Alliance (SNA), and Ali Mahdi Muhammad, of a different Hawiye subclan and leader of the Somali Salvation Alliance (SSA). In January 1991 Barre finally fled the country and was replaced by Ali Mahdi. In September Aidid, who had become chair of the United Somali Congress (USC), challenged Ali Mahdi for the presidency. This resulted in renewed fighting in Mogadishu and put an end even to the appearance of organized government.

In May 1991, with southern Somalia in complete anarchy, Muhammad Ibrahim Egal led the secession of northeastern Somalia, creating the breakaway Somaliland. After a brief interval of stability there, fighting broke out in the regional capital of Hargeysa, led by factions opposed to secession. The international community also generally refused to recognize the legitimacy of Somaliland.

The continual civil war devastated an already impoverished people. To compound matters, a severe drought brought some 1.5 to 2 million Somalis to the brink of starvation by the early 1990s. In 1992 U.S. president George H. W. Bush announced the U.S.-led and UN-sanctioned Operation Restore Hope to bring humanitarian aid and restore order to Somalia. In December 1992 the first of a contingent of 28,000 U.N. troops, including Americans, arrived to transport and distribute food and attempt to bring an end to the violence. By the end of March 1993—and the beginning of President Bill Clinton's first term—a great deal of food had been delivered, but the U.S.-led UN troops had not been successful in disarming the various warlords' militias.

In June–July 1993 Aidid went on the offensive, killing many Somalis and some UN peacekeepers. The Clinton administration called for broadening the UN mandate to include aggressive action against Aidid. This was met with dissension among the nations participating in Operation Restore Hope. During October 3–4, 1993, a U.S. Special Forces detachment, Task Force Ranger, entered Mogadishu to raid the Olympic Hotel in an effort to capture Aidid. The result was the downing of an American Black Hawk helicopter and the ambush of the task force detachment in a seventeen-hour battle in which sixteen U.S. soldiers were killed and fifty-four were wounded. One wounded helicopter pilot was also taken prisoner. The American media broadcast grisly images of a dead Special Forces soldier being dragged through the streets of Mogadishu. With this, the essential hopelessness of the intervention in Somalia became apparent to the American public and politicians alike. Popular pressure mounted to withdraw U.S. forces from Somalia, and by March

CHRONOLOGY OF U.S. INTERVENTION IN THE SOMALI CIVIL WAR

1988
Spring Rival Somali warlords begin a civil war.

1989
May UN and other relief workers are evacuated.
July 9 The assassination of the Catholic bishop of Mogadishu unleashes violence in the capital. President Siyaad Barre immediately calls for elections but is effectively neutralized (although not actually removed) by a coup d'état.

1990
• Mohamed Farrah Aidid (leader of the Somali National Alliance) and Ali Mahdi Muhammad (leader of the Somali Salvation Alliance) emerge as principal rivals for power.

1992
March 3 Warlords sign a UN-brokered cease-fire agreement
Aug. 15 The UN launches Operation Provide Relief.
Dec. 5 The UN accepts President George H. W. Bush's offer of military protection for UN humanitarian workers.

Dec. 9 The first U.S Marines land in Somalia as Operation Restore Hope begins.

1993
Mar. 15–28 The UN brokers new cease-fire agreements among the Somali warlords.
May 4 UN forces take over peacekeeping duties from U.S. troops.
June 5–6 Pakistani troops are ambushed; the UN calls for the apprehension of those responsible, which is interpreted as an order to capture Aidid.
Aug. 26 Task Force Ranger arrives in Somalia; its mission is to capture Aidid.
Oct. 3–4 Members of Task Force Ranger are ambushed. Televised images of the shocking aftermath raise a public cry in the United States for the immediate withdrawal of troops.

1994
Mar. 31 The deadline for U.S. withdrawal is met, thereby ending American involvement in the war.

Mohamed Farrah Aidid

(1934–1996)

A leader of the Habr Gidr subclan of the Hawiye clan in Somalia, Mohamed Farrah Aidid led a coup d'état against Maxamed Siyaad Barre and challenged UN and U.S. forces in his bid to maintain power in Somalia.

Aidid was educated in Rome and Moscow and served the Barre government as chief of intelligence. Barre suspected him of disloyalty and sent him to prison for six years, but in 1991 Aidid's clan overthrew Barre, and Aidid emerged as one of the dominant warlords in the country's civil war.

Aidid resisted efforts by UN and U.S. peacekeeping forces to bring sufficient order to the country to allow elections, and he managed to elude capture, effectively outlasting the Americans and the United Nations, who withdrew their troops from Somalia. In 1995, after the last UN soldiers had withdrawn, Aidid declared himself president of the country but failed to win recognition from any other nation. He succumbed on August 1, 1996, to wounds sustained in a gunfight with rival warlords.

1994 most U.S. and European troops had been withdrawn.

At about the time of the U.S. and European withdrawal, Aidid and Ali Mahdi met in Kenya to negotiate a coalition government for Somalia; however, the meeting only produced intensified fighting. In March 1995 the 19,000 remaining UN troops (all from African member nations) withdrew from Somalia, leaving Aidid and Ali Mahdi claiming leadership of the southern part of the country while the Somali Salvation Democratic Front (SSDF) controlled the northeast. The rest of the nation was divided among three lesser factions. Aidid died on August 1, 1996, from wounds received in a gunfight and was succeeded by Hussein Aidid, his son. Although the elder Aidid's death brought a lull in the fighting, Somalia remained in a state of low-level civil war.

Policy under President George H. W. Bush

Initially President George H. W. Bush continued the policy of the Reagan administration with regard to Somalia. The United States considered the country strategically valuable as a potential staging area for military operations in the Indian Ocean, the Red Sea, and the Persian Gulf. Under Reagan and at the start of the Bush administration, the United States provided economic, military, and diplomatic support to the Barre regime. By September 1989, however, reports of brutality and human rights abuses by Barre's regime became so frequent that the Bush administration began limiting aid to the government, which, without U.S. assistance, progressively disintegrated.

On March 3, 1992, leaders of warring factions signed a cease-fire agreement, which included provisions for a UN monitoring mission into Somalia. On April 24, the UN observers arrived, and Operation Provide Relief launched the humanitarian phase of the UN mission on August 15. Security rapidly deteriorated as warlords and armed gangs hijacked relief supplies and assaulted aid workers. The UN appealed to member nations for military aid to protect the humanitarian workers, and on December 5 the UN accepted President Bush's proposal to provide troops, 25,000 of whom were ordered into Somalia. The first contingent of U.S Marines landed on December 9.

In his December 4, 1992, **Address on Somalia,** President Bush explained that the troops' objective would be to provide a secure environment for

Bush's Address on Somalia, 1992

I want to talk to you today about the tragedy in Somalia and about a mission that can ease suffering and save lives. Every American has seen the shocking images from Somalia. The scope of suffering there is hard to imagine. Already, over a quarter-million people, as many people as live in Buffalo, New York, have died in the Somali famine. In the months ahead 5 times that number, 1 1/2 million people, could starve to death.

For many months now, the United States has been actively engaged in the massive international relief effort to ease Somalia's suffering. All told, America has sent Somalia 200,000 tons of food, more than half the world total. This summer, the distribution system broke down. Truck convoys from Somalia's ports were blocked. Sufficient food failed to reach the starving in the interior of Somalia. . . .

. . . There is no government in Somalia. Law and order have broken down. Anarchy prevails. . . .

. . . It's now clear that military support is necessary to ensure the safe delivery of the food Somalis need to survive. . . .

After consulting with my advisers, with world leaders, and the congressional leadership, I have today told Secretary-General Boutros-Ghali that America will answer the call. I have given the order to [Defense] Secretary Cheney to move a substantial American force into Somalia. . . .

We will not, however, be acting alone. I expect forces from about a dozen countries to join us in this mission. . . .

. . . Our mission has a limited objective: To open the supply routes, to get the food moving, and to prepare the way for a U.N. peacekeeping force to keep it moving. This operation is not open-ended. We will not stay one day longer than is absolutely necessary. . . .

. . . We will not fail.

Excerpted from George Bush, "Address to the Nation on the Situation in Somalia," December 4, 1992, in *Public Papers of the Presidents of the United States: George Bush, 1989–1993,* from the American Presidency Project, University of California, Santa Barbara, www.presidency.ucsb.edu.

---

humanitarian aid workers. Once this was established, the entire operation would be turned over to the UN peacekeeping forces. He announced that the troops would be home by the time President Bill Clinton was inaugurated in January. This US-led defense force was called Operation Restore Hope.

Policy under President Bill Clinton

Contrary to plans, American troops did not leave Somalia by Clinton's inauguration, and the new president, believing that the mission in Somalia would be better handled by UN troops from African nations, was anxious to scale down the U.S. military presence there. During March 15–28, 1993, the UN-organized Conference on National Reconciliation in Somalia convened in Addis Ababa, Ethiopia, and emerged with an agreement among the leaders of the various Somali factions. On May 4 UNOSOM II, a UN

peacekeeping operation, officially took over from the U.S. peacekeepers. President Clinton accordingly ordered a sharp reduction in U.S. troop strength, and by June only 1,200 American combat soldiers and 3,000 support troops remained in Somalia.

On June 5, twenty-four Pakistani soldiers (operating under UN authority) were ambushed and killed while on a weapons inspection mission. In an emergency resolution on June 6, the UN Security Council called for the apprehension of "those responsible." It was an order generally interpreted as a call to capture Aidid. During June and July U.S. (and UN) military activity escalated, as the hunt for Aidid was pressed. On August 26, a Special Forces unit, Task Force Ranger—440 elite troops from Delta Force and the Army Rangers—arrived in country with the specific mission of capturing Aidid.

During this manhunt, the Clinton administration in September authorized a secret initiative to negotiate with Aidid, and former president Jimmy Carter volunteered to serve as an intermediary. President Clinton did not inform military commanders of this effort, which came to nothing. Meanwhile, Secretary of Defense Les Aspin denied U.S. Army requests for reinforcements—especially tanks—to augment the U.S. force in Somalia. Acting according to Clinton's directions, Aspin was trying to avoid the appearance of a U.S. military buildup that might reduce the chances for a negotiated peace; however, the effect of the failure to supply an adequate armored force was to keep the U.S. military in Somalia undermanned and underequipped. Worse, the commanders in the field were never made fully aware of the administration's intention to maintain a low military profile. This led to resentment of the administration. Rela-

tions between the Clinton White House and the Pentagon became strained, and the Clinton administration was increasingly accused of both failing to define and to support the mission in Somalia adequately.

"Black Hawk Down," 1993

As mentioned in "The Conflict," above, Task Force Ranger's assault on the Olympic Hotel in Mogadishu to apprehend Aidid resulted in the downing of a U.S. Black Hawk helicopter, an ambush, and the seventeen-hour firefight during October 3–4, 1993. In addition to the sixteen American soldiers killed and fifty-four wounded in the battle (and the taking of a wounded prisoner), three more soldiers were killed and thirty-four more were wounded over the next

Call for Withdrawal of Troops, 1993

[Senator Phil Gramm, R-Texas]: I rise to speak about Somalia.

Mr. President, I believe, and I have always believed, that partisanship should end at the water's edge. As a result, I have tried to support our President in foreign affairs in each and every circumstance that I could.

I intend to support the President's decision to send reinforcements to Somalia, but only to protect the Americans that are there. . . .

We went to Somalia on December 9 in a great humanitarian effort to do one and only one thing, and that was to feed a hungry people. By any definition of the mission, that mission was finished by June of this year.

But, rather than saying that we had achieved what we went to Somalia to do, instead of taking the bow that was due Americans for their sacrifice and their commitment on behalf of a needy people halfway around the world, we started to change our mission. We, today, find ourselves in a combat role where Americans are being targeted, where Americans are being fired upon, and where Americans are dying.

Mr. President, I do not believe that the American people ever signed on to this new mission. I do not believe that Congress ever supported a mission in

Somalia other than feeding hungry people. I believe that mission is complete.

I am going to support the President in sending additional combat troops in order to, No. 1, protect the Americans that are there; and, No. 2, to do whatever we have to do to obtain the freedom of any American that is held hostage. I think it is imperative that we take actions to bring Americans home.

The President's decision to extend our presence for 6 more months is totally unacceptable to me and totally unacceptable, I believe, to the Congress.

If the people of Texas—who are calling my phones every moment, who are sending me letters and telegrams by the hour—are representative of the will of the American people, the American people do not believe that we should allow Americans to be targets in Somalia for 6 more months. I cannot see anything that we would achieve in 6 more months in Somalia being worth the precious lives of more Americans.

I want to help the President. I am concerned that the President has no coherent policy. If he has it, he has certainly kept it to himself.

Excerpted from "SOMALIA (Senate—October 07, 1993)," in *Congressional Record*, 103d Cong., 1st sess., October 7, 1993, S13208, at THOMAS, Library of Congress, http://thomas.loc.gov/home/r103query.html.

several days. (The prisoner was subsequently recovered.) Estimated Somali casualties were 500–1,500. Televised coverage of the aftermath of the Mogadishu ambush, including horrific images of a dead U.S. Special Forces soldier being dragged through the streets of Mogadishu, raised a cry in the United States for immediate withdrawal from Somalia. Senator Phil Gramm (R-Texas) was one among many in Congress who made a **Call for Withdrawal of Troops.** Gramm and other administration critics contended that emergency humanitarian relief was an appropriate goal for a U.S. expeditionary force, but longer-term nation building was not. They worried that a relatively small number of U.S. ground forces was being assigned the impossible role of playing referee among an array of anarchic warlords.

Although President Clinton sent substantial numbers of combat troops to Somalia as short-term reinforcements, he declared that all American forces would be withdrawn by March 31, 1994. On this date, the hunt for Aidid was ended, as was U.S. involvement in the Somali Civil War.

BIBLIOGRAPHY

Allard, Kenneth. *Somalia Operations: Lessons Learned.* Washington, D.C.: National Defense University Press, 1997.

Bowden, Mark. *Black Hawk Down: A Story of Modern War.* New York: Grove/Atlantic, 1999.

Stevenson, Jonathan. *Losing Mogadishu: Testing U.S. Policy in Somalia.* Annapolis, Md.: Naval Institute Press, 1995.

At Issue

The Dayton Accords, which ended the war in Bosnia and Herzegovina (see Chapters 39 and 44), failed to address the long-simmering problem of independence for the autonomous Yugoslav province of Kosovo. This failure convinced Kosovars who desired independence that only war would win it for them.

The Conflict

One of the many issues related to the war in Bosnia and Herzegovina (Chapter 44) was the question of total independence for Kosovo, an autonomous province of Serbian-dominated Yugoslavia. When the Dayton Accords (see Chapter 39), which ended the Bosnian war, failed to address this issue, the Kosovo Liberation Army (KLA)—a new militant organization that chiefly represented Kosovo's ethnic Albanians (the group most intensely seeking independence)—emerged in 1996 to launch guerrilla attacks on Serbian police forces. Over the next two years, the KLA attacked repeatedly, finally prompting Yugoslav president Slobodan Milošević in early 1998 to send troops to crush Kosovo's bid for independence once and for all. This resulted in a new civil war.

The North Atlantic Treaty Organization (NATO) and the United Nations attempted to broker peace; however, talks in Rambouillet, France, dissolved in March 1999 after the KLA accepted the settlement but the Serbs rejected key portions (see Chapter 39). Yugoslav Serb forces launched a new round of "ethnic cleansing" to drive out all of Kosovo's ethnic Albanians. This campaign, accompanied by all-too-familiar atrocities, created hundreds of thousands of refugees, who fled into Albania, Macedonia, and Montenegro.

On March 23, U.S. president Bill Clinton agreed with other NATO member nations that a military response was necessary. On March 24, the United States led NATO air strikes against Serbian Yugoslavia, targeting military positions in Serbia, Montenegro, and Kosovo. U.S. Navy ships also launched attacks using cruise missiles. The combined assault was the largest in Europe since World War II. It did not deter Milošević, however, who continued the campaign against the ethnic Albanians, even as the air war stretched over a ten-week period. Ultimately, about 35,000 sorties were flown, most of them directed against military targets, but also some against portions of the civilian infrastructure, including water, electric, and natural gas facilities. On June 3, 1999, Milošević finally backed down, declaring his acceptance of the international peace plan he had earlier rejected.

The war killed approximately 5,000 Yugoslav soldiers and 1,200 civilians. KLA, militia, and other casualties are unknown. Hundreds of thousands of refugees were displaced. Among NATO forces, two aircraft were lost, including one U.S. F-117 stealth fighter. (The American pilots were rescued.) The most serious instance of collateral damage was the accidental targeting and destruction of the Chinese embassy in Belgrade on May 7. The war did not include any U.S. or NATO ground attacks, although

U.S. troops formed part of the NATO peacekeeping contingent that entered Kosovo after the war.

U.S. Policy Evolves

As violence erupted in Kosovo in 1996, the Clinton administration, like many other Western governments, initially paid little attention, apparently hoping that the Dayton Accords had settled all Yugoslav issues. Few Americans, citizens and politicians alike, wanted to intervene in Yugoslav affairs again. Yet as the violence continued, a six-nation "Contact Group" was established in January 1997 among Britain, France, Germany, Italy, Russia, and the United States to formulate a coordinated and coherent response to the Kosovo crisis. The meetings of the group produced little.

Late in 1997 Sali Berisha, the progressive president of Albania, was voted out of office amid a massive economic scandal. The resulting chaos exposed

CHRONOLOGY OF THE KOSOVO CRISIS

1996–1998
- The Kosovo Liberation Army (KLA) is formed; guerrilla war begins in Kosovo.

1998
Feb. Yugoslav president Slobodan Milošević sends troops to Kosovo.
Oct. 12 Milošević agrees to a truce, but fighting resumes in December.

1999
Jan. 15 The Racak Incident motivates NATO to act.
Feb. Rambouillet conference
Mar. 18 Kosovar ethnic Albanians agree to the Rambouillet Accord, but the Serbs reject key parts of the agreement.
Mar. 24–June 11 NATO launches U.S.-led air strikes.
April–June Serb forces continue the "ethnic cleansing" of Albanians in Kosovo.
May 7 A NATO aircraft accidentally bombs the Chinese Embassy in Belgrade.
June 3 Milošević agrees to accept the Rambouillet Accords.

Albanian military stockpiles to looting, with much of the weaponry finding its way into the KLA arsenal. This escalated the conflict in Kosovo into a major guerrilla war, which came to involve Serbian police, special Serbian paramilitary police, and Serbian militia forces, thereby igniting a full-scale civil war.

As with the war in Bosnia and Herzegovina, media reports began bringing to the West stories and images of the horrors of ethnic violence. Of particular concern was the massive influx of Kosovar Albanian refugees into Macedonia, which threatened to bring civil war to that precariously poised country that had gained independence from Yugoslavia in 1991. NATO and the European Union (EU) believed that a civil war in Macedonia would also endanger Serbia, Albania, Greece, and Bulgaria; all four of these countries had territorial claims on Macedonia. There was even the possibility that Turkey would become involved in a greater Balkan conflict, because it claimed an interest in "protecting" the Albanians, who were its former subjects. In this dangerous climate, NATO and the EU decided that concerted action was required. The Clinton administration agreed.

The initial course of action was nothing more than a bid to persuade the KLA to stop seeking independence and simultaneously to convince Milošević to permit NATO peacekeeping troops to enter Kosovo. A cease-fire was negotiated, commencing on October 25, 1998, and a contingent of unarmed Organization for Security and Cooperation in Europe (OSCE) peace monitors was admitted into Kosovo. This proved entirely inadequate, and the cease-fire broke down almost immediately as fighting resumed in December 1998.

KLA attacks and Serbian reprisals continued through the winter of 1998–1999, culminating on January 15, 1999, with the so-called Racak Incident, a massacre of forty-five ethnic Albanians in a Kosovo village of about 350 inhabitants. The world had seen ethnic cleansing before, but this incident was widely perceived as a deliberate, cold-blooded massacre by Yugoslav security forces, and it therefore became the tipping point for NATO, which decided that a military peacekeeping force was now required.

President Clinton endorsed a January 30, 1999, **NATO Statement on Kosovo** declaring that the alliance was prepared to launch air strikes against Yugoslav targets "to compel compliance with the demands of the international community"; such use of force against Yugoslavia would depend on the "position and actions of the Kosovo Albanian leadership and all Kosovo Albanian armed elements in and around Kosovo."

Simultaneously with the NATO declaration, the six-nation Contact Group issued what it called "non-negotiable principles," including the restoration of Kosovo's pre-1990 autonomy within Serbia, the introduction of democracy into Kosovo, and supervision by international monitors. The Contact Group called for a peace conference to be held in February 1999 at the Château de Rambouillet, outside Paris. Those talks began on February 6 (see Chapter 39).

Operation Allied Force

After the Rambouillet talks collapsed, the OSCE international monitors withdrew on March 22 in anticipation of the NATO bombing campaign. On March 23, the Serbian assembly accepted the principle of autonomy for Kosovo and the nonmilitary portions of the Rambouillet agreement but refused to allow what it termed a "NATO occupation" of Yugoslav territory. On March 24, therefore, the U.S.-led NATO bombing began. Operation Allied Force would not end until June 11, 1999.

Public Response to an Air-Only War

Although most Americans supported President Clinton's decision to intervene in Kosovo, they were divided on the effectiveness of the Clinton administration's decision to wage an air-only war, and many believed that ground troops would eventually have to be committed to compel a definitive resolution to the conflict. The Clinton Administration perceived air strikes as safer for American troops. Critics objected

---

NATO Statement on Kosovo, 1999

NATO stands ready to act. We rule out no option to ensure full respect by both sides in Kosovo for the requirements of the international community. . . .

NATO's decisions today contribute to creating the conditions for a rapid and successful negotiation on an interim political settlement which provides for an enhanced status for Kosovo, preserves the territorial integrity of the Federal Republic of Yugoslavia and protects the rights of all ethnic groups. NATO is resolved to persevere until the violence in Kosovo has ended, and a political solution has been reached.

North Atlantic Treaty Organization, "Statement to the Press by NATO Secretary General Javier Solana," www.nato.int/docu/speech/1999/s990130a.htm.

---

that even in the age of precision-guided "smart weapons," collateral damage—in the form of civilian casualties—would be unacceptably high. (An estimated 2,500 to 5,000 civilians were killed, in fact, as a result of the NATO air campaign.)

Critics also argued that an air-only war was only half a commitment. Yet even among those who believed an air war would be insufficient to resolve the Kosovo crisis, only a minority favored actually committing U.S. ground troops. This public opinion conflict reflected an ongoing national ambivalence over military intervention in distant wars. The humanitarian impulse to help oppressed people was powerful, but there was also a profound reluctance to commit American lives to the struggle on the ground.

Resolution

By June the Milošević government agreed to a military withdrawal from Kosovo and pledged to abide by all of the Rambouillet Accords. President Clinton,

Clinton's Address on the End of the War, 1999

My fellow Americans, tonight for the first time in 79 days, the skies over Yugoslavia are silent. The Serb army and police are withdrawing from Kosovo. The one million men, women, and children driven from their land are preparing to return home. The demands of an outraged and united international community have been met.

I can report to the American people that we have achieved a victory for a safer world, for our democratic values, and for a stronger America. . . .

When I ordered our Armed Forces into combat, we had three clear goals: to enable the Kosovar people, the victims of some of the most vicious atrocities in Europe since the Second World War, to return to their homes with safety and self-government; to require Serbian forces responsible for those atrocities to leave Kosovo; and to deploy an international security force, with NATO at its core, to protect all the people of that troubled land, Serbs and Albanians, alike. Those goals will be achieved. A necessary conflict has been brought to a just and honorable conclusion. . . .

. . . This victory brings a new hope that when a people are singled out for destruction because of their heritage and religious faith and we can do something about it, the world will not look the other way.

Excerpted from William J. Clinton, "Address to the Nation on the Military Technical Agreement on Kosovo," June 10, 1999, in *Public Papers of the Presidents of the United States: William J. Clinton, 1993–2001,* from the American Presidency Project, University of California, Santa Barbara, www.presidency.ucsb.edu.

---

in his June 10, 1999, **Address on the End of the War,** proclaimed that the United States had "achieved a victory for a safer world, for our democratic values, and for a stronger America."

By UN Security Council Resolution 1244 (1999), Kosovo was defined as an autonomous province within the former Federal Republic of Yugoslavia under UN administration. Talks between Kosovar and Serbian negotiators on Kosovo's future status began in Vienna, Austria, on February 20, 2006. As of the summer of 2006, the government of Kosovo was conducted by Provisional Institutions of Self-Government and the UN Interim Administrative Mission in Kosovo (UNMIK). Security was maintained by NATO troops, including a contingent from the United States.

BIBLIOGRAPHY

Glenny, Misha. *The Balkans: Nationalism, War, and the Great Powers, 1804–1999.* New York: Penguin, 2001.

Judah, Tim. *Kosovo: War and Revenge,* 2d ed. New Haven, Ct.: Yale University Press, 2002.

Mertus, Julie A. *Kosovo: How Myths and Truths Started a War.* Berkeley: University of California Press, 1999.

CHAPTER 47

WAR IN AFGHANISTAN AND THE WAR ON TERROR (2001–)

At Issue

On September 11, 2001, Muslim extremists affiliated with al-Qaida hijacked commercial airliners and crashed them into the World Trade Center in New York City and the Pentagon in Arlington, Virginia. The United States responded by launching a war against al-Qaida bases in Afghanistan and against the Taliban, the Islamic fundamentalist regime that harbored and supported them. The war in Afghanistan developed as part of a wider "war on terror."

The Conflict

On September 11, 2001, four U.S. commercial airliners were hijacked. They were used as human-guided missiles: Two were flown into the twin towers of the World Trade Center in New York City and one was crashed into the Pentagon in Arlington, Virginia (outside Washington, D.C.). The fourth aircraft, which was apparently targeting the U.S. Capitol or the White House, crashed in rural Pennsylvania when passengers attempted to wrest control from the hijackers. Approximately 2,893 people were killed in the World Trade Center attack. An additional 189 people were killed in the attack on the Pentagon, and 44 passengers and crew members died in the Pennsylvania crash.

The hijackers were quickly identified as members of al-Qaida (Arabic for "the Base"), which was described as a terrorist organization by the U.S. government. At the time of the attacks, al-Qaida was led by Osama bin Laden, a multimillionaire Muslim

extremist. Although he was Saudi by nationality, he lived in Afghanistan, where he and al-Qaida enjoyed the protection of the radical Islamic Taliban government. Bin Laden and al-Qaida declared a *jihad* (holy war) against Israel and the West—in particular, the United States. Prior to the September 11 attacks, al-Qaida had been under surveillance by the U.S. government and was considered responsible for the

CHRONOLOGY OF THE WAR IN AFGHANISTAN

2001

Sept. 11 Al-Qaida operatives use hijacked airliners to attack the World Trade Center in New York City and the Pentagon in Arlington, Virginia. A fourth hijacked plane crashes in rural Pennsylvania.

Sept. 12 President George W. Bush announces "the first war of the twenty-first century."

Sept. 18 Congress passes a joint resolution authorizing the use of military force.

Sept. 20 President Bush defines the "war on terror" in a speech to a joint session of Congress.

Oct. 7 Air strikes are launched against the Taliban and al-Qaida in Afghanistan.

Oct. 20 U.S. Special Forces join with the Afghan Northern Alliance to stage the first ground raids on Taliban positions.

Nov. 12 U.S. and Northern Alliance forces take Mazar-e Sharif.

Nov. 13 The Northern Alliance occupies Kabul.

Dec. Kandahar, last major Taliban stronghold, falls

2002–

- Low-level guerrilla warfare continues in Afghanistan.

1993 bombing of the World Trade Center; the bombing of American embassies in Nairobi, Kenya, and Dar es Salaam, Tanzania, in 1998; and the 2001 suicide bombing of the U.S. destroyer *Cole* in Yemen. (In retaliation for the embassy bombings, in August 1998 the Clinton administration ordered missile strikes against alleged al-Qaida–related facilities in Sudan and Afghanistan, but bin Laden escaped serious injury.)

On September 12, 2001, President George W. Bush remarked, "We have just seen the first war of the twenty-first century," and on September 20, he made a televised **Address to a Joint Session of Congress** to announce the nation's new war footing and to pledge that the battle would be taken to the Taliban and al-Qaida.

In the days following September 11, U.S. military forces were deployed to strategic positions from which they could attack Afghanistan. The Bush administration made a successful diplomatic effort to secure the support of many nations in prosecuting a "war against terror." Even Pakistan, which shares a border with Afghanistan and had supported the Taliban regime, agreed to permit U.S. aircraft to fly within its air space and to use certain air base facilities. More remarkably, Iran—hostile to the United States since the fall of the shah and the hostage crisis of 1979–1981— agreed to permit flyovers and to accept emergency landings. Only Iraq refused to cooperate.

On October 7, the United States attacked Taliban targets in Afghanistan using B-1 bombers and the more advanced B-2 "stealth" bombers, as well as B-52s and cruise missiles. The air attacks continued until the Afghans' major air defenses had been wiped out and American and British aircraft could operate in Afghan air space with virtual impunity. Daylight raids were then added, and high-altitude bombers were replaced by lower-altitude strike aircraft, which searched for such "targets of opportunity" as vehicles, aircraft on the ground, and troops.

As U.S. and British aircraft targeted military objectives, including al-Qaida camps and Taliban installa-

Bush's Address to a Joint Session of Congress, September 20, 2001

On September 11th, enemies of freedom committed an act of war against our country. . . .

Americans have many questions tonight. Americans are asking, who attacked our country? The evidence we have gathered all points to a collection of loosely affiliated terrorist organizations known as Al Qaida. They are some of the murderers indicted for bombing American Embassies in Tanzania and Kenya, and responsible for bombing the U.S.S. *Cole*. Al Qaida is to terror what the Mafia is to crime. But its goal is not making money. Its goal is remaking the world and imposing its radical beliefs on people everywhere.

The terrorists practice a fringe form of Islamic extremism that has been rejected by Muslim scholars and the vast majority of Muslim clerics, a fringe movement that perverts the peaceful teachings of Islam. The terrorists' directive commands them to kill Christians and Jews, to kill all Americans, and make no distinctions among military and civilians, including women and children.

This group and its leader, a person named Osama bin Laden, are linked to many other organizations in different countries, including the Egyptian Islamic Jihad and the Islamic Movement of Uzbekistan. There are thousands of these terrorists in more than 60 countries. They are recruited from their own nations and neighborhoods and brought to camps in places like Afghanistan, where they are trained in the tactics of terror. They are sent back to their homes or sent to hide in countries around the world to plot evil and destruction.

The leadership of Al Qaida has great influence in Afghanistan and supports the Taliban regime in controlling most of that country. In Afghanistan, we see Al Qaida's vision for the world. . . .

tions, efforts were made to avoid killing civilians. Indeed, even as the air raids were being carried out, U.S. Air Force cargo transports dropped food packages and other supplies. The objective was to demonstrate support for the Afghan people while simultaneously destabilizing the Taliban by undercutting its popular support. With the Taliban neutralized, there would be an end to government support of al-Qaida and similar groups in Afghanistan. Another U.S. war objective was the capture or killing of bin Laden and others the government deemed to be terrorist leaders.

The air strikes were intended to prepare for action on the ground. Afghanistan's conventional military consisted of approximately 45,000 troops. The adversaries of more concern were the irregular forces associated with al-Qaida. For the ground war, the United States chose an unconventional approach. On October 20, approximately 100 U.S. Special Forces troops coordinated with the so-called Northern Alliance, a guerrilla army of about 15,000 Afghani opponents of the Taliban regime, to raid Tal-

iban facilities. It was the first of many such raids. By supplying and operating in concert with the Northern Alliance, the United States sought to hasten the collapse of the Taliban.

During November, U.S. and Northern Alliance attacks against Taliban positions made significant headway. On November 12, Mazar-e Sharif, a strategic gateway between Afghanistan and Pakistan, was captured by the Northern Alliance after preliminary bombardment by U.S. aircraft. On November 13, the Afghan capital city of Kabul was occupied by Northern Alliance troops, and by the end of November, the northern Taliban stronghold of Kunduz was also captured. Before the year ended, Kandahar, the only major city still held by the Taliban, fell to American and Northern Alliance troops after a long siege. But despite these victories, Osama bin Laden and many other al-Qaida leaders remained at large.

After the Taliban regime was removed, a pro-Western interim government was installed in

And tonight, the United States of America makes the following demands on the Taliban: Deliver to United States authorities all the leaders of Al Qaida who hide in your land. . . . Close immediately and permanently every terrorist training camp in Afghanistan, and hand over every terrorist and every person in their support structure to appropriate authorities. Give the United States full access to terrorist training camps, so we can make sure they are no longer operating. These demands are not open to negotiation or discussion. The Taliban must act and act immediately. They will hand over the terrorists, or they will share in their fate.

I also want to speak tonight directly to Muslims throughout the world. We respect your faith. . . .

Its teachings are good and peaceful. . . . The enemy of America is not our many Muslim friends; it is not our many Arab friends. Our enemy is a radical network of terrorists and every government that supports them.

Our response involves far more than instant retaliation and isolated strikes. Americans should not expect one battle but a lengthy campaign, unlike any other we have ever seen. . . . Every nation, in every region, now has a decision to make. Either you are with us, or you are with the terrorists. From this day forward, any nation that continues to harbor or support terrorism will be regarded by the United States as a hostile regime.

Excerpted from George W. Bush, "Address Before a Joint Session of the Congress on the United States Response to the Terrorist Attacks of September 11," September 20, 2001, in *Public Papers of the Presidents of the United States: George W. Bush, 2001–*, from the American Presidency Project, University of California, Santa Barbara, www.presidency.ucsb.edu.

Osama bin Laden

(1957–)

Osama bin Laden was born in Riyadh, Saudi Arabia, one of more than fifty children in a wealthy Saudi family. He went to Afghanistan to join the resistance after the Soviet Union invaded in 1979. Following the Soviet withdrawal a decade later, bin Laden returned to Saudi Arabia, where he was greeted as a hero. He, however, was appalled by what he saw as the corruption of the Saudi government and its close cooperation with the United States, including its hosting of U.S. troops during the Persian Gulf War (Chapter 43).

Bin Laden became increasingly fundamentalist in his practice of Islam and, probably by 1993, formed al-Qaida, which originally consisted of militant Muslims alongside whom bin Laden had fought in Afghanistan. Al-Qaida trained, planned, or funded numerous violent attacks worldwide, including the 1993 bombing of the World Trade Center in New York City. (This was followed by the bombing of American embassies in Nairobi, Kenya, and Dar es Salaam, Tanzania, in 1998; the suicide bombing of the

U.S. destroyer *Cole* in Yemen in 2001; and the attacks of September 11, 2001.)

In 1994 the Saudi government confiscated bin Laden's passport, accusing him of subversive activities. He fled to Sudan, in Africa, where he founded al-Qaida training camps. The Sudanese government expelled him in 1996, and he ultimately returned to Afghanistan, where he found support from the Taliban.

During 1996–1998, bin Laden issued *fatwas* (religious opinions) which constituted a declaration of *jihad* (holy war) against the United States. According to his own pronouncements, bin Laden's overriding goal was to embroil the United States in a major war with the entire Muslim world, which would result in the destruction of moderate Muslim governments and the elevation of radical Muslim powers. These would establish the Caliphate—a single vast Islamic state. Al-Qaida was to be an instrument of this transformation.

After the U.S.-led effort in Afghanistan removed the Taliban from power, bin Laden went into hiding.

Afghanistan, which was ratified in 2005 by the first free elections held in Afghanistan in thirty-three years. Despite this achievement, in 2006 Afghanistan remained a dangerous and unstable place, in which elements of the Taliban remained active.

Asymmetrical Warfare: Formulating Policy and Doctrine

The day after the attacks of September 11, 2001, President Bush identified the United States as the target of the "first war of the twenty-first century." The president defined terrorist attacks as acts of war. Rather than merely defending itself against future attacks, the United States would go on the offense to

fight a "war on terror." This new type of war was described as "asymmetrical," meaning that it pitted a large and powerful state (the United States) against much smaller forces, often based on ideology rather than affiliation with a state. Indeed, the president took pains to explain that the United States was not fighting Afghanistan or Muslims but the Taliban, a regime that supported terrorism. Afghanistan was a physical target in the war on terror because al-Qaida bases were concentrated there.

Bipartisan Support

By definition, the war on terror would be a global undertaking—combatants might operate from virtu-

Afghan women show their inked fingers after they voted during parliamentary elections in the Afghan capital of Kabul on September 18, 2005. Afghan president Hamid Karzai hailed the first national assembly and provincial elections in decades as a defining moment in the nation's struggle to rebuild.

for other purposes." Congress also approved on September 24, 2001, a $15 billion (subsequently increased to $20 billion) bailout for the airline industry, which had already been struggling financially when it was hard hit by a suspension of service following the September 11 attacks.

Of several laws quickly passed to expand the investigative powers of U.S. law enforcement agencies, the most important was the USA PATRIOT Act. Passed by the Senate on October 11, 2001, and the House on October 12, the act provided measures against money laundering to finance international terrorism; immunity against prosecution for the providers of government-requested wiretaps; expanded systems of personal identification, especially at ports of entry into the United States; a foreign student monitoring program; a mandate to improve passports and other documents to prevent forgery; a provision for so-called Sneak-and-Peek searches, authorizing surreptitious search warrants and seizures; expanded provisions for wiretaps and surveillance; and the authority to examine library records to determine who was reading what.

The USA PATRIOT Act drew a great deal of opposition from some politicians and from various advocacy groups on the grounds that it curtailed civil liberties and invaded individuals' privacy; despite these protests, it was renewed by Congress in 2006.

ally anywhere. It was less a war than a political military policy, analogous to the "containment" policy of the Cold War era (see Chapter 38). As such, it could not be a declared war—that is, a war formally authorized by Congress. But in a climate of bipartisan unity engendered by the events of September 11, President Bush readily secured from Congress a **Joint Resolution Authorizing Use of Military Force.**

The USA PATRIOT Act and Other Legislative Initiatives

The war in Afghanistan was the offensive phase of the war on terror. Defensive measures included a $40 billion emergency spending bill passed by Congress on September 14, 2001, that made "emergency supplemental appropriations for fiscal year 2001 for additional disaster assistance, for anti-terrorism initiatives, and for assistance in the recovery from the tragedy that occurred on September 11, 2001, and

Summary Detentions

Another effect of the September 11 attacks was a federal initiative to apprehend and detain persons who fit certain "terrorist" profiles, including the pro-

Joint Resolution Authorizing Use of Military Force, September 18, 2001

SEC. 2. AUTHORIZATION FOR USE OF UNITED STATES ARMED FORCES

(a) IN GENERAL—That the President is authorized to use all necessary and appropriate force against those nations, organizations, or persons he determines planned, authorized, committed, or aided the terrorist attacks that occurred on September 11, 2001, or harbored such organizations or persons, in order to prevent any future acts of international terrorism against the United States by such nations, organizations or persons.

(b) WAR POWERS RESOLUTION REQUIREMENTS.—

(1) SPECIFIC STATUTORY AUTHORIZATION.—Consistent with section 8(a)(1) of the War Powers Resolution, the Congress declares that this section is intended to constitute specific statutory authorization within the meaning of section 5(b) of the War Powers Resolution.

(2) APPLICABILITY OF OTHER REQUIREMENTS.—Nothing in this resolution supercedes any requirement of the War Powers Resolution.

Excerpted from *A Joint Resolution to Authorize the Use of United States Armed Forces against Those Responsible for the Recent Attacks Launched against the United States,* Public Law 107-40, *U.S. Statutes at Large* 115(2001): 224–225, from GPO Access, http://frwebgate.access.gpo.gov/cgi-bin/getdoc.cgi?dbname=107_cong_public_laws&docid=f:publ040.107.pdf.

file of the 9/11 hijackers. Within two months after the attacks, more than 1,200 people had been detained and held incommunicado within the United States, without hearings or trials. Most were subsequently released.

Homeland Security

On November 25, 2002, the Homeland Security Act of 2002 created the Department of Homeland Security (DHS) as the third-largest cabinet department, consisting of about 180,000 persons. The new department was designed to consolidate a variety of existing executive branch agencies related to homeland security. Although DHS began operations on January 24, 2003, most of the component agencies were not transferred to it until March 1.

From the beginning, DHS was plagued by controversy; issues included whether the Federal Bureau of Investigation and the Central Intelligence Agency should be integrated into it. (They were not.) Yet most Americans suffered the growing pains of DHS patiently, as they also tended to accept with little complaint or suspicion the provisions of the USA PATRIOT Act, the post-9/11 summary detentions, and the added security measures in airports and many public places and buildings. Among the American public, there was a widely perceived need for extraordinary measures to ensure security. If that meant giving the president added power to investigate individuals and to prosecute foreign wars, a majority of the public and politicians were willing to oblige. Indeed, although the election of President Bush in 2000 had been fraught with controversy—he received a minority of the popular vote, and the disputed Electoral College vote was ultimately settled by a Supreme Court decision—he was reelected in 2004 by a slim but solid majority. The implication was that most Americans believed the administration's approaches to the "war on terror" and "homeland security" were both necessary and effective.

BIBLIOGRAPHY

Gunararta, Rohan. *Inside Al-Qaeda.* New York: Columbia University Press, 2002.

Hoge, James F., and Gideon Rose, eds. *Understanding the War on Terror.* New York: Foreign Affairs, 2005.

Samon, Bill. *Fighting Back: The War on Terrorism from Inside the White House.* Chicago: Regnery, 2002.

Woodward, Bob. *Bush at War.* New York: Simon and Schuster, 2003.

CHAPTER 48

OPERATION IRAQI FREEDOM

(2003–)

At Issue

President George W. Bush stated that war with Iraq was justified by Iraq's possession of "weapons of mass destruction." Later, he also cited the need to remove Iraq's president, the dictator Saddam Hussein, from power in order to promote democracy in Iraq.

The Conflict

In his January 29, 2002, State of the Union Address, President George W. Bush identified Iraq as a supporter of terrorism and as part of an "axis of evil" along with Iran and North Korea. He made the case to the nation that the United States "must prevent the terrorists and regimes who seek chemical, biological or nuclear weapons from threatening the United States and the world." About Iraq, he stated:

> Iraq continues to flaunt its hostility toward America and to support terror. The Iraqi regime has plotted to develop anthrax, and nerve gas, and nuclear weapons for over a decade. This is a regime that has already used poison gas to murder thousands of its own citizens. . . . This is a regime that agreed to international inspections—then kicked out the inspectors. This is a regime that has something to hide from the civilized world.

As Saddam Hussein persisted in refusing to allow weapons inspectors to resume their work and the UN failed to enforce the thirteen resolutions on Iraqi disarmament and weapons inspections passed since the end of the Persian Gulf War, the president resolved to invade Iraq as part of the "war on terror" (Chapter 47). Instead of repeating demands concerning weapons inspectors, in a televised address on March 17, 2003, President Bush gave Saddam Hussein forty-eight hours to leave the country with his inner circle, including his sons Uday and Qusay. When the deadline passed, the president on March 19 authorized a "decapitation" attack on the Iraqi leadership—an aerial bombardment of a bunker in Baghdad believed to shelter Saddam. This attack was the beginning of Operation Iraqi Freedom, the undeclared war against Iraq. Saddam Hussein was not injured in the initial attack.

The first air attack was followed by a succession of carefully targeted air strikes, using satellite-guided Tomahawk Cruise Missiles fired from American warships, and bombardment by guided "smart weapons" deployed from aircraft. These surgical strikes pinpointed military and government targets and avoided most civilian structures.

As the air attacks continued, ground operations began on March 20 when U.S. Army and Marine units captured key oil fields. The ground war moved swiftly, as U.S. and allied British forces advanced against major Iraqi cities, including the capital, Baghdad. Fears that the Iraqis would retaliate with chemical or biological weapons proved unfounded.

On March 25, battles for the southern town of Najaf and the southern port city of Basra began. On March 26, American paratroops deployed in northern Iraq. On March 28, U.S. Marines fought fiercely for Nasiriya, and on April 2, U.S. forces began the conquest of Karbala, fifty miles from Baghdad.

The Karbala assault opened the Battle of Baghdad. After the fall of Karbala, U.S. Special Forces troops seized the Thar Thar presidential palace, just northwest of Baghdad, on April 3. At the same time, U.S. troops attacked Baghdad's Saddam International Airport. Also on April 3, Najaf fell to the U.S. 101st Airborne Division. The airport was secured on April 4, and U.S. forces renamed it Baghdad International Airport. It became the base of operations for the occupation of Baghdad.

On April 6, U.S. and British troops maneuvered to envelop the Iraqi capital. On April 7, U.S. forces advanced into the city and captured the presidential palaces. An air strike was called against a modest building in Baghdad believed to harbor Saddam Hussein, but Saddam again evaded death. While U.S. forces advanced through Baghdad, the British declared Basra secure.

On April 9, as the U.S. forces occupied Baghdad, people around the world saw television images of massive statues of Saddam Hussein toppled in Baghdad and other cities. In some places, U.S. and British soldiers were welcomed as liberators, but in others they were met with various forms of resis-

CHRONOLOGY OF OPERATION IRAQI FREEDOM

1997–2002

- Iraqi president Saddam Hussein repeatedly refuses to cooperate with United Nations weapons inspectors, thereby defying UN disarmament orders.

1998

Oct. 31 President Bill Clinton signs the Iraq Liberation Act, which declares "that it should be the policy of the United States to seek to remove the Saddam Hussein regime from power in Iraq and to replace it with a democratic government."

2002

Jan. 29 President George W. Bush identifies Iraq, Iran, and South Korea as an "axis of evil."

Sept. 12 Bush addresses the UN General Assembly; he states that if the UN fails to take action against Iraq, the United States will.

Oct. 10–11 The U.S. House and Senate authorize the use of force in Iraq.

2003

Jan. 28 Bush makes the case for war in his State of the Union Address.

Feb. 5 Secretary of State Colin Powell addresses the UN Security Council, presenting the administration's evidence of weapons of mass destruction in Iraq.

Mar. 17 Bush gives Saddam Hussein forty-eight hours to leave the country or suffer attack.

Mar. 19 The war begins with a "decapitation" attack against a building believed to house Saddam Hussein.

Mar. 20 The ground war begins.

Mar. 25 The battles for Najaf and Basra begin.

Mar. 26 American paratroops deploy in northern Iraq.

Mar. 28 U.S. Marines fight the Battle of Nasiriya.

Apr. 2 The Battle of Karbala opens the Battle of Baghdad.

Apr. 3 U.S. Special Forces troops seize the Thar Thar presidential palace. U.S. troops attack Baghdad's Saddam International Airport. Najaf falls to the U.S. 101st Airborne Division.

Apr. 4 U.S. forces capture Saddam International Airport and rename it Baghdad International Airport.

Apr. 7 U.S. forces capture Baghdad.

May 1 President Bush announces the end of "major combat."

July 22 Saddam Hussein's sons Uday and Qusay are killed in a raid.

Dec. 14 Saddam Hussein is captured.

2003–

- Despite the breakthrough legislative elections on January 30, 2005—Iraq's first democratic elections—the conflict continues as insurgents, extremists, Saddam loyalists, and rival religious sects fight on.

tance, including snipers' bullets and "improvised explosive devices" (IEDs).

After the occupation of Baghdad, U.S. forces turned to Tikrit, Saddam's hometown and a stronghold of his Baath political party. The American military issued and distributed to U.S. troops in the field decks of playing cards bearing the pictures and names of fifty-five of the Iraqi regime's most-wanted tyrants. These were intended to help soldiers identify the senior members of Saddam Hussein's regime and quickly became a collector's item.

On April 11, U.S. military officials announced that Baghdad had been secured. The city of Al Kut fell the next day, and Tikrit was put under heavy attack on April 13. The next day, the Pentagon announced that although some fighting continued, the major combat phase of Operation Iraqi Freedom had ended. Lieutenant General Jay Garner (U.S. Army, Ret.) was brought into Baghdad to lead U.S. occupation and reconstruction efforts in Iraq. (Garner would be replaced on May 11 by a new administrator, diplomat L. Paul Bremer.) On May 1, 2003, President Bush landed in an S-3 Viking on the deck of the aircraft carrier *Abraham Lincoln,* off the coast of California, to announce that major combat had been concluded in Iraq.

Saddam Hussein and his sons, however, were still at large. Uday and Qusay were killed in a July 22 raid. On December 14, 2003, U.S Special Forces soldiers captured Saddam, who was hiding in a cellar at a farmhouse ten miles south of Tikrit. He was detained for trial on charges of war crimes.

Despite the fall of the Saddam Hussein government and the capture of the dictator himself, Iraq was still swept by an insurgency made up of hardline Saddam loyalists and so-called foreign fighters (militant extremists from other countries) who targeted American forces and U.S.-trained Iraqi troops, generally using IEDs planted along the side of the road. Sectarian violence, especially between rival Shiite and Sunni factions, also took its toll on the Iraqi civilian population.

As of August 2, 2006, 2,582 U.S. military personnel had been killed, most of them after "major

President George W. Bush declares the end of major combat in Iraq as he speaks aboard the aircraft carrier USS Abraham Lincoln *off the California coast on May 1, 2003. The carrier's ten-month deployment had included Operation Iraqi Freedom.*

combat" had been declared to be at an end. Some 5,117 Iraqi police and military personnel had been killed by this date, and Iraqi civilian casualties were estimated at 11,495 between January 2005 and August 2, 2006. It is not known how many Iraqis perished in the phase of "major combat."

The Iraq Liberation Act of 1998

On October 31, 1998, President Bill Clinton signed into law the Iraq Liberation Act of 1998 (Public Law 105-338), which declared "that it should be the policy of the United States to seek to remove the Saddam Hussein regime from power in Iraq and to replace it with a democratic government." The act

George W. Bush

(1946–)

George W. Bush was born in New Haven, Connecticut, but grew up in Midland and Houston, Texas. After receiving a bachelor's degree in history from Yale University in 1968, he served in the Texas Air National Guard and then attended Harvard Business School, from which he received an MBA in 1975. After graduating, he returned to Midland and went to work for a family friend who was an oil and gas attorney. Bush then started his own oil and gas firm. He married Laura Welch, a Midland teacher and librarian, in 1977 (the couple would have twin daughters in 1981) and ran unsuccessfully for Congress in 1978. Bush's oil business failed in 1986, which was the same year he gave up alcohol and a year after a conversation with the Reverend Billy Graham had stirred in him strong Christian convictions.

Bush worked on his father's 1988 presidential campaign, then returned to the business world. He assembled a group of partners who purchased the Texas Rangers Major League Baseball franchise in 1989. In November 1994 Bush was elected governor of Texas, and in November 1998 he became the first Texas governor to be reelected to a consecutive term. He stepped down as governor when he became president in 2001, having defeated Democrat Al Gore in a disputed contest. Bush had received fewer popular votes but won a majority of the electoral votes. The Gore campaign contested Florida's electoral votes, however; ultimately the election was decided by the U.S. Supreme Court.

Bush entered office determined to carry out the conservative policies of his constituency but after the attacks of September 11, 2001, found his presidency almost wholly defined by what he called "the war on terror," the most prominent and controversial feature of which has been the war in Iraq.

---

authorized "the President . . . to provide to the Iraqi democratic opposition organizations: (1) grant assistance for radio and television broadcasting to Iraq; (2) Department of Defense (DOD) defense articles and services and military education and training (IMET); and (3) humanitarian assistance." The act prohibited "assistance to any group or organization that is engaged in military cooperation with the Hussein regime." The act also urged "the President to call upon the United Nations to establish an international criminal tribunal for the purpose of indicting, prosecuting, and imprisoning Saddam Hussein and other Iraqi officials who are responsible for crimes against humanity, genocide, and other criminal violations of international law."

The intent of the law was to redress what many in Congress felt was the failure of the administration of President George H. W. Bush at the end of the Per-

sian Gulf War to provide support to indigenous Iraqi (including Kurdish) resistance groups opposed to Saddam Hussein. Although President George W. Bush and other administration officials later cited the act as partial grounds for taking action against Saddam Hussein, the act did not explicitly authorize the president to go to war. It did express "the sense of the Congress that once the Saddam Hussein regime is removed from power in Iraq, the United States should support Iraq's transition to democracy by providing humanitarian assistance to the Iraqi people and democracy transition assistance to Iraqi parties and movements with democratic goals."

Bush at the United Nations

On September 12, 2002, President George W. Bush presented his case against Iraq in an **Address to the**

United Nations General Assembly. He appealed to the member nations for their support in opposing Iraq—with military force, if necessary—but made it clear that the United States was prepared to stand alone. The president declared Saddam and Iraq to be sponsors of terrorism and an ongoing threat to the world because of a stockpile of "weapons of mass destruction" (WMDs).

While waiting for the UN to act, the Bush administration secured from Congress on October 11, 2002, resolutions authorizing the use of military force against Iraq. On November 8, the United Nations approved Resolution 1441, pressuring Iraq to comply with its disarmament obligations or to prove that it had divested itself of all weapons of mass destruction.

State of the Union Address, January 28, 2003

On January 28, 2003, President Bush delivered his **State of the Union Address,** in which he made a case for taking military action against Iraq. He cited Saddam Hussein's refusal to comply with UN weapons inspectors and the administration's concern that Iraq might be hiding weapons of mass destruction. Bush also discussed the possibility that Saddam was developing nuclear weapons, stating that "[t]he International Atomic Energy Agency confirmed in the 1990s that Saddam Hussein had an advanced nuclear weapons development program." His next statement—"The British government has learned that Saddam Hussein recently sought significant quantities of uranium from Africa"— came under intense scrutiny from the press and from government offi-

cials, who asserted that the evidence cited had been discredited by U.S. intelligence agencies prior to the State of the Union speech. President Bush later (July 8, 2003) admitted that the "sixteen words" had been included in error. Critics used this incident to accuse the administration of willful manipulation of intelligence to build a case for war.

Colin Powell at the United Nations

Pursuant to Resolution 1441, the United Nations dispatched weapons inspectors to Iraq on November 13, 2002. Although the inspectors found nothing of significance, the 12,000-page weapons declaration Iraq filed on December 7 in compliance with Resolution 1441 proved to be little more than a reorganized version of documents submitted in 1997 and therefore revealed nothing about the current state of weapons in the Iraqi stockpile.

On February 5, 2003, U.S. Secretary of State Colin Powell presented the administration's **Case for the Existence of Weapons of Mass Destruction** to the UN Security Council. Powell presented images,

Secretary of State Colin Powell holds up a powder-filled vial to illustrate a teaspoon of anthrax as he presents evidence of Iraq's alleged weapons program to the UN Security Council on February 5, 2003.

Bush's Address to the United Nations General Assembly, 2002

We meet one year and one day after a terrorist attack brought grief to my country and brought grief to many citizens of our world. Yesterday we remembered the innocent lives taken that terrible morning. Today we turn to the urgent duty of protecting other lives, without illusion and without fear. . . .

We've accomplished much in the last year in Afghanistan and beyond. We have much yet to do. . . . Many nations represented here have joined in the fight against global terror, and the people of the United States are grateful.

Above all, our principles and our security are challenged today by outlaw groups and regimes that accept no law of morality and have no limit to their violent ambitions. . . . And our greatest fear is that terrorists will find a shortcut to their mad ambitions when an outlaw regime supplies them with the technologies to kill on a massive scale.

In one place—in one regime—we find all these dangers in their most lethal and aggressive forms, exactly the kind of aggressive threat the United Nations was born to confront.

Twelve years ago, Iraq invaded Kuwait without provocation, and the regime's forces were poised to continue their march to seize other countries and their resources. Had Saddam Hussein been appeased instead of stopped, he would have endangered the peace and stability of the world. Yet this aggression was stopped by the might of coalition forces and the will of the United Nations.

To suspend hostilities, to spare himself, Iraq's dictator accepted a series of commitments. The terms were clear to him and to all, and he agreed to prove he is complying with every one of those obligations.

He has proven instead only his contempt for the United Nations and for all his pledges. By breaking every pledge, by his deceptions, and by his cruelties, Saddam Hussein has made the case against himself.

[President Bush discusses the UN resolutions that Saddam had failed to abide by.]

Today, Iraq continues to withhold important information about its nuclear program, weapons design, procurement logs, experiment data, an accounting of nuclear materials, and documentation of foreign assistance. . . .

Iraq also possesses a force of Scud-type missiles with ranges beyond the 150 kilometers permitted by the U.N. . . .

As we meet today, it's been almost 4 years since the last U.N. inspectors set foot in Iraq, 4 years for the Iraqi regime to plan and to build and to test behind the cloak of secrecy.

We know that Saddam Hussein pursued weapons of mass murder even when inspectors were in his country. Are we to assume that he stopped when they left? The history, the logic, and the facts lead to one conclusion: Saddam Hussein's regime is a grave and gathering danger. To suggest otherwise is to hope against the evidence. To assume this regime's good faith is to bet the lives of millions and the peace of the world in a reckless gamble. And this is a risk we must not take.

Delegates to the General Assembly, we have been more than patient. We've tried sanctions. . . . But Saddam Hussein has defied all these efforts. . . . The first time we may be completely certain he has a — nuclear weapons is when, God forbids, he uses one. We owe it to all our citizens to do everything in our power to prevent that day from coming. . . .

---

diagrams, maps, and an audio recording of an intercepted conversation between Iraqi military officials, and he held up a vial of simulated weaponized anthrax spores in an effort to persuade the Security Council of the imminent threat posed by Iraq. Despite this presentation, the international community remained reluctant to support a war against Iraq.

When U.S. troops occupying Iraq did not find massive stockpiles of weapons of mass destruction, Powell was criticized for his statement to the UN. Powell responded to his critics on May 16, 2004, on television's *Meet the Press*:

> When I made that presentation in February 2003 it was based on the best

If the Iraqi regime wishes peace, it will immediately and unconditionally forswear, disclose, and remove or destroy all weapons of mass destruction, long-range missiles, and all related material.

If the Iraqi regime wishes peace, it will immediately end all support for terrorism and act to suppress it, as all states are required to do by U.N. Security Council resolutions. . . .

The United States has no quarrel with the Iraqi people. They've suffered too long in silent captivity. Liberty for the Iraqi people is a great moral cause and a great strategic goal. The people of Iraq deserve it; the security of all nations requires it. Free societies do not intimidate through cruelty and conquest, and open societies do not threaten the world with mass murder. The United States supports political and economic liberty in a unified Iraq.

We can harbor no illusions, and that's important today to remember. Saddam Hussein attacked Iran in 1980 and Kuwait in 1990. . . .

My Nation will work with the U.N. Security Council to meet our common challenge. If Iraq's regime defies us again, the world must move deliberately, decisively to hold Iraq to account. . . .

Events can turn in one of two ways: If we fail to act in the face of danger, the people of Iraq will continue to live in brutal submission; the regime will have new power to bully and dominate and conquer its neighbors, condemning the Middle East to more years of bloodshed and fear; the regime will remain unstable—the region will remain unstable, with little hope of freedom, and isolated from the progress of our times. With every step the Iraqi regime takes toward gaining and deploying the most terrible weapons, our own options to confront that regime will narrow. And if an emboldened regime were to supply these weapons to terrorist allies, then the attacks of September the 11th would be a prelude to far greater horrors.

If we meet our responsibilities, if we overcome this danger, we can arrive at a very different future. The people of Iraq can shake off their captivity. They can one day join a democratic Afghanistan and a democratic Palestine, inspiring reforms throughout the Muslim world. These nations can show by their example that honest government and respect for women and the great Islamic tradition of learning can triumph in the Middle East and beyond. And we will show that the promise of the United Nations can be fulfilled in our time. . . .

. . . We must choose between a world of fear and a world of progress. We cannot stand by and do nothing while dangers gather. We must stand up for our security and for the permanent rights and the hopes of mankind. By heritage and by choice, the United States of America will make that stand. And delegates to the United Nations, you have the power to make that stand as well.

Excerpted from George W. Bush, "Address to the United Nations General Assembly in New York City," September 12, 2002, in *Public Papers of the Presidents of the United States: George W. Bush, 2001–*, from the American Presidency Project, University of California, Santa Barbara, www.presidency.ucsb.edu.

information that the Central Intelligence Agency made available to me. We studied it carefully; we looked at the sourcing in the case of the mobile trucks and trains. There was multiple sourcing for that. Unfortunately, that multiple sourcing over time has turned out to be not accurate.

And so I'm deeply disappointed. But I'm also comfortable that at the time that I made the presentation, it reflected the collective judgment, the sound judgment of the intelligence community. But it turned out that the sourcing was inaccurate and wrong and in some cases, deliberately

Bush's State of the Union Address, 2003

Today, the gravest danger in the war on terror, the gravest danger facing America and the world, is outlaw regimes that seek and possess nuclear, chemical, and biological weapons. These regimes could use such weapons for blackmail, terror, and mass murder. They could also give or sell those weapons to terrorist allies, who would use them without the least hesitation.

This threat is new. America's duty is familiar. Throughout the 20th century, small groups of men seized control of great nations, built armies and arsenals, and set out to dominate the weak and intimidate the world. In each case, their ambitions of cruelty and murder had no limit. In each case, the ambitions of Hitlerism, militarism, and communism were defeated by the will of free peoples, by the strength of great alliances, and by the might of the United States of America.

Now, in this century, the ideology of power and domination has appeared again and seeks to gain the ultimate weapons of terror. Once again, this Nation and all our friends are all that stand between a world at peace and a world of chaos and constant alarm. Once again, we are called to defend the safety of our people and the hopes of all mankind. And we accept this responsibility.

America is making a broad and determined effort to confront these dangers. We have called on the United Nations to fulfill its charter and stand by its demand that Iraq disarm. We're strongly supporting the International Atomic Energy Agency in its mission to track and control nuclear materials around the world. We're working with other governments to secure nuclear materials in the former Soviet Union and to strengthen global treaties banning the production and shipment of missile technologies and weapons of mass destruction.

In all these efforts, however, America's purpose is more than to follow a process; it is to achieve a result, the end of terrible threats to the civilized world. All free nations have a stake in preventing sudden and catastrophic attacks. And we're asking them to join us, and many are doing so. Yet the course of this Nation does not depend on the decisions of others. Whatever action is required, whenever action is necessary, I will defend the freedom and security of the American people.

Excerpted from George W. Bush, "Address before a Joint Session of Congress on the State of the Union," January 28, 2003, in *Public Papers of the Presidents of the United States: George W. Bush, 2001–*, from the American Presidency Project, University of California, Santa Barbara, www.presidency.ucsb.edu.

---

misleading. And for that, I am disappointed and I regret it.

Powell resigned his position as secretary of state on November 14, 2004, stating that "it has always been my intention that I would serve one term."

A "Coalition of the Willing" or a Failure of Diplomacy?

On the eve of war, the Bush administration announced that it had assembled a forty-nine-member "coalition of the willing" to oppose Iraq.

(This number decreased to forty-eight when Costa Rica asked to be removed from the list before the outbreak of the war.) Yet 133,000—98 percent—of the troops committed to the Iraq war were American. Britain contributed the next largest share, 8,361 troops. South Korea contributed about 3,300 troops, Italy 2,600 troops, and Poland 900 troops. Twenty-two other nations each committed 130–830 troops. By the spring of 2006, seventeen nations had withdrawn from the coalition.

Some major powers, most notably France and Germany, actively opposed the Iraq war. Others did not directly oppose it but declined to commit substantive support. Still others, including Spain, voiced

Case for the Existence of Weapons of Mass Destruction, 2003

Underlying all that I have said, underlying all the facts and the patterns of behavior that I have identified, is Saddam Hussein's contempt for the will of this Council, his contempt for the truth, and, most damning of all, his utter contempt for human life. Saddam Hussein's use of mustard and nerve gas against the Kurds in 1988 was one of the 20th century's most horrible atrocities. Five thousand men, women and children died. His campaign against the Kurds from 1987 to '89 included mass summary executions, disappearances, arbitrary jailing and ethnic cleansing, and the destruction of some 2,000 villages. . . .

Nothing points more clearly to Saddam Hussein's dangerous intentions and the threat he poses to all of us than his calculated cruelty to his own citizens and to his neighbors. Clearly, Saddam Hussein and his regime will stop at nothing until something stops him.

. . . For Saddam Hussein, possession of the world's most deadly weapons is the ultimate trump card, the one he must hold to fulfill his ambition.

We know that Saddam Hussein is determined to keep his weapons of mass destruction, is determined to make more. Given Saddam Hussein's history of aggression, given what we know of his grandiose plans, given what we know of his terrorist associa-tions, and given his determination to exact revenge on those who oppose him, should we take the risk that he will not someday use these weapons at a time and a place and in a manner of his choosing, at a time when the world is in a much weaker position to respond?

The United States will not and cannot run that risk for the American people. Leaving Saddam Hussein in possession of weapons of mass destruction for a few more months or years is not an option, not in a post-September 11th world.

My colleagues, we have an obligation to our citizens, we have an obligation to this body to see that our resolutions are complied with. We wrote 1441 not in order to go to war. We wrote 1441 to try to preserve the peace. We wrote 1441 to give Iraq one last chance.

Iraq is not, so far, taking that one last chance.

We must not shrink from whatever is ahead of us. We must not fail in our duty and our responsibility to the citizens of the countries that are represented by this body.

Excerpted from Colin L. Powell, "Remarks to the United Nations Security Council," U.S. Department of State, www.state.gov/secretary/former/powell/remarks/2003/17300.htm.

support and pledged logistical and humanitarian assistance but withheld active military forces.

The United States and Britain largely stood alone in the war.

Deadline Set for Saddam

On March 17, 2003, in his televised **Address to the Nation on Iraq,** President Bush announced that action in Iraq was imminent and issued an ultimatum to Saddam Hussein, demanding that he and his immediate cohorts (including his sons, Uday and Qusay) permanently leave Iraq within forty-eight hours. It was after this deadline passed, on March 19, that the president authorized the aerial bombardment of a bunker in Baghdad believed to shelter Saddam.

Quagmire?

As discussed in "The Conflict," above, the military invasion of Iraq proceeded with astounding speed and at relatively little cost in terms of coalition casualties. Yet after the invasion was completed, Iraq became torn by violence and a state of chronic insurrection.

While the Bush administration and its allies pointed to progress in rebuilding and democratizing Iraq, the administration came under increasing criticism from those politicians (mostly Democrats) and

Bush's Address to the Nation on Iraq, 2003

Last September, I went to the U.N. General Assembly and urged the nations of the world to unite and bring an end to this danger. On November 8th, the Security Council unanimously passed Resolution 1441, finding Iraq in material breach of its obligations and vowing serious consequences if Iraq did not fully and immediately disarm.

Today, no nation can possibly claim that Iraq has disarmed, and it will not disarm so long as Saddam Hussein holds power. For the last 4 1/2 months, the United States and our allies have worked within the Security Council to enforce that Council's long-standing demands. Yet, some permanent members of the Security Council have publicly announced they will veto any resolution that compels the disarmament of Iraq. These governments share our assessment of the danger but not our resolve to meet it.

Many nations, however, do have the resolve and fortitude to act against this threat to peace, and a broad coalition is now gathering to enforce the just demands of the world. The United Nations Security Council has not lived up to its responsibilities, so we will rise to ours.

In recent days, some governments in the Middle East have been doing their part. They have delivered public and private messages urging the dictator to leave Iraq, so that disarmament can proceed peacefully. He has thus far refused.

All the decades of deceit and cruelty have now reached an end. Saddam Hussein and his sons must leave Iraq within 48 hours. Their refusal to do so will result in military conflict, commenced at a time of our choosing. For their own safety, all foreign nationals, including journalists and inspectors, should leave Iraq immediately.

Many Iraqis can hear me tonight in a translated radio broadcast, and I have a message for them: If we must begin a military campaign, it will be directed against the lawless men who rule your country and not against you. . . .

We are now acting because the risks of inaction would be far greater. . . .

. . . The security of the world requires disarming Saddam Hussein now.

Excerpted from George W. Bush, "Address to the Nation on Iraq," March 17, 2003, in *Public Papers of the Presidents of the United States: George W. Bush, 2001–*, from American Presidency Project, University of California, Santa Barbara, www.presidency.ucsb.edu.

news analysts who asserted that the nation was on the verge of civil war. On January 26, 2004, two days after he resigned as the top U.S. weapons inspector in Iraq, David Kay publicly reported that his group had found no evidence that Iraq had recently stockpiled unconventional weapons before the U.S.-led invasion. On April 28, 2004, the CBS television news magazine *60 Minutes* reported the shocking story of the abuse and torture by members of the U.S. military of Iraqi prisoners held in the Abu Ghraib Prison in Iraq. The story was reported in greater detail by Seymour Hersh in the *New Yorker*. The television and magazine stories were illustrated by lurid snapshots—taken by U.S. troops—of prisoner humiliation and torture. Although military offi-

cials testified that the instances of abuse were perpetrated by a few low-ranking troops, there was speculation both domestically and in the international community that abuse and torture might have been authorized by the military high command as legitimate interrogation techniques.

Despite these developments, at the time of President Bush's reelection in November 2004, a majority of Americans reported that they believed the war was necessary to the security of the United States. During Bush's second term, however, there was a precipitous erosion in public support for the war, likely due to the almost routine news stories of civil insurrection and violence in occupied Iraq; to ongoing debate concerning possible manipulation of prewar intelligence as well as tactics, strategy, manpower, and logistics; and to concern over the actions of some U.S. troops.

When the war began, a CBS News/*New York Times* poll reported that 69 percent of Americans approved of U.S. action against Iraq. Conversely, on July 25, 2006, a follow-up poll reported that 62 percent of respondents "disapproved" of the war in Iraq.

History Being Written

The Iraq war fomented a period of intense political, intellectual, and cultural debate in America. Recent authors have tried to document the Bush administration's reasons for waging war in Iraq, most notably Seymour Hersh (*Chain of Command: The Road from 9/11 to Abu Ghraib*, 2004), Bob Woodward (*Plan of Attack*, 2004), and Christopher Hitchens (*A Long Short War: The Postponed Liberation of Iraq*, 2003). Hersh and Woodward make the case that the Bush administration entered the White House in 2001 determined to "finish" the war with Iraq that (in the administration's view) had been left incomplete in the 1990–1991 Persian Gulf War (Chapter 43).

President Bush and his inner circle have often been characterized by political commentators as "neocons"—adherents to a neoconservative ideology that was first articulated in the 1960s by political scientist Irving Kristol (to whom Bush presented in July 2002 the Presidential Medal of Freedom) and that advocates an interventionist foreign policy, including the use of military force to remove and replace autocratic regimes with democratic ones. Woodward and Hersh argue that the events of September 11, 2001, provided a pretext for war. Another author critical of the Bush administration, James Bamford (*A Pretext for War: 9/11, Iraq, and the Abuse of America's Intelligence Agencies*, 2004)

claims that the president and his advisers deliberately manipulated intelligence information (especially relating to Iraq's possession of weapons of mass destruction) to make a case for conducting a war that was really motivated by neoconservative ideological objectives.

Although Hersh, Woodward, and Bamford are among those who have expressed varying degrees of skepticism of Bush and the war in Iraq, others believe that the war grew out of a bold and entirely legitimate vision of what President George H. W. Bush in the late 1980s and early 1990s characterized as a "new world order" in which America must assume moral and political leadership. Christopher Hitchens sees the democratization of the Middle East as crucial to the stability not only of the region, but also the world—-and as necessary for the survival of democracy itself.

BIBLIOGRAPHY

Bamford, James. *A Pretext for War: 9/11, Iraq, and the Abuse of America's Intelligence Agencies.* New York: Doubleday, 2004.

Hersh, Seymour M. *Chain of Command: The Road from 9/11 to Abu Ghraib.* New York: HarperCollins, 2004.

Hitchens, Christopher. *A Long Short War: The Postponed Liberation of Iraq.* New York: Penguin Putnam, 2003.

Sifry, Micah L., and Christopher Cerf, eds. *The Iraq War Reader: History, Documents, Opinions.* New York: Simon & Schuster, 2003.

Smith, Raymond L., and Bing West. *The March Up: Taking Baghdad with the 1st Marine Division.* New York: Bantam Doubleday Dell, 2003.

Woodward, Bob. *Plan of Attack.* New York: Simon and Schuster, 2004.

INDEX

References to boxes and documents are indicated by "b" and "d" after the page numbers.

PHOTO CREDITS

TEXT CREDITS

Page	Credit
11	Copyright © The Colonial Williamsburg Foundation 2006
14, 45, 52, 67, 68, 88, 95, 105, 120, 138, 139, 172, 206, 208, 215, 220, 241, 242, 321, 394, 395, 433, 434, 454, 455	Reprinted courtesy of William C. Fray, The Avalon Project at Yale Law School, www.yale.edu/lawweb/avalon/avalon.htm.
27	Reprinted courtesy of America's Home Page, Steven Thomas, curator, http://ahp.gatech.edu.
29, 319	Reprinted courtesy of Bartleby.com, Inc., www.bartleby.com.
55, 56, 145, 147, 148, 149, 150, 151, 154, 165, 166, 167, 240, 243, 249, 250, 251, 255, 262, 263, 268, 269, 270, 271, 272, 281, 282, 296, 297	Reprinted from *Documents of United States Indian Policy,* edited by Francis Paul Prucha. By permission of the University of Nebraska Press. © 1975, 1990, 2000 by the University of Nebraska Press.
89	Reprinted courtesy of the Carl Vinson Institute of Government, University of Georgia, www.cviog.uga.edu.
94	Reprinted courtesy of the University of North Texas Libraries, www.library.unt.edu.
108, 299	Reprinted courtesy of the Oklahoma State University Library, Electronic Publishing Center, http://digital.library.okstate.edu/about.html.
109, 178, 230	Reprinted courtesy of FindLaw, www.findlaw.com.
121, 130, 131, 134, 135, 175, 176, 177, 203, 204, 205, 305, 306, 314, 315, 317, 318, 319, 320, 342, 348, 357, 374, 375, 376, 419, 420, 477	Reprinted from *Annals of America* © 1968, 1976, 2003 Encyclopaedia Britannica, Inc.
181	Reprinted courtesy of Little Big Horn Associates and Jay Kanitz, www.lbha.org.
218	Reprinted courtesy of the Freedman and Southern Society Project, University of Maryland, www.history.umd.edu/Freedmen.
236	Transcribed with permission from the Colorado Historical Society.
303	Reprinted courtesy of Alan B. Howard and Michael Kidd, American Studies at the University of Virginia, http://xroads.virginia.edu/~HYPER/hypertex.html.
333	Reprinted courtesy of Joseph V. O'Brien, Department of History, John Jay College of Criminal Justice, CUNY, http://web.jjay.cuny.edu/~jobrien/.
334	Reprinted with permission of Current History, Inc.